BRIT[ISH]

LOCO[MOTIVES &]

COACHING STOCK

2015

The Complete Guide to all Locomotives & Coaching Stock which operate on the National Rail network and Eurotunnel

Robert Pritchard & Peter Hall

PLATFORM
5

Published by Platform 5 Publishing Ltd,
52 Broadfield Road, Sheffield, S8 0XJ, England.

Printed in England by Berforts Information Press, Eynsham, Oxford.

ISBN 978 1 909431 17 1

CONTENTS

Britain's Railway System 4
Provision of Information 11

SECTION 1 – LOCOMOTIVES

Introduction 12
General Information 14
1.1. Diesel Locomotives 18
1.2. Electro-Diesel & Electric Locomotives 58
1.3. Eurotunnel Locomotives 83
1.4. Former BR main line locos in industrial service 86
1.5. Locomotives awaiting disposal 88
1.6. Locomotives exported for use abroad 89

SECTION 2 – LOCO-HAULED COACHING STOCK

Introduction 93
General Information 96
2.1. BR Number Series Stock 100
2.2. High Speed Train Trailer Cars 130
2.3 HST set formations 161
2.4. Saloons 165
2.5. Pullman Car Company Series 168
2.6. Locomotive Support Carriages 171
2.7. 99xxx Range Number Conversion Table 173
2.8. Set formations 173
2.9. Service Stock 175
2.10 Coaching Stock Awaiting Disposal 182

SECTION 3 – DIESEL MULTIPLE UNITS

Introduction 184
General Information 185
3.1. Diesel Mechanical & Diesel Hydraulic Units 187
3.1.1. First Generation Units 187
    3.1.2. Parry People Movers 188
        3.1.3. Second Generation Units 188
3.2. Diesel-Electric Units 241
3.3. Service DMUs 246
3.4. DMUs Awaiting Disposal 247

CONTENTS

SECTION 4 – ELECTRIC MULTIPLE UNITS

Introduction 248
General Information 249
4.1. 25 kV AC 50 Hz Overhead & Dual-Voltage Units 251
4.2. 750 V DC Third Rail Units 303
4.3. Dual Voltage Thameslink Units 339
4.4. Eurostar Units 345
4.5. Service EMUs 348
4.6. EMU Vehicles in Industrial Service 348
4.7. EMUs Awaiting Disposal 348

SECTION 5 – ON-TRACK MACHINES

5. On-Track Machines 349

SECTION 6 – UK LIGHT RAIL & METRO SYSTEMS

6.1. Blackpool & Fleetwood Tramway 359
6.2. Docklands Light Railway 361
6.3. Edinburgh Tramway 363
6.4. Glasgow Subway 363
6.5. Greater Manchester Metrolink 364
6.6. London Tramlink 367
6.7. Nottingham Express Transit 368
6.8. Midland Metro 369
6.9. Sheffield Supertram 371
6.10. Tyne & Wear Metro 371

SECTION 7 – CODES

7.1. Livery Codes 373
7.2. Owner Codes 376
7.3. Locomotive Pool Codes 377
7.4. Operator Codes 380
7.5. Allocation & Location Codes 381
7.6. Abbreviations 383
7.7. Builders 384

COVER PHOTOGRAPHS

Front Cover: CrossCountry High Speed Train 43378/285 powers the 06.32 Dundee–Plymouth away from Sheffield on 3 May 2014.　**Robert Pritchard**

Back Cover: South West Trains 444 017 approaches Upwey with the 10.35 London Waterloo–Weymouth on 21 June 2014.　**Stephen A. Ginn**

BRITAIN'S RAILWAY SYSTEM

INFRASTRUCTURE & OPERATION

Britain's national railway infrastructure is owned by a "not for dividend" company, Network Rail. In September 2014 Network Rail was classified a public sector company, being described by the Government as a "public sector arm's-length body of the Department for Transport".

Many stations and maintenance depots are leased to and operated by Train Operating Companies (TOCs), but some larger stations are under Network Rail control. The only exception is the infrastructure on the Isle of Wight: Island Line was the only franchise that included the maintenance of the infrastructure as well as the provision of passenger services. As Island Line is now part of the South West Trains franchise, both the infrastructure and trains are operated by South West Trains.

Trains are operated by TOCs over Network Rail, regulated by access agreements between the parties involved. In general, TOCs are responsible for the provision and maintenance of the locomotives, rolling stock and staff necessary for the direct operation of services, whilst Network Rail is responsible for the provision and maintenance of the infrastructure and also for staff to regulate the operation of services.

The Department for Transport is the franchising authority for the national network, with Transport Scotland overseeing the award of the ScotRail franchise. Railway Franchise holders (TOCs) can take commercial risks, although some franchises are known as "management contracts", where ticket revenues pass directly to the DfT. Concessions (such as London Overground) see the operator paid a fee to run the service, usually within tightly specified guidelines. Operators running a Concession would not normally take commercial risks, although there are usually penalties and rewards in the contract.

During 2012 the letting of new franchises was suspended pending a review of the franchise system. The process was restarted in 2013 but it is taking a number of years to catch-up and several franchises are receiving short-term extensions (or "Direct Awards") in the meantime.

DOMESTIC PASSENGER TRAIN OPERATORS

The large majority of passenger trains are operated by the TOCs on fixed-term franchises or concessions. Franchise expiry dates are shown in the list of franchisees below:

Franchise	Franchisee	Trading Name
Caledonian Sleeper	Serco	**Caledonian Sleeper**

(*starts 1 April 2015*; runs until 31 March 2030)
A new franchise due to start in April 2015. The ScotRail and ScotRail Sleeper franchises are being split. Abellio has won the ScotRail franchise and Serco the Caledonian Sleeper franchise. Serco will introduce new rolling stock, to be manufactured by CAF, from 2018.

Chiltern
Arriva (Deutsche Bahn)
(until 31 December 2021)
Chiltern Railways

Chiltern Railways operates a frequent service between London Marylebone, Banbury and Birmingham Snow Hill, with some peak trains extending to Kidderminster. There are also regular services from Marylebone to Stratford-upon-Avon and to Aylesbury Vale Parkway via Amersham (along the London Underground Metropolitan Line). The fleet consists of DMUs of Classes 121 (used on the Princes Risborough–Aylesbury route), 165, 168 and 172 plus a number of loco-hauled rakes used on some of the Birmingham route trains, worked by Class 67s hired from DB Schenker. The Class 67s are being replaced by Class 68s at the time of writing, while the nine 170s operated by TransPennine Express will transfer to Chiltern Railways during 2015–16 to operate the new Marylebone–Oxford service.

Cross-Country
Arriva (Deutsche Bahn)
(until 31 March 2016)*
CrossCountry

Franchise extension to be negotiated to November 2019.

CrossCountry operates a network of long distance services between Scotland, North-East England and Manchester to the South-West of England, Reading, Southampton, Bournemouth and Guildford, centred on Birmingham New Street. These trains are mainly formed of diesel Class 220/221 Voyagers, supplemented by a small number of HSTs on the NE–SW route. Inter-urban services also link Nottingham, Leicester and Stansted Airport with Birmingham and Cardiff. These use Class 170 DMUs.

Crossrail
MTR
(*starts 31 May 2015*; runs until 30 May 2023)
Crossrail

A new concession due to start in May 2015. Initially Crossrail takes over the Liverpool Street–Shenfield stopping service from Greater Anglia. New Class 345 EMUs will be introduced from 2017 and from 2018–19 Crossrail will operate through new tunnels under construction in central London, from Shenfield and Abbey Wood in the east to Reading and Heathrow in the west. The contract runs for 8 years, with the option to extend it by a further 2 years.

East Midlands
Stagecoach Group
(until 31 March 2015)*
East Midlands Trains

Franchise extension to be negotiated to October 2017.

EMT operates a mix of long distance high speed services on the Midland Main Line (MML), from London St Pancras to Sheffield (Leeds at peak times and some extensions to York/Scarborough) and Nottingham, and local and regional services ranging from the Norwich–Liverpool route to Nottingham–Skegness, Nottingham–Mansfield–Worksop, Nottingham–Matlock and Derby–Crewe. It also operates local services in Lincolnshire. Trains on the MML are worked by a fleet of Class 222 DMUs and ten HSTs, whilst the local and regional fleet consists of DMU Classes 153, 156 and 158.

Essex Thameside
National Express Group
(until 8 November 2029)
c2c

c2c operates an intensive, principally commuter, service from London Fenchurch Street to Southend and Shoeburyness via both Upminster and Tilbury. The fleet consists entirely of Class 357 EMUs. In 2014 c2c won the new 15-year franchise that promised to introduce 17 new 4-car EMUs from 2019.

Greater Western   First Group
                                   (until 20 September 2015)   **First Great Western**

Franchise extension currently being negotiated.

First Great Western operates long distance trains from London Paddington to South Wales, the
West Country and Worcester and Hereford. In addition there are frequent trains along the Thames
Valley corridor to Newbury and Oxford, plus local and regional trains throughout the South-West
including the Cornish, Devon and Thames Valley branches, the Reading–Gatwick North Downs
line and Cardiff–Portsmouth Harbour and Bristol–Weymouth regional routes. A fleet of 53 HSTs
is used on the long-distance trains, with DMUs of Classes 165 and 166 used on the North
Downs and Thames Valley routes and Class 180s used alongside HSTs on the Cotswold Line to
Worcester and Hereford. Classes 143, 150, 153 and 158 are used on local and regional trains
in the South-West. A small fleet of four Class 57s is maintained to work the overnight "Cornish
Riviera" Sleeper service between London and Penzance.

Greater Anglia   Abellio (Netherlands Railways)
                                   (until 19 October 2016)   **Abellio Greater Anglia**

Abellio Greater Anglia operates main line trains between London Liverpool Street, Ipswich
and Norwich and local trains across Norfolk, Suffolk and parts of Cambridgeshire. It also runs
local and commuter services into Liverpool Street from the Great Eastern (including Southend,
Braintree and Clacton) and West Anglia (including Cambridge and Stansted Airport) routes. It
operates a varied fleet of Class 90s with loco-hauled Mark 3 sets, DMUs of Classes 153, 156
and 170 and EMUs of Classes 315, 317, 321, 360 and 379. London Overground and Crossrail
are due to take over some suburban services from Liverpool Street (to Chingford, Cheshunt,
Enfield and Shenfield) in May 2015.

Integrated Kent   Govia (Go-Ahead/Keolis)
                                   (until 24 June 2018)   **Southeastern**

Southeastern operates all services in the South-East London suburbs, the whole of Kent
and part of Sussex, which are primarily commuter services to London. It also operates
domestic high speed trains on HS1 from St Pancras to Ashford, Ramsgate, Dover and
Faversham with additional peak services on other routes. EMUs of Classes 375, 376, 465
and 466 are used, along with Class 395s on the High Speed trains.

InterCity East Coast   Directly Operated Railways
                                   (until 28 February 2015)   **East Coast**

*Currently run on an interim basis by DfT management company Directly Operated Railways
(trading as East Coast). In late 2014 DfT awarded a consortium of Stagecoach (90%) and
Virgin (10%) a new 8-year franchise (with the option of a 1-year extension), that will start on
1 March 2015. The new franchise will be branded Virgin Trains East Coast.*

East Coast operates frequent long distance trains on the East Coast Main Line between London
King's Cross, Leeds, York, Newcastle and Edinburgh, with less frequent services to Bradford,
Harrogate, Skipton, Hull, Lincoln, Glasgow, Aberdeen and Inverness. A mixed fleet of Class 91s
and 30 Mark 4 sets, and 14 HST sets, are used on these trains.

InterCity West Coast
Virgin Rail Group (Virgin/Stagecoach Group) **Virgin Trains**
(until 31 March 2017)
The DfT has the option to extend the franchise to 31 March 2018.

Virgin Trains operates long distance services along the West Coast Main Line from London Euston to Birmingham/Wolverhampton, Manchester, Liverpool and Glasgow using Class 390 Pendolino EMUs. It also operates Class 221 Voyagers on the Euston–Chester–Holyhead route, whilst a mixture of 221s and 390s are used on the Euston–Birmingham–Glasgow/Edinburgh route.

London Rail
MTR/Arriva (Deutsche Bahn) **London Overground**
(until 12 November 2016)
This is a Concession and is different from other rail franchises, as fares and service levels are set by Transport for London instead of by the DfT.

London Overground operates services on the Richmond–Stratford North London Line and the Willesden Junction–Clapham Junction West London Line, plus the East London Line from Highbury & Islington to New Cross and New Cross Gate, with extensions to Clapham Jn (via Denmark Hill), Crystal Palace and West Croydon. It also runs services from London Euston to Watford Junction. All these use Class 378 EMUs whilst Class 172 DMUs are used on the Gospel Oak–Barking route. London Overground will take over some suburban services from Liverpool Street from Greater Anglia in May 2015.

Merseyrail Electrics
Serco/Abellio (Netherlands Railways) **Merseyrail**
(until 19 July 2028)
Under the control of Merseytravel PTE instead of the DfT. Franchise reviewed every five years to fit in with the Merseyside Local Transport Plan.

Merseyrail operates services between Liverpool and Southport, Ormskirk, Kirkby, Hunts Cross, New Brighton, West Kirby, Chester and Ellesmere Port, all worked by EMUs of Classes 507 and 508.

Northern Rail
Serco/Abellio (Netherlands Railways) **Northern**
(until 1 February 2016)

Northern operates a range of inter-urban, commuter and rural services throughout the North of England, including those around the cities of Leeds, Manchester, Sheffield, Liverpool and Newcastle. The network extends from Chathill in the north to Nottingham in the south, and Cleethorpes in the east to St Bees in the west. Long distance services include Leeds–Carlisle, Middlesbrough–Carlisle and York–Blackpool North. The operator uses a large fleet of DMUs of Classes 142, 144, 150, 153, 155, 156 and 158 plus EMU Classes 319, 321, 322, 323 and 333.

ScotRail
First Group **ScotRail**
(until 31 March 2015)
Abellio has won the contract to operate the ScotRail franchise from April 2015. This franchise will run for 7 years with the option to extend it by a further 3 years. The Caledonian Sleeper will not form part of the new ScotRail franchise and will be operated separately by Serco.

ScotRail provides almost all passenger services within Scotland and also trains from Glasgow to Carlisle via Dumfries, some of which extend to Newcastle (jointly operated with Northern). The company also operates the overnight Caledonian Sleeper services between London and Glasgow, Edinburgh, Inverness, Aberdeen and Fort William. In addition to the Sleeper loco-hauled stock (hauled by Class 67s and 90s hired from DB Schenker), the company operates a large fleet of DMUs of Classes 156, 158 and 170 and EMU Classes 314, 318, 320, 334 and 380. One loco-hauled rake is also used on a Fife Circle commuter train, hauled by a Class 67.

South Central
Govia (Go-Ahead/Keolis)
(until 25 July 2015)

Southern

Upon termination of the Southern franchise in July 2015 it is to be combined with the new Thameslink, Southern & Great Northern franchise (also operated by Govia).

Southern operates predominantly commuter services between London, Surrey and Sussex, as well as services along the South Coast between Southampton, Brighton, Hastings and Ashford, and also the cross-London service linking South Croydon and Milton Keynes. It also operates metro services in South London and Gatwick Express, which is a premium non-stop service between London Victoria and Gatwick Airport. Class 171 DMUs are used on Brighton–Ashford and London Bridge–Uckfield services, whilst all other services are in the hands of EMUs of Classes 313, 377, 442 and 455.

South Western
Stagecoach Group
(until 3 February 2017)*

South West Trains

Franchise extension to be negotiated to April 2019.

South West Trains operates trains from London Waterloo to destinations across the South and South-West including Woking, Basingstoke, Southampton, Portsmouth, Salisbury, Exeter, Reading and Weymouth as well as suburban services from Waterloo. SWT also runs services between Ryde and Shanklin on the Isle of Wight, using former London Underground 1938 stock (Class 483). The rest of the fleet consists of DMU Classes 158 and 159 and EMU Classes 444, 450, 455, 456 and 458.

Thameslink & Great Northern
Govia (Go-Ahead/Keolis)
(until 19 September 2021)

Govia Thameslink Railway

The Southern franchise will be combined with Govia Thameslink Railway from July 2015.

Govia operates this franchise as a management contract. GTR operates trains on the Thameslink route between Bedford and Brighton via central London and also on the Sutton and Wimbledon loops. Some trains continue into Southeastern territory to Sevenoaks, Orpington and Ashford. GTR also runs services on the Great Northern route from London King's Cross and Moorgate to Welwyn Garden City, Hertford North, Peterborough, Cambridge and Kings Lynn. The fleet consists of EMU Classes 319, 377 and 387 (the Class 319s are being replaced by Class 387s during 2015) for the Thameslink route services and Classes 313, 317, 321 and 365 for the Great Northern route services.

Trans-Pennine Express
First Group/Keolis
(until 1 April 2015)

TransPennine Express

Franchise extension to be negotiated to February 2016.

TransPennine Express operates predominantly long distance inter-urban services linking major cities across the North of England, along with Edinburgh and Glasgow in Scotland. The main services are Manchester Airport/Manchester Piccadilly–Newcastle/Middlesbrough/ Hull plus Liverpool–Scarborough and Liverpool–Newcastle along the North Trans-Pennine route via Huddersfield, Leeds and York, and Manchester Airport–Cleethorpes along the South Trans-Pennine route via Sheffield. TPE also operates Manchester Airport–Blackpool/ Barrow/Windermere/Edinburgh/Glasgow. The fleet consists of DMU Classes 170 (used on the Hull and Cleethorpes routes) and 185 and also new Class 350 EMUs used on Manchester Airport–Scotland services. The Class 170s will transfer to Chiltern Railways during 2015–16, with Class 156s hired from Northern being used on some Manchester Airport–Blackpool North services.

| **Wales & Borders** | Arriva (Deutsche Bahn) (until 14 October 2018)* | **Arriva Trains Wales** |

The franchise agreement includes the provision for the term to be further extended by mutual agreement by up to five years beyond October 2018. Management of the franchise is devolved to the Welsh Government, but DfT is still the procuring authority.

Arriva Trains Wales operates a mix of long distance, regional and local services throughout Wales, including the Valley Lines network of lines around Cardiff, and also through services to the English border counties and to Manchester and Birmingham. The fleet consists of DMUs of Classes 142, 143, 150, 158 and 175 and two loco-hauled rakes: one used on a premium Welsh Government sponsored service on the Cardiff–Holyhead route, and one used between Manchester/Crewe and Holyhead (both are hauled by a Class 67).

| **West Midlands** | Govia (Go-Ahead/Keolis) (until 19 September 2015)* | **London Midland** |

Franchise extension to be negotiated to June 2017.

London Midland operates long distance and regional services from London Euston to Northampton and Birmingham/Crewe and also between Birmingham and Liverpool as well as local and regional services around Birmingham, including to Stratford-upon-Avon, Worcester, Redditch and Shrewsbury. It also operates the Bedford–Bletchley and Watford Jn–St Albans Abbey branches. The fleet consists of DMU Classes 150, 153, 170 and 172 and EMU Classes 321, 323 and 350.

* Franchise agreement includes provision for an extension of up to seven 4-week reporting periods.

The following operators run non-franchised services (* special summer services only):

Operator	Trading Name	Route
BAA	Heathrow Express	London Paddington–Heathrow Airport
First Hull Trains	First Hull Trains	London King's Cross–Hull
Grand Central	Grand Central	London King's Cross–Sunderland/ Bradford Interchange
North Yorkshire Moors Railway Enterprises	North Yorkshire Moors Railway	Pickering–Grosmont–Whitby/ Battersby
West Coast Railway Company	West Coast Railway Company	Birmingham–Stratford-upon-Avon* Fort William–Mallaig* York–Settle–Carlisle*

INTERNATIONAL PASSENGER OPERATORS

Eurostar International operates passenger services between the UK and mainland Europe. The company, established in 2010, is jointly owned by three shareholders – SNCF (the national operator of France), 55%, SNCB (the national operator of Belgium), 5% and HM Treasury, 40%. The 40% UK stake was transferred from London & Continental Railways (LCR) to HM Treasury in 2014. LCR had bought British Rail's interest in Eurostar at the time of the UK railway privatisation in 1996.

In addition, a service for the conveyance of accompanied road vehicles through the Channel Tunnel is provided by the tunnel operating company, Eurotunnel.

FREIGHT TRAIN OPERATORS

The following operators operate freight services or empty passenger stock workings under "Open Access" arrangements:

Colas Rail: Colas Rail operates a number of On-Track machines and also supplies infrastructure trains for Network Rail. It also now operates a number of different freight flows, including steel, coal, oil and timber. Colas Rail has a small but varied fleet consisting of Class 37s, 47s, 56s, 60s, 66s and 70s. The ten Class 60s were acquired from DBS in 2014 and are currently being returned to service.

DB Schenker Rail (UK): Still the biggest freight operator in the country, DBS (formerly EWS before being bought by DB) has seen some of its core traffic lost to competitors in recent years. It still provides a large number of infrastructure trains to Network Rail and operates coal, steel, intermodal and aggregate trains nationwide. The core fleet is Class 66s. Of the original 250 ordered 176 are still used in the UK, with the remainder having moved to DB's French and Polish operations, although some of the French locos do return to the UK when major maintenance is required. A fleet of around 25 Class 60s are also used on heavier trains.

DBS's six Class 59/2s are used alongside the Mendip Rail 59/0s and 59/1s on stone traffic from the Mendip quarries and around the South-East. DBS's fleet of Class 67s are mainly used on passenger or standby duties for Arriva Trains Wales, Chiltern Railways, East Coast and ScotRail. Class 90s are hired to ScotRail for use on the sleeping car services but see little use on freight, whilst the fleet of Class 92s are mainly used on intermodal duties, including a limited number of overnight trains on High Speed 1.

DBS also operates the Class 325 EMUs for Royal Mail and a number of excursion trains.

Devon & Cornwall Railways (a subsidiary of British American Railway Services): DCRail specialises in short-term freight haulage contracts, mainly in the scrap, coal and aggregates markets, using its fleet of Class 56s. It also provides locomotives from its fleet of 31s or 56s for stock moves or to move On-Track Machines or other equipment.

Direct Rail Services: DRS has built on its original nuclear flask traffic to operate a number of different services. The main flows are intermodal plus the provision of crews and locos to Network Rail for autumn Railhead Treatment Trains and also operates some NR infrastructure trains. Its Class 47s, 57s and 68s are used on excursion work.

DRS has the most varied fleet of locomotives, with Class 20s, 37s, 47s, 57s and 66s working alongside a fleet of Class 68s that are currently being delivered. The company has 25 Class 68s on order as well as ten new Vossloh electric locos (Class 88s), that will also feature a small diesel engine.

Freightliner: Freightliner has two divisions: Intermodal operates container trains from the main Ports at Southampton, Felixstowe, Tilbury and Thamesport to major cities including London, Manchester, Leeds and Birmingham. The Heavy Haul division covers the movement of coal, cement, infrastructure and aggregates nationwide. Most services are worked by Class 66s, with Class 70s used on some of the heavier intermodal trains and some Heavy Haul flows, principally coal, cement and ballast trains. A small fleet of Class 86 and 90 electrics is used on intermodal trains on the Great Eastern and West Coast Main Lines, the Class 86s mainly being used in pairs on the WCML between Crewe and Coatbridge.

GB Railfreight: GBRf, owned by Eurotunnel, operates a mixture of traffic types, mainly using Class 66s together with a small fleet of Class 73s on infrastructure duties in the South-East. A growing fleet of Class 92s is also used on some intermodal flows to/from Dollands Moor or through the Channel Tunnel to Calais. Traffic includes coal, intermodal, biomass, aggregates and gypsum as well as infrastructure services for Network Rail and London Underground.

GBRf also operates some excursion trains, including those using the preserved Class 201 "Hastings" DEMU.

West Coast Railway Company: WCRC has a freight licence but doesn't operate any freight as such – only empty stock movements. Its fleet of 47s, supplemented by a smaller number of 33s, 37s and 57s, is used on excursion work nationwide, including the prestigious Royal Scotsman.

In addition Amey, Balfour Beatty Rail, Harsco Rail, South West Trains, Swietelsky Babcock Rail (SB Rail) and VolkerRail operate trains formed of On-Track Machines.

PROVISION OF INFORMATION

This book has been compiled with care to be as accurate as possible, but in some cases information is not officially available and the publisher cannot be held responsible for any errors or omissions. The author would like to thank all those who have helped with the compilation of this book. These include individuals for their sightings, as well as Train Operating Companies, Freight Companies, Rolling Stock Leasing Companies, spot-hire companies and the Rolling Stock Library.

The authors of this book will be pleased to receive notification of any inaccuracies readers may find in the series, and also any additional information to supplement our records and thus enhance future editions.

Please send comments to: Robert Pritchard, Platform 5 Publishing Ltd, 52 Broadfield Road, Sheffield, S8 0XJ, England.

e-mail: robert@platform5.com   **Tel:** 0114 255 2625.

UPDATES

This book is updated to the start of January 2015. The Platform 5 railway magazine "Today's Railways UK" provides Stock Changes every month to update this book. The magazine also contains news and rolling stock information on the railways of Great Britain and Ireland and is published on the second Monday of every month. For further details of **Today's Railways UK**, please contact Platform 5 Publishing Ltd.

1. LOCOMOTIVES

INTRODUCTION

This section contains details of all locomotives which can run on Britain's national railway network, plus those of Eurotunnel.

Locomotives currently approved for use on the national railway network continue to fall into the four broad types: passenger, freight, mixed traffic and shunting.

Passenger

The number of dedicated passenger locomotives has not changed significantly in recent years. However, the number is expected to decline in the future as new multiple unit stock replaces some of the remaining loco-hauled or propelled trains. Classes 43 (HST) and 91 and some members of Classes 57, 67, 68 and 90 are dedicated to Franchised and Open Access Passenger operations. Excursion trains have a few dedicated locomotives but mainly use locomotives that are best described as mixed traffic.

Freight

By far the most numerous locomotives are those used solely for bulk commodity and intermodal freight. Since 1998 a large number of new Class 66 locomotives have replaced many former BR designs and in more recent years smaller numbers of Class 70s have also been introduced. There are however a significant number of BR era Class 20, 37, 47, 56, 60, 73, 86, 90 and 92 locomotives still in use; their number has increased slightly recently as some locomotives have been reinstated to cope with demand. In addition there is a small fleet of Class 59s acquired privately in the 1980s and 1990s and a small number of re-engined Class 57s in use.

Mixed Traffic

In addition to their use on passenger and commodity freight workings these locomotives are used for stock movements and specialist infrastructure and test trains. The majority, but not all, are fitted with Electric Train Supply. Locomotives from Classes 20, 31, 33, 37, 47, 57, 67, 68 and 90 fall into this category. Also included under this heading are preserved locomotives permitted to operate on the national railway network. Although these have in the past solely operated excursion trains they are increasingly seeing occasional use on other types of trains.

Shunting

Very few shunting locomotives are now permitted to operate freely on the National Railway network. The small number that are have to be fitted with a plethora of safety equipment in order to have engineering acceptance. They are mainly used for local workings such as trips between yards or stock movements between depots and stations. In the main section of this book all such shunting locomotives (Classes 08 and 09) in the fleets that have permitted locomotives are included. Otherwise, shunting locomotives are not permitted to venture from depots or yards onto the national railway network other than into defined limits within interface infrastructure. Generally such locomotives, which includes an increasing number of remotely controlled driverless types, are not included in this book. However, those of BR pedigree, such as Class 08s, can be found in the section Former BR Main Line Locos in Industrial Service.

Locomotives which are owned by, for example, DB Schenker or Freightliner which have been withdrawn from service and are awaiting disposal are listed in the main part of the book. Locomotives which are awaiting disposal at scrapyards are listed in the "Locomotives Awaiting Disposal" section.

Only preserved locomotives which are currently used on the National Rail network are included. Others, which may still be Network Rail registered but not at present certified for use, are not included, but will be found in the Platform 5 book, "Preserved Locomotives of British Railways".

LAYOUT OF INFORMATION

Locomotive classes are listed in numerical order of class. Principal details and dimensions are quoted for each class in metric and/or imperial units as considered appropriate bearing in mind common UK usage.

Where numbers actually carried are different from those officially allocated, these are noted in class headings where appropriate. Where locomotives have been recently renumbered, the most immediate previous number is shown in parentheses. Each locomotive entry is laid out as in the following example:

RSL No.	Detail	Livery	Owner	Pool	Allocn.	Name
59206 *b	**DB**	DB	WDAM	MD		John F. Yeoman Rail Pioneer

Detail Differences. Only detail differences which currently affect the areas and types of train which locomotives may work are shown. All other detail differences are excluded. Where such differences occur within a class or part class, they are shown in the "Detail" column alongside the individual locomotive number.

Codes: Codes are used to denote the livery, owner, pool and depot of each locomotive. Details of these will be found in section 7 of this book.

Depot allocation codes for all locomotives are shown in this book (apart from shunting locomotives (Class 08 & 09) where the actual location of each is shown). It should be noted that today much locomotive maintenance is undertaken away from these depots. This may be undertaken at fuelling points, berthing sidings or similar, or by mobile maintenance teams. Therefore locomotives in particular may not return to their former "home" depots as often as in the past.

(S) denotes that the locomotive is stored (the actual location is shown).

Names: Only names carried with official sanction are listed. Names are shown in UPPER/lower case characters as actually shown on the name carried on the locomotive.

Builders: These are shown in class headings. More details and a full list of builders can be found in section 7.7.

GENERAL INFORMATION

CLASSIFICATION AND NUMBERING

All locomotives are classified and allocated numbers by the Rolling Stock Library under the TOPS numbering system, introduced in 1972. This comprises a two-digit class number followed by a three-digit serial number. Where the actual number carried by a locomotive differs from the allocated number, or where an additional number is carried to the allocated number, this is shown by a note in the class heading.

For diesel locomotives, class numbers offer an indication of engine horsepower as shown in the table below.

Class No. Range	Engine hp
01–14	0–799
15–20	800–1000
21–31	1001–1499
32–39	1500–1999
40–54, 57	2000–2999
55–56, 58–70	3000+

For electric locomotives class numbers are allocated in ascending numerical order under the following scheme:

Class 71–80   Direct current and DC/diesel dual system locomotives.
Class 81 onwards Alternating current and AC/DC dual system locos.

Numbers in the 89xxx series are allocated by the Rolling Stock Library to locomotives which have been deregistered but subsequently re-registered for use on the national railway network and whose original number has already been reused. 89xxx numbers are normally only carried inside locomotive cabs and are not carried externally in normal circumstances.

WHEEL ARRANGEMENT

For main line locomotives the number of driven axles on a bogie or frame is denoted by a letter (A = 1, B = 2, C = 3 etc) and the number of non-powered axles is denoted by a number. The use of the letter "o" after a letter indicates each axle is individually powered, whilst the "+" symbol indicates bogies are inter-coupled.

For shunting locomotives, the Whyte notation is used. In this notation the number of leading wheels are given, followed by the number of driving wheels and then the trailing wheels.

UNITS OF MEASUREMENT

All dimensions and weights are quoted for locomotives in an "as new" condition with all necessary supplies (eg oil, water and sand) on board. Dimensions are quoted in the order length x width. Lengths quoted are over buffers or couplers as appropriate. All widths quoted are maxima. Where two different wheel diameter dimensions are shown, the first refers to powered wheels and the second refers to non-powered wheels. All weights are shown as metric tonnes (t = tonnes).

HAULAGE CAPABILITY OF DIESEL LOCOMOTIVES

The haulage capability of a diesel locomotive depends upon three basic factors:

1. Adhesive weight. The greater the weight on the driving wheels, the greater the adhesion and more tractive power can be applied before wheelslip occurs.

2. The characteristics of its transmission. To start a train the locomotive has to exert a pull at standstill. A direct drive diesel engine cannot do this, hence the need for transmission. This may be mechanical, hydraulic or electric. The present British Standard for locomotives is electric transmission. Here the diesel engine drives a generator or alternator and the current produced is fed to the traction motors. The force produced by each driven wheel depends on the current in its traction motor. In other words, the larger the current, the harder it pulls. As the locomotive speed increases, the current in the traction motor falls, hence the *Maximum Tractive Effort* is the maximum force at its wheels the locomotive can exert at a standstill. The electrical equipment cannot take such high currents for long without overheating. Hence the *Continuous Tractive Effort* is quoted which represents the current which the equipment can take continuously.

3. The power of its engine. Not all power reaches the rail, as electrical machines are approximately 90% efficient. As the electrical energy passes through two such machines (the generator or alternator and the traction motors), the *Power at Rail* is approximately 81% (90% of 90%) of the engine power, less a further amount used for auxiliary equipment such as radiator fans, traction motor blowers, air compressors, battery charging, cab heating, Electric Train Supply (ETS) etc. The power of the locomotive is proportional to the tractive effort times the speed. Hence when on full power there is a speed corresponding to the continuous tractive effort.

HAULAGE CAPABILITY OF ELECTRIC LOCOMOTIVES

Unlike a diesel locomotive, an electric locomotive does not develop its power on board and its performance is determined only by two factors, namely its weight and the characteristics of its electrical equipment. Whereas a diesel locomotive tends to be a constant power machine, the power of an electric locomotive varies considerably. Up to a certain speed it can produce virtually a constant tractive effort. Hence power rises with speed according to the formula given in section three above, until a maximum speed is reached at which tractive effort falls, such that the power also falls. Hence the power at the speed corresponding to the maximum tractive effort is lower than the maximum speed.

BRAKE FORCE

The brake force is a measure of the braking power of a locomotive. This is shown on the locomotive data panels so operating staff can ensure sufficient brake power is available on freight trains.

ELECTRIC TRAIN SUPPLY (ETS)

A number of locomotives are equipped to provide a supply of electricity to the train being hauled to power auxiliaries such as heating, cooling fans, air conditioning and kitchen equipment. ETS is provided from the locomotive by means of a separate alternator (except Class 33 locomotives, which have a DC generator). The ETS index of a locomotive is a measure of the electrical power available for train supply. Class 55 locomotives provide an ETS directly from one of their traction generators into the train line.

Similarly, most loco-hauled coaches also have an ETS index, which in this case is a measure of the power required to operate equipment mounted in the coach. The sum of the ETS indices of all the hauled vehicles in a train must not exceed the ETS index of the locomotive.

ETS is commonly (but incorrectly) known as ETH (Electric Train Heating), which is a throwback to the days before loco-hauled coaches were equipped with electrically powered auxiliary equipment other than for train heating.

ROUTE AVAILABILITY (RA)

This is a measure of a railway vehicle's axle load. The higher the axle load of a vehicle, the higher the RA number on a scale from 1 to 10. Each Network Rail route has a RA number and in general no vehicle with a higher RA number may travel on that route without special clearance.

MULTIPLE & PUSH-PULL WORKING

Multiple working between vehicles (ie two or more powered vehicles being driven from one cab) is facilitated by jumper cables connecting the vehicles. However, not all types are compatible with each other, and a number of different systems are in use, each system being incompatible with any other.

Association of American Railroads (AAR) System: Classes 59, 66, 67, 68 (some) and 70.
Blue Star Coupling Code: Classes 20, 25, 31, 33, 37 40 and 73.
DRS System: Classes 20/3, 37, 47 and 57.
Green Circle Coupling Code: Class 47 (not all equipped).
Orange Square Coupling Code: Class 50.
Red Diamond Coupling Code: Classes 56 and 58.
SR System: Classes 33/1, 73 and various electric multiple units.
Within Own Class only: Classes 43, 60, 68 (some).

Many locomotives use a time-division multiplex (TDM) system for push-pull and multiple working which utilises the existing RCH jumper cables fitted to coaching stock vehicles. Previously these cables had only been used to control train lighting and public address systems.

Class 47 locos 47701–47717 were equipped with an older non-standard TDM system.

ABBREVIATIONS

Standard abbreviations used for the locomotives section are:

a	Train air brake equipment only.
b	Drophead buckeye couplers.
c	Scharfenberg couplers.
d	Fitted with retracted Dellner couplers.
e	European Railway Traffic Management System (ERTMS) signalling equipment fitted.
i	Fitted with Tightlock couplers
k	Fitted with Swinghead Automatic "buckeye" combination couplers.
p	Train air, vacuum and electro-pneumatic brakes.
r	Radio Electric Token Block signalling equipment fitted.
s	Slow Speed Control equipment.
t	tonnes
v	Train vacuum brake only.
x	Train air and vacuum brakes ("Dual brakes").
+	Additional fuel tank capacity.
§	Sandite laying equipment.

In all cases use of the above abbreviations indicates the equipment in question is normally operable. The definition of non-standard abbreviations and symbols is detailed in individual class headings.

1.1. DIESEL LOCOMOTIVES

CLASS 08   BR/ENGLISH ELECTRIC   0-6-0

Built: 1955–62 by BR at Crewe, Darlington, Derby Locomotive, Doncaster or Horwich Works.
Engine: English Electric 6KT of 298 kW (400 hp) at 680 rpm.
Main Generator: English Electric 801.
Traction Motors: Two English Electric 506.
Maximum Tractive Effort: 156 kN (35000 lbf).
Continuous Tractive Effort: 49 kN (11100 lbf) at 8.8 mph.
Power at Rail: 194 kW (260 hp).   **Train Brakes:** Air & vacuum.
Brake Force: 19 t.   **Dimensions:** 8.92 x 2.59 m.
Weight: 49.6–50.4 t.   **Wheel Diameter:** 1372 mm.
Design Speed: 20 mph.   **Maximum Speed:** 15 mph.
Fuel Capacity: 3037 litres.   **RA:** 5.
Train Supply: Not equipped.
Multiple Working: m Equipped for multiple working. All others not equipped.

† – Fitted with remote control equipment.

For shunting locomotives, instead of the two-letter depot code, actual locations at the time of publication are given.

Class 08s that don't have current Network Rail engineering acceptance and are considered to be "in industrial service" can be found in section 1.4 of this book.

08850 has acceptance for use between Battersby and Whitby only, for rescue purposes.

Non-standard liveries/numbering:

08480	Yellow with a red bodyside band. Carries number "TOTON No 1".
08616	Carries number 3783.
08696	Carries no number.
08701	Carries number "Tyne 100".
08721	As **B**, but with a black roof & "Express parcels" branding with red & yellow stripe.
08824	Carries number "IEMD01".
08899	Crimson lake.

Originally numbered in series D3000–D4192.

Class 08/0. Standard Design.

08405	a†	**E**	DB	WQAA	Crewe International Depot (S)
08410	a	**FB**	FW	EFSH	RVEL Derby
08417	a	**Y**	NR	QADD	RVEL Derby
08428	ak	**E**	DB	WQAA	Carlisle Kingmoor Yard (S)
08451		**B**	AM	ATLO	Manchester Longsight Depot
08454		**K**	AM	ATLO	Wolverhampton Oxley Depot
08472	a	**WA**	WA	RFSH	Edinburgh Craigentinny Depot

08480 a	**0**	DB	WQBA	Toton Depot (S)
08483 a	**GL**	FW	EFSH	RVEL Derby
08495 †	**E**	DB	WQBA	Crewe International Depot (S)
08500	**E**	DB	WQCA	Tees Yard (S)
08523	**RS**	RL	MRSO	Inverness Depot
08525	**ST**	EM	EMSL	Leeds Neville Hill Depot
08530	**FL**	P	DFLS	LH Group, Barton-under-Needwood
08531 a	**FL**	P	DFLS	Felixstowe FLT
08567 †	**E**	DB	WQBA	Crewe International Depot (S)
08571 a	**WA**	WA	HBSH	Bounds Green Depot
08575	**FL**	P	DHLT	LH Group, Barton-under-Needwood (S)
08578 †	**E**	DB	WQCA	Toton Depot (S)
08580	**E**	DB	WQCA	Bescot Yards (S)
08585	**FL**	P	DFLS	Felixstowe FLT
08593	**E**	DB	WQCA	Crewe International Depot (S)
08596 a†	**WA**	WA	HBSH	Bounds Green Depot
08605 †	**E**	DB	WQBA	Toton Depot (S)
08611	**V**	AM	ATLO	Manchester Longsight Depot
08615	**WA**	WA	RFSH	Edinburgh Craigentinny Depot
08616	**LM**	LM	EJLO	Birmingham Tyseley Depot
08617	**K**	AM	ATLO	Wembley Depot
08623	**DB**	DB	WSSC	Warrington Yards
08624	**FL**	P	DFLS	Trafford Park FLT
08630	**E**	DB	WQCA	Toton Yards (S)
08632 †	**DB**	DB	WSRC	Mossend Yards
08633 †	**E**	DB	WQCA	Axiom Rail, Stoke-on-Trent Works
08641	**B**	FW	EFSH	Penzance Long Rock Depot
08644	**B**	FW	EFSH	Plymouth Laira Depot
08645	**DG**	FW	EFSH	Plymouth Laira Depot
08653	**E**	DB	WQCA	Toton Yards (S)
08663 a	**FB**	FW	EFSH	Old Oak Common HST Depot
08669 a	**WA**	WA	RFSH	Wabtec Rail, Doncaster Works
08676 †	**E**	DB	WQBA	Toton Depot (S)
08690	**ST**	EM	EMSL	Leeds Neville Hill Depot
08691	**FL**	FL	DFLS	Southampton Maritime FLT
08696 a	**G**	AM	ATLO	Glasgow Polmadie Depot
08701 a†	**RX**	DB	WQCA	Toton Yards (S)
08703 a	**E**	DB	WSSC	Knottingley Depot
08706 †	**E**	DB	WQCA	Crewe International Depot (S)
08709	**E**	DB	WQCA	Bescot Yards (S)
08711 k	**RX**	DB	WQCA	Tees Yard (S)
08714	**E**	DB	WQAA	Crewe International Depot (S)
08721	**0**	AM	ATLO	Liverpool Edge Hill Depot
08724	**WA**	WA	HBSH	Wabtec Rail, Doncaster Works
08735 †	**E**	DB	WQCA	Eastleigh Yards (S)
08737 a†	**E**	DB	WQBA	Crewe International Depot (S)
08738 m	**ECR**	DB	WQCA	Toton Yards (S)
08742 †	**RX**	DB	WSSC	Margam Yard
08752 †	**E**	DB	WSSC	Tyne Yard
08754	**B**	RL	MRSO	Norwich Crown Point Depot
08757 †	**RG**	DB	WQBA	Crewe International Depot (S)

08782 a†	**CU**	DB	WQAA	Doncaster Yards (S)
08784 †	**E**	DB	WQBA	Toton Depot (S)
08785 a	**FL**	P	DFLS	LH Group, Barton-under-Needwood
08788	**K**	RL	MRSO	Inverness Depot
08790	**B**	AM	ATLO	Eastleigh Works
08795	**K**	FW	EFSH	Swansea Landore Depot
08799 a	**E**	DB	WSSC	Westbury Yards
08802 †	**E**	DB	WQAA	Toton Depot (S)
08804 †	**E**	DB	WQBA	Crewe International Depot (S)
08805	**B**	LM	EJLO	Birmingham Soho Depot
08822	**FB**	FW	EFSH	Bristol St Philip's Marsh Depot
08824 ak	**K**	DB	WQAA	Crewe International Depot (S)
08836	**FB**	FW	EFSH	Old Oak Common HST Depot
08847	**CD**	RL	MRSO	RMS Locotec, Washwood Heath
08850	**B**	NY	MBDL	Grosmont Depot
08853 a	**WA**	WA	RFSH	Wabtec Rail, Doncaster Works
08865	**E**	DB	WQBA	Crewe International Depot (S)
08874	**SL**	RL	MRSO	Norwich Crown Point Depot
08877	**DG**	DB	WQCA	Wigan Springs Branch Depot
08879 †	**E**	DB	WSRC	Hinksey Yard
08886	**E**	DB	WQCA	Crewe International Depot (S)
08887 a	**B**	AM	ATLO	Wembley Depot
08888 †	**E**	DB	WQAA	Didcot Yards (S)
08891	**FL**	P	DHLT	LH Group, Barton-under-Needwood (S)
08899	**0**	EM	EMSL	Derby Etches Park Depot
08904	**E**	DB	WSGC	Eastleigh Yards
08907	**DB**	DB	WQAA	Bescot Yards (S)
08908	**ST**	EM	EMSL	Leeds Neville Hill Depot
08922	**DG**	DB	WQBA	Toton Depot (S)
08925	**G**	GB	GBWM	March Whitemoor Yard
08934 a	**VP**	GB	GBWM	Cardiff Tidal Steelworks
08939 m	**ECR**	DB	WQCA	Toton Yards (S)
08948 c	**EP**	EU	GPSS	Temple Mills Depot
08950	**ST**	EM	EMSL	Leeds Neville Hill Depot
08954	**B**	AM	ATLO	Glasgow Polmadie Depot

Class 08/9. Reduced height cab. Converted 1985–87 by BR at Landore.

08993	**E**	DB	WQBA	Axiom Rail, Stoke-on-Trent Works (S)
08994 a	**E**	DB	WQCA	Toton Depot (S)
08995 a	**E**	DB	WQBA	Crewe International Depot (S)

CLASS 09   BR/ENGLISH ELECTRIC   0-6-0

Built: 1959–62 by BR at Darlington or Horwich Works.
Engine: English Electric 6KT of 298 kW (400 hp) at 680 rpm.
Main Generator: English Electric 801.
Traction Motors: English Electric 506.
Maximum Tractive Effort: 111 kN (25000 lbf).
Continuous Tractive Effort: 39 kN (8800 lbf) at 11.6 mph.
Power at Rail: 201 kW (269 hp).   **Train Brakes:** Air & vacuum.
Brake Force: 19 t.   **Dimensions:** 8.92 x 2.59 m.
Weight: 49 t.   **Wheel Diameter:** 1372 mm.
Design Speed: 27 mph.   **Maximum Speed:** 27 mph.
Fuel Capacity: 3037 litres.   **RA:** 5.
Train Supply: Not equipped.   **Multiple Working:** Not equipped.

Class 09s that don't have current Network Rail engineering acceptance and are considered to be "in industrial service" can be found in section 1.4 of this book.

Class 09/0 were originally numbered D3665–D3671, D3719–D3721, D4099–D4114.

Class 09/0. Built as Class 09.

09002	**G**	GB	GBWM	March Whitemoor Yard
09006	**E**	DB	WQCA	Toton Depot (S)
09009	**G**	GB	GBWM	Dagenham Yard
09026 a	**G**	SN	HWSU	Brighton Lovers Walk Depot

Class 09/1. Converted from Class 08. 110 V electrical equipment.
Converted: 1992–1993 by RFS Industries, Kilnhurst.

| 09106 (08759) | **DB** | DB | WSSC | Warrington Yards |

Class 09/2. Converted from Class 08. 90 V electrical equipment.
Converted: 1992 by RFS Industries, Kilnhurst.

| 09201 (08421) ak† | **DG** | DB | WQBA | Toton Depot (S) |

Class 08 and Class 09 names:

08451	M.A. SMITH	08782	CASTLETON WORKS
08495	NOEL KIRTON OBE	08790	Steve Purser
08525	DUNCAN BEDFORD	08799	FRED
08585	Vicky	08805	CONCORDE
08616	TYSELEY 100	08822	John
08630	BOB BROWN	08874	Catherine
08645	Mike Baggott	08899	Midland Counties Railway
08669	Bob Machin		175 1839–2014
08690	DAVID THIRKILL	08908	IVAN STEPHENSON
08691	Terri	08950	DAVID LIGHTFOOT
08721	DOWNHILL C.S.	09026	Cedric Wares

CLASS 20   ENGLISH ELECTRIC   Bo-Bo

Built: 1957–68 by English Electric at Vulcan Foundry, Newton-le-Willows or by Robert Stephenson & Hawthorns at Darlington.
Engine: English Electric 8SVT Mk II of 746 kW (1000 hp) at 850 rpm.
Main Generator: English Electric 819/3C.
Traction Motors: English Electric 526/5D or 526/8D.
Maximum Tractive Effort: 187 kN (42000 lbf).
Continuous Tractive Effort: 111 kN (25000 lbf) at 11 mph.

Power at Rail: 574 kW (770 hp).	**Train Brakes:** Air & vacuum.
Brake Force: 35 t.	**Dimensions:** 14.25 x 2.67 m.
Weight: 73.4–73.5 t.	**Wheel Diameter:** 1092 mm.
Design Speed: 75 mph.	**Maximum Speed:** 75 mph.
Fuel Capacity: 1727 litres.	**RA:** 5.
Train Supply: Not equipped.	**Multiple Working:** Blue Star.

Class 20s that don't have current Network Rail engineering acceptance and are considered to be "in industrial service" can be found in section 1.4 of this book.

Originally numbered in series D8007–D8190, D8315–D8325.

Non-standard liveries/numbering:

20088 RFS grey (carries No. 2017).
20227 White, red & blue with London Underground roundels.

Class 20/0. Standard Design.

20016	**B**	HN	HNRS	LM (S)	
20081	**B**	HN	HNRS	LM (S)	
20088	**0**	HN	HNRS	LM (S)	
20092	**U**	HN	HNRS	LM (S)	
20096	**B**	HN	GBEE	BH	
20107	**B**	HN	GBEE	BH	
20118	**F0**	HN	GBEE	BH	Saltburn-by-the-Sea
20132	**F0**	HN	GBEE	BH	Barrow Hill Depot
20142	**BB**	20	GBEE	SK	
20189	**BB**	20	GBEE	SK	
20205	**B**	2L	MOLO	SK	
20227	**0**	2L	MOLO	SK	

Class 20/3. Direct Rail Services refurbished locos. Details as Class 20/0 except:

Refurbished: 15 locomotives were refurbished 1995–96 by Brush Traction at Loughborough (20301–305) or 1997–98 by RFS(E) at Doncaster (20306–315). Disc indicators or headcode panels removed.

Train Brakes: Air.	**Maximum Speed:** 60 mph (+ 75 mph).
Weight: 73 t (+ 76 t).	**Fuel Capacity:** 2909 (+ 4909) litres.
Brake Force: 35 t (+ 31 t).	**RA:** 5 (+ 6).
Multiple Working: DRS system.	

20301	(20047) r	**DS**	DR	XHSS	BH (S)	Max Joule 1958–1999
20302	(20084) r	**DS**	DR	XHSS	BH (S)	
20303	(20127) r	**DS**	DR	XHSS	BH (S)	
20304	(20120) r	**DS**	DR	XHNC	KM	

20305	(20095)	r	**DS**	DR	XHNC	KM	Gresty Bridge
20308	(20187)	r+	**DS**	DR	XHNC	KM	
20309	(20075)	r+	**DS**	DR	XHNC	KM	
20311	(20102)	r+	**HN**	HN	GBEE	BH	
20312	(20042)	r+	**DS**	DR	XHNC	KM	
20314	(20117)	r+	**HN**	HN	GBEE	BH	

Class 20/9. Harry Needle Railroad Company (former Hunslet-Barclay/ DRS) locos. Details as Class 20/0 except:

Refurbished: 1989 by Hunslet-Barclay at Kilmarnock.
Train Brakes: Air.   **Fuel Capacity:** 1727 (+ 4727) litres.
RA: 5 (+ 6).

20901	(20101)		**GB**	HN	GBEE	BH
20903	(20083)	+	**DR**	HN	HNRS	BO (S)
20904	(20041)	+	**DR**	HN	HNRS	BO (S)
20905	(20225)	+	**GB**	HN	GBEE	BH

CLASS 25   BR/BEYER PEACOCK/SULZER   Bo-Bo

Built: 1965 by Beyer Peacock at Gorton.
Engine: Sulzer 6LDA28-B of 930 kW (1250 hp) at 750 rpm.
Main Generator: AEI RTB15656.   **Traction Motors:** AEI 253AY.
Maximum Tractive Effort: 200 kN (45000 lbf).
Continuous Tractive Effort: 93 kN (20800 lbf) at 17.1 mph.
Power at Rail: 708 kW (949 hp).   **Train Brakes:** Air & vacuum.
Brake Force: 38 t.   **Dimensions:** 15.39 x 2.73 m.
Weight: 71.5 t.   **Wheel Diameter:** 1143 mm.
Design Speed: 90 mph.   **Maximum Speed:** 60 mph.
Fuel Capacity: 2270 litres.   **RA:** 5.
Train Supply: Not equipped.   **Multiple Working:** Blue Star.

Original number is D7628, which the loco currently carries.

Only certified for use on Network Rail metals between Whitby and Battersby, as an extension of North Yorkshire Moors Railway services.

25278		**GG**	NY	MBDL	NY	SYBILLA

CLASS 31   BRUSH/ENGLISH ELECTRIC   A1A-A1A

Built: 1958–62 by Brush Traction at Loughborough.
Engine: English Electric 12SVT of 1100 kW (1470 hp) at 850 rpm.
Main Generator: Brush TG160-48.   **Traction Motors:** Brush TM73-68.
Maximum Tractive Effort: 160 kN (35900 lbf).
Continuous Tractive Effort: 83 kN (18700 lbf) at 23.5 mph.
Power at Rail: 872 kW (1170 hp).   **Train Brakes:** Air & vacuum.
Brake Force: 49 t.   **Dimensions:** 17.30 x 2.67 m.
Weight: 106.7–111 t.   **Wheel Diameter:** 1092/1003 mm.
Design Speed: 90 mph.   **Maximum Speed:** 90 mph.
Fuel Capacity: 2409 litres.   **RA:** 5 or 6.
Train Supply: Not equipped.   **Multiple Working:** Blue Star.

Originally numbered D5520–D5699, D5800–D5862 (not in order).

Non-standard numbering: 31190 Also carries number D5613.

Class 31/1. Standard Design. RA: 5.

31105	**Y**	NR	QADD	ZA	
31106 a	**B**	HJ	RVLO	ZA (S)	
31128	**B**	NS	NRLO	NY	CHARYBDIS
31190	**G**	BA	HTLX	WH	
31233 a	**Y**	NR	QADD	ZA	
31285	**Y**	NR	QADD	ZA	

Class 31/4. Electric Train Supply equipment. RA: 6.
Train Supply: Electric, index 66.

31452	**DC**	BA	HTLX	ZA	
31454	**IC**	BA	HTLX	WH (S)	
31459	**K**	BA	RVLO	ZA (S)	CERBERUS
31465	**Y**	NR	QADD	ZA	
31468	**FR**	BA	RVLO	WO (S)	HYDRA

Class 31/6. ETS through wiring and controls. RA: 5.

31601 (31186)	**DC**	BA	HTLX	WH	
31602 (31191)	**Y**	BA	HTLX	WO (S)	

CLASS 33   BRCW/SULZER   Bo-Bo

Built: 1960–62 by the Birmingham Railway Carriage & Wagon Company at Smethwick.
Engine: Sulzer 8LDA28 of 1160 kW (1550 hp) at 750 rpm.
Main Generator: Crompton Parkinson CG391B1.
Traction Motors: Crompton Parkinson C171C2.
Maximum Tractive Effort: 200 kN (45000 lbf).
Continuous Tractive Effort: 116 kN (26000 lbf) at 17.5 mph.
Power at Rail: 906 kW (1215 hp).   **Train Brakes:** Air & vacuum.
Brake Force: 35 t.   **Dimensions:** 15.47 x 2.82 (2.64 m 33/2).
Weight: 76-78 t.   **Wheel Diameter:** 1092 mm.
Design Speed: 85 mph.   **Maximum Speed:** 85 mph.
Fuel Capacity: 3410 litres.   **RA:** 6.
Train Supply: Electric, index 48 (750 V DC only).
Multiple Working: Blue Star.

Originally numbered in series D6500–D6597 but not in order.

Non-standard numbering: 33012 Carries number D6515.

Class 33/0. Standard Design.

33012	**G**	71	MBDL	Swanage Rly	Lt Jenny Lewis RN
33025	**WC**	WC	AWCX	SH (S)	Glen Falloch
33029	**WC**	WC	AWCA	CS	
33030	**DR**	WC	AWCX	CS (S)	

Class 33/2. Built to former Loading Gauge of Tonbridge–Battle Line.
Equipped with slow speed control.

33207	**WC**	WC	AWCA	CS	Jim Martin

CLASS 37   ENGLISH ELECTRIC   Co-Co

Built: 1960–66 by English Electric at Vulcan Foundry, Newton-le-Willows or by Robert Stephenson & Hawthorns at Darlington.
Engine: English Electric 12CSVT of 1300 kW (1750 hp) at 850 rpm.
Main Generator: English Electric 822/10G.
Traction Motors: English Electric 538/A.
Maximum Tractive Effort: 247 kN (55500 lbf).
Continuous Tractive Effort: 156 kN (35000 lbf) at 13.6 mph.
Power at Rail: 932 kW (1250 hp).   **Train Brakes:** Air & vacuum.
Brake Force: 50 t.   **Dimensions:** 18.75 x 2.74 m.
Weight: 102.8–108.4 t.   **Wheel Diameter:** 1092 mm.
Design Speed: 90 mph.   **Maximum Speed:** 80 mph.
Fuel Capacity: 4046 (+ 7683) litres.   **RA:** 5 (§ 6).
Train Supply: Not equipped.
Multiple Working: Blue Star († DRS system).

Originally numbered D6600–D6608, D6700–D6999 (not in order).

Class 37/0. Standard Design. Details as above.

37038	a†	**DR**	DR	XHSS	LB (S)
37059	ar+†	**DI**	DR	XHNC	KM
37069	ar+†	**DS**	DR	XHSS	LB (S)
37116	+	**B**	CS	COTS	WH (S)
37165	a+	**CE**	WC	AWCX	CS (S)
37175	a	**CS**	CS	COTS	RU
37194	a+†	**DS**	DR	XHNC	KM
37198	+	**Y**	NR	MBDL	BO (S) CHIEF ENGINEER
37214		**WC**	WC	AWCX	CS (S)
37218	ar+†	**DI**	DR	XHNC	KM
37219		**CS**	CS	COTS	RU
37259	ar†	**DS**	DR	XHNC	KM

Class 37/4. Refurbished with electric train supply equipment. Main generator replaced by alternator. Regeared (CP7) bogies. Details as Class 37/0 except:
Main Alternator: Brush BA1005A.   **Power At Rail:** 935 kW (1254 hp).
Traction Motors: English Electric 538/5A.
Maximum Tractive Effort: 256 kN (57440 lbf).
Continuous Tractive Effort: 184 kN (41250 lbf) at 11.4 mph.
Weight: 107 t.   **Design Speed:** 80 mph.
Fuel Capacity: 7683 litres.
Train Supply: Electric, index 30.

37401	ar†	**BL**	DR	XHHP	ZA (S) Mary Queen of Scots
37402	a	**DS**	DR	XHAC	KM Stephen Middlemore 23.12.1954–8.6.2013
37405	ar	**DS**	DR	XHAC	KM
37409	ar†	**DS**	DR	XHAC	KM Lord Hinton
37419	ar	**DS**	DR	XHAC	KM Carl Haviland 1954–2012
37421		**CS**	CS	COTS	RU
37422	ar	**DS**	DR	XHHP	BH (S)
37423	ar†	**DI**	DR	XHAC	KM Spirit of the Lakes
37425	ar	**DS**	DR	XHAC	KM Sir Robert McAlpine/Concrete Bob

Class 37/5. Refurbished without train supply equipment. Main generator replaced by alternator. Regeared (CP7) bogies. Details as Class 37/4 except:
Power At Rail: 932 kW (1250 hp).
Maximum Tractive Effort: 248 kN (55590 lbf).
Continuous Tractive Effort: 184 kN (41250 lbf) at 11.4 mph.
Weight: 106.1–110.0 t.

37503	r§	**E**	DR	XHHP	BH (S)
37510	a	**DS**	DR	XHSS	BH (S)
37516	s	**WC**	WC	AWCA	CS	Loch Laidon
37517	as	**LH**	WC	AWCX	CS (S)
37518	ar	**IC**	WC	AWCA	CS	Fort William/An Gearasdan
37521	r§	**E**	DR	XHHP	BH (S)	English China Clays

Class 37/6. Originally refurbished for Nightstar services. Main generator replaced by alternator. UIC jumpers. Details as Class 37/5 except:
Maximum Speed: 90 mph.   **Train Brake:** Air.
Train Supply: Not equipped, but electric through wired.
Multiple Working: DRS system.

37601	a	**DS**	DR	XHNC	KM	Class 37-'Fifty'
37602	ar	**DS**	DR	XHNC	KM
37603	a	**DS**	DR	XHNC	KM
37604	a	**DS**	DR	XHNC	KM
37605	ar	**DS**	DR	XHNC	KM
37606	a	**DS**	DR	XHNC	KM
37607	ar	**DS**	DR	XHNC	KM
37608	ar	**DS**	DR	XHNC	KM
37609	a	**DI**	DR	XHNC	KM
37610	ar	**DS**	DR	XHNC	KM	T.S.(Ted) Cassady 14.5.61–6.4.08
37611	a	**DS**	DR	XHNC	KM
37612	a	**DS**	DR	XHNC	KM

Class 37/5 continued.

37667	arst	**DS**	DR	XHNC	KM
37668	s	**WC**	WC	AWCA	CS
37669	r	**WC**	WC	AWCA	CS
37670	r	**DB**	DR	XHSS	ZA (S)
37676	a	**WC**	WC	AWCA	CS (S)	Loch Rannoch
37682	ar	**DS**	DR	XHSS	KM (S)
37685	a	**WC**	WC	AWCA	CS	Loch Arkaig
37688	art	**DS**	DR	XHNC	KM	Kingmoor TMD

Class 37/7. Refurbished locos. Main generator replaced by alternator. Regeared (CP7) bogies. Ballast weights added. Details as Class 37/5 except:
Main Alternator: GEC G564AZ (37796–803) Brush BA1005A (others).
Maximum Tractive Effort: 276 kN (62000 lbf).
Weight: 120 t.   **RA:** 7.

37703		**DR**	DR	XHHP	Bo'ness
37706		**WC**	WC	AWCA	CS
37710		**LH**	WC	AWCX	CS (S)
37712	a	**WC**	WC	AWCX	CS (S)

37714	**DR**	DR	XHHP	BH (S)
37716	**DI**	DR	XHHP	ZA (S)
37718	**GIF**	DR	XHHP	ZA (S)
37800	**GIF**	EP	EPUK	BH (S)
37884	**EX**	EP	EPUK	WH

Class 97/3. Class 37s refurbished for Network Rail for use on the Cambrian Lines which are signalled by ERTMS. Details as Class 37/0.

97301 (37100) e	**Y**	NR	QETS	ZA	
97302 (37170) e	**Y**	NR	QETS	ZA	
97303 (37178) e	**Y**	NR	QETS	ZA	
97304 (37217) e	**Y**	NR	QETS	ZA	John Tiley

CLASS 40   ENGLISH ELECTRIC   1Co-Co1

Built: 1958–62 by English Electric at Vulcan Foundry, Newton-le-Willows.
Engine: English Electric 16SVT Mk2 of 1490 kW (2000 hp) at 850 rpm.
Main Generator: English Electric 822/4C.
Traction Motors: English Electric 526/5D or EE526/7D.
Maximum Tractive Effort: 231 kN (52000 lbf).
Continuous Tractive Effort: 137 kN (30900 lbf) at 18.8 mph.

Power at Rail: 1160 kW (1550 hp).	**Train Brakes:** Air & vacuum.
Brake Force: 51 t.	**Dimensions:** 21.18 x 2.78 m.
Weight: 132 t.	**Wheel Diameter:** 914/1143 mm.
Design Speed: 90 mph.	**Maximum Speed:** 90 mph.
Fuel Capacity: 3250 litres.	**RA:** 6.
Train Supply: Steam.	**Multiple Working:** Blue Star.

Originally numbered D345. Currently carries No. 345.

40145	**B**	40	ELRD	BQ

CLASS 43   BREL/PAXMAN   Bo-Bo

Built: 1975–82 by BREL at Crewe Works.
Engine: MTU 16V4000 R41R of 1680kW (2250 hp) at 1500 rpm.
(* Paxman 12VP185 of 1565 kW (2100 hp) at 1500 rpm.)
Main Alternator: Brush BA1001B.
Traction Motors: Brush TMH68–46 or GEC G417AZ (43124–152), frame mounted.
Maximum Tractive Effort: 80 kN (17980 lbf).
Continuous Tractive Effort: 46 kN (10340 lbf) at 64.5 mph.

Power at Rail: 1320 kW (1770 hp).	**Train Brakes:** Air.
Brake Force: 35 t.	**Dimensions:** 17.79 x 2.74 m.
Weight: 70.25–75.0 t.	**Wheel Diameter:** 1020 mm.
Design Speed: 125 mph.	**Maximum Speed:** 125 mph.
Fuel Capacity: 4500 litres.	**RA:** 5.
Train Supply: Three-phase electric.	

Multiple Working: Within class, jumpers at non-driving end only.

† Buffer fitted.

43013, 43014 & 43062 are fitted with measuring apparatus & front-end cameras.

Advertising livery: 43163 – Visit Plymouth (blue).

43002	**FB**	A	EFPC	LA	
43003	**FB**	A	EFPC	LA	ISAMBARD KINGDOM BRUNEL
43004	**FB**	A	EFPC	LA	First for the future/
					First ar gyfer y dyfodol
43005	**FB**	A	EFPC	LA	
43009	**FB**	A	EFPC	LA	
43010	**FB**	A	EFPC	LA	
43012	**FB**	A	EFPC	LA	
43013 †	**Y**	P	QCAR	EC	
43014 †	**Y**	P	QCAR	EC	The Railway Observer
43015	**FB**	A	EFPC	LA	
43016	**FB**	A	EFPC	LA	
43017	**FB**	A	EFPC	LA	Hannahs discoverhannahs.org
43018	**FB**	A	EFPC	LA	
43020	**FB**	A	EFPC	LA	MTU Power. Passion. Partnership
43021	**FB**	A	EFPC	LA	David Austin – Cartoonist
43022	**FB**	A	EFPC	LA	
43023	**FB**	A	EFPC	LA	
43024	**FB**	A	EFPC	LA	Great Western Society 1961–2011
					Didcot Railway Centre
43025	**FB**	A	EFPC	LA	IRO The Institution of Railway Operators
					2000–2010 TEN YEARS
					PROMOTING OPERATIONAL EXCELLENCE
43026	**FB**	A	EFPC	LA	
43027	**FB**	A	EFPC	LA	Glorious Devon
43028	**FB**	A	EFPC	LA	
43029	**FB**	A	EFPC	LA	
43030	**FB**	A	EFPC	LA	Christian Lewis Trust
43031	**FB**	A	EFPC	LA	
43032	**FB**	A	EFPC	LA	
43033	**FB**	A	EFPC	LA	Driver Brian Cooper
					15 June 1947–5 October 1999
43034	**FB**	A	EFPC	LA	TravelWatch SouthWest
43035	**FB**	A	EFPC	LA	
43036	**FB**	A	EFPC	LA	
43037	**FB**	A	EFPC	LA	PENYDARREN
43040	**FB**	A	EFPC	LA	Bristol St. Philip's Marsh
43041	**FB**	A	EFPC	LE	Meningitis Trust Support for Life
43042	**FB**	A	EFPC	LE	
43043 *	**ST**	P	EMPC	NL	
43044 *	**ST**	P	EMPC	NL	
43045 *	**ST**	P	EMPC	NL	
43046 *	**ST**	P	EMPC	NL	
43047 *	**ST**	P	EMPC	NL	
43048 *	**ST**	P	EMPC	NL	T.C.B. Miller MBE
43049 *	**ST**	P	EMPC	NL	Neville Hill
43050 *	**ST**	P	EMPC	NL	
43052 *	**ST**	P	EMPC	NL	
43053	**FB**	P	EFPC	LE	University of Worcester

43054	*	**ST**	P	EMPC	NL	
43055	*	**ST**	P	EMPC	NL	The Sheffield Star 125 Years
43056		**FB**	P	EFPC	LE	The Royal British Legion
43058	*	**ST**	P	EMPC	NL	
43059	*	**ST**	P	EMPC	NL	
43060	*	**ST**	P	EMPC	NL	
43061	*	**ST**	P	EMPC	NL	
43062		**Y**	P	QCAR	EC	John Armitt
43063		**FB**	P	EFPC	LE	
43064	*	**ST**	P	EMPC	NL	
43066	*	**ST**	P	EMPC	NL	
43069		**FB**	P	EFPC	LE	
43070		**FB**	P	EFPC	LE	The Corps of Royal Electrical and Mechanical Engineers
43071		**FB**	P	EFPC	LE	
43073	*	**ST**	P	EMPC	NL	
43075	*	**ST**	P	EMPC	NL	
43076	*	**ST**	P	EMPC	NL	IN SUPPORT OF HELP for HEROES
43078		**FB**	P	EFPC	LE	
43079		**FB**	P	EFPC	LE	
43081	*	**ST**	P	EMPC	NL	
43082	*	**ST**	P	EMPC	NL	RAILWAY children – THE VOICE FOR STREET CHILDREN WORLDWIDE
43083	*	**ST**	P	EMPC	NL	
43086		**FB**	P	EFPC	OO	
43087		**FB**	P	EFPC	OO	11 Explosive Ordnance Disposal Regiment Royal Logistic Corps
43088		**FB**	P	EFPC	OO	
43089	*	**ST**	P	EMPC	NL	
43091		**FB**	P	EFPC	OO	
43092		**FB**	FG	EFPC	OO	
43093		**FB**	FG	EFPC	OO	
43094		**FB**	FG	EFPC	OO	
43097		**FB**	FG	EFPC	OO	Environment Agency
43098		**FB**	FG	EFPC	OO	
43122		**FB**	FG	EFPC	OO	
43124		**FB**	A	EFPC	LE	
43125		**FB**	A	EFPC	LE	
43126		**FB**	A	EFPC	LE	
43127		**FB**	A	EFPC	LE	Sir Peter Parker 1924–2002 Cotswold Line 150
43128		**FB**	A	EFPC	LE	
43129		**FB**	A	EFPC	LE	
43130		**FB**	A	EFPC	LE	
43131		**FB**	A	EFPC	LE	
43132		**FB**	A	EFPC	LE	We Save the Children – Will You?
43133		**FB**	A	EFPC	LE	
43134		**FB**	A	EFPC	LE	
43135		**FB**	A	EFPC	LE	
43136		**FB**	A	EFPC	LE	
43137		**FB**	A	EFPC	LE	Newton Abbot 150

43138	**FB**	A	EFPC	LE	
43139	**FB**	A	EFPC	LE	Driver Stan Martin
					25 June 1950 – 6 November 2004
43140	**FB**	A	EFPC	LE	Landore Diesel Depot
					1963 Celebrating 50 years 2013/
					Depo Diesel Glandŵr
					1963 Dathlu 50 Mlynedd 2013
43141	**FB**	A	EFPC	LE	
43142	**FB**	A	EFPC	LE	Reading Panel Signal Box 1965–2010
43143	**FB**	A	EFPC	LE	Stroud 700
43144	**FB**	A	EFPC	LE	
43145	**FB**	A	EFPC	LE	
43146	**FB**	A	EFPC	LE	
43147	**FB**	A	EFPC	LE	Royal Marines
					Celebrating 350 Years
43148	**FB**	A	EFPC	LE	
43149	**FB**	A	EFPC	LE	University of Plymouth
43150	**FB**	A	EFPC	LE	
43151	**FB**	A	EFPC	LE	
43152	**FB**	A	EFPC	LE	
43153	**FB**	FG	EFPC	OO	
43154	**FB**	FG	EFPC	OO	
43155	**FB**	FG	EFPC	OO	The Red Arrows
					50 Seasons of Excellence
43156	**FB**	P	EFPC	OO	Dartington International Summer School
43158	**FB**	FG	EFPC	OO	
43159	**FB**	P	EFPC	OO	
43160	**FB**	P	EFPC	OO	Sir Moir Lockhead OBE
43161	**FB**	P	EFPC	OO	
43162	**FB**	P	EFPC	OO	
43163	**AL**	A	EFPC	OO	
43164	**FB**	A	EFPC	OO	
43165	**FB**	A	EFPC	OO	Prince Michael of Kent
43168	**FB**	A	EFPC	OO	
43169	**FB**	A	EFPC	OO	THE NATIONAL TRUST
43170	**FB**	A	EFPC	OO	
43171	**FB**	A	EFPC	OO	
43172	**FB**	A	EFPC	OO	
43174	**FB**	A	EFPC	OO	
43175	**FB**	A	EFPC	OO	GWR 175TH ANNIVERSARY
43176	**FB**	A	EFPC	OO	
43177	**FB**	A	EFPC	OO	
43179	**FB**	A	EFPC	OO	Pride of Laira
43180	**FB**	P	EFPC	OO	
43181	**FB**	A	EFPC	OO	
43182	**FB**	A	EFPC	OO	
43183	**FB**	A	EFPC	OO	
43185	**FB**	A	EFPC	OO	Great Western
43186	**FB**	A	EFPC	OO	
43187	**FB**	A	EFPC	OO	
43188	**FB**	A	EFPC	OO	

43189	**FB**	A	EFPC	OO	RAILWAY HERITAGE TRUST
43190	**FB**	A	EFPC	OO	
43191	**FB**	A	EFPC	OO	
43192	**FB**	A	EFPC	OO	
43193	**FB**	P	EFPC	OO	
43194	**FB**	FG	EFPC	OO	
43195	**FB**	P	EFPC	OO	
43196	**FB**	P	EFPC	OO	
43197	**FB**	P	EFPC	OO	
43198	**FB**	FG	EFPC	OO	Oxfordshire 2007

Class 43/2. Rebuilt East Coast, CrossCountry and Grand Central power cars. Power cars have been renumbered by adding 200 to their original number or 400 to their original number (Grand Central), except 43123 which became 43423.

43206 (43006)	**EC**	A	IECP	EC	
43207 (43007)	**XC**	A	EHPC	EC	
43208 (43008)	**NX**	A	IECP	EC	Lincolnshire Echo
43238 (43038)	**EC**	A	IECP	EC	
43239 (43039)	**EC**	A	IECP	EC	
43251 (43051)	**EC**	P	IECP	EC	
43257 (43057)	**EC**	P	IECP	EC	
43272 (43072)	**EC**	P	IECP	EC	
43274 (43074)	**EC**	P	IECP	EC	
43277 (43077)	**EC**	P	IECP	EC	
43285 (43085)	**XC**	P	EHPC	EC	
43290 (43090)	**EC**	P	IECP	EC	mtu fascination of power
43295 (43095)	**EC**	A	IECP	EC	
43296 (43096)	**EC**	A	IECP	EC	
43299 (43099)	**EC**	P	IECP	EC	
43300 (43100)	**EC**	P	IECP	EC	Craigentinny 100 YEARS 1914–2014
43301 (43101)	**XC**	P	EHPC	EC	
43302 (43102)	**EC**	P	IECP	EC	
43303 (43103)	**XC**	P	EHPC	EC	
43304 (43104)	**XC**	A	EHPC	EC	
43305 (43105)	**EC**	A	IECP	EC	
43306 (43106)	**EC**	A	IECP	EC	
43307 (43107)	**EC**	A	IECP	EC	
43308 (43108)	**EC**	A	IECP	EC	HIGHLAND CHIEFTAIN
43309 (43109)	**EC**	A	IECP	EC	
43310 (43110)	**EC**	A	IECP	EC	
43311 (43111)	**EC**	A	IECP	EC	
43312 (43112)	**EC**	A	IECP	EC	
43313 (43113)	**EC**	A	IECP	EC	
43314 (43114)	**EC**	A	IECP	EC	
43315 (43115)	**EC**	A	IECP	EC	
43316 (43116)	**EC**	A	IECP	EC	
43317 (43117)	**EC**	A	IECP	EC	
43318 (43118)	**EC**	A	IECP	EC	
43319 (43119)	**EC**	A	IECP	EC	

43320	(43120)	**NX**	A	IECP	EC
43321	(43121)	**XC**	P	EHPC	EC
43357	(43157)	**XC**	P	EHPC	EC
43366	(43166)	**XC**	A	EHPC	EC
43367	(43167)	**EC**	A	IECP	EC	DELTIC 50 1955–2005
43378	(43178)	**XC**	A	EHPC	EC
43384	(43184)	**XC**	A	EHPC	EC
43423	(43123) †	**GC**	A	GCHP	HT	'VALENTA' 1972–2010
43465	(43065) †	**GC**	A	GCHP	HT
43467	(43067) †	**GC**	A	GCHP	HT
43468	(43068) †	**GC**	A	GCHP	HT
43480	(43080) †	**GC**	A	GCHP	HT
43484	(43084) †	**GC**	A	GCHP	HT	PETER FOX 1942–2011 PLATFORM 5

CLASS 47   BR/BRUSH/SULZER   Co-Co

Built: 1963–67 by Brush Traction, at Loughborough or by BR at Crewe Works.
Engine: Sulzer 12LDA28C of 1920 kW (2580 hp) at 750 rpm.
Main Generator: Brush TG160-60 Mk4 or TM172-50 Mk1.
Traction Motors: Brush TM64-68 Mk1 or Mk1A.
Maximum Tractive Effort: 267 kN (60000 lbf).
Continuous Tractive Effort: 133 kN (30000 lbf) at 26 mph.
Power at Rail: 1550 kW (2080 hp).   **Train Brakes:** Air.
Brake Force: 61 t.   **Dimensions:** 19.38 x 2.79 m.
Weight: 111.5–120.6 t.   **Wheel Diameter:** 1143 mm.
Design Speed: 95 mph.
Maximum Speed: 95 mph (* 75 mph).
Fuel Capacity: 3273 (+ 5887).   **RA:** 6 or 7.
Train Supply: Not equipped.
Multiple Working: m Green Circle (operational locos only).

Originally numbered in series D1100–D1111, D1500–D1999 but not in order.

Non-standard liveries/numbering:

47270	Also carries the number 1971.
47773	Also carries the number D1755.
47798	Royal Train claret with Rail Express Systems markings.
47812	Also carries the number D1916.

Class 47/0 (Dual-braked locos) or Class 47/2 (Air-braked locos). Standard Design. Details as above.

47194	a+	**F**	WC	AWCX	CS (S)
47236	+	**FE**	WC	AWCX	CS (S)
47237	x+	**WC**	WC	AWCA	CS
47245	x+m	**WC**	WC	AWCA	CS
47270	a+	**B**	WC	AWCA	CS (S) SWIFT

Class 47/3 (Dual-braked locos) or Class 47/2 (Air-braked locos).
Details as Class 47/0 except: **Weight:** 113.7 t.

47355	am+	**K**	WC	AWCX	CS (S)
47368	x	**F**	WC	AWCX	CS (S)

Class 47/4. Electric Train Supply equipment.
Details as Class 47/0 except:

Weight: 120.4–125.1 t.   **Fuel Capacity:** 3273 (+ 5537) litres.
Train Supply: Electric, index 66.   **RA:** 7.

47492	x	**RX**	WC	AWCX	CS (S)
47500		**WC**	WC	AWCX	CS (S)
47501	xm+	**DS**	DR	XHSS	ZA (S)	Craftsman
47526	x	**BL**	WC	AWCX	CS (S)
47580	x	**BL**	47	MBDL	TM	County of Essex

Class 47/7. Former Railnet dedicated locos. All have twin fuel tanks.

47727	m	**CS**	CS	COLO	WH	Rebecca
47739	m	**CS**	CS	COLO	WH	Robin of Templecombe 1938–2013
47746	x	**WC**	WC	AWCA	CS
47749	m	**CS**	CS	COLO	WH	Demelza
47760	x	**WC**	WC	AWCA	CS
47768		**RX**	WC	AWCX	CS (S)
47769		**V**	HN	HNRS	BH (S)	Resolve
47772	x	**RX**	WC	AWCX	CS (S)
47773	x	**GG**	70	MBDL	TM
47776	x	**RX**	WC	AWCX	CS (S)
47786		**WC**	WC	AWCA	CS	Roy Castle OBE
47787		**WC**	WC	AWCX	CS (S)	Windsor Castle
47790	m	**VN**	DR	XHNB	KM	Galloway Princess

Class 47/4 continued. RA6. Most fitted with extended-range fuel tanks (+).

47798	x	**O**	NM	MBDL	YK	Prince William
47802	+m	**DS**	WC	AWCA	CS
47804		**WC**	WC	AWCA	CS
47805	+m	**DS**	DR	XHSS	CR (S)	John Scott 12.5.45–22.5.12
47810	+m	**DI**	DR	XHAC	KM	Peter Bath MBE 1927–2006
47811	+	**GL**	FL	DHLT	BA (S)
47812	+m	**GG**	RV	GBDF	BH
47813	+m	**DS**	DR	XHNB	KM	Solent
47815	+m	**RB**	RV	GBDF	BH	GREAT WESTERN
47816	+	**GL**	FL	DFLH	BA (S)
47818	+m	**DS**	DR	XHAC	KM
47826	+	**WC**	WC	AWCA	CS
47828	+m	**DS**	DR	XHSS	CR (S)
47830	+	**GL**	FL	DFLH	BH (S)
47832	+m	**WC**	WC	AWCA	CS
47841	+m	**DS**	DR	XHSS	CR (S)
47843	+m	**RB**	RV	GBDF	BH	VULCAN
47847	+m	**BL**	RV	GBDF	BH
47848	+m	**RB**	RV	GBDF	BH	TITAN STAR
47851	+	**WC**	WC	AWCA	CS
47853	+m	**DS**	DR	XHAC	KM	RAIL EXPRESS
47854	+	**WC**	WC	AWCA	CS	Diamond Jubilee

CLASS 50   ENGLISH ELECTRIC   Co-Co

Built: 1967–68 by English Electric at Vulcan Foundry, Newton-le-Willows.
Engine: English Electric 16CVST of 2010 kW (2700 hp) at 850 rpm.
Main Generator: English Electric 840/4B.
Traction Motors: English Electric 538/5A.
Maximum Tractive Effort: 216 kN (48500 lbf).
Continuous Tractive Effort: 147 kN (33000 lbf) at 23.5 mph.
Power at Rail: 1540 kW (2070 hp).   **Train Brakes:** Air & vacuum.
Brake Force: 59 t.   **Dimensions:** 20.88 x 2.78 m.
Weight: 116.9 t.   **Wheel Diameter:** 1092 mm.
Design Speed: 105 mph.   **Maximum Speed:** 90 mph.
Fuel Capacity: 4796 litres.   **RA:** 6.
Train Supply: Electric, index 61.   **Multiple Working:** Orange Square.

Originally numbered D407, D417, D444 & D449.

50007	B	NB	MBDL	WH	Hercules
50017	N	NB	MBDL	WH	Royal Oak
50044	B	50	CFOL	KR	Exeter
50049	BL	50	CFOL	KR	Defiance

CLASS 52   BR/MAYBACH   C-C

Built: 1961–64 by BR at Swindon Works.
Engine: Two Maybach MD655 of 1007 kW (1350 hp) at 1500 rpm.
Transmission: Hydraulic. Voith L630rV.
Maximum Tractive Effort: 297 kN (66700 lbf).
Continuous Tractive Effort: 201 kN (45200 lbf) at 14.5 mph.
Power at Rail: 1490 kW (2000 hp).   **Train Brakes:** Air & vacuum.
Brake Force: 83 t.   **Dimensions:** 20.7 m x 2.78 m.
Weight: 110 t.   **Wheel Diameter:** 1092 mm.
Design Speed: 90 mph.   **Maximum Speed:** 90 mph.
Fuel Capacity: 3900 litres.   **RA:** 6.
Train Supply: Steam.   **Multiple Working:** Not equipped.

Never allocated a number in the 1972 number series.

Registered on TOPS as No. 89416.

| D1015 | M | DT | MBDL | TM | WESTERN CHAMPION |

CLASS 55   ENGLISH ELECTRIC   Co-Co

Built: 1961 by English Electric at Vulcan Foundry, Newton-le-Willows.
Engine: Two Napier-Deltic D18-25 of 1230 kW (1650 hp) each at 1500 rpm.
Main Generators: Two English Electric 829/1A.
Traction Motors: English Electric 538/A.
Maximum Tractive Effort: 222 kN (50000 lbf).
Continuous Tractive Effort: 136 kN (30500 lbf) at 32.5 mph.
Power at Rail: 1969 kW (2640 hp).   **Train Brakes:** Air & vacuum.
Brake Force: 51 t.   **Dimensions:** 21.18 x 2.68 m.
Weight: 100 t.   **Wheel Diameter:** 1092 mm.

Design Speed: 105 mph.
Fuel Capacity: 3755 litres.
Train Supply: Electric, index 66.

Maximum Speed: 100 mph.
RA: 5.
Multiple Working: Not equipped.

Originally numbered D9002, D9009 & D9000.

55022 registered on TOPS as No. 89500.

55002	**B**	NM	MBDL	YK	THE KING'S OWN YORKSHIRE LIGHT INFANTRY
55009	**GG**	DP	MBDL	BH	ALYCIDON
55022	**B**	MW	MBDL	Bo'ness	ROYAL SCOTS GREY

CLASS 56   BRUSH/BR/RUSTON   Co-Co

Built: 1976–84 by Electroputere at Craiova, Romania (as sub contractors for Brush) or BREL at Doncaster or Crewe Works.
Engine: Ruston Paxman 16RK3CT of 2460 kW (3250 hp) at 900 rpm.
Main Alternator: Brush BA1101A.
Traction Motors: Brush TM73-62.
Maximum Tractive Effort: 275 kN (61800 lbf).
Continuous Tractive Effort: 240 kN (53950 lbf) at 16.8 mph.
Power at Rail: 1790 kW (2400 hp).   **Train Brakes:** Air.
Brake Force: 60 t.   **Dimensions:** 19.36 x 2.79 m.
Weight: 126 t.   **Wheel Diameter:** 1143 mm.
Design Speed: 80 mph.   **Maximum Speed:** 80 mph.
Fuel Capacity: 5228 litres.   **RA:** 7.
Train Supply: Not equipped.   **Multiple Working:** Red Diamond.

All equipped with Slow Speed Control.

Class 56s exported for use abroad are listed in section 1.6 of this book.

Non-standard liveries: 56009 All over blue.

56081, 56098 and 56104 Unbranded Railfreight grey.

56303 All over dark green.

56311 Light grey with yellow cabsides.

56007	**B**	UR	MBDL	LR (S)
56009	**O**	UR	MBDL	BL (S)
56018	**FER**	UR	MBDL	LB (S)
56031	**FER**	UR	MBDL	LR (S)
56032	**FER**	UR	MBDL	WH (S)
56037	**E**	UR	MBDL	BL (S)
56038	**FER**	UR	MBDL	LR (S)
56049	**FER**	CS	COLS	WH (S)
56051	**FER**	CS	COLS	WH (S)
56060	**FER**	UR	MBDL	WH (S)
56065	**FER**	UR	MBDL	LR (S)
56069	**FER**	UR	MBDL	LR (S)
56077	**LH**	UR	MBDL	BL (S)
56078	**CS**	CS	COFS	WH

56081	**0**	UR	DHLT	BA
56087	**CS**	CS	COFS	WH
56090	**FER**	CS	COLS	WH (S)
56091	**FER**	BA	HTLX	WH
56094	**CS**	CS	COFS	WH
56096	**CS**	CS	COFS	WH
56098	**0**	UR	MBDL	LR (S)
56103	**FER**	BA	HTLX	WH
56104	**0**	UR	MBDL	LR (S)
56105	**CS**	CS	COFS	WH
56106	**FER**	UR	MBDL	LR (S)
56113	**CS**	CS	COFS	WH
56128	**F**	BA	HTLX	WH (S)

56301	(56045)	**FA**	56	HTLX	WH
56302	(56124)	**CS**	CS	COFS	WH
56303	(56125)	**0**	BA	HTLX	WH
56311	(56057)	**0**	BA	HTLX	WH
56312	(56003)	**DC**	BA	HTLX	WH

Jeremiah Dixon Son of County Durham Surveyor of the Mason-Dixon Line U.S.A.

CLASS 57   BRUSH/GM   Co-Co

Built: 1964–65 by Brush Traction at Loughborough or BR at Crewe Works as Class 47. Rebuilt 1997–2004 by Brush Traction at Loughborough.
Engine: General Motors 12 645 E3 of 1860 kW (2500 hp) at 904 rpm.
Main Alternator: Brush BA1101D (recovered from Class 56).
Traction Motors: Brush TM64-68 Mark 1 or Mark 1a.
Maximum Tractive Effort: 244.5 kN (55000 lbf).
Continuous Tractive Effort: 140 kN (31500 lbf) at ?? mph.
Power at Rail: 1507 kW (2025 hp).   **Train Brakes:** Air.
Brake Force: 80 t.   **Dimensions:** 19.38 x 2.79 m.
Weight: 120.6 t.   **Wheel Diameter:** 1143 mm.
Design Speed: 75 mph.   **Maximum Speed:** 75 mph.
Fuel Capacity: 5550 litres.   **RA:** 6
Train Supply: Not equipped.   **Multiple Working:** † DRS system.

Class 57/0. No Train Supply Equipment. Rebuilt 1997–2000.

57001	(47356)		**WC**	WC	AWCA	CS
57002	(47322)	†	**DS**	P	XHCK	KM
57003	(47317)	†	**DI**	P	XHCK	KM
57004	(47347)	†	**DS**	DR	XHCK	KM
57005	(47350)		**AZ**	WC	AWCX	CS (S)
57006	(47187)		**WC**	WC	AWCA	CS (S)
57007	(47332)	†	**DS**	P	XHSS	ZG (S)
57008	(47060)	†	**DS**	P	XHCK	KM
57009	(47079)	†	**DS**	P	XHCK	KM
57010	(47231)	†	**DS**	P	XHCK	KM
57011	(47329)	†	**DS**	P	XHCK	KM
57012	(47204)	†	**DS**	P	XHCK	KM

Class 57/3. Electric Train Supply Equipment. Former Virgin Trains locos. Rebuilt 2002–04. Details as Class 57/0 except:

Engine: General Motors 12645F3B of 2050 kW (2750 hp) at 954 rpm.
Main Alternator: Brush BA1101F (recovered from a Class 56) or Brush BA1101G.
Fuel Capacity: 5887 litres.   **Train Supply:** Electric, index 100.
Design Speed: 95 mph.   **Maximum Speed:** 95 mph.
Brake Force: 60 t.   **Weight:** 117 t.

57301	(47845) i	**DI**	DR	XHAC	KM	Goliath
57302	(47827) d	**DS**	P	XHAC	KM	Chad Varah
57303	(47705) d	**DI**	DR	XHAC	KM	Pride of Carlisle
57304	(47807) d	**DS**	P	XHVT	KM	Pride of Cheshire
57305	(47822) d	**VN**	DR	XHAC	KM	Northern Princess
57306	(47814) i	**DI**	DR	XHAC	KM	
57307	(47225) d	**DR**	P	XHVT	KM	LADY PENELOPE
57308	(47846) d	**DS**	P	XHVT	KM	County of Staffordshire
57309	(47806) d	**DS**	P	XHVT	KM	Pride of Crewe
57310	(47831) d	**DI**	DR	XHAC	KM	Pride of Cumbria
57311	(47817) d	**DS**	P	XHVT	KM	Thunderbird
57312	(47330) d	**VN**	DR	XHAC	KM	Solway Princess
57313	(47371)	**WC**	WC	AWCA	CS	
57314	(47372)	**WC**	WC	AWCA	CS	
57315	(47234)	**WC**	WC	AWCA	CS	
57316	(47290)	**AB**	WC	AWCA	CS	

Class 57/6. Electric Train Supply Equipment. Prototype ETS loco. Rebuilt 2001. Details as Class 57/0 except:

Main Alternator: Brush BA1101E.   **Fuel Capacity:** 3273 litres.
Train Supply: Electric, index 95.   **Weight:** 113t.
Design Speed: 95 mph.   **Maximum Speed:** 95 mph.
Brake Force: 60 t.

57601	(47825)	**WC**	WC	AWCA	CS

Class 57/6. Electric Train Supply Equipment. First Great Western locos. Rebuilt 2004. Details as Class 57/3.

57602	(47337)	**FB**	P	EFOO	OO	Restormel Castle
57603	(47349)	**FB**	P	EFOO	OO	Tintagel Castle
57604	(47209)	**GW**	P	EFOO	OO	PENDENNIS CASTLE
57605	(47206)	**FB**	P	EFOO	OO	Totnes Castle

CLASS 58   BREL/RUSTON   Co-Co

Built: 1983–87 by BREL at Doncaster Works.
Engine: Ruston Paxman 12RK3ACT of 2460 kW (3300 hp) at 1000 rpm.
Main Alternator: Brush BA1101B.   **Traction Motors:** Brush TM73-62.
Maximum Tractive Effort: 275 kN (61800 lbf).
Continuous Tractive Effort: 240 kN (53950 lbf) at 17.4 mph.
Power at Rail: 1780 kW (2387 hp).   **Train Brakes:** Air.
Brake Force: 60 t.   **Dimensions:** 19.13 x 2.72 m.
Weight: 130 t.   **Wheel Diameter:** 1120 mm.

Design Speed: 80 mph.   **Maximum Speed:** 80 mph.
Fuel Capacity: 4214 litres.   **RA:** 7.
Train Supply: Not equipped.   **Multiple Working:** Red Diamond.

All equipped with Slow Speed Control.

Class 58s exported for use abroad are listed in section 1.6 of this book.

58008	**ML**	DB	WQDA	EH (S)
58012	**F**	DB	WQCA	TO (S)
58022	**F**	DB	WQCA	CE (S)
58023	**ML**	DB	WQCA	TO (S)
58048	**E**	DB	WQCA	CE (S)

CLASS 59   GENERAL MOTORS   Co-Co

Built: 1985 (59001–004) or 1989 (59005) by General Motors, La Grange, Illinois, USA or 1990 (59101–104), 1994 (59201) and 1995 (59202–206) by General Motors, London, Ontario, Canada.
Engine: General Motors 16-645E3C two stroke of 2460 kW (3300 hp) at 904 rpm.
Main Alternator: General Motors AR11 MLD-D14A.
Traction Motors: General Motors D77B.
Maximum Tractive Effort: 506 kN (113 550 lbf).
Continuous Tractive Effort: 291 kN (65 300 lbf) at 14.3 mph.
Power at Rail: 1889 kW (2533 hp).   **Train Brakes:** Air.
Brake Force: 69 t.   **Dimensions:** 21.35 x 2.65 m.
Weight: 121 t.   **Wheel Diameter:** 1067 mm.
Design Speed: 60 (* 75) mph.   **Maximum Speed:** 60 (* 75) mph.
Fuel Capacity: 4546 litres.   **RA:** 7.
Train Supply: Not equipped.   **Multiple Working:** AAR System.

Non-standard livery: 59003 Heavy Haul Power International (red & dark blue).

Class 59/0. Owned by Aggregate Industries and GB Railfreight.

59001	**AI**	AI	XYPO	MD	YEOMAN ENDEAVOUR
59002	**AI**	AI	XYPO	MD	ALAN J DAY
59003	**0**	GB	GBYH	PG	YEOMAN HIGHLANDER
59004	**FY**	AI	XYPO	MD	PAUL A HAMMOND
59005	**AI**	AI	XYPO	MD	KENNETH J PAINTER

Class 59/1. Owned by Hanson Quarry Products.

59101	**HA**	HA	XYPA	MD	Village of Whatley
59102	**HA**	HA	XYPA	MD	Village of Chantry
59103	**HA**	HA	XYPA	MD	Village of Mells
59104	**HA**	HA	XYPA	MD	Village of Great Elm

Class 59/2. Owned by DB Schenker.

59201	*	**DB**	DB	WDAM	MD
59202	*	**DB**	DB	WDAM	MD	Alan Meddows Taylor
					MD Mendip Rail Limited

59203	*	**DB**	DB	WDAM	MD
59204	*	**DB**	DB	WDAM	MD
59205	*b	**DB**	DB	WDAM	MD
59206	*b	**DB**	DB	WDAM	MD	John F. Yeoman Rail Pioneer

CLASS 60   BRUSH/MIRRLEES   Co-Co

Built: 1989–93 by Brush Traction at Loughborough.
Engine: Mirrlees 8MB275T of 2310 kW (3100 hp) at 1000 rpm.
Main Alternator: Brush BA1006A.
Traction Motors: Brush TM2161A.
Maximum Tractive Effort: 500 kN (106500 lbf).
Continuous Tractive Effort: 336 kN (71570 lbf) at 17.4 mph.
Power at Rail: 1800 kW (2415 hp).   **Train Brakes:** Air.
Brake Force: 74 (+ 62) t.   **Dimensions:** 21.34 x 2.64 m.
Weight: 129 (+ 131) t.   **Wheel Diameter:** 1118 mm.
Design Speed: 62 mph.   **Maximum Speed:** 60 mph.
Fuel Capacity: 4546 (+ 5225) litres.   **RA:** 8.
Train Supply: Not equipped.   **Multiple Working:** Within class.

All equipped with Slow Speed Control.

* Refurbished locos.

60034, 60064, 60072, 60073, 60077, 60084 and 60090 carry their names on one side only.

60500 originally carried the number 60016.

Advertising liveries: 60066 Powering Drax (silver).

60099 Tata Steel (silver).

60001	*	**DB**	DB	WCAT	TO
60002	+	**E**	CS	COLS	TO (S)
60003	+	**E**	DB	WQBA	TO (S) FREIGHT TRANSPORT ASSOCIATION
60004	+	**E**	DB	WQBA	TO (S)
60005	+	**E**	DB	WQBA	TO (S)
60006		**CU**	DB	WQBA	TO (S)
60007	+*	**DB**	DB	WQAA	TO (S) The Spirit of Tom Kendell
60008		**E**	DB	WQBA	TO (S) Sir William McAlpine
60009	+	**E**	DB	WQBA	TO (S)
60010	+*	**DB**	DB	WCBT	TO
60011		**DB**	DB	WCAT	TO
60012	+	**E**	DB	WQBA	TO (S)
60013		**EG**	DB	WQDA	TO (S) Robert Boyle
60014		**EG**	DB	WQBA	TO (S)
60015	+*	**DB**	DB	WCBT	TO
60017	+*	**DB**	DB	WCBT	TO
60018		**E**	DB	WQBA	TO (S)
60019	*	**DB**	DB	WCAT	TO Port of Grimsby & Immingham
60020	+*	**DB**	DB	WCBT	TO
60021	+*	**CS**	CS	COLO	RU
60022	+	**E**	DB	WQBA	TO (S)

60023 +	E	DB	WQBA	TO (S)	
60024 *	**DB**	DB	WCAT	TO	Clitheroe Castle
60025 +	E	DB	WQBA	TO (S)	
60026 +	E	CS	COLS	TO (S)	
60027 +	E	DB	WQBA	TO (S)	
60028 +	EG	DB	WQDA	CE (S)	
60029	E	DB	WQDA	CE (S)	
60030 +	E	DB	WQBA	TO (S)	
60031	E	DB	WQBA	TO (S)	
60032	F	DB	WQBA	TO (S)	
60033 +	**CU**	DB	WQDA	TO (S)	Tees Steel Express
60034	**EG**	DB	WQBA	TO (S)	Carnedd Llewelyn
60035	E	DB	WQBA	TO (S)	
60036	E	DB	WQBA	TO (S)	GEFCO
60037 +	E	DB	WQBA	TO (S)	
60038 +	E	DB	WQBA	CE (S)	
60039 *	**DB**	DB	WCAT	TO	
60040 *	**DB**	DB	WCAT	TO	The Territorial Army Centenary
60041 +	E	DB	WQDA	TO (S)	
60042	E	DB	WQBA	TO (S)	
60043	E	DB	WQBA	TO (S)	
60044 *	**DB**	DB	WCAT	TO	
60045	E	DB	WQAA	TO (S)	The Permanent Way Institution
60046 +	EG	DB	WQDA	CE (S)	
60047	E	CS	COLS	TO (S)	
60048	E	DB	WQDA	TO (S)	
60049	E	DB	WCAT	TO	
60050	E	DB	WQBA	TO (S)	
60051 +	E	DB	WQBA	TO (S)	
60052 +	E	DB	WQBA	TO (S)	Glofa Twr – The last deep mine in Wales – Tower Colliery
60053	E	DB	WQBA	TO (S)	
60054 +*	**DB**	DB	WCBT	TO	
60055	EG	DB	WQDA	CE (S)	
60056 +	EG	CS	COLS	TO (S)	
60057	EG	DB	WQBA	TO (S)	Adam Smith
60058 +	E	DB	WQBA	TO (S)	
60059 +*	**DB**	DB	WCBT	TO	Swinden Dalesman
60060	EG	DB	WQBA	TO (S)	
60061	F	DB	WQDA	TO (S)	
60062 *	**DB**	DB	WCAT	TO	Stainless Pioneer
60063 *	**DB**	DB	WCAT	TO	
60064 +	EG	DB	WQBA	TO (S)	Back Tor
60065	E	DB	WQBA	TO (S)	Spirit of JAGUAR
60066 *	**AL**	DB	WQAA	TO (S)	
60067	EG	DB	WQBA	TO (S)	
60068	EG	DB	WQBA	TO (S)	
60069	E	DB	WQBA	TO (S)	Slioch
60070 +	F	DB	WQBA	TO (S)	John Loudon McAdam
60071 +	E	DB	WQAA	TO (S)	Ribblehead Viaduct
60072	**EG**	DB	WQBA	TO (S)	Cairn Toul

60073	**EG**	DB	WQBA	TO (S)	Cairn Gorm
60074 *	**DB**	DB	WCAT	TO	
60075	**E**	DB	WQBA	TO (S)	
60076 *	**CS**	CS	COLO	RU	
60077 +	**EG**	DB	WQBA	TO (S)	Canisp
60078	**ML**	DB	WQBA	TO (S)	
60079 *	**DB**	DB	WCAT	TO	
60080 +	**E**	DB	WQBA	TO (S)	
60081 +	**GW**	DB	WQBA	TO (S)	
60082	**EG**	DB	WQBA	CE (S)	
60083	**E**	DB	WQBA	TO (S)	
60084	**EG**	DB	WQBA	TO (S)	Cross Fell
60085 *	**CS**	CS	COLO	RU	
60086	**EG**	DB	WQBA	TO (S)	
60087 *	**CS**	CS	COLO	RU	CLIC Sargent www.clicsargent.co.uk
60088	**F**	DB	WQBA	TO (S)	
60089 +	**E**	DB	WQBA	TO (S)	
60090 +	**EG**	DB	WQBA	TO (S)	Quinag
60091 +*	**DB**	DB	WCBT	TO	Barry Needham
60092 +*	**DB**	DB	WCBT	TO	
60093	**E**	DB	WQBA	TO (S)	
60094	**E**	DB	WQBA	TO (S)	Rugby Flyer
60095	**EG**	CS	COLS	TO (S)	
60096 +	**E**	CS	COLS	TO (S)	
60097 +	**E**	DB	WQBA	TO (S)	
60098 +	**E**	DB	WQBA	TO (S)	
60099	**AL**	DB	WQBA	TO (S)	
60100 *	**DB**	DB	WCAT	TO	
60500	**E**	DB	WQBA	TO (S)	

CLASS 66   GENERAL MOTORS/EMD   Co-Co

Built: 1998–2008 by General Motors/EMD, London, Ontario, Canada (Model JT42CWR (low emission locos Model JT42CWRM)) or 2013–15 by EMD/ Progress Rail, Muncie, Indiana (66752–779).
Engine: General Motors 12N-710G3B-EC two stroke of 2385 kW (3200 hp) at 904 rpm (low emission locos General Motors 12N-710G3B-T2).
Main Alternator: General Motors AR8/CA6.
Traction Motors: General Motors D43TR.
Maximum Tractive Effort: 409 kN (92000 lbf).
Continuous Tractive Effort: 260 kN (58390 lbf) at 15.9 mph.
Power at Rail: 1850 kW (2480 hp).   **Train Brakes:** Air.
Brake Force: 68 t.   **Dimensions:** 21.35 x 2.64 m.
Weight: 127 t.   **Wheel Diameter:** 1120 mm.
Design Speed: 87.5 mph.   **Maximum Speed:** 75 mph (unless stated).
Fuel Capacity: 6550 litres (unless stated). **RA:** 7.
Train Supply: Not equipped.   **Multiple Working:** AAR System.

All equipped with Slow Speed Control.

Class 66s previously used in the UK but now in use abroad are listed in section 1.6 of this book. Some of the 60 DBS 66s moved to France return to Great Britain from time to time for maintenance or operational requirements.

Advertising livery: 66048 Stobart Rail (two tone blue & white).

Class 66 delivery dates. The Class 66 design has evolved over a 16-year period, with over 400 locomotives delivered. For clarity the delivery dates (by year) for each batch of locos is as follows:

66001–250	EWS (now DB Schenker). 1998–2000 (some now in use in France or Poland).
66301–305	Fastline. 2008. Now used by DRS.
66401–410	DRS. 2003. Now in use with GB Railfreight or Colas Rail and renumbered 66733–737 and 66742–746 (66734 since scrapped).
66411–420	DRS. 2006. Now leased by Freightliner (66411/412/417 exported to Poland).
66421–430	DRS. 2007
66431–434	DRS. 2008
66501–505	Freightliner. 1999
66506–520	Freightliner. 2000
66521–525	Freightliner. 2000 (66521 since scrapped).
66526–531	Freightliner. 2001
66532–537	Freightliner. 2001
66538–543	Freightliner. 2001
66544–553	Freightliner. 2001
66554	Freightliner. 2002†
66555–566	Freightliner. 2002
66567–574	Freightliner. 2003. 66573–574 now used by Colas Rail and renumbered 66846–847.
66575–577	Freightliner. 2004. Now used by Colas Rail and renumbered 66848–850.
66578–581	Freightliner. 2005. Now used by GBRf and renumbered 66738–741.
66582–594	Freightliner. 2007 (66582/583/584/586 exported to Poland).
66595–599	Freightliner. 2008
66601–606	Freightliner. 2000
66607–612	Freightliner. 2002 (66607/609/611/612 exported to Poland)
66613–618	Freightliner. 2003
66619–622	Freightliner. 2005
66623–625	Freightliner. 2007 (66624/625 exported to Poland).
66701–707	GB Railfreight. 2001
66708–712	GB Railfreight. 2002
66713–717	GB Railfreight. 2003
66718–722	GB Railfreight. 2006
66723–727	GB Railfreight. 2006
66728–732	GB Railfreight. 2008
66747–749	Built in 2008 as 20078968-004/006/007 (DE 6313/15/16) for Crossrail AG in the Netherlands but never used. Sold to GB Railfreight in 2012.
66750–751	Built in 2003 as 20038513-01/04 and have worked in the Netherlands, Germany and Poland. GBRf secured these two locomotives on lease in 2013.

66752–772   GB Railfreight. 2014.
66773–779   GB Railfreight. On order for delivery 2015–16.
66951–952   Freightliner. 2004
66953–957   Freightliner. 2008

† Replacement for 66521, written off in the Great Heck accident in 2001.

Class 66/0. DB Schenker-operated locos.

All fitted with Swinghead Automatic "Buckeye" Combination Couplers except 66001 and 66002.

† Fitted with additional lights and drawgear for Lickey banking duties.

t Fitted with tripcocks for working over London Underground tracks between Harrow-on-the-Hill and Amersham.

66001 t	**DB**	A	WBAT	TO
66002	**E**	A	WBAT	TO
66003	**E**	A	WBAT	TO
66004	**E**	A	WBAT	TO
66005	**E**	A	WBAT	TO
66006	**E**	A	WBAT	TO
66007	**E**	A	WBAT	TO
66008	**E**	A	WBAT	TO
66009	**E**	A	WBAT	TO
66011	**E**	A	WBAT	TO
66012	**E**	A	WBAT	TO
66013	**E**	A	WBAT	TO
66014	**E**	A	WBAT	TO
66015	**E**	A	WBAT	TO
66016	**E**	A	WBAT	TO
66017 t	**E**	A	WBTT	TO
66018	**E**	A	WBAT	TO
66019 t	**E**	A	WBAT	TO
66020	**E**	A	WBAT	TO
66021	**E**	A	WBAT	TO
66023	**E**	A	WBAT	TO
66024	**E**	A	WBAT	TO
66025	**E**	A	WBAT	TO
66027	**E**	A	WBAT	TO
66030	**E**	A	WBAT	TO
66031	**E**	A	WBAT	TO
66034	**E**	A	WBAT	TO
66035	**E**	A	WBAT	TO
66037	**E**	A	WBAT	TO
66039	**E**	A	WBAT	TO
66040	**E**	A	WBAT	TO
66041	**E**	A	WBAT	TO
66043	**E**	A	WBAT	TO
66044	**E**	A	WBAI	TO
66046	**E**	A	WBAT	TO
66047	**E**	A	WBAT	TO
66048	**AL**	A	WQDA	TO (S) James the Engine

66050		E	A	WBAT	TO	EWS Energy
66051		E	A	WBAT	TO	
66053		E	A	WBAT	TO	
66054		E	A	WBAT	TO	
66055	†	E	A	WBLT	TO	
66056	†	E	A	WBLT	TO	
66057	†	E	A	WBLT	TO	
66058	†	E	A	WBLT	TO	
66059	†	E	A	WBLT	TO	
66060		E	A	WBAT	TO	
66061		E	A	WBAT	TO	
66063		E	A	WBAT	TO	
66065		E	A	WBAT	TO	
66066		E	A	WBAT	TO	
66067		E	A	WBAT	TO	
66068		E	A	WBAT	TO	
66069		E	A	WBAT	TO	
66070		E	A	WBAT	TO	
66074		E	A	WBAT	TO	
66075		E	A	WBAT	TO	
66076		E	A	WBAT	TO	
66077		E	A	WBAT	TO	Benjamin Gimbert G.C.
66078		E	A	WBAT	TO	
66079		E	A	WBAT	TO	James Nightall G.C.
66080		E	A	WBAT	TO	
66081		E	A	WBAT	TO	
66082		E	A	WBAT	TO	
66083		E	A	WBAT	TO	
66084		E	A	WBAT	TO	
66085		E	A	WBAT	TO	
66086		E	A	WBAT	TO	
66087		E	A	WBAT	TO	
66088		E	A	WBAT	TO	
66089		E	A	WBAT	TO	
66090		E	A	WBAT	TO	
66091		E	A	WBAT	TO	
66092		E	A	WBAT	TO	
66093		E	A	WBAT	TO	
66094		E	A	WBAT	TO	
66095		E	A	WBAT	TO	
66096		E	A	WBAI	TO	
66097		DB	A	WBAT	TO	
66098		E	A	WBAT	TO	
66099	r	E	A	WBBT	TO	
66100	r	E	A	WBBT	TO	
66101	r	DB	A	WBBT	TO	
66102	r	E	A	WBBT	TO	
66103	r	E	A	WBBT	TO	
66104	r	E	A	WBBT	TO	
66105	r	E	A	WBBT	TO	
66106	r	E	A	WBBT	TO	

66107 r	**E**	A	WBBT	TO	
66108 r	**E**	A	WBBT	TO	
66109	**E**	A	WBAT	TO	
66110 r	**E**	A	WBBT	TO	
66111 r	**E**	A	WBBT	TO	
66112 r	**E**	A	WBBT	TO	
66113 r	**E**	A	WBBT	TO	
66114 r	**DB**	A	WBBT	TO	
66115	**E**	A	WBAT	TO	
66116	**E**	A	WBAT	TO	
66117	**E**	A	WBAT	TO	
66118	**DB**	A	WBAT	TO	
66119	**E**	A	WBAT	TO	
66120	**E**	A	WBAT	TO	
66121	**E**	A	WBAT	TO	
66122	**E**	A	WBAT	TO	
66124	**E**	A	WBAT	TO	
66125	**E**	A	WBAT	TO	
66126	**E**	A	WBAT	TO	
66127	**E**	A	WBAT	TO	
66128	**E**	A	WBAT	TO	
66129	**E**	A	WBAT	TO	
66130	**E**	A	WBAT	TO	
66131	**E**	A	WBAT	TO	
66132	**E**	A	WBAT	TO	
66133	**E**	A	WBAT	TO	
66134	**E**	A	WBAT	TO	
66135	**E**	A	WBAT	TO	
66136	**E**	A	WBAT	TO	
66137	**E**	A	WBAT	TO	
66138	**E**	A	WBAT	TO	
66139	**E**	A	WBAT	TO	
66140	**E**	A	WBAT	TO	
66141	**E**	A	WQAA	TO (S)	
66142	**E**	A	WBAT	TO	
66143	**E**	A	WBAT	TO	
66144	**E**	A	WBAT	TO	
66145	**E**	A	WBAT	TO	
66147	**E**	A	WBAT	TO	
66148	**E**	A	WBAT	TO	
66149	**E**	A	WBAT	TO	
66150	**E**	A	WBAT	TO	
66151	**E**	A	WBAT	TO	
66152	**DB**	A	WBAT	TO	Derek Holmes Railway Operator
66154	**E**	A	WBAT	TO	
66155	**E**	A	WBAT	TO	
66156	**E**	A	WBAI	TO	
66158	**E**	A	WBAT	TO	
66160	**E**	A	WBAT	TO	
66161	**E**	A	WBAT	TO	
66162	**E**	A	WBAT	TO	

66164	E	A	WBAT	TO	
66165	E	A	WBAT	TO	
66167	E	A	WQAA	TO (S)	
66168	E	A	WBAT	TO	
66169	E	A	WBAT	TO	
66170	E	A	WBAT	TO	
66171	E	A	WBAT	TO	
66172	E	A	WBAT	TO	PAUL MELLENEY
66174	E	A	WBAT	TO	
66175	E	A	WBAT	TO	
66176	E	A	WBAK	TO	
66177	E	A	WBAT	TO	
66181	E	A	WBAT	TO	
66182	E	A	WBAI	TO	
66183	E	A	WBAT	TO	
66184	E	A	WQAA	LT (S)	
66185	DB	A	WBAT	TO	DP WORLD London Gateway
66186	E	A	WBAT	TO	
66187	E	A	WBAT	TO	
66188	E	A	WBAT	TO	
66192	E	A	WBAT	TO	
66193	E	A	WBAT	TO	
66194	E	A	WBAT	TO	
66197	E	A	WBAT	TO	
66198	E	A	WBAT	TO	
66199	E	A	WBAT	TO	
66200	E	A	WBAT	TO	RAILWAY HERITAGE COMMITTEE
66201	E	A	WBAT	TO	
66204	E	A	WBAT	TO	
66206	E	A	WBAT	TO	
66207	E	A	WBAT	TO	
66213	E	A	WBAT	TO	
66221	E	A	WBAT	TO	
66230	E	A	WBAT	TO	
66232	E	A	WBAT	TO	
66238	E	A	WBAT	TO	
66250	E	A	WBAT	TO	

Class 66/3. Former Fastline-operated loco now operated by DRS. Low emission. Details as Class 66/0 except:

Engine: EMD 12N-710G3B-U2 two stroke of 2420 kW (3245 hp) at 904 rpm.
Traction Motors: General Motors D43TRC.
Fuel Capacity: 5150 litres.

66301	DS	BN	XHIM	KM
66302	DS	BN	XHIM	KM
66303	DS	BN	XHIM	KM
66304	DS	BN	XHIM	KM
66305	DS	BN	XHIM	KM

66413–434. Low emission. Macquarie Group-owned. Details as Class 66/0 except:

Engine: EMD 12N-710G3B-U2 two stroke of 2420 kW (3245 hp) at 904 rpm.
Traction Motors: General Motors D43TRC.
Fuel Capacity: 5150 litres.

Non-standard livery: 66414 Two tone blue & white (formerly Stobart Rail).

66413	**DS**	MQ	DFHG	LD
66414	**O**	MQ	DFIN	LD
66415	**DS**	MQ	DFHG	LD
66416	**FH**	MQ	DFIN	LD
66418	**DS**	MQ	DFIN	LD
66419	**DS**	MQ	DFHG	LD
66420	**DS**	MQ	DFIN	LD
66421	**DS**	MQ	XHIM	KM
66422	**DS**	MQ	XHIM	KM
66423	**DS**	MQ	XHIM	KM
66424	**DS**	MQ	XHIM	KM
66425	**DS**	MQ	XHIM	KM
66426	**DS**	MQ	XHIM	KM
66427	**DS**	MQ	XHIM	KM
66428	**DS**	MQ	XHIM	KM
66429	**DS**	MQ	XHIM	KM
66430	**DS**	MQ	XHIM	KM
66431	**DS**	MQ	XHIM	KM
66432	**DS**	MQ	XHIM	KM
66433	**DS**	MQ	XHIM	KM
66434	**DR**	MQ	XHIM	KM

Class 66/5. Freightliner-operated locos. Details as Class 66/0.

Advertising livery: 66522 Shanks Waste (one half of loco Freightliner green and one half Shanks' Waste light green).

66501	**FL**	P	DFIM	LD	Japan 2001
66502	**FL**	P	DFIM	LD	Basford Hall Centenary 2001
66503	**FL**	P	DFIM	LD	The RAILWAY MAGAZINE
66504	**FH**	P	DFIM	LD	
66505	**FL**	P	DFIM	LD	
66506	**FL**	E	DFHH	LD	Crewe Regeneration
66507	**FL**	E	DFHH	LD	
66508	**FL**	E	DFHH	LD	
66509	**FL**	E	DFHH	LD	
66510	**FL**	E	DFHH	LD	
66511	**FL**	E	DFHH	LD	
66512	**FL**	E	DFHH	LD	
66513	**FL**	E	DFHH	LD	
66514	**FL**	E	DFHH	LD	
66515	**FL**	E	DFHH	LD	
66516	**FL**	E	DFIM	LD	
66517	**FL**	E	DFIM	LD	
66518	**FL**	E	DFHH	LD	

66519	**FL**	E	DFHH	LD	
66520	**FL**	E	DFHH	LD	
66522	**AL**	E	DFHH	LD	
66523	**FL**	E	DFHH	LD	
66524	**FL**	E	DFHH	LD	
66525	**FL**	E	DFHH	LD	
66526	**FL**	P	DFHH	LD	Driver Steve Dunn (George)
66527	**FL**	P	DFHH	LD	Don Raider
66528	**FL**	P	DFHH	LD	
66529	**FL**	P	DFHH	LD	
66530	**FL**	P	DFHH	LD	
66531	**FL**	P	DFHH	LD	
66532	**FL**	P	DFIM	LD	P&O Nedlloyd Atlas
66533	**FL**	P	DFIM	LD	Hanjin Express/Senator Express
66534	**FL**	P	DFIM	LD	OOCL Express
66535	**FL**	P	DFHH	LD	
66536	**FL**	P	DFHH	LD	
66537	**FL**	P	DFIM	LD	
66538	**FL**	E	DFIM	LD	
66539	**FL**	E	DFHH	LD	
66540	**FL**	E	DFIM	LD	Ruby
66541	**FL**	E	DFIM	LD	
66542	**FL**	E	DFIM	LD	
66543	**FL**	E	DFIM	LD	
66544	**FL**	P	DFHH	LD	
66545	**FL**	P	DFHH	LD	
66546	**FL**	P	DFHH	LD	
66547	**FL**	P	DFHH	LD	
66548	**FL**	P	DFHH	LD	
66549	**FL**	P	DFHH	LD	
66550	**FL**	P	DFHH	LD	
66551	**FL**	P	DFHH	LD	
66552	**FL**	P	DFHH	LD	Maltby Raider
66553	**FL**	P	DFHH	LD	
66554	**FL**	E	DFHH	LD	
66555	**FL**	E	DFHH	LD	
66556	**FL**	E	DFIM	LD	
66557	**FL**	E	DFHH	LD	
66558	**FL**	E	DFIM	LD	
66559	**FL**	E	DFHH	LD	
66560	**FL**	E	DFHH	LD	
66561	**FL**	E	DFHH	LD	
66562	**FL**	E	DFHH	LD	
66563	**FL**	E	DFHH	LD	
66564	**FL**	E	DFHH	LD	
66565	**FL**	E	DFHH	LD	
66566	**FL**	E	DFIM	LD	
66567	**FL**	E	DFIM	LD	
66568	**FL**	E	DFIM	LD	
66569	**FL**	E	DFIM	LD	
66570	**FL**	E	DFIM	LD	

| 66571 | **FL** | E | DFIM | LD |
| 66572 | **FL** | E | DFIM | LD |

Class 66/5. Freightliner-operated low emission locos. Details as Class 66/0 except:

Engine: EMD 12N-710G3B-U2 two stroke of 2420 kW (3245 hp) at 904 rpm.
Traction Motors: General Motors D43TRC.
Fuel Capacity: 5150 litres.

66585	**FL**	MQ	DFHG	LD	The Drax Flyer
66587	**FL**	MQ	DFIN	LD	
66588	**FL**	MQ	DFIN	LD	
66589	**FL**	MQ	DFIN	LD	
66590	**FL**	MQ	DFIN	LD	
66591	**FL**	MQ	DFIN	LD	
66592	**FL**	MQ	DFIN	LD	Johnson Stevens Agencies
66593	**FL**	MQ	DFIN	LD	3MG MERSEY MULTIMODAL GATEWAY
66594	**FL**	MQ	DFIN	LD	NYK Spirit of Kyoto
66595	**FL**	BN	DFHG	LD	
66596	**FL**	BN	DFHG	LD	
66597	**FL**	BN	DFHG	LD	Viridor
66598	**FL**	BN	DFHG	LD	
66599	**FL**	BN	DFHG	LD	

Class 66/6. Freightliner-operated locomotives with modified gear ratios.
Details as Class 66/0 except:

Maximum Tractive Effort: 467 kN (105080 lbf).
Continuous Tractive Effort: 296 kN (66630 lbf) at 14.0 mph.
Design Speed: 65 mph.   **Maximum Speed:** 65 mph.

66601	**FL**	P	DFHH	LD	The Hope Valley
66602	**FL**	P	DFHH	LD	
66603	**FL**	P	DFHH	LD	
66604	**FL**	P	DFHH	LD	
66605	**FL**	P	DFHH	LD	
66606	**FL**	P	DFHH	LD	
66607	**FL**	P	DFHH	LD	
66610	**FL**	P	DFHH	LD	
66613	**FL**	E	DFHH	LD	
66614	**FL**	E	DFHH	LD	
66615	**FL**	E	DFHH	LD	
66616	**FL**	E	DFHH	LD	
66617	**FL**	E	DFHH	LD	
66618	**FL**	E	DFHH	LD	Railways Illustrated Annual Photographic Awards Alan Barnes Derek W. Johnson MBE
66619	**FL**	E	DFHH	LD	
66620	**FL**	E	DFHH	LD	
66621	**FL**	E	DFHH	LD	
66622	**FL**	E	DFHH	LD	

Class 66/6. Freightliner-operated low emission loco with modified gear ratios.
Fuel Capacity: 5150 litres.

Advertising livery: 66623 Bardon Aggregates (blue).

| 66623 | **AL** | MQ | DFHG | | LD | | Bill Bolsover |

Class 66/7. GB Railfreight-operated locos. Details as Class 66/0.

Non-standard/advertising liveries:

66705 **GB** livery but with the addition of "Union Jack" bodyside vinyls.

66709 MSC – blue with images of a container ship.

66718 London Underground 150, black).

66720 Day and night (various colours, different on each side).

66721 London Underground 150 (white with tube map images).

66750 Rush Rail all over blue.

66701	**GB**	E	GBCM	RR	
66702	**GB**	E	GBCM	RR	Blue Lightning
66703	**GB**	E	GBCM	RR	Doncaster PSB 1981–2002
66704	**GB**	E	GBCM	RR	Colchester Power Signalbox
66705	**GB**	E	GBCM	RR	Golden Jubilee
66706	**GB**	E	GBCM	RR	Nene Valley
66707	**GB**	E	GBCM	RR	Sir Sam Fay GREAT CENTRAL RAILWAY
66708	**GB**	E	GBCM	RR	Jayne
66709	**AL**	E	GBCM	RR	Sorrento
66710	**GB**	E	GBCM	RR	Phil Packer BRIT
66711	**GB**	E	GBCM	RR	
66712	**GB**	E	GBCM	RR	Peterborough Power Signalbox
66713	**GB**	E	GBCM	RR	Forest City
66714	**GB**	E	GBCM	RR	Cromer Lifeboat
66715	**GB**	E	GBCM	RR	VALOUR – IN MEMORY OF ALL RAILWAY EMPLOYEES WHO GAVE THEIR LIVES FOR THEIR COUNTRY
66716	**GB**	E	GBCM	RR	LOCOMOTIVE & CARRIAGE INSTITUTION CENTENARY 1911–2011
66717	**GB**	E	GBCM	RR	Good Old Boy

66718–746. Low emission. GB Railfreight locos. 66733–737 renumbered from former DRS locos 66401–405. 66738–741 renumbered from former Freightliner locos 66578–581. 66742–746 renumbered from former DRS/Colas Rail locos 66406–410/841–845.

All details as Class 66/0 except 66718–732/747–749 as below:

Engine: EMD 12N-710G3B-U2 two stroke of 2420 kW (3245 hp) at 904 rpm.
Traction Motors: General Motors D43TRC.
Fuel Capacity: 5546 litres (66718–722) or 5150 litres (66723–732/747–749).

66747–749 were originally built for Crossrail AG in the Netherlands.

66750/751 were originally built for mainland Europe in 2003.

66718	**AL**	E	GBCM		RR	Sir Peter Hendy CBE
66719	**GB**	E	GBCM		RR	METRO-LAND
66720	**O**	E	GBCM		RR	
66721	**AL**	E	GBCM		RR	Harry Beck
66722	**GB**	E	GBCM		RR	Sir Edward Watkin
66723	**FS**	E	GBSD		RR	Chinook
66724	**FS**	E	GBSD		RR	Drax Power Station
66725	**FS**	E	GBSD		RR	SUNDERLAND
66726	**FS**	E	GBSD		RR	SHEFFIELD WEDNESDAY
66727	**FS**	E	GBSD		RR	Andrew Scott CBE
66728	**GB**	P	GBCM		RR	Institution of Railway Operators
66729	**GB**	P	GBCM		RR	DERBY COUNTY
66730	**GB**	P	GBCM		RR	Whitemoor
66731	**GB**	P	GBCM		RR	interhub GB
66732	**GB**	P	GBCM		RR	GBRf The First Decade 1999–2009
						John Smith – MD

66733	(66401)	r	**GB**	P	GBFM	RR		Cambridge PSB
66735	(66403)	r	**GB**	P	GBFM	RR		
66736	(66404)	r	**GB**	P	GBFM	RR		WOLVERHAMPTON WANDERERS
66737	(66405)	r	**GB**	P	GBFM	RR		Lesia
66738	(66578)		**GB**	BN	GBCM	RR		HUDDERSFIELD TOWN
66739	(66579)		**GB**	BN	GBCM	RR		Bluebell Railway
66740	(66580)		**GB**	BN	GBCM	RR		Sarah
66741	(66581)		**GB**	BN	GBCM	RR		

66742	(66406, 66841)	**GB**	BN	GBRT	RR	ABP Port of Immingham
						Centenary 1912–2012
66743	(66407, 66842)	**GB**	BN	GBRT	RR	
66744	(66408, 66843)	**GB**	BN	GBRT	RR	Crossrail
66745	(66409, 66844)	**GB**	BN	GBRT	RR	Modern Railways
						The first 50 Years
66746	(66410, 66845)	**GB**	BN	GBRT	RR	

66747	(20078968-007)	**U**	GB	GBNL	RR	
66748	(20078968-004)	**U**	GB	GBNL	RR	
66749	(20078968-006)	**U**	GB	GBNL	RR	
66750	(20038513-01)	**O**	BN	GBDR	RR	
66751	(20038513-04)	**GB**	BN	GBDR	RR	

66752–779. Low emission. New build locomotives (66772–779 on order).

Engine: EMD 12N-710G3B-U2 two stroke of 2420 kW (3245 hp) at 904 rpm.
Traction Motors: General Motors D43TRC.
Fuel Capacity: 5150 litres.

66752	**GB**	GB	GBNB		RR	The Hoosier State
66753	**GB**	GB	GBNB		RR	EMD Roberts Road
66754	**GB**	GB	GBNB		RR	
66755	**GB**	GB	GBNB		RR	
66756	**GB**	GB	GBNB		RR	
66757	**GB**	GB	GBNB		RR	
66758	**GB**	GB	GBNB		RR	
66759	**GB**	GB	GBNB		RR	

66760	**GB**	GB	GBNB	RR
66761	**GB**	GB	GBNB	RR
66762	**GB**	GB	GBNB	RR
66763	**GB**	GB	GBNB	RR
66764	**GB**	GB	GBNB	RR
66765	**GB**	GB	GBNB	RR
66766	**GB**	GB	GBNB	RR
66767	**GB**	GB	GBNB	RR
66768	**GB**	GB	GBNB	RR
66769	**GB**	GB	GBNB	RR
66770	**GB**	GB	GBNB	RR
66771	**GB**	GB	GBNB	RR
66772	**GB**	GB	GBNB	RR
66573				
66574				
66775				
66776				
66777				
66778				
66779				

Class 66/8. Colas Rail locos. Renumbered from former Freightliner locos 66573–577. Details as Class 66/0.

66846	(66573)	**CS**	CS	COLO	RU	
66847	(66574)	**CS**	CS	COLO	RU	
66848	(66575)	**CS**	CS	COLO	RU	
66849	(66576)	**CS**	CS	COLO	RU	Wylam Dilly
66850	(66577)	**CS**	CS	COLO	RU	David Maidment OBE

Class 66/9. Freightliner locos. Low emission "demonstrator" locos. Details as Class 66/0 except:

Engine: EMD 12N-710G3B-U2 two stroke of 2420 kW (3245 hp) at 904 rpm.
Traction Motors: General Motors D43TRC.
Fuel Capacity: 5905/5150 litres.

66951	**FL**	E	DFHG	LD	
66952	**FL**	E	DFHG	LD	

Class 66/9. Freightliner-operated low emission locos. Owing to the 665xx number range being full, subsequent deliveries of 66/5s were numbered from 66953 onwards. Details as Class 66/5 (low emission).

66953	**FL**	BN	DFHG	LD	
66954	**FL**	BN	DFIN	LD	
66955	**FL**	BN	DFIN	LD	
66956	**FL**	BN	DFHG	LD	
66957	**FL**	BN	DFHG	LD	Stephenson Locomotive Society 1909–2009

CLASS 67   ALSTOM/GENERAL MOTORS EMD Bo-Bo

Built: 1999–2000 by Alstom at Valencia, Spain, as sub-contractors for General Motors (General Motors model JT42 HW-HS).
Engine: GM 12N-710G3B-EC two stroke of 2385 kW (3200 hp) at 904 rpm.
Main Alternator: General Motors AR9A/HEP7/CA6C.
Traction Motors: General Motors D43FM.
Maximum Tractive Effort: 141 kN (31770 lbf).
Continuous Tractive Effort: 90 kN (20200 lbf) at 46.5 mph.

Power at Rail: 1860 kW.	**Train Brakes:** Air.
Brake Force: 78 t.	**Dimensions:** 19.74 x 2.72 m.
Weight: 90 t.	**Wheel Diameter:** 965 mm.
Design Speed: 125 mph.	**Maximum Speed:** 125 mph.
Fuel Capacity: 4927 litres.	**RA:** 8.
Train Supply: Electric, index 66.	**Multiple Working:** AAR System.

All equipped with Slow Speed Control and Swinghead Automatic "Buckeye" Combination Couplers.

67001/002/029 have been modified to operate in push-pull mode on the Arriva Trains Wales loco-hauled sets.

67004, 67007, 67009 and 67011 are fitted with cast iron brake blocks for working the Fort William Sleeper. **Maximum Speed:** 80 mph.

67008/010/012–015/017/018/023/025 have been modified to operate in push-pull mode on the Chiltern Railways loco-hauled sets.

Non-standard liveries: 67026 Diamond Jubilee silver.

67029 All over silver with DB logos.

67001	**AB**	A	WAWC	CE	
67002	**AB**	A	WAWC	CE	
67003	**AB**	A	WAAC	CE	
67004 r	**E**	A	WABC	CE	
67005	**RZ**	A	WAAC	CE	Queen's Messenger
67006	**RZ**	A	WQAA	CE (S)	Royal Sovereign
67007 r	**E**	A	WQAA	CE (S)	
67008	**E**	A	WACC	CE	
67009 r	**E**	A	WABC	CE	
67010	**CM**	A	WACC	CE	
67011 r	**E**	A	WABC	CE	
67012	**CM**	A	WAAC	CE	A Shropshire Lad
67013	**CM**	A	WACC	CE	
67014	**CM**	A	WACC	CE	Thomas Telford
67015	**CM**	A	WAAC	CE	David J. Lloyd
67016	**E**	A	WAAC	CE	
67017	**E**	A	WACC	CE	Arrow
67018	**DB**	A	WACC	CE	Keith Heller
67019	**E**	A	WAAC	CE	
67020	**E**	A	WACC	CE	
67021	**E**	A	WAAC	CE	
67022	**E**	A	WAAC	CE	

67023		E	A	WACC	CE	
67024		E	A	WAAC	CE	
67025		E	A	WAAC	CE	Western Star
67026		0	A	WAAC	CE	Diamond Jubilee
67027		DB	A	WAAC	CE	
67028		E	A	WAAC	CE	
67029		0	A	WAWC	CE	Royal Diamond
67030	r	E	A	WABC	CE	

CLASS 68   VOSSLOH   Bo-Bo

New Vossloh mixed-traffic locos currently being delivered to DRS. 68010–015 will be dedicated to operating the Chiltern Railways loco-hauled trains.

Built: 2012–14 by Vossloh, Valencia, Spain.
Engine: Caterpillar C175-16 of 2800 kW (3750 hp) at 1740 rpm.
Main Alternator: ABB WGX560.
Traction Motors: 4 x AC frame mounted ABB 4FRA6063.
Maximum Tractive Effort: 317 kN (71 260 lbf).
Continuous Tractive Effort:
Power at Rail: **Train Brakes:** Air.
Brake Force: 65.2 t.   **Dimensions:** 20.50 x 2.69 m.
Weight: 86 t.   **Wheel Diameter:** 1100 mm.
Design Speed: 100 mph.   **Maximum Speed:** 100 mph.
Fuel Capacity: 6000 litres.   **RA:** 7.
Train Supply: Electric, index 100.
Multiple Working: Within class and with Class 88. 68008–015 AAR system.

68001	DI	BN	XHVE	CR	Evolution
68002	DI	BN	XHVE	CR	Intrepid
68003	DI	BN	XHVE	CR	Astute
68004	DI	BN	XHVE	CR	Rapid
68005	DI	BN	XHVE	CR	Defiant
68006	DI	BN	XHVE	CR	Daring
68007	DI	BN	XHVE	CR	Valiant
68008	DI	BN	XHVE	CR	Avenger
68009	DI	BN	XHVE	CR	Titan
68010	CM	BN	XHCE	CR	
68011	CM	BN	XHCE	CR	
68012	CM	BN	XHCE	CR	
68013	CM	BN	XHCE	CR	
68014	CM	BN	XHCE	CR	
68015	CM	BN	XHCE	CR	
68016		BN			
68017		BN			
68018		BN			
68019		BN			
68020		BN			

68021	BN
68022	BN
68023	BN
68024	BN
68025	BN

CLASS 70   GENERAL ELECTRIC   Co-Co

New GE "PowerHaul" locomotives. 70012 was badly damaged whilst being unloaded in 2011 and was returned to Pennsylvania.

70801 (built as 70099) is a Turkish-built demonstrator that arrived in Britain in October 2012. Colas Rail leased this locomotive and then in 2013 ordered a further nine locomotives (70802–810) that were delivered in 2014.

Built: 2009–14 by General Electric, Erie, Pennsylvania, USA or by TÜLOMSAS, Eskişehir, Turkey (70801).
Engine: General Electric PowerHaul P616LDA1 of 2848 kW (3820 hp) at 1500 rpm.
Main Alternator: General Electric GTA series.
Traction Motors: AC-GE 5GEB30.
Maximum Tractive Effort: 544 kN (122 000 lbf).
Continuous Tractive Effort: 427 kN (96000 lbf) at ?? m.p.h.

Power at Rail:	**Train Brakes:** Air.
Brake Force: 96.7t.	**Dimensions:** 21.71 x 2.64 m.
Weight: 129 t.	**Wheel Diameter:** 1066 mm.
Design Speed: 75 mph.	**Maximum Speed:** 75 mph.
Fuel Capacity: 6000 litres.	**RA:** 7.
Train Supply: Not equipped.	**Multiple Working:** AAR System.

Class 70/0. Freightliner locomotives.

70001	FH	MQ	DFGI	LD	PowerHaul
70002	FH	MQ	DFGH	LD	
70003	FH	MQ	DFGH	LD	
70004	FH	MQ	DFGH	LD	The Coal Industry Society
70005	FH	MQ	DFGH	LD	
70006	FH	MQ	DFGH	LD	
70007	FH	MQ	DFGI	LD	
70008	FH	MQ	DFGI	LD	
70009	FH	MQ	DFGI	LD	
70010	FH	MQ	DFGH	LD	
70011	FH	MQ	DFGH	LD	
70013	FH	MQ	DFGI	LD	
70014	FH	MQ	DFGI	LD	
70015	FH	MQ	DFGI	LD	
70016	FH	MQ	DFGI	LD	
70017	FH	MQ	DFGI	LD	
70018	FH	MQ	DFGI	LD	
70019	FH	MQ	DFGI	LD	
70020	FH	MQ	DFGI	LD	

Class 70/8. Colas Rail locomotives.

70801	**CS** LF	COLO	RU
70802	**CS** LF	COLO	RU
70803	**CS** LF	COLO	RU
70804	**CS** LF	COLO	RU
70805	**CS** LF	COLO	RU
70806	**CS** LF	COLO	RU
70807	**CS** LF	COLO	RU
70808	**CS** LF	COLO	RU
70809	**CS** LF	COLO	RU
70810	**CS** LF	COLO	RU

1.2. ELECTRO-DIESEL & ELECTRIC LOCOMOTIVES

CLASS 73   BR/ENGLISH ELECTRIC   Bo-Bo

Electro-diesel locomotives which can operate either from a DC supply or using power from a diesel engine.

Built: 1965–67 by English Electric Co. at Vulcan Foundry, Newton-le-Willows.
Engine: English Electric 4SRKT of 447 kW (600 hp) at 850 rpm.
Main Generator: English Electric 824/5D.
Electric Supply System: 750 V DC from third rail.
Traction Motors: English Electric 546/1B.
Maximum Tractive Effort (Electric): 179 kN (40000 lbf).
Maximum Tractive Effort (Diesel): 160 kN (36000 lbf).
Continuous Rating (Electric): 1060 kW (1420 hp) giving a tractive effort of 35 kN (7800 lbf) at 68 mph.
Continuous Tractive Effort (Diesel): 60 kN (13600 lbf) at 11.5 mph.
Maximum Rail Power (Electric): 2350 kW (3150 hp) at 42 mph.
Train Brakes: Air, vacuum & electro-pneumatic († Air & electro-pneumatic).

Brake Force: 31 t.	**Dimensions:** 16.36 x 2.64 m.
Weight: 77 t.	**Wheel Diameter:** 1016 mm.
Design Speed: 90 mph.	**Maximum Speed:** 90 mph.
Fuel Capacity: 1409 litres.	**RA:** 6.

Train Supply: Electric, index 66 (on electric power only).
Multiple Working: SR 27-way System & Blue Star.

Formerly numbered E6001–E6020/E6022–E6026/E6028–E6049 (not in order).

Locomotives numbered in the 732xx series are classed as 73/2 and were originally dedicated to Gatwick Express services.

Two separate rebuild projects are underway. For GBRf at least 11 locomotives are being rebuilt at Brush, Loughborough with a 1600 hp MTU engine (these will be renumbered in the 73961 onwards series). For Network Rail 73104/211 are being rebuilt at RVEL, Derby with a pair of QSK19 750 hp engines (these will become 73951/952).

Non-standard liveries:

73107 and 73128 Two-tone grey.
73109 Mid blue.
73139 Weardale Railway brown & cream.

73101	**PC**	RE	RVLO	ZA (S)	
73107	**O**	GB	GBED	SE	Redhill 1844–1994
73109	**O**	GB	GBED	SE	
73119	**B**	GB	GBED	SE	Borough of Eastleigh
73128	**O**	20	MBED	SE	OVS Bulleid CBE
73133	**TT**	TT	MBED	BM	
73136	**GB**	GB	GBED	SE	

73138	**Y**	NR	QADD	ZA	
73139	**0**	RE	RVLO	ZA (S)	
73141	**GB**	GB	GBED	SE	Charlotte
73201 †	**B**	GB	GBED	SE	Broadlands
73202 †	**SN**	P	MBED	SL	
73207 †	**BL**	GB	GBED	SE	
73212 †	**GB**	GB	GBED	SE	Fiona
73213 †	**GB**	GB	GBED	SE	Rhodalyn
73235 †	**SD**	P	HYWD	BM	

CLASS 73/9 (RVEL)　　　BR/RVEL　　　Bo-Bo

The 7395x number series is reserved for rebuilt Network Rail locomotives.

Rebuilt: Re-engineered by RVEL Derby 2013–15.
Engine: 2 x QSK19 of 560 kw (750 hp) at 1800 rpm (total 1120 kw (1500 hp)).
Main Alternator: 2 x Marathon Magnaplus.
Electric Supply System: 750 V DC from third rail.
Traction Motors: English Electric 546/1B.
Maximum Tractive Effort (Electric): 179 kN (40000 lbf).
Maximum Tractive Effort (Diesel): 179 kN (40000 lbf).
Continuous Rating (Electric): 1060 kW (1420 hp) giving a tractive effort of 35 kN (7800 lbf) at 68 mph.
Continuous Tractive Effort (Diesel): 990 kW (1328 hp) giving a tractive effort of 33 kN (7420 lbf) at 68 mph.
Maximum Rail Power (Electric): 2350 kW (3150 hp) at 42 mph.

Train Brakes: Air.		**Brake Force:** 31 t.
Weight: 77 t.		**Dimensions:** 16.36 x 2.64 m.
Maximum Speed: 90 mph.		**Wheel Diameter:** 1016 mm.
Fuel Capacity: 2260 litres.		**RA:** 6.
Train Supply: None.		**Multiple Working:** SR 27-way System.

| 73951 (73104) | **Y** | RE | RVLO | ZA (S) |
| 73952 (73211) | **Y** | RE | RVLO | ZA (S) |

CLASS 73/9 (GBRf)　　　BR/BRUSH　　　Bo-Bo

GBRf Class 73s are being rebuilt at Brush Loughborough. 73961–965 are earmarked for Network Rail contracts and 73966–971 for the Caledonian Sleeper contract.

Rebuilt: Re-engineered by Brush, Loughborough 2014– .
Engine: MTU 8V4000 R43L of 1195 kW (1600 hp) at 1800 rpm.
Main Alternator: Lechmotoren SDV 87.53-12.
Electric Supply System: 750 V DC from third rail.
Traction Motors: English Electric 546/1B.
Maximum Tractive Effort (Electric): 179 kN (40000 lbf).
Maximum Tractive Effort (Diesel): 179 kN (40000 lbf).
Continuous Rating (Electric): 1060 kW (1420 hp) giving a tractive effort of 35 kN (7800 lbf) at 68 mph.
Continuous Tractive Effort (Diesel): awaited.
Maximum Rail Power (Electric): 2350 kW (3150 hp) at 42 mph.

Train Brakes: Air.   **Brake Force:** 31 t.
Weight: 77 t.   **Dimensions:** 16.36 x 2.64 m.
Maximum Speed: 90 mph.   **Wheel Diameter:** 1016 mm.
Fuel Capacity: 1409 litres.   **RA:** 6.
Train Supply: Electric, index 38 (electric & diesel).
Multiple Working: SR 27-way System & AAR (diesel only).

When converted 73966–971 will have a higher Train Supply index (96) and a slightly higher fuel capacity of 1509 litres.

73961	(73209)	**GB**	GB	GBBR	SE	Alison
73962	(73204)	**GB**	GB	GBBR	SE	Dick Mabbutt
73963	(73206)	**GB**	GB	GBBR	LB (S)	Janice
73964	(73205)	**GB**	GB	GBBR	LB (S)	Jeanette
73965	(73208)		GB	GBBR	LB (S)	
73966	(73005)		GB	GBBR	LB (S)	
73967	(73006)		GB	GBBR	LB (S)	
73968	(73117)		GB	GBBR	LB (S)	
73969	(73105)		GB	GBBR	LB (S)	
73970	(73103)		GB	GBBR	LB (S)	
73971	(73207)					

CLASS 86   BR/ENGLISH ELECTRIC   Bo-Bo

Built: 1965–66 by English Electric Co at Vulcan Foundry, Newton-le-Willows or by BR at Doncaster Works.
Electric Supply System: 25 kV AC 50 Hz overhead.
Train Brakes: Air.   **Brake Force:** 40 t.
Dimensions: 17.83 x 2.65 m.   **Weight:** 83–86.8 t.
RA: 6.   **Multiple Working:** TDM system.
Train Supply: Electric, index 66.

Formerly numbered E3101–E3200 (not in order).

Class 86s exported for use abroad are listed in section 1.6 of this book.

Class 86/1. Class 87-type bogies & motors.

Details as above except:
Traction Motors: GEC 412AZ frame mounted.
Maximum Tractive Effort: 258 kN (58000 lbf).
Continuous Rating: 3730 kW (5000 hp) giving a tractive effort of 95 kN (21300 lbf) at 87 mph.
Maximum Rail Power: 5860 kW (7860 hp) at 50.8 mph.
Wheel Diameter: 1150 mm.   **Weight:** 86.8 t.
Design Speed: 110 mph.   **Maximum Speed:** 110 mph.

86101	**B**	EL	ACAC	WN	Sir William A Stanier FRS

Class 86/2. Standard design rebuilt with resilient wheels & Flexicoil suspension.

Traction Motors: AEI 282BZ axle hung.
Maximum Tractive Effort: 207 kN (46500 lbf).
Continuous Rating: 3010 kW (4040 hp) giving a tractive effort of 85 kN (19200 lbf) at 77.5 mph.

Maximum Rail Power: 4550 kW (6100 hp) at 49.5 mph.
Wheel Diameter: 1156 mm.   **Weight:** 85–86.2 t.
Design Speed: 125 mph.   **Maximum Speed:** 100 mph.

Non-standard livery: 86259 BR "Electric blue".

86229	**V**	EP	EPEX	LM (S)	
86231	**V**	EP	EPEX	LM (S)	
86234	**AR**	EP	EPEX	LM (S)	
86235	**AR**	EP	EPUK	LM (S)	
86246	**AR**	EP	EPEX	LM (S)	
86247	**EX**	P	DHLT	BA (S)	
86251	**V**	EP	EPEX	LM (S)	
86259 x	**0**	PP	MBEL	WN	Les Ross

Class 86/4.

Traction Motors: AEI 282AZ axle hung.
Maximum Tractive Effort: 258 kN (58000 lbf).
Continuous Rating: 2680 kW (3600 hp) giving a tractive effort of 89 kN (20000 lbf) at 67 mph.
Maximum Rail Power: 4400 kW (5900 hp) at 38 mph.
Wheel Diameter: 1156 mm.   **Weight:** 83–83.9 t.
Design Speed: 100 mph.   **Maximum Speed:** 100 mph.

86401	**N**	EL	ACXX	WN (S) Northampton Town	

Class 86/5. Regeared locomotive operated by Freightliner.

Details as Class 86/4 except:

Continuous Rating: 2680 kW (3600 hp) giving a tractive effort of 117 kN (26300 lbf) at 67 mph.
Maximum Speed: 75 mph.   **Train Supply:** Electric, isolated.

86501 (86608)	**FL**	FL	DFMC	CP

Class 86/6. Freightliner-operated locomotives.

Details as Class 86/4 except:

Maximum Speed: 75 mph.   **Train Supply:** Electric, isolated.

86604	**FL**	FL	DFNC	CP
86605	**FL**	FL	DFNC	CP
86607	**FL**	FL	DFNC	CP
86609	**FL**	FL	DFNC	CP
86610	**FL**	FL	DFNC	CP
86612	**FL**	P	DFNC	CP
86613	**FL**	P	DFNC	CP
86614	**FL**	P	DFNC	CP
86622	**FH**	P	DFNC	CP
86627	**FL**	P	DFNC	CP
86628	**FL**	P	DFNC	CP
86632	**FL**	P	DFNC	CP
86637	**FH**	P	DFNC	CP
86638	**FL**	P	DFNC	CP
86639	**FL**	P	DFNC	CP

Class 86/7. Europhoenix-owned locomotives. Refurbished Class 86/2s for the UK spot-hire market. Details as Class 86/2 unless stated.

Maximum Speed: 110 mph.   **Weight:** 85t.
Train Supply: Electric, index 74.

```
86701 (86205)  CS EP EPUK    WN (S)  Orion
86702 (86260)  EL EP EPUK    WN (S)  Cassiopeia
```

CLASS 87   BREL/GEC   Bo-Bo

Built: 1973–75 by BREL at Crewe Works.
Electric Supply System: 25 kV AC 50 Hz overhead.
Traction Motors: GEC G412AZ frame mounted.
Maximum Tractive Effort: 258 kN (58000 lbf).
Continuous Rating: 3730 kW (5000 hp) giving a tractive effort of 95 kN (21300 lbf) at 87 mph.
Maximum Rail Power: 5860 kW (7860 hp) at 50.8 mph.
Train Brakes: Air.   **Brake Force:** 40 t.
Dimensions: 17.83 x 2.65 m.   **Weight:** 83.3 t.
Wheel Diameter: 1150 mm.   **Design Speed:** 110 mph.
Maximum Speed: 110 mph.   **Train Supply:** Electric, index 95.
RA: 6.   **Multiple Working:** TDM system.

Class 87s exported for use abroad are listed in section 1.6 of this book.

```
87002    B    EL  ETLO     WN    Royal Sovereign
```

CLASS 88   VOSSLOH   Bo-Bo

Ten new Vossloh bi-mode locomotives on order for DRS and due for delivery 2015–16. Full details awaited.
Built: 2014–15 by Vossloh, Valencia, Spain.
Electric Supply System: 25 kV AC 50 Hz overhead.
Engine: Caterpillar 12-cylinder 700 kW (940 hp) at 1800 rpm.
Traction Motors: ABB.
Maximum Tractive Effort (Electric):
Maximum Tractive Effort (Diesel):
Continuous Rating: 4000 kW (5360 hp).
Maximum Rail Power: **Dimensions:**
Train Brakes: Air.   **Brake Force:**
Weight: **Wheel Diameter:**
Fuel capacity: **Train Supply:**
Design Speed: 100 mph.   **Maximum Speed:** 100 mph.
RA:
Multiple Working: Within class and with Class 68.

```
88001        BN
88002        BN
88003        BN
88004        BN
88005        BN
88006        BN
```

88007	BN
88008	BN
88009	BN
88010	BN

CLASS 90   GEC   Bo-Bo

Built: 1987–90 by BREL at Crewe Works (as sub contractors for GEC).
Electric Supply System: 25 kV AC 50 Hz overhead.
Traction Motors: GEC G412CY frame mounted.
Maximum Tractive Effort: 258 kN (58000 lbf).
Continuous Rating: 3730 kW (5000 hp) giving a tractive effort of 95 kN (21300 lbf) at 87 mph.
Maximum Rail Power: 5860 kW (7860 hp) at 68.3 mph.
Train Brakes: Air.

Brake Force: 40 t.	**Dimensions:** 18.80 x 2.74 m.
Weight: 84.5 t.	**Wheel Diameter:** 1150 mm.
Design Speed: 110 mph.	**Maximum Speed:** 110 mph.
Train Supply: Electric, index 95.	**RA:** 7.
Multiple Working: TDM system.	

90001	b	GA	P	IANA	NC	Crown Point
90002	b	1	P	IANA	NC	Eastern Daily Press 1870–2010 SERVING NORFOLK FOR 140 YEARS
90003	b	NX	P	IANA	NC	Rædwald of East Anglia
90004	b	1	P	IANA	NC	City of Chelmsford
90005	b	GA	P	IANA	NC	Vice-Admiral Lord Nelson
90006	b	1	P	IANA	NC	Modern Railways Magazine/ Roger Ford
90007	b	1	P	IANA	NC	Sir John Betjeman
90008	b	NX	P	IANA	NC	The East Anglian
90009	b	1	P	IANA	NC	Diamond Jubilee
90010	b	GA	P	IANA	NC	
90011	b	GA	P	IANA	NC	East Anglian Daily Times Suffolk & Proud
90012	b	1	P	IANA	NC	Royal Anglian Regiment
90013	b	GA	P	IANA	NC	
90014	b	GA	P	IANA	NC	Norfolk and Norwich Festival
90015	b	NX	P	IANA	NC	Colchester Castle
90016		FL	P	DFLC	CP	
90017		E	DB	WQBA	CE (S)	
90018		DB	DB	WEAC	CE	
90019		FS	DB	WEAC	CE	
90020		E	DB	WEAC	CE	Collingwood
90021		FS	DB	WEAC	CE	
90022		EG	DB	WQBA	CE (S)	Freightconnection
90023		E	DB	WQBA	CE (S)	
90024		FS	DB	WEAC	CE	
90025		F	DB	WQBA	CE (S)	
90026		E	DB	WQAA	CE (S)	
90027		F	DB	WQBA	CE (S)	Allerton T&RS Depot
90028		E	DB	WQAA	CE (S)	

90029	**DB**	DB	WEAC	CE	
90030	**E**	DB	WQBA	CE (S)	
90031	**E**	DB	WQBA	CE (S)	The Railway Children Partnership
					Working For Street Children Worldwide
90032	**E**	DB	WQBA	CE (S)	
90033	**FE**	DB	WQBA	CE (S)	
90034	**DR**	DB	WEAC	CE	
90035	**E**	DB	WEAC	CE	
90036	**DB**	DB	WEAC	CE	Driver Jack Mills
90037	**E**	DB	WEAC	CE	Spirit of Dagenham
90038	**FE**	DB	WQBA	CE (S)	
90039	**E**	DB	WEAC	CE	
90040	**E**	DB	WQAA	CE (S)	The Railway Mission
90041	**FL**	P	DFLC	CP	
90042	**FH**	P	DFLC	CP	
90043	**FF**	P	DFLC	CP	Freightliner Coatbridge
90044	**FF**	P	DFLC	CP	
90045	**FH**	P	DFLC	CP	
90046	**FL**	P	DFLC	CP	
90047	**FF**	P	DFLC	CP	
90048	**FF**	P	DFLC	CP	
90049	**FH**	P	DFLC	CP	
90050	**FF**	AV	MBEL	BA (S)	

CLASS 91　　　　　GEC　　　　　Bo-Bo

Built: 1988–91 by BREL at Crewe Works (as sub contractors for GEC).
Electric Supply System: 25 kV AC 50 Hz overhead.
Traction Motors: GEC G426AZ.
Maximum Tractive Effort: 190 kN (43 000 lbf).
Continuous Rating: 4540 kW (6090 hp) giving a tractive effort of 170 kN at 96 mph.
Maximum Rail Power: 4700 kW (6300 hp) at ?? mph.
Train Brakes: Air.
Brake Force: 45 t.
Weight: 84 t.
Design Speed: 140 mph.
Train Supply: Electric, index 95.
Multiple Working: TDM system.

Dimensions: 19.41 x 2.74 m.
Wheel Diameter: 1000 mm.
Maximum Speed: 125 mph.
RA: 7.

Locomotives originally numbered in the 910xx series, but renumbered upon completion of overhauls at Bombardier, Doncaster by the addition of 100 to their original number. The exception to this rule was 91023 which was renumbered 91132.

91114 has been fitted with a second pantograph for evaluation purposes.

Advertising liveries: 91101 Flying Scotsman (purple).

91110 Battle of Britain (black and grey).

91111 For the fallen (various with poppy and Union Jack vinyls).

▲ 08649 shunts two Greater Anglia Mark 3s at Knorr Bremse Rail Services' Wolverton site on 16/04/14. **John Pink**

▼ Harry Needle Railroad Company 08943 is seen at the Bombardier Transportation depot at Central Rivers on 08/10/13. **Paul Abell**

▲ BR Railfreight grey-liveried 20132 and 20118 are seen stabled at Derby on 13/09/14. **Robert Pritchard**

▼ Devon & Cornwall Railways green-liveried 31601 passes Shipton-by-Benningborough with a Darlington–York engineers train on 18/05/14.
Andrew Mason

▲ West Coast Railway Company-liveried 33029 passes Shrivenham with a train of empty coaching stock from Southall to Bristol on 26/07/14.   **Jamie Squibbs**

▼ Newly restored to main line action, BR Blue-liveried 40145 passes Horbury Bridge, east of Healey Mills, with a 13.14 Carnforth–Castleton railtour on 06/06/14.   **Andrew Wills**

▲ In the latest DRS livery, 37423 runs off the Deepcar branch at Nunnery, Sheffield, with an 09.49 Doncaster West Yard–Derby test train on 01/07/14. 37667 was on the rear of the train. **Andrew Wills**

▲ The Network Rail New Measurement Train HST, with power cars 43014/013, passes Cleghorn with a 12.07 Glasgow Central–Crewe on 15/04/14. **Robin Ralston**

▼ East Midlands Trains HST 43073/044 passes through the Mere Valley shortly after departure from Scarborough with the 17.03 Scarborough–London St Pancras on 09/08/14. **Andrew Mason**

▲ Riviera Trains-liveried 47843 leads the 06.58 Doncaster–Great Yarmouth GBRf charter near Syston on 24/08/14. **Louis Hurst**

▼ Back on the main line in 2014 was BR blue-liveried 50007, seen here double-heading the 08.59 Washwood Heath–Boston Docks steel train with Colas Rail 56105 at Hemington, near Castle Donington, on 17/05/14. **Paul Biggs**

▲ BR Maroon-liveried D1015 "Western Champion" rounds the curve at Marazion with an 05.00 Tame Bridge Parkway–Penzance railtour on 28/06/14. **Ron Westwater**

▼ Colas Rail 56105 passes Caverswall, near Blythe Bridge, with 6S96 13.15 Sinfin–Grangemouth empty tanks on 12/06/14. **Cliff Beeton**

▲ West Coast Railway Company-liveried 57601 passes Plean with the 14.30 Stirling–London Euston Statesman railtour on 17/08/13. **Ian Lothian**

▼ Aggregate Industries-liveried 59001 passes Berkley, near Frome, with 6C76 14.40 Acton–Merehead stone empties on 13/06/13. **Roger Geach**

▲ Colas Rail-liveried 60087 exits Chipping Sodbury Tunnel with 6V62 11.22 Tilbury–Llanwern steel empties on 06/08/14. **Jamie Squibbs**

▼ DRS-liveried 66303 is seen stabled at Crewe Gresty Bridge depot on 11/03/14. **Robert Pritchard**

▲ GBRf-liveried 66738 heads north at Slindon, Staffordshire, with 4F01 16.07 Ironbridge–Seaforth empty biomass as Pendolino 390 107 overtakes with the 16.07 London Euston–Liverpool Lime Street on 14/05/14. **Brad Joyce**

▲ Diamond Jubilee silver-liveried 67026 passes Inverkeithing East Jn with the 18.14 Glenrothes–Edinburgh ScotRail loco-hauled train on 09/07/14. **Ian Lothian**

▼ One of the new Vossloh Class 68s, 68006, stands at Inverness container terminal on 25/08/14. DRS has ordered 25 of these locomotives which carry the latest DRS livery. **Alexander Colley**

▲ Colas Rail-liveried 70803 (on hire to Freightliner) passes Bentley, Suffolk with 4M81 08.01 Felixstowe–Crewe Intermodal on 12/08/14. **Antony Guppy**

▼ Network Rail yellow-liveried 73138 trails a Crewe–Derby test train (led by 73141) at Longport on 25/07/14. **Cliff Beeton**

▲ The first of the rebuilt GBRf Class 73s, 73961, is seen on test at Quorn & Woodhouse on the Great Central Railway with preserved Class 31 D5830 on 17/09/14. **Keith Satterly**

▼ BR Blue-liveried 87002 passes Cromwell, between Retford and Newark, with an 07.09 Newcastle–London King's Cross GBRf charter on 09/08/14. **Lindsay Atkinson**

Ashton, south of Roade, with 4L89 04.10 Crewe–Felixstowe intermodal
Nigel Gibbs

91101	**AL**	E	IECA	BN	
91102	**EC**	E	IECA	BN	City of York
91103	**EC**	E	IECA	BN	
91104	**EC**	E	IECA	BN	
91105	**EC**	E	IECA	BN	
91106	**EC**	E	IECA	BN	
91107	**EC**	E	IECA	BN	SKYFALL
91108	**EC**	E	IECA	BN	
91109	**EC**	E	IECA	BN	Sir Bobby Robson
91110	**AL**	E	IECA	BN	BATTLE OF BRITAIN MEMORIAL FLIGHT
91111	**AL**	E	IECA	BN	For the Fallen
91112	**EC**	E	IECA	BN	
91113	**EC**	E	IECA	BN	
91114	**EC**	E	IECA	BN	Durham Cathedral
91115	**EC**	E	IECA	BN	Blaydon Races
91116	**EC**	E	IECA	BN	
91117	**EC**	E	IECA	BN	WEST RIDING LIMITED
91118	**EC**	E	IECA	BN	
91119	**EC**	E	IECA	BN	
91120	**EC**	E	IECA	BN	
91121	**EC**	E	IECA	BN	
91122	**EC**	E	IECA	BN	
91124	**EC**	E	IECA	BN	
91125	**EC**	E	IECA	BN	
91126	**EC**	E	IECA	BN	
91127	**EC**	E	IECA	BN	
91128	**EC**	E	IECA	BN	
91129	**EC**	E	IECA	BN	
91130	**EC**	E	IECA	BN	
91131	**EC**	E	IECA	BN	
91132	**EC**	E	IECA	BN	

CLASS 92   BRUSH   Co-Co

Built: 1993–96 by Brush Traction at Loughborough.
Electric Supply System: 25 kV AC 50 Hz overhead or 750 V DC third rail.
Traction Motors: Asea Brown Boveri design. Model 6FRA 7059B (Asynchronous 3-phase induction motors).
Maximum Tractive Effort: 400 kN (90 000 lbf).
Continuous Rating: 5040 kW (6760 hp) on AC, 4000 kW (5360 hp) on DC.
Maximum Rail Power: **Train Brakes:** Air.
Brake Force: 63 t.   **Dimensions:** 21.34 x 2.67 m.
Weight: 126 t.   **Wheel Diameter:** 1070 mm.
Design Speed: 140 km/h (87 mph).   **Maximum Speed:** 145 km/h (90 mph).
Train Supply: Electric, index 108 (AC), 70 (DC).
RA: 7.

* Modified to operate on High Speed 1.

Class 92s exported for use abroad are listed in section 1.6 of this book.

Advertising livery: 92017 Stobart Rail (two-tone blue & white).

92002	**EG**	DB	WGEE	CE (S)	H.G. Wells
92003 *	**EG**	DB	WFBC	CE	Beethoven
92004	**EG**	DB	WGEE	CE (S)	Jane Austen
92005 *	**EG**	DB	WFBC	CE	Mozart
92006	**EP**	GB	PTXX	LB (S)	Louis Armand
92007	**EG**	DB	WQBA	CE (S)	Schubert
92008	**EG**	DB	WQBA	CE (S)	Jules Verne
92009 *	**DB**	DB	WQBA	CE (S)	Marco Polo
92010	**EP**	GB	GBET	CO	Molière
92011	**EG**	DB	WFAC	CE	Handel
92013	**EG**	DB	WQAA	CE (S)	Puccini
92014	**EP**	GB	GBET	LB (S)	Emile Zola
92015 *	**DB**	DB	WFBC	CE	
92016 *	**DB**	DB	WFDC	CE	
92017	**AL**	DB	WQBA	CE (S)	Bart the Engine
92018	**EP**	GB	GBET	LB (S)	Stendhal
92019	**EG**	DB	WFBC	CE	Wagner
92020	**EP**	GB	PTXX	LB (S)	Milton
92021	**EP**	GB	PTXX	CO (S)	Purcell
92022	**EG**	DB	WQBA	CE (S)	Charles Dickens
92023	**EP**	GB	GBET	LB (S)	Ravel
92024	**EG**	DB	WFAC	CE	J.S. Bach
92026	**EG**	DB	WGEE	CE (S)	Britten
92028	**EP**	GB	GBET	CO	Saint Saëns
92029	**EG**	DB	WFCC	CE	Dante
92030	**EG**	DB	WGEE	CE (S)	Ashford
92031 *	**DB**	DB	WFBC	CE	
92032	**GB**	GB	GBET	CO	IMechE Railway Division
92033	**EP**	GB	GBET	LB (S)	Berlioz
92035	**EP**	DB	WQBA	CE (S)	Mendelssohn
92036 *	**EG**	DB	WFBC	CE	Bertolt Brecht
92037	**EG**	DB	WQAA	ME (S)	Sullivan
92038	**EP**	GB	GBET	CO	Voltaire
92039	**EG**	DB	WFAC	CE	Johann Strauss
92040	**EP**	GB	PTXX	CO (S)	Goethe
92041 *	**EG**	DB	WFBC	CE	Vaughan Williams
92042 *	**DB**	DB	WFBC	CE	
92043	**EP**	GB	GBET	CO	Debussy
92044	**EP**	GB	GBET	CO	Couperin
92045	**EP**	GB	GBET	LB (S)	Chaucer
92046	**EP**	GB	GBET	LB (S)	Sweelinck

1.3. EUROTUNNEL LOCOMOTIVES

DIESEL LOCOMOTIVES

0001–0007   MaK   Bo-Bo

Built: 1991–92 by MaK at Kiel, Germany (Model DE1004).
Engine: MTU 12V 396 TC13 of 940 kW (1260 hp) at 1800 rpm.
Main Alternator: ABB.   **Traction Motors:** ABB.
Maximum Tractive Effort: 305 kN (68600 lbf).
Continuous Tractive Effort: 140 kN (31500 lbf) at 20 mph.
Power At Rail: 750 kW (1012 hp).   **Dimensions:** 14.40 x ?? m.
Brake Force: 120 kN.   **Wheel Diameter:** 1000 mm.
Weight: 82 t.   **Maximum Speed:** 100 km/h.
Design Speed: 120 km/h.   **Train Brakes:** Air.
Fuel Capacity: 3500 litres.   **Multiple Working:** Within class.
Train Supply: Not equipped.   **Signalling System:** TVM430 cab signalling.

Registered on TOPS as 21901–907.

0001	**GY**	ET	CO
0002	**GY**	ET	CO
0003	**GY**	ET	CO
0004	**GY**	ET	CO
0005	**GY**	ET	CO

The following two locos were rebuilt from NS 6400 Class 6456 and 6457 (built 1991) and added to the Eurotunnel fleet in 2011.

0006	**GY**	ET	CO
0007	**GY**	ET	CO

0031–0042   HUNSLET/SCHÖMA   0-4-0

Built: 1989–90 by Hunslet Engine Company at Leeds as 900 mm gauge.
Rebuilt: 1993–94 by Schöma in Germany to 1435 mm gauge.
Engine: Deutz FL10L 413FW of 170 kW (230 hp) at 2300 rpm.
Transmission: Mechanical Clark 5000 series.
Maximum Tractive Effort:
Continuous Tractive Effort:
Power At Rail:
Brake Force: **Dimensions:** 6.63 x 2.69 m.
Weight: 26–28 t.   **Wheel Diameter:**
Design Speed: 48 km/h.   **Maximum Speed:** 50 km/h.
Fuel Capacity: **Train Brakes:** Air.
Train Supply: Not equipped.   **Multiple Working:** Not equipped.

* Rebuilt with inspection platforms to check overhead catenary.

0031	**GY**	ET	CO	FRANCES

0032		**GY**	ET	CO	ELISABETH
0033		**GY**	ET	CO	SILKE
0034		**GY**	ET	CO	AMANDA
0035		**GY**	ET	CO	MARY
0036		**GY**	ET	CO	LAURENCE
0037		**GY**	ET	CO	LYDIE
0038		**GY**	ET	CO	JENNY
0039	*	**GY**	ET	CO	PACITA
0040		**GY**	ET	CO	JILL
0041	*	**GY**	ET	CO	KIM
0042		**GY**	ET	CO	NICOLE

ELECTRIC LOCOMOTIVES

9005–9840   BRUSH/ABB   Bo-Bo-Bo

Built: 1993–2002 by Brush Traction at Loughborough.
Supply System: 25 kV AC 50 Hz overhead.
Traction Motors: Asea Brown Boveri design. Asynchronous 3-phase motors.
Model 6FHA 7059 (as built). Model 6FHA 7059C (7000 kW rated locos).
Maximum Tractive Effort: 400kN (90 000 lbf).
Continuous Rating: Class 9/0 and 9/1: 5760 kW (7725 hp). Class 9/7 and 9/8:
7000 kW (9387 hp).

Maximum Rail Power:	**Multiple Working:** TDM system.
Brake Force: 50 t.	**Dimensions:** 22.01 x 2.97 x 4.20 m.
Weight: 136 t.	**Wheel Diameter:** 1250 mm.
Design Speed: 100 mph.	**Maximum Speed:** 100 mph.
Train Supply: Electric.	**Train Brakes:** Air.

Class 9/0 Original build locos. Built 1993–94.

9005	**EB**	ET	CO	JESSYE NORMAN
9007	**EB**	ET	CO	DAME JOAN SUTHERLAND
9011	**EB**	ET	CO	JOSÉ VAN DAM
9013	**EB**	ET	CO	MARIA CALLAS
9015	**EB**	ET	CO	LÖTSCHBERG 1913
9018	**EB**	ET	CO	WILHELMENIA FERNANDEZ
9022	**EB**	ET	CO	DAME JANET BAKER
9024	**EB**	ET	CO	GOTTHARD 1882
9026	**EB**	ET	CO	FURKATUNNEL 1982
9029	**EB**	ET	CO	THOMAS ALLEN
9033	**EB**	ET	CO	MONTSERRAT CABALLE
9036	**EB**	ET	CO	ALAIN FONDARY
9037	**EB**	ET	CO	GABRIEL BACQUIER

Class 9/7. Increased power freight shuttle locos. Built 2001–02 (9711–23
built 1998–2001 as 9101–13 and rebuilt as 9711–23 2010–12).

9701	**EB**	ET	CO	
9702	**EB**	ET	CO	
9703	**EB**	ET	CO	

9704	**EB**	ET	CO	
9705	**EB**	ET	CO	
9706	**EB**	ET	CO	
9707	**EB**	ET	CO	
9711	(9101)	**EB**	ET	CO
9712	(9102)	**EB**	ET	CO
9713	(9103)	**EB**	ET	CO
9714	(9104)	**EB**	ET	CO
9715	(9105)	**EB**	ET	CO
9716	(9106)	**EB**	ET	CO
9717	(9107)	**EB**	ET	CO
9718	(9108)	**EB**	ET	CO
9719	(9109)	**EB**	ET	CO
9720	(9110)	**EB**	ET	CO
9721	(9111)	**EB**	ET	CO
9722	(9112)	**EB**	ET	CO
9723	(9113)	**EB**	ET	CO

Class 9/8 Locos rebuilt from Class 9/0 by adding 800 to the loco number. Uprated to 7000 kW.

9801	**EB**	ET	CO	LESLEY GARRETT
9802	**EB**	ET	CO	STUART BURROWS
9803	**EB**	ET	CO	BENJAMIN LUXON
9804	**EB**	ET	CO	VICTORIA DE LOS ANGELES
9806	**EB**	ET	CO	REGINE CRESPIN
9808	**EB**	ET	CO	ELISABETH SODERSTROM
9809	**EB**	ET	CO	FRANÇOISE POLLET
9810	**EB**	ET	CO	JEAN-PHILIPPE COURTIS
9812	**EB**	ET	CO	LUCIANO PAVAROTTI
9814	**EB**	ET	CO	LUCIA POPP
9816	**EB**	ET	CO	WILLARD WHITE
9817	**EB**	ET	CO (S)	JOSÉ CARRERAS
9819	**EB**	ET	CO	MARIA EWING
9820	**EB**	ET	CO	NICOLAI GHIAROV
9821	**EB**	ET	CO	TERESA BERGANZA
9823	**EB**	ET	CO	DAME ELISABETH LEGGE-SCHWARZKOPF
9825	**EB**	ET	CO	
9827	**EB**	ET	CO	BARBARA HENDRICKS
9828	**EB**	ET	CO	DAME KIRI TE KANAWA
9831	**EB**	ET	CO	
9832	**EB**	ET	CO	RENATA TEBALDI
9834	**EB**	ET	CO	MIRELLA FRENI
9835	**EB**	ET	CO	NICOLAI GEDDA
9838	**EB**	ET	CO	HILDEGARD BEHRENS
9840	**EB**	ET	CO	

1.4. FORMER BR MAIN LINE LOCOS IN INDUSTRIAL SERVICE

Former British Rail main line locomotives considered to be in "industrial use" are listed here. These locomotives do not currently have Network Rail engineering acceptance for operation on the national railway network.

Number Other no./name   Location

Class 03

03084	HELEN-LOUISE	West Coast Railway Company, Carnforth
03179	CLIVE	First Capital Connect, Hornsey Depot, London
03196	JOYCE/GLYNIS	West Coast Railway Company, Carnforth
D2381		West Coast Railway Company, Carnforth

Class 07

D2991	07007	Arlington Fleet Services, Eastleigh Works, Hampshire

Class 08

08202	CHUFFER	Chasewater Light Railway, Brownhills, Staffordshire
08220		EMD, Longport Works, Stoke-on-Trent
		(on loan from Nottingham Transport Heritage Centre)
08308	23	PD Ports, Teesport, Grangetown, Middlesbrough
08331		Midland Railway-Butterley, Derbyshire
08375	21	Hanson Cement, Ketton Cement Works, nr Stamford
08389		Barrow Hill Roundhouse, Chesterfield, Derbyshire
08393		LH Group, Barton-under-Needwood, Staffordshire
08401		Celsa Steel (UK), Castle Works, Cardiff
08411		Colne Valley Railway, Halstead, Essex
08418		West Coast Railway Company, Carnforth
08423	H011 14	PD Ports, Teesport, Grangetown, Middlesbrough
08441		RSS, Rye Farm, Wishaw, Sutton Coldfield
08442	RICHARD J. WENHAM	
	EASTLEIGH DEPOT	LNWR, Eastleigh Depot, Hampshire
08445		Daventry International Railfreight Terminal, Crick
08447		John G Russell (Transport), Hillington, Glasgow
08460		RSS, Rye Farm, Wishaw, Sutton Coldfield
08484	CAPTAIN NATHANIEL	
	DARELL	RSS, Rye Farm, Wishaw, Sutton Coldfield
08485		West Coast Railway Company, Carnforth
08499		Colas Rail, Canton Depot, Cardiff
08502		Barrow Hill Roundhouse, Chesterfield, Derbyshire
08503		Barry Island Railway, Vale of Glamorgan
08507		Riviera Trains, Crewe Down Holding Sidings
08511		Felixstowe Dock & Railway Company, Felixstowe
08516		LNWR, Barton Hill Depot, Bristol
08527		Northern Rail, Allerton Depot, Liverpool
08536		RVEL, RTC Business Park, Derby
08568	St. Rollox	Knorr-Bremse Rail Systems, Springburn Depot, Glasgow
08573		Bombardier Transportation, Ilford Works, London

Number	Name	Location
08588		Cemex UK, Washwood Heath, Birmingham
08598	H016 HERCULES	Chasewater Light Railway, Brownhills, Staffordshire
08600		AV Dawson, Ayrton Rail Terminal, Middlesbrough
08602	004 BOMBER	Bombardier Transportation, Derby Works
08613	H064	Celtic Energy, Onllwyn Coal & Distribution Centre, West Glamorgan
08622	H028 19	Hanson Cement, Ketton Cement Works, nr Stamford
08629	Wolverton	Knorr-Bremse Rail Systems, Wolverton Works, Milton Keynes
08631		Bombardier Transportation, Derby Works *(on loan from the Mid Norfolk Railway)*
08643		Aggregate Industries, Merehead Rail Terminal
08648		Northern Rail, Heaton Depot, Newcastle-upon-Tyne
08649	Bradwell	Knorr-Bremse Rail Systems, Wolverton Works, Milton Keynes
08650	ISLE OF GRAIN	Bardon Aggregates, Isle of Grain, Kent
08652		Hanson Aggregates, Whatley Quarry, near Frome
08670		RSS, Rye Farm, Wishaw, Sutton Coldfield
08678	ARTILA	West Coast Railway Company, Carnforth
08682	Lionheart	Bombardier Transportation, Derby Works
08683		RSS, Rye Farm, Wishaw, Sutton Coldfield
08685		Barrow Hill Roundhouse, Chesterfield, Derbyshire
08699		Weardale Railway, Wolsingham, County Durham
08700		Barrow Hill Roundhouse, Chesterfield, Derbyshire
08704		Riviera Trains, Crewe Down Holding Sidings
08730	The Caley	Knorr-Bremse Rail Systems, Springburn Depot, Glasgow
08743	Bryan Turner	SembCorp Utilities Teesside, Wilton, Middlesbrough
08750		Weardale Railway, Wolsingham, County Durham
08756		Tata Steel, Shotton Works, Deeside, Flintshire
08762		Cemex UK, Washwood Heath, Birmingham
08764		Stonebridge Park Heavy Repair depot, Wembley, London
08765		Nemesis Rail, Burton-upon-Trent, Staffordshire
08774	ARTHUR VERNON DAWSON	AV Dawson, Ayrton Rail Terminal, Middlesbrough
08786		Barrow Hill Roundhouse, Chesterfield, Derbyshire
08787	"08296"	Hanson Aggregates, Machen Quarry, nr Newport
08807		AV Dawson, Ayrton Rail Terminal, Middlesbrough
08809	24	PD Ports, Teesport, Grangetown, Middlesbrough
08810		LNWR, Eastleigh Depot, Hampshire
08818	MOLLY	GB Railfreight, Trafford Park Euroterminal, Gtr Manchester
08823	LIBBIE	Daventry International Railfreight Terminal, Crick
08834		Bombardier Transportation, Old Dalby Test Centre, Asfordby
08846	003	Bombardier Transportation, Derby Works
08868		LNWR, Crewe Carriage Depot, Crewe, Cheshire
08870	H024	Weardale Railway, Wolsingham, County Durham
08871	22	Weardale Railway, Wolsingham, County Durham
08873		Hams Hall Distribution Park, Coleshill, Warwickshire
08885	H042 18	Weardale Railway, Wolsingham, County Durham
08892		First Capital Connect, Hornsey Depot, London
08903	JOHN W. ANTILL	SembCorp Utilities Teesside, Wilton, Middlesbrough
08905		Hope Construction Materials, Hope Cement Works, Derbyshire
08912		AV Dawson, Ayrton Rail Terminal, Middlesbrough
08913		LH Group, Barton-under-Needwood, Staffordshire

08918		Nemesis Rail, Burton-upon-Trent, Staffordshire
08924	1	GB Railfreight, Garston Car Terminal, Liverpool
08927	D4157	EMD, Roberts Road Depot, Doncaster
08933		Aggregate Industries, Merehead Rail Terminal
08936		Tata Steel, Shotton Works, Deeside, Flintshire
08937	D4167 BLUEBELL MEL	Bardon Aggregates, Meldon Quarry, near Okehampton
08943		Bombardier Transportation, Central Rivers Depot, Barton-under-Needwood
08947	HOWIE	Arlington Fleet Services, Eastleigh Works, Hampshire
08956		Bombardier Transportation, Old Dalby Test Centre, Asfordby

Class 09

09007	D3671	London Overground, Willesden Depot, London
09014		Nemesis Rail, Burton-upon-Trent, Staffordshire
09022		Victoria Group, Port of Boston, Boston
09204		LNWR, Crewe Carriage Depot, Crewe, Cheshire

Class 14

| D9504 | | Kent & East Sussex Railway |
| D9529 | 14029 | Nene Valley Railway |

Class 20

20056	81	Tata Steel, Appleby-Frodingham Works, Scunthorpe
20066	82	Tata Steel, Appleby-Frodingham Works, Scunthorpe
20110	D8110	Tata Steel, Appleby-Frodingham Works, Scunthorpe
20121		Barrow Hill Roundhouse, Chesterfield, Derbyshire
20166		Wensleydale Railway, Leeming Bar, North Yorkshire
20168	2 SIR GEORGE EARLE	Hope Construction Materials, Hope Cement Works, Derbyshire
20906	3	Hope Construction Materials, Hope Cement Works, Derbyshire

Class 47

| 47703 | | Wabtec Rail, Doncaster Works |
| 47714 | | Bombardier Transportation, Old Dalby Test Centre, Asfordby |

1.5. LOCOMOTIVES AWAITING DISPOSAL

Locomotives that are still extant but at scrapyards are listed here.

Class 08

08646	F	European Metal Recycling, Kingsbury
08783	E	European Metal Recycling, Kingsbury
08798	E	European Metal Recycling, Attercliffe
08872	E	European Metal Recycling, Attercliffe
08921	E	European Metal Recycling, Kingsbury

Class 09

| 09023 | E | European Metal Recycling, Attercliffe |
| 09107 | E | European Metal Recycling, Kingsbury |

Class 86

| 86901 | Y | CF Booth, Rotherham |
| 86902 | Y | CF Booth, Rotherham |

1.6. LOCOMOTIVES EXPORTED FOR USE ABROAD

This section details former BR (plus privatisation era) diesel and electric locomotives that have been exported from the UK for use in industrial locations or by a main line operator abroad. Not included are locos that are "preserved" abroad, which are included in our "Preserved Locomotives of British Railways" publication. (S) denotes locomotives that are stored.

Number Other no./name   Location

Class 03

D2xxx		Ferramento Pugliesse, Terlizzi, Bari, Italy

Class 04

D2289		Lonato SpA, Lonato Steelworks, Lonato, Brescia, Italy

Class 56

56101	0659 001-5	FLOYD, Hungary
56115	0659 002-3	FLOYD, Hungary
56117	0659 003-1	FLOYD, Hungary

Class 58

58001		Axiom Rail, France, (S) Alizay
58004		Axiom Rail, France, (S) Alizay
58005		Axiom Rail, France, (S) Alizay
58006		Axiom Rail, France, (S) Alizay
58007		Axiom Rail, France, (S) Alizay
58009		Axiom Rail, France, (S) Alizay
58010		Axiom Rail, France, (S) Alizay
58011		Axiom Rail, France, (S) Alizay
58013		Axiom Rail, France, (S) Alizay
58015		Transfesa, Spain, (S) Monforte del Cid, Alicante
58018		Axiom Rail, France, (S) Alizay
58020	L43	Transfesa, Spain, (S) Monforte del Cid, Alicante
58021		Axiom Rail, France, (S) Alizay
58024	L42	Transfesa, Spain, (S) Monforte del Cid, Alicante
58025		DB Schenker, Spain, (S) Albacete
58026		Axiom Rail, France, (S) Alizay
58027	L52	DB Schenker, Spain, (S) Albacete
58029	L44	Transfesa, Spain, (S) Monforte del Cid, Alicante
58030	L46	Transfesa, Spain, (S) Monforte del Cid, Alicante
58031	L45	Transfesa, Spain, (S) Monforte del Cid, Alicante
58032		Axiom Rail, France, (S) Alizay
58033		Axiom Rail, France, (S) Alizay
58034		Axiom Rail, France, (S) Alizay
58035		Axiom Rail, France, (S) Alizay
58036		Axiom Rail, France, (S) Alizay
58038		Axiom Rail, France, (S) Alizay

58039		Axiom Rail, France, (S) Alizay
58040		Axiom Rail, France, (S) Alizay
58041	L36	Transfesa, Spain, (S) Albacete
58042		Axiom Rail, France, (S) Alizay
58043	L37	Transfesa, Spain, (S) Monforte del Cid, Alicante
58044		Axiom Rail, France, (S) Woippy, Metz
58046		Axiom Rail, France, (S) Alizay
58047	L51	Transfesa, Spain, (S) Monforte del Cid, Alicante
58049		Axiom Rail, France, (S) Alizay
58050	L53	DB Schenker, Spain, (S) Albacete

Class 66

66010	Euro Cargo Rail, France
66022	Euro Cargo Rail, France
66026	Euro Cargo Rail, France
66028	Euro Cargo Rail, France
66029	Euro Cargo Rail, France
66032	Euro Cargo Rail, France
66033	Euro Cargo Rail, France
66036	Euro Cargo Rail, France
66038	Euro Cargo Rail, France
66042	Euro Cargo Rail, France
66045	Euro Cargo Rail, France
66049	Euro Cargo Rail, France
66052	Euro Cargo Rail, France
66062	Euro Cargo Rail, France
66064	Euro Cargo Rail, France
66071	Euro Cargo Rail, France
66072	Euro Cargo Rail, France
66073	Euro Cargo Rail, France
66123	Euro Cargo Rail, France
66146	DB Schenker Rail Polska, Poland
66153	DB Schenker Rail Polska, Poland
66157	DB Schenker Rail Polska, Poland
66159	DB Schenker Rail Polska, Poland
66163	DB Schenker Rail Polska, Poland
66166	DB Schenker Rail Polska, Poland
66173	DB Schenker Rail Polska, Poland
66178	DB Schenker Rail Polska, Poland
66179	Euro Cargo Rail, France
66180	DB Schenker Rail Polska, Poland
66189	DB Schenker Rail Polska, Poland
66190	Euro Cargo Rail, France
66191	Euro Cargo Rail, France
66195	Euro Cargo Rail, France
66196	DB Schenker Rail Polska, Poland
66202	Euro Cargo Rail, France
66203	Euro Cargo Rail, France
66205	Euro Cargo Rail, France
66208	Euro Cargo Rail, France
66209	Euro Cargo Rail, France

66210		Euro Cargo Rail, France
66211		Euro Cargo Rail, France
66212		Euro Cargo Rail, France
66214		Euro Cargo Rail, France
66215		Euro Cargo Rail, France
66216		Euro Cargo Rail, France
66217		Euro Cargo Rail, France
66218		Euro Cargo Rail, France
66219		Euro Cargo Rail, France
66220		DB Schenker Rail Polska, Poland
66222		Euro Cargo Rail, France
66223		Euro Cargo Rail, France
66224		Euro Cargo Rail, France
66225		Euro Cargo Rail, France
66226		Euro Cargo Rail, France
66227		DB Schenker Rail Polska, Poland
66228		Euro Cargo Rail, France
66229		Euro Cargo Rail, France
66231		Euro Cargo Rail, France
66233		Euro Cargo Rail, France
66234		Euro Cargo Rail, France
66235		Euro Cargo Rail, France
66236		Euro Cargo Rail, France
66237		DB Schenker Rail Polska, Poland
66239		Euro Cargo Rail, France
66240		Euro Cargo Rail, France
66241		Euro Cargo Rail, France
66242		Euro Cargo Rail, France
66243		Euro Cargo Rail, France
66244		Euro Cargo Rail, France
66245		Euro Cargo Rail, France
66246		Euro Cargo Rail, France
66247		Euro Cargo Rail, France
66248		DB Schenker Rail Polska, Poland
66249		Euro Cargo Rail, France
66411	66013	Freightliner, Poland
66412	66015	Freightliner, Poland
66417	66014	Freightliner, Poland
66582	66009	Freightliner, Poland
66583	66010	Freightliner, Poland
66584	66011	Freightliner, Poland
66586	66008	Freightliner, Poland
66608	66603	Freightliner, Poland
66609	66604	Freightliner, Poland
66611	66605	Freightliner, Poland
66612	66606	Freightliner, Poland
66624	66602	Freightliner, Poland
66625	66601	Freightliner, Poland

Class 86

86215	91 55 0450 005-8	FLOYD, Hungary
86217	91 55 0450 006-6	FLOYD, Hungary
86218	91 55 0450 004-1	FLOYD, Hungary
86228	91 55 0450 007-4	FLOYD, Hungary
86232	91 55 0450 003-3	FLOYD, Hungary
86233		Bulmarket, Bulgaria (S)
86242	91 55 0450 008-2	FLOYD, Hungary
86248	91 55 0450 001-7	FLOYD, Hungary
86250	91 55 0450 002-5	FLOYD, Hungary
86424	91 55 0450 009-0	FLOYD, Hungary (S)

Class 87

87003	87003-0	BZK, Bulgaria
87004	87004-8 Britannia	BZK, Bulgaria
87006	87006-3	BZK, Bulgaria
87007	87007-1	BZK, Bulgaria
87008	87008-9	BZK, Bulgaria (S)
87009		Bulmarket, Bulgaria
87010	87010-5	BZK, Bulgaria
87012	87012-1	BZK, Bulgaria
87013	87013-9	BZK, Bulgaria
87014	87014-7	BZK, Bulgaria (S)
87017	Iron Duke	Bulmarket, Bulgaria
87019	87019-6	BZK, Bulgaria
87020	87020-4	BZK, Bulgaria
87022	87022-0	BZK, Bulgaria
87023	Velocity	Bulmarket, Bulgaria
87025		Bulmarket, Bulgaria
87026	87026-1	BZK, Bulgaria
87028	87028-7	BZK, Bulgaria
87029	87029-5	BZK, Bulgaria
87033	87033-7	BZK, Bulgaria
87034	87034-5	BZK, Bulgaria

Class 92

92001	91 53 0472 002-1 Mircea Eliade	DB Schenker, Romania
92012	91 53 0472 001-3 Mihai Eminescu	DB Schenker, Romania
92025	Oscar Wilde	DB Schenker, Bulgaria
92027	George Eliot	DB Schenker, Bulgaria
92034	Kipling	DB Schenker, Bulgaria

2. LOCO-HAULED COACHING STOCK

INTRODUCTION

This section contains details of all locomotive-hauled or propelled coaching stock, often referred to as carriages, which can run on Britain's national railway network.

The number of locomotive-hauled or propelled carriages in use on the national railway network is much fewer than was once the case and their number is expected to reduce further as more new multiple units are delivered. Those that remain fall into two distinct groups.

Firstly, there are those used by franchised and open access operators for regular timetabled services. Most of these are formed in fixed or semi-fixed formations with either locomotives or a locomotive and Driving Brake Van at either end which allows for push-pull operation. There are also a small number of mainly overnight trains with variable formations that use conventional locomotive haulage.

Secondly there are those used for what can best be described as excursion trains. These include a wide range of carriage types ranging from luxurious saloons to those more suited to the "bucket and spade" seaside type of excursion. These are formed into sets to suit the requirements of the day. From time to time some see limited use with franchised and open access operators to cover for stock shortages and times of exceptional demand such as major sporting events.

In addition there remain a small number of carriages referred to as "Service Stock" which are used internally within the railway industry and are not used to convey passengers.

FRANCHISED & OPEN ACCESS OPERATORS

For each operator regularly using locomotive-hauled carriages brief details are given here of the sphere if operation. For details of operators using HSTs see Section 2.2.

Arriva Trains Wales
The Monday–Friday Welsh Assembly Government sponsored train between Cardiff and Holyhead uses Mark 3 carriages in push-pull mode with a Class 67. A second similarly formed set is used for weekday trains between Crewe or Manchester and Chester/North Wales. These carriages are also used for relief trains, particularly in connection with sports fixtures at Cardiff and busy ferry sailings to/from Holyhead.

Chiltern Railways
Chiltern operates four sets of Mark 3 carriages with Class 67 locomotives (to be replaced with Class 68s in 2015) on its Mainline services between London Marylebone and Birmingham Moor Street/Kidderminster. Another set is used on a peak-hour commuter service between Marylebone and

Banbury (already hauled by a Class 68 from December 2014). All trains operate as push-pull sets.

East Coast
East Coast operates 30 sets of Mark 4 carriages with Class 91 locomotives in push-pull formations on its Inter-City services between London King's Cross and Yorkshire, North-East England and Scotland.

First Great Western
The "Night Riviera" seating and sleeping car service between London Paddington and Penzance uses sets of Mark 3 carriages hauled by Class 57/6 locomotives. The seating carriages are also used in Devon and Cornwall for local services on summer Saturdays.

Greater Anglia
The Inter-City service between London Liverpool Street and Norwich is operated using 12 sets of Mark 3 carriages with Class 90 locomotives in push-pull formations. On summer Saturdays some of these trains are extended to Great Yarmouth, hauled beyond Norwich by Class 47s. In addition local trains between Norwich and Great Yarmouth or Lowestoft are sometimes Class 47 hauled using spare Mark 3s or hired Mark 2 carriages from DRS.

North Yorkshire Moors Railway
In addition to operating the North Yorkshire Moors Railway between Pickering and Grosmont the company operates through services to Whitby and occasionally Battersby. A fleet of Mark 1 passenger carriages and Pullman Cars are used for these services.

ScotRail
The Caledonian Sleeper seating and sleeping car service between London Euston and Scotland uses sets of Mark 3 Sleeping Cars and Mark 2 seating and catering carriages. These are hauled by Class 90 locomotives between London and Edinburgh/Glasgow and Class 67 locomotives between Edinburgh and Aberdeen, Inverness and Fort William. In addition, a Class 67 is used to haul a hired set of Mark 2 excursion stock on peak hour services between Edinburgh and Fife. The Sleeper operation is due to be split from the ScotRail franchise and transfer to a new operator, Serco, in April 2015.

EXCURSION TRAIN OPERATORS

Usually, three types of companies will be involved in the operation of an excursion train. There will be the promoter, the rolling stock provider and the train operator. In many cases two or more of these roles may be undertaken by the same or associated companies. Only a small number of Train Operating Companies facilitate the operation of excursion trains. This takes various forms ranging from the complete package of providing and operating the train, through offering a "hook up and haul" service, to operating the train for a third party rolling stock custodian.

DB Schenker Rail UK
DBS currently operates its own luxurious train of Mark 3 carriages, called the company train. It also offers a hook up and haul service and regularly operates the Royal Train and the Belmond British Pullman as well as trains

for Riviera Trains and its client promoters. An excursion train fleet of Mark 2 carriages is owned by DBS but only a very small number of these currently see use being hired to ScotRail for Edinburgh–Fife peak-hour trains.

Direct Rail Services

DRS operates a small fleet of Mark 2 carriages which see occasional use on excursion trains. These are also hired to franchised operators to cover stock shortages or periods of exceptional passenger demand. The company also offers a hook up and haul service operating the Belmond Northern Belle as well as trains for Riviera Trains and their client promoters.

GB Railfreight

GBRf Initially operated excursion trains using the preserved Class 201 "Hastings" DEMU. It now also operates a small number of company excursions using hired carriages and trains for Riviera Trains and its client promoters.

West Coast Railway Company

This vertically integrated company has its own fleet of steam and diesel locomotives as well as a full range of different carriage types. It operates its own regular trains, such as the "Jacobite" steam service between Fort William and Mallaig and numerous excursion trains for itself and client promoters. In addition it offers a hook up and haul service operating the Royal Scotsman and Statesman trains as well as trains for Vintage Trains, The Princess Royal Locomotive Trust and the Scottish Railway Preservation Society.

LAYOUT OF INFORMATION

Carriages are listed in numerical order of painted number in batches according to type.

Where a carriage has been renumbered, the former number is shown in parentheses. If a carriage has been renumbered more than once, the original number is shown first in parentheses, followed by the most recent previous number.

Each carriage entry is laid out as in the following example (previous number(s) column may be omitted where not applicable):

No.	Prev. No.	Notes	Livery	Owner	Operator	Depot/Location
42346	(41053)	*h	**FD**	A	GW	LA

Codes: Codes are used to denote the livery, owner and depot/location of each carriage. Details of these will be found in section 7 of this book.

The owner is the responsible custodian of the carriage and this may not always be the legal owner.

The operator is the organisation which facilitates the use of the carriage and may not be the actual train operating company which runs the train. If no operator is shown the carriage is considered to be not in use.

The depot is the facility primarily responsible for the carriages maintenance. Light maintenance and heavy overhauls may be carried out elsewhere.

The location is where carriages not in use are currently being kept/stored.

GENERAL INFORMATION

CLASSIFICATION AND NUMBERING

Seven different numbering systems were in use on British Rail. These were the British Rail series, the four pre-nationalisation companies' series', the Pullman Car Company's series and the UIC (International Union of Railways) series. In this book BR number series carriages and former Pullman Car Company series are listed separately. There is also a separate listing of "Saloon" type carriages, that includes pre-nationalisation survivors, which are registered to run on the national railway system, Locomotive Support Carriages and Service Stock. Please note the Mark 2 Pullman carriages were ordered after the Pullman Car Company had been nationalised and are therefore numbered in the British Rail series.

Also listed separately are the British Rail and Pullman Car Company number series carriages used on North Yorkshire Moors Railway services on the national railway system. This is due to their very restricted sphere of operation.

The BR number series grouped carriages of a particular type together in chronological order. Major modifications affecting type of accommodation resulted in renumbering into a more appropriate or new number series. Since privatisation such renumbering has not always taken place resulting in renumbering which has been more haphazard and greater variations within numbering groups.

With the introduction of the TOPS numbering system, coaching stock (including multiple unit vehicles) retained their original BR number unless this conflicted with a locomotive number. Carriages can be one–five digits, although no one or two digit examples remain in use on the national network.

UNITS OF MEASUREMENT

All dimensions and weights are quoted for carriages in an "as new" condition or after a major modification, such as fitting with new bogies etc. Dimensions are quoted in the order length x width. Lengths quoted are over buffers or couplers as appropriate. All widths quoted are maxima. All weights are shown as metric tonnes (t = tonnes).

DETAILED INFORMATION & CODES

Under each type heading, the following details are shown:

- "Mark" of carriage (see below).
- Descriptive text.
- Number of First Class seats, Standard Class seats, lavatory compartments and wheelchair spaces shown as F/S nT nW respectively.
- Bogie type (see below).
- Additional features.
- ETS Index.
- Weight: All weights are shown as metric tonnes (t = tonnes).

BOGIE TYPES

BR Mark 1 (BR1). Double bolster leaf spring bogie. Generally 90 mph, but Mark 1 bogies may be permitted to run at 100 mph with special maintenance. Weight: 6.1 t.

BR Mark 2 (BR2). Single bolster leaf-spring bogie used on certain types of non-passenger stock and suburban stock (all now withdrawn). Weight: 5.3 t.

COMMONWEALTH (C). Heavy, cast steel coil spring bogie. 100 mph. Weight: 6.75 t.

B4. Coil spring fabricated bogie. Generally 100 mph, but B4 bogies may be permitted to run at 110 mph with special maintenance. Weight: 5.2 t.

B5. Heavy duty version of B4. 100 mph. Weight: 5.3 t.

B5 (SR). A bogie originally used on Southern Region EMUs, similar in design to B5. Now also used on locomotive-hauled carriages. 100 mph.

BT10. A fabricated bogie designed for 125 mph. Air suspension.

T4. A 125 mph bogie designed by BREL (now Bombardier Transportation).

BT41. Fitted to Mark 4 carriages, designed by SIG in Switzerland. At present limited to 125 mph, but designed for 140 mph.

BRAKES

Air braking is now standard on British main line trains. Carriages with other equipment are denoted:

b   Air braked, through vacuum pipe.
v   Vacuum braked.
x   Dual braked (air and vacuum).

HEATING & VENTILATION

Electric heating and ventilation is now standard on British main-line trains. Certain carriages for use on excursion services may also have steam heating facilities, or be steam heated only. All carriages used on North Yorkshire Moors Railway trains have steam heating.

NOTES ON ELECTRIC TRAIN SUPPLY

The sum of ETS indices in a train must not be more than the ETS index of the locomotive. The normal voltage on British trains is 1000 V. Suffix "X" denotes 600 amp wiring instead of 400 amp. Trains whose ETS index is higher than 66 must be formed completely of 600 amp wired stock. Class 33 and 73 locomotives cannot provide a suitable electric train supply for Mark 2D, Mark 2E, Mark 2F, Mark 3, Mark 3A, Mark 3B or Mark 4 carriages. Class 55 locomotives provide an ETS directly from one of their traction generators into the train line. Consequently voltage fluctuations can result in motor-alternator flashover. Thus these locomotives are not suitable for use with Mark 2D, Mark 2E, Mark 2F, Mark 3, Mark 3A, Mark 3B or Mark 4 carriages unless modified motor-alternators are fitted. Such motor alternators were fitted to Mark 2D and 2F carriages used on the East Coast Main Line, but few remain fitted.

PUBLIC ADDRESS

It is assumed all carriages are now fitted with public address equipment, although certain stored carriages may not have this feature. In addition, it is assumed all carriages with a conductor's compartment have public address transmission facilities, as have catering carriages.

COOKING EQUIPMENT

It is assumed that Mark 1 catering carriages have gas powered cooking equipment, whilst Mark 2, 3 and 4 catering carriages have electric powered cooking equipment unless stated otherwise.

ADDITIONAL FEATURE CODES

d	Central Door Locking.
dg	Driver–Guard communication equipment.
f	Facelifted or fluorescent lighting.
h	"High density" seating
k	Composition brake blocks (instead of cast iron).
n	Day/night lighting.
pg	Public address transmission and driver-guard communication.
pt	Public address transmission facility.
q	Catering staff to shore telephone.
w	Wheelchair space.
★	Blue star multiple working cables fitted.

BUILD DETAILS

Lot Numbers
Carriages ordered under the auspices of BR were allocated a lot (batch) number when ordered and these are quoted in class headings and sub-headings.

Builders
These are shown for each lot. More details and a full list of builders can be found in section 7.7.

Information on sub-contracting works which built parts of carriages eg the underframes etc is not shown.

In addition to the above, certain vintage Pullman cars were built or rebuilt at the following works:

Metropolitan Carriage & Wagon Company, Birmingham (later Alstom).
Midland Carriage & Wagon Company, Birmingham.
Pullman Car Company, Preston Park, Brighton.
Conversions have also been carried out at the Railway Technical Centre, Derby, LNWR Crewe and Blakes Fabrications, Edinburgh.

2.1. BR NUMBER SERIES COACHING STOCK

KITCHEN FIRST

Mark 1. Spent most of its life as a Royal Train vehicle and was numbered 2907 for a time. 24/–. B5 bogies. ETS 2.

Lot No. 30633 Swindon 1961. 41 t.

325	**VN** BE *NB*	CP	DUART

PULLMAN KITCHEN

Mark 2. Pressure Ventilated. Built with First Class seating but this has been replaced with a servery area. Gas cooking. 2T. B5 bogies. ETS 6.

Lot No. 30755 Derby 1966. 40 t.

| 504 | **PC** WC *WC* | CS | ULLSWATER |
| 506 | **PC** WC *WC* | CS | WINDERMERE |

PULLMAN OPEN FIRST

Mark 2. Pressure Ventilated. 36/– 2T. B4 bogies. ETS 5.

Lot No. 30754 Derby 1966. 35 t.

Non-standard livery: 546 Maroon & beige.

546	**0** WC	CS	CITY OF MANCHESTER
548	**PC** WC *WC*	CS	GRASMERE
549	**PC** WC *WC*	CS	BASSENTHWAITE
550	**PC** WC *WC*	CS	RYDAL WATER
551	**PC** WC *WC*	CS	BUTTERMERE
552	**PC** WC *WC*	CS	ENNERDALE WATER
553	**PC** WC *WC*	CS	CRUMMOCK WATER

PULLMAN OPEN BRAKE FIRST

Mark 2. Pressure Ventilated. 30/– 2T. B4 bogies. ETS 4.

Lot No. 30753 Derby 1966. 35 t.

| 586 | **PC** WC *WC* | CS | DERWENTWATER |

BUFFET FIRST

Mark 2F. Air conditioned. Converted 1988–89/91 at BREL, Derby from Mark 2F Open Firsts. 1200/01/03/11/20/21 have Stones equipment, others have Temperature Ltd. 25/– 1T 1W. B4 bogies. d. ETS 6X.

1200/03/11/20. Lot No. 30845 Derby 1973. 33 t.
1201/07/10/12/21/54. Lot No. 30859 Derby 1973–74. 33 t.

1200	(3287, 6459)	**RV** RV	*RV*	EH	AMBER
1201	(3361, 6445)	**CH** VT	*WC*	CS	
1203	(3291)	**IC** RV	*RV*	EH	
1207	(3328, 6422)	**V** BE		ZG	
1210	(3405, 6462)	**FS** E	*SR*	IS	
1211	(3305)	**PC** RA	*ST*	CS	
1212	(3427, 6453)	**V** RV	*RV*	EH	
1220	(3315, 6432)	**FS** E	*SR*	IS	
1221	(3371)	**IC** BE		ZG	
1254	(3391)	**BG** DR		BH	

KITCHEN WITH BAR

Mark 1. Built with no seats but three Pullman-style seats now fitted in bar area. B5 bogies. ETS 1.

Lot No. 30624 Cravens 1960–61. 41 t.

1566		**VN** BE	*NB*	CP

KITCHEN BUFFET UNCLASSIFIED

Mark 1. Built with 23 loose chairs. All remaining vehicles refurbished with 23 fixed polypropylene chairs and fluorescent lighting. 1683/91/92/99 were further refurbished with 21 chairs, wheelchair space and carpets. ETS 2 (* 2X).

Now used on excursion trains with the seating area adapted to various uses including servery and food preparation areas, with some or all seating removed.

1651–99. Lot No. 30628 Pressed Steel 1960–61. Commonwealth bogies. 39 t.
1730. Lot No. 30512 BRCW 1960–61. B5 bogies. 37 t.

1651		**CC** RV	*RV*	EH		1683		**RB** RV	*RV*	EH
1657		**CH** RV		ZG		1691		**CC** RV	*RV*	EH
1659		**PC** RA	*ST*	CS		1692		**CH** RV		EH
1666	x	**M** RP	*WC*	CS		1699		**RB** RV		EH
1671	x*	**CH** RV	*RV*	EH		1730	x	**M** BK	*BK*	BT

BUFFET STANDARD

Mark 1. These carriages are basically an open standard with two full window spaces removed to accommodate a buffet counter, and four seats removed to allow for a stock cupboard. All remaining vehicles now have fluorescent lighting. –/44 2T. Commonwealth bogies. ETS 3.

1861 has had its toilets replaced with store cupboards.

1813–32. Lot No. 30520 Wolverton 1960. 38 t.
1840. Lot No. 30507 Wolverton 1960. 37 t.
1859–63. Lot No. 30670 Wolverton 1961–62. 38 t.
1882. Lot No. 30702 Wolverton 1962. 38 t.

1813	x	**CH**	RV	*RV*	EH	1860	x	**M**	WC	*WC*	CS
1832	x	**CC**	RV	*RV*	EH	1861	x	**M**	WC	*WC*	CS
1840	v	**M**	WC	*WC*	CS	1863	x	**CH**	LS		CM
1859	x	**M**	BK	*BK*	BT	1882	x	**M**	WC	*WC*	CS

KITCHEN UNCLASSIFIED

Mark 1. These carriages were built as Unclassified Restaurants. They were rebuilt with buffet counters and 23 fixed polypropylene chairs, then further refurbished by fitting fluorescent lighting. Further modified for use as servery vehicle with seating removed and kitchen extended. ETS 2X.

1953. Lot No. 30575 Swindon 1960. B4/B5 bogies. 36.5 t.
1961. Lot No. 30632 Swindon 1961. Commonwealth bogies. 39 t.

1953		**VN**	BE	*NB*	CP	1961	x	**M**	WC	*WC*	CS

HM THE QUEEN'S SALOON

Mark 3. Converted from an Open First built 1972. Consists of a lounge, bedroom and bathroom for HM The Queen, and a combined bedroom and bathroom for the Queen's dresser. One entrance vestibule has double doors. Air conditioned. BT10 bogies. ETS 9X.

Lot No. 30886 Wolverton 1977. 36 t.

2903	(11001)	**RP**	NR	*RP*	ZN

HRH THE DUKE OF EDINBURGH'S SALOON

Mark 3. Converted from an Open Standard built 1972. Consists of a combined lounge/dining room, a bedroom and a shower room for the Duke, a kitchen and a valet's bedroom and bathroom. Air conditioned. BT10 bogies. ETS 15X.

Lot No. 30887 Wolverton 1977. 36 t.

2904	(12001)	**RP**	NR	*RP*	ZN

ROYAL HOUSEHOLD SLEEPING CAR

Mark 3A. Built to similar specification as Sleeping Cars 10647–729. 12 sleeping compartments for use of Royal Household with a fixed lower berth and a hinged upper berth. 2T plus shower room. Air conditioned. BT10 bogies. ETS 11X.

Lot No. 31002 Derby/Wolverton 1985. 44 t.

| 2915 | | **RP** NR *RP* | ZN |

HRH THE PRINCE OF WALES'S DINING CAR

Mark 3. Converted from HST TRUK built 1976. Large kitchen retained, but dining area modified for Royal use seating up to 14 at central table(s). Air conditioned. BT10 bogies. ETS 13X.

Lot No. 31059 Wolverton 1988. 43 t.

| 2916 | (40512) | **RP** NR *RP* | ZN |

ROYAL KITCHEN/HOUSEHOLD DINING CAR

Mark 3. Converted from HST TRUK built 1977. Large kitchen retained and dining area slightly modified with seating for 22 Royal Household members. Air conditioned. BT10 bogies. ETS 13X.

Lot No. 31084 Wolverton 1990. 43 t.

| 2917 | (40514) | **RP** NR *RP* | ZN |

ROYAL HOUSEHOLD CARS

Mark 3. Converted from HST TRUKs built 1976/77. Air conditioned. BT10 bogies. ETS 10X.

Lot Nos. 31083 (* 31085) Wolverton 1989. 41.05 t.

| 2918 | (40515) | **RP** NR | ZN |
| 2919 | (40518) * | **RP** NR | ZN |

ROYAL HOUSEHOLD COUCHETTES

Mark 2B. Converted from Corridor Brake First built 1969. Consists of luggage accommodation, guard's compartment, workshop area, 350 kW diesel generator and staff sleeping accommodation. B5 bogies. ETS 2X.

Lot No. 31044 Wolverton 1986. 48 t.

| 2920 | (14109, 17109) | **RP** NR *RP* | ZN |

Mark 2B. Converted from Corridor Brake First built 1969. Consists of luggage accommodation, kitchen, brake control equipment and staff accommodation. B5 bogies. ETS 7X.

Lot No. 31086 Wolverton 1990. 41.5 t.

2921   (14107, 17107)   **RP**   NR   *RP*   ZN

HRH THE PRINCE OF WALES'S SLEEPING CAR

Mark 3B. Air conditioned. BT10 bogies. ETS 7X.

Lot No. 31035 Derby/Wolverton 1987.

2922   **RP**   NR   *RP*   ZN

ROYAL SALOON

Mark 3B. Air conditioned. BT10 bogies. ETS 6X.

Lot No. 31036 Derby/Wolverton 1987.

2923   **RP**   NR   *RP*   ZN

OPEN FIRST

Mark 1. 42/– 2T. ETS 3. Many now fitted with table lamps.

3058 was numbered DB 975313, 3068 was numbered DB 975606 and 3093 was numbered DB 977594 for a time when in departmental service for BR.

3058–69. Lot No. 30169 Doncaster 1955. B4 bogies. 33 t (* Commonwealth bogies 35 t).
3093. Lot No. 30472 BRCW 1959. B4 bogies. 33 t.
3096–3100. Lot No. 30576 BRCW 1959. B4 bogies. 33 t.

3058	*x **M**	WC *WC*	CS	FLORENCE	3096	x **M**	BK *BK*	BT	
3066	**CC**	RV *RV*	EH		3097	**CC**	RV *RV*	EH	
3068	**CC**	RV *RV*	EH		3098	x **CH**	RV *RV*	EH	
3069	**CC**	RV *RV*	EH		3100	x **CH**	RV *RV*	EH	
3093	x **M**	WC *WC*	CS	FLORENCE					

Later design with fluorescent lighting, aluminium window frames and Commonwealth bogies.

3128/36/41/43/44/46/47/48 were renumbered 1058/60/63/65/66/68/69/70 when reclassified Restaurant Open First, then 3600/05/08/09/02/06/04/10 when declassified to Open Standard, but have since regained their original numbers. 3136 was numbered DB 977970 for a time when in use with Serco Railtest as a Brake Force Runner.

3105 has had its luggage racks removed and has tungsten lighting.

3105–28. Lot No. 30697 Swindon 1962–63. 36 t.
3130–50. Lot No. 30717 Swindon 1963. 36 t.

3105	x	**M**	WC	*WC*	CS
3106	x	**M**	WC	*WC*	CS
3107	x	**CH**	RV	*RV*	EH
3110	x	**CH**	RV	*RV*	EH
3112	x	**CH**	RV	*RV*	EH
3113	x	**M**	WC	*WC*	CS
3115	x	**M**	BK	*BK*	BT
3117	x	**M**	WC	*WC*	CS
3119		**CC**	RV	*RV*	EH
3120		**CC**	RV	*RV*	EH
3121		**CH**	RV	*RV*	EH
3122	x	**CH**	RV	*RV*	EH
3123		**CC**	RV	*RV*	EH
3125	x	**CH**	LS	*RV*	EH

3128	x	**M**	WC	*WC*	CS
3130	x	**M**	WC	*WC*	CS
3133	x	**M**	RV		EH
3136	x	**M**	WC	*WC*	CS
3140	x	**CH**	RV	*RV*	EH
3141		**M**	RV		CD
3143	x	**M**	WC	*WC*	CS
3144	x	**M**	RV		BQ
3146		**M**	RV		EH
3147		**CH**	RV	*RV*	EH
3148		**M**	LS		CL
3149		**CC**	RV	*RV*	EH
3150		**M**	BK	*BK*	BT

Names:

3105	JULIA
3106	ALEXANDRA
3113	JESSICA
3117	CHRISTINA

3128	VICTORIA
3130	PAMELA
3136	DIANA
3143	PATRICIA

OPEN FIRST

Mark 2D. Air conditioned. Stones equipment. 42/– 2T. B4 bogies. ETS 5.

† Interior modified to Pullman Car standards with new seating, new panelling, tungsten lighting and table lights for the Belmond Northern Belle.

Lot No. 30821 Derby 1971–72. 34 t.

3174	†	**VN**	BE	*NB*	CP	GLAMIS
3182	†	**VN**	BE	*NB*	CP	WARWICK
3188		**PC**	RA	*ST*	CS	CADAIR IDRIS

OPEN FIRST

Mark 2E. Air conditioned. Stones equipment. 42/– 2T (p 36/– 2T). B4 bogies. ETS 5.

r Refurbished with new seats.
† Interior modified to Pullman Car standards with new seating, new panelling, tungsten lighting and table lights for the Belmond Northern Belle.

Lot No. 30843 Derby 1972–73. 32.5 t. († 35.8 t).

3223		**RV**	RA		BO	DIAMOND
3231	p	**PC**	RA	*ST*	CS	BEN CRUACHAN
3232	dr	**BG**	BE		CD	
3240		**RV**	RA		BO	SAPPHIRE
3247	†	**VN**	BE	*NB*	CP	CHATSWORTH
3267	†	**VN**	BE	*NB*	CP	BELVOIR
3273	†	**VN**	BE	*NB*	CP	ALNWICK
3275	†	**VN**	BE	*NB*	CP	HARLECH

OPEN FIRST

Mark 2F. Air conditioned. 3277–3318/3358–79 have Stones equipment, others have Temperature Ltd. All refurbished in the 1980s with power-operated vestibule doors, new panels and new seat trim. 42/– 2T. B4 bogies. d. ETS 5X.

r Further refurbished with table lamps and modified seats with burgundy seat trim.
u Fitted with power supply for Mark 1 Kitchen Buffet Unclassified.

3277–3318. Lot No. 30845 Derby 1973. 33.5 t.
3325–3426. Lot No. 30859 Derby 1973–74. 33.5 t.
3431–3438. Lot No. 30873 Derby 1974–75. 33.5 t.

3277		**AR**	RV	*RV*	EH	3356	r	**RV**	RV	*RV*	EH
3278	r	**BP**	RV	*RV*	EH	3358		**M**	DB		MH
3279	u	**M**	DB		MH	3359	r	**M**	WC	*WC*	CS
3292		**M**	DB		MH	3360	r	**PC**	WC	*WC*	CS
3295		**AR**	RV	*RV*	EH	3362	r	**PC**	WC	*WC*	CS
3304	r	**V**	RV	*RV*	EH	3364	r	**RV**	RV	*RV*	EH
3312		**PC**	RA	*ST*	CS	3366	r	**BG**	DR		ZG
3313	r	**M**	WC	*WC*	CS	3374		**BG**	DR		BH
3314	r	**V**	RV	*RV*	EH	3379	u	**AR**	RV	*RV*	EH
3318		**M**	DB		MH	3384	r	**RV**	RV	*RV*	EH
3325	r	**V**	RV	*RV*	EH	3386	r	**V**	RV	*RV*	EH
3326	r	**M**	WC	*WC*	CS	3388		**M**	DB		FA
3330	r	**RV**	RV	*RV*	EH	3390	r	**RV**	RV	*RV*	EH
3331		**M**	DB		MH	3392	r	**M**	WC	*WC*	CS
3333	r	**V**	RV	*RV*	EH	3395	r	**M**	WC	*WC*	CS
3334		**AR**	RV	*RV*	EH	3397	r	**RV**	RV	*RV*	EH
3336	u	**AR**	RV	*RV*	EH	3399	u	**M**	DB		FA
3340	r	**V**	RV	*RV*	EH	3400		**M**	DB		MH
3344	r	**V**	RV	*RV*	EH	3417		**AR**	RV	*RV*	EH
3345	r	**V**	RV	*RV*	EH	3424		**M**	DB		MH
3348	r	**RV**	RV	*RV*	EH	3426	r	**RV**	RV	*RV*	EH
3350	r	**M**	WC	*WC*	CS	3431	r	**M**	WC	*WC*	CS
3351		**CH**	VT	*WC*	CS	3438	r	**PC**	RA	*ST*	CS
3352	r	**M**	WC	*WC*	CS						

Names:

3312	HELVELLYN		3384	DICKENS
3330	BRUNEL		3390	CONSTABLE
3348	GAINSBOROUGH		3397	WORDSWORTH
3356	TENNYSON		3426	ELGAR
3364	SHAKESPEARE		3438	BEN LOMOND

OPEN STANDARD

Mark 1. –/64 2T. ETS 4.

4831–36. Lot No. 30506 Wolverton 1959. Commonwealth bogies. 33 t.
4856. Lot No. 30525 Wolverton 1959–60. B4 bogies. 33 t.

4831	x	**M**	BK	*BK*	BT		4836	x	**M**	BK	*BK*	BT
4832	x	**M**	BK	*BK*	BT		4856	x	**M**	BK	*BK*	BT

OPEN STANDARD

Mark 1. Commonwealth bogies. –/64 2T. ETS 4.

4905. Lot No. 30646 Wolverton 1961. 36 t.
4927–5044. Lot No. 30690 Wolverton 1961–62. 37 t.

4905	x	**M**	WC	*WC*	CS		4994	x	**M**	WC	*WC*	CS
4927	x	**CC**	RV	*RV*	EH		4998		**CH**	RV	*RV*	EH
4931	v	**M**	WC	*WC*	CS		5007		**G**	RV		EH
4940	x	**M**	WC	*WC*	CS		5008	x	**M**	RV		EH
4946	x	**CH**	RV	*RV*	EH		5009	x	**CH**	RV		EH
4949	x	**CH**	RV	*RV*	EH		5027		**G**	RV		EH
4951	x	**M**	WC	*WC*	CS		5028	x	**CC**	BK	*BK*	BT
4954	v	**M**	WC	*WC*	CS		5032	x	**M**	WC	*WC*	CS
4959		**CH**	RV	*RV*	EH		5033	x	**M**	WC	*WC*	CS
4960	x	**M**	WC	*WC*	CS		5035	x	**M**	WC	*WC*	CS
4973	x	**M**	WC	*WC*	CS		5040	x	**CH**	RV	*RV*	EH
4984	x	**M**	WC	*WC*	CS		5044	x	**M**	WC	*WC*	CS
4991		**CH**	RV	*RV*	EH							

OPEN STANDARD

Mark 2. Pressure ventilated. –/64 2T. B4 bogies. ETS 4.

Lot No. 30751 Derby 1965–67. 32 t.

5157	v	**CH**	VT	*VT*	TM		5200	v	**M**	WC	*WC*	CS
5171	v	**M**	WC	*WC*	CS		5212	v	**CH**	VT	*VT*	TM
5177	v	**CH**	VT	*VT*	TM		5216	v	**M**	WC	*WC*	CS
5191	v	**CH**	VT	*VT*	TM		5222	v	**M**	WC	*WC*	CS
5198	v	**CH**	VT	*VT*	TM							

OPEN STANDARD

Mark 2. Pressure ventilated. –/48 2T. B4 bogies. ETS 4.

Lot No. 30752 Derby 1966. 32 t.

5229		**M**	WC	*WC*	CS		5239		**M**	WC	*WC*	CS
5236	v	**M**	WC	*WC*	CS		5249	v	**M**	WC	*WC*	CS
5237	v	**M**	WC	*WC*	CS							

OPEN STANDARD

Mark 2A. Pressure ventilated. –/64 2T (w –/62 2T). B4 bogies. ETS 4.

f Facelifted vehicles.

5276–5341. Lot No. 30776 Derby 1967–68. 32 t.
5366–5419. Lot No. 30787 Derby 1968. 32 t.

5276	f	**RV**	RV		BQ	5341	f	**CC**	RV *RV*	EH
5278		**M**	WC *WC*		CS	5366	f	**CH**	RV *RV*	EH
5292	f	**CC**	RV *RV*		EH	5419	w	**M**	WC *WC*	CS

OPEN STANDARD

Mark 2D. Air conditioned. Stones equipment. Refurbished with new seats and end luggage stacks. –/58 2T. B4 bogies. d. ETS 5.

Lot No. 30822 Derby 1971. 33 t.

5631	**M**	DB *SR*	TO	5700	**FP**	DR		ZG
5632	**M**	DB *SR*	TO	5710	**FP**	DR		BH
5657	**M**	DB *SR*	TO					

OPEN STANDARD

Mark 2E. Air conditioned. Stones equipment. –/64 2T. B4 bogies. d. ETS 5.

r Refurbished with new interior panelling.
s Refurbished with new interior panelling, modified design of seat headrest and centre luggage stack. –/60 2T.

5787–97. Lot No. 30837 Derby 1972. 33.5 t.
5810. Lot No. 30844 Derby 1972–73. 33.5 t.

5787	s	**V**	DR		BH	5810	s	**DS** DR *DR*	KM
5797	r★	**IC**	RA		BO				

OPEN STANDARD

Mark 2F. Air conditioned. Temperature Ltd equipment. InterCity 70 seats. All were refurbished in the 1980s with power-operated vestibule doors, new panels and seat trim. –/64 2T. B4 bogies. d. ETS 5X.

* Early Mark 2 style seats. These vehicles have undergone a second refurbishment with carpets and new seat trim.
q Fitted with two wheelchair spaces. –/60 2T 2W.
s Fitted with centre luggage stack. –/60 2T.
t Fitted with centre luggage stack and wheelchair space. –/58 2T 1W.

5910–55. Lot No. 30846 Derby 1973. 33 t.
5959–6158. Lot No. 30860 Derby 1973–74. 33 t.
6173–83. Lot No. 30874 Derby 1974–75. 33 t.

5910	q	**V**	RV	*RV*	EH
5912		**PC**	RA	*ST*	CS
5919	s pt	**DS**	DR	*GA*	KM
5921		**AR**	RV	*GA*	EH
5922		**M**	DB		BS
5924		**M**	DB		BS
5928		**CH**	VT	*WC*	CS
5929		**AR**	RV	*RV*	EH
5937		**V**	RV	*RV*	EH
5945		**V**	RV	*RV*	EH
5950		**AR**	RV	*RV*	EH
5952		**V**	RV	*RV*	EH
5954		**M**	DB	*SR*	TO
5955		**V**	RV	*RV*	EH
5959	n	**M**	DB		BS
5961	s pt	**V**	RV	*RV*	EH
5964		**AR**	RV	*RV*	EH
5965	t	**AW**	RV	*RV*	EH
5971		**DS**	DR	*GA*	KM
5976	t	**AW**	RV	*RV*	EH
5985		**AR**	RV	*RV*	EH
5987		**V**	RV	*RV*	EH
5991		**PC**	RA	*ST*	CS
5995		**DS**	DR	*GA*	KM
5998		**AR**	RV	*RV*	EH
6000	t	**M**	WC	*WC*	CS
6001		**DS**	DR	*GA*	KM
6006		**AR**	RV	*RV*	EH
6008		**DS**	DR	*GA*	KM
6012		**M**	WC	*WC*	CS
6021		**M**	WC	*WC*	CS
6022	s	**M**	WC	*WC*	CS
6024	s	**V**	RV	*RV*	EH
6027	q	**V**	RV	*RV*	EH
6036	*	**M**	DB		BS
6042		**AR**	RV	*RV*	EH
6046		**DS**	DR	*DR*	KM
6051		**V**	RV	*RV*	EH
6054		**V**	RV	*RV*	EH
6064	s	**DS**	DR	*DR*	KM
6067	s pt	**V**	RV	*RV*	EH
6103		**M**	WC	*WC*	CS
6110		**M**	DB	*SR*	TO
6115	s	**M**	WC	*WC*	CS
6117	★	**DS**	DR	*GA*	KM
6122	★	**DS**	DR	*DR*	KM
6137	s pt	**AW**	RV	*RV*	EH
6139	n*	**M**	DB		MH
6141	q	**V**	RV	*RV*	EH
6152	*	**M**	DB		BS
6158		**V**	RV	*RV*	EH
6173	★	**DS**	DR	*DR*	KM
6176	t	**V**	RV	*RV*	EH
6177	s	**V**	RV	*RV*	EH
6183	s	**AW**	RV	*RV*	EH

BRAKE GENERATOR VAN

Mark 1. Renumbered 1989 from BR departmental series. Converted from Gangwayed Brake Van in 1973 to three-phase supply brake generator van for use with HST trailers. Modified 1999 for use with loco-hauled stock. B5 bogies.

Lot No. 30400 Pressed Steel 1958.

6310	(81448, 975325)	**CH**	RV	*RV*	EH

GENERATOR VAN

Mark 1. Converted from Gangwayed Brake Vans in 1992. B4 bogies. ETS 75.

6311. Lot No. 30162 Pressed Steel 1958. 37.25 t.
6312. Lot No. 30224 Cravens 1956. 37.25 t.
6313. Lot No. 30484 Pressed Steel 1958. 37.25 t.

6311	(80903, 92911)	**B**	DB		TO
6312	(81023, 92925)	**M**	WC	*WC*	CS
6313	(81553, 92167)	**PC**	BE	*BP*	SL

BUFFET STANDARD

Mark 2C. Converted from Open Standard by removal of one seating bay and replacing this by a counter with a space for a trolley, now replaced with a more substantial buffet. Adjacent toilet removed and converted to steward's washing area/store. Pressure ventilated. –/55 1T. B4 bogies. ETS 4.

Lot No. 30795 Derby 1969–70. 32.5 t.

6528	(5592)	**M**	WC	*WC*		CS

SLEEPER RECEPTION CAR

Mark 2F. Converted from Open First. These vehicles consist of pantry, microwave cooking facilities, seating area for passengers (with loose chairs, staff toilet plus two bars). Now refurbished again with new "sofa" seating as well as the loose chairs. Converted at RTC, Derby (6700), Ilford (6701–05) and Derby (6706–08). Air conditioned. 6700/01/03/05–08 have Stones equipment and 6702/04 have Temperature Ltd equipment. The number of seats per coach can vary but typically is 25/– 1T (12 seats as "sofa" seating and 13 loose chairs). B4 bogies. d. ETS 5X.

6700–02/04/08. Lot No. 30859 Derby 1973–74. 33.5 t.
6703/05–07. Lot No. 30845 Derby 1973. 33.5 t.

6700	(3347)	**FS**	E	*SR*	IS
6701	(3346)	**FS**	E	*SR*	IS
6702	(3421)	**FS**	E	*SR*	IS
6703	(3308)	**FS**	E	*SR*	IS
6704	(3341)	**FS**	E	*SR*	IS
6705	(3310, 6430)	**FS**	E	*SR*	IS
6706	(3283, 6421)	**FS**	E	*SR*	IS
6707	(3276, 6418)	**FS**	E	*SR*	IS
6708	(3370)	**FS**	E	*SR*	IS

BUFFET FIRST

Mark 2D. Converted from Buffet Standard by the removal of another seating bay and fitting a more substantial buffet counter with boiler and microwave oven. Now converted to First Class with new seating and end luggage stacks. Air conditioned. Stones equipment. 30/– 1T. B4 bogies. d. ETS 5.

Lot No. 30822 Derby 1971. 33 t.

6720	(5622, 6652)	**M**	DB		FA
6722	(5736, 6661)	**FP**	E		LM
6723	(5641, 6662)	**M**	WC		CS
6724	(5721, 6665)	**M**	WC	*WC*	CS

OPEN BRAKE STANDARD WITH TROLLEY SPACE

Mark 2. This vehicle uses the same bodyshell as the Mark 2 Corridor Brake First. Converted from Open Brake Standard by removal of one seating bay and replacing this with a counter with a space for a trolley. Adjacent toilet removed and converted to a steward's washing area/store. –/23. B4 bogies. ETS 4.

Lot No. 30757 Derby 1966. 31 t.

| 9101 | (9398) | v | **CH** | VT | *VT* | | TM |

OPEN BRAKE STANDARD

Mark 2. These vehicles use the same body shell as the Mark 2 Corridor Brake First and have First Class seat spacing and wider tables. Pressure ventilated. –/31 1T. B4 bogies. ETS 4.

9104 was originally numbered 9401. It was renumbered when converted to Open Brake Standard with trolley space. Now returned to original layout.

Lot No. 30757 Derby 1966. 31.5 t.

| 9104 | v | **M** | WC | *WC* | CS | | 9392 | v | **M** | WC | *WC* | CS |
| 9391 | | **M** | WC | *WC* | CS | | | | | | | |

OPEN BRAKE STANDARD

Mark 2C. Pressure ventilated. –/31 1T. B4 bogies. d. ETS 4.

Lot No. 30798 Derby 1970. 32 t.

| 9440 | | **M** | WC | | SH |

OPEN BRAKE STANDARD

Mark 2D. Air conditioned. Stones Equipment. All now refurbished with new seating –/22 1TD. B4 bogies. d. pg. ETS 5.

Lot No. 30824 Derby 1971. 33 t.

| 9488 | **FP** | DR | | ZG | | 9494 | **M** | DB | | MH |
| 9493 | **M** | WC | *WC* | CS | | | | | | |

OPEN BRAKE STANDARD

Mark 2E. Air conditioned. Stones Equipment. –/32 1T. B4 bogies. d. pg. ETS 5.

Lot No. 30838 Derby 1972. 33 t.

Non-standard livery: 9502 Pullman umber & cream.

r Refurbished with new interior panelling.
s Refurbished with modified design of seat headrest and new interior panelling.

9496	r	IC	VT	WC	CS
9502	s	0	BE	BP	SL
9504	s	V	RV	RV	EH
9506	s★	BG	DR		MH

9507	s	V	RV	SR	EH
9508	s	BG	DR		BH
9509	s	AV	RV		CD

OPEN BRAKE STANDARD

Mark 2F. Air conditioned. Temperature Ltd equipment. All were refurbished in the 1980s with power-operated vestibule doors, new panels and seat trim. All now further refurbished with carpets. –/32 1T. B4 bogies. d. pg. ETS 5X.

9537 has had all its seats removed for the purpose of carrying luggage.

Advertising livery: 9537 CruiseSaver Express (dark blue).

Lot No. 30861 Derby 1974. 34 t.

9520	n	AR	RV	RV	EH
9521	★	AW	RV	RV	EH
9522		M	DB	SR	TO
9525		DS	DR	GA	KM
9526	n★	IC	RV	RV	EH

9527	n	AR	RV	RV	EH
9529	n	M	DB		BS
9531		M	DB		BS
9537	n	AL	RV		EH
9539		AW	RV	RV	EH

DRIVING OPEN BRAKE STANDARD

Mark 2F. Air conditioned. Temperature Ltd equipment. Push & pull (tdm system). Converted from Open Brake Standard, these vehicles originally had half cabs at the brake end. They have since been refurbished and have had their cabs widened and the cab-end gangways removed. Five vehicles (9701–03/08/14) have been converted for use in Network Rail test trains and can be found in the Service Stock section of this book. –/30 1W 1T. B4 bogies. d. pg. Cowcatchers. ETS 5X.

9704–10. Lot No. 30861 Derby 1974. Converted Glasgow 1979. Disc brakes. 34 t.
9711/13. Lot No. 30861 Derby 1974. Converted Glasgow 1985. 34 t.

9704	(9512)	AR	BA	ZG
9705	(9519)	DS	DR	ZA
9707	(9511)	DS	DR	ZA
9709	(9515)	AR	BA	ZG

9710	(9518)	1	BA	ZG
9711	(9532)	AR	VT	TM
9713	(9535)	AR	NR	ZA

OPEN BRAKE UNCLASSIFIED

Mark 2E. Converted from Open Standard with new seating for use on Anglo-Scottish overnight services by Railcare, Wolverton. Air conditioned. Stones equipment. –/31 2T. B4 bogies. d. ETS 4X.

9801–03. Lot No. 30837 Derby 1972. 33.5 t.
9804–10. Lot No. 30844 Derby 1972–73. 33.5 t.

9800	(5751)	**FS**	E	*SR*	IS		9806	(5840)	**FS**	E	*SR*	IS
9801	(5760)	**FS**	E	*SR*	IS		9807	(5851)	**FS**	E	*SR*	IS
9802	(5772)	**FS**	E	*SR*	IS		9808	(5871)	**FS**	E	*SR*	IS
9803	(5799)	**FS**	E	*SR*	IS		9809	(5890)	**FS**	E	*SR*	IS
9804	(5826)	**FS**	E	*SR*	IS		9810	(5892)	**FS**	E	*SR*	IS
9805	(5833)	**FS**	E	*SR*	IS							

KITCHEN BUFFET FIRST

Mark 3A. Air conditioned. Converted from HST catering vehicles and Mark 3 Open Firsts. Refurbished with table lamps and burgundy seat trim (except *). 18/– plus two seats for staff use (* 24/–, † 24/–, § 24/–, t 23/– 1W). BT10 bogies. d. ETS 14X.

§ First Great Western Sleeper "day coaches" that have been fitted with former HST First Class seats to a 2+1 layout.

Non-standard livery: 10211 EWS dark maroon.

10200–211. Lot No. 30884 Derby 1977. 39.8 t.
10212–229. Lot No. 30878 Derby 1975–76. 39.8 t.
10232–259. Lot No. 30890 Derby 1979. 39.8 t.

10200	(40519)	*	**1**	P	*GA*	NC	10228	(11035)	*	**GA**	P	*GA*	NC
10202	(40504)	†	**BG**	AV		LM	10229	(11059)	*	**GA**	P	*GA*	NC
10203	(40506)	*	**GA**	P	*GA*	NC	10232	(10027)	§	**FD**	P	*GW*	PZ
10211	(40510)		**0**	DB	*DB*	TO	10233	(10013)		**V**	AV		LM
10212	(11049)		**VT**	P	*GA*	NC	10235	(10015)	†	**BG**	AV		LM
10214	(11034)	*	**GA**	P	*GA*	NC	10237	(10022)		**DR**	AV		LM
10215	(11032)		**BG**	AV		LM	10241	(10009)	*	**1**	P		IL
10216	(11041)	*	**GA**	P	*GA*	NC	10242	(10002)		**BG**	AV		LM
10217	(11051)		**VT**	P		ZH	10246	(10014)	†	**BG**	AV		LM
10219	(11047)	§	**FD**	P	*GW*	PZ	10247	(10011)	*	**NX**	P	*GA*	NC
10222	(11063)		**BG**	AV		LM	10249	(10012)		**AW**	AV	*AW*	CF
10223	(11043)	*	**GA**	P	*GA*	NC	10250	(10020)		**V**	AV		LM
10225	(11014)	§	**FD**	P	*GW*	PZ	10257	(10007)	†	**BG**	AV		LM
10226	(11015)		**V**	AV		LM	10259	(10025)	t	**AW**	AV	*AW*	CF

KITCHEN BUFFET FIRST

Mark 3A. Air conditioned. Rebuilt for Chiltern Railways 2011–12 and fitted with sliding plug doors. Interiors originally refurbished for Wrexham & Shropshire with Primarius seating, a new kitchen area and universal-access toilet. 30/– 1TD 1W. BT10 bogies. ETS 14X.

10271/273/274. Lot No. 30890 Derby 1979. 41.3 t.
10272. Lot No. 30884 Derby 1977. 41.3 t.

10271	(10018, 10236)	**CM**	AV	*CR*	AL
10272	(40517, 10208)	**CM**	AV	*CR*	AL
10273	(10021, 10230)	**CM**	AV	*CR*	AL
10274	(10010, 10255)	**CM**	AV	*CR*	AL

KITCHEN BUFFET STANDARD

Mark 4. Air conditioned. Rebuilt from First to Standard Class with bar adjacent to seating area instead of adjacent to end of coach. –/30 1T. BT41 bogies. ETS 6X.

Lot No. 31045 Metro-Cammell 1989–92. 43.2 t.

10300	**EC**	E	*EC*	BN	10317	**EC**	E	*EC*	BN
10301	**EC**	E	*EC*	BN	10318	**EC**	E	*EC*	BN
10302	**EC**	E	*EC*	BN	10319	**EC**	E	*EC*	BN
10303	**EC**	E	*EC*	BN	10320	**EC**	E	*EC*	BN
10304	**EC**	E	*EC*	BN	10321	**EC**	E	*EC*	BN
10305	**EC**	E	*EC*	BN	10323	**EC**	E	*EC*	BN
10306	**EC**	E	*EC*	BN	10324	**EC**	E	*EC*	BN
10307	**EC**	E	*EC*	BN	10325	**EC**	E	*EC*	BN
10308	**EC**	E	*EC*	BN	10326	**EC**	E	*EC*	BN
10309	**EC**	E	*EC*	BN	10328	**EC**	E	*EC*	BN
10310	**EC**	E	*EC*	BN	10329	**EC**	E	*EC*	BN
10311	**EC**	E	*EC*	BN	10330	**EC**	E	*EC*	BN
10312	**EC**	E	*EC*	BN	10331	**EC**	E	*EC*	BN
10313	**EC**	E	*EC*	BN	10332	**EC**	E	*EC*	BN
10315	**EC**	E	*EC*	BN	10333	**EC**	E	*EC*	BN

BUFFET STANDARD

Mark 3A. Air conditioned. Converted from Mark 3 Open Standards at Derby 2006. –/52 1T (including 6 Compin Pegasus seats for "priority" use). BT10 bogies. d. ETS 13X.

Lot No. 30877 Derby 1975–77. 37.8 t.

10401	(12168)	**NX**	P	*GA*	NC	10404	(12068)	**1**	P	*GA*	NC
10402	(12010)	**1**	P	*GA*	NC	10405	(12157)	**1**	P	*GA*	NC
10403	(12135)	**1**	P	*EA*	NC	10406	(12020)	**1**	P	*GA*	NC

SLEEPING CAR WITH PANTRY

Mark 3A. Air conditioned. Retention toilets. 12 compartments with a fixed lower berth and a hinged upper berth, plus an attendants compartment. 2T. BT10 bogies. d. ETS 7X.

Non-standard livery: 10546 EWS dark maroon.

Lot No. 30960 Derby 1981–83. 41 t.

10501	**FS**	P	*SR*	IS	10513	**FS**	P	*SR*	IS
10502	**FS**	P	*SR*	IS	10516	**FS**	P	*SR*	IS
10504	**FS**	P	*SR*	IS	10519	**FS**	P	*SR*	IS
10506	**FS**	P	*SR*	IS	10520	**FS**	P	*SR*	IS
10507	**FS**	P	*SR*	IS	10522	**FS**	P	*SR*	IS
10508	**FS**	P	*SR*	IS	10523	**FS**	P	*SR*	IS

10526	**FS**	P	*SR*	IS
10527	**FS**	P	*SR*	IS
10529	**FS**	P	*SR*	IS
10531	**FS**	P	*SR*	IS
10532	**FD**	P	*GW*	PZ
10534	**FD**	P	*GW*	PZ
10542	**FS**	P	*SR*	IS
10543	**FS**	P	*SR*	IS
10544	**FS**	P	*SR*	IS
10546	**0**	DB	*DB*	TO
10548	**FS**	P	*SR*	IS
10551	**FS**	P	*SR*	IS
10553	**FS**	P	*SR*	IS
10561	**FS**	P	*SR*	IS
10562	**FS**	P	*SR*	IS
10563	**FD**	P	*GW*	PZ
10565	**FS**	P	*SR*	IS
10580	**FS**	P	*SR*	IS

10584	**FD**	P	*GW*	PZ
10589	**FD**	P	*GW*	PZ
10590	**FD**	P	*GW*	PZ
10594	**FD**	P	*GW*	PZ
10596	**U**	P		ZH
10597	**FS**	P	*SR*	IS
10598	**FS**	P	*SR*	IS
10600	**FS**	P	*SR*	IS
10601	**FD**	P	*GW*	PZ
10605	**FS**	P	*SR*	IS
10607	**FS**	P	*SR*	IS
10610	**FS**	P	*SR*	IS
10612	**FD**	P	*GW*	PZ
10613	**FS**	P	*SR*	IS
10614	**FS**	P	*SR*	IS
10616	**FD**	P	*GW*	PZ
10617	**FS**	P	*SR*	IS

SLEEPING CAR

Mark 3A. Air conditioned. Retention toilets. 13 compartments with a fixed lower berth and a hinged upper berth (* 11 compartments with a fixed lower berth and a hinged upper berth + one compartment for a disabled person. 1TD). 2T. BT10 bogies. ETS 6X.

10734 was originally 2914 and used as a Royal Train staff sleeping car. It has 12 berths and a shower room and is ETS 11X.

10648–729. Lot No. 30961 Derby 1980–84. 43.5 t.
10734. Lot No. 31002 Derby/Wolverton 1985. 42.5 t.

10648	d*	**FS**	P	*SR*	IS
10650	d*	**FS**	P	*SR*	IS
10666	d*	**FS**	P	*SR*	IS
10675	d	**FS**	P	*SR*	IS
10680	d*	**FS**	P	*SR*	IS
10683	d	**FS**	P	*SR*	IS
10688	d	**FS**	P	*SR*	IS
10689	d*	**FS**	P	*SR*	IS
10690	d	**FS**	P	*SR*	IS
10693	d	**FS**	P	*SR*	IS

10699	d*	**FS**	P	*SR*	IS
10703	d	**FS**	P	*SR*	IS
10706	d*	**FS**	P	*SR*	IS
10714	d*	**FS**	P	*SR*	IS
10718	d*	**FS**	P	*SR*	IS
10719	d*	**FS**	P	*SR*	IS
10722	d*	**FS**	P	*SR*	IS
10723	d*	**FS**	P	*SR*	IS
10729		**VN**	BE	*NB*	CP
10734		**VN**	BE	*NB*	CP

Names:

| 10729 | CREWE | | 10734 | BALMORAL |

OPEN FIRST

Mark 3A. Air conditioned. All refurbished with table lamps and new seat cushions and trim. 48/– 2T (* 48/– 1T 1TD, † 47/– 2T 1W). BT10 bogies. d. ETS 6X.

§ 11029 has been reseated with Standard Class seats: –/68 2T 2W.

11006/007 were open composites 11906/907 for a time.

Non-standard livery: 11039 EWS dark maroon.

Lot No. 30878 Derby 1975–76. 34.3 t.

11006		**V**	DR		BH		11029 §	**BG**	AV	*CR*	AL
11007		**VT**	P	*GA*	NC		11031 †	**BG**	AV	*CR*	AL
11011	*	**V**	DR		BH		11033		**DR**	AV		LM
11018		**VT**	P	*GA*	NC		11039		**0**	DB	*DB*	TO
11028		**V**	AV		ZB		11048		**VT**	P	*GA*	NC

OPEN FIRST

Mark 3B. Air conditioned. InterCity 80 seats. All refurbished with table lamps and new seat cushions and trim. 48/– 2T. BT10 bogies. d. ETS 6X.

† Greater Anglia vehicles fitted with disabled toilet and reduced seating including three Compin "Pegasus" seats of the same type as used in Standard Class (but regarded as First Class!). 34/3 1T 1TD 2W.

Lot No. 30982 Derby 1985. 36.5 t.

11066	**1**	P	*GA*	NC		11085 †	**1**	P	*GA*	NC
11067	**GA**	P	*GA*	NC		11087 †	**GA**	P	*GA*	NC
11068	**1**	P	*GA*	NC		11088 †	**GA**	P	*GA*	NC
11069	**GA**	P	*GA*	NC		11090 †	**1**	P	*GA*	NC
11070	**1**	P	*GA*	NC		11091	**GA**	P	*GA*	NC
11072	**1**	P	*GA*	NC		11092 †	**GA**	P	*GA*	NC
11073	**1**	P	*GA*	NC		11093 †	**GA**	P	*GA*	NC
11075	**GA**	P	*GA*	NC		11094 †	**1**	P	*GA*	NC
11076	**1**	P	*GA*	NC		11095 †	**1**	P	*GA*	NC
11077	**1**	P	*GA*	NC		11096 †	**GA**	P	*GA*	NC
11078 †	**1**	P	*GA*	NC		11097	**V**	AV		LM
11079	**V**	AV		LM		11098 †	**1**	P	*GA*	NC
11080	**1**	P	*GA*	NC		11099 †	**1**	P	*GA*	NC
11081	**1**	P	*GA*	NC		11100 †	**1**	P	*GA*	NC
11082	**GA**	P	*GA*	NC		11101 †	**1**	P	*GA*	NC

OPEN FIRST

Mark 4. Air conditioned. Rebuilt with new interior by Bombardier Wakefield 2003–05 (some converted from Standard Class vehicles) 41/– 1T (plus 2 seats for staff use). BT41 bogies. ETS 6X.

11201–11273. Lot No. 31046 Metro-Cammell 1989–92. 41.3 t.
11277–11299. Lot No. 31049 Metro-Cammell 1989–92. 41.3 t.

11201		**EC**	E	*EC*	BN		11284	(12487)	**EC**	E	*EC*	BN
11219		**EC**	E	*EC*	BN		11285	(12537)	**EC**	E	*EC*	BN
11229		**EC**	E	*EC*	BN		11286	(12482)	**EC**	E	*EC*	BN
11237		**EC**	E	*EC*	BN		11287	(12527)	**EC**	E	*EC*	BN
11241		**EC**	E	*EC*	BN		11288	(12517)	**EC**	E	*EC*	BN
11244		**EC**	E	*EC*	BN		11289	(12528)	**EC**	E	*EC*	BN
11273		**EC**	E	*EC*	BN		11290	(12530)	**EC**	E	*EC*	BN
11277	(12408)	**EC**	E	*EC*	BN		11291	(12535)	**EC**	E	*EC*	BN
11278	(12479)	**EC**	E	*EC*	BN		11292	(12451)	**EC**	E	*EC*	BN
11279	(12521)	**EC**	E	*EC*	BN		11293	(12536)	**EC**	E	*EC*	BN
11280	(12523)	**EC**	E	*EC*	BN		11294	(12529)	**EC**	E	*EC*	BN
11281	(12418)	**EC**	E	*EC*	BN		11295	(12475)	**EC**	E	*EC*	BN
11282	(12524)	**EC**	E	*EC*	BN		11298	(12416)	**EC**	E	*EC*	BN
11283	(12435)	**EC**	E	*EC*	BN		11299	(12532)	**EC**	E	*EC*	BN

OPEN FIRST (DISABLED)

Mark 4. Air conditioned. Rebuilt from Open First by Bombardier Wakefield 2003–05. 42/– 1W 1TD. BT41 bogies. ETS 6X.

Lot No. 31046 Metro-Cammell 1989–92. 40.7 t.

11301	(11215)	**EC**	E	*EC*	BN		11316	(11227)	**EC**	E	*EC*	BN
11302	(11203)	**EC**	E	*EC*	BN		11317	(11223)	**EC**	E	*EC*	BN
11303	(11211)	**EC**	E	*EC*	BN		11318	(11251)	**EC**	E	*EC*	BN
11304	(11257)	**EC**	E	*EC*	BN		11319	(11247)	**EC**	E	*EC*	BN
11305	(11261)	**EC**	E	*EC*	BN		11320	(11255)	**EC**	E	*EC*	BN
11306	(11276)	**EC**	E	*EC*	BN		11321	(11245)	**EC**	E	*EC*	BN
11307	(11217)	**EC**	E	*EC*	BN		11322	(11228)	**EC**	E	*EC*	BN
11308	(11263)	**EC**	E	*EC*	BN		11323	(11235)	**EC**	E	*EC*	BN
11309	(11259)	**EC**	E	*EC*	BN		11324	(11253)	**EC**	E	*EC*	BN
11310	(11272)	**EC**	E	*EC*	BN		11325	(11231)	**EC**	E	*EC*	BN
11311	(11221)	**EC**	E	*EC*	BN		11326	(11206)	**EC**	E	*EC*	BN
11312	(11225)	**EC**	E	*EC*	BN		11327	(11236)	**EC**	E	*EC*	BN
11313	(11210)	**EC**	E	*EC*	BN		11328	(11274)	**EC**	E	*EC*	BN
11314	(11207)	**EC**	E	*EC*	BN		11329	(11243)	**EC**	E	*EC*	BN
11315	(11238)	**EC**	E	*EC*	BN		11330	(11249)	**EC**	E	*EC*	BN

OPEN FIRST

Mark 4. Air conditioned. Rebuilt from Open First by Bombardier Wakefield 2003–05. Separate area for 7 smokers, although smoking is no longer allowed. 46/– 1W 1TD. BT41 bogies. ETS 6X.

Lot No. 31046 Metro-Cammell 1989–92. 42.1 t.

11401	(11214)	**EC**	E	*EC*	BN		11408	(11218)	**EC**	E	*EC*	BN
11402	(11216)	**EC**	E	*EC*	BN		11409	(11262)	**EC**	E	*EC*	BN
11403	(11258)	**EC**	E	*EC*	BN		11410	(11260)	**EC**	E	*EC*	BN
11404	(11202)	**EC**	E	*EC*	BN		11411	(11240)	**EC**	E	*EC*	BN
11405	(11204)	**EC**	E	*EC*	BN		11412	(11209)	**EC**	E	*EC*	BN
11406	(11205)	**EC**	E	*EC*	BN		11413	(11212)	**EC**	E	*EC*	BN
11407	(11256)	**EC**	E	*EC*	BN		11414	(11246)	**EC**	E	*EC*	BN

11415	(11208)	**EC**	E	*EC*	BN	11423	(11230)	**EC**	E *EC* BN
11416	(11254)	**EC**	E	*EC*	BN	11424	(11239)	**EC**	E *EC* BN
11417	(11226)	**EC**	E	*EC*	BN	11425	(11234)	**EC**	E *EC* BN
11418	(11222)	**EC**	E	*EC*	BN	11426	(11252)	**EC**	E *EC* BN
11419	(11250)	**EC**	E	*EC*	BN	11427	(11200)	**EC**	E *EC* BN
11420	(11242)	**EC**	E	*EC*	BN	11428	(11233)	**EC**	E *EC* BN
11421	(11220)	**EC**	E	*EC*	BN	11429	(11275)	**EC**	E *EC* BN
11422	(11232)	**EC**	E	*EC*	BN	11430	(11248)	**EC**	E *EC* BN

OPEN FIRST

Mark 4. Air conditioned. Converted from Kitchen Buffet Standard with new interior by Bombardier Wakefield 2005. 46/– 1T. BT41 bogies. ETS 6X.

Lot No. 31046 Metro-Cammell 1989–92. 41.3 t.

11998	(10314)	**EC**	E	*EC*	BN	11999	(10316)	**EC**	E *EC* BN

OPEN STANDARD

Mark 3A. Air conditioned. All refurbished with modified seat backs and new layout and further refurbished with new seat trim. –/76 2T (s –/70 2T 1W, t –/72 2T, z –/70 1TD 1T 2W. BT10 bogies. d. ETS 6X.

h   Greater Anglia modified coaches with 8 Compin Pegasus seats at saloon ends for "priority" use and more unidirectional seating. –/80 2T.

§   First Great Western Sleeper "day coaches" that have been fitted with former HST First Class seats to a 2+1 layout and are effectively unclassified. –/45(2) 2T 1W.

12170/171 were converted from Open Composites 11909/910, formerly Open Firsts 11009/010.

Non-standard livery: 12142 GWR brown (trial livery).

12005–167. Lot No. 30877 Derby 1975–77. 34.3 t.
12170/171. Lot No. 30878 Derby 1975–76. 34.3 t.

12005	h	**1**	P	*GA*	NC	12034		**1**	P	*GA*	NC
12009	h	**GA**	P	*GA*	NC	12035	h	**GA**	P	*GA*	NC
12011		**VT**	P	*GA*	NC	12037	h	**1**	P	*GA*	NC
12012	h	**GA**	P	*GA*	NC	12040	h	**GA**	P	*GA*	NC
12013	h	**GA**	P	*GA*	NC	12041		**1**	P	*GA*	NC
12015	h	**GA**	P	*GA*	NC	12042	h	**1**	P	*GA*	NC
12016		**1**	P	*GA*	NC	12043	s	**BG**	AV	*CR*	AL
12017		**BG**	AV	*CR*	AL	12046	h	**GA**	P	*GA*	NC
12019	h	**GA**	P	*GA*	NC	12047	z	**V**	DR		BH
12021		**GA**	P	*GA*	NC	12049		**1**	P	*GA*	NC
12024	h	**1**	P	*GA*	NC	12051	h	**GA**	P	*GA*	NC
12026	h	**GA**	P	*GA*	NC	12054	s	**BG**	AV	*CR*	AL
12027	h	**GA**	P	*GA*	NC	12056	h	**1**	P	*GA*	NC
12030	h	**GA**	P	*GA*	NC	12057	h	**1**	P	*GA*	NC
12031		**1**	P	*GA*	NC	12058		**V**	AV		LM
12032		**1**	P	*GA*	NC	12060	h	**1**	P	*GA*	NC

12061	h	**1**	P	*GA*	NC	12116	h	**GA**	P	*GA*	NC
12062	h	**1**	P	*GA*	NC	12118		**GA**	P	*GA*	NC
12063		**1**	DR		BH	12119	t	**BG**	AV	*CR*	AL
12064		**1**	P	*GA*	NC	12120	h	**1**	P	*GA*	NC
12065		**1**	DR		BH	12122	z	**VT**	P	*GA*	NC
12066	h	**1**	P	*GA*	NC	12125		**1**	P	*GA*	NC
12067		**1**	P	*GA*	NC	12126	h	**GA**	P	*GA*	NC
12073	h	**1**	P	*GA*	NC	12129	h	**GA**	P	*GA*	NC
12078		**VT**	P	*VW*	WB	12130	h	**1**	P	*GA*	NC
12079		**1**	P	*GA*	NC	12132		**GA**	P	*GA*	NC
12081		**1**	P	*GA*	NC	12133		**VT**	P	*GA*	NC
12082	h	**GA**	P	*GA*	NC	12134		**V**	DR		BH
12084	h	**1**	P	*GA*	NC	12137	h	**1**	P	*GA*	NC
12087	s	**V**	DR		BH	12138		**VT**	P	*GA*	NC
12089		**1**	P	*GA*	NC	12139		**NC**	P	*GA*	NC
12090	h	**GA**	P	*GA*	NC	12141		**1**	P	*GA*	NC
12091	h	**GA**	P	*GA*	NC	12142	z	**0**	P		ZH
12093		**1**	P	*GA*	NC	12143		**1**	P	*GA*	NC
12094		**V**	AV	*CR*	AL	12146		**GA**	P	*GA*	NC
12097		**1**	P	*GA*	NC	12147		**GA**	P	*GA*	NC
12098		**1**	P	*GA*	NC	12148		**GA**	P	*GA*	NC
12099	h	**1**	P	*GA*	NC	12150	h	**GA**	P	*GA*	NC
12100	§	**FD**	P	*GW*	PZ	12151		**1**	P	*GA*	NC
12103		**1**	P	*GA*	NC	12153		**GA**	P	*GA*	NC
12104		**V**	AV		LM	12154	h	**GA**	P	*GA*	NC
12105	h	**1**	P	*GA*	NC	12159		**GA**	P	*GA*	NC
12107	h	**1**	P	*GA*	NC	12161	§	**FD**	P	*GW*	PZ
12108		**1**	P	*GA*	NC	12164		**1**	P	*GA*	NC
12109	h	**1**	P	*GA*	NC	12165		**V**	AV		LM
12110	h	**1**	P	*GA*	NC	12166		**1**	P	*GA*	NC
12111		**1**	P	*GA*	NC	12167	h	**1**	P	*GA*	NC
12114	h	**1**	P	*GA*	NC	12170		**GA**	P	*GA*	NC
12115	h	**1**	P	*GA*	NC	12171		**GA**	P	*GA*	NC

OPEN STANDARD

Mark 3A (†) or Mark 3B. Air conditioned. BT10 bogies. d. ETS 6X. Converted from Mark 3A or 3B Open Firsts. Fitted with new Grammer seating. –/70 2T 1W. 12182/183 under conversion.

12176–181/185. Mark 3B. Lot No. 30982 Derby 1985. 38.5 t.
12182–184. Mark 3A. Lot No. 30878 Derby 1975–76. t .

12176 (11064)	**AW**	AV	*AW*	CF
12177 (11065)	**AW**	AV	*AW*	CF
12178 (11071)	**AW**	AV	*AW*	CF
12179 (11083)	**AW**	AV	*AW*	CF
12180 (11084)	**AW**	AV	*AW*	CF
12181 (11086)	**AW**	AV	*AW*	CF
12182 (11013) †		AV		CP
12183 (11027) †		AV		CP
12184 (11044) †	**AW**	AV	*AW*	CF
12185 (11089)	**AW**	AV	*AW*	CF

OPEN STANDARD (END)

Mark 4. Air conditioned. Rebuilt with new interior by Bombardier Wakefield 2003–05. Separate area for 26 smokers, although smoking is no longer allowed. –/76 1T. BT41 bogies. ETS 6X.

12232 was converted from the original 12405.

12200–231. Lot No. 31047 Metro-Cammell 1989–91. 39.5 t.
12232. Lot No. 31049 Metro-Cammell 1989–92. 39.5 t.

12200	**EC**	E	*EC*	BN	12217	**EC**	E	*EC*	BN
12201	**EC**	E	*EC*	BN	12218	**EC**	E	*EC*	BN
12202	**EC**	E	*EC*	BN	12219	**EC**	E	*EC*	BN
12203	**EC**	E	*EC*	BN	12220	**EC**	E	*EC*	BN
12204	**EC**	E	*EC*	BN	12222	**EC**	E	*EC*	BN
12205	**EC**	E	*EC*	BN	12223	**EC**	E	*EC*	BN
12207	**EC**	E	*EC*	BN	12224	**EC**	E	*EC*	BN
12208	**EC**	E	*EC*	BN	12225	**EC**	E	*EC*	BN
12209	**EC**	E	*EC*	BN	12226	**EC**	E	*EC*	BN
12210	**EC**	E	*EC*	BN	12227	**EC**	E	*EC*	BN
12211	**EC**	E	*EC*	BN	12228	**EC**	E	*EC*	BN
12212	**EC**	E	*EC*	BN	12229	**EC**	E	*EC*	BN
12213	**EC**	E	*EC*	BN	12230	**EC**	E	*EC*	BN
12214	**EC**	E	*EC*	BN	12231	**EC**	E	*EC*	BN
12215	**EC**	E	*EC*	BN	12232	**EC**	E	*EC*	BN
12216	**EC**	E	*EC*	BN					

OPEN STANDARD (DISABLED)

Mark 4. Air conditioned. Rebuilt with new interior by Bombardier Wakefield 2003–05. –/68 2W 1TD. BT41 bogies. ETS 6X.

12331 was converted from Open Standard 12531.

12300–330. Lot No. 31048 Metro-Cammell 1989–91. 39.4 t.
12331. Lot No. 31049 Metro-Cammell 1989–92. 39.4 t.

12300	**EC**	E	*EC*	BN	12317	**EC**	E	*EC*	BN
12301	**EC**	E	*EC*	BN	12318	**EC**	E	*EC*	BN
12302	**EC**	E	*EC*	BN	12319	**EC**	E	*EC*	BN
12303	**EC**	E	*EC*	BN	12320	**EC**	E	*EC*	BN
12304	**EC**	E	*EC*	BN	12321	**EC**	E	*EC*	BN
12305	**EC**	E	*EC*	BN	12322	**EC**	E	*EC*	BN
12307	**EC**	E	*EC*	BN	12323	**EC**	E	*EC*	BN
12308	**EC**	E	*EC*	BN	12324	**EC**	E	*EC*	BN
12309	**EC**	E	*EC*	BN	12325	**EC**	E	*EC*	BN
12310	**EC**	E	*EC*	BN	12326	**EC**	E	*EC*	BN
12311	**EC**	E	*EC*	BN	12327	**EC**	E	*EC*	BN
12312	**EC**	E	*EC*	BN	12328	**EC**	E	*EC*	BN
12313	**EC**	E	*EC*	BN	12329	**EC**	E	*EC*	BN
12315	**EC**	E	*EC*	BN	12330	**EC**	E	*EC*	BN
12316	**EC**	E	*EC*	BN	12331	**EC**	E	*EC*	BN

OPEN STANDARD

Mark 4. Air conditioned. Rebuilt with new interior by Bombardier Wakefield 2003–05. –/76 1T. BT41 bogies. ETS 6X.

12405 is the second coach to carry that number. It was built from the bodyshell originally intended for 12221. The original 12405 is now 12232.

Lot No. 31049 Metro-Cammell 1989–92. 40.8 t.

12400	**EC**	E	*EC*	BN	12448	**EC**	E	*EC*	BN
12401	**EC**	E	*EC*	BN	12449	**EC**	E	*EC*	BN
12402	**EC**	E	*EC*	BN	12450	**EC**	E	*EC*	BN
12403	**EC**	E	*EC*	BN	12452	**EC**	E	*EC*	BN
12404	**EC**	E	*EC*	BN	12453	**EC**	E	*EC*	BN
12405	**EC**	E	*EC*	BN	12454	**EC**	E	*EC*	BN
12406	**EC**	E	*EC*	BN	12455	**EC**	E	*EC*	BN
12407	**EC**	E	*EC*	BN	12456	**EC**	E	*EC*	BN
12409	**EC**	E	*EC*	BN	12457	**EC**	E	*EC*	BN
12410	**EC**	E	*EC*	BN	12458	**EC**	E	*EC*	BN
12411	**EC**	E	*EC*	BN	12459	**EC**	E	*EC*	BN
12414	**EC**	E	*EC*	BN	12460	**EC**	E	*EC*	BN
12415	**EC**	E	*EC*	BN	12461	**EC**	E	*EC*	BN
12417	**EC**	E	*EC*	BN	12462	**EC**	E	*EC*	BN
12419	**EC**	E	*EC*	BN	12463	**EC**	E	*EC*	BN
12420	**EC**	E	*EC*	BN	12464	**EC**	E	*EC*	BN
12421	**EC**	E	*EC*	BN	12465	**EC**	E	*EC*	BN
12422	**EC**	E	*EC*	BN	12466	**EC**	E	*EC*	BN
12423	**EC**	E	*EC*	BN	12467	**EC**	E	*EC*	BN
12424	**EC**	E	*EC*	BN	12468	**EC**	E	*EC*	BN
12425	**EC**	E	*EC*	BN	12469	**EC**	E	*EC*	BN
12426	**EC**	E	*EC*	BN	12470	**EC**	E	*EC*	BN
12427	**EC**	E	*EC*	BN	12471	**EC**	E	*EC*	BN
12428	**EC**	E	*EC*	BN	12472	**EC**	E	*EC*	BN
12429	**EC**	E	*EC*	BN	12473	**EC**	E	*EC*	BN
12430	**EC**	E	*EC*	BN	12474	**EC**	E	*EC*	BN
12431	**EC**	E	*EC*	BN	12476	**EC**	E	*EC*	BN
12432	**EC**	E	*EC*	BN	12477	**EC**	E	*EC*	BN
12433	**EC**	E	*EC*	BN	12478	**EC**	E	*EC*	BN
12434	**EC**	E	*EC*	BN	12480	**EC**	E	*EC*	BN
12436	**EC**	E	*EC*	BN	12481	**EC**	E	*EC*	BN
12437	**EC**	E	*EC*	BN	12483	**EC**	E	*EC*	BN
12438	**EC**	E	*EC*	BN	12484	**EC**	E	*EC*	BN
12439	**EC**	E	*EC*	BN	12485	**EC**	E	*EC*	BN
12440	**EC**	E	*EC*	BN	12486	**EC**	E	*EC*	BN
12441	**EC**	E	*EC*	BN	12488	**EC**	E	*EC*	BN
12442	**EC**	E	*EC*	BN	12489	**EC**	E	*EC*	BN
12443	**EC**	E	*EC*	BN	12513	**EC**	E	*EC*	BN
12444	**EC**	E	*EC*	BN	12514	**EC**	E	*EC*	BN
12445	**EC**	E	*EC*	BN	12515	**EC**	E	*EC*	BN
12446	**EC**	E	*EC*	BN	12518	**EC**	E	*EC*	BN
12447	**EC**	E	*EC*	BN	12519	**EC**	E	*EC*	BN

12520	**EC**	E	*EC*	BN		12533	**EC**	E	*EC*	BN
12522	**EC**	E	*EC*	BN		12534	**EC**	E	*EC*	BN
12526	**EC**	E	*EC*	BN		12538	**EC**	E	*EC*	BN

OPEN STANDARD

Mark 3A. Air conditioned. Rebuilt for Chiltern Railways 2011–13 and fitted with sliding plug doors and toilets with retention tanks. Original InterCity 70 seating retained but mainly arranged around tables. –/72(6) or * –/69(4) 1T. BT10 bogies. ETS 6X.

12602–609/614–616/618/620. Lot No. 30877 Derby 1975–77. 36.2 t (* 37.1 t).
12601/613/617–619/621/623/625/627. Lot No. 30878 Derby 1975–76. 36.2 t (* 37.1 t).

12602	(12072)		**CM**	AV	*CR*	AL
12603	(12053)	*	**CM**	AV	*CR*	AL
12604	(12131)		**CM**	AV	*CR*	AL
12605	(11040)	*	**CM**	AV	*CR*	AL
12606	(12048)		**CM**	AV	*CR*	AL
12607	(12038)	*	**CM**	AV	*CR*	AL
12608	(12069)		**CM**	AV	*CR*	AL
12609	(12014)	*	**CM**	AV	*CR*	AL
12610	(12117)		**CM**	AV	*CR*	AL
12613	(11042, 12173)	*	**CM**	AV	*CR*	AL
12614	(12145)		**CM**	AV	*CR*	AL
12615	(12059)	*	**CM**	AV	*CR*	AL
12616	(12127)		**CM**	AV	*CR*	AL
12617	(11052, 12174)	*	**CM**	AV	*CR*	AL
12618	(11008, 12169)		**CM**	AV	*CR*	AL
12619	(11058, 12175)	*	**CM**	AV	*CR*	AL
12620	(12124)		**CM**	AV	*CR*	AL
12621	(11046)	*	**CM**	AV	*CR*	AL
12623	(11019)	*	**CM**	AV	*CR*	AL
12625	(11030)	*	**CM**	AV	*CR*	AL
12627	(11054)	*	**CM**	AV	*CR*	AL

CORRIDOR FIRST

Mark 1. Seven compartments. 42/– 2T. B4 bogies. ETS 3.

Lot No. 30381 Swindon 1959. 33 t.

| 13227 | x | **CH** | LS | | CL | | 13230 | xk | **M** | BK | *BK* | BT |
| 13229 | xk | **M** | BK | *BK* | BT |

OPEN FIRST

Mark 1 converted from Corridor First in 2013–14. 42/– 2T. Commonwealth bogies. ETS 3.

Lot No. 30667 Swindon 1962. 35 t.

| 13320 | x | **M** | WC | *WC* | CS | ANNA |

CORRIDOR FIRST

Mark 2A. Seven compartments. Pressure ventilated. 42/– 2T. B4 bogies. ETS 4.

Lot No. 30774 Derby 1968. 33 t.

13440 v   **M**   WC   *WC*   CS

CORRIDOR BRAKE FIRST

Mark 1. Four compartments. 24/– 1T. Commonwealth bogies. ETS 2.

Lot No. 30668 Swindon 1961. 36 t.

17013 (14013)	x	**PC**	LS		CM
17018 (14018)	v	**CH**	VT	*VT*	TM BOTAURUS

CORRIDOR BRAKE FIRST

Mark 2A. Four compartments. Pressure ventilated. 24/– 1T. B4 bogies. ETS 4.

17080/090 were numbered 35516/503 for a time when declassified.

17056/077. Lot No. 30775 Derby 1967–68. 32 t.
17080–102. Lot No. 30786 Derby 1968. 32 t.

17056 (14056)		**M**	RV		CD
17077 (14077)		**RV**	RV		BQ
17080 (14080)		**PC**	RA	*ST*	CS
17090 (14090)	v	**CH**	VT		TM
17102 (14102)		**M**	WC	*WC*	CS

COUCHETTE/GENERATOR COACH

Mark 2B. Formerly part of Royal Train. Converted from Corridor Brake First built 1969. Consists of luggage accommodation, guard's compartment, 350 kW diesel generator and staff sleeping accommodation. Pressure ventilated. B5 bogies. ETS 5X.

Lot No. 30888 Wolverton 1977. 46 t.

17105 (14105, 2905)   **RB**   RV   *RV*   EH

CORRIDOR BRAKE FIRST

Mark 2D. Four compartments. Air conditioned. Stones equipment. 24/– 1T. B4 Bogies. ETS 5.

Lot No. 30823 Derby 1971–72. 33.5 t.

17159 (14159)	d	**DS**	DR	*DR*	KM
17167 (14167)		**VN**	BE	*NB*	CP MOW COP

OPEN BRAKE UNCLASSIFIED

Mark 3B. Air conditioned. Fitted with hydraulic handbrake. Used by First Great Western as Sleeper "day coaches" that have been fitted with former HST First Class seats to a 2+1 layout and are effectively unclassified. 36/–1T. BT10 bogies. pg. d. ETS 5X.

Lot No. 30990 Derby 1986. 35.81 t.

| 17173 | **FD** | P | *GW* | PZ | 17175 | **FD** | P | *GW* | PZ |
| 17174 | **FD** | P | *GW* | PZ | | | | | |

CORRIDOR STANDARD

Mark 1. –/48 2T. Eight Compartments. Commonwealth bogies. ETS 4.

Lot No. 30685 Derby 1961–62. 36 t.

| 18756 (25756) | x | **M** | WC | *WC* | CS |

CORRIDOR BRAKE COMPOSITE

Mark 1. There are two variants depending upon whether the Standard Class compartments have armrests. Each vehicle has two First Class and three Standard Class compartments. 12/18 2T (* 12/24 2T). Commonwealth bogies. ETS 2.

21241–245. Lot No. 30669 Swindon 1961–62. 36 t.
21256. Lot No. 30731 Derby 1963. 37 t.
21266–272. Lot No. 30732 Derby 1964. 37 t.

21241	x	**M**	BK	*BK*	BT	21266	x*	**M**	WC	*WC*	CS
21245	x	**M**	RV	*RV*	EH	21269	*	**CC**	RV	*RV*	EH
21256	x	**M**	WC	*WC*	CS	21272	x*	**CH**	RV	*RV*	EH

CORRIDOR BRAKE STANDARD

Mark 1. Four compartments. –/24 1T. ETS 2.

35185. Lot No. 30427 Wolverton 1959. B4 bogies. 33 t.
35459. Lot No. 30721 Wolverton 1963. Commonwealth bogies. 37 t.

| 35185 | x | **M** | BK | *BK* | BT |
| 35459 | x | **M** | WC | *WC* | CS |

CORRIDOR BRAKE GENERATOR STANDARD

Mark 1. Four compartments. –/24 1T. Fitted with an ETS generator in the former luggage compartment.

Lot No. 30721 Wolverton 1963. Commonwealth bogies. 37 t.

| 35469 | x | **CC** | RV | *RV* | EH |

BRAKE/POWER KITCHEN

Mark 2C. Pressure ventilated. Converted from Corridor Brake First (declassified to Corridor Brake Standard) built 1970. Converted by West Coast Railway Company 2000–01. Consists of 60 kVA generator, guard's compartment and electric kitchen. B5 bogies. ETS 4.

Non-standard livery: British Racing Green with gold lining.

Lot No. 30796 Derby 1969–70. 32.5 t.

35511 (14130, 17130)	**0**	RA		BO

KITCHEN CAR

Mark 1. Converted 1989/2006 from Kitchen Buffet Unclassified. Buffet and seating area replaced with additional kitchen and food preparation area. Fluorescent lighting. Commonwealth bogies. ETS 2X.

Lot No. 30628 Pressed Steel 1960–61. 39 t.

80041 (1690)	x	**M**	RV		EH
80042 (1646)		**BG**	RV	*RV*	EH

DRIVING BRAKE VAN (110 mph)

Mark 3B. Air conditioned. T4 bogies. dg. ETS 5X. Driving Brake Vans converted for use by Network Rail can be found in the Service Stock section of this book.

Non-standard livery: 82146 All over silver with DB logos.

Lot No. 31042 Derby 1988. 45.2 t.

82101	**V**	DR		BH	82123	**V**	AV		LM
82102	**1**	P	*GA*	NC	82126	**VT**	P	*GA*	NC
82103	**GA**	P	*GA*	NC	82127	**1**	P	*GA*	NC
82105	**GA**	P	*GA*	NC	82132	**1**	P	*GA*	NC
82106	**V**	AV		LB	82133	**1**	P	*GA*	NC
82107	**GA**	P	*GA*	NC	82136	**GA**	P	*GA*	NC
82110	**V**	AV		LM	82137	**V**	AV		LM
82112	**GA**	P	*GA*	NC	82138	**V**	AV		LM
82113	**V**	AV		LM	82139	**1**	P	*GA*	NC
82114	**1**	P	*GA*	NC	82141	**V**	AV		LM
82115	**B**	NR		ZN	82143	**1**	P	*GA*	NC
82116	**V**	AV		LM	82146	**0**	DB	*DB*	TO
82118	**GA**	P	*GA*	NC	82148	**V**	AV		LM
82120	**V**	AV		LM	82150	**V**	AV		LM
82121	**GA**	P	*GA*	NC	82152	**GA**	P	*GA*	NC
82122	**V**	AV		LM					

DRIVING BRAKE VAN (140 mph)

Mark 4. Air conditioned. Swiss-built (SIG) bogies. dg. ETS 6X.

Advertising livery: 82205 Flying Scotsman (purple).

Lot No. 31043 Metro-Cammell 1988. 43.5 t.

82200	**EC**	E	*EC*	BN	82216	**EC**	E	*EC*	BN
82201	**EC**	E	*EC*	BN	82217	**EC**	E	*EC*	BN
82202	**EC**	E	*EC*	BN	82218	**EC**	E	*EC*	BN
82203	**EC**	E	*EC*	BN	82219	**EC**	E	*EC*	BN
82204	**EC**	E	*EC*	BN	82220	**EC**	E	*EC*	BN
82205	**AL**	E	*EC*	BN	82222	**EC**	E	*EC*	BN
82206	**EC**	E	*EC*	BN	82223	**EC**	E	*EC*	BN
82207	**EC**	E	*EC*	BN	82224	**EC**	E	*EC*	BN
82208	**EC**	E	*EC*	BN	82225	**EC**	E	*EC*	BN
82209	**EC**	E	*EC*	BN	82226	**EC**	E	*EC*	BN
82210	**EC**	E	*EC*	BN	82227	**EC**	E	*EC*	BN
82211	**EC**	E	*EC*	BN	82228	**EC**	E	*EC*	BN
82212	**EC**	E	*EC*	BN	82229	**EC**	E	*EC*	BN
82213	**EC**	E	*EC*	BN	82230	**EC**	E	*EC*	BN
82214	**EC**	E	*EC*	BN	82231	**EC**	E	*EC*	BN
82215	**EC**	E	*EC*	BN					

DRIVING BRAKE VAN (110 mph)

Mark 3B. Air conditioned. T4 bogies. dg. ETS 6X.

82301–305 originally converted 2008 for use by Wrexham & Shropshire. Now operated by Chiltern Railways. 82306–308 converted for Arriva Trains Wales 2011–12. 82309 converted for Chiltern Railways 2013.

g   Fitted with a diesel generator.

Lot No. 31042 Derby 1988. 45.2 t.

82301	(82117)	g	**CM**	AV	*CR*	AL
82302	(82151)	g	**CM**	AV	*CR*	AL
82303	(82135)	g	**CM**	AV	*CR*	AL
82304	(82130)	g	**CM**	AV	*CR*	AL
82305	(82134)	g	**CM**	AV	*CR*	AL
82306	(82144)		**AW**	AV	*AW*	CF
82307	(82131)		**AW**	AV	*AW*	CF
82308	(82108)		**AW**	AV	*AW*	CF
82309	(82104)	g	**CM**	AV	*CR*	AL

GANGWAYED BRAKE VAN (100 mph)

Mark 1. Short frame (57 ft). Load 10 t. Adapted 199? for use as Brake Luggage Van. Guard's compartment retained and former baggage area adapted for secure stowage of passengers' luggage. B4 bogies. 100 mph. ETS 1X.

Lot No. 30162 Pressed Steel 1956–57. 30.5 t.

92904 (80867, 99554)		**VN**	BE	*NB*		CP

GENERAL UTILITY VAN (100 mph)

Mark 1. Short frame. Load 14 t. Screw couplers. Adapted 2013/2010 for use as a water carrier with 3000 gallon capacity. ETS 0.

Non-standard livery: 96100 GWR Brown.

96100. Lot No. 30565 Pressed Steel 1959. 30 t. B5 bogies.
96175. Lot No. 30403 York/Glasgow 1958–60. 30 t. Commonwealth bogies.

96100 (86734, 93734)	x	**0**	VT	*VT*	TM
96175 (86628, 93628)	x	**M**	WC	*WC*	CS

KITCHEN CAR

Mark 1 converted from Corridor First in 2008 with staff accommodation. Commonwealth bogies. ETS 3.

Lot No. 30667 Swindon 1961. 35 t.

99316 (13321)	x	**M**	WC	*WC*	CS

BUFFET STANDARD

Mark 1 converted from Open Standard in 2013 by the removal of two seating bays and fitting of a buffet. –/48 2T. Commonwealth bogies. ETS 4.

Lot No. 30646 Wolverton 1961. 36 t.

99318 (4912)	x	**M**	WC	*WC*	CS

KITCHEN CAR

Mark 1 converted from Corridor Standard in 2011 with staff accommodation. Commonwealth bogies. ETS 3.

Lot No. 30685 Derby 1961–62. 34 t.

99712 (18893)	x	**M**	WC	*WC*	CS

OPEN STANDARD

Mark 1 Corridor Standard rebuilt in 1997 as Open Standard using components from 4936. –/64 2T. Commonwealth bogies. ETS 4.

Lot No. 30685 Derby 1961–62. 36 t.

99722 (25806, 18806)	x	**M**	WC	*WC*	CS

NYMR REGISTERED CARRIAGES

These carriages are permitted to operate on the national railway network but may only be used to convey fare-paying passengers between Middlesbrough and Whitby on the Esk Valley branch as an extension of North Yorkshire Moors Railway services between Pickering and Grosmont. Only NYMR coaches currently registered for use on the national railway network are listed.

RESTAURANT FIRST

Mark 1. 24/–. Commonwealth bogies. Lot No. 30633 Swindon 1961. 42.5 t.

| 324 | x | **PC** | NY | *NY* | | NY | | JOS de CRAU |

BUFFET STANDARD

Mark 1. –/44 2T. Commonwealth bogies.
Lot No. 30520 Wolverton 1960. 38 t.

| 1823 | v | **M** | NY | *NY* | | NY |

OPEN STANDARD

Mark 1. –/64 2T (* –/60 2W 2T, † –/60 3W 1T). BR Mark 1 bogies.

3798/3801. Lot No. 30079 York 1953. 33 t.
3860/72. Lot No. 30080 York 1954. 33 t.
3948. Lot No. 30086 Eastleigh 1954–55. 33 t.
4198/4252. Lot No. 30172 York 1956. 33 t.
4286/90. Lot No. 30207 BRCW 1956. 33 t.
4455. Lot No. 30226 BRCW 1957. 33 t.

3798	v	**M**	NY	*NY*	NY		4198	v	**CC**	NY	*NY*	NY
3801	v	**CC**	NY	*NY*	NY		4252	v*	**CC**	NY	*NY*	NY
3860	v*	**M**	NY	*NY*	NY		4286	v	**CC**	NY	*NY*	NY
3872	v†	**BG**	NY	*NY*	NY		4290	v	**M**	NY	*NY*	NY
3948	v	**CC**	NY	*NY*	NY		4455	v	**CC**	NY	*NY*	NY

OPEN STANDARD

Mark 1. –/48 2T. BR Mark 1 bogies.

4786. Lot No. 30376 York 1957. 33 t.
4817. Lot No. 30473 BRCW 1959. 33 t.

| 4786 | v | **CH** | NY | *NY* | NY | | 4817 | v | **M** | NY | *NY* | NY |

OPEN STANDARD

Mark 1. Later vehicles built with Commonwealth bogies. –/64 2T.
Lot No. 30690 Wolverton 1961–62. Aluminium window frames. 37 t.

| 4990 | v | **M** | NY | *NY* | NY | | 5029 | v | **CH** | NY | *NY* | NY |
| 5000 | v | **M** | NY | *NY* | NY | | | | | | |

OPEN BRAKE STANDARD

Mark 1. –/39 1T. BR Mark 1 bogies.

Lot No. 30170 Doncaster 1956. 34 t.

| 9225 | v | **M** | NY | *NY* | NY | | 9274 | v | **M** | NY | *NY* | NY |
| 9267 | v | **BG** | NY | *NY* | NY | | | | | | | |

CORRIDOR COMPOSITE

Mark 1. 24/18 1T. BR Mark 1 bogies.

15745. Lot No. 30179 Metro Cammell 1956. 36 t.
16156. Lot No. 30665 Derby 1961. 36 t.

| 15745 | v | **M** | NY | *NY* | NY | | 16156 | v | **CC** | NY | *NY* | NY |

CORRIDOR BRAKE COMPOSITE

Mark 1. Two First Class and three Standard Class compartments. 12/18 2T. BR Mark 1 bogies.

Lot No. 30185 Metro Cammell 1956. 36 t.

| 21100 | v | **CC** | NY | *NY* | NY |

CORRIDOR BRAKE STANDARD

Mark 1. –/24 1T. BR Mark 1 bogies.

Lot No. 30233 Gloucester 1957. 35 t.

| 35089 | v | **CC** | NY | *NY* | NY |

PULLMAN BRAKE THIRD

Built 1928 by Metropolitan Carriage & Wagon Company. –/30. Gresley bogies. 37.5 t.

| 232 | v | **PC** | NY | *NY* | NY | CAR No. 79 |

PULLMAN KITCHEN FIRST

Built by Metro-Cammell 1960–61 for ECML services. 20/– 2T. Commonwealth bogies. 41.2 t.

| 318 | x | **PC** | NY | *NY* | NY | ROBIN |

PULLMAN PARLOUR FIRST

Built by Metro-Cammell 1960–61 for ECML services. 29/– 2T. Commonwealth bogies. 38.5 t.

| 328 | x | **PC** | NY | *NY* | NY | OPAL |

2.2. HIGH SPEED TRAIN TRAILER CARS

HSTs consist of a number of trailer cars (usually between six and nine) with a power car at each end. All trailers are classified Mark 3 and have BT10 bogies with disc brakes and central door locking. Heating is by a 415 V three-phase supply and vehicles have air conditioning. Maximum speed is 125 mph.

The trailer cars have one standard bodyshell for both First and Standard Class, thus facilitating easy conversion from one class to the other. As built all cars had facing seating around tables with Standard Class carriages having nine bays of seats per side which did not line up with the eight windows per side. This created a new unwelcome trend in British rolling stock of seats not lining up with windows.

All vehicles underwent a mid-life refurbishment in the 1980s with Standard Class seating layouts revised to incorporate unidirectional seating in addition to facing, in a somewhat higgledy-piggledy layout where seats did not line up either side of the aisle.

A further refurbishment programme was completed in November 2000, with each Train Operating Company having a different scheme as follows:

Great Western Trains (later First Great Western). Green seat covers and extra partitions between seat bays.

Great North Eastern Railway. New ceiling lighting panels and brown seat covers. First Class vehicles had table lamps and imitation walnut plastic end panels.

Virgin CrossCountry. Green seat covers. Standard Class vehicles had four seats in the centre of each carriage replaced with a luggage stack. All have now passed to other operators.

Midland Mainline. Grey seat covers, redesigned seat squabs, side carpeting and two seats in the centre of each Standard Class carriage and one in First Class carriages replaced with a luggage stack.

Since then the remaining three operators of HSTs embarked on separate, and very different, refurbishment projects:

Midland Mainline was first to refurbish its vehicles a second time during 2003–04. This involved fitting new fluorescent and halogen ceiling lighting, although the original seats were retained in First and Standard Class, but with blue upholstery.

London St Pancras–Sheffield/Leeds and Nottingham services are now operated by **East Midlands Trains** and in late 2009 this operator embarked on another, less radical, refurbishment which included retention of the original seats but with red upholstery in Standard Class and blue in First Class. This programme was completed in 2010.

First Great Western started a major rebuild of its HST sets in late 2006, with the programme completed in 2008. With an increased fleet of 54 sets (since reduced to 53) the new interiors feature new lighting and seating throughout. First Class seats have leather upholstery, and are made by Primarius UK. Standard Class seats are of high-back design by Grammer. A number of sets operate without a full buffet or kitchen car, instead using one of 19 TS vehicles converted to include a "mini buffet" counter for use on shorter distance services. During 2012 15 402xx or 407xx buffet vehicles were converted to Trailer Standards to make the rakes formed as 7-cars up to 8-cars. During 2014–15 further changes to the FGW sets include the conversion of one First Class carriage from each set to Standard Class.

GNER modernised its buffet cars with new corner bars in 2004 and at the same time each HST set was made up to 9-cars with an extra Standard Class vehicle added with a disabled person's toilet.

At the end of 2006 **GNER** embarked on a major rebuild of its sets, with the work being carried out at Wabtec, Doncaster. All vehicles will have similar interiors to the Mark 4 "Mallard" fleet, with new Primarius seats throughout. The refurbishment of the 13 sets was completed by **National Express East Coast** in late 2009, these trains are now operated by **East Coast**.

Ten sets ex-Virgin CrossCountry, and some spare vehicles, were temporarily allocated to Midland Mainline for the interim service to Manchester during 2003–04 and had a facelift. Buffet cars were converted from TSB to TFKB and renumbered in the 408xx series. Most of these vehicles are now in use with First Great Western.

Open access operator **Grand Central** started operation in December 2007 with a new service from Sunderland to London King's Cross. This operator has three sets mostly using stock converted from loco-hauled Mark 3s. The seats in Standard Class have First Class spacing and in most vehicles are all facing. Increases in the number of passengers on its services has seen rakes lengthened from 5-cars to 6-cars and they can run as 7-cars at busy times.

CrossCountry reintroduced HSTs to the Cross-Country network from 2008. Five sets were refurbished at Wabtec, Doncaster principally for use on the Plymouth–Edinburgh route. Three of these sets use stock mostly converted from loco-hauled Mark 3s and two are sets ex-Midland Mainline. The interiors are similar to refurbished East Coast sets, although the seating layout is different and one toilet per carriage has been removed in favour of a luggage stack.

Operator Codes

Operator codes are shown in the heading before each set of vehicles. The first letter is always "T" for HST carriages, denoting a Trailer vehicle. The second letter denotes the passenger accommodation in that vehicle, for example "F" for First. "GS" denotes Guards accommodation and Standard Class seating. This is followed by catering provision, with "B" for buffet, and "K" for a kitchen and buffet:

TCK	Trailer Composite Kitchen	TFKB	Trailer Kitchen Buffet First
TF	Trailer First	TSB	Trailer Buffet Standard
TFB	Trailer Buffet First	TS	Trailer Standard
TGS	Trailer Guard's Standard		

TRAILER STANDARD BUFFET   TSB

19 vehicles converted at Laira 2009–10 from HST TSs for First Great Western. Refurbished with Grammer seating.

40101–119. For Lot No. details see TS. –/70 1T. 35.5 t.

40101 (42170)	**FD**	P	*GW*	LA
40102 (42223)	**FD**	P	*GW*	LA
40103 (42316)	**FD**	P	*GW*	LA
40104 (42254)	**FD**	P	*GW*	LA
40105 (42084)	**FD**	P	*GW*	LA
40106 (42162)	**FD**	P	*GW*	LA
40107 (42334)	**FD**	P	*GW*	LA
40108 (42314)	**FD**	P	*GW*	LA
40109 (42262)	**FD**	P	*GW*	LA
40110 (42187)	**FD**	P	*GW*	LA
40111 (42248)	**FD**	P	*GW*	LA
40112 (42336)	**FD**	P	*GW*	LA
40113 (42309)	**FD**	P	*GW*	LA
40114 (42086)	**FD**	P	*GW*	LA
40115 (42320)	**FD**	P	*GW*	LA
40116 (42147)	**FD**	P	*GW*	LA
40117 (42249)	**FD**	P	*GW*	LA
40118 (42338)	**FD**	P	*GW*	LA
40119 (42090)	**FD**	P	*GW*	LA

TRAILER BUFFET FIRST   TFB

Converted from TSB by fitting First Class seats. Renumbered from 404xx series by subtracting 200. All refurbished by First Great Western and fitted with Primarius leather seating. 23/–.

40204–221. Lot No. 30883 Derby 1976–77. 36.12 t.
40231. Lot No. 30899 Derby 1978–79. 36.12 t.

40204	**FD**	A	*GW*	LA	40210	**FD**	A	*GW*	LA
40205	**FD**	A	*GW*	LA	40221	**FD**	A	*GW*	LA
40207	**FD**	A	*GW*	LA	40231	**FD**	A	*GW*	LA

TRAILER BUFFET STANDARD   TSB

Renumbered from 400xx series by adding 400. –/33 1W.

40433 was numbered 40233 for a time when fitted with 23 First Class seats.

40402–426. Lot No. 30883 Derby 1976–77. 36.12 t.
40433. Lot No. 30899 Derby 1978–79. 36.12 t.

40402	**V**	AV		LM	40426	**GC**	A	*GC*	HT
40419	**V**	AV		LM	40433	**GC**	A	*GC*	HT
40424	**GC**	A	*GC*	HT					

TRAILER KITCHEN BUFFET FIRST   TFKB

These vehicles have larger kitchens than the 402xx and 404xx series
vehicles, and are used in trains where a full meal service is required.
They were renumbered from the 403xx series (in which the seats were
unclassified) by adding 400 to the previous number. 17/–.

*   Refurbished First Great Western vehicles. Primarius leather seating.
m   Refurbished East Coast vehicles with Primarius seating.

40700–721. Lot No. 30921 Derby 1978–79. 38.16 t.
40722–735. Lot No. 30940 Derby 1979–80. 38.16 t.
40737–753. Lot No. 30948 Derby 1980–81. 38.16 t.
40754–757. Lot No. 30966 Derby 1982. 38.16 t.

40700		**ST**	P	*EM*	NL			
40701	m	**NX**	P	*EC*	EC			
40702	m	**NX**	P	*EC*	EC			
40703	*	**FD**	A	*GW*	LA			
40704	m	**NX**	A	*EC*	EC			
40705	m	**NX**	A	*EC*	EC			
40706	m	**NX**	A	*EC*	EC			
40707	*	**FD**	A	*GW*	LA			
40708	m	**NX**	P	*EC*	EC			
40710	*	**FD**	A	*GW*	LA			
40711	m	**NX**	A	*EC*	EC			
40713	*	**FD**	A	*GW*	LA			
40715	*	**FD**	A	*GW*	LA			
40716	*	**FD**	A	*GW*	LA			
40718	*	**FD**	A	*GW*	LA			
40720	m	**NX**	A	*EC*	EC			
40721	*	**FD**	A	*GW*	LA			
40722	*	**FD**	A	*GW*	LA			
40727	*	**FD**	A	*GW*	LA			
40728		**ST**	P	*EM*	NL			
40730		**ST**	P	*EM*	NL			

40732		**EC**	P	*EC*	EC
40733	*	**FD**	A	*GW*	LA
40734	*	**FD**	A	*GW*	LA
40735	m	**NX**	A	*EC*	EC
40737	m	**NX**	A	*EC*	EC
40739	*	**FD**	A	*GW*	LA
40740	m	**NX**	A	*EC*	EC
40741		**ST**	P	*EM*	NL
40742	m	**NX**	A	*EC*	EC
40743	*	**FD**	A	*GW*	LA
40746		**ST**	P	*EM*	NL
40748	m	**NX**	A	*EC*	EC
40749		**ST**	P	*EM*	NL
40750	m	**NX**	A	*EC*	EC
40751		**ST**	P	*EM*	NL
40752	*	**FD**	A	*GW*	LA
40753		**ST**	P	*EM*	NL
40754		**ST**	P	*EM*	NL
40755	*	**FD**	A	*GW*	LA
40756		**ST**	P	*EM*	NL
40757	*	**FD**	A	*GW*	LA

TRAILER KITCHEN BUFFET FIRST   TFKB

These vehicles have been converted from TSBs in the 404xx series to be
similar to the 407xx series vehicles. 17/–.

40802/804/811 were numbered 40212/232/211 for a time when fitted with
23 First Class seats.

*   Refurbished First Great Western vehicles. Primarius leather seating.
m   Refurbished East Coast vehicle with Primarius seating.

40801–803/805/808/809/811. Lot No. 30883 Derby 1976–77. 38.16 t.
40804/806/807/810. Lot No. 30899 Derby 1978–79. 38.16 t.

40801	(40027, 40427)	*	**FD**	P	*GW*	LA
40802	(40012, 40412)	*	**FD**	P	*GW*	LA

40803	(40018, 40418)	*	**FD**	P	*GW*	LA
40804	(40032, 40432)	*	**FD**	P	*GW*	LA
40805	(40020, 40420)	m	**NX**	P		EC
40806	(40029, 40429)	*	**FD**	P	*GW*	LA
40807	(40035, 40435)	*	**FD**	P	*GW*	LA
40808	(40015, 40415)	*	**FD**	P	*GW*	LA
40809	(40014, 40414)	*	**FD**	P	*GW*	LA
40810	(40030, 40430)	*	**FD**	P	*GW*	LA
40811	(40011, 40411)	*	**FD**	P	*GW*	LA

TRAILER BUFFET FIRST   TFB

Vehicles owned by First Group. Converted from TSB by First Great Western.
Refurbished with Primarius leather seating. 23/–.

40900/902/904. Lot No. 30883 Derby 1976–77. 36.12 t.
40901/903. Lot No. 30899 Derby 1978–79. 36.12 t.

40900	(40022, 40422)	**FD**	FG	*GW*	LA
40901	(40036, 40436)	**FD**	FG	*GW*	LA
40902	(40023, 40423)	**FD**	FG	*GW*	LA
40903	(40037, 40437)	**FD**	FG	*GW*	LA
40904	(40001, 40401)	**FD**	FG	*GW*	LA

TRAILER FIRST   TF

As built and m 48/– 2T (m† 48/– 1T – one toilet removed for trolley space).
*   Refurbished First Great Western vehicles. Primarius leather seating.
c   Refurbished CrossCountry vehicles with Primarius seating and 2 tip-up
    seats. One toilet removed. 40/– 1TD 1W.
m   Refurbished East Coast vehicles with Primarius seating.
s   Fitted with centre luggage stack, disabled toilet and wheelchair space.
    46/– 1T 1TD 1W.
w   Wheelchair space. 47/– 2T 1W. (41154 47/– 1TD 1T 1W).
x   Toilet removed for trolley space (FGW). 48/– 1T.

41004–056. Lot No. 30881 Derby 1976–77. 33.66 t.
41057–120. Lot No. 30896 Derby 1977–78. 33.66 t.
41122–148. Lot No. 30938 Derby 1979–80. 33.66 t.
41149–166. Lot No. 30947 Derby 1980. 33.66 t.
41167–169. Lot No. 30963 Derby 1982. 33.66 t.
41170. Lot No. 30967 Derby 1982. Former prototype vehicle. 33.66 t.
41176. Lot No. 30897 Derby 1977. 33.66 t.
41180. Lot No. 30884 Derby 1976–77. 33.66 t.
41181–184/189. Lot No. 30939 Derby 1979–80. 33.66 t.
41185–187/191. Lot No. 30969 Derby 1982. 33.66 t.
41190. Lot No. 30882 Derby 1976–77. 33.60 t.
41192. Lot No. 30897 Derby 1977–79. 33.66 t.
41193–195/201–206. Lot No. 30878 Derby 1975–76. 34.3 t. Converted from
Mark 3A Open First.

41004	*x	**FD**	A	*GW*	LA	41089	*w	**FD**	A	*GW*	LA
41005	*x	**FD**	A	*GW*	LA	41090	mt	**NX**	A	*EC*	EC
41006	*w	**FD**	A	*GW*	LA	41091	mt	**NX**	A	*EC*	EC
41008	*w	**FD**	A	*GW*	LA	41092	mw	**NX**	A	*EC*	EC
41010	*w	**FD**	A	*GW*	LA	41094	*w	**FD**	A	*GW*	LA
41012	*w	**FD**	A	*GW*	LA	41095	mw	**NX**	P	*EC*	EC
41016	*w	**FD**	A	*GW*	LA	41096	*x	**FD**	P	*GW*	LA
41018	*w	**FD**	A	*GW*	LA	41097	mt	**NX**	A	*EC*	EC
41020	*w	**FD**	A	*GW*	LA	41098	mw	**NX**	A	*EC*	EC
41022	*w	**FD**	A	*GW*	LA	41099	mt	**NX**	A	*EC*	EC
41024	*w	**FD**	A	*GW*	LA	41100	mw	**NX**	A	*EC*	EC
41026	c	**XC**	A	*XC*	EC	41102	*w	**FD**	A	*GW*	LA
41028	*w	**FD**	A	*GW*	LA	41103	*x	**FD**	A	*GW*	LA
41029	*x	**FD**	A	*GW*	LA	41104	*w	**FD**	A	*GW*	LA
41030	*w	**FD**	A	*GW*	LA	41106	*w	**FD**	A	*GW*	LA
41032	*w	**FD**	A	*GW*	LA	41108	*w	**FD**	P	*GW*	LA
41033	*w	**FD**	A	*GW*	LA	41109	*x	**FD**	P	*GW*	LA
41034	*w	**FD**	A	*GW*	LA	41110	*w	**FD**	A	*GW*	LA
41035	c	**XC**	A	*XC*	EC	41111		**ST**	P	*EM*	NL
41038	*w	**FD**	A	*GW*	LA	41112		**ST**	P	*EM*	NL
41039	mt	**NX**	A	*EC*	EC	41113	s	**ST**	P	*EM*	NL
41040	mw	**NX**	A	*EC*	EC	41115	mt	**NX**	P	*EC*	EC
41041	s	**ST**	P	*EM*	NL	41116	*x	**FD**	A	*GW*	LA
41044	mw	**NX**	A	*EC*	EC	41117		**ST**	P	*EM*	NL
41046	s	**ST**	P	*EM*	NL	41118	mw	**NX**	A	*EC*	EC
41052	*w	**FD**	A	*GW*	LA	41119	*x	**FD**	A	*GW*	LA
41055	*x	**FD**	A	*GW*	LA	41120	mt	**NX**	A	*EC*	EC
41056	*w	**FD**	A	*GW*	LA	41122	*w	**FD**	A	*GW*	LA
41057		**ST**	P	*EM*	NL	41124	*w	**FD**	A	*GW*	LA
41059	*w	**FD**	FG	*GW*	LA	41126	*w	**FD**	A	*GW*	LA
41061	w	**ST**	P	*EM*	NL	41128	*w	**FD**	A	*GW*	LA
41062		**EC**	P	*EC*	EC	41130	*w	**FD**	A	*GW*	LA
41063		**ST**	P	*EM*	NL	41132	*w	**FD**	A	*GW*	LA
41064	s	**ST**	P	*EM*	NL	41134	*w	**FD**	A	*GW*	LA
41065	*x	**FD**	A	*GW*	LA	41135	*w	**FD**	A	*GW*	LA
41066	mt	**NX**	A	*EC*	EC	41136	*w	**FD**	A	*GW*	LA
41067	s	**ST**	P	*EM*	NL	41137	*x	**FD**	A	*GW*	LA
41068	s	**ST**	P	*EM*	NL	41138	*w	**FD**	A	*GW*	LA
41069	s	**ST**	P	*EM*	NL	41140	*w	**FD**	A	*GW*	LA
41070	s	**ST**	P	*EM*	NL	41142	*w	**FD**	A	*GW*	LA
41071		**ST**	P	*EM*	NL	41144	*w	**FD**	A	*GW*	LA
41072	s	**ST**	P	*EM*	NL	41146	*w	**FD**	A	*GW*	LA
41075		**ST**	P	*EM*	NL	41147	*x	**FD**	P	*GW*	LA
41076	s	**ST**	P	*EM*	NL	41148	*x	**FD**	P	*GW*	LA
41077		**ST**	P	*EM*	NL	41149	*w	**FD**	P	*GW*	LA
41079		**ST**	P	*EM*	NL	41150	mw	**NX**	A	*EC*	EC
41081	*x	**FD**	P	*GW* ·	LA	41151	mt	**NX**	A	*EC*	EC
41083	mw	**NX**	P	*EC*	EC	41152	mw	**NX**	A	*EC*	EC
41084	s	**ST**	P	*EM*	NL	41154	w	**EC**	P	*EC*	EC
41087	mt	**NX**	A	*EC*	EC	41156		**ST**	P	*EM*	NL
41088	mw	**NX**	A	*EC*	EC	41158	*w	**FD**	A	*GW*	LA

41159		m†	**NX**	P	*EC*	EC		41165		mw	**NX**	P	*EC*	EC
41160		*w	**FD**	FG	*GW*	LA		41166		*w	**FD**	FG	*GW*	LA
41161		*w	**FD**	P	*GW*	LA		41167		*w	**FD**	FG	*GW*	LA
41162		*w	**FD**	FG	*GW*	LA		41168		*x	**FD**	P	*GW*	LA
41164		mw	**NX**	A	*EC*	EC		41169		*w	**FD**	P	*GW*	LA

41170	(41001)	m†	**NX**	A	*EC*	EC
41176	(42142, 42352)	*w	**FD**	P	*GW*	LA
41180	(40511)	*w	**FD**	A	*GW*	LA
41181	(42282)	*x	**FD**	P	*GW*	LA
41182	(42278)	*w	**FD**	P	*GW*	LA
41183	(42274)	*w	**FD**	P	*GW*	LA
41184	(42270)	*x	**FD**	P	*GW*	LA
41185	(42313)	m†	**NX**	P	*EC*	EC
41186	(42312)	*w	**FD**	P	*GW*	LA
41187	(42311)	*w	**FD**	P	*GW*	LA
41189	(42298)	*w	**FD**	P	*GW*	LA
41190	(42088)	m†	**NX**	P	*EC*	EC
41191	(42318)	*x	**FD**	P	*GW*	LA
41192	(42246)	*w	**FD**	P	*GW*	LA

The following carriages have been converted from loco-hauled Mark 3 vehicles for CrossCountry or Grand Central.

41193	(11060)	c	**XC**	P	*XC*	EC
41194	(11016)	c	**XC**	P	*XC*	EC
41195	(11020)	c	**XC**	P	*XC*	EC

41201	(11045)		**GC**	A	*GC*	HT
41202	(11017)		**GC**	A	*GC*	HT
41203	(11038)		**GC**	A	*GC*	HT
41204	(11023)		**GC**	A	*GC*	HT
41205	(11036)		**GC**	A	*GC*	HT
41206	(11055)		**GC**	A	*GC*	HT

TRAILER STANDARD   TS

42158 was numbered 41177 for a time when fitted with First Class seats.
42310 was numbered 41188 for a time when fitted with First Class seats.

Standard seating and m –/76 2T.
* Refurbished First Great Western vehicles. Grammer seating. –/80 2T (unless h – high density).
c Refurbished CrossCountry vehicles with Primarius seating. One toilet removed. –/82 1T.
§c Refurbished CrossCountry vehicles with Primarius seating and 2 tip-up seats. One toilet removed. –/66 1TD 2W. 42379/380 are –/71 1TD 1T 2W.
d FGW vehicles with disabled persons toilet and 5, 6 or 7 tip-up seats. –/68 1T 1TD 2W.
h "High density" FGW vehicles. –/84 2T.
k "High density" FGW refurbished vehicle with disabled persons toilet and 5, 6 or 7 tip-up seats. –/72 1T 1TD 2W.
m Refurbished East Coast vehicles with Primarius seating.

u Centre luggage stack (EMT) –/74 2T.
w Centre luggage stack and wheelchair space (EMT) –72 2T 1W.
† Disabled persons toilet (East Coast) –/62 1T 1TD 1W.

42003–089/362. Lot No. 30882 Derby 1976–77. 33.6 t.
42091–250. Lot No. 30897 Derby 1977–79. 33.6 t.
42251–305. Lot No. 30939 Derby 1979–80. 33.6 t.
42306–322. Lot No. 30969 Derby 1982. 33.6 t.
42323–341. Lot No. 30983 Derby 1984–85. 33.6 t.
42342/360. Lot No. 30949 Derby 1982. 33.47 t. Converted from TGS.
42343/345. Lot No. 30970 Derby 1982. 33.47 t. Converted from TGS.
42344/361. Lot No. 30964 Derby 1982. 33.47 t. Converted from TGS.
42246/347/350/351/379/380/551–564. Lot No. 30881 Derby 1976–77. 33.66 t. Converted from TF.
42348/349/363–365/381/565–570. Lot No. 30896 Derby 1977–78. 33.66 t. Converted from TF.
42354. Lot No. 30897 Derby 1977. Was TF from 1983 to 1992. 33.66 t.
42353/355–357. Lot No. 30967 Derby 1982. Ex-prototype vehicles. 33.66 t.
42366–378/382/383/401–409. Lot No. 30877 Derby 1975–77. 34.3 t. Converted from Mark 3A Open Standard.
42384. Lot No. 30896 Derby 1977–78. 33.66 t. Converted from TF.
42385/580–583. Lot No. 30947 Derby 1980. 33.66 t. Converted from TF.
42501/509/513/515/517. Lot No. 30948 Derby 1980–81. 34.8 t. Converted from TFKB.
42502/506/508/514/516. Lot No. 30940 Derby 1979–80. 34.8 t. Converted from TFKB.
42503/504/510/511. Lot No. 30921 Derby 1978–79. 34.8 t. Converted from TFKB.
42505/507/512/518/519. Lot No. 30883 Derby 1976–77. 34.8 t. Converted from TSB.
42520. Lot No. 30899 Derby 1978–79. 34.8 t. Converted from TSB.
42571–579. Lot No. 30938 Derby 1979–80. 33.66 t. Converted from TF.

42003	*h	FD	A	GW	LA	42028	*h	FD	A	GW	LA
42004	*d	FD	A	GW	LA	42029	*h	FD	A	GW	LA
42005	*h	FD	A	GW	LA	42030	*k	FD	A	GW	LA
42006	*h	FD	A	GW	LA	42031	*h	FD	A	GW	LA
42007	*d	FD	A	GW	LA	42032	*h	FD	A	GW	LA
42008	*k	FD	A	GW	LA	42033	*	FD	A	GW	LA
42009	*h	FD	A	GW	LA	42034	*	FD	A	GW	LA
42010	*h	FD	A	GW	LA	42035	*	FD	A	GW	LA
42012	*k	FD	A	GW	LA	42036	c	XC	A	XC	EC
42013	*h	FD	A	GW	LA	42037	c	XC	A	XC	EC
42014	*h	FD	A	GW	LA	42038	c	XC	A	XC	EC
42015	*k	FD	A	GW	LA	42039	*h	FD	A	GW	LA
42016	*h	FD	A	GW	LA	42040	*h	FD	A	GW	LA
42019	*	FD	A	GW	LA	42041	*h	FD	A	GW	LA
42021	*k	FD	A	GW	LA	42042	*h	FD	A	GW	LA
42023	*k	FD	A	GW	LA	42043	*h	FD	A	GW	LA
42024	*k	FD	A	GW	LA	42044	*h	FD	A	GW	LA
42025	*h	FD	A	GW	LA	42045	*	FD	A	GW	LA
42026	*h	FD	A	GW	LA	42046	*	FD	A	GW	LA
42027	*h	FD	A	GW	LA	42047	*	FD	A	GW	LA

42048	*h	**FD**	A	*GW*	LA	42104	m	**NX**	A	*EC*	EC
42049	*h	**FD**	A	*GW*	LA	42105	*k	**FD**	FG	*GW*	LA
42050	*h	**FD**	A	*GW*	LA	42106	m	**NX**	A	*EC*	EC
42051	c	**XC**	A	*XC*	EC	42107	*	**FD**	A	*GW*	LA
42052	c	**XC**	A	*XC*	EC	42108	*h	**FD**	FG	*GW*	LA
42053	c	**XC**	A	*XC*	EC	42109	m	**NX**	P	*EC*	EC
42054	*	**FD**	A	*GW*	LA	42110	m	**NX**	P	*EC*	EC
42055	*	**FD**	A	*GW*	LA	42111	u	**ST**	P	*EM*	NL
42056	*	**FD**	A	*GW*	LA	42112	u	**ST**	P	*EM*	NL
42057	m	**NX**	A	*EC*	EC	42113	u	**ST**	P	*EM*	NL
42058	m	**NX**	A	*EC*	EC	42115	*h	**FD**	P	*GW*	LA
42059	m	**NX**	A	*EC*	EC	42116	m†	**NX**	A	*EC*	EC
42060	*h	**FD**	A	*GW*	LA	42117	m	**NX**	P	*EC*	EC
42061	*h	**FD**	A	*GW*	LA	42118	*h	**FD**	A	*GW*	LA
42062	*k	**FD**	A	*GW*	LA	42119	u	**ST**	P	*EM*	NL
42063	m	**NX**	A	*EC*	EC	42120	u	**ST**	P	*EM*	NL
42064	m	**NX**	A	*EC*	EC	42121	u	**ST**	P	*EM*	NL
42065	m	**NX**	A	*EC*	EC	42122	m	**NX**	A	*EC*	EC
42066	*k	**FD**	A	*GW*	LA	42123		**EC**	P	*EC*	EC
42067	*h	**FD**	A	*GW*	LA	42124	u	**ST**	P	*EM*	NL
42068	*h	**FD**	A	*GW*	LA	42125		**EC**	P	*EC*	EC
42069	*k	**FD**	A	*GW*	LA	42126	*h	**FD**	A	*GW*	LA
42070	*h	**FD**	A	*GW*	LA	42127	m†	**NX**	A	*EC*	EC
42071	*h	**FD**	A	*GW*	LA	42128	m†	**NX**	A	*EC*	EC
42072	*	**FD**	A	*GW*	LA	42129	*	**FD**	A	*GW*	LA
42073	*h	**FD**	A	*GW*	LA	42130	m	**NX**	P	*EC*	EC
42074	*h	**FD**	A	*GW*	LA	42131	u	**ST**	P	*EM*	NL
42075	*	**FD**	A	*GW*	LA	42132	w	**ST**	P	*EM*	NL
42076	*	**FD**	A	*GW*	LA	42133	u	**ST**	P	*EM*	NL
42077	*	**FD**	A	*GW*	LA	42134	m	**NX**	A	*EC*	EC
42078	*	**FD**	A	*GW*	LA	42135	u	**ST**	P	*EM*	NL
42079	*h	**FD**	A	*GW*	LA	42136	u	**ST**	P	*EM*	NL
42080	*h	**FD**	A	*GW*	LA	42137	u	**ST**	P	*EM*	NL
42081	*k	**FD**	A	*GW*	LA	42138	*k	**FD**	A	*GW*	LA
42083	*h	**FD**	A	*GW*	LA	42139	u	**ST**	P	*EM*	NL
42085	*h	**FD**	P	*GW*	LA	42140	u	**ST**	P	*EM*	NL
42087	*h	**FD**	P	*GW*	LA	42141	u	**ST**	P	*EM*	NL
42089	*h	**FD**	A	*GW*	LA	42143	*	**FD**	A	*GW*	LA
42091	m†	**NX**	A	*EC*	EC	42144	*	**FD**	A	*GW*	LA
42092	*k	**FD**	FG	*GW*	LA	42145	*	**FD**	A	*GW*	LA
42093	*h	**FD**	FG	*GW*	LA	42146	m	**NX**	A	*EC*	EC
42094	*h	**FD**	FG	*GW*	LA	42148	u	**ST**	P	*EM*	NL
42095	*	**FD**	FG	*GW*	LA	42149	u	**ST**	P	*EM*	NL
42096	*h	**FD**	A	*GW*	LA	42150	m	**NX**	A	*EC*	EC
42097	c	**XC**	A	*XC*	EC	42151	w	**ST**	P	*EM*	NL
42098	*h	**FD**	A	*GW*	LA	42152	u	**ST**	P	*EM*	NL
42099	*h	**FD**	A	*GW*	LA	42153	u	**ST**	P	*EM*	NL
42100	u	**ST**	P	*EM*	NL	42154	m	**NX**	A	*EC*	EC
42101	*h	**FD**	P	*GW*	LA	42155	w	**ST**	P	*EM*	NL
42102	*h	**FD**	P	*GW*	LA	42156	u	**ST**	P	*EM*	NL
42103	*k	**FD**	FG	*GW*	LA	42157	u	**ST**	P	*EM*	NL

42158	m	NX	A	EC	EC		42212	*h	FD	A	GW	LA

Number	Flag	Code	Col	Code2	Code3
42158	m	NX	A	*EC*	EC
42159	m†	NX	P	*EC*	EC
42160	m	NX	P	*EC*	EC
42161	m†	NX	A	*EC*	EC
42163	m	NX	P	*EC*	EC
42164		ST	P	*EM*	NL
42165		ST	P	*EM*	NL
42166	*h	FD	P	*GW*	LA
42167	*h	FD	FG	*GW*	LA
42168	*h	FD	FG	*GW*	LA
42169	*h	FD	FG	*GW*	LA
42171	m	NX	A	*EC*	EC
42172	m	NX	A	*EC*	EC
42173	*k	FD	P	*GW*	LA
42174	*k	FD	P	*GW*	LA
42175	*h	FD	FG	*GW*	LA
42176	*h	FD	FG	*GW*	LA
42177	*h	FD	FG	*GW*	LA
42178	*h	FD	P	*GW*	LA
42179	m	NX	A	*EC*	EC
42180	m	NX	A	*EC*	EC
42181	m	NX	A	*EC*	EC
42182	m	NX	A	*EC*	EC
42183	*d	FD	A	*GW*	LA
42184	*	FD	A	*GW*	LA
42185	*	FD	A	*GW*	LA
42186	m	NX	A	*EC*	EC
42188	m†	NX	P	*EC*	EC
42189	m†	NX	A	*EC*	EC
42190	m	NX	A	*EC*	EC
42191	m	NX	A	*EC*	EC
42192	m	NX	A	*EC*	EC
42193	m	NX	A	*EC*	EC
42194	w	ST	P	*EM*	NL
42195	*k	FD	P	*GW*	LA
42196	*h	FD	A	*GW*	LA
42197	*h	FD	A	*GW*	LA
42198	m	NX	A	*EC*	EC
42199	m	NX	A	*EC*	EC
42200	*d	FD	A	*GW*	LA
42201	*k	FD	A	*GW*	LA
42202	*k	FD	A	*GW*	LA
42203	*h	FD	A	*GW*	LA
42204	*h	FD	A	*GW*	LA
42205		EC	P	*EC*	EC
42206	*d	FD	A	*GW*	LA
42207	*d	FD	A	*GW*	LA
42208	*	FD	A	*GW*	LA
42209	*	FD	A	*GW*	LA
42210		EC	P	*EC*	EC
42211	*k	FD	A	*GW*	LA
42212	*h	FD	A	*GW*	LA
42213	*h	FD	A	*GW*	LA
42214	*h	FD	A	*GW*	LA
42215	m	NX	A	*EC*	EC
42216	*h	FD	A	*GW*	LA
42217	*k	FD	P	*GW*	LA
42218	*k	FD	P	*GW*	LA
42219	m	NX	A	*EC*	EC
42220	w	ST	P	*EM*	NL
42221	*h	FD	A	*GW*	LA
42222	*h	FD	P	*GW*	LA
42224	*k	FD	P	*GW*	LA
42225	u	ST	P	*EM*	NL
42226	m	NX	A	*EC*	EC
42227	u	ST	P	*EM*	NL
42228	m	NX	P	*EC*	EC
42229	u	ST	P	*EM*	NL
42230	u	ST	P	*EM*	NL
42231	*h	FD	FG	*GW*	LA
42232	*h	FD	FG	*GW*	LA
42233	*h	FD	FG	*GW*	LA
42234	c	XC	P	*XC*	EC
42235	m	NX	A	*EC*	EC
42236	*h	FD	A	*GW*	LA
42237	m	NX	P	*EC*	EC
42238	m†	NX	A	*EC*	EC
42239	m†	NX	A	*EC*	EC
42240		NX	A	*EC*	EC
42241	m	NX	A	*EC*	EC
42242	m	NX	A	*EC*	EC
42243	m	NX	A	*EC*	EC
42244	m	NX	A	*EC*	EC
42245	*	FD	A	*GW*	LA
42247	*h	FD	P	*GW*	LA
42250	*	FD	A	*GW*	LA
42251	*k	FD	A	*GW*	LA
42252	*	FD	A	*GW*	LA
42253	*	FD	A	*GW*	LA
42255	*d	FD	A	*GW*	LA
42256	*	FD	A	*GW*	LA
42257	*	FD	A	*GW*	LA
42258	*h	FD	P	*GW*	LA
42259	*k	FD	A	*GW*	LA
42260	*h	FD	A	*GW*	LA
42261	*h	FD	A	*GW*	LA
42263	*	FD	A	*GW*	LA
42264	*k	FD	A	*GW*	LA
42265	*	FD	A	*GW*	LA
42266	*k	FD	P	*GW*	LA
42267	*d	FD	A	*GW*	LA
42268	*d	FD	A	*GW*	LA

42269	*	**FD**	A	*GW*	LA
42271	*k	**FD**	A	*GW*	LA
42272	*h	**FD**	A	*GW*	LA
42273	*h	**FD**	A	*GW*	LA
42275	*d	**FD**	A	*GW*	LA
42276	*	**FD**	A	*GW*	LA
42277	*	**FD**	A	*GW*	LA
42279	*d	**FD**	A	*GW*	LA
42280	*	**FD**	A	*GW*	LA
42281	*	**FD**	A	*GW*	LA
42283	*h	**FD**	A	*GW*	LA
42284	*h	**FD**	A	*GW*	LA
42285	*h	**FD**	A	*GW*	LA
42286	m†	**NX**	P	*EC*	EC
42287	*k	**FD**	A	*GW*	LA
42288	*h	**FD**	A	*GW*	LA
42289	*h	**FD**	A	*GW*	LA
42290	c	**XC**	P	*XC*	EC
42291	*d	**FD**	A	*GW*	LA
42292	*d	**FD**	A	*GW*	LA
42293	*	**FD**	A	*GW*	LA
42294	*	**FD**	P	*GW*	LA
42295	*d	**FD**	A	*GW*	LA
42296	*	**FD**	A	*GW*	LA
42297	*	**FD**	A	*GW*	LA
42299	*d	**FD**	A	*GW*	LA
42300	*	**FD**	A	*GW*	LA
42301	*	**FD**	A	*GW*	LA

42302	*k	**FD**	FG	*GW*	LA
42303	*h	**FD**	FG	*GW*	LA
42304	*h	**FD**	FG	*GW*	LA
42305	*h	**FD**	FG	*GW*	LA
42306	m	**NX**	P	*EC*	EC
42307	m	**NX**	P	*EC*	EC
42308	*h	**FD**	P	*GW*	LA
42310	*k	**FD**	P	*GW*	LA
42315	*h	**FD**	P	*GW*	LA
42317	*k	**FD**	P	*GW*	LA
42319	*h	**FD**	P	*GW*	LA
42321	*h	**FD**	P	*GW*	LA
42322	m	**NX**	P	*EC*	EC
42323	m	**NX**	A	*EC*	EC
42325	*	**FD**	A	*GW*	LA
42326	m	**NX**	P	*EC*	EC
42327	w	**ST**	P	*EM*	NL
42328	w	**ST**	P	*EM*	NL
42329	w	**ST**	P	*EM*	NL
42330	m	**NX**	P	*EC*	EC
42331	u	**ST**	P	*EM*	NL
42332	*	**FD**	A	*GW*	LA
42333	*	**FD**	A	*GW*	LA
42335	w	**EC**	P	*EC*	EC
42337	w	**ST**	P	*EM*	NL
42339	w	**ST**	P	*EM*	NL
42340	m	**NX**	A	*EC*	EC
42341	u	**ST**	P	*EM*	NL

42342	(44082)		c	**XC**	A	*XC*	EC
42343	(44095)		*	**FD**	A	*GW*	LA
42344	(44092)		*k	**FD**	A	*GW*	LA
42345	(44096)		*d	**FD**	A	*GW*	LA
42346	(41053)		*h	**FD**	A	*GW*	LA
42347	(41054)		*k	**FD**	A	*GW*	LA
42348	(41073)		*k	**FD**	A	*GW*	LA
42349	(41074)		*h	**FD**	A	*GW*	LA
42350	(41047)		*	**FD**	A	*GW*	LA
42351	(41048)		*	**FD**	A	*GW*	LA
42353	(42001, 41171)		*k	**FD**	FG	*GW*	LA
42354	(42114, 41175)	m		**NX**	A	*EC*	EC
42355	(42000, 41172)	m		**NX**	A	*EC*	EC
42356	(42002, 41173)		*k	**FD**	A	*GW*	LA
42357	(41002, 41174)	m		**NX**	A	*EC*	EC
42360	(44084, 45084)		*h	**FD**	A	*GW*	LA
42361	(44099, 42000)		*h	**FD**	A	*GW*	LA
42362	(42011, 41178)		*h	**FD**	A	*GW*	LA
42363	(41082)		m†	**NX**	A	*EC*	EC
42364	(41080)		*k	**FD**	P	*GW*	LA
42365	(41107)		*h	**FD**	P	*GW*	LA

42366–378 have been converted from loco-hauled Mark 3 vehicles for CrossCountry and 42382/383 for First Great Western.

42366	(12007)	§c **XC**	P	*XC*	EC
42367	(12025)	c **XC**	P	*XC*	EC
42368	(12028)	c **XC**	P	*XC*	EC
42369	(12050)	c **XC**	P	*XC*	EC
42370	(12086)	c **XC**	P	*XC*	EC
42371	(12052)	§c **XC**	P	*XC*	EC
42372	(12055)	c **XC**	P	*XC*	EC
42373	(12071)	c **XC**	P	*XC*	EC
42374	(12075)	c **XC**	P	*XC*	EC
42375	(12113)	c **XC**	P	*XC*	EC
42376	(12085)	§c **XC**	P	*XC*	EC
42377	(12102)	c **XC**	P	*XC*	EC
42378	(12123)	c **XC**	P	*XC*	EC
42379	(41036)	§c **XC**	A	*XC*	EC
42380	(41025)	§c **XC**	A	*XC*	EC
42381	(41058)	*k **FD**	P	*GW*	LA
42382	(12128)	*h **FD**	P	*GW*	LA
42383	(12172)	*h **FD**	P	*GW*	LA
42384	(41078)	w **ST**	P	*EM*	NL
42385	(41153)	*h **FD**	P	*GW*	LA

The following carriages have been converted from loco-hauled Mark 3 vehicles for Grand Central. They have a lower density seating layout (most seats arranged around tables). –/64 2T († –/60 1TD 1T 2W).

42401	(12149)	**GC**	A	*GC*	HT
42402	(12155)	**GC**	A	*GC*	HT
42403	(12033) †	**GC**	A	*GC*	HT
42404	(12152)	**GC**	A	*GC*	HT
42405	(12136)	**GC**	A	*GC*	HT
42406	(12112) †	**GC**	A	*GC*	HT
42407	(12044)	**GC**	A	*GC*	HT
42408	(12121)	**GC**	A	*GC*	HT
42409	(12088) †	**GC**	A	*GC*	HT

These carriages have been converted from TFKB or TSB buffet cars to TS vehicles in 2011–12 (42501–515) and 2013–14 (42516–520) at Wabtec Kilmarnock for FGW. Refurbished with Grammer seating.–/84 1T. 34.8 t.

42501	(40344, 40744)	**FD**	A	*GW*	LA
42502	(40331, 40731)	**FD**	A	*GW*	LA
42503	(40312, 40712)	**FD**	A	*GW*	LA
42504	(40314, 40714)	**FD**	A	*GW*	LA
42505	(40428, 40228)	**FD**	A	*GW*	LA
42506	(40324, 40724)	**FD**	A	*GW*	LA
42507	(40409, 40209)	**FD**	A	*GW*	LA
42508	(40325, 40725)	**FD**	A	*GW*	LA
42509	(40336, 40736)	**FD**	A	*GW*	LA
42510	(40317, 40717)	**FD**	A	*GW*	LA
42511	(40309, 40709)	**FD**	A	*GW*	LA

42512	(40408, 40208)	**FD**	A	*GW*	LA
42513	(40338, 40738)	**FD**	A	*GW*	LA
42514	(40326, 40726)	**FD**	A	*GW*	LA
42515	(40347, 40747)	**FD**	A	*GW*	LA
42516	(40323, 40723)	**FD**	A	*GW*	LA
42517	(40345, 40745)	**FD**	A	*GW*	LA
42518	(40003, 40403)	**FD**	P	*GW*	LA
42519	(40016, 40416)	**FD**	P	*GW*	LA
42520	(40234, 40434)	**FD**	P	*GW*	LA

These carriages have been converted from TF to TS vehicles in 2014 at Wabtec Kilmarnock for FGW. Refurbished with Grammer seating. –/80 1T. 35.5 t.

42551	(41003)	**FD**	A	*GW*	LA
42552	(41007)	**FD**	A	*GW*	LA
42553	(41009)	**FD**	A	*GW*	LA
42554	(41011)	**FD**	A	*GW*	LA
42555	(41015)	**FD**	A	*GW*	LA
42556	(41017)	**FD**	A	*GW*	LA
42557	(41019)	**FD**	A	*GW*	LA
42558	(41021)	**FD**	A	*GW*	LA
42559	(41023)	**FD**	A	*GW*	LA
42560	(41027)	**FD**	A	*GW*	LA
42561	(41031)	**FD**	A	*GW*	LA
42562	(41037)	**FD**	A	*GW*	LA
42563	(41045)	**FD**	FG	*GW*	LA
42564	(41051)	**FD**	A	*GW*	LA
42565	(41085)	**FD**	FG	*GW*	LA
42566	(41086)	**FD**	FG	*GW*	LA
42567	(41093)	**FD**	A	*GW*	LA
42568	(41101)	**FD**	A	*GW*	LA
42569	(41105)	**FD**	A	*GW*	LA
42570	(41114)	**FD**	FG	*GW*	LA
42571	(41121)	**FD**	A	*GW*	LA
42572	(41123)	**FD**	A	*GW*	LA
42573	(41127)	**FD**	A	*GW*	LA
42574	(41129)	**FD**	A	*GW*	LA
42575	(41131)	**FD**	A	*GW*	LA
42576	(41133)	**FD**	A	*GW*	LA
42577	(41141)	**FD**	A	*GW*	LA
42578	(41143)	**FD**	A	*GW*	LA
42579	(41145)	**FD**	A	*GW*	LA
42580	(41155)	**FD**	P	*GW*	LA
42581	(41157)	**FD**	A	*GW*	LA
42582	(41163)	**FD**	FG	*GW*	LA
42583	(41153, 42385)	**FD**	P		

TRAILER GUARD'S STANDARD   TGS

As built and m –/65 1T.
* Refurbished First Great Western vehicles. Grammer seating and toilet removed for trolley store. –/67 (unless h).

† Contains a mix of original seats and 20 new Grammer seats. –/65 1T.
c Refurbished CrossCountry vehicles with Primarius seating. –/67 1T.
h "High density" FGW vehicles. –/71.
m Refurbished East Coast vehicles with Primarius seating.
s Fitted with centre luggage stack (EMT) –/63 1T.
t Fitted with centre luggage stack –/61 1T.

44000. Lot No. 30953 Derby 1980. 33.47 t.
44001–090. Lot No. 30949 Derby 1980–82. 33.47 t.
44091–094. Lot No. 30964 Derby 1982. 33.47 t.
44097–101. Lot No. 30970 Derby 1982. 33.47 t.

44000	*h	**FD**	P	*GW*	LA	44041	s	**ST**	P	*EM*	NL
44001	*	**FD**	A	*GW*	LA	44042	*h	**FD**	P	*GW*	LA
44002	*h	**FD**	A	*GW*	LA	44043	*h	**FD**	A	*GW*	LA
44003	*h	**FD**	A	*GW*	LA	44044	s	**ST**	P	*EM*	NL
44004	*h	**FD**	A	*GW*	LA	44045	m	**NX**	A	*EC*	EC
44005	*h	**FD**	A	*GW*	LA	44046	s	**ST**	P	*EM*	NL
44007	*h	**FD**	A	*GW*	LA	44047	s	**ST**	P	*EM*	NL
44008	*h	**FD**	A	*GW*	LA	44048	s	**ST**	P	*EM*	NL
44009	*h	**FD**	A	*GW*	LA	44049	*	**FD**	A	*GW*	LA
44010	*h	**FD**	A	*GW*	LA	44050	m	**NX**	P	*EC*	EC
44011	*	**FD**	A	*GW*	LA	44051	s	**ST**	P	*EM*	NL
44012	c	**XC**	A	*XC*	EC	44052	c	**XC**	P	*XC*	EC
44013	*h	**FD**	A	*GW*	LA	44054	s	**ST**	P	*EM*	NL
44014	*h	**FD**	A	*GW*	LA	44055	*h	**FD**	FG	*GW*	LA
44015	*	**FD**	A	*GW*	LA	44056	m	**NX**	A	*EC*	EC
44016	*h	**FD**	A	*GW*	LA	44057	m	**NX**	P	*EC*	EC
44017	c	**XC**	A	*XC*	EC	44058	m	**NX**	A	*EC*	EC
44018	*	**FD**	A	*GW*	LA	44059	*	**FD**	A	*GW*	LA
44019	m	**NX**	A	*EC*	EC	44060	*h	**FD**	P	*GW*	LA
44020	*h	**FD**	A	*GW*	LA	44061	m	**NX**	A	*EC*	EC
44021	c	**XC**	P	*XC*	EC	44063	m	**NX**	A	*EC*	EC
44022	*h	**FD**	A	*GW*	LA	44064	*h	**FD**	A	*GW*	LA
44023	*h	**FD**	A	*GW*	LA	44065	t	**V**	AV		LM
44024	*h	**FD**	A	*GW*	OO	44066	*	**FD**	A	*GW*	LA
44025	*	**FD**	A	*GW*	LA	44067	*h	**FD**	A	*GW*	LA
44026	*h	**FD**	A	*GW*	LA	44068	*h	**FD**	FG	*GW*	LA
44027	s	**ST**	P	*EM*	NL	44069	*h	**FD**	P	*GW*	LA
44028	*	**FD**	A	*GW*	LA	44070	s	**ST**	P	*EM*	NL
44029	*	**FD**	A	*GW*	LA	44071	s	**ST**	P	*EM*	NL
44030	*h	**FD**	A	*GW*	LA	44072	c	**XC**	P	*XC*	EC
44031	m	**NX**	A	*EC*	EC	44073	†	**EC**	P	*EC*	EC
44032	*	**FD**	A	*GW*	LA	44074	*h	**FD**	FG	*GW*	LA
44033	*h	**FD**	A	*GW*	LA	44075	m	**NX**	P	*EC*	EC
44034	*	**FD**	A	*GW*	LA	44076	*h	**FD**	FG	*GW*	LA
44035	*	**FD**	A	*GW*	LA	44077	m	**NX**	A	*EC*	EC
44036	*h	**FD**	A	*GW*	LA	44078	*h	**FD**	P	*GW*	LA
44037	*h	**FD**	A	*GW*	LA	44079	*h	**FD**	P	*GW*	LA
44038	*	**FD**	A	*GW*	LA	44080	m	**NX**	A	*EC*	EC
44039	*	**FD**	A	*GW*	LA	44081	*h	**FD**	FG	*GW*	LA
44040	*	**FD**	A	*GW*	LA	44083	*h	**FD**	P	*GW*	LA

44085	s	**ST**	P	*EM*	NL
44086	*	**FD**	A	*GW*	LA
44088	t	**V**	AV		LM
44089	t	**V**	AV		LM
44090	*h	**FD**	P	*GW*	LA
44091	*h	**FD**	P	*GW*	LA

44093	*h	**FD**	A	*GW*	LA
44094	m	**NX**	A	*EC*	EC
44097	*h	**FD**	P	*GW*	LA
44098	m	**NX**	A	*EC*	EC
44100	*h	**FD**	FG	*GW*	PM
44101	*h	**FD**	P	*GW*	LA

TRAILER COMPOSITE KITCHEN   TCK

Converted from Mark 3A Open Standard. Refurbished CrossCountry vehicles with Primarius seating. Small kitchen for the preparation of hot food and stowage space for two trolleys between First and Standard Class. One toilet removed. 30/10 1T.

45001–005. Lot No. 30877 Derby 1975–77. 34.3 t.

45001	(12004)	**XC**	P	*XC*	EC
45002	(12106)	**XC**	P	*XC*	EC
45003	(12076)	**XC**	P	*XC*	EC
45004	(12077)	**XC**	P	*XC*	EC
45005	(12080)	**XC**	P	*XC*	EC

TRAILER COMPOSITE   TC

Converted from TF for First Great Western 2014–15. Refurbished with Grammer seating. 24/39 1T.

46001–004. Lot No. 30881 Derby 1976–77.   t. Converted from TF.
46005–009. Lot No. 30896 Derby 1977–78.   t. Converted from TF.
46010–013. Lot No. 30938 Derby 1979–80.   t. Converted from TF.
46014. Lot No. 30963 Derby 1982.   t. Converted from TF.
46015. Lot No. 30884 Derby 1976–77.   t. Converted from TF.
46016/017. Lot No. 30939 Derby 1979–80.   t. Converted from TF.
46018. Lot No. 30969 Derby 1982.   t. Converted from TF.

46001	(41005)	**FD**	A		
46002	(41029)	**FD**	A		
46003	(41033)	**FD**	A		
46004	(41055)	**FD**	A		
46005	(41065)	**FD**	A		
46006	(41081)	**FD**	P		
46007	(41096)	**FD**	P		
46008	(41109)	**FD**	P		
46009	(41119)	**FD**	P		
46010	(41125)	**FD**	A	*GW*	LA
46011	(41139)	**FD**	A	*GW*	LA
46012	(41147)	**FD**	P		
46013	(41148)	**FD**	P		
46014	(41168)	**FD**	P		
46015	(40505, 41179)	**FD**	A	*GW*	LA
46016	(42282, 41181)	**FD**	P		
46017	(42270, 41184)	**FD**	P		
46018	(42318, 41191)	**FD**	P		

▲ Pullman Car Company-liveried Mark 2 Pullman Open First 550 "RYDAL WATER" at Kirkby-in-Furness on 13/04/13. **Andrew Mason**

▼ Riviera Trains Oxford blue-liveried Mark 1 Kitchen Buffet Unclassified 1683 near Scarborough on 10/05/14. **Andrew Mason**

▲ BR maroon-liveried Mark 1 Buffet Standard 1882 (carrying the number 99311) at Stoneycombe on 09/06/13.
Tony Christie

▼ HRH The Prince of Wales's Sleeping Car Mark 3B 2922 at Wolverton on 23/03/12.
Mark Beal

▲ BR Carmine & Cream-liveried Mark 1 Open First 3097 at Soulbury on 07/08/14.
Mark Beal

▼ BR Western Region/GWR chocolate & cream-liveried Mark 1 Open First 3125 at Exeter St Davids on 25/08/14.
Tony Christie

▲ Riviera Trains Great Briton-liveried Mark 2F Open First 3348 "GAINSBOROUGH" at Docker on 17/05/14. **Andrew Mason**

▼ BR maroon-liveried Mark 1 Open Standard 3766 (carrying the number 99317) at Worcester Shrub Hill on 07/06/14. **Steve Widdowson**

▲ BR Western Region/GWR chocolate & cream-liveried Mark 2 Open Standard 5212 near Scarborough on 12/07/14. **Andrew Mason**

▼ BR maroon-liveried Mark 2D Open Standard 5657 near Inverkeithing on 09/07/14. **Ian Lothian**

▲ First Group-liveried Mark 2E Open Brake Unclassified 9804, used in the ScotRail Caledonian Sleeper trains, at Carluke on 20/06/14.　　　　**Robin Ralston**

▼ Chiltern Mainline-liveried Mark 3A Kitchen Buffet First 10274 at Birmingham Moor Street on 05/09/14.　　　　**Robert Pritchard**

▲ First Group Dynamic Lines-liveried Mark 3A Sleeping Car With Pantry 10532 at Plymouth on 06/08/14. **Tony Christie**

▼ Abellio Greater Anglia-liveried Mark 3B Open First 11096 at Stratford on 29/04/14. **Robert Pritchard**

▲ East Coast-liveried Mark 4 Open Standard 12465 at Doncaster on 09/09/14.
Robert Pritchard

▼ Revised Direct Rail Services-liveried Mark 2D Corridor Brake First 17159 at North Staffs Junction on 26/08/13.
Andrew Mason

▲ First Group Dynamic Lines-liveried Mark 3B Open Brake Unclassified 17174 at Exeter St Davids on 26/07/14. **Stewart Armstrong**

▼ BR carmine & cream-liveried Mark 1 Corridor Brake Generator Standard 35469 at Carluke on 21/06/14. **Robin Ralston**

▲ Abellio Greater Anglia-liveried Mark 3B Driving Brake Van 82152 arrives at Colchester leading the 10.00 London Liverpool Street–Norwich on 15/04/14.
Antony Guppy

▼ Stagecoach East Midlands Trains-liveried HST Trailer First 41067 at Nottingham on 03/08/14. **Robert Pritchard**

▲ Grand Central-liveried HST Trailer Standard 42402 at Hitchin on 09/05/14.
Mark Beal

▼ First Great Western Dynamic Lines-liveried HST Trailer Standard 42561 (converted in 2014 from Trailer First 41031) at Newport on 29/07/14.
Stewart Armstrong

▲ BR maroon-liveried First Class Queen of Scots Saloon No. 41 at Cleghorn on 30/09/13 on the rear of a Carnforth–Glenfinnan charter. **Robin Ralston**

▼ Royal Scotsman Saloon 99964 "STATE CAR 4" at Kinneil on 15/04/14.
Ian Lothian

▲ Pullman Car Company-liveried Pullman Parlour First 254 "ZENA" at Newton Abbot on 25/04/14.   **Tony Christie**

▼ Porterbrook-liveried EMU Translator Vehicle 6376 at Wimbledon depot on 30/06/14.   **Brian Garvin**

▲ Network Rail Driving Trailer Coach 9701 leads a Perth–Stirling test train (powered by 37601) on the approaches to Alloa on 10/04/14. **Ian Lothian**

▼ Network Rail Ultrasonic Test Coach 62384 (converted from a Class 421 EMU MBSO) at Torquay on 17/06/14. **Tony Christie**

▲ BR Southern Region green-liveried Inspection Saloon 975025 "CAROLINE" passes Loughborough, being propelled by 37409, on 14/04/12. **Paul Biggs**

▼ Overhead Line Equipment Test Coach 975091 "MENTOR" (converted from a Mark 1 Corridor Brake Standard) at Totnes on 25/07/14. **Tony Christie**

▲ New Measurement Train Lecture Coach 975984 (converted from a prototype HST catering vehicle) at Stoke-on-Trent on 07/08/14. **Robert Pritchard**

▼ NMT Overhead Line Equipment Test Coast 977993 (converted from an HST TGS and fitted with a pantograph) at Cleghorn on 10/09/13. **Robin Ralston**

2.3. HST SET FORMATIONS

FIRST GREAT WESTERN

The largest operator of HSTs is First Great Western with 53 sets to cover 49 diagrams (of these one is a "hot spare" at Old Oak Common and one a "hot spare" at Bristol St Philip's Marsh).

The sets are split into three types, as shown below. These are 16 "low density" sets mainly used on West Country services, 19 "high density" sets with a full kitchen or buffet vehicle and 18 "super high density" sets including a TSB vehicle (with just a small corner buffet counter).

Although some sets are prefixed "OC" for Old Oak Common, for maintenance purposes all trailers are now based at Laira apart from two spare vehicles.

Set formations were in a state of flux as this book closed for press. A programme to reduce each set to just one TF instead of two is due for completion in summer 2015. Sets LA01–LA16/OC30–OC38/LA60–LA75 had been completed by the start of 2015, while sets OC40–OC57 were mostly still running with two TF vehicles, pending the arrival of their converted Trailer Composite vehicles (46001–018). All sets are shown as they will be formed at the conclusion of the programme.

Number of sets: 53.
Maximum number of daily diagrams: 49.
Formations: 8-cars.
Allocation: Laira (Plymouth).
Other maintenance and servicing depots: Landore (Swansea), St Philip's Marsh (Bristol), Long Rock (Penzance).
Operation: London Paddington–Exeter/Paignton/Plymouth/(Newquay in the summer)/Penzance, Bristol, Cardiff/Swansea/West Wales, Oxford/Hereford/Great Malvern/Cheltenham Spa.

Set	L	K	F	E	D	C	B	A	density
LA01	41024	40755	42034	42559	42033	42007	42035	44011	L
LA02	41032	40727	42046	42561	42045	42207	42047	44015	L
LA03	41038	40757	42055	42562	42343	42292	42056	44018	L
LA04	41052	40710	42077	42564	42076	42004	42078	44025	L
LA05	41094	40707	42185	42567	42184	42183	42107	44001	L
LA06	41104	40713	42208	42505	42054	42206	42209	44066	L
LA07	41122	40722	42252	42571	42019	42345	42253	44028	L
LA08	41124	40739	42256	42572	42263	42255	42257	44029	L
LA09	41130	40716	42072	42574	42325	42267	42269	44032	L
LA10	41134	40721	42276	42576	42332	42275	42277	44034	L
LA11	41135	40703	42280	42580	42265	42279	42281	44035	L
LA12	41136	40752	42144	42551	42143	42268	42145	44049	L
LA13	41142	40734	42333	42577	42075	42291	42293	44038	L
LA14	41144	40733	42296	42578	42350	42295	42297	44039	L
LA15	41146	40715	42300	42579	42351	42299	42301	44040	L
LA16	41158	40743	42245	42581	42129	42200	42250	44086	L

Set	L	K	F	E	D	C	B	A	density
OC30	41008	40807	42079	42552	42236	42251	42080	44026	H
OC31	41128	40804	42060	42573	42197	42347	42061	44020	H
OC32	41018	40801	42025	42556	42362	42024	42026	44008	H
OC33	41028	40806	42040	42560	42039	42348	42041	44013	H
OC34	41102	40803	42203	42568	42027	42201	42204	44064	H
OC35	41106	40808	42213	42569	42212	42211	42214	44067	H
OC36	41110	40809	42346	42511	42349	42138	42089	44003	H
OC37	41132	40802	42272	42575	42073	42271	42273	44033	H
OC38	41138	40810	42284	42517	42003	42202	42285	44036	H
LA60	41162	40900	42231	42570	42232	42353	42233	44074	H
LA61	41160	40901	42304	42566	42303	42302	42305	44068	H
LA62	41167	40902	42167	42565	42168	42103	42169	44055	H
LA63	41059	40903	42175	42563	42176	42105	42177	44081	H
LA64	41166	40904	42094	42582	42093	42092	42108	44076	H
LA71	41010	40204	42013	42553	42360	42012	42014	44004	H
LA72	41012	40205	42016	42554	42005	42015	42361	44005	H
LA73	41016	40207	42006	42555	42096	42021	42023	44007	H
LA74	41020	40221	42028	42557	42009	42259	42029	44009	H
LA75	41022	40210	42031	42558	42010	42030	42032	44010	H

Set	*L*	*K*	*F*	*E*	*D*	*C*	*B*	*A*	*density*
OC40	41149	46016	40106	42502	42166	42218	42071	44079	SH
OC41	41182	46008	40107	42520	42222	42224	42382	44101	SH
OC42	41183	46014	40108	42519	42315	42317	42383	44090	SH
OC43	41186	46012	40109	42515	42258	42266	42365	44000	SH
OC44	41192	46018	40110	42514	42115	42174	42288	44097	SH
OC45	41187	46009	40111	42501	42247	42173	42260	44078	SH
OC46	41161	46007	40112	42512	42178	42195	42043	44042	SH
OC47	41108	46006	40113	42509	42308	42217	42067	44060	SH
OC48	41189	46017	40114	42518	42085	42310	42087	44069	SH
OC49	41169	46013	40115	42385	42319	42364	42321	44091	SH
OC50	41180	46015	40101	42516	42098	42264	42283	44093	SH
OC51	41006	46001	40103	42513	42070	42069	42118	44023	SH
OC52	41030	46002	40102	42510	42042	42008	42044	44014	SH
OC53	41034	46003	40118	42506	42048	42066	42050	44016	SH
OC54	41056	46004	40117	42503	42074	42081	42126	44043	SH
OC55	41089	46005	40104	42504	42221	42062	42068	44022	SH
OC56	41126	46010	40116	42508	42216	42344	42261	44030	SH
OC57	41140	46011	40105	42507	42099	42287	42289	44037	SH

L = Low density; H = High density; SH = Super High density.

Spares:

LA:	40119	40231	40718	40811	41004	41103	41116	41137	41176
	42049	42083	42095	42101	42102	42196	42294	42356	42381
	44002	44059	44083						
OO:	44024								
PM:	44100								

EAST COAST

East Coast operates 14 refurbished HST sets on the ECML. As well as serving non-electrified destinations such as Hull and Inverness the East Coast HSTs also work alongside Class 91s and Mark 4 sets on services to Leeds, Newcastle and Edinburgh. Set EC64 (ex-NL05) transferred from East Midlands Trains in 2011.

Number of sets: 14.
Maximum number of daily diagrams: 13.
Formations: 9-cars.
Allocation: Craigentinny (Edinburgh).
Other maintenance depot: Neville Hill (Leeds).
Operation: London King's Cross–Leeds/Harrogate/Skipton/Hull/Lincoln/Newcastle/Edinburgh/Aberdeen/Inverness.

Set	M	L	J	G	F	E	D	C	B
EC51	41120	41150	40748	42215	42091	42146	42150	42154	44094
EC52	41039	41040	40735	42323	42189	42057	42058	42059	44019
EC53	41090	41044	40737	42340	42127	42063	42064	42065	44045
EC54	41087	41088	40706	42104	42161	42171	42172	42219	44056
EC55	41091	41092	40704	42179	42188	42180	42181	42106	44058
EC56	41170	41118	40720	42241	42363	42242	42243	42244	44098
EC57	41151	41152	40740	42226	42128	42182	42186	42190	44080
EC58	41097	41098	40750	42158	42238	42191	42192	42193	44061
EC59	41099	41100	40711	42235	42239	42240	42198	42199	44063
EC60	41066	41164	40742	42122	42116	42357	42134	42355	44031
EC61	41115	41165	40702	42117	42159	42160	42109	42110	44057
EC62	41185	41095	40701	42306	42326	42330	42237	42307	44075
EC63	41159	41083	40708	42163	42286	42228	42130	42322	44050
EC64	41062	41154	40732	42125	42335	42123	42205	42210	44073

Spares:

EC: 40705   41190   42354   44077

GRAND CENTRAL

GC operates HSTs between Sunderland and King's Cross. Formations are flexible: there are enough vehicles to form three 6-car sets or one set can be disbanded to enable the sets to run as 7-cars at times of high demand.

Number of sets: 3.
Maximum number of daily diagrams: 2.
Formations: 6-cars or 7-cars.
Allocation: Heaton (Newcastle).
Operation: London King's Cross–Sunderland.

Set	TF	TSB	TS	TS	TS	TF*
GC01	41201	40424	42403	42402	42401	41204
GC02	41202	40426	42406	42405	42404	41205
GC03	41203	40433	42409	42408	42407	41206

* declassified.

EAST MIDLANDS TRAINS

East Midlands Trains HSTs are concentrated on the Nottingham corridor during the day, with early morning and evening services to Leeds for servicing at Neville Hill.

Number of sets: 10.
Maximum number of daily diagrams: 9.
Formations: 8-cars.
Allocation: Neville Hill (Leeds).
Other maintenance depot: Derby Etches Park.
Operation: London St Pancras–Nottingham, Sheffield/Leeds.

Set	J	G	F	E	D	C	B	A
NL01	41057	41084	40730	42327	42111	42112	42113	44041
NL02	41112	41067	40754	42194	42229	42227	42225	44027
NL03	41061	41068	40741	42337	42119	42120	42121	44054
NL04	41077	41064	40749	42151	42164	42165	42153	44047
NL06	41156	41041	40746	42132	42131	42331	42133	44046
NL07	41111	41070	40751	42339	42135	42136	42137	44044
NL08	41071	41072	40753	42329	42140	42141	42141	44048
NL10	41075	41076	40756	42328	42341	42148	42149	44051
NL11	41117	41046	40728	42220	42100	42230	42124	44085
NL12	41079	41069	40700	42155	42156	42157	42152	44070

Spares:

NL: 41063   41113   42384   44071

CROSSCOUNTRY

CrossCountry reintroduced regular HST diagrams on its services from the December 2008 timetable. Trains run in 7-car formation with the spare TS coaches regularly used in traffic as coaches "C", "D" or "E".

Number of sets: 5.
Maximum number of daily diagrams: 4.
Formations: 7-cars.
Allocation: Craigentinny (Edinburgh).
Other maintenance depots: Laira (Plymouth) or Neville Hill (Leeds).
Operation: Edinburgh–Leeds–Plymouth is the core route with some services extending to Dundee or Penzance.

Set	A	B	C	D	E	F	G
XC01	41193	45001	42368	42369	42367	42366	44021
XC02	41194	45002	42375	42373	42374	42371	44072
XC03	41195	45003	42290	42378	42377	42376	44052
XC04	41026	45004	42038	42037	42036	42380	44012
XC05	41035	45005	42051	42053	42052	42379	44017

Spares:

EC: 42097   42234   42342   42370   42372

2.4. SALOONS

Several specialist passenger carrying carriages, normally referred to as saloons are permitted to run on the national railway system. Many of these are to pre-nationalisation designs.

WCJS FIRST CLASS SALOON

Built 1892 by LNWR, Wolverton. Originally dining saloon mounted on six-wheel bogies. Rebuilt with new underframe with four-wheel bogies in 1927. Rebuilt 1960 as observation saloon with DMU end. Gangwayed at other end. The interior has a saloon, kitchen, guards vestibule and observation lounge. 19/– 1T. Gresley bogies. 28.5 t. 75 mph. ETS x.

41   (484, 45018) x   **M**   WC *WC*   CS

LNWR DINING SALOON

Built 1890 by LNWR, Wolverton. Mounted on the underframe of LMS General Utility Van 37908 in the 1980s. Contains kitchen and dining area seating 12 at tables for two. 12/–. Gresley bogies. 75 mph. 25.4 t. ETS x.

159   (5159)   x   **M**   WC *WC*   CS

GNR FIRST CLASS SALOON

Built 1912 by GNR, Doncaster. Contains entrance vestibule, lavatory, two separate saloons, library and luggage space. 19/– 1T. Gresley bogies. 75 mph. 29.4 t. ETS x.

Non-standard livery: Teak.

807   (4807)   x   **0**   WC *WC*   CS

LNER GENERAL MANAGERS SALOON

Built 1945 by LNER, York. Gangwayed at one end with a veranda at the other. The interior has a dining saloon seating 12, kitchen, toilet, office and nine seat lounge. 21/– 1T. B4 bogies. 75 mph. 35.7 t. ETS 3.

1999   (902260)   **M**   BE   CS   DINING CAR No. 2

GENERAL MANAGER'S SALOON

Renumbered 1989 from London Midland Region departmental series.
Formerly the LMR General Manager's saloon. Rebuilt from LMS period 1
Corridor Brake First M5033M to dia 1654 and mounted on the underframe of
BR suburban Brake Standard M43232. Screw couplings have been removed.
B4 bogies. 100 mph. ETS 2X.

LMS Lot No. 326 Derby 1927. 27.5 t.

6320   (5033, DM 395707)   x   **M**   62   *62*   SK

BELMOND BRITISH PULLMAN SUPPORT CAR

Converted 199? from Courier vehicle converted from Mark 1 Corridor Brake
Standard 1986–87. Toilet retained and former compartment area replaced
with train manager's office, crew locker room, linen store and dry goods
store. The former luggage area has been adapted for use as an engineers'
compartment and workshop. Commonwealth bogies. 100 mph. ETS 2.

Lot No. 30721 Wolverton 1963. 37 t.

99545   (35466, 80207)   **PC**   BE   *BP*   SL   BAGGAGE CAR No. 11

SERVICE CAR

Converted from BR Mark 1 Corridor Brake Standard. Commonwealth
bogies. 100 mph. ETS 2.

Lot No. 30721 Wolverton 1963.

99886   (35407)   x   **M**   WC   *WC*   CS   SERVICE CAR No. 86

ROYAL SCOTSMAN SALOONS

Built 1960 by Metro-Cammell as Pullman Kitchen First for East Coast Main
Line services. Rebuilt 2013 as dining car. Commonwealth bogies. 38.5 t.
ETS x.

99960   (321 SWIFT)   **M**   BE   *RS*   CS   DINING CAR No. 2

Built 1960 by Metro-Cammell as Pullman Parlour First (§ Pullman Kitchen
First) for East Coast Main Line services. Rebuilt 1990 as sleeping cars with
four twin sleeping rooms (*§ three twin sleeping rooms and two single
sleeping rooms at each end). Commonwealth bogies. 38.5 t. ETS x.

99961	(324 AMBER) *	**M**	BE	*RS*	CS	STATE CAR 1
99962	(329 PEARL)	**M**	BE	*RS*	CS	STATE CAR 2
99963	(331 TOPAZ)	**M**	BE	*RS*	CS	STATE CAR 3
99964	(313 FINCH) §	**M**	BE	*RS*	CS	STATE CAR 4

Built 1960 by Metro-Cammell as Pullman Kitchen First for East Coast Main Line services. Rebuilt 1990 as observation car with open verandah seating 32. Commonwealth bogies. 38.5 t. ETS x.

| 99965 (319 SNIPE) | M | BE | *RS* | CS | OBSERVATION CAR |

Built 1960 by Metro-Cammell as Pullman Kitchen First for East Coast Main Line services. Rebuilt 1993 as dining car. Commonwealth bogies. 38.5 t. ETS x.

| 99967 (317 RAVEN) | M | BE | *RS* | CS | DINING CAR No. 1 |

Mark 3A. Converted 1997 from a Sleeping Car at Carnforth Railway Restoration & Engineering Services. BT10 bogies. Attendant's and adjacent two sleeping compartments converted to generator room containing a 160 kW Volvo unit. In 99968 four sleeping compartments remain for staff use with another converted for use as a staff shower and toilet. The remaining five sleeping compartments have been replaced by two passenger cabins. In 99969 seven sleeping compartments remain for staff use. A further sleeping compartment, along with one toilet, have been converted to store rooms. The other two sleeping compartments have been combined to form a crew mess. 41.5 t. ETS 7X.

Lot No. 30960 Derby 1981–83.

| 99968 (10541) | | M | BE | *RS* | CS | STATE CAR 5 |
| 99969 (10556) | | M | BE | *RS* | CS | SERVICE CAR |

RAILFILMS "LMS CLUB CAR"

Converted from BR Mark 1 Open Standard at Carnforth Railway Restoration & Engineering Services in 1994. Contains kitchen, pantry and two dining saloons. 20/– 1T. Commonwealth bogies. 100 mph. ETS 4.

Lot No. 30724 York 1963. 37 t.

| 99993 (5067) | x | M | RA | *ST* | CS | LMS CLUB CAR |

BR INSPECTION SALOON

Mark 1. Short frames. Non-gangwayed. Observation windows at each end. The interior layout consists of two saloons interspersed by a central lavatory/kitchen/guards/luggage section. 90 mph. ETS x.

BR Wagon Lot No. 3095 Swindon 1957. B4 bogies. 30.5 t.

| 999506 | | M | WC | *WC* | CS | |

2.5. PULLMAN CAR COMPANY SERIES

Pullman cars have never generally been numbered as such, although many have carried numbers, instead they have carried titles. However, a scheme of schedule numbers exists which generally lists cars in chronological order. In this section those numbers are shown followed by the car's title. Cars described as "kitchen" contain a kitchen in addition to passenger accommodation and have gas cooking unless otherwise stated. Cars described as "parlour" consist entirely of passenger accommodation. Cars described as "brake" contain a compartment for the use of the guard and a luggage compartment in addition to passenger accommodation.

PULLMAN PARLOUR FIRST

Built 1927 by Midland Carriage & Wagon Company. 26/– 2T. Gresley bogies. 41 t. ETS 2.

| 213 | MINERVA | **PC** | BE | *BP* | SL |

PULLMAN KITCHEN FIRST

Built 1928 by Metropolitan Carriage & Wagon Company. 20/– 1T. Gresley bogies. 42 t. ETS 4.

| 238 | PHYLISS | **PC** | BE | | SL |

PULLMAN PARLOUR FIRST

Built 1928 by Metropolitan Carriage & Wagon Company. 24/– 2T. Gresley bogies. 40 t. ETS 4.

| 239 | AGATHA | **PC** | BE | | SL |
| 243 | LUCILLE | **PC** | BE | *BP* | SL |

PULLMAN KITCHEN FIRST

Built 1925 by BRCW. Rebuilt by Midland Carriage & Wagon Company in 1928. 20/– 1T. Gresley bogies. 41 t. ETS 4.

| 245 | IBIS | **PC** | BE | *BP* | SL |

PULLMAN PARLOUR FIRST

Built 1928 by Metropolitan Carriage & Wagon Company. 24/– 2T. Gresley bogies. ETS 4.

| 254 | ZENA | **PC** | BE | *BP* | SL |

PULLMAN KITCHEN FIRST

Built 1928 by Metropolitan Carriage & Wagon Company. 20/– 1T. Gresley bogies. 42 t. ETS 4.

255   IONE   **PC**   BE   *BP*   SL

PULLMAN KITCHEN COMPOSITE

Built 1932 by Metropolitan Carriage & Wagon Company. Originally included in 6-Pul EMU. Electric cooking. 12/16 1T. EMU bogies. ETS x.

264   RUTH   **PC**   BE   SL

PULLMAN KITCHEN FIRST

Built 1932 by Metropolitan Carriage & Wagon Company. Originally included in "Brighton Belle" EMUs but now used as hauled stock. Electric cooking. 20/– 1T. B5 (SR) bogies (§ EMU bogies). 44 t. ETS 2.

280	AUDREY		**PC**	BE	*BP*	SL
281	GWEN		**PC**	BE	*BP*	SL
283	MONA	§	**PC**	BE		SL
284	VERA		**PC**	BE	*BP*	SL

PULLMAN PARLOUR THIRD

Built 1932 by Metropolitan Carriage & Wagon Company. Originally included in "Brighton Belle" EMUs. –/56 2T. EMU bogies. ETS x.

Non-standard livery: BR Revised Pullman (blue & white lined out in white).

286   CAR No. 86   **0**   BE   SL

PULLMAN BRAKE THIRD

Built 1932 by Metropolitan Carriage & Wagon Company. Originally driving motor cars in "Brighton Belle" EMUs. Traction and control equipment removed for use as hauled stock. –/48 1T. EMU bogies. ETS x.

| 292 | CAR No. 92 | **PC** | BE | SL |
| 293 | CAR No. 93 | **PC** | BE | SL |

PULLMAN PARLOUR FIRST

Built 1951 by Birmingham Railway Carriage & Wagon Company. 32/– 2T. Gresley bogies. 39 t. ETS 3.

301   PERSEUS   **PC**   BE   *BP*   SL

Built 1952 by Pullman Car Company, Preston Park using underframe and bogies from 176 RAINBOW, the body of which had been destroyed by fire. 26/– 2T. Gresley bogies. 38 t. ETS 4.

302   PHOENIX   **PC**   BE   *BP*   SL

PULLMAN PARLOUR FIRST

Built 1951 by Birmingham Railway Carriage & Wagon Company. 32/– 2T. Gresley bogies. 39 t. ETS 3.

308   CYGNUS   **PC**   BE   *BP*   SL

PULLMAN BAR FIRST

Built 1951 by Birmingham Railway Carriage & Wagon Company. Rebuilt 1999 by Blake Fabrications, Edinburgh with original timber-framed body replaced by a new fabricated steel body. Contains kitchen, bar, dining saloon and coupé. Electric cooking. 14/– 1T. Gresley bogies. ETS 3.

310   PEGASUS   x   **PC**   LS   BO

Also carries "THE TRIANON BAR" branding.

PULLMAN PALOUR FIRST

Built 1960–61 by Metro-Cammell for East Coast Main Line services. –/36 2T. Commonwealth bogies. 38.5 t. ETS x.

326   EMERALD   x   **PC**   WC   *WC*   CS

PULLMAN KITCHEN SECOND

Built 1960–61 by Metro-Cammell for East Coast Main Line services. Commonwealth bogies. –/30 1T. 40 t. ETS x.

335   CAR No. 335   x   **PC**   VT   *VT*   TM

PULLMAN PARLOUR SECOND

Built 1960–61 by Metro-Cammell for East Coast Main Line services. 347, 348 and 350 are used as Open Firsts. –/42 2T. Commonwealth bogies. 38.5 t. ETS x.

347	CAR No. 347	x	**M**	WC	*WC*	CS	
348	CAR No. 348	x	**M**	WC	*WC*	CS	
349	CAR No. 349	x	**PC**	VT	*VT*	TM	
350	CAR No. 350	x	**M**	WC	*WC*	CS	
351	CAR No. 351	x	**PC**	WC	*WC*	CS	
352	CAR No. 352	x	**PC**	WC	*WC*	CS	AMETHYST
353	CAR No. 353	x	**PC**	VT	*VT*	TM	

PULLMAN SECOND BAR

Built 1960–61 by Metro-Cammell for East Coast Main Line services. –/24+17 bar seats. Commonwealth bogies. 38.5 t. ETS x.

354   THE HADRIAN BAR   x   **PC**   WC   *WC*   CS

2.6. LOCOMOTIVE SUPPORT CARRIAGES

These carriages have been adapted from Mark 1s and Mark 2s for use as support carriages for heritage steam and diesel locomotives. Some seating is retained for the use of personnel supporting the locomotives operation with the remainder of the carriage adapted for storage, workshop, dormitory and catering purposes. These carriages can spend considerable periods of time off the national railway system when the locomotives they support are not being used on that system. No owner or operator details are included in this section. After the depot code, the locomotive(s) each carriage is usually used to support is given.

CORRIDOR BRAKE FIRST

Mark 1. Commonwealth bogies. ETS 2.

14007. Lot No. 30382 Swindon 1959. 35 t.
17015. Lot No. 30668 Swindon 1961. 36 t.
17025. Lot No. 30718 Swindon 1963. Metal window frames. 36 t.

14007 (14007, 17007)	x	M	NY	LNER 61264
17015 (14015)	x	CC	TM	Tyseley Locomotive Works-based locos
17025 (14025)	v	M	CS	LMS 45690

CORRIDOR BRAKE FIRST

Mark 2A. Pressure ventilated. B4 bogies. ETS 4.

14064. Lot No. 30775 Derby 1967–68. 32 t.
14099/17096. Lot No. 30786 Derby 1968. 32 t.

14064 (14064, 17064)	x	M	CS	LMS 45305/BR 70013	
14099 (14099, 17099)	v	M	CS	LMS 45305/BR 70013	
17096 (14096)		PC	SL	SR 35028	MERCATOR

CORRIDOR BRAKE COMPOSITE

Mark 1. ETS 2.

21096. Lot No. 30185 Metro-Cammell 1956. BR Mark 1 bogies. 32.5 t.
21232. Lot No. 30574 GRCW 1960. B4 bogies. 34 t.
21249. Lot No. 30669 Swindon 1961–62. Commonwealth bogies. 36 t.

21096	x	M	NY	LNER 60007
21232	x	M	SK	LMS 46233
21249	x	CC	BH	New Build 60163

CORRIDOR BRAKE STANDARD

Mark 1. Metal window frames and melamine interior panelling. ETS 2.

35317–322. Lot No. 30699 Wolverton 1962–63. Commonwealth bogies. 37 t.
35449. Lot No. 30728 Wolverton 1963. Commonwealth bogies. 37 t.
35451–486. Lot No. 30721 Wolverton 1963. Commonwealth bogies. 37 t.

35317	x	**CC**	SH	LNER 60019
35322	x	**M**	CS	WCRC Carnforth-based locomotives
35449	x	**M**	BQ	LMS 45231
35451	x	**CC**	SH	SR 34046
35461	x	**CH**	SH	GWR 5029
35463	v	**M**	CS	WCRC Carnforth-based locomotives
35465	x	**CC**	SH	BR 70000
35468	x	**M**	YK	National Railway Museum locomotives
35470	v	**CH**	TM	Tyseley Locomotive Works-based locos
35476	x	**M**	SK	LMS 46233
35486	x	**M**	TN	LNER 60009/61994

CORRIDOR BRAKE FIRST

Mark 2C. Pressure ventilated. Renumbered when declassified. B4 bogies. ETS 4.

Lot No. 30796 Derby 1969–70. 32.5 t.

35508 (14128, 17128)	**M**	BQ	LMS 44871/45407

CORRIDOR BRAKE FIRST

Mark 2A. Pressure ventilated. Renumbered when declassified. B4 bogies. ETS 4.

Lot No. 30786 Derby 1968. 32 t.

35517 (14088, 17088)	b	**M**	BQ	LMS 44871/45407
35518 (14097, 17097)	b	**G**	SH	SR 34067

COURIER VEHICLE

Mark 1. Converted 1986–87 from Corridor Brake Standards. ETS 2.

80204/217. Lot No. 30699 Wolverton 1962. Commonwealth bogies. 37 t.
80220. Lot No. 30573 Gloucester 1960. B4 bogies. 33 t.

80204 (35297)	**M**	CS	WCRC Carnforth-based locomotives
80217 (35299)	**M**	CS	WCRC Carnforth-based locomotives
80220 (35276)	**M**	NY	LNER 62005

2.7. 95xxx & 99xxx RANGE NUMBER CONVERSION TABLE

The following table is presented to help readers identify carriages which may still carry numbers in the 95xxx and 99xxx number ranges of the former private owner number series, which is no longer in general use.

9xxxx	BR No.	9xxxx	BR No.	9xxxx	BR No.
95402	Pullman 326	99350	Pullman 350	99673	550
99035	35322	99351	Pullman 351	99674	551
99040	21232	99352	Pullman 352	99675	552
99041	35476	99353	Pullman 353	99676	553
99052	Saloon 41	99354	Pullman 354	99677	586
99121	3105	99361	Pullman 335	99678	504
99122	3106	99371	3128	99679	506
99125	3113	99405	35486	99680	17102
99127	3117	99530	Pullman 301	99710	18767
99128	3130	99531	Pullman 302	99716 *	18808
99131	Saloon 1999	99532	Pullman 308	99718	18862
99241	35449	99534	Pullman 245	99721	18756
99302	13323	99535	Pullman 213	99723	35459
99304	21256	99536	Pullman 254	99880	Saloon 159
99311	1882	99537	Pullman 280	99881	Saloon 807
99312	35463	99539	Pullman 255	99883	2108
99319	17168	99541	Pullman 243	99885	2110
99326	4954	99543	Pullman 284	99887	2127
99327	5044	99546	Pullman 281	99953	35468
99328	5033	99547	Pullman 292	99966	34525
99329	4931	99548	Pullman 293	99970	Pullman 232
99347	Pullman 347	99670	546	99972	Pullman 318
99348	Pullman 348	99671	548	99973	324
99349	Pullman 349	99672	549	99974	Pullman 328

* The number 99716 has also been applied to 3416 for filming purposes.

2.8. SET FORMATIONS

CHILTERN RAILWAYS MARK 3 SET FORMATIONS

Chiltern Railways uses a number of loco-hauled rakes on services principally between London Marylebone and Birmingham Moor Street. Rake AL06 is used on a commuter train between Marylebone and Banbury. All coaches apart from rake AL06 and spare 12094 have been rebuilt at Wabtec, Doncaster and fitted with sliding plug doors.

Set							DVT
AL01	12610	12613	12614	12615	12602	10273	82301
AL02	12603	12606	12607	12608	12609	10272	82302
AL03	12616	12617	12618	12619	12604	10274	82303
AL04	12623	12605	12621	12627	12625	10271	82304
AL06	12043	12119	12017	11029	11031	12054	82305

Spare 12094 12620 82309

EAST COAST MARK 4 SET FORMATIONS

The East Coast Mark 4 sets generally run in fixed formations since their refurbishment at Bombardier, Wakefield in 2003–05. These rakes are listed below. Class 91 locomotives are positioned next to Coach B.

Set	B	C	D	E	F	H	K	L	M	DVT
BN01	12207	12417	12415	12414	12307	10307	11298	11301	11401	82207
BN02	12232	12402	12450	12448	12302	10302	11299	11302	11402	82202
BN03	12201	12401	12459	12478	12301	10320	11277	11303	11403	82219
BN04	12202	12480	12421	12518	12327	10303	11278	11304	11404	82209
BN05	12209	12486	12520	12522	12300	10326	11219	11305	11405	82210
BN06	12208	12406	12420	12422	12313	10309	11279	11306	11406	82208
BN07	12231	12411	12405	12489	12329	10323	11280	11307	11407	82204
BN08	12205	12481	12485	12407	12328	10300	11229	11308	11408	82211
BN09	12230	12513	12483	12514	12308	10304	11281	11309	11409	82215
BN10	12214	12419	12488	12443	12305	10331	11282	11310	11410	82205
BN11	12203	12437	12436	12484	12315	10308	11283	11311	11411	82218
BN12	12212	12431	12404	12426	12330	10333	11284	11312	11412	82212
BN13	12228	12469	12430	12424	12311	10313	11285	11313	11413	82213
BN14	12229	12410	12526	12423	12312	10332	12201	11314	11414	82206
BN15	12226	12442	12409	12515	12309	10306	11286	11315	11415	82214
BN16	12213	12428	12445	12433	12304	10315	11287	11316	11416	82222
BN17	12223	12444	12427	12432	12303	10324	11288	11317	11417	82225
BN18	12215	12453	12468	12467	12324	10305	11289	11318	11418	82220
BN19	12211	12434	12400	12470	12310	10318	11290	11319	11419	82201
BN20	12224	12477	12439	12440	12326	10321	11241	11320	11420	82200
BN21	12222	12461	12441	12476	12323	10330	11244	11321	11421	82227
BN22	12210	12452	12460	12473	12316	10301	11291	11322	11422	82230
BN23	12225	12454	12456	12455	12318	10325	11292	11323	11423	82226
BN24	12219	12447	12425	12403	12319	10328	11293	11324	11424	82229
BN25	12217	12446	12519	12464	12322	10312	11294	11325	11425	82216
BN26	12220	12474	12465	12429	12325	10311	11295	11326	11426	82223
BN27	12216	12449	12466	12538	12317	10319	11237	11327	11427	82228
BN28	12218	12458	12463	12533	12320	10310	11273	11328	11428	82217
BN29	12204	12462	12457	12438	12321	10317	11998	11329	11429	82231
BN30	12227	12471	12534	12472	12331	10329	11999	11330	11430	82203
Spare	12200									82224

2.9. SERVICE STOCK

Carriages in this section are used for internal purposes within the railway industry, ie they do not generate revenue from outside the industry. Most are numbered in the former BR departmental number series.

BARRIER, ESCORT & TRANSLATOR VEHICLES

These vehicles are used to move multiple unit, HST and other vehicles around the national railway system.

HST Barrier Vehicles. Mark 1/2A. Renumbered from BR departmental series, or converted from various types. B4 bogies (* Commonwealth bogies).

Non-standard livery: 6340, 6344, 6346 All over dark blue.

6330. Mark 2A. Lot No. 30786 Derby 1968.
6336/38/44. Mark 1. Lot No. 30715 Gloucester 1962.
6340. Mark 1. Lot No. 30669 Swindon 1962.
6346. Mark 2A. Lot No. 30777 Derby 1967.
6348. Mark 1. Lot No. 30163 Pressed Steel 1957.

6330	(14084, 975629)		**FB**	A	*GW*	LA
6336	(81591, 92185)		**FB**	A	*GW*	LA
6338	(81581, 92180)		**FB**	A	*GW*	LA
6340	(21251, 975678)	*	**0**	A	*EC*	EC
6344	(81263, 92080)		**0**	A	*EC*	EC
6346	(9422)		**0**	A	*EC*	EC
6348	(81233, 92963)		**FB**	A	*GW*	LA

Mark 4 Barrier Vehicles. Mark 2A/2C. Converted from Corridor First (*) or Open Brake Standard. B4 bogies.

Non-standard livery: 6358 All over dark blue.

6352/53. Mark 2A. Lot No. 30774 Derby 1968.
6354/55. Mark 2C. Lot No. 30820 Derby 1970.
6358/59. Mark 2A. Lot No. 30788 Derby 1968.

6352	(13465, 19465)	*	**GN**	E	*EC*	BN
6353	(13478, 19478)	*	**GN**	E	*EC*	BN
6354	(9459)		**GN**	E	*EC*	BN
6355	(9477)		**GN**	E	*EC*	BN
6358	(9432)		**0**	E	*EC*	BN
6359	(9429)		**GN**	E	*EC*	BN

EMU Translator Vehicles. Mark 1. Converted 1980 from Restaurant Unclassified Opens. Commonwealth bogies.

Lot No. 30647 Wolverton 1959–61.

6376	(1021, 975973)	**PB**	P	*CS*	RU *(works with 6377)*
6377	(1042, 975975)	**PB**	P	*CS*	RU *(works with 6376)*
6378	(1054, 975971)	**PB**	P	*CS*	RU *(works with 6379)*
6379	(1059, 975972)	**PB**	P	*CS*	RU *(works with 6378)*

HST Barrier Vehicles. Mark 1. Converted from Gangwayed Brake Vans in 1994–95. B4 bogies.

6392. Lot No. 30715 Gloucester 1962.
6393/97. Lot No. 30716 Gloucester 1962.
6394. Lot No. 30162 Pressed Steel 1956–57.
6398/99. Lot No. 30400 Pressed Steel 1957–58.

6392	(81588, 92183)	**PB**	P		LM
6393	(81609, 92196)	**PB**	P	*EC*	EC
6394	(80878, 92906)	**P**	P	*EC*	EC
6397	(81600, 92190)	**PB**	P		LM
6398	(81471, 92126)	**PB**	EM	*EM*	NL
6399	(81367, 92994)	**PB**	EM	*EM*	NL

Escort Coaches. Converted from Mark 2A Open Brake Standards. These vehicles use the same bodyshell as the Mark 2A Corridor Brake First. B4 bogies.

9419. Lot No.30777 Derby 1970.
9428. Lot No.30820 Derby 1970.

9419		**DS**	DR	*DR*	KM
9428		**DS**	DR	*DR*	KM

EMU Translator Vehicles. Converted from Class 508 driving cars.

64664. Lot No. 30979 York 1979–80.
64707. Lot No. 30981 York 1979–80.

64664	**AG**	A	*GB*	PG	James D. Rowlands	*(works with 64707)*
64707	**AG**	A	*GB*	PG	Sir David Rowlands	*(works with 64664)*

Eurostar Barrier Vehicles. Mark 1. Converted from General Utility Vans with bodies removed. Fitted with B4 bogies for use as Eurostar barrier vehicles.

96380/381. Lot No. 30417 Pressed Steel 1958–59.
96383. Lot No. 30565 Pressed Steel 1959.
96384. Lot No. 30616 Pressed Steel 1959–60.

96380	(86386, 6380)	**B**	EU	*EU*	TI
96381	(86187, 6381)	**B**	EU	*EU*	TI
96383	(86664, 6383)	**B**	EU	*EU*	TI
96384	(86955, 6384)	**B**	EU	*EU*	TI

EMU Translator Vehicles. Converted from various Mark 1s.

Non-standard livery: All over blue.

975864. Lot No. 30054 Eastleigh 1951–54. Commonwealth bogies.
975867. Lot No. 30014 York 1950–51. Commonwealth bogies.
975875. Lot No. 30143 Charles Roberts 1954–55. Commonwealth bogies.
975974/978. Lot No. 30647 Wolverton 1959–61. B4 bogies.
977087. Lot No. 30229 Metro–Cammell 1955–57. Commonwealth bogies.

975864	(3849)	**HB**	E	*GB*	PG	*(works with 975867)*
975867	(1006)	**HB**	E	*GB*	PG	*(works with 975864)*
975875	(34643)	**0**	E	*GB*	PG	*(works with 977087)*

975974	(1030)	**AG**	A	*GB*	PG	Paschar	*(works with 975978)*
975978	(1025)	**AG**	A	*GB*	PG	Perpetiel	*(works with 975974)*
977087	(34971)	**0**	E	*GB*	PG		*(works with 975875)*

LABORATORY, TESTING & INSPECTION COACHES

These coaches are used for research, development, testing and inspection on the national railway system. Many are fitted with sophisticated technical equipment.

Plain Line Pattern Recognition Coaches. Converted from BR Mark 2F Buffet First (*) or Open Standard. B4 bogies.

1256. Lot No. 30845 Derby 1973.
5981. Lot No. 30860 Derby 1973–74.

| 1256 | (3296) | * | **Y** | NR | *DB* | ZA |
| 5981 | | | **Y** | NR | *DB* | ZA |

Generator Vans. Mark 1. Converted from BR Mark 1 Gangwayed Brake Vans. B5 bogies.

6260. Lot No. 30400 Pressed Steel 1957–58.
6261. Lot No. 30323 Pressed Steel 1957.
6262. Lot No. 30228 Metro-Cammell 1957–58.
6263. Lot No. 30163 Pressed Steel 1957.
6264. Lot No. 30173 York 1956.

6260	(81450, 92116)	**NR**	NR		ZA
6261	(81284, 92988)	**Y**	NR	*DB*	ZA
6262	(81064, 92928)	**Y**	NR	*DB*	ZA
6263	(81231, 92961)	**Y**	NR	*DB*	ZA
6264	(80971, 92923)	**Y**	NR	*DB*	ZA

Staff Coaches. Mark 2D/2F. Converted from BR Mark 2D/2F Open Brake Standard. B4 bogies.

9481. Lot No. 30824 Derby 1971.
9516/23. Lot No. 30861 Derby 1974.

9481		**Y**	NR	*DB*	ZA
9516		**Y**	NR	*DB*	ZA
9523		**Y**	NR	*DB*	ZA

Driving Trailer Coaches. Converted 2008 at Serco, Derby from Mark 2F Driving Open Brake Standards. Fitted with generator and modified to work in Blue Star push-pull mode. Disc brakes. B4 bogies.

9701–08. Lot No. 30861 Derby 1974. Converted to Driving Open Brake Standard Glasgow 1974.
9714. Lot No. 30861 Derby 1974. Converted to Driving Open Brake Standard Glasgow 1986.

9701	(9528)	**Y**	NR	*DB*	ZA
9702	(9510)	**Y**	NR	*DB*	ZA
9703	(9517)	**Y**	NR	*DB*	ZA

| 9708 | (9530) | Y | NR | *DB* | ZA |
| 9714 | (9536) | Y | NR | *DB* | ZA |

Ultrasonic Test Coach. Converted from Class 421 EMU MBSO.

62287. Lot No. 30808. York 1970. SR Mark 6 bogies.
62384. Lot No. 30816. York 1970. SR Mark 6 bogies.

| 62287 | Y | NR | *DB* | ZA |
| 62384 | Y | NR | *DB* | ZA |

Test Train Brake Force Runners. Converted from Mark 2F Open Standard converted to Class 488/3 EMU TSOLH. These vehicles are included in test trains to provide brake force and are not used for any other purposes. Lot No. 30860 Derby 1973–74. B4 bogies.

| 72612 | (6156) | Y | NR | *DB* | ZA |
| 72616 | (6007) | Y | NR | *DB* | ZA |

Structure Gauging Train Coach. Converted from Mark 2F Open Standard converted to Class 488/3 EMU TSOLH. Lot No. 30860 Derby 1973–74. B4 bogies.

| 72630 | (6094) | Y | NR | *DB* | ZA *(works with 99666)* |

Plain Line Pattern Recognition Coaches. Converted from BR Mark 2F Open Standard converted to Class 488/3 EMU TSOLH. Lot No. 30860 Derby 1973–74. B4 bogies.

| 72631 | (6096) | Y | NR | *DB* | ZA |
| 72639 | (6070) | Y | NR | *DB* | ZA |

Driving Trailer Coaches. Converted from Mark 3B 110 mph Driving Brake Vans. Fitted with diesel generator. Lot No. 31042 Derby 1988.

82111	Y	NR	*DB*	ZA
82124	Y	NR		ZA
82129	Y	NR	*DB*	ZA
82145	Y	NR	*DB*	ZA

Structure Gauging Train Coach. Converted from BR Mark 2E Open First then converted to exhibition van. Lot No. 30843 Derby 1972–73. B4 bogies.

| 99666 | (3250) | Y | NR | *DB* | ZA *(works with 72630)* |

Inspection Saloon. Converted from Class 202 DEMU TRB at Stewarts Lane for use as a BR Southern Region General Manager's Saloon. Overhauled at FM Rail, Derby in 2004–05 for use as a New Trains Project Saloon. Can be used in push-pull mode with suitably equipped locomotives. Eastleigh 1958. SR Mark 4 bogies.

| 975025 | (60755) | G | NR | *DB* | ZA | CAROLINE |

Overhead Line Equipment Test Coach ("MENTOR"). Converted from BR Mark 1 Corridor Brake Standard. Lot No. 30142 Gloucester 1954–55. Fitted with pantograph. B4 bogies.

| 975091 | (34615) | Y | NR | *DB* | ZA |

New Measurement Train Conference Coach. Converted from prototype HST TF Lot No. 30848 Derby 1972. BT10 bogies.

975814 (11000, 41000)	Y	NR	*DB*	EC

New Measurement Train Lecture Coach. Converted from prototype HST catering vehicle. Lot No. 30849 Derby 1972–73. BT10 bogies.

975984 (10000, 40000)	Y	NR	*DB*	EC

Radio Survey Coach. Converted from BR Mark 2E Open Standard. Lot No. 30844 Derby 1972–73. B4 bogies.

977868 (5846)	Y	NR	*DB*	ZA

Staff Coach. Converted from Royal Household couchette Lot No. 30889, which in turn had been converted from BR Mark 2B Corridor Brake First. Lot No. 30790 Derby 1969. B5 bogies.

977969 (14112, 2906)	Y	NR	*DB*	ZA

Track Inspection Train Coach. Converted from BR Mark 2E Open Standard. Lot No. 30844 Derby 1972–73. B4 bogies.

977974 (5854)	Y	NR	*DB*	ZA

Electrification Measurement Coach. Converted from BR Mark 2F Open First converted to Class 488/2 EMU TFOH. Lot No. 30859 Derby 1973–74. B4 bogies.

977983 (3407, 72503)	Y	NR	*DB*	ZA

New Measurement Train Staff Coach. Converted from HST catering vehicle. Lot No. 30884 Derby 1976–77. BT10 bogies.

977984 (40501)	Y	P	*DB*	EC

Structure Gauging Train Coaches. Converted from Mark 2F Open Standard converted to Class 488/3 EMU TSOLH or from BR Mark 2D Open First subsequently declassified to Open Standard and then converted to exhibition van. B4 bogies.
977985. Lot No. 30860 Derby 1973–74.
977986. Lot No. 30821 Derby 1971.

977985 (6019, 72715)	Y	NR	*DB*	ZA *(works with 977986)*
977986 (3189, 99664)	Y	NR	*DB*	ZA *(works with 977985)*

New Measurement Train Overhead Line Equipment Test Coach. Converted from HST TGS. Lot No. 30949 Derby 1982. Fitted with pantograph. BT10 bogies.

977993 (44053)	Y	P	*DB*	EC

New Measurement Train Track Recording Coach. Converted from HST TGS. Lot No. 30949 Derby 1982. BT10 bogies.

977994 (44087)	Y	P	*DB*	EC

New Measurement Train Coach. Converted from HST catering vehicle. Lot No. 30921 Derby 1978–79. BT10 bogies. Fitted with generator.

977995 (40719, 40619)	Y	P	*DB*	EC

Radio Survey Coach. Converted from Mark 2F Open Standard converted to Class 488/3 EMU TSOLH. Lot No. 30860 Derby 1973–74.

977997	(72613, 6126)	**Y**	NR	*DB*	ZA		

Track Recording Coach. Purpose built Mark 2. B4 bogies.

999550	**Y**	NR	*DB*	ZA	

Ultrasonic Test Coaches. Converted from Class 421 EMU MBSO and Class 432 EMU MSO.

999602/605. Lot No. 30862 York 1974. SR Mk 6 bogies.
999606. Lot No. 30816. York 1970. SR Mk 6 bogies.

999602	(62483)	**Y**	NR	*DB*	ZA
999605	(62482)	**Y**	NR	*DB*	ZA
999606	(62356)	**Y**	NR	*DB*	ZA

BREAKDOWN TRAIN COACHES

These coaches are formed in trains used for the recovery of derailed railway vehicles and were converted from BR Mark 1 Corridor Brake Standard and General Utility Van. The current use of each vehicle is given.

971001/003/004. Lot No. 30403 York/Glasgow 1958–60. Commonwealth bogies.
971002. Lot No. 30417 Pressed Steel 1958–59. Commonwealth bogies.
975087. Lot No. 30032 Wolverton 1951–52. BR Mark 1 bogies.
975464. Lot No. 30386 Charles Roberts 1956–58. Commonwealth bogies.
975471. Lot No. 30095 Wolverton 1953–55. Commonwealth bogies.
975477. Lot No. 30233 GRCW 1955–57. BR Mark 1 bogies.
975486. Lot No. 30025 Wolverton 1950–52. Commonwealth bogies.

971001	(86560, 94150)	**Y**	NR	*DB*	SP	Tool & Generator Van
971002	(86624, 94190)	**Y**	NR	*DB*	SP	Tool Van
971003	(86596, 94191)	**Y**	NR	*DB*	SP	Tool Van
971004	(86194, 94168)	**Y**	NR	*DB*	KY	Tool Van
975087	(34289)	**Y**	NR	*DB*	KY	Tool & Generator Van
975464	(35171)	**Y**	NR	*DB*	SP	Staff Coach
975471	(34543)	**Y**	NR	*DB*	SP	Staff Coach
975477	(35108)	**Y**	NR	*DB*	KY	Staff Coach
975486	(34100)	**Y**	NR	*DB*	SP	Tool & Generator Van

INFRASTRUCTURE MAINTENANCE COACHES

De-Icing Coaches

These coaches are used for removing ice from the conductor rail of DC lines. They were converted from Class 489 DMLVs that had originally been Class 414/3 DMBSOs.

Lot No. 30452 Ashford/Eastleigh 1959. Mk 4 bogies.

68501	(61281)	**Y**	NR	*GB*	TW
68504	(61286)	**Y**	NR	*GB*	TW
68505	(61299)	**Y**	NR	*GB*	TW

Winterisation Train Coach. Converted from BR Mark 2E Open Standard. Lot No. 30844 Derby 1972–73. B4 bogies.

977869 (5858)	**Y**	NR	*DR*	Edinburgh Slateford

INTERNAL USER VEHICLES

These vehicles are confined to yards and depots or do not normally move at all. Details are given of the internal user number (if allocated), type, former identity, current use and location. Many no longer see regular use.

975403 carries its original number 4598.

041379	LMS CCT 35527	Stores van	Leeman Road EY, York
041947	BR GUV 93425	Stores van	IL
042154	BR GUV 93975	Stores van	Ipswich Upper Yard
061061	BR CCT 94135	Stores van	Oxford Station
061223	BR GUV 93714	Stores van	Oxford Station
083439	BR CCT 94752	Stores van	WD
083602	BR CCT 94494	Stores van	Three Bridges Station
083637	BR NW 99203	Stores van	SL
083644	BR Ferry Van 889201	Stores van	EH
083664	BR Ferry Van 889203	Stores van	EH
–	BR Open First 3186	Instruction Coach	DY
–	BR Open First 3381	Instruction Coach	HE
–	BR Open Standard 5636	Instruction Coach	PM
–	BR BV 6360	Barrier vehicle	NL
–	BR BV 6396	Stores van	MA
–	BR RFKB 10256	Instruction Coach	Yoker
–	BR RFKB 10260	Instruction Coach	Yoker
–	BR BFK 17156	Instruction Coach	DY
–	BR BG 92901	Stores van	WB
–	BR NL 94003	Stores van	OO
–	BR NL 94006	Stores van	OO
–	BR NK 94121	Stores van	TO
–	BR NB 94438	Stores van	TO
–	BR GUV 96139	Stores van	MA
–	BR Ferry Van 889200	Stores van	SL
–	BR Ferry Van 889202	Stores van	SL
–	BR Open Standard 975403	Cinema Coach	PM

Abbreviations:
BFK = Corridor Brake First
BG = Gangwayed Brake Van
BV = Barrier Vehicle
CCT = Covered Carriage Truck (a 4-wheeled van similar to a GUV)
GUV = General Utility Van
NB = High Security Brake Van (converted from BG)
NK= High Security General Utility Van
NL = Newspaper Van (converted from a GUV)
NW = Bullion Van (converted from a Corridor Brake Standard)
RFKB = Kitchen Buffet First

2.10. COACHING STOCK AWAITING DISPOSAL

This list contains the last known locations of carriages awaiting disposal. The definition of which vehicles are "awaiting disposal" is somewhat vague, but generally speaking these are vehicles of types not now in normal service, those not expected to see further use or carriages which have been damaged by fire, vandalism or collision.

1252	SH	5221	TM	10540	LM	92159	CS
1253	SH	5331	FA	10554	LM	92303	CD
1258	CS	5386	FA	10588	ZH	92400	CD
1644	CS	5420	TM	10647	LM	92908	CS
1650	CS	5453	SH	10681	LM	92936	CD
1652	CS	5463	CS	10682	LM	93723	BY
1655	CS	5478	SH	10701	LM	94101	CS
1658	ZN	5487	CS	10710	LM	94104	TO
1663	CS	5491	CS	10727	LM	94106	BO
1670	CS	5569	CS	10731	LM	94116	BO
1679	ZN	5737	CS	11005	LM	94137	CS
1680	EH	5740	CS	11021	LM	94147	CS
1696	ZN	5756	CS	12008	LM	94153	WE
1800	SH	5815	SH	12022	LM	94160	BT
2108	CS	5876	SH	12029	LM	94166	BS
2110	CS	5888	SH	12036	LM	94170	BO
2127	CS	5925	SH	12095	LM	94176	BS
2131	CS	5943	SH	12096	ZN	94177	TO
2833	CS	5958	SH	12101	LM	94192	CS
2834	EH	5978	SH	12144	LM	94195	BS
2909	CS	6009	SH	12156	LM	94196	CS
3241	CS	6029	SH	12160	LM	94197	BS
3255	FA	6041	CS	12163	LM	94199	BT
3303	TO	6045	SH	13306	CS	94207	TO
3309	CS	6050	CS	13323	CS	94208	TO
3368	FA	6073	SH	13508	BO	94214	CS
3408	CS	6134	SH	17168	CS	94217	BT
3416	CS	6151	SH	18767	SH	94222	CS
4362	BO	6154	SH	18808	SH	94225	SH
4849	CS	6175	SH	18862	SH	94227	Tees Yard
4854	CS	6179	CS	34525	CS	94229	BO
4860	CS	6324	CP	40729	NL	94302	Hellifield
4932	CS	6361	NL	41043	LB	94303	Hellifield
4997	CS	6364	WH	80212	CS	94304	MH
5148	TM	6365	WH	80403	CS	94306	Hellifield
5179	TM	6412	BO	80404	CS	94308	CS
5183	TM	9489	CS	80414	SL	94310	WE
5186	TM	10201	LM	82125	LM	94311	WE
5193	TM	10245	CS	84519	CD	94313	WE
5194	TM	10530	ZH	92114	ZA	94316	TO

94317	TO	94482	CS	95301	CS	99884	CS
94322	CS	94488	CD	95400	BO	889400	ZA
94323	Hellifield	94490	BO	95410	CS	975081	ZA
94326	Hellifield	94492	WE	95727	WE	975280	ZA
94332	CS	94495	Hellifield	95754	CS	975454	TO
94333	Hellifield	94497	BT	95761	WE	975484	CS
94335	BO	94498	CS	95763	BS	975639	CS
94336	BO	94501	TO	96110	CS	975681	Portobello
94337	WE	94504	Hellifield	96132	CS	975682	Portobello
94338	WE	94512	CS	96135	CS	975685	Portobello
94344	TO	94514	BT	96164	CS	975686	Portobello
94401	CS	94515	**	96165	CS	975687	Portobello
94406	CS	94517	CD	96170	CS	975688	Portobello
94408	CS	94520	BO	96178	CS	975918	ME
94410	WE	94522	BO	96182	CS	975920	Portobello
94420	CS	94525	Hellifield	96191	CS	977077	**
94422	TO	94526	Hellifield	96192	CS	977085	BO
94423	BS	94527	Hellifield	96371	WB	977095	CS
94427	WE	94528	CS	96372	LM	977111	**
94428	CS	94530	CS	96373	LM	977112	**
94429	Tees Yard	94531	BO	96374	ZB	977169	BO
94431	CS	94538	CD	96375	LM	977618	BY
94433	BO	94539	CS	96602	RU	977989	ZA
94434	BO	94540	TJ	96603	CF	999508	ZA
94435	TO	94542	Hellifield	96604	CF		
94445	WE	94544	BT	96605	RU	DS 70220	**
94450	WE	94545	Tees Yard	96606	RU		
94451	WE	94546	Hellifield	96607	RU	Pullman 315	CS
94462	CD	94547	CS	96608	RU	Pullman 316	CS
94470	TO	94548	CS	96609	RU	Pullman 325	CS
94479	TO	95300	CS	99019	**	Pullman 337	CS

** Other locations:

94515	Eastleigh East Yard
99019	York Klondyke Yard
977077	Ripple Lane Yard
977111	Ripple Lane Yard
977112	Ripple Lane Yard
DS 70220	Western Trading Estate Siding, North Acton

3. DIESEL MULTIPLE UNITS

INTRODUCTION

This section contains details of all Diesel Multiple Units, usually referred to as DMUs, which can run on Britain's national railway network.

The number of DMUs used on the national railway network has increased dramatically since the 1980s as they have replaced more traditional locomotive hauled trains on many routes. DMUs today work a wide variety of services, from long distance Intercity to inter-urban and suburban duties.

In addition to DMUs used for passenger services there are a small number used as Service Stock and these are listed in section 3.3.

LAYOUT OF INFORMATION

DMUs are listed in numerical order of set – using current numbers as allocated by the RSL. Individual "loose" vehicles are listed in numerical order after vehicles formed into fixed formations. Where sets or vehicles have been renumbered in recent years, former numbering detail is shown in parentheses. Each entry is laid out as in the following example:

RSL Set No.	Detail	Livery	Owner	Operator	Depot	Formation	Name
153 309	cr	**GA**	P	*GA*	NC	52309	GERALD FIENNES

Codes: Codes are used to denote the livery, owner, operator and depot allocation of each Diesel Multiple Unit. Details of these can be found in section 7 of this book. Where a unit or spare car is off-lease, the operator column is left blank.

Detail Differences: Detail differences which currently affect the areas and types of train which vehicles may work are shown, plus differences in interior layout. Where such differences occur within a class, these are shown either in the heading information or alongside the individual set or vehicle number. The following standard abbreviations are used:

e   European Railway Traffic Management System (ERTMS) signalling equipment fitted.

r   Radio Electric Token Block signalling equipment fitted.

Use of the above abbreviations indicates the equipment fitted is normally operable. Meaning of non-standard abbreviations is detailed in individual class headings.

Set Formations: Regular set formations are shown where these are normally maintained. Readers should note set formations might be temporarily varied from time to time to suit maintenance and/or operational requirements. Vehicles shown as "Spare" are not formed in any regular set formation.

Names: Only names carried with official sanction are listed. Names are shown in UPPER/lower case characters as actually shown on the name carried on the vehicle(s). Unless otherwise shown, complete units are regarded as named rather than just the individual car(s) which carry the name.

GENERAL INFORMATION

CLASSIFICATION AND NUMBERING

DMU Classes are listed in class number order.

First generation ("Heritage") DMUs were classified in the series 100–139.
Parry People Movers (not actually technically DMUs) are classified in the series 139.
Second generation DMUs are classified in the series 140–199.
Diesel Electric Multiple Units are classified in the series 200–249.
Service units are classified in the series 930–999.

First and second generation individual cars are numbered in the series 50000–59999 and 79000–79999.

Parry People Mover cars are numbered in the 39000 series.

DEMU individual cars are numbered in the series 60000–60999, except for a few former EMU vehicles which retain their EMU numbers.

Service Stock individual cars are numbered in the series 975000–975999 and 977000–977999, although this series is not exclusively used for DMU vehicles.

UNITS OF MEASUREMENT

Principal details and dimensions are quoted for each class in metric and/or imperial units as considered appropriate bearing in mind common usage in the UK.

All dimensions and weights are quoted for vehicles in an "as new" condition with all necessary supplies (eg oil, water, sand) on board. Dimensions are quoted in the order Length – Width. All lengths quoted are over buffers or couplers as appropriate. Where two lengths are quoted, the first refers to outer vehicles in a set and the second to inner vehicles. All width dimensions quoted are maxima. All weights are shown as metric tonnes (t = tonnes).

OPERATING CODES

These codes are used by train operating company staff to describe the various different types of vehicles and normally appear on data panels on the inner (ie non driving) ends of vehicles.

The first part of the code describes whether or not the car has a motor or a driving cab as follows:

DM Driving motor   M   Motor
DT Driving trailer   T   Trailer

The next letter is a "B" for cars with a brake compartment.

This is followed by the saloon details:

F   First
S   Standard
C   Composite
L   denotes a vehicle with a toilet.
W   denotes a Wheelchair space.
Finally vehicles with a buffet or kitchen area are suffixed RB or RMB for a miniature buffet counter.

Where two vehicles of the same type are formed within the same unit, the above codes may be suffixed by (A) and (B) to differentiate between the vehicles.

A composite is a vehicle containing both First and Standard Class accommodation, whilst a brake vehicle is a vehicle containing separate specific accommodation for the conductor.

Where vehicles have been declassified, the correct operating code which describes the actual vehicle layout is quoted in this publication.

BUILD DETAILS

Lot Numbers

Vehicles ordered under the auspices of BR were allocated a Lot (batch) number when ordered and these are quoted in class headings and sub-headings. Vehicles ordered since 1995 have no Lot Numbers, but the manufacturer and location that they were built is given.

Builders

These are shown for each lot. More details and a full list of builders can be found in section 7.7.

Information on sub-contracting works which built parts of carriages eg the underframes etc is not shown.

ACCOMMODATION

The information given in class headings and sub-headings is in the form F/S nT (or TD) nW. For example 12/54 1T 1W denotes 12 First Class and 54 Standard Class seats, one toilet and one space for a wheelchair. A number in brackets (ie (2)) denotes tip-up seats (in addition to the fixed seats). Tip-up seats in vestibules do not count. The seating layout of open saloons is shown as 2+1, 2+2 or 3+2 as the case may be. Where units have First Class accommodation as well as Standard Class and the layout is different for each class then these are shown separately prefixed by "1:" and "2:". TD denotes a toilet suitable for use by a disabled person.

3.1. DIESEL MECHANICAL & DIESEL HYDRAULIC UNITS

3.1.1 FIRST GENERATION UNITS

CLASS 121   PRESSED STEEL SUBURBAN

First generation units. One set is used on weekdays by Chiltern Railways on peak-hour Aylesbury–Princes Risborough services.
Construction: Steel.
Engines: Two Leyland 1595 of 112 kW (150 hp) at 1800 rpm.
Transmission: Mechanical. Cardan shaft and freewheel to a four-speed epicyclic gearbox and final drive.
Bogies: DD10.
Brakes: Vacuum.
Couplers: Screw.
Dimensions: 20.45 x 2.82 m.
Gangways: Non gangwayed single cars with cabs at each end.
Wheel arrangement: 1-A + A-1.
Doors: Manually-operated slam.
Maximum Speed: 70 mph.
Seating Layout: 3+2 facing.
Multiple Working: "Blue Square" coupling code. First Generation vehicles cannot be coupled to Second Generation units.

Fitted with central door locking.

121 020 formerly in departmental use as unit 960 002 (977722).

121 034 returned to service with Chiltern Railways in 2011. Formerly in departmental use as 977828.

Non-standard livery: 121 020 All over Chiltern blue with a silver stripe.

DMBS. Lot No. 30518 1960–61. –/65. 38.0 t.

121 020	**0**	CR	*CR*	AL	55020
121 034	**G**	CR	*CR*	AL	55034

3.1.2 PARRY PEOPLE MOVERS

CLASS 139   PPM-60

Gas/flywheel hybrid drive Railcars used on the Stourbridge Junction–Stourbridge Town branch.

Body construction: Stainless steel framework.
Chassis construction: Welded mild steel box section.
Primary Drive: Ford MVH420 2.3 litre 64 kW (86 hp) LPG fuel engine driving through Newage marine gearbox, Tandler bevel box and 4 "V" belt driver to flywheel.
Flywheel Energy Store: 500 kg, 1 m diameter, normal operational speed range 1000–1500 rpm.
Final transmission: 4 "V" belt driver from flywheel to Tandler bevel box, Linde hydrostatic transmission and spiral bevel gearbox at No. 2 end axle.
Braking: Normal service braking by regeneration to flywheel (1 m/s/s); emergency/parking braking by sprung-on, air-off disc brakes (3 m/s/s).
Maximum Speed: 45 mph.
Dimensions: 8.7 x 2.4 m.
Doors: Deans powered doors, double-leaf folding (one per side).
Seating Layout: 1+1 unidirectional/facing.
Multiple Working: Not applicable.

39001–002. DMS. Main Road Sheet Metal, Leyland 2007–08. –/17(4) 1W. 12.5 t.

| 139 001 | **LM** | P | *LM* | SJ | 39001 |
| 139 002 | **LM** | P | *LM* | SJ | 39002 |

3.1.3 SECOND GENERATION UNITS

All units in this section have air brakes and are equipped with public address, with transmission equipment on driving vehicles and flexible diaphragm gangways. Except where otherwise stated, transmission is Voith 211r hydraulic with a cardan shaft to a Gmeinder GM190 final drive.

CLASS 142   PACER   BREL DERBY/LEYLAND

DMS–DMSL.

Construction: Steel underframe, rivetted steel body and roof. Built from Leyland National bus parts on Leyland Bus four-wheeled underframes.
Engines: One Cummins LT10-R of 165 kW (225 hp) at 1950 rpm.
Couplers: BSI at outer ends, bar within unit.
Dimensions: 15.55 x 2.80 m.
Gangways: Within unit only.   **Wheel Arrangement:** 1-A + A-1.
Doors: Twin-leaf inward pivoting.   **Maximum Speed:** 75 mph.
Seating Layout: 3+2 mainly unidirectional bus/bench style unless stated.
Multiple Working: Within class and with Classes 143, 144, 150, 153, 155, 156, 158 and 159.

c Refurbished Arriva Trains Wales units. Fitted with 2+2 individual Chapman seating.
s Fitted with 2+2 individual high-back seating.
t Former First North Western facelifted units – DMS fitted with a luggage/bicycle rack and wheelchair space.
u Merseytravel units – Fitted with 3+2 individual low-back seating.

55542–591. DMS. Lot No. 31003 1985–86. –/62 (c –/46(6) 2W, s –/56, t –/53 or 55 1W, u –/52 or 54 1W). 24.5 t.
55592–641. DMSL. Lot No. 31004 1985–86. –/59 1T (c –/44(6) 1T 2W, s –/50 1T, u –/60 1T). 25.0 t.
55701–746. DMS. Lot No. 31013 1986–87. –/62 (c –/46(6) 2W, s –/56, t –/53 or 55 1W, u –/52 or 54 1W). 24.5 t.
55747–792. DMSL. Lot No. 31014 1986–87. –/59 1T (c –/44(6) 1T 2W, s –/50 1T, u –/60 1T). 25.0 t.

142 001	t	**NO**	A	*NO*	NH	55542 55592
142 002	c	**AV**	A	*AW*	CF	55543 55593
142 003		**NO**	A	*NO*	NH	55544 55594
142 004	t	**NO**	A	*NO*	NH	55545 55595
142 005	t	**NO**	A	*NO*	NH	55546 55596
142 006	c	**AV**	A	*AW*	CF	55547 55597
142 007	t	**NO**	A	*NO*	NH	55548 55598
142 009	t	**NO**	A	*NO*	HT	55550 55600
142 010	c	**AV**	A	*AW*	CF	55551 55601
142 011	t	**NO**	A	*NO*	NH	55552 55602
142 012	t	**NO**	A	*NO*	NH	55553 55603
142 013		**NO**	A	*NO*	NH	55554 55604
142 014	t	**NO**	A	*NO*	NH	55555 55605
142 015	s	**NO**	A	*NO*	HT	55556 55606
142 016	s	**NO**	A	*NO*	HT	55557 55607
142 017	s	**NO**	A	*NO*	HT	55558 55608
142 018	s	**NO**	A	*NO*	HT	55559 55609
142 019	s	**NO**	A	*NO*	HT	55560 55610
142 020	s	**NO**	A	*NO*	HT	55561 55611
142 021	s	**NO**	A	*NO*	HT	55562 55612
142 022	s	**NO**	A	*NO*	HT	55563 55613
142 023	t	**NO**	A	*NO*	HT	55564 55614
142 024	s	**NO**	A	*NO*	HT	55565 55615
142 025	s	**NO**	A	*NO*	HT	55566 55616
142 026	s	**NO**	A	*NO*	HT	55567 55617
142 027	t	**NO**	A	*NO*	HT	55568 55618
142 028	t	**NO**	A	*NO*	NH	55569 55619
142 029		**NO**	A	*NO*	HT	55570 55620
142 030		**NO**	A	*NO*	NH	55571 55621
142 031	t	**NO**	A	*NO*	NH	55572 55622
142 032	t	**NO**	A	*NO*	NH	55573 55623
142 033	t	**NO**	A	*NO*	NH	55574 55624
142 034	t	**NO**	A	*NO*	NH	55575 55625
142 035	t	**NO**	A	*NO*	NH	55576 55626
142 036	t	**NO**	A	*NO*	NH	55577 55627
142 037	t	**NO**	A	*NO*	NH	55578 55628

142 038	t	**NO**	A	*NO*	NH	55579	55629
142 039	t	**NO**	A	*NO*	NH	55580	55630
142 040	t	**NO**	A	*NO*	NH	55581	55631
142 041	u	**NO**	A	*NO*	NH	55582	55632
142 042	u	**NO**	A	*NO*	NH	55583	55633
142 043	u	**NO**	A	*NO*	NH	55584	55634
142 044	u	**NO**	A	*NO*	NH	55585	55635
142 045	u	**NO**	A	*NO*	NH	55586	55636
142 046	u	**NO**	A	*NO*	NH	55587	55637
142 047	u	**NO**	A	*NO*	NH	55588	55638
142 048	u	**NO**	A	*NO*	NH	55589	55639
142 049	u	**NO**	A	*NO*	NH	55590	55640
142 050	s	**NO**	A	*NO*	HT	55591	55641
142 051	u	**NO**	A	*NO*	NH	55701	55747
142 052	u	**NO**	A	*NO*	NH	55702	55748
142 053	u	**NO**	A	*NO*	NH	55703	55749
142 054	u	**NO**	A	*NO*	NH	55704	55750
142 055	u	**NO**	A	*NO*	NH	55705	55751
142 056	u	**NO**	A	*NO*	NH	55706	55752
142 057	u	**NO**	A	*NO*	NH	55707	55753
142 058	u	**NO**	A	*NO*	NH	55708	55754
142 060	t	**NO**	A	*NO*	NH	55710	55756
142 061	t	**NO**	A	*NO*	NH	55711	55757
142 062	t	**NO**	A	*NO*	NH	55712	55758
142 063	t	**NO**	A	*NO*	NH	55713	55759
142 064	t	**NO**	A	*NO*	HT	55714	55760
142 065	s	**NO**	A	*NO*	HT	55715	55761
142 066	s	**NO**	A	*NO*	HT	55716	55762
142 067		**NO**	A	*NO*	HT	55717	55763
142 068	t	**NO**	A	*NO*	HT	55718	55764
142 069	c	**AV**	A	*AW*	CF	55719	55765
142 070	t	**NO**	A	*NO*	HT	55720	55766
142 071	s	**NO**	A	*NO*	HT	55721	55767
142 072	c	**AV**	A	*AW*	CF	55722	55768
142 073	c	**AV**	A	*AW*	CF	55723	55769
142 074	c	**AV**	A	*AW*	CF	55724	55770
142 075	c	**AV**	A	*AW*	CF	55725	55771
142 076	c	**AV**	A	*AW*	CF	55726	55772
142 077	c	**AV**	A	*AW*	CF	55727	55773
142 078	s	**NO**	A	*NO*	HT	55728	55774
142 079	s	**NO**	A	*NO*	HT	55729	55775
142 080	c	**AV**	A	*AW*	CF	55730	55776
142 081	c	**AV**	A	*AW*	CF	55731	55777
142 082	c	**AV**	A	*AW*	CF	55732	55778
142 083	c	**AV**	A	*AW*	CF	55733	55779
142 084	s	**NO**	A	*NO*	HT	55734	55780
142 085	c	**AV**	A	*AW*	CF	55735	55781
142 086	s	**NO**	A	*NO*	HT	55736	55782
142 087	s	**NO**	A	*NO*	HT	55737	55783
142 088	s	**NO**	A	*NO*	HT	55738	55784
142 089	s	**NO**	A	*NO*	HT	55739	55785

142 090	s	**NO**	A	*NO*	HT	55740	55786
142 091	s	**NO**	A	*NO*	HT	55741	55787
142 092	s	**NO**	A	*NO*	HT	55742	55788
142 093	s	**NO**	A	*NO*	HT	55743	55789
142 094	s	**NO**	A	*NO*	HT	55744	55790
142 095	s	**NO**	A	*NO*	HT	55745	55791
142 096	s	**NO**	A	*NO*	HT	55746	55792

CLASS 143   PACER   ALEXANDER/BARCLAY

DMS–DMSL. Similar design to Class 142, but bodies built by W Alexander with Barclay underframes.

Construction: Steel underframe, aluminium alloy body and roof. Alexander bus bodywork on four-wheeled underframes.
Engines: One Cummins LT10-R of 165 kW (225 hp) at 1950 rpm.
Couplers: BSI at outer ends, bar within unit.
Dimensions: 15.45 x 2.80 m.
Gangways: Within unit only.   **Wheel Arrangement:** 1-A + A-1.
Doors: Twin-leaf inward pivoting.   **Maximum Speed:** 75 mph.
Seating Layout: 2+2 high-back Chapman seating, mainly unidirectional.
Multiple Working: Within class and with Classes 142, 144, 150, 153, 155, 156, 158 and 159.

DMS. Lot No. 31005 Andrew Barclay 1985–86. –/48(6) 2W. 24.0 t.
DMSL. Lot No. 31006 Andrew Barclay 1985–86. –/44(6) 1T 2W. 24.5 t.

143 601	**AV**	MG	*AW*	CF	55642	55667	
143 602	**AV**	P	*AW*	CF	55651	55668	
143 603	**FI**	P	*GW*	EX	55658	55669	
143 604	**AV**	P	*AW*	CF	55645	55670	
143 605	**AW**	P	*AW*	CF	55646	55671	
143 606	**AV**	P	*AW*	CF	55647	55672	
143 607	**AV**	P	*AW*	CF	55648	55673	
143 608	**AW**	P	*AW*	CF	55649	55674	
143 609	**AV**	SG	*AW*	CF	55650	55675	Sir Tom Jones
143 610	**AV**	MG	*AW*	CF	55643	55676	
143 611	**FI**	P	*GW*	EX	55652	55677	
143 612	**FI**	P	*GW*	EX	55653	55678	
143 614	**AV**	MG	*AW*	CF	55655	55680	
143 616	**AV**	P	*AW*	CF	55657	55682	
143 617	**FI**	FW	*GW*	EX	55644	55683	
143 618	**FI**	FW	*GW*	EX	55659	55684	
143 619	**FI**	FW	*GW*	EX	55660	55685	
143 620	**FI**	P	*GW*	EX	55661	55686	
143 621	**FI**	P	*GW*	EX	55662	55687	
143 622	**AV**	P	*AW*	CF	55663	55688	
143 623	**AV**	P	*AW*	CF	55664	55689	
143 624	**AW**	P	*AW*	CF	55665	55690	
143 625	**AV**	P	*AW*	CF	55666	55691	

CLASS 144   PACER   ALEXANDER/BREL DERBY

DMS–DMSL or DMS–MS–DMSL. As Class 143, but underframes built by BREL.

Construction: Steel underframe, aluminium alloy body and roof. Alexander bus bodywork on four-wheeled underframes.
Engines: One Cummins LT10-R of 165 kW (225 hp) at 1950 rpm.
Couplers: BSI at outer ends, bar within unit.
Dimensions: 15.45/15.43 x 2.80 m.
Gangways: Within unit only.   **Wheel Arrangement:** 1-A + A-1.
Doors: Twin-leaf inward pivoting.   **Maximum Speed:** 75 mph.
Seating Layout: 2+2 high-back Richmond seating, mainly unidirectional.
Multiple Working: Within class and with Classes 142, 143, 150, 153, 155, 156, 158 and 159.

DMS. Lot No. 31015 BREL Derby 1986–87. –/45(3) 1W 24.0 t.
MS. Lot No. BREL Derby 31037 1987. –/58. 23.5 t.
DMSL. Lot No. BREL Derby 31016 1986–87. –/41(3) 1T. 24.5 t.

144 001	**NO**	P	*NO*	NL	55801		55824
144 002	**NO**	P	*NO*	NL	55802		55825
144 003	**NO**	P	*NO*	NL	55803		55826
144 004	**NO**	P	*NO*	NL	55804		55827
144 005	**NO**	P	*NO*	NL	55805		55828
144 006	**NO**	P	*NO*	NL	55806		55829
144 007	**NO**	P	*NO*	NL	55807		55830
144 008	**NO**	P	*NO*	NL	55808		55831
144 009	**NO**	P	*NO*	NL	55809		55832
144 010	**NO**	P	*NO*	NL	55810		55833
144 011	**NO**	P	*NO*	NL	55811		55834
144 012	**NO**	P	*NO*	NL	55812		55835
144 013	**NO**	P	*NO*	NL	55813		55836
144 014	**NO**	P	*NO*	NL	55814	55850	55837
144 015	**NO**	P	*NO*	NL	55815	55851	55838
144 016	**NO**	P	*NO*	NL	55816	55852	55839
144 017	**NO**	P	*NO*	NL	55817	55853	55840
144 018	**NO**	P	*NO*	NL	55818	55854	55841
144 019	**NO**	P	*NO*	NL	55819	55855	55842
144 020	**NO**	P	*NO*	NL	55820	55856	55843
144 021	**NO**	P	*NO*	NL	55821	55857	55844
144 022	**NO**	P	*NO*	NL	55822	55858	55845
144 023	**NO**	P	*NO*	NL	55823	55859	55846

Name: 144 001 THE PENISTONE LINE PARTNERSHIP

CLASS 150/0   SPRINTER   BREL YORK

DMSL–MS–DMS. Prototype Sprinter.

Construction: Steel.
Engines: One Cummins NT855R5 of 213 kW (285 hp) at 2100 rpm.
Bogies: BX8P (powered), BX8T (non-powered).
Couplers: BSI at outer end of driving vehicles, bar non-driving ends.

▲ One of the two Class 121 "bubble cars" used on the Princes Risborough–Aylesbury line, BR green-liveried 121 034, approaches Little Kimble with the 11.11 Princes Risborough–Aylesbury on 25/05/11.　**Robert Pritchard**

▼ London Midland-liveried Parry People Mover 139 002 leaves Stourbridge Town with the 10.35 shuttle to Stourbridge Junction on 21/09/14.　**Robert Pritchard**

▲ Arriva Trains liveried 142 073 and 143 623 arrive at Radyr with the 10.47 Treherbert–Cardiff Central on 17/10/12. **Robert Pritchard**

▼ First Great Western "Local Lines"-liveried 143 603 and 153 373 at Exeter St Davids with the 17.50 to Exmouth on 06/04/13. **Robert Pritchard**

▲ Northern-liveried 144 021 heads away from Morecambe with the 10.19 Leeds–Heysham Port on 15/06/13. **Dave McAlone**

▼ 150 133 and an unidentified 156 arrive at Preston with the 18.20 Manchester Victoria–Blackpool North on 08/06/13. **Robin Ralston**

▲ London Midland-liveried 153 366 awaits departure from Bletchley with the 11.05 to Bedford on 11/04/14. **Harry Savage**

▼ Northern-liveried 155 345 passes Hambleton West Junction with the 12.54 Selby–Huddersfield on 05/08/14. **Lindsay Atkinson**

▲ ScotRail Saltire-liveried 156 514, the last of the 114-strong class to be built, leaves Glasgow Central empty stock on 02/06/13. **Robert Pritchard**

▼ First Great Western 3-car hybrid 158 960 pauses at Filton Abbey Wood with the 16.35 Cardiff Central–Brighton on 18/08/13. **Robert Pritchard**

▲ South West Trains 159 005 leaves Exeter St Davids with the 14.26 to London Waterloo on 26/07/13. **Stewart Armstrong**

▼ Chiltern Railways 165 012 leaves Bicester North with the 16.48 Banbury–London Marylebone on 25/05/12. **Robert Pritchard**

▲ The first of the FGW Class 166s to receive the all over blue livery, 166 221, passes Old Linslade on the WCML on 12/07/14 on its way back from Wolverton to Reading following overhaul. **Mark Beal**

▼ In the new Chiltern Mainline livery, 168 003 passes Hatton North Jn with the 16.18 London Marylebone–Birmingham Snow Hill on 19/08/14. **Dave Gommersall**

▲ ScotRail Saltire-liveried 170 470 passes Plean with the 14.18 Dunblane–Glasgow Queen Street on 23/08/14. **Ian Lothian**

▼ London Midland 172 215 arrives at Birmingham Moor Street with the 14.29 Stratford-upon-Avon–Worcester Foregate Street on 29/09/13. **Robert Pritchard**

▲ Arriva Trains-liveried 175 007 arrives at Stockport with the 14.30 Manchester Piccadilly–Milford Haven on 11/03/14. **Robert Pritchard**

▼ First Great Western Dynamic Lines-liveried 180 102 passes Didcot North Junction with a London Paddington–Oxford train on 01/08/13. **Andrew Mason**

▲ TransPennine Express 185 126 approaches Rotherham Masborough on 23/07/14 with the 17.26 Cleethorpes–Manchester Airport. **Robert Pritchard**

▼ Hastings Diesels preserved Class 201 DEMU 1001 rounds the Queensville Curve into Stafford with a 17.16 Crewe–Hastings railtour on 12/07/14. **Chris Morrison**

▲ CrossCountry 220 003 leaves Stafford on 20/08/13 with the 13.07 Manchester Piccadilly–Bristol Temple Meads. **Cliff Beeton**

▼ 221 126 passes Tyseley with the 14.40 Reading–Newcastle on 29/09/13. **Robert Pritchard**

▲ East Midlands Trains-liveried 222 016 leaves Sheffield with the 16.49 to London St Pancras on 23/07/14. **Robert Pritchard**

▼ Colas Rail Plasser & Theurer 08-4x4/4S-RT Tamper DR 73936 passes Exeter St Thomas running from Kings Norton to Tavistock Junction on 14/02/14. **David Hunt**

▲ Volker Rail Matisa R 24 S Ballast Regulator DR 77802 passes Normanton-on-Soar, near Loughborough, working from Trent Sidings to Doncaster on 27/03/14. **Paul Biggs**

▼ Network Rail Loram SPML 17 Rail Grinding Train DR 79201 at Carlisle Upperby on 11/07/14. **Craig Millar**

▲ Network Rail Pandrol Jackson Plain Line Stoneblower DR 80201 heads north at Normanton working from Huntingdon to Lichfield City on 11/04/14. **Paul Biggs**

▼ The structural equipment section of the new Network Rail Electrification Train formation consisting of 99 70 9131 013-3 (leading) and 99 70 9131 011-7 (tailing) that also carry identities DR 76913 and DR 76911 respectively, are seen just south of Abbotswood Junction running from Tuxford to Swindon on 06/08/14.

Steve Widdowson

▲ Network Rail Independent Drift Snowploughs ADB 965243 and ADB 965234 are seen either end of DRS 37218 and 37606 at Feabuie on their way from Culloden to Inverness on 25/02/14. **Alexander Colley**

▼ Manchester Metrolink Bombardier Flexity Swift tram 3001 leaves East Didsbury with a service to Rochdale via Oldham on 25/05/13. **Robert Pritchard**

▲ One of the new Alstom Citadis Nottingham trams, 221, approaches High School stop with a Station Street service on 03/08/14.　　**Robert Pritchard**

▼ The first of the 20 new Midland Metro CAF trams entered service in September 2014. On 05/09/14 23 arrives at The Hawthorns for Birmingham Snow Hill.

Robert Pritchard

Dimensions: 19.93/19.92 x 2.73 m.
Gangways: Within unit only.   **Wheel Arrangement:** 2-B + 2-B + B-2.
Doors: Twin-leaf sliding.   **Maximum Speed:** 75 mph.
Seating Layout: 3+2 (mainly unidirectional).
Multiple Working: Within class and with Classes 142, 143, 144, 153, 155, 156, 158, 159, 170 and 172.

DMSL. Lot No. 30984 1984. –/72 1T. 35.4 t.
MS. Lot No. 30986 1984. –/92. 35.0 t.
DMS. Lot No. 30985 1984. –/69(6). 34.7 t.

| 150 001 | **FB** | A | *GW* | RG | 55200 | 55400 | 55300 |
| 150 002 | **FB** | A | *GW* | RG | 55201 | 55401 | 55301 |

CLASS 150/1   SPRINTER   BREL YORK

DMSL–DMS.

Construction: Steel.
Engines: One Cummins NT855R5 of 213 kW (285 hp) at 2100 rpm.
Bogies: BP38 (powered), BT38 (non-powered).
Couplers: BSI.
Dimensions: 19.74 x 2.82 m.
Gangways: Within unit only.   **Wheel Arrangement:** 2-B (+ 2-B) + B-2.
Doors: Twin-leaf sliding.   **Maximum Speed:** 75 mph.
Seating Layout: 3+2 facing as built but Centro units were reseated with mainly unidirectional seating.
Multiple Working: Within class and with Classes 142, 143, 144, 153, 155, 156, 158, 159, 170 and 172.

c 3+2 Chapman seating.

DMSL. Lot No. 31011 1985–86. –/72 1T (c –/59 1TD (except 52144 which is –/62 1TD), t –/71 1T, u –/71 1T). 38.3 t.
DMS. Lot No. 31012 1985–86. –/76 (c –/65, t –/73, u –/70 (6)). 38.1 t.

150 101	u	**FB**	A	*GW*	PM	52101	57101
150 102	u	**FB**	A	*GW*	PM	52102	57102
150 103	u	**NO**	A	*NO*	NH	52103	57103
150 104	u	**FB**	A	*GW*	PM	52104	57104
150 105	u	**LM**	A	*LM*	TS	52105	57105
150 106	u	**FB**	A	*GW*	PM	52106	57106
150 107	u	**LM**	A	*LM*	TS	52107	57107
150 108	u	**FB**	A	*GW*	PM	52108	57108
150 109	u	**LM**	A	*LM*	TS	52109	57109
150 110	u	**NO**	A	*NO*	NH	52110	57110
150 111	u	**NO**	A	*NO*	NH	52111	57111
150 112	u	**NO**	A	*NO*	NH	52112	57112
150 113	u	**NO**	A	*NO*	NH	52113	57113
150 114	u	**NO**	A	*NO*	NH	52114	57114
150 115	u	**NO**	A	*NO*	NH	52115	57115
150 116	u	**NO**	A	*NO*	NH	52116	57116
150 117	u	**NO**	A	*NO*	NH	52117	57117
150 118	u	**NO**	A	*NO*	NH	52118	57118

150 119	u	**NO**	A	*NO*	NH	52119	57119
150 120	t	**FB**	A	*GW*	EX	52120	57120
150 121	u	**FB**	A	*GW*	EX	52121	57121
150 122	u	**FB**	A	*GW*	EX	52122	57122
150 123	t	**FB**	A	*GW*	EX	52123	57123
150 124	u	**FB**	A	*GW*	EX	52124	57124
150 127	u	**FB**	A	*GW*	EX	52127	57127
150 128	t	**FB**	A	*GW*	EX	52128	57128
150 129	t	**FB**	A	*GW*	EX	52129	57129
150 130	t	**FB**	A	*GW*	EX	52130	57130
150 131	t	**FB**	A	*GW*	EX	52131	57131
150 132	u	**NO**	A	*NO*	NH	52132	57132
150 133	c	**NO**	A	*NO*	NH	52133	57133
150 134	c	**NO**	A	*NO*	NH	52134	57134
150 135	c	**NO**	A	*NO*	NH	52135	57135
150 136	c	**NO**	A	*NO*	NH	52136	57136
150 137	c	**NO**	A	*NO*	NH	52137	57137
150 138	c	**NO**	A	*NO*	NH	52138	57138
150 139	c	**NO**	A	*NO*	NH	52139	57139
150 140	c	**NO**	A	*NO*	NH	52140	57140
150 141	c	**NO**	A	*NO*	NH	52141	57141
150 142	c	**NO**	A	*NO*	NH	52142	57142
150 143	c	**NO**	A	*NO*	NH	52143	57143
150 144	c	**NO**	A	*NO*	NH	52144	57144
150 145	c	**NO**	A	*NO*	NH	52145	57145
150 146	c	**NO**	A	*NO*	NH	52146	57146
150 147	c	**NO**	A	*NO*	NH	52147	57147
150 148	c	**NO**	A	*NO*	NH	52148	57148
150 149	c	**NO**	A	*NO*	NH	52149	57149
150 150	c	**NO**	A	*NO*	NH	52150	57150

Names:

| 150 129 | Devon & Cornwall RAIL PARTNERSHIP |
| 150 130 | Severnside Community Rail Partnership |

CLASS 150/2   SPRINTER   BREL YORK

DMSL–DMS.

Construction: Steel.
Engines: One Cummins NT855R5 of 213 kW (285 hp) at 2100 rpm.
Bogies: BP38 (powered), BT38 (non-powered).
Couplers: BSI.
Dimensions: 19.74 x 2.82 m.
Gangways: Throughout.   **Wheel Arrangement:** 2-B + B-2.
Doors: Twin-leaf sliding.   **Maximum Speed:** 75 mph.
Seating Layout: 3+2 mainly unidirectional seating as built, but most units
have now been refurbished with new 2+2 seating.
Multiple Working: Within class and with Classes 142, 143, 144, 153, 155,
156, 158, 159, 170 and 172.

c 3+2 Chapman seating (former First North Western units).
p Refurbished Arriva Trains Wales units with 2+2 Primarius seating.
v Units refurbished for Valley Lines with 2+2 Chapman seating.
w Units refurbished for First Great Western with 2+2 Chapman seating.

Northern promotional vinyls:

150 203/205/207/215/218/222/223/225/228/268–271/273–277 Welcome
to Yorkshire.
150 272 R&B Festival week, Colne.

DMSL. Lot No. 31017 1986–87. † –/68 1T 1W, c –/62 1TD, p –/60(4) 1T, u –/71
1T), v –/60(8) 1T, w –/60(8) 1T. 37.5 t.
DMS. Lot No. 31018 1986–87. † –/71(3), c –/70, p –/56(10) 1W, u –/70(6),
v –/56(15) 2W, w –/56(17) 2W, z –/68. 36.5 t.

150 201	c	**NO**	A	*NO*	NH	52201	57201
150 202	u	**FB**	A	*GW*	PM	52202	57202
150 203	c	**NO**	A	*NO*	NH	52203	57203
150 204	u	**NO**	A	*NO*	NH	52204	57204
150 205	u	**NO**	A	*NO*	NH	52205	57205
150 206	u	**NO**	A	*NO*	NH	52206	57206
150 207	c	**NO**	A	*NO*	NH	52207	57207
150 208	p	**AV**	P	*AW*	CF	52208	57208
150 210	u	**NO**	A	*NO*	NH	52210	57210
150 211	c	**NO**	A	*NO*	NH	52211	57211
150 213	p	**AW**	P	*AW*	CF	52213	57213
150 214	u	**NO**	A	*NO*	NH	52214	57214
150 215	c	**NO**	A	*NO*	NH	52215	57215
150 216	u	**FB**	A	*GW*	PM	52216	57216
150 217	p	**AV**	P	*AW*	CF	52217	57217
150 218	c	**NO**	A	*NO*	NH	52218	57218
150 219	w	**FI**	P	*GW*	PM	52219	57219
150 220	u	**NO**	A	*NO*	NH	52220	57220
150 221	w	**FI**	P	*GW*	PM	52221	57221
150 222	c	**NO**	A	*NO*	NH	52222	57222
150 223	c	**NO**	A	*NO*	NH	52223	57223
150 224	c	**NO**	A	*NO*	NH	52224	57224
150 225	c	**NO**	A	*NO*	NH	52225	57225
150 226	u	**NO**	A	*NO*	NH	52226	57226
150 227	p	**AW**	P	*AW*	CF	52227	57227
150 228	†	**NO**	P	*NO*	NH	52228	57228
150 229	p	**AV**	P	*AW*	CF	52229	57229
150 230	w	**AW**	P	*AW*	CF	52230	57230
150 231	p	**AV**	P	*AW*	CF	52231	57231
150 232	w	**FI**	P	*GW*	PM	52232	57232
150 233	w	**FI**	P	*GW*	PM	52233	57233
150 234	w	**FI**	P	*GW*	PM	52234	57234
150 235	p	**AV**	P	*AW*	CF	52235	57235
150 236	w	**AW**	P	*AW*	CF	52236	57236
150 237	p	**AW**	P	*AW*	CF	52237	57237
150 238	w	**FI**	P	*GW*	PM	52238	57238
150 239	w	**FI**	P	*GW*	PM	52239	57239

150 240	w	**AV**	P	*AW*	CF	52240	57240
150 241	w	**AV**	P	*AW*	CF	52241	57241
150 242	w	**AV**	P	*AW*	CF	52242	57242
150 243	w	**FI**	P	*GW*	PM	52243	57243
150 244	w	**FI**	P	*GW*	PM	52244	57244
150 245	p	**AV**	P	*AW*	CF	52245	57245
150 246	w	**FI**	P	*GW*	PM	52246	57246
150 247	w	**FI**	P	*GW*	PM	52247	57247
150 248	w	**FI**	P	*GW*	PM	52248	57248
150 249	w	**FI**	P	*GW*	PM	52249	57249
150 250	p	**AW**	P	*AW*	CF	52250	57250
150 251	w	**AW**	P	*AW*	CF	52251	57251
150 252	p	**AV**	P	*AW*	CF	52252	57252
150 253	w	**AW**	P	*AW*	CF	52253	57253
150 254	w	**AV**	P	*AW*	CF	52254	57254
150 255	p	**AW**	P	*AW*	CF	52255	57255
150 256	p	**AV**	P	*AW*	CF	52256	57256
150 257	p	**AW**	P	*AW*	CF	52257	57257
150 258	p	**AV**	P	*AW*	CF	52258	57258
150 259	p	**AV**	P	*AW*	CF	52259	57259
150 260	p	**AV**	P	*AW*	CF	52260	57260
150 261	w	**FB**	P	*GW*	PM	52261	57261
150 262	p	**AV**	P	*AW*	CF	52262	57262
150 263	w	**FI**	P	*GW*	PM	52263	57263
150 264	p	**AV**	P	*AW*	CF	52264	57264
150 265	w	**FI**	P	*GW*	PM	52265	57265
150 266	w	**FI**	P	*GW*	PM	52266	57266
150 267	v	**AV**	P	*AW*	CF	52267	57267
150 268	†	**NO**	P	*NO*	NH	52268	57268
150 269	†	**NO**	P	*NO*	NH	52269	57269
150 270	†	**NO**	P	*NO*	NH	52270	57270
150 271	†	**NO**	P	*NO*	NH	52271	57271
150 272	†	**NO**	P	*NO*	NH	52272	57272
150 273	†	**NO**	P	*NO*	NH	52273	57273
150 274	†	**NO**	P	*NO*	NH	52274	57274
150 275	†	**NO**	P	*NO*	NH	52275	57275
150 276	†	**NO**	P	*NO*	NH	52276	57276
150 277	†	**NO**	P	*NO*	NH	52277	57277
150 278	v	**AW**	P	*AW*	CF	52278	57278
150 279	v	**AW**	P	*AW*	CF	52279	57279
150 280	v	**AV**	P	*AW*	CF	52280	57280
150 281	v	**AW**	P	*AW*	CF	52281	57281
150 282	v	**AV**	P	*AW*	CF	52282	57282
150 283	p	**AV**	P	*AW*	CF	52283	57283
150 284	p	**AW**	P	*AW*	CF	52284	57284
150 285	p	**AV**	P	*AW*	CF	52285	57285

Name:

150 261   THE TARKA LINE THE FIRST 25 YEARS 1989–2014

CLASS 150/9   SPRINTER   BREL YORK

3-car First Great Western hybrids formed of a Class 150/1 with a 150/2 centre vehicle. DMSL–DMS–DMS. For details see Class 150/1 or Class 150/2.

| 150 925 | u | FB | A | GW | PM | 52125 | 57209 | 57125 |
| 150 926 | u | FB | A | GW | PM | 52126 | 57212 | 57126 |

Name:

150 925   THE HEART OF WESSEX LINE

CLASS 153   SUPER SPRINTER   LEYLAND BUS

DMSL. Converted by Hunslet-Barclay, Kilmarnock from Class 155 2-car units.

Construction: Steel underframe, rivetted steel body and roof. Built from Leyland National bus parts on Leyland Bus bogied underframes.
Engine: One Cummins NT855R5 of 213 kW (285 hp) at 2100 rpm.
Bogies: One P3-10 (powered) and one BT38 (non-powered).
Couplers: BSI.
Dimensions: 23.21 x 2.70 m.
Gangways: Throughout.   **Wheel Arrangement:** 2-B.
Doors: Single-leaf sliding plug.   **Maximum Speed:** 75 mph.
Seating Layout: 2+2 facing/unidirectional.
Multiple Working: Within class and with Classes 142, 143, 144, 150, 155, 156, 158, 159, 170 and 172.

Cars numbered in the 573xx series were renumbered by adding 50 to their original number so that the last two digits correspond with the set number.

c Chapman seating.
d Richmond seating.

52301–52335. DMSL. Lot No. 31026 1987–88. Converted under Lot No. 31115 1991–92. –/72(3) 1T 1W. (s –/72 1T 1W, t –/72(2) 1T 1W). 41.2 t.
57301–57335. DMSL. Lot No. 31027 1987–88. Converted under Lot No. 31115 1991–92. –/72(3) 1T 1W (s –/72 1T 1W). 41.2 t.

153 301	d	NO	A	NO	NL	52301	
153 302	c	EM	A	EM	NM	52302	
153 303	c	AW	A	AW	CF	52303	
153 304	ds	NO	A	NO	NL	52304	
153 305	d	FI	A	GW	EX	52305	
153 306	cr	GA	P	GA	NC	52306	
153 307	d	NO	A	NO	NL	52307	
153 308	c	EM	A	EM	NM	52308	
153 309	cr	GA	P	GA	NC	52309	GERARD FIENNES
153 310	c	EM	P	EM	NM	52310	
153 311	c	EM	P	EM	NM	52311	
153 312	s	AV	A	AW	CF	52312	
153 313	cs	EM	P	EM	NM	52313	
153 314	cr	GA	P	GA	NC	52314	
153 315	ds	NO	A	NO	NL	52315	

153 316	c	NO	P	*NO*	NL	52316	John "Logitude" Harrison Inventor of the Marine Chronometer
153 317	ds	NO	A	*NO*	NL	52317	
153 318	d	FI	A	*GW*	EX	52318	
153 319	c	EM	A	*EM*	NM	52319	
153 320	c	AV	P	*AW*	CF	52320	
153 321	ct	EM	P	*EM*	NM	52321	
153 322	cr	GA	P	*GA*	NC	52322	BENJAMIN BRITTEN
153 323	c	AV	P	*AW*	CF	52323	
153 324	c	NO	A	*NO*	NL	52324	
153 325	c	LM	P	*GW*	EX	52325	
153 326	c	EM	P	*EM*	NM	52326	
153 327	c	AV	A	*AW*	CF	52327	
153 328	ds	NO	A	*NO*	NL	52328	
153 329	c	FB	P	*GW*	EX	52329	
153 330	cs	NO	P	*NO*	NL	52330	
153 331	d	NO	A	*NO*	NL	52331	
153 332	c	NO	P	*NO*	NL	52332	
153 333	cs	LM	P	*GW*	EX	52333	
153 334	ct	LM	P	*LM*	TS	52334	
153 335	cr	GA	P	*GA*	NC	52335	MICHAEL PALIN
153 351	d	NO	A	*NO*	NL	57351	
153 352	ds	NO	A	*NO*	NL	57352	
153 353	c	AW	A	*AW*	CF	57353	
153 354	c	LM	P	*LM*	TS	57354	
153 355	c	EM	A	*EM*	NM	57355	
153 356	c	LM	P	*LM*	TS	57356	
153 357	c	EM	A	*EM*	NM	57357	
153 358	c	NO	P	*NO*	NL	57358	
153 359	c	NO	P	*NO*	NL	57359	
153 360	c	NO	P	*NO*	NL	57360	
153 361	cs	FB	P	*GW*	EX	57361	
153 362	cs	AW	A	*AW*	CF	57362	
153 363	cs	NO	P	*NO*	NL	57363	
153 364	c	LM	P	*LM*	TS	57364	
153 365	c	LM	P	*LM*	TS	57365	
153 366	c	LM	P	*LM*	TS	57366	
153 367	cs	AV	P	*AW*	CF	57367	
153 368	d	FI	A	*GW*	EX	57368	
153 369	c	FB	P	*GW*	EX	57369	
153 370	d	FI	A	*GW*	EX	57370	
153 371	c	LM	P	*LM*	TS	57371	
153 372	d	FI	A	*GW*	EX	57372	
153 373	d	FI	A	*GW*	EX	57373	
153 374	c	EM	A	*EM*	NM	57374	
153 375	c	LM	P	*LM*	TS	57375	
153 376	c	EM	P	*EM*	NM	57376	X24-EXPEDITIOUS
153 377	d	FI	A	*GW*	EX	57377	
153 378	d	NO	A	*NO*	NL	57378	
153 379	c	EM	P	*EM*	NM	57379	
153 380	d	FI	A	*GW*	EX	57380	

153 381	c	**EM**	P	*EM*	NM	57381
153 382	d	**FI**	A	*GW*	EX	57382
153 383	c	**EM**	P	*EM*	NM	57383
153 384	c	**EM**	P	*EM*	NM	57384
153 385	c	**EM**	P	*EM*	NM	57385

CLASS 155 SUPER SPRINTER   LEYLAND BUS

DMSL–DMS.

Construction: Steel underframe, rivetted steel body and roof. Built from Leyland National bus parts on Leyland Bus bogied underframes.
Engines: One Cummins NT855R5 of 213 kW (285 hp) at 2100 rpm.
Bogies: One P3-10 (powered) and one BT38 (non-powered).
Couplers: BSI.
Dimensions: 23.21 x 2.70 m.
Gangways: Throughout.   **Wheel Arrangement:** 2-B + B-2.
Doors: Single-leaf sliding plug.   **Maximum Speed:** 75 mph.
Seating Layout: 2+2 facing/unidirectional Chapman seating.
Multiple Working: Within class and with Classes 142, 143, 144, 150, 153, 156, 158, 159, 170 and 172.

Northern promotional vinyls:

155 341–347 Leeds–Bradford–Manchester route (the "Calder Valley").

DMSL. Lot No. 31057 1988. –/76 1TD 1W. 39.0 t.
DMS. Lot No. 31058 1988. –/80. 38.6 t.

155 341	**NO**	P	*NO*	NL	52341	57341
155 342	**NO**	P	*NO*	NL	52342	57342
155 343	**NO**	P	*NO*	NL	52343	57343
155 344	**NO**	P	*NO*	NL	52344	57344
155 345	**NO**	P	*NO*	NL	52345	57345
155 346	**NO**	P	*NO*	NL	52346	57346
155 347	**NO**	P	*NO*	NL	52347	57347

CLASS 156 SUPER SPRINTER METRO-CAMMELL

DMSL–DMS.

Construction: Steel.
Engines: One Cummins NT855R5 of 213 kW (285 hp) at 2100 rpm.
Bogies: One P3-10 (powered) and one BT38 (non-powered).
Couplers: BSI.
Dimensions: 23.03 x 2.73 m.
Gangways: Throughout.   **Wheel Arrangement:** 2-B + B-2.
Doors: Single-leaf sliding.   **Maximum Speed:** 75 mph.
Seating Layout: 2+2 facing/unidirectional.
Multiple Working: Within class and with Classes 142, 143, 144, 150, 153, 155, 158, 159, 170 and 172.

† Abellio Greater Anglia units fitted with new universal access toilet to meet the 2020 accessibility regulations.
c Chapman seating.
d Richmond seating.

Northern promotional vinyls:

156 441	Manchester and Liverpool
156 461	Ravenglass & Eskdale Railway.
156 464	Lancashire DalesRail
156 484	Settle & Carlisle line.

DMSL. Lot No. 31028 1988–89. –/74 1TD 1W (* –/72, c & t –/70, u –/68, † –/62 1TD 2W). 38.6 t.
DMS. Lot No. 31029 1987–89. –/76 (d –/78, † –/74, t & u –/72). 36.1 t.

156 401	c*	**EM**	P	*EM*	DY	52401	57401
156 402	†cr	**GA**	P	*GA*	NC	52402	57402
156 403	c*	**EM**	P	*EM*	DY	52403	57403
156 404	c*	**EM**	P	*EM*	DY	52404	57404
156 405	c*	**EM**	P	*EM*	DY	52405	57405
156 406	c*	**EM**	P	*EM*	DY	52406	57406
156 407	†cr	**GA**	P	*GA*	NC	52407	57407
156 408	c*	**EM**	P	*EM*	DY	52408	57408
156 409	†cr	**GA**	P	*GA*	NC	52409	57409
156 410	c*	**EM**	P	*EM*	DY	52410	57410
156 411	c*	**EM**	P	*EM*	DY	52411	57411
156 412	†cr	**GA**	P	*GA*	NC	52412	57412
156 413	c*	**EM**	P	*EM*	DY	52413	57413
156 414	c*	**EM**	P	*EM*	DY	52414	57414
156 415	c*	**EM**	P	*EM*	DY	52415	57415
156 416	†cr	**GA**	P	*GA*	NC	52416	57416
156 417	†cr	**GA**	P	*GA*	NC	52417	57417
156 418	†cr	**GA**	P	*GA*	NC	52418	57418
156 419	†cr	**GA**	P	*GA*	NC	52419	57419
156 420	c	**NO**	P	*NO*	AN	52420	57420
156 421	c	**NO**	P	*NO*	AN	52421	57421
156 422	†cr	**GA**	P	*GA*	NC	52422	57422
156 423	c	**NO**	P	*NO*	AN	52423	57423
156 424	c	**NO**	P	*NO*	AN	52424	57424
156 425	c	**NO**	P	*NO*	AN	52425	57425
156 426	c	**NO**	P	*NO*	AN	52426	57426
156 427	c	**NO**	P	*NO*	AN	52427	57427
156 428	c	**NO**	P	*NO*	AN	52428	57428
156 429	c	**NO**	P	*NO*	AN	52429	57429
156 430	t	**SR**	A	*SR*	CK	52430	57430
156 431	t	**SR**	A	*SR*	CK	52431	57431
156 432	t	**SR**	A	*SR*	CK	52432	57432
156 433	t	**SR**	A	*SR*	CK	52433	57433
156 434	t	**SR**	A	*SR*	CK	52434	57434
156 435	t	**SR**	A	*SR*	CK	52435	57435
156 436	†	**SR**	A	*SR*	CK	52436	57436
156 437	t	**SR**	A	*SR*	CK	52437	57437

156 438	d	**NO**	A	*NO*	HT	52438	57438
156 439	t	**SR**	A	*SR*	CK	52439	57439
156 440	c	**NO**	P	*NO*	AN	52440	57440
156 441	c	**NO**	P	*NO*	AN	52441	57441
156 442	t	**SR**	A	*SR*	CK	52442	57442
156 443	d	**NO**	A	*NO*	HT	52443	57443
156 444	d	**NO**	A	*NO*	HT	52444	57444
156 445	ru	**SR**	A	*SR*	CK	52445	57445
156 446	t	**FS**	A	*SR*	CK	52446	57446
156 447	ru	**FS**	A	*SR*	CK	52447	57447
156 448	d	**NO**	A	*NO*	HT	52448	57448
156 449	u	**FS**	A	*SR*	CK	52449	57449
156 450	ru	**FS**	A	*SR*	CK	52450	57450
156 451	d	**NO**	A	*NO*	HT	52451	57451
156 452	c	**NO**	P	*NO*	AN	52452	57452
156 453	ru	**FS**	A	*SR*	CK	52453	57453
156 454	d	**NO**	A	*NO*	HT	52454	57454
156 455	c	**NO**	P	*NO*	AN	52455	57455
156 456	rt	**FS**	A	*SR*	CK	52456	57456
156 457	rt	**FS**	A	*SR*	CK	52457	57457
156 458	rt	**FS**	A	*SR*	CK	52458	57458
156 459	c	**NO**	P	*NO*	AN	52459	57459
156 460	c	**NO**	P	*NO*	AN	52460	57460
156 461	c	**NO**	P	*NO*	AN	52461	57461
156 462		**FS**	A	*SR*	CK	52462	57462
156 463	d	**NO**	A	*NO*	HT	52463	57463
156 464	c	**NO**	P	*NO*	AN	52464	57464
156 465	ru	**FS**	A	*SR*	CK	52465	57465
156 466	c	**NO**	P	*NO*	AN	52466	57466
156 467	r	**FS**	A	*SR*	CK	52467	57467
156 468	d	**NO**	A	*NO*	AN	52468	57468
156 469	d	**NO**	A	*NO*	HT	52469	57469
156 470	c	**EM**	A	*EM*	DY	52470	57470
156 471	d	**NO**	A	*NO*	AN	52471	57471
156 472	d	**NO**	A	*NO*	AN	52472	57472
156 473	c	**EM**	A	*EM*	DY	52473	57473
156 474	rt	**FS**	A	*SR*	CK	52474	57474
156 475	d	**NO**	A	*NO*	HT	52475	57475
156 476	rt	**FS**	A	*SR*	CK	52476	57476
156 477	t	**FS**	A	*SR*	CK	52477	57477
156 478	rt	**FS**	A	*SR*	CK	52478	57478
156 479	d	**NO**	A	*NO*	HT	52479	57479
156 480	d	**NO**	A	*NO*	HT	52480	57480
156 481	d	**NO**	A	*NO*	HT	52481	57481
156 482	d	**NO**	A	*NO*	AN	52482	57482
156 483	d	**NO**	A	*NO*	AN	52483	57483
156 484	d	**NO**	A	*NO*	HT	52484	57484
156 485	ru	**FS**	A	*SR*	CK	52485	57485
156 486	d	**NO**	A	*NO*	AN	52486	57486
156 487	d	**NO**	A	*NO*	AN	52487	57487
156 488	d	**NO**	A	*NO*	AN	52488	57488

156 489	d	**NO**	A	*NO*	AN	52489	57489
156 490	d	**NO**	A	*NO*	HT	52490	57490
156 491	d	**NO**	A	*NO*	AN	52491	57491
156 492	r*	**SR**	A	*SR*	CK	52492	57492
156 493	rt	**FS**	A	*SR*	CK	52493	57493
156 494	u	**SR**	A	*SR*	CK	52494	57494
156 495	u	**SR**	A	*SR*	CK	52495	57495
156 496	u	**FS**	A	*SR*	CK	52496	57496
156 497	c	**EM**	A	*EM*	DY	52497	57497
156 498	c	**EM**	A	*EM*	DY	52498	57498
156 499	rt	**SR**	A	*SR*	CK	52499	57499
156 500	ru	**SR**	A	*SR*	CK	52500	57500
156 501		**SR**	A	*SR*	CK	52501	57501
156 502		**SR**	A	*SR*	CK	52502	57502
156 503		**SR**	A	*SR*	CK	52503	57503
156 504		**SR**	A	*SR*	CK	52504	57504
156 505		**SR**	A	*SR*	CK	52505	57505
156 506		**SR**	A	*SR*	CK	52506	57506
156 507		**SR**	A	*SR*	CK	52507	57507
156 508		**SR**	A	*SR*	CK	52508	57508
156 509		**SR**	A	*SR*	CK	52509	57509
156 510		**SR**	A	*SR*	CK	52510	57510
156 511		**SR**	A	*SR*	CK	52511	57511
156 512		**SR**	A	*SR*	CK	52512	57512
156 513		**SR**	A	*SR*	CK	52513	57513
156 514		**SR**	A	*SR*	CK	52514	57514

Names:

156 416	Saint Edmund
156 420	LA' AL RATTY Ravenglass & Eskdale Railway
156 438	Timothy Hackworth
156 440	George Bradshaw
156 441	William Huskisson MP
156 444	Councillor Bill Cameron
156 448	Bram Stoker Creator of Dracula
156 459	Benny Rothman – The Manchester Rambler
156 460	Driver John Axon G.C.
156 464	Lancashire DalesRail
156 466	Gracie Fields
156 482	Elizabeth Gaskell
156 490	Captain James Cook Master Mariner

CLASS 158/0   BREL

DMSL(B)–DMSL(A) or DMCL–DMSL or DMSL–MSL–DMSL.

Construction: Welded aluminium.
Engines: 158 701–813/158 880–890/158 950–961: One Cummins NTA855R1 of 260 kW (350 hp) at 2100 rpm.
158 815–862: One Perkins 2006-TWH of 260 kW (350 hp) at 2100 rpm.
158 863–872: One Cummins NTA855R3 of 300 kW (400 hp) at 1900 rpm.
Bogies: One BREL P4 (powered) and one BREL T4 (non-powered) per car.
Couplers: BSI.   **Dimensions:** 22.57 x 2.70 m.
Gangways: Throughout.   **Wheel Arrangement:** 2-B + B-2.
Doors: Twin-leaf swing plug.   **Maximum Speed:** 90 mph.
Seating Layout: 2+2 facing/unidirectional in all Standard and First Class except 2+1 in South West Trains First Class.
Multiple Working: Within class and with Classes 142, 143, 144, 150, 153, 155, 156, 159, 170 and 172.

ScotRail 158s 158 701–741 are "fitted" for RETB. When a unit arrives at Inverness the cab display unit is clipped on and plugged in.

Arriva Trains Wales units have ERTMS plugged in at Machynlleth for working the Cambrian Lines.

*   Refurbished ScotRail units fitted with Grammer seating, additional luggage racks and cycle stowage areas.
     ScotRail units 158 726–741 are fitted with Richmond seating.
†   Refurbished East Midlands Trains units with Grammer seating.
c   Chapman seating.
s   Refurbished Arriva Trains Wales units with Grammer seating.
u   Refurbished former South West Trains units with Class 159-style interiors, including First Class seating.
w   Refurbished First Great Western units. Units 158 745–749/751/762/767 (now formed into 3-car sets) have been fitted with Richmond seating.

Advertising liveries:

158 798   Gunwharf Quays, Portsmouth (blue).
158 849   Tour de France (yellow).

Northern promotional vinyls:

158 784 PTEG: 40 years.
158 787, 158 792–796 Sheffield–Leeds fast service.
158 790 Rugby League (Northern Rail Cup).
158 860 Keighley & Brontë Country.
158 901–910 Leeds–Bradford–Manchester route (the "Calder Valley").

DMSL(B). Lot No. 31051 BREL Derby 1989–92. –/68 1TD 1W. († –/72 1TD 1W, c, w –/66 1TD 1W, s –/64(4) 1TD 2W, t –/64 1TD 1W). 38.5 t.
MSL. Lot No. 31050 BREL Derby 1991. –/66(3) 1T. 38.5 t.
DMSL(A). Lot No. 31052 BREL Derby 1989–92. –/70 1T († –/74, c, w –/68 1T, * –/64(2) 1T plus cycle stowage area, s –/70 1T, t –/66 1T). 38.5 t.

The above details refer to the "as built" condition. The following DMSL(B) have now been converted to DMCL as follows:

52701–736/738–741 (ScotRail). 15/53 1TD 1W (* refurbished sets 14/46(6) 1TD 1W plus cycle stowage area).
52786/789 (Former South West Trains units). 13/44 1TD 1W.

158 701	*	**FS**	P	*SR*	IS	52701	57701
158 702	*	**FS**	P	*SR*	IS	52702	57702
158 703	*	**FS**	P	*SR*	IS	52703	57703
158 704	*	**FS**	P	*SR*	IS	52704	57704
158 705	*	**FS**	P	*SR*	IS	52705	57705
158 706	*	**FS**	P	*SR*	IS	52706	57706
158 707	*	**FS**	P	*SR*	IS	52707	57707
158 708	*	**FS**	P	*SR*	IS	52708	57708
158 709	*	**FS**	P	*SR*	IS	52709	57709
158 710	*	**FS**	P	*SR*	IS	52710	57710
158 711	*	**FS**	P	*SR*	IS	52711	57711
158 712	*	**FS**	P	*SR*	IS	52712	57712
158 713	*	**FS**	P	*SR*	IS	52713	57713
158 714	*	**FS**	P	*SR*	IS	52714	57714
158 715	*	**FS**	P	*SR*	IS	52715	57715
158 716	*	**FS**	P	*SR*	IS	52716	57716
158 717	*	**FS**	P	*SR*	IS	52717	57717
158 718	*	**FS**	P	*SR*	IS	52718	57718
158 719	*	**FS**	P	*SR*	IS	52719	57719
158 720	*	**FS**	P	*SR*	IS	52720	57720
158 721	*	**FS**	P	*SR*	IS	52721	57721
158 722	*	**FS**	P	*SR*	IS	52722	57722
158 723	*	**FS**	P	*SR*	IS	52723	57723
158 724	*	**FS**	P	*SR*	IS	52724	57724
158 725	*	**FS**	P	*SR*	IS	52725	57725
158 726		**FS**	P	*SR*	HA	52726	57726
158 727		**FS**	P	*SR*	HA	52727	57727
158 728		**FS**	P	*SR*	HA	52728	57728
158 729		**FS**	P	*SR*	HA	52729	57729
158 730		**FS**	P	*SR*	HA	52730	57730
158 731		**FS**	P	*SR*	HA	52731	57731
158 732		**FS**	P	*SR*	HA	52732	57732
158 733		**FS**	P	*SR*	HA	52733	57733
158 734		**FS**	P	*SR*	HA	52734	57734
158 735		**FS**	P	*SR*	HA	52735	57735
158 736		**FS**	P	*SR*	HA	52736	57736
158 738		**FS**	P	*SR*	HA	52738	57738
158 739		**FS**	P	*SR*	HA	52739	57739
158 740		**FS**	P	*SR*	HA	52740	57740
158 741		**FS**	P	*SR*	HA	52741	57741
158 752		**NO**	P	*NO*	NL	52752	58716	57752
158 753		**NO**	P	*NO*	NL	52753	58710	57753
158 754		**NO**	P	*NO*	NL	52754	58708	57754
158 755		**NO**	P	*NO*	NL	52755	58702	57755
158 756		**NO**	P	*NO*	NL	52756	58712	57756
158 757		**NO**	P	*NO*	NL	52757	58706	57757
158 758		**NO**	P	*NO*	NL	52758	58714	57758

158 759		**NO**	P	*NO*	NL	52759	58713	57759
158 763	w	**FI**	P	*GW*	PM	52763	57763	
158 766	w	**FI**	P	*GW*	PM	52766	57766	
158 770	†	**ST**	P	*EM*	NM	52770	57770	
158 773	†	**ST**	P	*EM*	NM	52773	57773	
158 774	†	**ST**	P	*EM*	NM	52774	57774	
158 777	†	**ST**	P	*EM*	NM	52777	57777	
158 780	†	**ST**	A	*EM*	NM	52780	57780	
158 782		**SR**	A	*SR*	HA	52782	57782	
158 783	†	**ST**	A	*EM*	NM	52783	57783	
158 784		**NO**	A	*NO*	NL	52784	57784	
158 785	†	**ST**	A	*EM*	NM	52785	57785	
158 786	u	**SR**	A	*SR*	HA	52786	57786	
158 787		**NO**	A	*NO*	NL	52787	57787	
158 788	†	**ST**	A	*EM*	NM	52788	57788	
158 789	u	**SR**	A	*SR*	HA	52789	57789	
158 790		**NO**	A	*NO*	NL	52790	57790	
158 791		**NO**	A	*NO*	NL	52791	57791	
158 792		**NO**	A	*NO*	NL	52792	57792	
158 793		**NO**	A	*NO*	NL	52793	57793	
158 794		**NO**	A	*NO*	NL	52794	57794	
158 795		**NO**	A	*NO*	NL	52795	57795	
158 796		**NO**	A	*NO*	NL	52796	57796	
158 797		**NO**	A	*NO*	NL	52797	57797	
158 798	w	**AL**	P	*GW*	PM	52798	58715	57798
158 799	†	**ST**	P	*EM*	NM	52799	57799	
158 806	†	**ST**	P	*EM*	NM	52806	57806	
158 810	†	**ST**	P	*EM*	NM	52810	57810	
158 812	†	**ST**	P	*EM*	NM	52812	57812	
158 813	†	**ST**	P	*EM*	NM	52813	57813	
158 815	c	**NO**	A	*NO*	NL	52815	57815	
158 816	c	**NO**	A	*NO*	NL	52816	57816	
158 817	c	**NO**	A	*NO*	NL	52817	57817	
158 818	es	**AW**	A	*AW*	MN	52818	57818	
158 819	es	**AW**	A	*AW*	MN	52819	57819	
158 820	es	**AW**	A	*AW*	MN	52820	57820	
158 821	es	**AW**	A	*AW*	MN	52821	57821	
158 822	es	**AW**	A	*AW*	MN	52822	57822	
158 823	es	**AW**	A	*AW*	MN	52823	57823	
158 824	es	**AW**	A	*AW*	MN	52824	57824	
158 825	es	**AW**	A	*AW*	MN	52825	57825	
158 826	es	**AW**	A	*AW*	MN	52826	57826	
158 827	es	**AW**	A	*AW*	MN	52827	57827	
158 828	es	**AW**	A	*AW*	MN	52828	57828	
158 829	es	**AW**	A	*AW*	MN	52829	57829	
158 830	es	**AW**	A	*AW*	MN	52830	57830	
158 831	es	**AW**	A	*AW*	MN	52831	57831	
158 832	es	**AW**	A	*AW*	MN	52832	57832	
158 833	es	**AW**	A	*AW*	MN	52833	57833	
158 834	es	**AW**	A	*AW*	MN	52834	57834	
158 835	es	**AW**	A	*AW*	MN	52835	57835	

158 836	es	**AW**	A	*AW*	MN	52836	57836
158 837	es	**AW**	A	*AW*	MN	52837	57837
158 838	es	**AW**	A	*AW*	MN	52838	57838
158 839	es	**AW**	A	*AW*	MN	52839	57839
158 840	es	**AW**	A	*AW*	MN	52840	57840
158 841	es	**AW**	A	*AW*	MN	52841	57841
158 842	c	**NO**	A	*NO*	NL	52842	57842
158 843	c	**NO**	A	*NO*	NL	52843	57843
158 844		**NO**	A	*NO*	NL	52844	57844
158 845		**NO**	A	*NO*	NL	52845	57845
158 846	†	**ST**	A	*EM*	NM	52846	57846
158 847	†	**ST**	A	*EM*	NM	52847	57847
158 848		**NO**	A	*NO*	NL	52848	57848
158 849		**AL**	A	*NO*	NL	52849	57849
158 850		**NO**	A	*NO*	NL	52850	57850
158 851		**NO**	A	*NO*	NL	52851	57851
158 852	†	**ST**	A	*EM*	NM	52852	57852
158 853		**NO**	A	*NO*	NL	52853	57853
158 854	†	**ST**	A	*EM*	NM	52854	57854
158 855		**NO**	A	*NO*	NL	52855	57855
158 856	†	**ST**	A	*EM*	NM	52856	57856
158 857	†	**ST**	A	*EM*	NM	52857	57857
158 858	†	**ST**	A	*EM*	NM	52858	57858
158 859		**NO**	A	*NO*	NL	52859	57859
158 860		**NO**	A	*NO*	NL	52860	57860
158 861		**NO**	A	*NO*	NL	52861	57861
158 862	†	**ST**	A	*EM*	NM	52862	57862
158 863	†	**ST**	A	*EM*	NM	52863	57863
158 864	†	**ST**	A	*EM*	NM	52864	57864
158 865	†	**ST**	A	*EM*	NM	52865	57865
158 866	†	**ST**	A	*EM*	NM	52866	57866
158 867	c	**SR**	A	*SR*	HA	52867	57867
158 868	c	**SR**	A	*SR*	HA	52868	57868
158 869	c	**SR**	A	*SR*	HA	52869	57869
158 870	c	**SR**	A	*SR*	HA	52870	57870
158 871	c	**SR**	A	*SR*	HA	52871	57871
158 872	c	**NO**	A	*NO*	NL	52872	57872

Names (ScotRail units carry their names on the unit ends):

158 702	BBC Scotland 75 years
158 707	Far North Line 125th ANNIVERSARY
158 715	Haymarket
158 720	Inverness & Nairn Railway – 150 years
158 784	Barbara Castle
158 791	County of Nottinghamshire
158 796	Fred Trueman Cricketing Legend
158 797	Jane Tomlinson
158 860	Ian Dewhirst

Class 158/8. Refurbished South West Trains units. Converted from former TransPennine Express units at Wabtec, Doncaster in 2007. 2+1 seating in First Class. Details as Class 158/0 except:

DMCL. Lot No. 31051 BREL Derby 1989–92. 13/44 1TD 1W. 38.5 t.
DMSL. Lot No. 31052 BREL Derby 1989–92. –/70 1T. 38.5 t.

158 880	(158 737)	**ST**	P	*SW*	SA	52737	57737
158 881	(158 742)	**ST**	P	*SW*	SA	52742	57742
158 882	(158 743)	**ST**	P	*SW*	SA	52743	57743
158 883	(158 744)	**ST**	P	*SW*	SA	52744	57744
158 884	(158 772)	**ST**	P	*SW*	SA	52772	57772
158 885	(158 775)	**ST**	P	*SW*	SA	52775	57775
158 886	(158 779)	**ST**	P	*SW*	SA	52779	57779
158 887	(158 781)	**ST**	P	*SW*	SA	52781	57781
158 888	(158 802)	**ST**	P	*SW*	SA	52802	57802
158 889	(158 808)	**ST**	P	*SW*	SA	52808	57808
158 890	(158 814)	**ST**	P	*SW*	SA	52814	57814

CLASS 158/9   BREL

DMSL–DMS. Units leased by West Yorkshire PTE but managed by Eversholt Rail. Details as Class 158/0 except for seating and toilets.

DMSL. Lot No. 31051 BREL Derby 1990–92. –/70 1TD 1W. 38.5 t.
DMS. Lot No. 31052 BREL Derby 1990–92. –/72 and parcels area. 38.5 t.

158 901	**NO**	E	*NO*	NL	52901	57901	
158 902	**NO**	E	*NO*	NL	52902	57902	
158 903	**NO**	E	*NO*	NL	52903	57903	
158 904	**NO**	E	*NO*	NL	52904	57904	
158 905	**NO**	E	*NO*	NL	52905	57905	
158 906	**NO**	E	*NO*	NL	52906	57906	
158 907	**NO**	E	*NO*	NL	52907	57907	
158 908	**NO**	E	*NO*	NL	52908	57908	
158 909	**NO**	E	*NO*	NL	52909	57909	
158 910	**NO**	E	*NO*	NL	52910	57910	William Wilberforce

CLASS 158/0   BREL

DMSL–DMSL–DMSL. Refurbished units reformed for First Great Western. For vehicle details see above. Formations can be flexible depending on when unit exams become due.

158 950	w	**FI**	P	*GW*	PM	57751	52761	57761
158 951	w	**FI**	P	*GW*	PM	52751	52764	57764
158 952	w	**FI**	P	*GW*	PM	57745	52762	57762
158 953	w	**FI**	P	*GW*	PM	52745	52750	57750
158 954	w	**FI**	P	*GW*	PM	57747	52760	57760
158 955	w	**FI**	P	*GW*	PM	52747	52765	57765
158 956	w	**FI**	P	*GW*	PM	52748	52768	57768
158 957	w	**FI**	P	*GW*	PM	57748	52771	57771

158 958	w	**FI**	P	*GW*	PM	57746	52776	57776
158 959	w	**FI**	P	*GW*	PM	52746	52778	57778
158 960	w	**FI**	P	*GW*	PM	57749	52769	57769
158 961	w	**FI**	P	*GW*	PM	52749	52767	57767

CLASS 159/0   BREL

DMCL–MSL–DMSL. Built as Class 158. Converted before entering passenger service to Class 159 by Rosyth Dockyard.

Construction: Welded aluminium.
Engines: One Cummins NTA855R3 of 300 kW (400 hp) at 1900 rpm.
Bogies: One BREL P4 (powered) and one BREL T4 (non-powered) per car.
Couplers: BSI.   **Dimensions:** 22.16 x 2.70 m.
Gangways: Throughout.   **Wheel Arrangement:** 2-B + B-2 + B-2.
Doors: Twin-leaf swing plug.   **Maximum Speed:** 90 mph.
Seating Layout: 1: 2+1 facing, 2: 2+2 facing/unidirectional.
Multiple Working: Within class and with Classes 142, 143, 144, 150, 153, 155, 156, 158 and 170.

DMCL. Lot No. 31051 BREL Derby 1992–93. 23/28 1TD 1W. 38.5 t.
MSL. Lot No. 31050 BREL Derby 1992–93. –/70(6) 1T. 38.5 t.
DMSL. Lot No. 31052 BREL Derby 1992–93. –/72 1T. 38.5 t.

159 001	**ST**	P	*SW*	SA	52873	58718	57873	CITY OF EXETER
159 002	**ST**	P	*SW*	SA	52874	58719	57874	CITY OF SALISBURY
159 003	**ST**	P	*SW*	SA	52875	58720	57875	TEMPLECOMBE
159 004	**ST**	P	*SW*	SA	52876	58721	57876	BASINGSTOKE AND DEANE
159 005	**ST**	P	*SW*	SA	52877	58722	57877	WEST OF ENGLAND LINE
159 006	**ST**	P	*SW*	SA	52878	58723	57878	THE SEATON TRAMWAY Seaton–Colyford–Colyton
159 007	**ST**	P	*SW*	SA	52879	58724	57879	
159 008	**ST**	P	*SW*	SA	52880	58725	57880	
159 009	**ST**	P	*SW*	SA	52881	58726	57881	
159 010	**ST**	P	*SW*	SA	52882	58727	57882	
159 011	**ST**	P	*SW*	SA	52883	58728	57883	
159 012	**ST**	P	*SW*	SA	52884	58729	57884	
159 013	**ST**	P	*SW*	SA	52885	58730	57885	
159 014	**ST**	P	*SW*	SA	52886	58731	57886	
159 015	**ST**	P	*SW*	SA	52887	58732	57887	
159 016	**ST**	P	*SW*	SA	52888	58733	57888	
159 017	**ST**	P	*SW*	SA	52889	58734	57889	
159 018	**ST**	P	*SW*	SA	52890	58735	57890	
159 019	**ST**	P	*SW*	SA	52891	58736	57891	
159 020	**ST**	P	*SW*	SA	52892	58737	57892	
159 021	**ST**	P	*SW*	SA	52893	58738	57893	
159 022	**ST**	P	*SW*	SA	52894	58739	57894	

CLASS 159/1   BREL

DMCL–MSL–DMSL. Units converted from Class 158s at Wabtec, Doncaster in 2006–07 for South West Trains.

Details as Class 158/0 except:
Seating Layout: 1: 2+1 facing, 2: 2+2 facing/unidirectional.

DMCL. Lot No. 31051 BREL Derby 1989–92. 24/28 1TD 1W. 38.5 t.
MSL. Lot No. 31050 BREL Derby 1989–92. –/70 1T. 38.5 t.
DMSL. Lot No. 31052 BREL Derby 1989–92. –/72 1T.38.5 t.

159 101	(158 800)	**ST**	P	*SW*	SA	52800	58717	57800
159 102	(158 803)	**ST**	P	*SW*	SA	52803	58703	57803
159 103	(158 804)	**ST**	P	*SW*	SA	52804	58704	57804
159 104	(158 805)	**ST**	P	*SW*	SA	52805	58705	57805
159 105	(158 807)	**ST**	P	*SW*	SA	52807	58707	57807
159 106	(158 809)	**ST**	P	*SW*	SA	52809	58709	57809
159 107	(158 811)	**ST**	P	*SW*	SA	52811	58711	57811
159 108	(158 801)	**ST**	P	*SW*	SA	52801	58701	57801

CLASS 165/0   NETWORK TURBO   BREL

DMSL–DMS and DMSL–MS–DMS. Chiltern Railways units. Refurbished 2003–05 with First Class seats removed and air conditioning fitted.
Construction: Welded aluminium.
Engines: One Perkins 2006-TWH of 260 kW (350 hp) at 2100 rpm.
Bogies: BREL P3-17 (powered), BREL T3-17 (non-powered).
Couplers: BSI.
Dimensions: 23.50/23.25 x 2.81 m.
Gangways: Within unit only.   **Wheel Arrangement:** 2-B (+ B-2) + B-2.
Doors: Twin-leaf swing plug.   **Maximum Speed:** 75 mph.
Seating Layout: 2+2/3+2 facing/unidirectional.
Multiple Working: Within class and with Classes 166, 168, 170 and 172.

Fitted with tripcocks for working over London Underground tracks between Harrow-on-the-Hill and Amersham.

58801–822/58873–878. DMSL. Lot No. 31087 BREL York 1990. –/82(7) 1T 2W. 40.1 t.
58823–833. DMSL. Lot No. 31089 BREL York 1991–92. –/82(7) 1T 2W. 40.1 t.
MS. Lot No. 31090 BREL York 1991–92. –/106. 37.0 t.
DMS. Lot No. 31088 BREL York 1991–92. –/94. 39.4 t.

165 001	**CR**	A	*CR*	AL	58801	58834
165 002	**CR**	A	*CR*	AL	58802	58835
165 003	**CR**	A	*CR*	AL	58803	58836
165 004	**CR**	A	*CR*	AL	58804	58837
165 005	**CR**	A	*CR*	AL	58805	58838
165 006	**CR**	A	*CR*	AL	58806	58839
165 007	**CR**	A	*CR*	AL	58807	58840
165 008	**CR**	A	*CR*	AL	58808	58841
165 009	**CR**	A	*CR*	AL	58809	58842

165 010	**CR**	A	*CR*	AL	58810		58843
165 011	**CR**	A	*CR*	AL	58811		58844
165 012	**CR**	A	*CR*	AL	58812		58845
165 013	**CR**	A	*CR*	AL	58813		58846
165 014	**CR**	A	*CR*	AL	58814		58847
165 015	**CR**	A	*CR*	AL	58815		58848
165 016	**CR**	A	*CR*	AL	58816		58849
165 017	**CR**	A	*CR*	AL	58817		58850
165 018	**CR**	A	*CR*	AL	58818		58851
165 019	**CR**	A	*CR*	AL	58819		58852
165 020	**CR**	A	*CR*	AL	58820		58853
165 021	**CR**	A	*CR*	AL	58821		58854
165 022	**CR**	A	*CR*	AL	58822		58855
165 023	**CR**	A	*CR*	AL	58873		58867
165 024	**CR**	A	*CR*	AL	58874		58868
165 025	**CR**	A	*CR*	AL	58875		58869
165 026	**CR**	A	*CR*	AL	58876		58870
165 027	**CR**	A	*CR*	AL	58877		58871
165 028	**CR**	A	*CR*	AL	58878		58872
165 029	**CR**	A	*CR*	AL	58823	55404	58856
165 030	**CR**	A	*CR*	AL	58824	55405	58857
165 031	**CR**	A	*CR*	AL	58825	55406	58858
165 032	**CR**	A	*CR*	AL	58826	55407	58859
165 033	**CR**	A	*CR*	AL	58827	55408	58860
165 034	**CR**	A	*CR*	AL	58828	55409	58861
165 035	**CR**	A	*CR*	AL	58829	55410	58862
165 036	**CR**	A	*CR*	AL	58830	55411	58863
165 037	**CR**	A	*CR*	AL	58831	55412	58864
165 038	**CR**	A	*CR*	AL	58832	55413	58865
165 039	**CR**	A	*CR*	AL	58833	55414	58866

CLASS 165/1   NETWORK TURBO   BREL

First Great Western units. DMCL–MS–DMS or DMCL–DMS.

Construction: Welded aluminium.
Engines: One Perkins 2006-TWH of 260 kW (350 hp) at 2100 rpm.
Bogies: BREL P3-17 (powered), BREL T3-17 (non-powered).
Couplers: BSI.
Dimensions: 23.50/23.25 x 2.81 m.
Gangways: Within unit only.   **Wheel Arrangement:** 2-B (+ B-2) + B-2.
Doors: Twin-leaf swing plug.   **Maximum Speed:** 90 mph.
Seating Layout: 1: 2+2 facing, 2: 3+2 facing/unidirectional.
Multiple Working: Within class and with Classes 166, 168, 170 and 172.

58953–969. DMCL. Lot No. 31098 BREL York 1992. 16/66 1T. 38.0 t.
58879–898. DMCL. Lot No. 31096 BREL York 1992. 16/72 1T. 38.0 t.
MS. Lot No. 31099 BREL 1992. –/106. 37.0 t.
DMS. Lot No. 31097 BREL 1992. –/98. 37.0 t.

165 101	**FD**	A	*GW*	RG	58953	55415	58916
165 102	**FD**	A	*GW*	RG	58954	55416	58917

165 103	**FD**	A	*GW*	RG	58955	55417	58918
165 104	**FD**	A	*GW*	RG	58956	55418	58919
165 105	**FD**	A	*GW*	RG	58957	55419	58920
165 106	**FD**	A	*GW*	RG	58958	55420	58921
165 107	**FD**	A	*GW*	RG	58959	55421	58922
165 108	**FD**	A	*GW*	RG	58960	55422	58923
165 109	**FD**	A	*GW*	RG	58961	55423	58924
165 110	**FD**	A	*GW*	RG	58962	55424	58925
165 111	**FD**	A	*GW*	RG	58963	55425	58926
165 112	**FD**	A	*GW*	RG	58964	55426	58927
165 113	**FD**	A	*GW*	RG	58965	55427	58928
165 114	**FD**	A	*GW*	RG	58966	55428	58929
165 116	**FD**	A	*GW*	RG	58968	55430	58931
165 117	**FD**	A	*GW*	RG	58969	55431	58932
165 118	**FD**	A	*GW*	RG	58879		58933
165 119	**FD**	A	*GW*	RG	58880		58934
165 120	**FD**	A	*GW*	RG	58881		58935
165 121	**FD**	A	*GW*	RG	58882		58936
165 122	**FD**	A	*GW*	RG	58883		58937
165 123	**FD**	A	*GW*	RG	58884		58938
165 124	**FD**	A	*GW*	RG	58885		58939
165 125	**FD**	A	*GW*	RG	58886		58940
165 126	**FD**	A	*GW*	RG	58887		58941
165 127	**FD**	A	*GW*	RG	58888		58942
165 128	**FD**	A	*GW*	RG	58889		58943
165 129	**FD**	A	*GW*	RG	58890		58944
165 130	**FD**	A	*GW*	RG	58891		58945
165 131	**FD**	A	*GW*	RG	58892		58946
165 132	**FD**	A	*GW*	RG	58893		58947
165 133	**FD**	A	*GW*	RG	58894		58948
165 134	**FD**	A	*GW*	RG	58895		58949
165 135	**FD**	A	*GW*	RG	58896		58950
165 136	**FD**	A	*GW*	RG	58897		58951
165 137	**FD**	A	*GW*	RG	58898		58952

CLASS 166   NETWORK EXPRESS TURBO   ABB

DMSL–MS–DMCL. First Great Western units, built for Paddington–Oxford/
Newbury services. Air conditioned and with additional luggage space
compared to the Class 165s. The DMSL vehicles have had their 16 First
Class seats declassified.

Construction: Welded aluminium.
Engines: One Perkins 2006-TWH of 260 kW (350 hp) at 2100 rpm.
Bogies: BREL P3-17 (powered), BREL T3-17 (non-powered).
Couplers: BSI.
Dimensions: 23.50 x 2.81 m.
Gangways: Within unit only.   **Wheel Arrangement:** 2-B + B-2 + B-2.
Doors: Twin-leaf swing plug.   **Maximum Speed:** 90 mph.
Seating Layout: 1: 2+2 facing, 2: 2+2/3+2 facing/unidirectional.
Multiple Working: Within class and with Classes 165, 168, 170 and 172.

* Refurbished with a new universal access toilet to comply with the 2020 accessibility regulations. Full details awaited.

DMSL. Lot No. 31116 ABB York 1992–93. –/84 1T. 39.6 t.
MS. Lot No. 31117 ABB York 1992–93. –/91. 38.0 t.
DMCL. Lot No. 31116 ABB York 1992–93. 16/68 1T. 39.6 t.

166 201	*	**FB**	A	*GW*	RG	58101	58601 58122
166 202	*	**FB**	A	*GW*	RG	58102	58602 58123
166 203		**FD**	A	*GW*	RG	58103	58603 58124
166 204		**FD**	A	*GW*	RG	58104	58604 58125
166 205		**FD**	A	*GW*	RG	58105	58605 58126
166 206		**FD**	A	*GW*	RG	58106	58606 58127
166 207		**FD**	A	*GW*	RG	58107	58607 58128
166 208		**FD**	A	*GW*	RG	58108	58608 58129
166 209		**FD**	A	*GW*	RG	58109	58609 58130
166 210		**FD**	A	*GW*	RG	58110	58610 58131
166 211		**FD**	A	*GW*	RG	58111	58611 58132
166 212		**FD**	A	*GW*	RG	58112	58612 58133
166 213		**FD**	A	*GW*	RG	58113	58613 58134
166 214		**FD**	A	*GW*	RG	58114	58614 58135
166 215	*	**FB**	A	*GW*	RG	58115	58615 58136
166 216		**FD**	A	*GW*	RG	58116	58616 58137
166 217		**FD**	A	*GW*	RG	58117	58617 58138
166 218		**FD**	A	*GW*	RG	58118	58618 58139
166 219		**FD**	A	*GW*	RG	58119	58619 58140
166 220		**FD**	A	*GW*	RG	58120	58620 58141
166 221	*	**FB**	A	*GW*	RG	58121	58621 58142

Name: 166 221 Reading Train Care Depot/READING TRAIN CARE DEPOT *(alt sides)*

CLASS 168 CLUBMAN ADTRANZ/BOMBARDIER

Air conditioned.

Construction: Welded aluminium bodies with bolt-on steel ends.
Engines: One MTU 6R183TD13H of 315 kW (422 hp) at 1900 rpm.
Transmission: Hydraulic. Voith T211rzze to ZF final drive.
Bogies: One Adtranz P3–23 and one BREL T3–23 per car.
Couplers: BSI at outer ends, bar within unit.
Dimensions: Class 168/0: 24.10/23.61 x 2.69 m. Others: 23.62/23.61 x 2.69 m.
Gangways: Within unit only.   **Wheel Arrangement:** 2-B (+ B-2 + B-2) + B-2.
Doors: Twin-leaf swing plug.   **Maximum Speed:** 100 mph.
Seating Layout: 2+2 facing/unidirectional.
Multiple Working: Within class and with Classes 165 and 166.

Fitted with tripcocks for working over London Underground tracks between Harrow-on-the-Hill and Amersham.

Class 168/0. Original Design. DMSL(A)–MS–MSL–DMSL(B) or DMSL(A)–MSL–MS–DMSL(B).

58451–455 were numbered 58656–660 for a time when used in 168 106–110.

58151–155. DMSL(A). Adtranz Derby 1997–98. –/57 1TD 1W. 44.0 t.
58651–655. MSL. Adtranz Derby 1998. –/73 1T. 41.0 t.
58451–455. MS. Adtranz Derby 1998. –/77. 41.0 t.
58251–255. DMSL(B). Adtranz Derby 1998. –/68 1T. 43.6 t.

168 001	**CL**	P	*CR*	AL	58151	58451	58651	58251
168 002	**CL**	P	*CR*	AL	58152	58652	58452	58252
168 003	**CL**	P	*CR*	AL	58153	58453	58653	58253
168 004	**CL**	P	*CR*	AL	58154	58654	58454	58254
168 005	**CL**	P	*CR*	AL	58155	58455	58655	58255

Class 168/1. These units are effectively Class 170s. DMSL(A)–MSL–MS–DMSL(B) or DMSL(A)–MS–DMSL(B).

58461–463 have been renumbered from 58661–663.

58156–163. DMSL(A). Adtranz Derby 2000. –/57 1TD 2W. 45.2 t.
58456–460. MS. Bombardier Derby 2002. –/76. 41.8 t.
58756–757. MSL. Bombardier Derby 2002. –/73 1T. 42.9 t.
58461–463. MS. Adtranz Derby 2000. –/76. 42.4 t.
58256–263. DMSL(B). Adtranz Derby 2000. –/69 1T. 45.2 t.

168 106	**CL**	P	*CR*	AL	58156	58456	58756	58256
168 107	**CL**	P	*CR*	AL	58157	58757	58457	58257
168 108	**CL**	P	*CR*	AL	58158		58458	58258
168 109	**CL**	P	*CR*	AL	58159		58459	58259
168 110	**CL**	P	*CR*	AL	58160		58460	58260
168 111	**CR**	E	*CR*	AL	58161		58461	58261
168 112	**CL**	E	*CR*	AL	58162		58462	58262
168 113	**CL**	E	*CR*	AL	58163		58463	58263

Class 168/2. These units are effectively Class 170s. DMSL(A)–(MS)–MS–DMSL(B).

58164–169. DMSL(A). Bombardier Derby 2003–04. –/57 1TD 2W. 45.4 t.
58365–367. MS. Bombardier Derby 2006. –/76. 43.3 t.
58464/468/469. MS. Bombardier Derby 2003–04. –/76. 44.0 t.
58465–467. MS. Bombardier Derby 2006. –/76. 43.3 t.
58264–269. DMSL(B). Bombardier Derby 2003–04. –/69 1T. 45.5 t.

168 214	**CL**	P	*CR*	AL	58164		58464	58264
168 215	**CL**	P	*CR*	AL	58165	58365	58465	58265
168 216	**CL**	P	*CR*	AL	58166	58366	58466	58266
168 217	**CL**	P	*CR*	AL	58167	58367	58467	58267
168 218	**CL**	P	*CR*	AL	58168		58468	58268
168 219	**CL**	P	*CR*	AL	58169		58469	58269

CLASS 170 TURBOSTAR ADTRANZ/BOMBARDIER

Various formations. Air conditioned.

Construction: Welded aluminium bodies with bolt-on steel ends.
Engines: One MTU 6R183TD13H of 315 kW (422 hp) at 1900 rpm.
Transmission: Hydraulic. Voith T211rzze to ZF final drive.
Bogies: One Adtranz P3–23 and one BREL T3–23 per car.
Couplers: BSI at outer ends, bar within later build units.
Dimensions: 23.62/23.61 x 2.69 m.
Gangways: Within unit only.   **Wheel Arrangement:** 2-B (+ B-2) + B-2.
Doors: Twin-leaf sliding plug.   **Maximum Speed:** 100 mph.
Seating Layout: 1: 2+1 facing/unidirectional. 2: 2+2 unidirectional/facing.
Multiple Working: Within class and with Classes 150, 153, 155, 156, 158, 159 and 172.

Class 170/1. CrossCountry (former Midland Mainline) units. Lazareni seating. DMSL–MS–DMCL/DMSL–DMCL.

DMSL. Adtranz Derby 1998–99. –/59 1TD 2W. 45.0 t.
MS. Adtranz Derby 2001. –/80. 43.0 t.
DMCL. Adtranz Derby 1998–99. 9/52 1T. 44.8 t

170 101	**XC**	P	*XC*	TS	50101	55101	79101
170 102	**XC**	P	*XC*	TS	50102	55102	79102
170 103	**XC**	P	*XC*	TS	50103	55103	79103
170 104	**XC**	P	*XC*	TS	50104	55104	79104
170 105	**XC**	P	*XC*	TS	50105	55105	79105
170 106	**XC**	P	*XC*	TS	50106	55106	79106
170 107	**XC**	P	*XC*	TS	50107	55107	79107
170 108	**XC**	P	*XC*	TS	50108	55108	79108
170 109	**XC**	P	*XC*	TS	50109	55109	79109
170 110	**XC**	P	*XC*	TS	50110	55110	79110
170 111	**XC**	P	*XC*	TS	50111		79111
170 112	**XC**	P	*XC*	TS	50112		79112
170 113	**XC**	P	*XC*	TS	50113		79113
170 114	**XC**	P	*XC*	TS	50114		79114
170 115	**XC**	P	*XC*	TS	50115		79115
170 116	**XC**	P	*XC*	TS	50116		79116
170 117	**XC**	P	*XC*	TS	50117		79117

Class 170/2. Abellio Greater Anglia 3-car units. Chapman seating. DMCL–MSL–DMSL.

Advertising livery: 170 208 Breckland Line (Norwich–Cambridge).

DMCL. Adtranz Derby 1999. 7/39 1TD 2W. 45.0 t.
MSL. Adtranz Derby 1999. –/68 1T. Guard's office. 45.3 t.
DMSL. Adtranz Derby 1999. –/66 1T. 43.4 t.

170 201	r	**1**	P	*GA*	NC	50201	56201	79201
170 202	r	**1**	P	*GA*	NC	50202	56202	79202
170 203	r	**1**	P	*GA*	NC	50203	56203	79203
170 204	r	**1**	P	*GA*	NC	50204	56204	79204
170 205	r	**1**	P	*GA*	NC	50205	56205	79205

170 206	r	**1**	P	*GA*	NC	50206	56206	79206
170 207	r	**1**	P	*GA*	NC	50207	56207	79207
170 208	r	**AL**	P	*GA*	NC	50208	56208	79208

Class 170/2. Abellio Greater Anglia 2-car units. Chapman seating. DMSL–DMCL.

DMSL. Bombardier Derby 2002. –/57 1TD 2W. 45.7 t.
DMCL. Bombardier Derby 2002. 9/53 1T. 45.7 t.

170 270	r	**1**	P	*GA*	NC	50270	79270
170 271	r	**AN**	P	*GA*	NC	50271	79271
170 272	r	**AN**	P	*GA*	NC	50272	79272
170 273	r	**AN**	P	*GA*	NC	50273	79273

Class 170/3. TransPennine Express units. Chapman seating. DMCL–DMSL.
170 309 renumbered from 170 399.

These units are due to transfer to Chiltern Railways in 2015–16 and will be renumbered as Class 168s in the series 168 301–309.

50301–308/399. DMCL. Adtranz Derby 2000–01. 8/43 1TD 2W. 45.8 t.
79301–308/399. DMSL. Adtranz Derby 2000–01. –/65 1T. 45.8 t.

170 301	**FT**	P	*TP*	XW	50301	79301
170 302	**FT**	P	*TP*	XW	50302	79302
170 303	**FT**	P	*TP*	XW	50303	79303
170 304	**FT**	P	*TP*	XW	50304	79304
170 305	**FT**	P	*TP*	XW	50305	79305
170 306	**FT**	P	*TP*	XW	50306	79306
170 307	**FT**	P	*TP*	XW	50307	79307
170 308	**FT**	P	*TP*	XW	50308	79308
170 309	**FT**	P	*TP*	XW	50399	79399

Class 170/3. Units built for Hull Trains, now in use with ScotRail. Chapman seating. DMSL–MSLRB–DMSL.

DMSL(A). Bombardier Derby 2004. –/55 1TD 2W. 46.5 t.
MSLRB. Bombardier Derby 2004. –/57 1T. Buffet and guard's office 44.7 t.
DMSL(B). Bombardier Derby 2004. –/67 1T. 47.0 t.

170 393	**SR**	P	*SR*	HA	50393	56393	79393
170 394	**SR**	P	*SR*	HA	50394	56394	79394
170 395	**SR**	P	*SR*	HA	50395	56395	79395
170 396	**SR**	P	*SR*	HA	50396	56396	79396

Class 170/3. CrossCountry units. Lazareni seating. DMSL–MS–DMCL.

DMSL. Bombardier Derby 2002. –/59 1TD 2W. 45.4 t.
MS. Bombardier Derby 2002. –/80. 43.0 t.
DMCL. Bombardier Derby 2002. 9/52 1T. 45.8 t.

| 170 397 | **XC** | P | *XC* | TS | 50397 | 56397 | 79397 |
| 170 398 | **XC** | P | *XC* | TS | 50398 | 56398 | 79398 |

Class 170/4. ScotRail "express" units. Chapman seating. DMCL–MS–DMCL.

DMCL(A). Adtranz Derby 1999–2001. 9/43 1TD 2W. 45.2 t.
MS. Adtranz Derby 1999–2001. –/76. 42.5 t.
DMCL(B). Adtranz Derby 1999–2001. 9/49 1T. 45.2 t.

170 401	**FS**	P	*SR*	HA	50401	56401	79401
170 402	**SR**	P	*SR*	HA	50402	56402	79402
170 403	**FS**	P	*SR*	HA	50403	56403	79403
170 404	**FS**	P	*SR*	HA	50404	56404	79404
170 405	**FS**	P	*SR*	HA	50405	56405	79405
170 406	**FS**	P	*SR*	HA	50406	56406	79406
170 407	**FS**	P	*SR*	HA	50407	56407	79407
170 408	**FS**	P	*SR*	HA	50408	56408	79408
170 409	**FS**	P	*SR*	HA	50409	56409	79409
170 410	**FS**	P	*SR*	HA	50410	56410	79410
170 411	**FS**	P	*SR*	HA	50411	56411	79411
170 412	**SR**	P	*SR*	HA	50412	56412	79412
170 413	**FS**	P	*SR*	HA	50413	56413	79413
170 414	**FS**	P	*SR*	HA	50414	56414	79414
170 415	**SR**	P	*SR*	HA	50415	56415	79415
170 416	**FS**	E	*SR*	HA	50416	56416	79416
170 417	**FS**	E	*SR*	HA	50417	56417	79417
170 418	**SR**	E	*SR*	HA	50418	56418	79418
170 419	**FS**	E	*SR*	HA	50419	56419	79419
170 420	**FS**	E	*SR*	HA	50420	56420	79420
170 421	**FS**	E	*SR*	HA	50421	56421	79421
170 422	**FS**	E	*SR*	HA	50422	56422	79422
170 423	**FS**	E	*SR*	HA	50423	56423	79423
170 424	**FS**	E	*SR*	HA	50424	56424	79424

Names (carried on end cars):

170 401	Sir Moir Lockhead OBE
170 405	Riverside Museum
170 407	UNIVERSITY OF ABERDEEN

Class 170/4. ScotRail "express" units. Chapman seating. DMCL–MS–DMCL.

DMCL. Bombardier Derby 2003–05. 9/43 1TD 2W. 46.8 t.
MS. Bombardier Derby 2003–05. –/76. 43.7 t.
DMCL. Bombardier Derby 2003–05. 9/49 1T. 46.5 t.

170 425	**SR**	P	*SR*	HA	50425	56425	79425
170 426	**SR**	P	*SR*	HA	50426	56426	79426
170 427	**SR**	P	*SR*	HA	50427	56427	79427
170 428	**SR**	P	*SR*	HA	50428	56428	79428
170 429	**SR**	P	*SR*	HA	50429	56429	79429
170 430	**SR**	P	*SR*	HA	50430	56430	79430
170 431	**SR**	P	*SR*	HA	50431	56431	79431
170 432	**SR**	P	*SR*	HA	50432	56432	79432
170 433	**SR**	P	*SR*	HA	50433	56433	79433
170 434	**SR**	P	*SR*	HA	50434	56434	79434

Class 170/4. ScotRail units. Originally built as Standard Class only units. 170 450–457 have been retro-fitted with First Class. Chapman seating. DMSL–MS–DMSL or † DMCL–MS–DMCL.

DMSL. Bombardier Derby 2004–05. –/55 1TD 2W († 9/47 1TD 2W). 46.3 t.
MS. Bombardier Derby 2004–05. –/76. 43.4 t.
DMSL. Bombardier Derby 2004–05. –/67 1T († 9/49 1T 1W). 46.4 t.

170 450	†	**SR**	P	*SR*	HA	50450	56450	79450
170 451	†	**SR**	P	*SR*	HA	50451	56451	79451
170 452	†	**SR**	P	*SR*	HA	50452	56452	79452
170 453	†	**SR**	P	*SR*	HA	50453	56453	79453
170 454	†	**SR**	P	*SR*	HA	50454	56454	79454
170 455	†	**SR**	P	*SR*	HA	50455	56455	79455
170 456	†	**SR**	P	*SR*	HA	50456	56456	79456
170 457	†	**SR**	P	*SR*	HA	50457	56457	79457
170 458		**SR**	P	*SR*	HA	50458	56458	79458
170 459		**SR**	P	*SR*	HA	50459	56459	79459
170 460		**SR**	P	*SR*	HA	50460	56460	79460
170 461		**SR**	P	*SR*	HA	50461	56461	79461

Class 170/4. ScotRail units. Standard Class only units. Chapman seating. DMSL–MS–DMSL.

50470–471. DMSL(A). Adtranz Derby 2001. –/55 1TD 2W. 45.1 t.
50472–478. DMSL(A). Bombardier Derby 2004–05. –/57 1TD 2W. 46.3 t.
56470–471. MS. Adtranz Derby 2001. –/76. 42.4 t.
56472–478. MS. Bombardier Derby 2004–05. –/76. 43.4 t.
79470–471. DMSL(B). Adtranz Derby 2001. –/67 1T. 45.1 t.
79472–478. DMSL(B). Bombardier Derby 2004–05. –/67 1T. 46.4 t.

170 470	**SR**	P	*SR*	HA	50470	56470	79470
170 471	**SR**	P	*SR*	HA	50471	56471	79471
170 472	**SR**	P	*SR*	HA	50472	56472	79472
170 473	**SR**	P	*SR*	HA	50473	56473	79473
170 474	**SR**	P	*SR*	HA	50474	56474	79474
170 475	**SR**	P	*SR*	HA	50475	56475	79475
170 476	**SR**	P	*SR*	HA	50476	56476	79476
170 477	**SR**	P	*SR*	HA	50477	56477	79477
170 478	**SR**	P	*SR*	HA	50478	56478	79478

Class 170/5. London Midland and CrossCountry 2-car units. Lazareni seating. DMSL–DMSL or * DMSL–DMCL (CrossCountry).

DMSL(A). Adtranz Derby 1999–2000. –/55 1TD 2W (* –/59 1TD 2W). 45.8 t.
DMSL(B). Adtranz Derby 1999–2000. –/67 1T (* DMCL 9/52 1T). 45.9 t.

170 501	**LM**	P	*LM*	TS	50501	79501
170 502	**LM**	P	*LM*	TS	50502	79502
170 503	**LM**	P	*LM*	TS	50503	79503
170 504	**LM**	P	*LM*	TS	50504	79504
170 505	**LM**	P	*LM*	TS	50505	79505
170 506	**LM**	P	*LM*	TS	50506	79506
170 507	**LM**	P	*LM*	TS	50507	79507
170 508	**LM**	P	*LM*	TS	50508	79508
170 509	**LM**	P	*LM*	TS	50509	79509
170 510	**LM**	P	*LM*	TS	50510	79510
170 511	**LM**	P	*LM*	TS	50511	79511
170 512	**LM**	P	*LM*	TS	50512	79512
170 513	**LM**	P	*LM*	TS	50513	79513
170 514	**LM**	P	*LM*	TS	50514	79514
170 515	**LM**	P	*LM*	TS	50515	79515

170 516		**LM**	P	*LM*	TS	50516		79516
170 517		**LM**	P	*LM*	TS	50517		79517
170 518	*	**XC**	P	*XC*	TS	50518		79518
170 519	*	**XC**	P	*XC*	TS	50519		79519
170 520	*	**XC**	P	*XC*	TS	50520		79520
170 521	*	**XC**	P	*XC*	TS	50521		79521
170 522	*	**XC**	P	*XC*	TS	50522		79522
170 523	*	**XC**	P	*XC*	TS	50523		79523

Class 170/6. London Midland and CrossCountry 3-car units. Lazareni seating. DMSL–MS–DMSL or * DMSL–MS–DMCL (CrossCountry).

DMSL(A). Adtranz Derby 2000. –/55 1TD 2W (* –/59 1TD 2W). 45.8 t.
MS. Adtranz Derby 2000. –/74 (* –/80). 42.4 t.
DMSL(B). Adtranz Derby 2000. –/67 1T (* DMCL 9/52 1T). 45.9 t.

170 630		**LM**	P	*LM*	TS	50630	56630	79630
170 631		**LM**	P	*LM*	TS	50631	56631	79631
170 632		**LM**	P	*LM*	TS	50632	56632	79632
170 633		**LM**	P	*LM*	TS	50633	56633	79633
170 634		**LM**	P	*LM*	TS	50634	56634	79634
170 635		**LM**	P	*LM*	TS	50635	56635	79635
170 636	*	**XC**	P	*XC*	TS	50636	56636	79636
170 637	*	**XC**	P	*XC*	TS	50637	56637	79637
170 638	*	**XC**	P	*XC*	TS	50638	56638	79638
170 639	*	**XC**	P	*XC*	TS	50639	56639	79639

CLASS 171   TURBOSTAR   BOMBARDIER

DMCL–DMSL or DMCL–MS–MS–DMCL. Southern units. Air conditioned. Chapman seating.

Construction: Welded aluminium bodies with bolt-on steel ends.
Engines: One MTU 6R183TD13H of 315 kW (422 hp) at 1900 rpm.
Transmission: Hydraulic. Voith T211rzze to ZF final drive.
Bogies: One Adtranz P3–23 and one BREL T3–23 per car.
Couplers: Dellner 12 at outer ends, bar within unit (Class 171/8s).
Dimensions: 23.62/23.61 x 2.69 m.
Gangways: Within unit only.   **Wheel Arrangement:** 2-B (+ B-2 + B-2) + B-2.
Doors: Twin-leaf swing plug.   **Maximum Speed:** 100 mph.
Seating Layout: 1: 2+1 facing/unidirectional. 2: 2+2 facing/unidirectional.
Multiple Working: Within class and with EMU Classes 375 and 377 in an emergency.

Class 171/7. 2-car units. DMCL–DMSL.

171 721–726 were built as Class 170s (170 721–726), but renumbered as Class 171s on fitting with Dellner couplers.

171 730 was formerly South West Trains unit 170 392, before transferring to Southern in 2007.

50721–726. DMCL. Bombardier Derby 2003. 9/43 1TD 2W. 47.6 t.
50727–729. DMCL. Bombardier Derby 2005. 9/43 1TD 2W. 46.3 t.
50392. DMCL. Bombardier Derby 2003. 9/43 1TD 2W. 46.6 t.
79721–726. DMSL. Bombardier Derby 2003. –/64 1T. 47.8 t.
79727–729. DMSL. Bombardier Derby 2005. –/64 1T. 46.2 t.
79392. DMSL. Bombardier Derby 2003. –/64 1T. 46.5 t.

171 721	**SN**	P	*SN*	SU	50721	79721
171 722	**SN**	P	*SN*	SU	50722	79722
171 723	**SN**	P	*SN*	SU	50723	79723
171 724	**SN**	P	*SN*	SU	50724	79724
171 725	**SN**	P	*SN*	SU	50725	79725
171 726	**SN**	P	*SN*	SU	50726	79726
171 727	**SN**	P	*SN*	SU	50727	79727
171 728	**SN**	P	*SN*	SU	50728	79728
171 729	**SN**	P	*SN*	SU	50729	79729
171 730	**SN**	P	*SN*	SU	50392	79392

Class 171/8. 4-car units. DMCL(A)–MS–MS–DMCL(B).

DMCL(A). Bombardier Derby 2004. 9/43 1TD 2W. 46.5 t.
MS. Bombardier Derby 2004. –/74. 43.7 t.
DMCL(B). Bombardier Derby 2004. 9/50 1T. 46.5 t.

171 801	**SN**	P	*SN*	SU	50801	54801	56801	79801
171 802	**SN**	P	*SN*	SU	50802	54802	56802	79802
171 803	**SN**	P	*SN*	SU	50803	54803	56803	79803
171 804	**SN**	P	*SN*	SU	50804	54804	56804	79804
171 805	**SN**	P	*SN*	SU	50805	54805	56805	79805
171 806	**SN**	P	*SN*	SU	50806	54806	56806	79806

CLASS 172   TURBOSTAR   BOMBARDIER

New generation London Overground, Chiltern Railways and London Midland Turbostars. Air conditioned.

Construction: Welded aluminium bodies with bolt-on steel ends.
Engines: One MTU 6H1800R83 of 360 kW (483 hp) at 1800 rpm.
Transmission: Mechanical. Supplied by ZF, Germany.
Bogies: B5006 type "lightweight" bogies.
Couplers: BSI at outer ends, bar within unit.
Dimensions: 23.62/23.0 x 2.69 m.
Gangways: London Overground & Chiltern units: Within unit only. London Midland units: Throughout.
Wheel Arrangement: 2-B (+ B-2) + B-2.
Doors: Twin-leaf sliding plug.
Maximum Speed: 100 mph (London Overground units 75 mph).
Seating Layout: 2+2 facing/unidirectional.
Multiple Working: Within class and with Classes 150, 153, 155, 156, 158, 159, 165, 166 and 170.

Class 172/0. London Overground units. Used on the Gospel Oak–Barking line. DMS–DMS.

59311–318. DMS(W). Bombardier Derby 2009–10. –/60 2W. 41.6 t.
59411–418. DMS. Bombardier Derby 2009–10. –/64. 41.5 t.

172 001	**LO**	A	*LO*	WN	59311	59411
172 002	**LO**	A	*LO*	WN	59312	59412
172 003	**LO**	A	*LO*	WN	59313	59413
172 004	**LO**	A	*LO*	WN	59314	59414
172 005	**LO**	A	*LO*	WN	59315	59415
172 006	**LO**	A	*LO*	WN	59316	59416
172 007	**LO**	A	*LO*	WN	59317	59417
172 008	**LO**	A	*LO*	WN	59318	59418

Class 172/1. Chiltern Railways units. DMSL–DMS.

59111–114. DMSL. Bombardier Derby 2009–10. –/60(5) 1TD 2W. 42.4 t.
59211–214. DMS. Bombardier Derby 2009–10. –/80. 41.8 t.

172 101	**CR**	A	*CR*	AL	59111	59211
172 102	**CR**	A	*CR*	AL	59112	59212
172 103	**CR**	A	*CR*	AL	59113	59213
172 104	**CR**	A	*CR*	AL	59114	59214

Class 172/2. London Midland 2-car units. DMSL–DMS. Used on local services via Birmingham Snow Hill.

50211–222. DMSL. Bombardier Derby 2010–11. –/52(11) 1TD 2W. 42.5 t.
79211–222. DMS. Bombardier Derby 2010–11. –/68(8). 41.9 t.

172 211	**LM**	P	*LM*	TS	50211	79211
172 212	**LM**	P	*LM*	TS	50212	79212
172 213	**LM**	P	*LM*	TS	50213	79213
172 214	**LM**	P	*LM*	TS	50214	79214
172 215	**LM**	P	*LM*	TS	50215	79215
172 216	**LM**	P	*LM*	TS	50216	79216
172 217	**LM**	P	*LM*	TS	50217	79217
172 218	**LM**	P	*LM*	TS	50218	79218
172 219	**LM**	P	*LM*	TS	50219	79219
172 220	**LM**	P	*LM*	TS	50220	79220
172 221	**LM**	P	*LM*	TS	50221	79221
172 222	**LM**	P	*LM*	TS	50222	79222

Class 172/3. London Midland 3-car units. DMSL–MS–DMS. Used on local services via Birmingham Snow Hill.

50331–345. DMSL. Bombardier Derby 2010–11. –/52(11) 1TD 2W. 42.5 t.
56331–345. MS. Bombardier Derby 2010–11. –/72(8). 38.8 t.
79331–345. DMS. Bombardier Derby 2010–11. –/68(8). 41.9 t.

172 331	**LM**	P	*LM*	TS	50331	56331	79331
172 332	**LM**	P	*LM*	TS	50332	56332	79332
172 333	**LM**	P	*LM*	TS	50333	56333	79333
172 334	**LM**	P	*LM*	TS	50334	56334	79334
172 335	**LM**	P	*LM*	TS	50335	56335	79335
172 336	**LM**	P	*LM*	TS	50336	56336	79336
172 337	**LM**	P	*LM*	TS	50337	56337	79337
172 338	**LM**	P	*LM*	TS	50338	56338	79338

172 339	**LM**	P	*LM*	TS	50339	56339	79339
172 340	**LM**	P	*LM*	TS	50340	56340	79340
172 341	**LM**	P	*LM*	TS	50341	56341	79341
172 342	**LM**	P	*LM*	TS	50342	56342	79342
172 343	**LM**	P	*LM*	TS	50343	56343	79343
172 344	**LM**	P	*LM*	TS	50344	56344	79344
172 345	**LM**	P	*LM*	TS	50345	56345	79345

CLASS 175   CORADIA 1000   ALSTOM

Air conditioned.

Construction: Steel.
Engines: One Cummins N14 of 335 kW (450 hp).
Transmission: Hydraulic. Voith T211rzze to ZF Voith final drive.
Bogies: ACR (Alstom FBO) – LTB-MBS1, TB-MB1, MBS1-LTB.
Couplers: Scharfenberg outer ends and bar within unit (Class 175/1).
Dimensions: 23.7 x 2.73 m.
Gangways: Within unit only.   **Wheel Arrangement:** 2-B (+ B-2) + B-2.
Doors: Single-leaf swing plug.   **Maximum Speed:** 100 mph.
Seating Layout: 2+2 facing/unidirectional.
Multiple Working: Within class and with Class 180.

Class 175/0. DMSL–DMSL. 2-car units.

DMSL(A). Alstom Birmingham 1999–2000. –/54 1TD 2W. 48.8 t.
DMSL(B). Alstom Birmingham 1999–2000. –/64 1T. 50.7 t.

175 001	**AV**	A	*AW*	CH	50701	79701
175 002	**AV**	A	*AW*	CH	50702	79702
175 003	**AV**	A	*AW*	CH	50703	79703
175 004	**AV**	A	*AW*	CH	50704	79704
175 005	**AV**	A	*AW*	CH	50705	79705
175 006	**AV**	A	*AW*	CH	50706	79706
175 007	**AV**	A	*AW*	CH	50707	79707
175 008	**AV**	A	*AW*	CH	50708	79708
175 009	**AV**	A	*AW*	CH	50709	79709
175 010	**AV**	A	*AW*	CH	50710	79710
175 011	**AV**	A	*AW*	CH	50711	79711

Class 175/1. DMSL–MSL–DMSL. 3-car units.

DMSL(A). Alstom Birmingham 1999–2001. –/54 1TD 2W. 50.7 t.
MSL. Alstom Birmingham 1999–2001. –/68 1T. 47.5 t.
DMSL(B). Alstom Birmingham 1999–2001. –/64 1T. 49.5 t.

175 101	**AV**	A	*AW*	CH	50751	56751	79751
175 102	**AV**	A	*AW*	CH	50752	56752	79752
175 103	**AV**	A	*AW*	CH	50753	56753	79753
175 104	**AV**	A	*AW*	CH	50754	56754	79754
175 105	**AV**	A	*AW*	CH	50755	56755	79755
175 106	**AV**	A	*AW*	CH	50756	56756	79756
175 107	**AV**	A	*AW*	CH	50757	56757	79757
175 108	**AV**	A	*AW*	CH	50758	56758	79758

175 109	**AV**	A	*AW*	CH	50759	56759	79759
175 110	**AV**	A	*AW*	CH	50760	56760	79760
175 111	**AV**	A	*AW*	CH	50761	56761	79761
175 112	**AV**	A	*AW*	CH	50762	56762	79762
175 113	**AV**	A	*AW*	CH	50763	56763	79763
175 114	**AV**	A	*AW*	CH	50764	56764	79764
175 115	**AV**	A	*AW*	CH	50765	56765	79765
175 116	**AV**	A	*AW*	CH	50766	56766	79766

CLASS 180   ADELANTE   ALSTOM

Air conditioned.

Construction: Steel.
Engines: One Cummins QSK19 of 560 kW (750 hp) at 2100 rpm.
Transmission: Hydraulic. Voith T312br to Voith final drive.
Bogies: ACR (Alstom FBO): LTB1-MBS2, TB1-MB2, TB1-MB2, TB2-MB2, MBS2-LTB1.
Couplers: Scharfenberg outer ends, bar within unit.
Dimensions: 23.71/23.03 x 2.73 m.
Gangways: Within unit only.
Wheel Arrangement: 2-B + B-2 + B-2 + B-2 + B-2.
Doors: Single-leaf swing plug.   **Maximum Speed:** 125 mph.
Seating Layout: 1: 2+1 facing/unidirectional, 2: 2+2 facing/unidirectional.
Multiple Working: Within class and with Class 175.

DMSL(A). Alstom Birmingham 2000–01. –/46 2W 1TD. 51.7 t.
MFL. Alstom Birmingham 2000–01. 42/– 1T 1W + catering point. 49.6 t.
MSL. Alstom Birmingham 2000–01. –/68 1T. 49.5 t.
MSLRB. Alstom Birmingham 2000–01. –/56 1T. 50.3 t.
DMSL(B). Alstom Birmingham 2000–01. –/56 1T. 51.4 t.

180 101	**GC**	A	*GC*	HT	50901	54901	55901	56901	59901
180 102	**FD**	A	*GW*	OO	50902	54902	55902	56902	59902
180 103	**FD**	A	*GW*	OO	50903	54903	55903	56903	59903
180 104	**FD**	A	*GW*	OO	50904	54904	55904	56904	59904
180 105	**GC**	A	*GC*	HT	50905	54905	55905	56905	59905
180 106	**FD**	A	*GW*	OO	50906	54906	55906	56906	59906
180 107	**GC**	A	*GC*	HT	50907	54907	55907	56907	59907
180 108	**FD**	A	*GW*	OO	50908	54908	55908	56908	59908
180 109	**FD**	A	*HT*	OO	50909	54909	55909	56909	59909
180 110	**FD**	A	*HT*	OO	50910	54910	55910	56910	59910
180 111	**FD**	A	*HT*	OO	50911	54911	55911	56911	59911
180 112	**GC**	A	*GC*	HT	50912	54912	55912	56912	59912
180 113	**FD**	A	*HT*	OO	50913	54913	55913	56913	59913
180 114	**GC**	A	*GC*	HT	50914	54914	55914	56914	59914

Names (carried on DMSL(A):

180 105	THE YORKSHIRE ARTIST ASHLEY JACKSON
180 107	HART OF THE NORTH
180 112	JAMES HERRIOT

CLASS 185   DESIRO UK   SIEMENS

Air conditioned. Grammer seating.

Construction: Aluminium.
Engines: One Cummins QSK19 of 560 kW (750 hp) at 2100 rpm.
Transmission: Voith.
Bogies: Siemens.
Couplers: Dellner 12.   **Dimensions:** 23.76/23.75 x 2.66 m.
Gangways: Within unit only.   **Wheel Arrangement:** 2-B + 2-B + B-2.
Doors: Double-leaf sliding plug.   **Maximum Speed:** 100 mph.
Seating Layout: 1: 2+1 facing/unidirectional, 2: 2+2 facing/unidirectional.
Multiple Working: Within class only.

DMCL. Siemens Krefeld 2005–06. 15/18(8) 2W 1TD + catering point. 55.4 t.
MSL. Siemens Krefeld 2005–06. –/72 1T. 52.7 t.
DMS. Siemens Krefeld 2005–06. –/64(4). 54.9 t.

185 101	**FT**	E	*TP*	AK	51101	53101	54101
185 102	**FT**	E	*TP*	AK	51102	53102	54102
185 103	**FT**	E	*TP*	AK	51103	53103	54103
185 104	**FT**	E	*TP*	AK	51104	53104	54104
185 105	**FT**	E	*TP*	AK	51105	53105	54105
185 106	**FT**	E	*TP*	AK	51106	53106	54106
185 107	**FT**	E	*TP*	AK	51107	53107	54107
185 108	**FT**	E	*TP*	AK	51108	53108	54108
185 109	**FT**	E	*TP*	AK	51109	53109	54109
185 110	**FT**	E	*TP*	AK	51110	53110	54110
185 111	**FT**	E	*TP*	AK	51111	53111	54111
185 112	**FT**	E	*TP*	AK	51112	53112	54112
185 113	**FT**	E	*TP*	AK	51113	53113	54113
185 114	**FT**	E	*TP*	AK	51114	53114	54114
185 115	**FT**	E	*TP*	AK	51115	53115	54115
185 116	**FT**	E	*TP*	AK	51116	53116	54116
185 117	**FT**	E	*TP*	AK	51117	53117	54117
185 118	**FT**	E	*TP*	AK	51118	53118	54118
185 119	**FT**	E	*TP*	AK	51119	53119	54119
185 120	**FT**	E	*TP*	AK	51120	53120	54120
185 121	**FT**	E	*TP*	AK	51121	53121	54121
185 122	**FT**	E	*TP*	AK	51122	53122	54122
185 123	**FT**	E	*TP*	AK	51123	53123	54123
185 124	**FT**	E	*TP*	AK	51124	53124	54124
185 125	**FT**	E	*TP*	AK	51125	53125	54125
185 126	**FT**	E	*TP*	AK	51126	53126	54126
185 127	**FT**	E	*TP*	AK	51127	53127	54127
185 128	**FT**	E	*TP*	AK	51128	53128	54128
185 129	**FT**	E	*TP*	AK	51129	53129	54129
185 130	**FT**	E	*TP*	AK	51130	53130	54130
185 131	**FT**	E	*TP*	AK	51131	53131	54131
185 132	**FT**	E	*TP*	AK	51132	53132	54132
185 133	**FT**	E	*TP*	AK	51133	53133	54133
185 134	**FT**	E	*TP*	AK	51134	53134	54134

185 135	**FT**	E	*TP*	AK	51135	53135	54135
185 136	**FT**	E	*TP*	AK	51136	53136	54136
185 137	**FT**	E	*TP*	AK	51137	53137	54137
185 138	**FT**	E	*TP*	AK	51138	53138	54138
185 139	**FT**	E	*TP*	AK	51139	53139	54139
185 140	**FT**	E	*TP*	AK	51140	53140	54140
185 141	**FT**	E	*TP*	AK	51141	53141	54141
185 142	**FT**	E	*TP*	AK	51142	53142	54142
185 143	**FT**	E	*TP*	AK	51143	53143	54143
185 144	**FT**	E	*TP*	AK	51144	53144	54144
185 145	**FT**	E	*TP*	AK	51145	53145	54145
185 146	**FT**	E	*TP*	AK	51146	53146	54146
185 147	**FT**	E	*TP*	AK	51147	53147	54147
185 148	**FT**	E	*TP*	AK	51148	53148	54148
185 149	**FT**	E	*TP*	AK	51149	53149	54149
185 150	**FT**	E	*TP*	AK	51150	53150	54150
185 151	**FT**	E	*TP*	AK	51151	53151	54151

3.2. DIESEL ELECTRIC UNITS

CLASS 201/202   PRESERVED "HASTINGS" UNIT   BR

DMBS–TSL–TSL–TSRB–TSL–DMBS.

Preserved unit made up from two Class 201 short-frame cars and three Class 202 long-frame cars. The "Hastings" units were made with narrow body-profiles for use on the section between Tonbridge and Battle which had tunnels of restricted loading gauge. These tunnels were converted to single track operation in the 1980s thus allowing standard loading gauge stock to be used. The set also contains a Class 411 EMU trailer (not Hastings line gauge) and a Class 422 EMU buffet car.

Construction: Steel.
Engine: One English Electric 4SRKT Mk. 2 of 450 kW (600 hp) at 850 rpm.
Main Generator: English Electric EE824.
Traction Motors: Two English Electric EE507 mounted on the inner bogie.
Bogies: SR Mk 4. (Former EMU TSL vehicles have Commonwealth bogies).
Couplers: Drophead buckeye.
Dimensions: 18.40 x 2.50 m (60000), 20.35 x 2.50 m (60116/118/529), 18.36 x 2.50 m (60501), 20.35 x 2.82 (69337), 20.30 x 2.82 (70262).
Gangways: Within unit only.   **Doors:** Manually operated slam.
Brakes: Electro-pneumatic and automatic air.
Maximum Speed: 75 mph.   **Seating Layout:** 2+2 facing.
Multiple Working: Other ex-BR Southern Region DEMU vehicles.

60000. DMBS. Lot No. 30329 Eastleigh 1957. –/22. 55.0 t.
60116. DMBS. Lot No. 30395 Eastleigh 1957. –/31. 56.0 t.
60118. DMBS. Lot No. 30395 Eastleigh 1957. –/30. 56.0 t.
60501. TSL. Lot No. 30331 Eastleigh 1957. –/52 2T. 29.5 t.
60529. TSL. Lot No. 30397 Eastleigh 1957. –/60 2T. 30.5 t.
69337. TSRB (ex-Class 422 EMU). Lot No. 30805 York 1970. –/40. 35.0 t.
70262. TSL (ex-Class 411/5 EMU). Lot No. 30455 Eastleigh 1958. –/64 2T. 31.5 t.

201 001	**G**	HD	*HD*	SE	60116	60529	70262	69337	60501	60118
Spare	**G**	HD	*HD*	SE	60000					

Names:

60000	Hastings
60116	Mountfield
60118	Tunbridge Wells

CLASS 220   VOYAGER   BOMBARDIER

DMS–MS–MS–DMF. All engines have been derated from 750 hp to 700 hp.

Construction: Steel.
Engine: Cummins QSK19 of 520 kW (700 hp) at 1800 rpm.
Transmission: Two Alstom Onix 800 three-phase traction motors of 275 kW.
Braking: Rheostatic and electro-pneumatic.

Bogies: Bombardier B5005.
Couplers: Dellner 12 at outer ends, bar within unit.
Dimensions: 23.85/23.00 (602xx) x 2.73 m.
Gangways: Within unit only.
Wheel Arrangement: 1A-A1 + 1A-A1 + 1A-A1 + 1A-A1.
Doors: Single-leaf swing plug.
Maximum Speed: 125 m.p.h.
Seating Layout: 1: 2+1 facing/unidirectional, 2: 2+2 mainly unidirectional.
Multiple Working: Within class and with Classes 221 and 222 (in an emergency). Also can be controlled from Class 57/3 locomotives.

DMS. Bombardier Bruges/Wakefield 2000–01. –/42 1TD 1W. 51.1 t.
MS(A). Bombardier Bruges/Wakefield 2000–01. –/66. 45.9 t.
MS(B). Bombardier Bruges/Wakefield 2000–01. –/66 1TD. 46.7 t.
DMF. Bombardier Bruges/Wakefield 2000–01. 26/– 1TD 1W. 50.9 t.

220 001	**XC**	VL	*XC*	CZ	60301	60701	60201	60401
220 002	**XC**	VL	*XC*	CZ	60302	60702	60202	60402
220 003	**XC**	VL	*XC*	CZ	60303	60703	60203	60403
220 004	**XC**	VL	*XC*	CZ	60304	60704	60204	60404
220 005	**XC**	VL	*XC*	CZ	60305	60705	60205	60405
220 006	**XC**	VL	*XC*	CZ	60306	60706	60206	60406
220 007	**XC**	VL	*XC*	CZ	60307	60707	60207	60407
220 008	**XC**	VL	*XC*	CZ	60308	60708	60208	60408
220 009	**XC**	VL	*XC*	CZ	60309	60709	60209	60409
220 010	**XC**	VL	*XC*	CZ	60310	60710	60210	60410
220 011	**XC**	VL	*XC*	CZ	60311	60711	60211	60411
220 012	**XC**	VL	*XC*	CZ	60312	60712	60212	60412
220 013	**XC**	VL	*XC*	CZ	60313	60713	60213	60413
220 014	**XC**	VL	*XC*	CZ	60314	60714	60214	60414
220 015	**XC**	VL	*XC*	CZ	60315	60715	60215	60415
220 016	**XC**	VL	*XC*	CZ	60316	60716	60216	60416
220 017	**XC**	VL	*XC*	CZ	60317	60717	60217	60417
220 018	**XC**	VL	*XC*	CZ	60318	60718	60218	60418
220 019	**XC**	VL	*XC*	CZ	60319	60719	60219	60419
220 020	**XC**	VL	*XC*	CZ	60320	60720	60220	60420
220 021	**XC**	VL	*XC*	CZ	60321	60721	60221	60421
220 022	**XC**	VL	*XC*	CZ	60322	60722	60222	60422
220 023	**XC**	VL	*XC*	CZ	60323	60723	60223	60423
220 024	**XC**	VL	*XC*	CZ	60324	60724	60224	60424
220 025	**XC**	VL	*XC*	CZ	60325	60725	60225	60425
220 026	**XC**	VL	*XC*	CZ	60326	60726	60226	60426
220 027	**XC**	VL	*XC*	CZ	60327	60727	60227	60427
220 028	**XC**	VL	*XC*	CZ	60328	60728	60228	60428
220 029	**XC**	VL	*XC*	CZ	60329	60729	60229	60429
220 030	**XC**	VL	*XC*	CZ	60330	60730	60230	60430
220 031	**XC**	VL	*XC*	CZ	60331	60731	60231	60431
220 032	**XC**	VL	*XC*	CZ	60332	60732	60232	60432
220 033	**XC**	VL	*XC*	CZ	60333	60733	60233	60433
220 034	**XC**	VL	*XC*	CZ	60334	60734	60234	60434

CLASS 221   SUPER VOYAGER   BOMBARDIER

* DMS–MS–MS–MSRMB–DMF (Virgin Trains units) or DMS–MS–MS–
MS–DMF (CrossCountry units). Built as tilting units but tilt now isolated on
CrossCountry sets. All engines have been derated from 750 hp to 700 hp.

Construction: Steel.
Engine: Cummins QSK19 of 520 kW (700 hp) at 1800 rpm.
Transmission: Two Alstom Onix 800 three-phase traction motors of 275 kW.
Braking: Rheostatic and electro-pneumatic.
Bogies: Bombardier HVP.
Couplers: Dellner 12 at outer ends, bar within unit.
Dimensions: 23.67 x 2.73 m.
Gangways: Within unit only.
Wheel Arrangement: 1A-A1 + 1A-A1 + 1A-A1 (+ 1A-A1) + 1A-A1.
Doors: Single-leaf swing plug.
Maximum Speed: 125 mph.
Seating Layout: 1: 2+1 facing/unidirectional, 2: 2+2 mainly unidirectional.
Multiple Working: Within class and with Classes 220 and 222 (in an
emergency). Also can be controlled from Class 57/3 locomotives.

* Virgin Trains units. MSRMB moved adjacent to the DMF. The seating in
this vehicle (2+2 facing) can be used by First or Standard Class passengers
depending on demand.

Advertising livery: 221 115 Dark grey Bombardier branding on end vehicles.

DMS. Bombardier Bruges/Wakefield 2001–02. –/42 1TD 1W. 58.5 t (* 58.9 t.)
60751–794 MS (* MSRMB). Bombardier Bruges/Wakefield 2001–02. –/66
(* –/52). 54.1 t (* 55.9 t.)
60951–994. MS. Bombardier Bruges/Wakefield 2001–02. –/66 1TD (* –/68
1TD). 54.8 t (* 54.3 t.)
60851–890. MS. Bombardier Bruges/Wakefield 2001–02. –/62 1TD (* –/68
1TD). 54.4 t (* 55.0 t.)
DMF. Bombardier Bruges/Wakefield 2001–02. 26/– 1TD 1W. 58.9 t (* 59.1 t.)

221 101	*	**VT**	VL	*VW*	CZ	60351	60951	60851	60751	60451
221 102	*	**VT**	VL	*VW*	CZ	60352	60952	60852	60752	60452
221 103	*	**VT**	VL	*VW*	CZ	60353	60953	60853	60753	60453
221 104	*	**VT**	VL	*VW*	CZ	60354	60954	60854	60754	60454
221 105	*	**VT**	VL	*VW*	CZ	60355	60955	60855	60755	60455
221 106	*	**VT**	VL	*VW*	CZ	60356	60956	60856	60756	60456
221 107	*	**VT**	VL	*VW*	CZ	60357	60957	60857	60757	60457
221 108	*	**VT**	VL	*VW*	CZ	60358	60958	60858	60758	60458
221 109	*	**VT**	VL	*VW*	CZ	60359	60959	60859	60759	60459
221 110	*	**VT**	VL	*VW*	CZ	60360	60960	60860	60760	60460
221 111	*	**VT**	VL	*VW*	CZ	60361	60961	60861	60761	60461
221 112	*	**VT**	VL	*VW*	CZ	60362	60962	60862	60762	60462
221 113	*	**VT**	VL	*VW*	CZ	60363	60963	60863	60763	60463
221 114	*	**VT**	VL	*VW*	CZ	60364	60764	60964	60864	60464
221 115	*	**AL**	VL	*VW*	CZ	60365	60765	60965	60865	60465
221 116	*	**VT**	VL	*VW*	CZ	60366	60766	60966	60866	60466
221 117	*	**VT**	VL	*VW*	CZ	60367	60767	60967	60867	60467

221 118	*	**VT**	VL	*VW*	CZ	60368	60768	60968	60868	60468
221 119		**XC**	VL	*XC*	CZ	60369	60769	60969	60869	60469
221 120		**XC**	VL	*XC*	CZ	60370	60770	60970	60870	60470
221 121		**XC**	VL	*XC*	CZ	60371	60771	60971	60871	60471
221 122		**XC**	VL	*XC*	CZ	60372	60772	60972	60872	60472
221 123		**XC**	VL	*XC*	CZ	60373	60773	60973	60873	60473
221 124		**XC**	VL	*XC*	CZ	60374	60774	60974	60874	60474
221 125		**XC**	VL	*XC*	CZ	60375	60775	60975	60875	60475
221 126		**XC**	VL	*XC*	CZ	60376	60776	60976	60876	60476
221 127		**XC**	VL	*XC*	CZ	60377	60777	60977	60877	60477
221 128		**XC**	VL	*XC*	CZ	60378	60778	60978	60878	60478
221 129		**XC**	VL	*XC*	CZ	60379	60779	60979	60879	60479
221 130		**XC**	VL	*XC*	CZ	60380	60780	60980	60880	60480
221 131		**XC**	VL	*XC*	CZ	60381	60781	60981	60881	60481
221 132		**XC**	VL	*XC*	CZ	60382	60782	60982	60882	60482
221 133		**XC**	VL	*XC*	CZ	60383	60783	60983	60883	60483
221 134		**XC**	VL	*XC*	CZ	60384	60784	60984	60884	60484
221 135		**XC**	VL	*XC*	CZ	60385	60785	60985	60885	60485
221 136		**XC**	VL	*XC*	CZ	60386	60786	60986	60886	60486
221 137		**XC**	VL	*XC*	CZ	60387	60787	60987	60887	60487
221 138		**XC**	VL	*XC*	CZ	60388	60788	60988	60888	60488
221 139		**XC**	VL	*XC*	CZ	60389	60789	60989	60889	60489
221 140		**XC**	VL	*XC*	CZ	60390	60790	60990	60890	60490
221 141		**XC**	VL	*XC*	CZ	60391	60791	60991		60491
221 142	*	**VT**	VL	*VW*	CZ	60392	60992	60994	60792	60492
221 143	*	**VT**	VL	*VW*	CZ	60393	60993	60794	60793	60493
Spare	*	**VT**	VL		CZ	60394				60494

Names (carried on MS No. 609xx):

221 101	Louis Bleriot	221 110	James Cook
221 102	John Cabot	221 111	Roald Amundsen
221 103	Christopher Columbus	221 112	Ferdinand Magellan
221 104	Sir John Franklin	221 113	Sir Walter Raleigh
221 105	William Baffin	221 115	Polmadie Depot
221 106	Willem Barents	221 117	The Wrekin Giant
221 107	Sir Martin Frobisher	221 142	BOMBARDIER Voyager
221 108	Sir Ernest Shackleton	221 143	Auguste Picard
221 109	Marco Polo		

CLASS 222   MERIDIAN   BOMBARDIER

Construction: Steel.
Engine: Cummins QSK19 of 560 kW (750 hp) at 1800 rpm.
Transmission: Two Alstom Onix 800 three-phase traction motors of 275 kW.
Braking: Rheostatic and electro-pneumatic.
Bogies: Bombardier B5005. **Dimensions:** 23.85/23.00 x 2.73 m.
Couplers: Dellner at outer ends, bar within unit.
Gangways: Within unit only. **Wheel Arrangement:** All cars 1A-A1.
Doors: Single-leaf swing plug. **Maximum Speed:** 125 mph.
Seating Layout: 1: 2+1, 2: 2+2 facing/unidirectional.
Multiple Working: Within class and with Classes 220 and 221 (in an emergency).

222 001–006. 7-car units. DMF–MF–MF–MSRMB–MS–MS–DMS.

The 7-car units were built as 9-car units, before being reduced to 8-car sets and then later to 7-car sets to strengthen all 4-car units to 5-cars. 222 007 was built as a 9-car unit but later reduced to a 5-car unit.

DMRF. Bombardier Bruges 2004–05. 22/– 1TD 1W. 52.8 t.
MF. Bombardier Bruges 2004–05. 42/– 1T. 46.8 t.
MSRMB. Bombardier Bruges 2004–05. –/62. 48.0 t.
MS. Bombardier Bruges 2004–05. –/68 1T. 47.0 t.
DMS. Bombardier Bruges 2004–05. –/38 1TD 1W. 49.4 t.

222 001	**ST**	E	*EM*	DY	60241	60445	60341	60621
					60561	60551	60161	
222 002	**ST**	E	*EM*	DY	60242	60346	60342	60622
					60562	60544	60162	
222 003	**ST**	E	*EM*	DY	60243	60446	60343	60623
					60563	60553	60163	
222 004	**ST**	E	*EM*	DY	60244	60345	60344	60624
					60564	60554	60164	
222 005	**ST**	E	*EM*	DY	60245	60347	60443	60625
					60555	60565	60165	
222 006	**ST**	E	*EM*	DY	60246	60447	60441	60626
					60566	60556	60166	

Names (carried on MSRMB or DMS (222 003)):

222 001   THE ENTREPRENEUR EXPRESS
222 002   THE CUTLERS' COMPANY
222 003   TORNADO
222 004   CHILDREN'S HOSPITAL SHEFFIELD
222 006   THE CARBON CUTTER

222 007–023. 5-car units. DMF–MC–MSRMB–MS–DMS.

DMRF. Bombardier Bruges 2003–04. 22/– 1TD 1W. 52.8 t.
MC. Bombardier Bruges 2003–04. 28/22 1T. 48.6 t.
MSRMB. Bombardier Bruges 2003–04. –/62. 49.6 t.
MS. Bombardier Bruges 2004–05. –/68 1T. 47.0 t.
DMS. Bombardier Bruges 2003–04. –/40 1TD 1W. 51.0 t.

222 007	**ST**	E	*EM*	DY	60247	60442	60627	60567	60167
222 008	**ST**	E	*EM*	DY	60248	60918	60628	60545	60168
222 009	**ST**	E	*EM*	DY	60249	60919	60629	60557	60169
222 010	**ST**	E	*EM*	DY	60250	60920	60630	60546	60170
222 011	**ST**	E	*EM*	DY	60251	60921	60631	60531	60171
222 012	**ST**	E	*EM*	DY	60252	60922	60632	60532	60172
222 013	**ST**	E	*EM*	DY	60253	60923	60633	60533	60173
222 014	**ST**	E	*EM*	DY	60254	60924	60634	60534	60174
222 015	**ST**	E	*EM*	DY	60255	60925	60635	60535	60175
222 016	**ST**	E	*EM*	DY	60256	60926	60636	60536	60176
222 017	**ST**	E	*EM*	DY	60257	60927	60637	60537	60177
222 018	**ST**	E	*EM*	DY	60258	60928	60638	60444	60178
222 019	**ST**	E	*EM*	DY	60259	60929	60639	60547	60179
222 020	**ST**	E	*EM*	DY	60260	60930	60640	60543	60180

222 021	**ST**	E	*EM*	DY	60261	60931	60641	60552	60181
222 022	**ST**	E	*EM*	DY	60262	60932	60642	60542	60182
222 023	**ST**	E	*EM*	DY	60263	60933	60643	60541	60183

Names (carried on MSRMB or DMS):

222 008 Derby Etches Park
222 011 Sheffield City Battalion 1914–1918
222 015 175 YEARS OF DERBY'S RAILWAYS 1839–2014
222 022 INVEST IN NOTTINGHAM

222 101–104. 4-car former Hull Trains units. DMF–MC–MSRMB–DMS.

DMRF. Bombardier Bruges 2005. 22/– 1TD 1W. 52.8 t.
MC. Bombardier Bruges 2005. 11/46 1T. 47.1 t.
MSRMB. Bombardier Bruges 2005. –/62. 48.0 t.
DMS. Bombardier Bruges 2005. –/40 1TD 1W. 49.4 t.

222 101	**ST**	E	*EM*	DY	60271	60571	60681	60191
222 102	**ST**	E	*EM*	DY	60272	60572	60682	60192
222 103	**ST**	E	*EM*	DY	60273	60573	60683	60193
222 104	**ST**	E	*EM*	DY	60274	60574	60684	60194

3.3. SERVICE DMUS

This section lists vehicles not used for passenger-carrying purposes. Vehicles are numbered in the special service stock number series.

CLASS 950   TRACK ASSESSMENT UNIT

DM–DM. Purpose built service unit based on the Class 150/1 design. Gangwayed within unit.

Construction: Steel.
Engine: One Cummins NT-855-RT5 of 213 kW (285 hp) at 2100 rpm per power car.
Transmission: Hydraulic. Voith T211r with cardan shafts to Gmeinder GM190 final drive.
Maximum Speed: 75 mph.   **Couplers:** BSI automatic.
Bogies: BP38 (powered), BT38 (non-powered).
Brakes: Electro-pneumatic.   **Dimensions:** 20.06 x 2.82 m.
Doors: Manually operated slam & power operated sliding.
Multiple Working: Classes 142, 143, 144, 150, 153, 155, 156, 158, 159 and 170.

999600. DM. Lot No. 4060 BREL York 1987. 35.0 t.
999601. DM. Lot No. 4061 BREL York 1987. 35.0 t.

| 950 001 | **Y** | NR | *DB* | ZA | 999600 999601 |

CLASS 960   ROUTE LEARNING UNIT

DMB. Converted from Class 121. Non-gangwayed.

For details see Page 187.

This unit is available for hire to other operators for route learning if required.

Lot No. 30518 Pressed Steel 1960. 38.0 t.

960 014   **BG** CR *CR*   AL   977873 (55022)

CLASS 960   WATER-JETTING UNIT

DMB–MS–DMB. Converted 2003–04 from Class 117. Non-gangwayed.

Construction: Steel.
Engines: Two Leyland 1595 of 112 kW (150 hp) at 1800 rpm.
Transmission: Mechanical. Cardan shaft and freewheel to a four-speed epicyclic gearbox with a further cardan shaft to the final drive, each engine driving the inner axle of one bogie.
Maximum Speed: 70 mph.
Bogies: DD10.   **Couplers:** Screw.
Brakes: Twin pipe vacuum.   **Multiple Working:** Blue Square.
Doors: Manually operated slam.   **Dimensions:** 20.45 x 2.84 m.

977987/988. DMB. Lot No. 30546/30548 Pressed Steel 1959–60. 36.5 t.
977992. MS. Lot No. 30548 Pressed Steel 1959–60. 36.5 t.

960 301   **G**   CR *CR*   AL   977987 (51371) 977992 (51375)
                                          977988 (51413)

3.4. DMUS AWAITING DISPOSAL

The list below comprises vehicles which are stored awaiting disposal.

Class 121

121 032   **AV** CR AL   55032

Class 960

Converted from Class 121.

960 011   **RK** CR TM   977859   (55025)

4. ELECTRIC MULTIPLE UNITS

INTRODUCTION

This section contains details of all Electric Multiple Units, usually referred to as EMUs, which can run on Britain's national railway network.

The number of EMUs in operation has been steadily increasing in recent years as both more lines have been opened or electrified and as the number of passengers travelling on the network has increased. EMUs work a wide variety of services, from long distance Intercity (such as the Class 390 Pendolinos) to inter-urban and suburban duties.

LAYOUT OF INFORMATION

25 kV AC 50 Hz overhead EMUs and dual voltage EMUs are listed in numerical order of set numbers. Individual "loose" vehicles are listed in numerical order after vehicles formed into fixed formations.

750 V DC third rail EMUs are listed in numerical order of class number, then in numerical order of set number. Some of these use the former Southern Region four-digit set numbers. These are derived from theoretical six digit set numbers which are the four-digit set number prefixed by the first two numbers of the class.

Where sets or vehicles have been renumbered in recent years, former numbering detail is shown alongside current detail. Each entry is laid out as in the following example:

Set No.	Detail	Livery	Owner	Operator	Allocation	Formation
315803	†	**GA**	E	*GA*	IL	64465 71283 71391 64466

Codes: Codes are used to denote the livery, owner, operator and depot allocation of each Electric Multiple Unit. Details of these can be found in section 7 of this book. Where a unit or spare car is off-lease, the operator column is left blank.

Detail Differences: Detail differences which currently affect the areas and types of train which vehicles may work are shown, plus differences in interior layout. Where such differences occur within a class, these are shown either in the heading information or alongside the individual set or vehicle number.

Set Formations: Regular set formations are shown where these are normally maintained. Readers should note set formations might be temporarily varied from time to time to suit maintenance and/or operational requirements. Vehicles shown as "Spare" are not formed in any regular set formation.

Names: Only names carried with official sanction are listed. Names are shown in UPPER/lower case characters as actually shown on the name carried on the vehicle(s). Unless otherwise shown, complete units are regarded as named rather than just the individual car(s) which carry the name.

GENERAL INFORMATION

CLASSIFICATION AND NUMBERING

25 kV AC 50 Hz overhead and "Versatile" EMUs are classified in the series 300–399.

750 V DC third rail EMUs are classified in the series 400–599.

Service units are classified in the series 900–949.

Until 2014 EMU individual cars were numbered in the series 61000–78999, except for vehicles used on the Isle of Wight – which are numbered in a separate series, and the Class 378s, 380s and 395s, which took up the 38xxx and 39xxx series'.

For all new vehicles delivered from 2014 6-digit vehicle numbers are being used. So far this applies to Classes 387 and 700.

Any vehicle constructed or converted to replace another vehicle following accident damage and carrying the same number as the original vehicle is denoted by the suffix[II] in this publication.

UNITS OF MEASUREMENT

Principal details and dimensions are quoted for each class in metric and/or imperial units as considered appropriate bearing in mind common usage in the UK.

All dimensions and weights are quoted for vehicles in an "as new" condition with all necessary supplies (eg oil, water, sand) on board. Dimensions are quoted in the order Length – Width. All lengths quoted are over buffers or couplers as appropriate. Where two lengths are quoted, the first refers to outer vehicles in a set and the second to inner vehicles. All width dimensions quoted are maxima. All weights are shown as metric tonnes (t = tonnes).

Bogie Types are quoted in the format motored/non-motored (eg BP20/BT13 denotes BP20 motored bogies and BT non-motored bogies).

Unless noted to the contrary, all vehicles listed have bar couplers at non-driving ends.

OPERATING CODES

These codes are used by train operating company staff to describe the various different types of vehicles and normally appear on data panels on the inner (ie non driving) ends of vehicles.

A "B" prefix indicates a battery vehicle.
A "P" prefix indicates a trailer vehicle on which is mounted the pantograph, instead of the default case where the pantograph is mounted on a motor vehicle.

The first part of the code describes whether or not the car has a motor or a driving cab as follows:

DM Driving motor	M Motor	T Trailer
DT Driving trailer		

The next letter is a "B" for cars with a brake compartment.
This is followed by the saloon details:

F First	S Standard	C Composite

The next letter denotes the style of accommodation, which is "O" for Open for all EMU vehicles still in service.

Finally vehicles with a buffet or kitchen area are suffixed RB or RMB for a miniature buffet counter.

Where two vehicles of the same type are formed within the same unit, the above codes may be suffixed by (A) and (B) to differentiate between vehicles.

A composite is a vehicle containing both First and Standard Class accommodation, whilst a brake vehicle is a vehicle containing separate specific accommodation for the conductor.

BUILD DETAILS

Lot Numbers: Vehicles ordered under the auspices of BR were allocated a Lot (batch) number when ordered and these are quoted in class headings and sub-headings. Vehicles ordered since 1995 have no Lot Numbers, but the manufacturer and location that they were built is given.

Builders: These are shown for each lot. More details and a full list of builders can be found in section 7.7.

ACCOMMODATION

The information given in class headings and sub-headings is in the form F/S nT (or TD) nW. For example 12/54 1T 1W denotes 12 First Class and 54 Standard Class seats, one toilet and one space for a wheelchair. A number in brackets (ie (2)) denotes tip-up seats (in addition to the fixed seats). Tip-up seats in vestibules do not count. The seating layout of open saloons is shown as 2+1, 2+2 or 3+2 as the case may be. Where units have First Class accommodation as well as Standard Class and the layout is different for each class then these are shown separately prefixed by "1:" and "2:". TD denotes a toilet suitable for use by a disabled person.

CLASSES 800 AND 801

As this book closed for press the number series for the new Hitachi Class 800 and 801 InterCity Express Project (IEP) trains (due for delivery 2015–20) had not yet been confirmed. The following units have been ordered:

Class 800 Bi-mode DMU/EMU	**Class 801 EMU**
800/0: 36 x 5-car for Greater Western	**801/0:** 21 x 9-car for Greater Western
800/1: 13 x 9-car for East Coast	**801/1:** 12 x 5-car for East Coast
800/2: 10 x 5-car for East Coast	**801/2:** 30 x 9-car for East Coast

4.1. 25 kV AC 50 Hz OVERHEAD & DUAL VOLTAGE UNITS

Except where otherwise stated, all units in this section operate on 25 kV AC 50 Hz overhead only.

CLASS 313   BREL YORK

Inner suburban units.

Formation: DMSO–PTSO–BDMSO or DMSO–TSO–BDMSO.
Systems: 25 kV AC overhead/750 V DC third rail.
Construction: Steel underframe, aluminium alloy body and roof.
Traction Motors: Four GEC G310AZ of 82.125 kW.
Wheel Arrangement: Bo-Bo + 2-2 + Bo-Bo.
Braking: Disc & rheostatic.   **Dimensions:** 20.33/20.18 x 2.82 m.
Bogies: BX1.   **Couplers:** Tightlock.
Gangways: Within unit + end doors.   **Control System:** Camshaft.
Doors: Sliding.   **Maximum Speed:** 75 mph.
Seating Layout: Various, see sub-class headings.
Multiple Working: Within class.

DMSO. Lot No. 30879 1976–77. –/74. 36.0 t.
PTSO. Lot No. 30880 1976–77. –/83. 31.0 t.
BDMSO. Lot No. 30885 1976–77. –/74. 37.5 t.

Class 313/0. Standard Design. Refurbished with high back seats (3+2 facing).

313018	**FU**	E	*GT*	HE	62546	71230	62610
313024	**FU**	E	*GT*	HE	62552	71236	62616
313025	**FU**	E	*GT*	HE	62553	71237	62617
313026	**FU**	E	*GT*	HE	62554	71238	62618
313027	**FU**	E	*GT*	HE	62555	71239	62619
313028	**FU**	E	*GT*	HE	62556	71240	62620
313029	**FU**	E	*GT*	HE	62557	71241	62621
313030	**FU**	E	*GT*	HE	62558	71242	62622
313031	**FU**	E	*GT*	HE	62559	71243	62623
313032	**FU**	E	*GT*	HE	62560	71244	62643
313033	**FU**	E	*GT*	HE	62561	71245	62625
313035	**FU**	E	*GT*	HE	62563	71247	62627
313036	**FU**	E	*GT*	HE	62564	71248	62628
313037	**FU**	E	*GT*	HE	62565	71249	62629
313038	**FU**	E	*GT*	HE	62566	71250	62630
313039	**FU**	E	*GT*	HE	62567	71251	62631
313040	**FU**	E	*GT*	HE	62568	71252	62632
313041	**FU**	E	*GT*	HE	62569	71253	62633
313042	**FU**	E	*GT*	HE	62570	71254	62634
313043	**FU**	E	*GT*	HE	62571	71255	62635
313044	**FU**	E	*GT*	HE	62572	71256	62636
313045	**FU**	E	*GT*	HE	62573	71257	62637
313046	**FU**	E	*GT*	HE	62574	71258	62638

313047	**FU**	E	*GT*	HE	62575	71259	62639
313048	**FU**	E	*GT*	HE	62576	71260	62640
313049	**FU**	E	*GT*	HE	62577	71261	62641
313050	**FU**	E	*GT*	HE	62578	71262	62649
313051	**FU**	E	*GT*	HE	62579	71263	62624
313052	**FU**	E	*GT*	HE	62580	71264	62644
313053	**FU**	E	*GT*	HE	62581	71265	62645
313054	**FU**	E	*GT*	HE	62582	71266	62646
313055	**FU**	E	*GT*	HE	62583	71267	62647
313056	**FU**	E	*GT*	HE	62584	71268	62648
313057	**FU**	E	*GT*	HE	62585	71269	62642
313058	**FU**	E	*GT*	HE	62586	71270	62650
313059	**FU**	E	*GT*	HE	62587	71271	62651
313060	**FU**	E	*GT*	HE	62588	71272	62652
313061	**FU**	E	*GT*	HE	62589	71273	62653
313062	**FU**	E	*GT*	HE	62590	71274	62654
313063	**FU**	E	*GT*	HE	62591	71275	62655
313064	**FU**	E	*GT*	HE	62592	71276	62656

Name (carried on PTSO): 313054   Captain William Leefe Robinson V.C.

Class 313/1. Former London Overground units. Original low back seats (3+2 facing). Details as Class 313/0.

313122	**FU**	E	*GT*	HE	62550	71234	62614
313123	**FU**	E	*GT*	HE	62551	71235	62615
313134	**FU**	E	*GT*	HE	62562	71246	62626

Names (carried on PTSO):

313122   Eric Roberts 1946–2012 "The Flying Nottsman"
313134   City of London

Class 313/2. Southern units. Units refurbished for Southern for Brighton Coastway services. Fitted with 2+2 mainly facing high-back seating. 750 V DC only (pantographs removed).

DMSO. Lot No. 30879 1976–77. –/64. 36.0 t.
TSO. Lot No. 30880 1976–77. –/68.   . t.
BDMSO. Lot No. 30885 1976–77. –/64. 37.5 t.

313201	(313101)	**SN**	BN	*SN*	BI	62529	71213	62593
313202	(313102)	**SN**	BN	*SN*	BI	62530	71214	62594
313203	(313103)	**SN**	BN	*SN*	BI	62531	71215	62595
313204	(313104)	**SN**	BN	*SN*	BI	62532	71216	62596
313205	(313105)	**SN**	BN	*SN*	BI	62533	71217	62597
313206	(313106)	**SN**	BN	*SN*	BI	62534	71218	62598
313207	(313107)	**SN**	BN	*SN*	BI	62535	71219	62599
313208	(313108)	**SN**	BN	*SN*	BI	62536	71220	62600
313209	(313109)	**SN**	BN	*SN*	BI	62537	71221	62601
313210	(313110)	**SN**	BN	*SN*	BI	62538	71222	62602
313211	(313111)	**SN**	BN	*SN*	BI	62539	71223	62603
313212	(313112)	**SN**	BN	*SN*	BI	62540	71224	62604
313213	(313113)	**SN**	BN	*SN*	BI	62541	71225	62605
313214	(313114)	**SN**	BN	*SN*	BI	62542	71226	62606

313215	(313115)	**SN**	BN	*SN*	Bl	62543	71227	62607
313216	(313116)	**SN**	BN	*SN*	Bl	62544	71228	62608
313217	(313117)	**SN**	BN	*SN*	Bl	62545	71229	62609
313219	(313119)	**SN**	BN	*SN*	Bl	62547	71231	62611
313220	(313120)	**SN**	BN	*SN*	Bl	62548	71232	62612

CLASS 314   BREL YORK

Inner suburban units.

Formation: DMSO–PTSO–DMSO.
Construction: Steel underframe, aluminium alloy body and roof.
Traction Motors: Four GEC G310AZ (* Brush TM61-53) of 82.125 kW.
Wheel Arrangement: Bo-Bo + 2-2 + Bo-Bo.
Braking: Disc & rheostatic.   **Dimensions:** 20.33/20.18 x 2.82 m.
Bogies: BX1.   **Couplers:** Tightlock.
Gangways: Within unit + end doors. **Control System:** Thyristor.
Doors: Sliding.   **Maximum Speed:** 70 mph.
Seating Layout: 3+2 low-back facing.
Multiple Working: Within class and with Class 315.

DMSO. Lot No. 30912 1979. –/68. 34.5 t.
64588[II]**. DMSO.** Lot No. 30908 1978–80. Rebuilt Railcare Glasgow 1996 from Class 507 No. 64426. The original 64588 was scrapped. –/74. 34.5 t.
PTSO. Lot No. 30913 1979. –/76. 33.0 t.

314201	*	**SC**	A	*SR*	GW	64583	71450	64584
314202	*	**SC**	A	*SR*	GW	64585	71451	64586
314203	*	**SR**	A	*SR*	GW	64587	71452	64588[II]
314204	*	**SR**	A	*SR*	GW	64589	71453	64590
314205	*	**SC**	A	*SR*	GW	64591	71454	64592
314206	*	**SC**	A	*SR*	GW	64593	71455	64594
314207		**SC**	A	*SR*	GW	64595	71456	64596
314208		**SR**	A	*SR*	GW	64597	71457	64598
314209		**SC**	A	*SR*	GW	64599	71458	64600
314210		**SC**	A	*SR*	GW	64601	71459	64602
314211		**SR**	A	*SR*	GW	64603	71460	64604
314212		**SR**	A	*SR*	GW	64605	71461	64606
314213		**SC**	A	*SR*	GW	64607	71462	64608
314214		**SC**	A	*SR*	GW	64609	71463	64610
314215		**SC**	A	*SR*	GW	64611	71464	64612
314216		**SC**	A	*SR*	GW	64613	71465	64614

CLASS 315   BREL YORK

Inner suburban units.

Formation: DMSO–TSO–PTSO–DMSO.
Construction: Steel underframe, aluminium alloy body and roof.
Traction Motors: Four Brush TM61-53 (* GEC G310AZ) of 82.125 kW.
Wheel Arrangement: Bo-Bo + 2-2 + 2-2 + Bo-Bo.
Braking: Disc & rheostatic.   **Dimensions:** 20.18 x 2.82 m.
Bogies: BX1.   **Couplers:** Tightlock.

Gangways: Within unit + end doors. **Control System:** Thyristor.
Doors: Sliding.   **Maximum Speed:** 75 mph.
Seating Layout: 3+2 low-back facing.
Multiple Working: Within class and with Class 314.

DMSO. Lot No. 30902 1980–81. –/74. 35.0 t († 38.2 t).
TSO. Lot No. 30904 1980–81. –/86. 25.5 t († 27.4 t).
PTSO. Lot No. 30903 1980–81. –/84 († –/75(7) 2W). 32.0 t († 33.8 t).

315801	†	**GA**	E	*GA*	IL	64461	71281	71389	64462
315802	†	**GA**	E	*GA*	IL	64463	71282	71390	64464
315803	†	**GA**	E	*GA*	IL	64465	71283	71391	64466
315804	†	**GA**	E	*GA*	IL	64467	71284	71392	64468
315805	†	**GA**	E	*GA*	IL	64469	71285	71393	64470
315806	†	**GA**	E	*GA*	IL	64471	71286	71394	64472
315807	†	**GA**	E	*GA*	IL	64473	71287	71395	64474
315808	†	**GA**	E	*GA*	IL	64475	71288	71396	64476
315809		**GA**	E	*GA*	IL	64477	71289	71397	64478
315810	†	**GA**	E	*GA*	IL	64479	71290	71398	64480
315811	†	**GA**	E	*GA*	IL	64481	71291	71399	64482
315812	†	**GA**	E	*GA*	IL	64483	71292	71400	64484
315813	†	**GA**	E	*GA*	IL	64485	71293	71401	64486
315814	†	**GA**	E	*GA*	IL	64487	71294	71402	64488
315815	†	**GA**	E	*GA*	IL	64489	71295	71403	64490
315816	†	**GA**	E	*GA*	IL	64491	71296	71404	64492
315817	†	**GA**	E	*GA*	IL	64493	71297	71405	64494
315818	†	**GA**	E	*GA*	IL	64495	71298	71406	64496
315819	†	**GA**	E	*GA*	IL	64497	71299	71407	64498
315820	†	**GA**	E	*GA*	IL	64499	71300	71408	64500
315821	†	**GA**	E	*GA*	IL	64501	71301	71409	64502
315822	†	**GA**	E	*GA*	IL	64503	71302	71410	64504
315823	†	**GA**	E	*GA*	IL	64505	71303	71411	64506
315824	†	**GA**	E	*GA*	IL	64507	71304	71412	64508
315825	†	**GA**	E	*GA*	IL	64509	71305	71413	64510
315826	†	**GA**	E	*GA*	IL	64511	71306	71414	64512
315827	†	**GA**	E	*GA*	IL	64513	71307	71415	64514
315828	†	**GA**	E	*GA*	IL	64515	71308	71416	64516
315829	†	**GA**	E	*GA*	IL	64517	71309	71417	64518
315830	†	**GA**	E	*GA*	IL	64519	71310	71418	64520
315831	†	**GA**	E	*GA*	IL	64521	71311	71419	64522
315832	†	**GA**	E	*GA*	IL	64523	71312	71420	64524
315833	†	**GA**	E	*GA*	IL	64525	71313	71421	64526
315834	†	**GA**	E	*GA*	IL	64527	71314	71422	64528
315835	†	**GA**	E	*GA*	IL	64529	71315	71423	64530
315836		**1**	E	*GA*	IL	64531	71316	71424	64532
315837	†	**GA**	E	*GA*	IL	64533	71317	71425	64534
315838	†	**GA**	E	*GA*	IL	64535	71318	71426	64536
315839	†	**GA**	E	*GA*	IL	64537	71319	71427	64538
315840	†	**GA**	E	*GA*	IL	64539	71320	71428	64540
315841	†	**GA**	E	*GA*	IL	64541	71321	71429	64542
315842	*	**1**	E	*GA*	IL	64543	71322	71430	64544
315843	*	**1**	E	*GA*	IL	64545	71323	71431	64546

315 844	*† **GA**	E	*GA*	IL	64547	71324	71432	64548
315 845	*† **GA**	E	*GA*	IL	64549	71325	71433	64550
315 846	*† **GA**	E	*GA*	IL	64551	71326	71434	64552
315 847	*† **GA**	E	*GA*	IL	64553	71327	71435	64554
315 848	* **1**	E	*GA*	IL	64555	71328	71436	64556
315 849	*† **GA**	E	*GA*	IL	64557	71329	71437	64558
315 850	* **1**	E	*GA*	IL	64559	71330	71438	64560
315 851	*† **GA**	E	*GA*	IL	64561	71331	71439	64562
315 852	*† **GA**	E	*GA*	IL	64563	71332	71440	64564
315 853	* **1**	E	*GA*	IL	64565	71333	71441	64566
315 854	*† **GA**	E	*GA*	IL	64567	71334	71442	64568
315 855	*† **GA**	E	*GA*	IL	64569	71335	71443	64570
315 856	* **1**	E	*GA*	IL	64571	71336	71444	64572
315 857	* **1**	E	*GA*	IL	64573	71337	71445	64574
315 858	*† **GA**	E	*GA*	IL	64575	71338	71446	64576
315 859	*† **GA**	E	*GA*	IL	64577	71339	71447	64578
315 860	* **1**	E	*GA*	IL	64579	71340	71448	64580
315 861	* **1**	E	*GA*	IL	64581	71341	71449	64582

Names (carried on DMSO):

315817	Transport for London
315829	London Borough of Havering Celebrating 40 years
315845	Herbie Woodward
315857	Stratford Connections

CLASS 317   BREL YORK/DERBY

Outer suburban units.

Formation: Various, see sub-class headings.
Construction: Steel.
Traction Motors: Four GEC G315BZ of 247.5 kW (except 317 722, see below).
Wheel Arrangement: 2-2 + Bo-Bo + 2-2 + 2-2.
Braking: Disc.　　　　　　　　　　　**Dimensions:** 19.83/20.18 x 2.82 m.
Bogies: BP20 (MSO), BT13 (others).　**Couplers:** Tightlock.
Gangways: Throughout　　　　　　　**Control System:** Thyristor.
Doors: Sliding.　　　　　　　　　　　**Maximum Speed:** 100 mph.
Seating Layout: Various, see sub-class headings.
Multiple Working: Within class & with Classes 318, 319, 320, 321, 322 and 323.

Class 317/1. Pressure ventilated.

Formation: DTSO–MSO–TCO–DTSO.
Seating Layout: 1: 2+2 facing, 2: 3+2 facing.

DTSO(A) Lot No. 30955 York 1981–82. –/74. 29.5 t.
MSO. Lot No. 30958 York 1981–82. –/79. 49.0 t.
TCO. Lot No. 30957 Derby 1981–82. 22/46 2T. 29.0 t.
DTSO(B) Lot No. 30956 York 1981–82. –/71. 29.5 t.

317 337	**FU**	A	*GT*	HE	77036	62671	71613	77084
317 338	**FU**	A	*GT*	HE	77037	62698	71614	77085
317 339	**FU**	A	*GT*	HE	77038	62699	71615	77086

317340	**FU**	A	*GT*	HE	77039	62700	71616	77087
317341	**FU**	A	*GT*	HE	77040	62701	71617	77088
317342	**FU**	A	*GT*	HE	77041	62702	71618	77089
317343	**FU**	A	*GT*	HE	77042	62703	71619	77090
317344	**FU**	A	*GT*	HE	77029	62690	71620	77091
317345	**FU**	A	*GT*	HE	77044	62705	71621	77092
317346	**FU**	A	*GT*	HE	77045	62706	71622	77093
317347	**FU**	A	*GT*	HE	77046	62707	71623	77094
317348	**FU**	A	*GT*	HE	77047	62708	71624	77095

Names (carried on TCO):

317345 Driver John Webb | 317348 Richard A Jenner

Class 317/5. Pressure ventilated. Units renumbered from Class 317/1 in 2005 for West Anglia Metro services. Refurbished with new upholstery and Passenger Information Systems. Details as Class 317/1.

The original DTSO 77048 was written off after the Cricklewood accident of 1983. A replacement vehicle was built (at Wolverton) in 1987 and given the same number.

317501	**NX**	A	*GA*	IL	77024	62661	71577	77048
317502	**NX**	A	*GA*	IL	77001	62662	71578	77049
317503	**NX**	A	*GA*	IL	77002	62663	71579	77050
317504	**NX**	A	*GA*	IL	77003	62664	71580	77051
317505	**NX**	A	*GA*	IL	77004	62665	71581	77052
317506	**NX**	A	*GA*	IL	77005	62666	71582	77053
317507	**NX**	A	*GA*	IL	77006	62667	71583	77054
317508	**NX**	A	*GA*	IL	77010	62697	71587	77058
317509	**NX**	A	*GA*	IL	77011	62672	71588	77059
317510	**NX**	A	*GA*	IL	77012	62673	71589	77060
317511	**NC**	A	*GA*	IL	77014	62675	71591	77062
317512	**NC**	A	*GA*	IL	77015	62676	71592	77063
317513	**NX**	A	*GA*	IL	77016	62677	71593	77064
317514	**NX**	A	*GA*	IL	77017	62678	71594	77065
317515	**NX**	A	*GA*	IL	77019	62680	71596	77067

Name (carried on TCO):

317507 University of Cambridge 800 Years 1209–2009

Class 317/6. Convection heating. Units converted from Class 317/2 by Railcare, Wolverton 1998–99 with new Chapman seating.

Formation: DTSO–MSO–TSO–DTCO.
Seating Layout: 2+2 facing.

77200–219. DTSO. Lot No. 30994 York 1985–86. –/64. 29.5 t.
77280–283. DTSO. Lot No. 31007 York 1987. –/64. 29.5 t.
62846–865. MSO. Lot No. 30996 York 1985–86. –/70. 49.0 t.
62886–889. MSO. Lot No. 31009 York 1987. –/70. 49.0 t.
71734–753. TSO. Lot No. 30997 York 1985–86. –/62 2T. 29.0 t.
71762–765. TSO. Lot No. 31010 York 1987. –/62 2T. 29.0 t.
77220–239. DTCO. Lot No. 30995 York 1985–86. 24/48. 29.5 t.
77284–287. DTCO. Lot No. 31008 York 1987. 24/48. 29.5 t.

317649	**NC**	A	*GA*	IL	77200	62846	71734	77220
317650	**NC**	A	*GA*	IL	77201	62847	71735	77221
317651	**NC**	A	*GA*	IL	77202	62848	71736	77222
317652	**NC**	A	*GA*	IL	77203	62849	71739	77223
317653	**NC**	A	*GA*	IL	77204	62850	71738	77224
317654	**NC**	A	*GA*	IL	77205	62851	71737	77225
317655	**GA**	A	*GA*	IL	77206	62852	71740	77226
317656	**NC**	A	*GA*	IL	77207	62853	71742	77227
317657	**NC**	A	*GA*	IL	77208	62854	71741	77228
317658	**GA**	A	*GA*	IL	77209	62855	71743	77229
317659	**GA**	A	*GA*	IL	77210	62856	71744	77230
317660	**GA**	A	*GA*	IL	77211	62857	71745	77231
317661	**GA**	A	*GA*	IL	77212	62858	71746	77232
317662	**GA**	A	*GA*	IL	77213	62859	71747	77233
317663	**GA**	A	*GA*	IL	77214	62860	71748	77234
317664	**GA**	A	*GA*	IL	77215	62861	71749	77235
317665	**GA**	A	*GA*	IL	77216	62862	71750	77236
317666	**NC**	A	*GA*	IL	77217	62863	71752	77237
317667	**GA**	A	*GA*	IL	77218	62864	71751	77238
317668	**GA**	A	*GA*	IL	77219	62865	71753	77239
317669	**NC**	A	*GA*	IL	77280	62886	71762	77284
317670	**GA**	A	*GA*	IL	77281	62887	71763	77285
317671	**NC**	A	*GA*	IL	77282	62888	71764	77286
317672	**GA**	A	*GA*	IL	77283	62889	71765	77287

Name (carried on DTCO): 317654   Richard Wells

Class 317/7. Units converted from Class 317/1 by Railcare, Wolverton 2000 for Stansted Express services between London Liverpool Street and Stansted. Air conditioning. Fitted with luggage stacks. Displaced from Stansted services in 2011 by Class 379s.

* 317722 has received new Bombardier MJA 280-8 AC traction motors as part of an Angel trial. Two vehicles (77021 and 62682, now in **GA** livery) have also received an interior refurbishment with new Fainsa seating whilst the other two vehicles have been left in their former Stansted Express condition (and are still in **NX** livery). The unit returned to use with Abellio Greater Anglia as a demonstrator in 2014.

Formation: DTSO–MSO–TSO–DTCO.
Seating Layout: 1: 2+1 facing, 2: 2+2 facing.

DTSO Lot No. 30955 York 1981–82. –/52 + catering point. 31.4 t.
MSO. Lot No. 30958 York 1981–82. –/62 (* –/64). 51.3 t.
TSO. Lot No. 30957 Derby 1981–82. –/42(5) 1W 1T 1TD. 30.2 t.
DTCO Lot No. 30956 York 1981–82. 22/16 + catering point. 31.6 t.

317708		**GA**	A		ZG	77007	62668	71584	77055
317709		**NX**	A	*GA*	IL	77008	62669	71585	77056
317710		**NX**	A		ZI	77009	62670	71586	77057
317714		**GA**	A		ZG	77013	62674	71590	77061
317719		**NX**	A	*GA*	IL	77018	62679	71595	77066
317722	*	**GA/NX**	A	*GA*	IL	77021	62682	71598	77069
317723		**NX**	A		ZI	77022	62683	71599	77070

| 317 729 | **GA** | A | | ZG | 77028 | 62689 | 71605 | 77076 |
| 317 732 | **NX** | A | | ZI | 77031 | 62692 | 71608 | 77079 |

Name (carried on DTCO):

317 723 The Tottenham Flyer

Class 317/8. Pressure Ventilated. Units refurbished and renumbered from Class 317/1 in 2005–06 at Wabtec, Doncaster for use on Stansted Express services. Displaced from Stansted services in 2011.

Formation: DTSO–MSO–TCO–DTSO.
Seating Layout: 1: 2+2 facing, 2: 3+2 facing.

DTSO(A) Lot No. 30955 York 1981–82. –/66. 29.5 t.
MSO. Lot No. 30958 York 1981–82. –/71. 49.0 t.
TCO. Lot No. 30957 Derby 1981–82. 20/42 2T. 29.0 t.
DTSO(B) Lot No. 30956 York 1981–82. –/66. 29.5 t.

317 881	**NX**	A	*GA*	IL	77020	62681	71597	77068	
317 882	**NC**	A	*GA*	IL	77023	62684	71600	77071	
317 883	**NC**	A	*GA*	IL	77000	62685	71601	77072	
317 884	**NC**	A	*GA*	IL	77025	62686	71602	77073	
317 885	**NC**	A	*GA*	IL	77026	62687	71603	77074	
317 886	**NC**	A	*GA*	IL	77027	62688	71604	77075	
317 887	**NX**	A	*GA*	IL	77043	62704	71606	77077	
317 888	**NX**	A	*GA*	IL	77030	62691	71607	77078	
317 889	**NX**	A	*GA*	IL	77032	62693	71609	77080	
317 890	**NX**	A	*GA*	IL	77033	62694	71610	77081	
317 891	**NX**	A	*GA*	IL	77034	62695	71611	77082	
317 892	**NX**	A	*GA*	IL	77035	62696	71612	77083	Ilford Depot

CLASS 318   BREL YORK

Outer suburban units. An overhaul programme is underway that is seeing a new universal access toilet (to comply with the 2020 accessibility regulations) fitted (units in **SR** livery).

Formation: DTSO–MSO–DTSO.
Construction: Steel.
Traction Motors: Four Brush TM 2141 of 268 kW.
Wheel Arrangement: 2-2 + Bo-Bo + 2-2.
Braking: Disc.   **Dimensions:** 19.83/19.92 x 2.82 m.
Bogies: BP20 (MSO), BT13 (others).   **Couplers:** Tightlock.
Gangways: Within unit.   **Control System:** Thyristor.
Doors: Sliding.   **Maximum Speed:** 90 mph.
Seating Layout: 3+2 facing.
Multiple Working: Within class & with Classes 317, 319, 320, 321, 322 and 323.

77240–259. DTSO. Lot No. 30999 1985–86. –/64 1T (–/55 1TD 2W). 30.0 t (* 32.0 t).
77288. DTSO. Lot No. 31020 1987. –/64 1T. 30.0 t.
62866–885. MSO. Lot No. 30998 1985–86. –/77 (*–/79). 50.9 t (* 53.0 t).
62890. MSO. Lot No. 31019 1987. –/77. 50.9 t.
77260–279. DTSO. Lot No. 31000 1985–86. –/72 (* –/74). 29.6 t (* 31.6 t).
77289. DTSO. Lot No. 31021 1987. –/72. 29.6 t.

318250	**SC**	E	*SR*	GW	77240	62866	77260
318251	* **SR**	E	*SR*	GW	77241	62867	77261
318252	**SC**	E	*SR*	GW	77242	62868	77262
318253	**SC**	E	*SR*	GW	77243	62869	77263
318254	* **SR**	E	*SR*	GW	77244	62870	77264
318255	**SC**	E	*SR*	GW	77245	62871	77265
318256	**SC**	E	*SR*	GW	77246	62872	77266
318257	* **SR**	E	*SR*	GW	77247	62873	77267
318258	**SC**	E	*SR*	GW	77248	62874	77268
318259	* **SR**	E	*SR*	GW	77249	62875	77269
318260	**SC**	E	*SR*	GW	77250	62876	77270
318261	**SC**	E	*SR*	GW	77251	62877	77271
318262	**SC**	E	*SR*	GW	77252	62878	77272
318263	**SC**	E	*SR*	GW	77253	62879	77273
318264	* **SR**	E	*SR*	GW	77254	62880	77274
318265	**SC**	E	*SR*	GW	77255	62881	77275
318266	**SC**	E	*SR*	GW	77256	62882	77276	STRATHCLYDER
318267	**SC**	E	*SR*	GW	77257	62883	77277
318268	**SC**	E	*SR*	GW	77258	62884	77278
318269	**SC**	E	*SR*	GW	77259	62885	77279
318270	**SC**	E	*SR*	GW	77288	62890	77289

CLASS 319   BREL YORK

Express and outer suburban units. Units are currently being refurbished and fitted with a new universal access toilet to comply with the 2020 accessibility regulations (shown as *).

Formation: Various, see sub-class headings.
Systems: 25 kV AC overhead/750 V DC third rail.
Construction: Steel.
Traction Motors: Four GEC G315BZ of 268 kW.
Wheel Arrangement: 2-2 + Bo-Bo + 2-2 + 2-2.
Braking: Disc.   **Dimensions:** 20.17/20.16 x 2.82 m.
Bogies: P7-4 (MSO), T3-7 (others).   **Couplers:** Tightlock.
Gangways: Within unit + end doors.   **Control System:** GTO chopper.
Doors: Sliding.   **Maximum Speed:** 100 mph.
Seating Layout: Various, see sub-class headings.
Multiple Working: Within class & with Classes 317, 318, 320, 321, 322 and 323.

Class 319/0. DTSO–MSO–TSO–DTSO.

Seating Layout: 3+2 facing.

DTSO(A). Lot No. 31022 (odd nos.) 1987–88. –/82 (* –/79). 28.2 t.
MSO. Lot No. 31023 1987–88. –/82 (* –/81). 49.2 t.
TSO. Lot No. 31024 1987–88. –/77 2T (* –/63 1TD 2W). 31.0 t.
DTSO(B). Lot No. 31025 (even nos.) 1987–88. –/78 (* –/79). 28.1 t.

319001	**TL**	P	*GT*	BF	77291	62891	71772	77290
319002	**FU**	P	*GT*	BF	77293	62892	71773	77292
319003	**FU**	P	*GT*	BF	77295	62893	71774	77294
319004	**TL**	P	*GT*	BF	77297	62894	71775	77296
319005	* **TL**	P	*GT*	BF	77299	62895	71776	77298

319006	*	**TL**	P	*GT*	BF	77301	62896	71777	77300
319007		**FU**	P	*GT*	BF	77303	62897	71778	77302
319008		**SN**	P	*GT*	BF	77305	62898	71779	77304
319009		**TL**	P	*GT*	BF	77307	62899	71780	77306
319010		**TL**	P	*GT*	BF	77309	62900	71781	77308
319011		**TL**	P	*GT*	BF	77311	62901	71782	77310
319012		**SN**	P	*GT*	BF	77313	62902	71783	77312
319013		**SN**	P	*GT*	BF	77315	62903	71784	77314

Names (carried on TSO):

319001	Driver Mick Winnett	319011	John Ruskin College
319008	Cheriton	319013	The Surrey Hills
319009	Coquelles		

Class 319/2. DTSO–MSO–TSO–DTCO. Units converted from Class 319/0.

Seating Layout: 1: 2+1 facing, 2: 2+2 facing.

Advertising liveries: 319215 Visit Switzerland (red).
319 218 Lycamobile (white).

DTSO. Lot No. 31022 (odd nos.) 1987–88. –/64. 28.2 t.
MSO. Lot No. 31023 1987–88. –/73. 49.2 t.
TSO. Lot No. 31024 1987–88. –/52 1T 1TD. 31.0 t.
DTCO. Lot No. 31025 (even nos.) 1987–88. 18/36. 28.1 t.

319214	**SN**	P	*GT*	BF	77317	62904	71785	77316	
319215	**AL**	P	*GT*	BF	77319	62905	71786	77318	
319216	**SN**	P	*GT*	BF	77321	62906	71787	77320	
319217	**SN**	P	*GT*	BF	77323	62907	71788	77322 Brighton
319218	**AL**	P	*GT*	BF	77325	62908	71789	77324 Croydon
319219	**SN**	P	*GT*	BF	77327	62909	71790	77326	
319220	**SN**	P	*GT*	BF	77329	62910	71791	77328	

Class 319/3. DTSO–MSO–TSO–DTSO. Converted from Class 319/1 by replacing First Class seats with Standard Class seats.

14 units (319 361–367/369/371/374–378) are currently being refurbished for Northern and will enter service on newly electrified lines in the North-West during 2015. Another six, as yet unidentified, Class 319s will also move to Northern later in 2015.

Seating Layout: 3+2 facing.   **Dimensions:** 19.33 x 2.82 m.

DTSO(A). Lot No. 31063 1990. –/70. 29.0 t.
MSO. Lot No. 31064 1990. –/78. 50.6 t.
TSO. Lot No. 31065 1990. –/74 2T. 31.0 t.
DTSO(B). Lot No. 31066 1990. –/75. 29.7 t.

319361	**FU**	P	*NO*	AN	77459	63043	71929	77458
319362	**NP**	P	*NO*	AN	77461	63044	71930	77460
319363	**NP**	P	*NO*	AN	77463	63045	71931	77462
319364	**NP**	P	*NO*	AN	77465	63046	71932	77464
319365	**NP**	P	*NO*	AN	77467	63047	71933	77466
319366	**FU**	P	*GT*	BF	77469	63048	71934	77468
319367	**FU**	P	*GT*	BF	77471	63049	71935	77470

319368	**FU**	P	*GT*	BF	77473	63050	71936	77472
319369	**FU**	P	*GT*	BF	77475	63051	71937	77474
319370	**FU**	P	*GT*	BF	77477	63052	71938	77476
319371	**FU**	P	*GT*	BF	77479	63053	71939	77478
319372	**FU**	P	*GT*	BF	77481	63054	71940	77480
319373	**TL**	P	*GT*	BF	77483	63055	71941	77482
319374	**FU**	P	*GT*	BF	77485	63056	71942	77484
319375	**FU**	P	*GT*	BF	77487	63057	71943	77486
319376	**FU**	P	*GT*	BF	77489	63058	71944	77488
319377	**FU**	P	*GT*	BF	77491	63059	71945	77490
319378	**FU**	P	*GT*	BF	77493	63060	71946	77492
319379	**FU**	P	*GT*	BF	77495	63061	71947	77494
319380	**FU**	P	*GT*	BF	77497	63062	71948	77496
319381	**FU**	P	*GT*	BF	77973	63093	71979	77974
319382	**FU**	P	*GT*	BF	77975	63094	71980	77976
319383	**FU**	P	*GT*	BF	77977	63095	71981	77978
319384	**FU**	P	*GT*	BF	77979	63096	71982	77980
319385	**FU**	P	*GT*	BF	77981	63097	71983	77982
319386	**FU**	P	*GT*	BF	77983	63098	71984	77984

Name (carried on TSO): 319374   Bedford Cauldwell TMD

Class 319/4. DTCO–MSO–TSO–DTSO. Converted from Class 319/0. Refurbished with carpets. DTSO(A) converted to composite.

Seating Layout: 1: 2+1 facing 2: 2+2/3+2 facing.

77331–381. DTCO. Lot No. 31022 (odd nos.) 1987–88. 12/51. 28.2t.
77431–457. DTCO. Lot No. 31038 (odd nos.) 1988. 12/51. 28.2t.
62911–936. MSO. Lot No. 31023 1987–88. –/74. 49.2t.
62961–974. MSO. Lot No. 31039 1988. –/74. 49.2t.
71792–817. TSO. Lot No. 31024 1987–88. –/67 2T. 31.0t.
71866–879. TSO. Lot No. 31040 1988. –/67 2T. 31.0t.
77330–380. DTSO. Lot No. 31025 (even nos.) 1987–88. –/71 1W. 28.1t.
77430–456. DTSO. Lot No. 31041 (even nos.) 1988. –/71 1W. 28.1t.

319421	**FU**	P	*GT*	BF	77331	62911	71792	77330
319422	**FU**	P	*GT*	BF	77333	62912	71793	77332
319423	**FU**	P	*GT*	BF	77335	62913	71794	77334
319424	**FU**	P	*GT*	BF	77337	62914	71795	77336
319425	**FU**	P	*GT*	BF	77339	62915	71796	77338
319426	**TL**	P	*GT*	BF	77341	62916	71797	77340
319427	**FU**	P	*GT*	BF	77343	62917	71798	77342
319428	**FU**	P	*GT*	BF	77345	62918	71799	77344
319429	**FU**	P	*GT*	BF	77347	62919	71800	77346
319430	**FU**	P	*GT*	BF	77349	62920	71801	77348
319431	**TL**	P	*GT*	BF	77351	62921	71802	77350
319432	**FU**	P	*GT*	BF	77353	62922	71803	77352
319433	**FU**	P	*GT*	BF	77355	62923	71804	77354
319434	**FU**	P	*GT*	BF	77357	62924	71805	77356
319435	**FU**	P	*GT*	BF	77359	62925	71806	77358
319436	**FU**	P	*GT*	BF	77361	62926	71807	77360
319437	**FU**	P	*GT*	BF	77363	62927	71808	77362

319438	**TL**	P	*GT*	BF	77365	62928	71809	77364
319439	**FU**	P	*GT*	BF	77367	62929	71810	77366
319440	**FU**	P	*GT*	BF	77369	62930	71811	77368
319441	**FU**	P	*GT*	BF	77371	62931	71812	77370
319442	**FU**	P	*GT*	BF	77373	62932	71813	77372
319443	**TL**	P	*GT*	BF	77375	62933	71814	77374
319444	**FU**	P	*GT*	BF	77377	62934	71815	77376
319445	**FU**	P	*GT*	BF	77379	62935	71816	77378
319446	**FU**	P	*GT*	BF	77381	62936	71817	77380
319447	**FU**	P	*GT*	BF	77431	62961	71866	77430
319448	**FU**	P	*GT*	BF	77433	62962	71867	77432
319449	**FU**	P	*GT*	BF	77435	62963	71868	77434
319450	**FU**	P	*GT*	BF	77437	62964	71869	77436
319451	**FU**	P	*GT*	BF	77439	62965	71870	77438
319452	**FU**	P	*GT*	BF	77441	62966	71871	77440
319453	**FU**	P	*GT*	BF	77443	62967	71872	77442
319454	**FU**	P	*GT*	BF	77445	62968	71873	77444
319455	**FU**	P	*GT*	BF	77447	62969	71874	77446
319456	**FU**	P	*GT*	BF	77449	62970	71875	77448
319457	**FU**	P	*GT*	BF	77451	62971	71876	77450
319458	**FU**	P	*GT*	BF	77453	62972	71877	77452
319459	**FU**	P	*GT*	BF	77455	62973	71878	77454
319460	**FU**	P	*GT*	BF	77457	62974	71879	77456

Names (carried on TSO):

319425 Transforming Travel
319435 Adrian Jackson-Robbins Chairman 1987–2007 Association of Public
          Transport Users
319444 City of St Albans
319446 St Pancras International
319448 Elstree Studios The Home of British Film and Television production
319449 King's Cross Thameslink

CLASS 320   BREL YORK

Suburban units. All refurbished 2011–13 and fitted with a new universal access toilet to comply with the 2020 accessibility regulations.

Formation: DTSO–MSO–DTSO.
Construction: Steel
Traction Motors: Four Brush TM2141B of 268 kW.
Wheel Arrangement: 2-2 + Bo-Bo + 2-2.
Braking: Disc.   **Dimensions:** 19.95 x 2.82 m.
Bogies: P7-4 (MSO), T3-7 (others).   **Couplers:** Tightlock.
Gangways: Within unit.   **Control System:** Thyristor.
Doors: Sliding.   **Maximum Speed:** 90 mph.
Seating Layout: 3+2 facing.
Multiple Working: Within class & with Classes 317, 318, 319, 321, 322 and 323.

DTSO (A). Lot No. 31060 1990. –/51(4) 1TD 2W. 31.7 t.
MSO. Lot No. 31062 1990. –/78. 52.6 t.
DTSO (B). Lot No. 31061 1990. –/77. 31.6 t.

320301	**SR**	E	*SR*	GW	77899	63021	77921
320302	**SR**	E	*SR*	GW	77900	63022	77922
320303	**SR**	E	*SR*	GW	77901	63023	77923
320304	**SR**	E	*SR*	GW	77902	63024	77924
320305	**SR**	E	*SR*	GW	77903	63025	77925
320306	**SR**	E	*SR*	GW	77904	63026	77926
320307	**SR**	E	*SR*	GW	77905	63027	77927
320308	**SR**	E	*SR*	GW	77906	63028	77928
320309	**SR**	E	*SR*	GW	77907	63029	77929
320310	**SR**	E	*SR*	GW	77908	63030	77930
320311	**SR**	E	*SR*	GW	77909	63031	77931
320312	**SR**	E	*SR*	GW	77910	63032	77932
320313	**SR**	E	*SR*	GW	77911	63033	77933
320314	**SR**	E	*SR*	GW	77912	63034	77934
320315	**SR**	E	*SR*	GW	77913	63035	77935
320316	**SR**	E	*SR*	GW	77914	63036	77936
320317	**SR**	E	*SR*	GW	77915	63037	77937
320318	**SR**	E	*SR*	GW	77916	63038	77938
320319	**SR**	E	*SR*	GW	77917	63039	77939
320320	**SR**	E	*SR*	GW	77918	63040	77940
320321	**SR**	E	*SR*	GW	77919	63041	77941
320322	**SR**	E	*SR*	GW	77920	63042	77942

CLASS 321   BREL YORK

Outer suburban units.

Formation: DTCO (DTSO on Class 321/9)–MSO–TSO–DTSO.
Construction: Steel.
Traction Motors: Four Brush TM2141C of 268 kW.
Wheel Arrangement: 2-2 + Bo-Bo + 2-2 + 2-2.
Braking: Disc.   **Dimensions:** 19.95 x 2.82 m.
Bogies: P7-4 (MSO), T3-7 (others).   **Couplers:** Tightlock.
Gangways: Within unit.   **Control System:** Thyristor.
Doors: Sliding.   **Maximum Speed:** 100 mph.
Seating Layout: 1: 2+2 facing, 2: 3+2 facing.
Multiple Working: Within class & with Classes 317, 318, 319, 320, 322 and 323.

Class 321/3.

DTCO. Lot No. 31053 1988–90. 16/57 (321 347–366 16/56). 29.7 t.
MSO. Lot No. 31054 1988–90. –/82. 51.5 t.
TSO. Lot No. 31055 1988–90. –/75 2T. 29.1 t.
DTSO. Lot No. 31056 1988–90. –/78. 29.7 t.

321301	**NX**	E	*GA*	IL	78049	62975	71880	77853
321302	**NX**	E	*GA*	IL	78050	62976	71881	77854
321303	**NX**	E	*GA*	IL	78051	62977	71882	77855
321304	**NX**	E	*GA*	IL	78052	62978	71883	77856
321305	**NX**	E	*GA*	IL	78053	62979	71884	77857
321306	**NX**	E	*GA*	IL	78054	62980	71885	77858
321307	**NX**	E	*GA*	IL	78055	62981	71886	77859
321308	**NX**	E	*GA*	IL	78056	62982	71887	77860

321 309	**NX**	E	*GA*	IL	78057	62983	71888	77861
321 310	**NX**	E	*GA*	IL	78058	62984	71889	77862
321 311	**NX**	E	*GA*	IL	78059	62985	71890	77863
321 312	**NX**	E	*GA*	IL	78060	62986	71891	77864
321 313	**NX**	E	*GA*	IL	78061	62987	71892	77865
321 314	**NX**	E	*GA*	IL	78062	62988	71893	77866
321 315	**NX**	E	*GA*	IL	78063	62989	71894	77867
321 316	**NX**	E	*GA*	IL	78064	62990	71895	77868
321 317	**NX**	E	*GA*	IL	78065	62991	71896	77869
321 318	**NX**	E	*GA*	IL	78066	62992	71897	77870
321 319	**NX**	E	*GA*	IL	78067	62993	71898	77871
321 320	**NX**	E	*GA*	IL	78068	62994	71899	77872
321 321	**NX**	E	*GA*	IL	78069	62995	71900	77873
321 322	**NX**	E	*GA*	IL	78070	62996	71901	77874
321 323	**NX**	E	*GA*	IL	78071	62997	71902	77875
321 324	**NX**	E	*GA*	IL	78072	62998	71903	77876
321 325	**NX**	E	*GA*	IL	78073	62999	71904	77877
321 326	**NX**	E	*GA*	IL	78074	63000	71905	77878
321 327	**NC**	E	*GA*	IL	78075	63001	71906	77879
321 328	**NX**	E	*GA*	IL	78076	63002	71907	77880
321 329	**NX**	E	*GA*	IL	78077	63003	71908	77881
321 330	**NC**	E	*GA*	IL	78078	63004	71909	77882
321 331	**NC**	E	*GA*	IL	78079	63005	71910	77883
321 332	**NC**	E	*GA*	IL	78080	63006	71911	77884
321 333	**NC**	E	*GA*	IL	78081	63007	71912	77885
321 334	**NC**	E	*GA*	IL	78082	63008	71913	77886
321 335	**NC**	E	*GA*	IL	78083	63009	71914	77887
321 336	**NC**	E	*GA*	IL	78084	63010	71915	77888
321 337	**NC**	E	*GA*	IL	78085	63011	71916	77889
321 338	**NC**	E	*GA*	IL	78086	63012	71917	77890
321 339	**NC**	E	*GA*	IL	78087	63013	71918	77891
321 340	**NC**	E	*GA*	IL	78088	63014	71919	77892
321 341	**NC**	E	*GA*	IL	78089	63015	71920	77893
321 342	**NC**	E	*GA*	IL	78090	63016	71921	77894
321 343	**NC**	E	*GA*	IL	78091	63017	71922	77895
321 344	**NC**	E	*GA*	IL	78092	63018	71923	77896
321 345	**NC**	E	*GA*	IL	78093	63019	71924	77897
321 346	**NC**	E	*GA*	IL	78094	63020	71925	77898
321 347	**NC**	E	*GA*	IL	78131	63105	71991	78280
321 348	**NC**	E	*GA*	IL	78132	63106	71992	78281
321 349	**NC**	E	*GA*	IL	78133	63107	71993	78282
321 350	**NC**	E	*GA*	IL	78134	63108	71994	78283
321 351	**NC**	E	*GA*	IL	78135	63109	71995	78284
321 352	**NC**	E	*GA*	IL	78136	63110	71996	78285
321 353	**NC**	E	*GA*	IL	78137	63111	71997	78286
321 354	**NC**	E	*GA*	IL	78138	63112	71998	78287
321 355	**NC**	E	*GA*	IL	78139	63113	71999	78288
321 356	**NC**	E	*GA*	IL	78140	63114	72000	78289
321 357	**NC**	E	*GA*	IL	78141	63115	72001	78290
321 358	**NC**	E	*GA*	IL	78142	63116	72002	78291
321 359	**GA**	E	*GA*	IL	78143	63117	72003	78292

321360	**NC**	E	*GA*	IL	78144	63118	72004	78293
321361	**GA**	E	*GA*	IL	78145	63119	72005	78294
321362	**GA**	E	*GA*	IL	78146	63120	72006	78295
321363	**GA**	E	*GA*	IL	78147	63121	72007	78296
321364	**GA**	E	*GA*	IL	78148	63122	72008	78297
321365	**GA**	E	*GA*	IL	78149	63123	72009	78298
321366	**GA**	E	*GA*	IL	78150	63124	72010	78299

Names (carried on TSO):

321312 Southend-on-Sea
321313 University of Essex
321321 NSPCC ESSEX FULL STOP
321334 Amsterdam
321336 GEOFFREY FREEMAN ALLEN
321342 R. Barnes
321343 RSA RAILWAY STUDY ASSOCIATION
321351 London Southend Airport
321361 Phoenix

Class 321/4.

The original vehicles 71966 and 77960 from 321418 and 78114 and 63082 from 321420 were written off after the Watford Junction accident in 1996. The undamaged vehicles were formed together as 321418 whilst four new vehicles were built in 1997, taking the same numbers as the scrapped vehicles, and these became the second 321420.

The DTCOs of 321421–437 have had 12 First Class seats declassified.

* 321448 has received an interior refurbishment as an Eversholt demonstrator unit. It has been fitted with two different types of interior using seats supplied by ATD. 78130 and 63104 have a "suburban" interior with a 3+2 seating layout and 78279 and 71990 have a "metro" interior with 2+2 seating. The unit is in normal service with Abellio Greater Anglia.

Non-standard livery: 321448 Eversholt demonstrator (silver with blue doors and multi-coloured stripes).

DTCO. Lot No. 31067 1989–90. 28/40 (321 421–437 16/52, 321 438–447 16/56). 29.8 t. (* 16/30(4) 1TD 2W 33.9 t).
MSO. Lot No. 31068 1989–90. –/79 (321 438–447 –/82). 51.6 t (* –/82. 54.0 t).
TSO. Lot No. 31069 1989–90. –/74 2T (321 438–447 –/75 2T). 29.2 t (* –/62 1T. 31.7 t).
DTSO. Lot No. 31070 1989–90. –/78. 29.8 t. (* –/58. 33.2 t).

321401	**FU**	E	*GT*	HE	78095	63063	71949	77943
321402	**FU**	E	*GT*	HE	78096	63064	71950	77944
321403	**FU**	E	*GT*	HE	78097	63065	71951	77945
321404	**FU**	E	*GT*	HE	78098	63066	71952	77946
321405	**FU**	E	*GT*	HE	78099	63067	71953	77947
321406	**FU**	E	*GT*	HE	78100	63068	71954	77948
321407	**FU**	E	*GT*	HE	78101	63069	71955	77949
321408	**FU**	E	*GT*	HE	78102	63070	71956	77950
321409	**FU**	E	*GT*	HE	78103	63071	71957	77951
321410	**FU**	E	*GT*	HE	78104	63072	71958	77952
321411	**LM**	E	*LM*	NN	78105	63073	71959	77953

321412	**LM**	E	*LM*	NN	78106	63074	71960	77954
321413	**LM**	E	*LM*	NN	78107	63075	71961	77955
321414	**LM**	E	*LM*	NN	78108	63076	71962	77956
321415	**LM**	E	*LM*	NN	78109	63077	71963	77957
321416	**LM**	E	*LM*	NN	78110	63078	71964	77958
321417	**LM**	E	*LM*	NN	78111	63079	71965	77959
321418	**FU**	E	*GT*	HE	78112	63080	71968	77962
321419	**FU**	E	*GT*	HE	78113	63081	71967	77961
321420	**FU**	E	*GT*	HE	78114	63082	71966	77960
321421	**NC**	E	*GA*	IL	78115	63083	71969	77963
321422	**NC**	E	*GA*	IL	78116	63084	71970	77964
321423	**NC**	E	*GA*	IL	78117	63085	71971	77965
321424	**NX**	E	*GA*	IL	78118	63086	71972	77966
321425	**NC**	E	*GA*	IL	78119	63087	71973	77967
321426	**NX**	E	*GA*	IL	78120	63088	71974	77968
321427	**NX**	E	*GA*	IL	78121	63089	71975	77969
321428	**NX**	E	*GA*	IL	78122	63090	71976	77970
321429	**NX**	E	*GA*	IL	78123	63091	71977	77971
321430	**NX**	E	*GA*	IL	78124	63092	71978	77972
321431	**NX**	E	*GA*	IL	78151	63125	72011	78300
321432	**NC**	E	*GA*	IL	78152	63126	72012	78301
321433	**NC**	E	*GA*	IL	78153	63127	72013	78302
321434	**NC**	E	*GA*	IL	78154	63128	72014	78303
321435	**NC**	E	*GA*	IL	78155	63129	72015	78304
321436	**NC**	E	*GA*	IL	78156	63130	72016	78305
321437	**NC**	E	*GA*	IL	78157	63131	72017	78306
321438	**GA**	E	*GA*	IL	78158	63132	72018	78307
321439	**GA**	E	*GA*	IL	78159	63133	72019	78308
321440	**GA**	E	*GA*	IL	78160	63134	72020	78309
321441	**GA**	E	*GA*	IL	78161	63135	72021	78310
321442	**GA**	E	*GA*	IL	78162	63136	72022	78311
321443	**GA**	E	*GA*	IL	78125	63099	71985	78274
321444	**NC**	E	*GA*	IL	78126	63100	71986	78275
321445	**NC**	E	*GA*	IL	78127	63101	71987	78276
321446	**NC**	E	*GA*	IL	78128	63102	71988	78277
321447	**GA**	E	*GA*	IL	78129	63103	71989	78278
321448	* **0**	E	*GA*	IL	78130	63104	71990	78279

Names (carried on TSO):

321403 Stewart Fleming Signalman King's Cross
321409 Dame Alice Owen's School 400 Years of Learning
321428 The Essex Commuter
321442 Crouch Valley 1889–2014
321444 Essex Lifeboats
321446 George Mullings

Class 321/9. DTSO(A)–MSO–TSO–DTSO(B).

DTSO(A). Lot No. 31108 1991. –/70(8). 29.2 t.
MSO. Lot No. 31109 1991. –/79. 51.1 t.
TSO. Lot No. 31110 1991. –/74 2T. 29.0 t.
DTSO(B). Lot No. 31111 1991. –/70(7) 1W. 29.2 t.

321901	**YR**	E	*NO*	NL	77990	63153	72128	77993
321902	**YR**	E	*NO*	NL	77991	63154	72129	77994
321903	**YR**	E	*NO*	NL	77992	63155	72130	77995

CLASS 322   BREL YORK

Units built for use on Stansted Airport services, used for a number of years with ScotRail before transfer to Northern. Refurbished 2014–15 with a universal access toilet to comply with the 2020 accessibility regulations.

Formation: DTSO–MSO–TSO–DTSO.
Construction: Steel.
Traction Motors: Four Brush TM2141C of 268 kW.
Wheel Arrangement: 2-2 + Bo-Bo + 2-2 + 2-2.
Braking: Disc.   **Dimensions:** 19.95/19.92 x 2.82 m.
Bogies: P7-4 (MSO), T3-7 (others).   **Couplers:** Tightlock.
Gangways: Within unit.   **Control System:** Thyristor.
Doors: Sliding.   **Maximum Speed:** 100 mph.
Seating Layout: 3+2 facing.
Multiple Working: Within class & with Classes 317, 318, 319, 320, 321 and 323.

DTSO(A). Lot No. 31094 1990. –/54(4) 1TD 2W. 31.7 t.
MSO. Lot No. 31092 1990. –/83. 52.1 t.
TSO. Lot No. 31093 1990. –/80 1T. 30.6 t.
DTSO(B). Lot No. 31091 1990. –/79. 30.6 t.

322481	**NB**	E	*NO*	NL	78163	63137	72023	77985
322482	**NB**	E	*NO*	NL	78164	63138	72024	77986
322483	**NB**	E	*NO*	NL	78165	63139	72025	77987
322484	**NB**	E	*NO*	NL	78166	63140	72026	77988
322485	**NB**	E	*NO*	NL	78167	63141	72027	77989

CLASS 323   HUNSLET TRANSPORTATION PROJECTS

Suburban units.

Formation: DMSO–PTSO–DMSO.
Construction: Welded aluminium alloy.
Traction Motors: Four Holec DMKT 52/24 asynchronous of 146 kW.
Wheel Arrangement: Bo-Bo + 2-2 + Bo-Bo.
Braking: Disc.   **Dimensions:** 23.37/23.44 x 2.80 m.
Bogies: SRP BP62 (DMSO), BT52 (PTSO). **Couplers:** Tightlock.
Gangways: Within unit.   **Control System:** GTO Inverter.
Doors: Sliding plug.   **Maximum Speed:** 90 mph.
Seating Layout: 3+2 facing/unidirectional.
Multiple Working: Within class & with Classes 317, 318, 319, 320, 321 and 322.

DMSO(A). Lot No. 31112 Hunslet 1992–93. –/98 (* –/82). 41.0 t.
TSO. Lot No. 31113 Hunslet 1992–93. –/88(5) 1T 2W. (* –/80 1T 2W). 39.4 t.
DMSO(B). Lot No. 31114 Hunslet 1992–93. –/98 (* –/82). 41.0 t.

323201	**LM**	P	*LM*	SO	64001	72201	65001
323202	**LM**	P	*LM*	SO	64002	72202	65002
323203	**LM**	P	*LM*	SO	64003	72203	65003

323 204		**LM**	P	*LM*	SO	64004	72204	65004
323 205		**LM**	P	*LM*	SO	64005	72205	65005
323 206		**LM**	P	*LM*	SO	64006	72206	65006
323 207		**LM**	P	*LM*	SO	64007	72207	65007
323 208		**LM**	P	*LM*	SO	64008	72208	65008
323 209		**LM**	P	*LM*	SO	64009	72209	65009
323 210		**LM**	P	*LM*	SO	64010	72210	65010
323 211		**LM**	P	*LM*	SO	64011	72211	65011
323 212		**LM**	P	*LM*	SO	64012	72212	65012
323 213		**LM**	P	*LM*	SO	64013	72213	65013
323 214		**LM**	P	*LM*	SO	64014	72214	65014
323 215		**LM**	P	*LM*	SO	64015	72215	65015
323 216		**LM**	P	*LM*	SO	64016	72216	65016
323 217		**LM**	P	*LM*	SO	64017	72217	65017
323 218		**LM**	P	*LM*	SO	64018	72218	65018
323 219		**LM**	P	*LM*	SO	64019	72219	65019
323 220		**LM**	P	*LM*	SO	64020	72220	65020
323 221		**LM**	P	*LM*	SO	64021	72221	65021
323 222		**LM**	P	*LM*	SO	64022	72222	65022
323 223	*	**NO**	P	*NO*	LG	64023	72223	65023
323 224	*	**NO**	P	*NO*	LG	64024	72224	65024
323 225	*	**NO**	P	*NO*	LG	64025	72225	65025
323 226		**NO**	P	*NO*	LG	64026	72226	65026
323 227		**NO**	P	*NO*	LG	64027	72227	65027
323 228		**NO**	P	*NO*	LG	64028	72228	65028
323 229		**NO**	P	*NO*	LG	64029	72229	65029
323 230		**NO**	P	*NO*	LG	64030	72230	65030
323 231		**NO**	P	*NO*	LG	64031	72231	65031
323 232		**NO**	P	*NO*	LG	64032	72232	65032
323 233		**NO**	P	*NO*	LG	64033	72233	65033
323 234		**NO**	P	*NO*	LG	64034	72234	65034
323 235		**NO**	P	*NO*	LG	64035	72235	65035
323 236		**NO**	P	*NO*	LG	64036	72236	65036
323 237		**NO**	P	*NO*	LG	64037	72237	65037
323 238		**NO**	P	*NO*	LG	64038	72238	65038
323 239		**NO**	P	*NO*	LG	64039	72239	65039
323 240		**LM**	P	*LM*	SO	64040	72340	65040
323 241		**LM**	P	*LM*	SO	64041	72341	65041
323 242		**LM**	P	*LM*	SO	64042	72342	65042
323 243		**LM**	P	*LM*	SO	64043	72343	65043

CLASS 325   ABB DERBY

Postal units based on Class 319s. Compatible with diesel or electric
locomotive haulage.

Formation: DTPMV–MPMV–TPMV–DTPMV.
System: 25 kV AC overhead/750 V DC third rail.
Construction: Steel.
Traction Motors: Four GEC G315BZ of 268 kW.
Wheel Arrangement: 2-2 + Bo-Bo + 2-2 + 2-2.

Braking: Disc.
Bogies: P7-4 (MSO), T3-7 (others).
Gangways: None.
Doors: Roller shutter.
Multiple Working: Within class.

Dimensions: 19.33 x 2.82 m.
Couplers: Drop-head buckeye.
Control System: GTO Chopper.
Maximum Speed: 100 mph.

DTPMV. Lot No. 31144 1995. 29.1 t.
MPMV. Lot No. 31145 1995. 49.5 t.
TPMV. Lot No. 31146 1995. 30.7 t.

325 001	**RM**	RM	*DB*	CE	68300	68340	68360	68301
325 002	**RM**	RM	*DB*	CE	68302	68341	68361	68303
325 003	**RM**	RM	*DB*	CE	68304	68342	68362	68305
325 004	**RM**	RM	*DB*	CE	68306	68343	68363	68307
325 005	**RM**	RM	*DB*	CE	68308	68344	68364	68309
325 006	**RM**	RM	*DB*	CE	68310	68345	68365	68311
325 007	**RM**	RM	*DB*	CE	68312	68346	68366	68313
325 008	**RM**	RM	*DB*	CE	68314	68347	68367	68315
325 009	**RM**	RM	*DB*	CE	68316	68349	68368	68317
325 011	**RM**	RM	*DB*	CE	68320	68350	68370	68321
325 012	**RM**	RM	*DB*	CE	68322	68351	68371	68323
325 013	**RM**	RM	*DB*	CE	68324	68352	68372	68325
325 014	**RM**	RM	*DB*	CE	68326	68353	68373	68327
325 015	**RM**	RM	*DB*	CE	68328	68354	68374	68329
325 016	**RM**	RM	*DB*	CE	68330	68355	68375	68331

Names (carried on one side of each DTPMV):

325 002 Royal Mail North Wales & North West
325 006 John Grierson
325 008 Peter Howarth CBE

CLASS 332   HEATHROW EXPRESS CAF/SIEMENS

Dedicated Heathrow Express units. Five units were increased from 4-car to 5-car in 2002. Usually operate in coupled pairs.

Formations: DMSO–TSO–PTSO–(TSO)–DMFO.
Construction: Steel.
Traction Motors: Two Siemens monomotors asynchronous of 350 kW.
Wheel Arrangement: B-B + 2-2 + 2-2 (+ 2-2) + B-B.
Braking: Disc.
Bogies: CAF.
Gangways: Within unit.
Doors: Sliding plug.
Heating & ventilation: Air conditioning.
Seating: 1: 1+1 facing/unidirectional, 2: 2+2 mainly unidirectional.
Multiple Working: Within class.

Dimensions: 23.74/23.35/23.14 x 2.75 m.
Couplers: Scharfenberg 10L.
Control System: IGBT Inverter.
Maximum Speed: 100 mph.

DMSO. CAF 1997–98. –/43 (8). 49.9 t.
72400–413. TSO. CAF 1997–98. –/64 (11). 38.4 t.
72414–418. TSO. CAF 2002. –/56 35.8 t.

PTSO. CAF 1997–98. –/39 (11) 1TD 2W. 47.6 t.
DMFO. CAF 1997–98. 20/–. 49.5 t.

332 001	**HE**	HE	*HE*	OH	78400	72412	63400		78401
332 002	**HE**	HE	*HE*	OH	78402	72409	63406		78403
332 003	**HE**	HE	*HE*	OH	78404	72407	63402		78405
332 004	**HE**	HE	*HE*	OH	78406	72405	63403		78407
332 005	**HE**	HE	*HE*	OH	78408	72411	63404	72417	78409
332 006	**HE**	HE	*HE*	OH	78410	72410	63405	72415	78411
332 007	**HE**	HE	*HE*	OH	78412	72401	63401	72414	78413
332 008	**HE**	HE	*HE*	OH	78414	72413	63407	72418	78415
332 009	**HE**	HE	*HE*	OH	78416	72400	63408	72416	78417
332 010	**HE**	HE	*HE*	OH	78418	72402	63409		78419
332 011	**HE**	HE	*HE*	OH	78420	72403	63410		78421
332 012	**HE**	HE	*HE*	OH	78422	72404	63411		78423
332 013	**HE**	HE	*HE*	OH	78424	72406	63412		78425
332 014	**HE**	HE	*HE*	OH	78426	72406	63413		78427

CLASS 333   CAF/SIEMENS

West Yorkshire area suburban units.

Formation: DMSO–PTSO–TSO–DMSO.
Construction: Steel.
Traction Motors: Two Siemens monomotors asynchronous of 350 kW.
Wheel Arrangement: B-B + 2-2 + 2-2 + B-B.
Braking: Disc.
Dimensions: 23.74 (outer ends)/23.35 (TSO) x 2.75 m.
Bogies: CAF.   **Couplers:** Dellner 10L.
Gangways: Within unit.   **Control System:** IGBT Inverter.
Doors: Sliding plug.   **Maximum Speed:** 100 mph.
Heating & ventilation: Air conditioning.
Seating Layout: 3+2 facing/unidirectional.
Multiple Working: Within class.

333001–008 were made up to 4-car units from 3-car units in 2002.

333009–016 were made up to 4-car units from 3-car units in 2003.

DMSO(A). (Odd Nos.) CAF 2001. –/90. 50.6 t.
PTSO. CAF 2001. –/73(6) 1TD 2W. 46.0 t.
TSO. CAF 2002–03. –/100. 38.5 t.
DMSO(B). (Even Nos.) CAF 2001. –/90. 50.0 t.

333 001	**YR**	A	*NO*	NL	78451	74461	74477	78452
333 002	**YR**	A	*NO*	NL	78453	74462	74478	78454
333 003	**YR**	A	*NO*	NL	78455	74463	74479	78456
333 004	**YR**	A	*NO*	NL	78457	74464	74480	78458
333 005	**YR**	A	*NO*	NL	78459	74465	74481	78460
333 006	**YR**	A	*NO*	NL	78461	74466	74482	78462
333 007	**YR**	A	*NO*	NL	78463	74467	74483	78464
333 008	**YR**	A	*NO*	NL	78465	74468	74484	78466
333 009	**YR**	A	*NO*	NL	78467	74469	74485	78468
333 010	**YR**	A	*NO*	NL	78469	74470	74486	78470

333011	**YR**	A	*NO*	NL	78471	74471	74487	78472
333012	**YR**	A	*NO*	NL	78473	74472	74488	78474
333013	**YR**	A	*NO*	NL	78475	74473	74489	78476
333014	**YR**	A	*NO*	NL	78477	74474	74490	78478
333015	**YR**	A	*NO*	NL	78479	74475	74491	78480
333016	**YR**	A	*NO*	NL	78481	74476	74492	78482

Name (carried on end cars):

333007 Alderman J Arthur Godwin First Lord Mayor of Bradford 1907

CLASS 334   JUNIPER   ALSTOM BIRMINGHAM

Outer suburban units.

Formation: DMSO–PTSO–DMSO.
Construction: Steel.
Traction Motors: Two Alstom ONIX 800 asynchronous of 270 kW.
Wheel Arrangement: 2-Bo + 2-2 + Bo-2.
Braking: Disc.   **Dimensions:** 21.01/19.94 x 2.80 m.
Bogies: Alstom LTB3/TBP3.   **Couplers:** Tightlock.
Gangways: Within unit.   **Control System:** IGBT Inverter.
Doors: Sliding plug.   **Maximum Speed:** 90 mph.
Heating & ventilation: Pressure heating and ventilation.
Seating Layout: 2+2 facing/unidirectional (3+2 in PTSO).
Multiple Working: Within class.

DMSO(A). Alstom Birmingham 1999–2001. –/64. 42.6 t.
PTSO. Alstom Birmingham 1999–2001. –/55 1TD 1W. 39.4 t.
DMSO(B). Alstom Birmingham 1999–2001. –/64. 42.6 t.

334001	**SR**	E	*SR*	GW	64101	74301	65101
334002	**SR**	E	*SR*	GW	64102	74302	65102
334003	**SR**	E	*SR*	GW	64103	74303	65103
334004	**SR**	E	*SR*	GW	64104	74304	65104
334005	**SR**	E	*SR*	GW	64105	74305	65105
334006	**SR**	E	*SR*	GW	64106	74306	65106
334007	**SR**	E	*SR*	GW	64107	74307	65107
334008	**SR**	E	*SR*	GW	64108	74308	65108
334009	**SR**	E	*SR*	GW	64109	74309	65109
334010	**SR**	E	*SR*	GW	64110	74310	65110
334011	**SR**	E	*SR*	GW	64111	74311	65111
334012	**SR**	E	*SR*	GW	64112	74312	65112
334013	**SR**	E	*SR*	GW	64113	74313	65113
334014	**SR**	E	*SR*	GW	64114	74314	65114
334015	**SR**	E	*SR*	GW	64115	74315	65115
334016	**SR**	E	*SR*	GW	64116	74316	65116
334017	**SR**	E	*SR*	GW	64117	74317	65117
334018	**SR**	E	*SR*	GW	64118	74318	65118
334019	**SR**	E	*SR*	GW	64119	74319	65119
334020	**SR**	E	*SR*	GW	64120	74320	65120
334021	**SR**	E	*SR*	GW	64121	74321	65121
334022	**SR**	E	*SR*	GW	64122	74322	65122

334023	**SR**	E	*SR*	GW	64123	74323	65123
334024	**SR**	E	*SR*	GW	64124	74324	65124
334025	**SR**	E	*SR*	GW	64125	74325	65125
334026	**SR**	E	*SR*	GW	64126	74326	65126
334027	**SR**	E	*SR*	GW	64127	74327	65127
334028	**SR**	E	*SR*	GW	64128	74328	65128
334029	**SR**	E	*SR*	GW	64129	74329	65129
334030	**SR**	E	*SR*	GW	64130	74330	65130
334031	**SR**	E	*SR*	GW	64131	74331	65131
334032	**SR**	E	*SR*	GW	64132	74332	65132
334033	**SR**	E	*SR*	GW	64133	74333	65133
334034	**SR**	E	*SR*	GW	64134	74334	65134
334035	**SR**	E	*SR*	GW	64135	74335	65135
334036	**SR**	E	*SR*	GW	64136	74336	65136
334037	**SR**	E	*SR*	GW	64137	74337	65137
334038	**SR**	E	*SR*	GW	64138	74338	65138
334039	**SR**	E	*SR*	GW	64139	74339	65139
334040	**SR**	E	*SR*	GW	64140	74340	65140

CLASS 350   DESIRO UK   SIEMENS

Outer suburban and long distance units.

Formation: DMCO–TCO–PTSO–DMCO.
Systems: 25 kV AC overhead (350/1s built with 750 V DC).
Construction: Welded aluminium.
Traction Motors: 4 Siemens 1TB2016-0GB02 asynchronous of 250 kW.
Wheel Arrangement: Bo-Bo + 2-2 + 2-2 + Bo-Bo.
Braking: Disc & regenerative.   **Dimensions:** 20.34 x 2.79 m.
Bogies: SGP SF5000.   **Couplers:** Dellner 12.
Gangways: Throughout.   **Control System:** IGBT Inverter.
Doors: Sliding plug.
Maximum Speed: 110 mph (350/1, 350/3 & 350/4) or 100 mph (350/2).
Heating & ventilation: Air conditioning.
Seating Layout: Various, see sub-class headings.
Multiple Working: Within class.

Class 350/1. Original build units owned by Angel Trains. Formerly part of an aborted South West Trains 5-car Class 450/2 order. 2+2 seating.

Seating Layout: 1: 2+2 facing, 2: 2+2 facing/unidirectional.

Advertising livery: 350 110 Project 110 (silver centre cars).

DMSO(A). Siemens Krefeld 2004–05. –/60. 48.7 t.
TCO. Siemens Krefeld/Prague 2004–05. 24/32 1T. 36.2 t.
PTSO. Siemens Krefeld/Prague 2004–05. –/50(9) 1TD 2W. 45.2 t.
DMSO(B). Siemens Krefeld 2004–05. –/60. 49.2 t.

350101	**LM**	A	*LM*	NN	63761	66811	66861	63711
350102	**LM**	A	*LM*	NN	63762	66812	66862	63712
350103	**LM**	A	*LM*	NN	63765	66813	66863	63713
350104	**LM**	A	*LM*	NN	63764	66814	66864	63714

350 105	**LM**	A	*LM*	NN	63763	66815	66868	63715
350 106	**LM**	A	*LM*	NN	63766	66816	66866	63716
350 107	**LM**	A	*LM*	NN	63767	66817	66867	63717
350 108	**LM**	A	*LM*	NN	63768	66818	66865	63718
350 109	**LM**	A	*LM*	NN	63769	66819	66869	63719
350 110	**AL**	A	*LM*	NN	63770	66820	66870	63720
350 111	**LM**	A	*LM*	NN	63771	66821	66871	63721
350 112	**LM**	A	*LM*	NN	63772	66822	66872	63722
350 113	**LM**	A	*LM*	NN	63773	66823	66873	63723
350 114	**LM**	A	*LM*	NN	63774	66824	66874	63724
350 115	**LM**	A	*LM*	NN	63775	66825	66875	63725
350 116	**LM**	A	*LM*	NN	63776	66826	66876	63726
350 117	**LM**	A	*LM*	NN	63777	66827	66877	63727
350 118	**LM**	A	*LM*	NN	63778	66828	66878	63728
350 119	**LM**	A	*LM*	NN	63779	66829	66879	63729
350 120	**LM**	A	*LM*	NN	63780	66830	66880	63730
350 121	**LM**	A	*LM*	NN	63781	66831	66881	63731
350 122	**LM**	A	*LM*	NN	63782	66832	66882	63732
350 123	**LM**	A	*LM*	NN	63783	66833	66883	63733
350 124	**LM**	A	*LM*	NN	63784	66834	66884	63734
350 125	**LM**	A	*LM*	NN	63785	66835	66885	63735
350 126	**LM**	A	*LM*	NN	63786	66836	66886	63736
350 127	**LM**	A	*LM*	NN	63787	66837	66887	63737
350 128	**LM**	A	*LM*	NN	63788	66838	66888	63738
350 129	**LM**	A	*LM*	NN	63789	66839	66889	63739
350 130	**LM**	A	*LM*	NN	63790	66840	66890	63740

Class 350/2. Owned by Porterbrook Leasing.

Seating Layout: 1: 2+2 facing, 2: 3+2 facing/unidirectional.

DMSO(A). Siemens Krefeld 2008–09. –/70. 43.7 t.
TCO. Siemens Prague 2008–09. 24/42 1T. 35.3 t.
PTSO. Siemens Prague 2008–09. –/61(9) 1TD 2W. 42.9 t.
DMSO(B). Siemens Krefeld 2008–09. –/70. 44.2 t.

350 231	**LM**	P	*LM*	NN	61431	65231	67531	61531
350 232	**LM**	P	*LM*	NN	61432	65232	67532	61532
350 233	**LM**	P	*LM*	NN	61433	65233	67533	61533
350 234	**LM**	P	*LM*	NN	61434	65234	67534	61534
350 235	**LM**	P	*LM*	NN	61435	65235	67535	61535
350 236	**LM**	P	*LM*	NN	61436	65236	67536	61536
350 237	**LM**	P	*LM*	NN	61437	65237	67537	61537
350 238	**LM**	P	*LM*	NN	61438	65238	67538	61538
350 239	**LM**	P	*LM*	NN	61439	65239	67539	61539
350 240	**LM**	P	*LM*	NN	61440	65240	67540	61540
350 241	**LM**	P	*LM*	NN	61441	65241	67541	61541
350 242	**LM**	P	*LM*	NN	61442	65242	67542	61542
350 243	**LM**	P	*LM*	NN	61443	65243	67543	61543
350 244	**LM**	P	*LM*	NN	61444	65244	67544	61544
350 245	**LM**	P	*LM*	NN	61445	65245	67545	61545
350 246	**LM**	P	*LM*	NN	61446	65246	67546	61546
350 247	**LM**	P	*LM*	NN	61447	65247	67547	61547

350 248	**LM**	P	*LM*	NN	61448	65248	67548	61548
350 249	**LM**	P	*LM*	NN	61449	65249	67549	61549
350 250	**LM**	P	*LM*	NN	61450	65250	67550	61550
350 251	**LM**	P	*LM*	NN	61451	65251	67551	61551
350 252	**LM**	P	*LM*	NN	61452	65252	67552	61552
350 253	**LM**	P	*LM*	NN	61453	65253	67553	61553
350 254	**LM**	P	*LM*	NN	61454	65254	67554	61554
350 255	**LM**	P	*LM*	NN	61455	65255	67555	61555
350 256	**LM**	P	*LM*	NN	61456	65256	67556	61556
350 257	**LM**	P	*LM*	NN	61457	65257	67557	61557
350 258	**LM**	P	*LM*	NN	61458	65258	67558	61558
350 259	**LM**	P	*LM*	NN	61459	65259	67559	61559
350 260	**LM**	P	*LM*	NN	61460	65260	67560	61560
350 261	**LM**	P	*LM*	NN	61461	65261	67561	61561
350 262	**LM**	P	*LM*	NN	61462	65262	67562	61562
350 263	**LM**	P	*LM*	NN	61463	65263	67563	61563
350 264	**LM**	P	*LM*	NN	61464	65264	67564	61564
350 265	**LM**	P	*LM*	NN	61465	65265	67565	61565
350 266	**LM**	P	*LM*	NN	61466	65266	67566	61566
350 267	**LM**	P	*LM*	NN	61467	65267	67567	61567

Name (carried on one side of PTSO): 350 232   Chad Varah

Class 350/3. Owned by Angel Trains. London Midland units built for 110 mph operation.

Seating Layout: 1: 2+2 facing, 2: 2+2 facing/unidirectional.

DMSO(A). Siemens Krefeld 2014. –/60. 44.2 t.
TCO. Siemens Krefeld 2014. 24/36 1T. 36.3 t.
PTSO. Siemens Krefeld 2014. –/50(9) 1TD 2W. 44.0 t.
DMSO(B). Siemens Krefeld 2014. –/60. 45.0 t.

350 368	**LM**	A	*LM*	NN	60141	60511	60651	60151
350 369	**LM**	A	*LM*	NN	60142	60512	60652	60152
350 370	**LM**	A	*LM*	NN	60143	60513	60653	60153
350 371	**LM**	A	*LM*	NN	60144	60514	60654	60154
350 372	**LM**	A	*LM*	NN	60145	60515	60655	60155
350 373	**LM**	A	*LM*	NN	60146	60516	60656	60156
350 374	**LM**	A	*LM*	NN	60147	60517	60657	60157
350 375	**LM**	A	*LM*	NN	60148	60518	60658	60158
350 376	**LM**	A	*LM*	NN	60149	60519	60659	60159
350 377	**LM**	A	*LM*	NN	60150	60520	60660	60160

Class 350/4. Owned by Angel Trains. TransPennine Express units used on the Manchester Airport–Edinburgh/Glasgow route.

Seating Layout: 1: 2+1 facing, 2: 2+2 facing/unidirectional.

DMSO(A). Siemens Krefeld 2013–14. –/56. 44.2 t.
TCO. Siemens Krefeld 2013–14. 19/24 1T. 36.2 t.
PTSO. Siemens Krefeld 2013–14. –/42 1TD 1T. 44.6 t.
DMSO(B). Siemens Krefeld 2013–14. –/56. 45.0 t.

350401	**FT**	A	*TP*	AK	60691	60901	60941	60671
350402	**FT**	A	*TP*	AK	60692	60902	60942	60672
350403	**FT**	A	*TP*	AK	60693	60903	60943	60673
350404	**FT**	A	*TP*	AK	60694	60904	60944	60674
350405	**FT**	A	*TP*	AK	60695	60905	60945	60675
350406	**FT**	A	*TP*	AK	60696	60906	60946	60676
350407	**FT**	A	*TP*	AK	60697	60907	60947	60677
350408	**FT**	A	*TP*	AK	60698	60908	60948	60678
350409	**FT**	A	*TP*	AK	60699	60909	60949	60679
350410	**FT**	A	*TP*	AK	60700	60910	60950	60680

CLASS 357 ELECTROSTAR
ADTRANZ/BOMBARDIER DERBY

Provision for 750 V DC supply if required.

Formation: DMSO–MSO–PTSO–DMSO.
Construction: Welded aluminium alloy underframe, sides and roof with steel ends. All sections bolted together.
Traction Motors: Two Adtranz asynchronous of 250 kW.
Wheel Arrangement: 2-Bo + 2-Bo + 2-2 + Bo-2.
Braking: Disc & regenerative.   **Dimensions:** 20.40/19.99 x 2.80 m.
Bogies: Adtranz P3-25/T3-25.   **Couplers:** Tightlock.
Gangways: Within unit.   **Control System:** IGBT Inverter.
Doors: Sliding plug.   **Maximum Speed:** 100 mph.
Heating & ventilation: Air conditioning.
Seating Layout: 3+2 facing/unidirectional.
Multiple Working: Within class.

Class 357/0. Owned by Porterbrook Leasing.

DMSO(A). Adtranz Derby 1999–2001. –/71. 40.7 t.
MSO. Adtranz Derby 1999–2001. –/78. 36.7 t.
PTSO. Adtranz Derby 1999–2001. –/58(4) 1TD 2W. 39.5 t.
DMSO(B). Adtranz Derby 1999–2001. –/71. 40.7 t.

357001	**NC**	P	*C2*	EM	67651	74151	74051	67751
357002	**NC**	P	*C2*	EM	67652	74152	74052	67752
357003	**NC**	P	*C2*	EM	67653	74153	74053	67753
357004	**NC**	P	*C2*	EM	67654	74154	74054	67754
357005	**NC**	P	*C2*	EM	67655	74155	74055	67755
357006	**NC**	P	*C2*	EM	67656	74156	74056	67756
357007	**NC**	P	*C2*	EM	67657	74157	74057	67757
357008	**NC**	P	*C2*	EM	67658	74158	74058	67758
357009	**NC**	P	*C2*	EM	67659	74159	74059	67759
357010	**NC**	P	*C2*	EM	67660	74160	74060	67760
357011	**NC**	P	*C2*	EM	67661	74161	74061	67761
357012	**NC**	P	*C2*	EM	67662	74162	74062	67762
357013	**NC**	P	*C2*	EM	67663	74163	74063	67763
357014	**NC**	P	*C2*	EM	67664	74164	74064	67764
357015	**NC**	P	*C2*	EM	67665	74165	74065	67765
357016	**NC**	P	*C2*	EM	67666	74166	74066	67766

357017	**NC**	P	*C2*	EM	67667	74167	74067	67767
357018	**NC**	P	*C2*	EM	67668	74168	74068	67768
357019	**NC**	P	*C2*	EM	67669	74169	74069	67769
357020	**NC**	P	*C2*	EM	67670	74170	74070	67770
357021	**NC**	P	*C2*	EM	67671	74171	74071	67771
357022	**NC**	P	*C2*	EM	67672	74172	74072	67772
357023	**NC**	P	*C2*	EM	67673	74173	74073	67773
357024	**NC**	P	*C2*	EM	67674	74174	74074	67774
357025	**NC**	P	*C2*	EM	67675	74175	74075	67775
357026	**NC**	P	*C2*	EM	67676	74176	74076	67776
357027	**NC**	P	*C2*	EM	67677	74177	74077	67777
357028	**NC**	P	*C2*	EM	67678	74178	74078	67778
357029	**NC**	P	*C2*	EM	67679	74179	74079	67779
357030	**NC**	P	*C2*	EM	67680	74180	74080	67780
357031	**NC**	P	*C2*	EM	67681	74181	74081	67781
357032	**NC**	P	*C2*	EM	67682	74182	74082	67782
357033	**NC**	P	*C2*	EM	67683	74183	74083	67783
357034	**NC**	P	*C2*	EM	67684	74184	74084	67784
357035	**NC**	P	*C2*	EM	67685	74185	74085	67785
357036	**NC**	P	*C2*	EM	67686	74186	74086	67786
357037	**NC**	P	*C2*	EM	67687	74187	74087	67787
357038	**NC**	P	*C2*	EM	67688	74188	74088	67788
357039	**NC**	P	*C2*	EM	67689	74189	74089	67789
357040	**NC**	P	*C2*	EM	67690	74190	74090	67790
357041	**NC**	P	*C2*	EM	67691	74191	74091	67791
357042	**NC**	P	*C2*	EM	67692	74192	74092	67792
357043	**NC**	P	*C2*	EM	67693	74193	74093	67793
357044	**NC**	P	*C2*	EM	67694	74194	74094	67794
357045	**NC**	P	*C2*	EM	67695	74195	74095	67795
357046	**NC**	P	*C2*	EM	67696	74196	74096	67796

Names (carried on DMSO(A) and DMSO(B) (one plate on each)):

357001 BARRY FLAXMAN
357002 ARTHUR LEWIS STRIDE 1841–1922
357003 SOUTHEND city.on.sea
357004 TONY AMOS
357006 DIAMOND JUBILEE 1952–2012
357011 JOHN LOWING
357028 London, Tilbury & Southend Railway 1854–2004
357029 THOMAS WHITELEGG 1840–1922
357030 ROBERT HARBEN WHITELEGG 1871–1957

Class 357/2. Owned by Angel Trains.

DMSO(A). Bombardier Derby 2001–02. –/71. 40.7 t.
MSO. Bombardier Derby 2001–02. –/78. 36.7 t.
PTSO. Bombardier Derby 2001–02. –/58(4) 1TD 2W. 39.5 t.
DMSO(B). Bombardier Derby 2001–02. –/71. 40.7 t.

357201	**NC**	A	*C2*	EM	68601	74701	74601	68701
357202	**NC**	A	*C2*	EM	68602	74702	74602	68702
357203	**NC**	A	*C2*	EM	68603	74703	74603	68703

357 204	**NC**	A	*C2*	EM	68604	74704	74604	68704
357 205	**NC**	A	*C2*	EM	68605	74705	74605	68705
357 206	**NC**	A	*C2*	EM	68606	74706	74606	68706
357 207	**NC**	A	*C2*	EM	68607	74707	74607	68707
357 208	**NC**	A	*C2*	EM	68608	74708	74608	68708
357 209	**NC**	A	*C2*	EM	68609	74709	74609	68709
357 210	**NC**	A	*C2*	EM	68610	74710	74610	68710
357 211	**NC**	A	*C2*	EM	68611	74711	74611	68711
357 212	**NC**	A	*C2*	EM	68612	74712	74612	68712
357 213	**NC**	A	*C2*	EM	68613	74713	74613	68713
357 214	**NC**	A	*C2*	EM	68614	74714	74614	68714
357 215	**NC**	A	*C2*	EM	68615	74715	74615	68715
357 216	**NC**	A	*C2*	EM	68616	74716	74616	68716
357 217	**NC**	A	*C2*	EM	68617	74717	74617	68717
357 218	**NC**	A	*C2*	EM	68618	74718	74618	68718
357 219	**NC**	A	*C2*	EM	68619	74719	74619	68719
357 220	**NC**	A	*C2*	EM	68620	74720	74620	68720
357 221	**NC**	A	*C2*	EM	68621	74721	74621	68721
357 222	**NC**	A	*C2*	EM	68622	74722	74622	68722
357 223	**NC**	A	*C2*	EM	68623	74723	74623	68723
357 224	**NC**	A	*C2*	EM	68624	74724	74624	68724
357 225	**NC**	A	*C2*	EM	68625	74725	74625	68725
357 226	**NC**	A	*C2*	EM	68626	74726	74626	68726
357 227	**NC**	A	*C2*	EM	68627	74727	74627	68727
357 228	**NC**	A	*C2*	EM	68628	74728	74628	68728

Names (carried on DMSO(A) and DMSO(B) (one plate on each)):

357 201	KEN BIRD	357 207	JOHN PAGE
357 202	KENNY MITCHELL	357 208	DAVE DAVIS
357 203	HENRY PUMFRETT	357 209	JAMES SNELLING
357 204	DEREK FOWERS	357 213	UPMINSTER I.E.C.C.
357 205	JOHN D'SILVA	357 217	ALLAN BURNELL
357 206	MARTIN AUNGIER	357 227	SOUTHEND UNITED

CLASS 360/0　　　DESIRO UK　　　SIEMENS

Outer suburban/express units.

Formation: DMCO–PTSO–TSO–DMCO.
Construction: Welded aluminium.
Traction Motors: Four Siemens 1TB2016-0GB02 asynchronous of 250 kW.
Wheel Arrangement: Bo-Bo + 2-2 + 2-2 + Bo-Bo.
Braking: Disc & regenerative. **Dimensions:** 20.34 x 2.80 m.
Bogies: SGP SF5000. **Couplers:** Dellner 12.
Gangways: Within unit. **Control System:** IGBT Inverter.
Doors: Sliding plug. **Maximum Speed:** 100 mph.
Heating & ventilation: Air conditioning.
Seating Layout: 1: 2+2 facing, 2: 3+2 facing/unidirectional.
Multiple Working: Within class.

DMCO(A). Siemens Krefeld 2002–03. 8/59. 45.0 t.
PTSO. Siemens Vienna 2002–03. –/60(9) 1TD 2W. 43.0 t.
TSO. Siemens Vienna 2002–03. –/78. 35.0 t.
DMCO(B). Siemens Krefeld 2002–03. 8/59. 45.0 t.

360 101	**FB**	A	*GA*	IL	65551	72551	74551	68551
360 102	**FB**	A	*GA*	IL	65552	72552	74552	68552
360 103	**FB**	A	*GA*	IL	65553	72553	74553	68553
360 104	**FB**	A	*GA*	IL	65554	72554	74554	68554
360 105	**FB**	A	*GA*	IL	65555	72555	74555	68555
360 106	**FB**	A	*GA*	IL	65556	72556	74556	68556
360 107	**FB**	A	*GA*	IL	65557	72557	74557	68557
360 108	**FB**	A	*GA*	IL	65558	72558	74558	68558
360 109	**FB**	A	*GA*	IL	65559	72559	74559	68559
360 110	**FB**	A	*GA*	IL	65560	72560	74560	68560
360 111	**FB**	A	*GA*	IL	65561	72561	74561	68561
360 112	**FB**	A	*GA*	IL	65562	72562	74562	68562
360 113	**FB**	A	*GA*	IL	65563	72563	74563	68563
360 114	**FB**	A	*GA*	IL	65564	72564	74564	68564
360 115	**FB**	A	*GA*	IL	65565	72565	74565	68565
360 116	**FB**	A	*GA*	IL	65566	72566	74566	68566
360 117	**FB**	A	*GA*	IL	65567	72567	74567	68567
360 118	**FB**	A	*GA*	IL	65568	72568	74568	68568
360 119	**FB**	A	*GA*	IL	65569	72569	74569	68569
360 120	**FB**	A	*GA*	IL	65570	72570	74570	68570
360 121	**FB**	A	*GA*	IL	65571	72571	74571	68571

CLASS 360/2   DESIRO UK   SIEMENS

4-car Class 350 testbed units rebuilt for use by Heathrow Express on Paddington–Heathrow Airport stopping services ("Heathrow Connect").

Original 4-car sets 360 201–204 were made up to 5-cars during 2007 using additional TSOs. A fifth unit (360 205) was delivered in late 2005 as a 5-car set. This set is normally used on Terminals 1&3–Terminal 4 shuttle services.

Formation: DMSO–PTSO–TSO–TSO–DMSO.
Construction: Welded aluminium.
Traction Motors: Four Siemens 1TB2016-0GB02 asynchronous of 250 kW.
Wheel Arrangement: Bo-Bo + 2-2 + 2-2 + 2-2 + Bo-Bo.
Braking: Disc & regenerative.   **Dimensions:** 20.34 x 2.80 m.
Bogies: SGP SF5000.   **Couplers:** Dellner 12.
Gangways: Within unit.   **Control System:** IGBT Inverter.
Doors: Sliding plug.   **Maximum Speed:** 100 mph.
Heating & ventilation: Air conditioning.
Seating Layout: 3+2 (* 2+2) facing/unidirectional.
Multiple Working: Within class.

DMSO(A). Siemens Krefeld 2002–06. –/63 (* –/54). 44.8 t.
PTSO. Siemens Krefeld 2002–06. –/57(9) 1TD 2W (* –/48(9) 2W). 44.2 t.
TSO. Siemens Krefeld 2005–06. –/74 (* –/62). 35.3 t.
TSO. Siemens Krefeld 2002–06. –/74 (* –/62). 34.1 t.
DMSO(B). Siemens Krefeld 2002–06. –/63 (* –/54). 44.4 t.

360 201		**HC**	HE	*HC*	OH	78431	63421	72431	72421	78441
360 202		**HC**	HE	*HC*	OH	78432	63422	72432	72422	78442
360 203		**HC**	HE	*HC*	OH	78433	63423	72433	72423	78443
360 204		**HC**	HE	*HC*	OH	78434	63424	72434	72424	78444
360 205	*	**HE**	HE	*HE*	OH	78435	63425	72435	72425	78445

CLASS 365   NETWORKER EXPRESS   ABB YORK

Outer suburban units.

Formations: DMCO–TSO–PTSO–DMCO.
Systems: 25 kV AC overhead but with 750 V DC third rail capability (units marked * were formerly used on DC lines in the South-East).
Construction: Welded aluminium alloy.
Traction Motors: Four GEC-Alsthom G354CX asynchronous of 157 kW.
Wheel Arrangement: Bo-Bo + 2-2 + 2-2 + Bo-Bo.
Braking: Disc & rheostatic.
Dimensions: 20.89/20.06 x 2.81 m.
Bogies: ABB P3-16/T3-16.
Gangways: Within unit.
Doors: Sliding plug.

Couplers: Tightlock.
Control System: GTO Inverter.
Maximum Speed: 100 mph.

Seating Layout: 1: 2+2 facing, 2: 2+2 facing.
Multiple Working: Within class only.

Advertising liveries:

365510 Cambridge & Ely; Cathedral cities (blue & white with various images).
365519 Peterborough; environment capital (blue & white with various images).
365531 Nelson's County; Norfolk (blue & white with various images).

DMCO(A). Lot No. 31133 1994–95. 12/56. 41.7 t.
TSO. Lot No. 31134 1994–95. –/65 1TD (* –/64 1TD) 32.9 t.
PTSO. Lot No. 31135 1994–95. –/68 1T. 34.6 t.
DMCO(B). Lot No. 31136 1994–95. 12/56. 41.7 t.

365 501	*	**FU**	E	*GT*	HE	65894	72241	72240	65935
365 502	*	**FU**	E	*GT*	HE	65895	72243	72242	65936
365 503	*	**FU**	E	*GT*	HE	65896	72245	72244	65937
365 504	*	**FU**	E	*GT*	HE	65897	72247	72246	65938
365 505	*	**FU**	E	*GT*	HE	65898	72249	72248	65939
365 506	*	**FU**	E	*GT*	HE	65899	72251	72250	65940
365 507	*	**FU**	E	*GT*	HE	65900	72253	72252	65941
365 508	*	**FU**	E	*GT*	HE	65901	72255	72254	65942
365 509	*	**FU**	E	*GT*	HE	65902	72257	72256	65943
365 510	*	**AL**	E	*GT*	HE	65903	72259	72258	65944
365 511	*	**FU**	E	*GT*	HE	65904	72261	72260	65945
365 512	*	**FU**	E	*GT*	HE	65905	72263	72262	65946
365 513	*	**FU**	E	*GT*	HE	65906	72265	72264	65947
365 514	*	**FU**	E	*GT*	HE	65907	72267	72266	65948
365 515	*	**FU**	E	*GT*	HE	65908	72269	72268	65949
365 516	*	**FU**	E	*GT*	HE	65909	72271	72270	65950
365 517		**TL**	E	*GT*	HE	65910	72273	72272	65951
365 518		**FU**	E	*GT*	HE	65911	72275	72274	65952

365519	AL	E	GT	HE	65912	72277	72276	65953
365520	TL	E	GT	HE	65913	72279	72278	65954
365521	FU	E	GT	HE	65914	72281	72280	65955
365522	TL	E	GT	HE	65915	72283	72282	65956
365523	TL	E	GT	HE	65916	72285	72284	65957
365524	TL	E	GT	HE	65917	72287	72286	65958
365525	TL	E	GT	HE	65918	72289	72288	65959
365527	FU	E	GT	HE	65920	72293	72292	65961
365528	TL	E	GT	HE	65921	72295	72294	65962
365529	FU	E	GT	HE	65922	72297	72296	65963
365530	FU	E	GT	HE	65923	72299	72298	65964
365531	AL	E	GT	HE	65924	72301	72300	65965
365532	FU	E	GT	HE	65925	72303	72302	65966
365533	TL	E	GT	HE	65926	72305	72304	65967
365534	FU	E	GT	HE	65927	72307	72306	65968
365535	FU	E	GT	HE	65928	72309	72308	65969
365536	FU	E	GT	HE	65929	72311	72310	65970
365537	TL	E	GT	HE	65930	72313	72312	65971
365538	TL	E	GT	HE	65931	72315	72314	65972
365539	FU	E	GT	HE	65932	72317	72316	65973
365540	TL	E	GT	HE	65933	72319	72318	65974
365541	FU	E	GT	HE	65934	72321	72320	65975

Names (carried on each DMCO):

365506 The Royston Express
365513 Hornsey Depot
365514 Captain George Vancouver
365517 Supporting Red Balloon
365518 The Fenman
365527 Robert Stripe Passengers' Champion
365530 The Intalink Partnership promoting integrated transport in
        Hertfordshire since 1999
365533 Max Appeal
365536 Rufus Barnes Chief Executive of London TravelWatch for 25 years
365537 Daniel Edwards (1974–2010) Cambridge Driver

CLASS 375 ELECTROSTAR
ADTRANZ/BOMBARDIER DERBY

Express and outer suburban units.

Formations: Various.
Systems: 25 kV AC overhead/750 V DC third rail (some third rail only with provision for retro-fitting of AC equipment).
Construction: Welded aluminium alloy underframe, sides and roof with steel ends. All sections bolted together.
Traction Motors: Two Adtranz asynchronous of 250 kW.
Wheel Arrangement: 2-Bo (+ 2-Bo) + 2-2 + Bo-2.
Braking: Disc & regenerative.   **Dimensions:** 20.40/19.99 x 2.80 m.
Bogies: Adtranz P3-25/T3-25.   **Couplers:** Dellner 12.

Gangways: Throughout.
Doors: Sliding plug.
Heating & ventilation: Air conditioning.
Control System: IGBT Inverter.
Maximum Speed: 100 mph.
Seating Layout: 1: 2+2 facing/unidirectional (seats behind drivers cab in each DMCO). 2: 2+2 facing/unidirectional (except 375/9 – 3+2 facing/unidirectional).
Multiple Working: Within class and with Classes 376, 377, 378 and 379.

Class 375/3. Express units. 750 V DC only. DMCO–TSO–DMCO.

DMCO(A). Bombardier Derby 2001–02. 12/48. 43.8 t.
TSO. Bombardier Derby 2001–02. –/56 1TD 2W. 35.5 t.
DMCO(B). Bombardier Derby 2001–02. 12/48. 43.8 t.

375301	**CN**	E	*SE*	RM	67921	74351	67931
375302	**CN**	E	*SE*	RM	67922	74352	67932
375303	**CN**	E	*SE*	RM	67923	74353	67933
375304	**CN**	E	*SE*	RM	67924	74354	67934
375305	**CN**	E	*SE*	RM	67925	74355	67935
375306	**CN**	E	*SE*	RM	67926	74356	67936
375307	**CN**	E	*SE*	RM	67927	74357	67937
375308	**SE**	E	*SE*	RM	67928	74358	67938
375309	**CN**	E	*SE*	RM	67929	74359	67939
375310	**CN**	E	*SE*	RM	67930	74360	67940

Name (carried on TSO): 375 304 Medway Valley Line 1856–2006

Class 375/6. Express units. 25 kV AC/750 V DC. DMCO–MSO–PTSO–DMCO.

DMCO(A). Adtranz Derby 1999–2001. 12/48. 46.2 t.
MSO. Adtranz Derby 1999–2001. –/66 1T. 40.5 t.
PTSO. Adtranz Derby 1999–2001. –/56 1TD 2W. 40.7 t.
DMCO(B). Adtranz Derby 1999–2001. 12/48. 46.2 t.

375601	**CN**	E	*SE*	RM	67801	74251	74201	67851
375602	**CN**	E	*SE*	RM	67802	74252	74202	67852
375603	**CN**	E	*SE*	RM	67803	74253	74203	67853
375604	**CN**	E	*SE*	RM	67804	74254	74204	67854
375605	**CN**	E	*SE*	RM	67805	74255	74205	67855
375606	**CN**	E	*SE*	RM	67806	74256	74206	67856
375607	**CN**	E	*SE*	RM	67807	74257	74207	67857
375608	**CN**	E	*SE*	RM	67808	74258	74208	67858
375609	**SE**	E	*SE*	RM	67809	74259	74209	67859
375610	**CN**	E	*SE*	RM	67810	74260	74210	67860
375611	**CN**	E	*SE*	RM	67811	74261	74211	67861
375612	**CN**	E	*SE*	RM	67812	74262	74212	67862
375613	**CN**	E	*SE*	RM	67813	74263	74213	67863
375614	**CN**	E	*SE*	RM	67814	74264	74214	67864
375615	**CN**	E	*SE*	RM	67815	74265	74215	67865
375616	**CN**	E	*SE*	RM	67816	74266	74216	67866
375617	**CN**	E	*SE*	RM	67817	74267	74217	67867
375618	**CN**	E	*SE*	RM	67818	74268	74218	67868
375619	**CN**	E	*SE*	RM	67819	74269	74219	67869
375620	**CN**	E	*SE*	RM	67820	74270	74220	67870
375621	**CN**	E	*SE*	RM	67821	74271	74221	67871

375622	**CN**	E	*SE*	RM	67822	74272	74222	67872
375623	**CN**	E	*SE*	RM	67823	74273	74223	67873
375624	**SE**	E	*SE*	RM	67824	74274	74224	67874
375625	**CN**	E	*SE*	RM	67825	74275	74225	67875
375626	**CN**	E	*SE*	RM	67826	74276	74226	67876
375627	**CN**	E	*SE*	RM	67827	74277	74227	67877
375628	**CN**	E	*SE*	RM	67828	74278	74228	67878
375629	**CN**	E	*SE*	RM	67829	74279	74229	67879
375630	**CN**	E	*SE*	RM	67830	74280	74230	67880

Names (carried on one side of each MSO or PTSO):

375608 Bromley Travelwise	375619 Driver John Neve
375610 Royal Tunbridge Wells	375623 Hospice in the Weald
375611 Dr. William Harvey	

Class 375/7. Express units. 750 V DC only. DMCO–MSO–TSO–DMCO.

DMCO(A). Bombardier Derby 2001–02. 12/48. 43.8 t.
MSO. Bombardier Derby 2001–02. –/66 1T. 36.4 t.
TSO. Bombardier Derby 2001–02. –/56 1TD 2W. 34.1 t.
DMCO(B). Bombardier Derby 2001–02. 12/48. 43.8 t.

375701	**CN**	E	*SE*	RM	67831	74281	74231	67881
375702	**CN**	E	*SE*	RM	67832	74282	74232	67882
375703	**CN**	E	*SE*	RM	67833	74283	74233	67883
375704	**CN**	E	*SE*	RM	67834	74284	74234	67884
375705	**SE**	E	*SE*	RM	67835	74285	74235	67885
375706	**CN**	E	*SE*	RM	67836	74286	74236	67886
375707	**CN**	E	*SE*	RM	67837	74287	74237	67887
375708	**CN**	E	*SE*	RM	67838	74288	74238	67888
375709	**CN**	E	*SE*	RM	67839	74289	74239	67889
375710	**CN**	E	*SE*	RM	67840	74290	74240	67890
375711	**CN**	E	*SE*	RM	67841	74291	74241	67891
375712	**CN**	E	*SE*	RM	67842	74292	74242	67892
375713	**CN**	E	*SE*	RM	67843	74293	74243	67893
375714	**CN**	E	*SE*	RM	67844	74294	74244	67894
375715	**CN**	E	*SE*	RM	67845	74295	74245	67895

Name (carried on one side of each MSO or TSO):

375701 Kent Air Ambulance Explorer

Class 375/8. Express units. 750 V DC only. DMCO–MSO–TSO–DMCO.

375 801–820 are fitted with de-icing equipment. TSO weighs 36.5 t.

DMCO(A). Bombardier Derby 2004. 12/48. 43.3 t.
MSO. Bombardier Derby 2004. –/66 1T. 39.8 t.
TSO. Bombardier Derby 2004. –/52 1TD 2W. 35.9 t.
DMCO(B). Bombardier Derby 2004. 12/52. 43.3 t.

375801	**CN**	E	*SE*	RM	73301	79001	78201	73701
375802	**CN**	E	*SE*	RM	73302	79002	78202	73702
375803	**CN**	E	*SE*	RM	73303	79003	78203	73703
375804	**CN**	E	*SE*	RM	73304	79004	78204	73704

375805	**CN**	E	*SE*	RM	73305	79005	78205	73705
375806	**CN**	E	*SE*	RM	73306	79006	78206	73706
375807	**CN**	E	*SE*	RM	73307	79007	78207	73707
375808	**CN**	E	*SE*	RM	73308	79008	78208	73708
375809	**CN**	E	*SE*	RM	73309	79009	78209	73709
375810	**CN**	E	*SE*	RM	73310	79010	78210	73710
375811	**CN**	E	*SE*	RM	73311	79011	78211	73711
375812	**CN**	E	*SE*	RM	73312	79012	78212	73712
375813	**CN**	E	*SE*	RM	73313	79013	78213	73713
375814	**CN**	E	*SE*	RM	73314	79014	78214	73714
375815	**CN**	E	*SE*	RM	73315	79015	78215	73715
375816	**CN**	E	*SE*	RM	73316	79016	78216	73716
375817	**CN**	E	*SE*	RM	73317	79017	78217	73717
375818	**CN**	E	*SE*	RM	73318	79018	78218	73718
375819	**CN**	E	*SE*	RM	73319	79019	78219	73719
375820	**CN**	E	*SE*	RM	73320	79020	78220	73720
375821	**CN**	E	*SE*	RM	73321	79021	78221	73721
375822	**CN**	E	*SE*	RM	73322	79022	78222	73722
375823	**CN**	E	*SE*	RM	73323	79023	78223	73723
375824	**CN**	E	*SE*	RM	73324	79024	78224	73724
375825	**CN**	E	*SE*	RM	73325	79025	78225	73725
375826	**CN**	E	*SE*	RM	73326	79026	78226	73726
375827	**CN**	E	*SE*	RM	73327	79027	78227	73727
375828	**CN**	E	*SE*	RM	73328	79028	78228	73728
375829	**CN**	E	*SE*	RM	73329	79029	78229	73729
375830	**CN**	E	*SE*	RM	73330	79030	78230	73730

Name (carried on one side of each MSO or TSO):

375830 City of London

Class 375/9. Outer suburban units. 750 V DC only. DMCO–MSO–TSO–DMCO.

DMCO(A). Bombardier Derby 2003–04. 12/59. 43.4 t.
MSO. Bombardier Derby 2003–04. –/73 1T. 39.3 t.
TSO. Bombardier Derby 2003–04. –/59 1TD 2W. 35.6 t.
DMCO(B). Bombardier Derby 2003–04. 12/59. 43.4 t.

375901	**CN**	E	*SE*	RM	73331	79031	79061	73731
375902	**CN**	E	*SE*	RM	73332	79032	79062	73732
375903	**CN**	E	*SE*	RM	73333	79033	79063	73733
375904	**CN**	E	*SE*	RM	73334	79034	79064	73734
375905	**CN**	E	*SE*	RM	73335	79035	79065	73735
375906	**CN**	E	*SE*	RM	73336	79036	79066	73736
375907	**CN**	E	*SE*	RM	73337	79037	79067	73737
375908	**CN**	E	*SE*	RM	73338	79038	79068	73738
375909	**CN**	E	*SE*	RM	73339	79039	79069	73739
375910	**CN**	E	*SE*	RM	73340	79040	79070	73740
375911	**CN**	E	*SE*	RM	73341	79041	79071	73741
375912	**CN**	E	*SE*	RM	73342	79042	79072	73742
375913	**CN**	E	*SE*	RM	73343	79043	79073	73743
375914	**CN**	E	*SE*	RM	73344	79044	79074	73744
375915	**CN**	E	*SE*	RM	73345	79045	79075	73745

375916	CN	E	*SE*	RM	73346	79046	79076	73746
375917	CN	E	*SE*	RM	73347	79047	79077	73747
375918	CN	E	*SE*	RM	73348	79048	79078	73748
375919	CN	E	*SE*	RM	73349	79049	79079	73749
375920	CN	E	*SE*	RM	73350	79050	79080	73750
375921	CN	E	*SE*	RM	73351	79051	79081	73751
375922	CN	E	*SE*	RM	73352	79052	79082	73752
375923	CN	E	*SE*	RM	73353	79053	79083	73753
375924	CN	E	*SE*	RM	73354	79054	79084	73754
375925	CN	E	*SE*	RM	73355	79055	79085	73755
375926	CN	E	*SE*	RM	73356	79056	79086	73756
375927	CN	E	*SE*	RM	73357	79057	79087	73757

CLASS 376 ELECTROSTAR BOMBARDIER DERBY

Inner suburban units.

Formation: DMSO–MSO–TSO–MSO–DMSO.
System: 750 V DC third rail.
Construction: Welded aluminium alloy underframe, sides and roof with steel ends. All sections bolted together.
Traction Motors: Two Bombardier asynchronous of 200 kW.
Wheel Arrangement: 2-Bo + 2-Bo + 2-2 + Bo-2 + Bo-2.

Braking: Disc & regenerative.	**Dimensions:** 20.40/19.99 x 2.80 m.
Bogies: Bombardier P3-25/T3-25.	**Couplers:** Dellner 12.
Gangways: Within unit.	**Control System:** IGBT Inverter.
Doors: Sliding.	**Maximum Speed:** 75 mph.

Heating & ventilation: Pressure heating and ventilation.
Seating Layout: 2+2 low density facing.
Multiple Working: Within class and with Classes 375, 377, 378 and 379.

DMSO(A). Bombardier Derby 2004–05. –/36(6) 1W. 42.1 t.
MSO. Bombardier Derby 2004–05. –/48. 36.2 t.
TSO. Bombardier Derby 2004–05. –/48. 36.3 t.
DMSO(B). Bombardier Derby 2004–05. –/36(6) 1W. 42.1 t.

376001	CN	E	*SE*	SG	61101	63301	64301	63501	61601
376002	CN	E	*SE*	SG	61102	63302	64302	63502	61602
376003	CN	E	*SE*	SG	61103	63303	64303	63503	61603
376004	CN	E	*SE*	SG	61104	63304	64304	63504	61604
376005	CN	E	*SE*	SG	61105	63305	64305	63505	61605
376006	CN	E	*SE*	SG	61106	63306	64306	63506	61606
376007	CN	E	*SE*	SG	61107	63307	64307	63507	61607
376008	CN	E	*SE*	SG	61108	63308	64308	63508	61608
376009	CN	E	*SE*	SG	61109	63309	64309	63509	61609
376010	CN	E	*SE*	SG	61110	63310	64310	63510	61610
376011	CN	E	*SE*	SG	61111	63311	64311	63511	61611
376012	CN	E	*SE*	SG	61112	63312	64312	63512	61612
376013	CN	E	*SE*	SG	61113	63313	64313	63513	61613
376014	CN	E	*SE*	SG	61114	63314	64314	63514	61614
376015	CN	E	*SE*	SG	61115	63315	64315	63515	61615
376016	CN	E	*SE*	SG	61116	63316	64316	63516	61616

375 805	**CN**	E	*SE*	RM	73305	79005	78205	73705
375 806	**CN**	E	*SE*	RM	73306	79006	78206	73706
375 807	**CN**	E	*SE*	RM	73307	79007	78207	73707
375 808	**CN**	E	*SE*	RM	73308	79008	78208	73708
375 809	**CN**	E	*SE*	RM	73309	79009	78209	73709
375 810	**CN**	E	*SE*	RM	73310	79010	78210	73710
375 811	**CN**	E	*SE*	RM	73311	79011	78211	73711
375 812	**CN**	E	*SE*	RM	73312	79012	78212	73712
375 813	**CN**	E	*SE*	RM	73313	79013	78213	73713
375 814	**CN**	E	*SE*	RM	73314	79014	78214	73714
375 815	**CN**	E	*SE*	RM	73315	79015	78215	73715
375 816	**CN**	E	*SE*	RM	73316	79016	78216	73716
375 817	**CN**	E	*SE*	RM	73317	79017	78217	73717
375 818	**CN**	E	*SE*	RM	73318	79018	78218	73718
375 819	**CN**	E	*SE*	RM	73319	79019	78219	73719
375 820	**CN**	E	*SE*	RM	73320	79020	78220	73720
375 821	**CN**	E	*SE*	RM	73321	79021	78221	73721
375 822	**CN**	E	*SE*	RM	73322	79022	78222	73722
375 823	**CN**	E	*SE*	RM	73323	79023	78223	73723
375 824	**CN**	E	*SE*	RM	73324	79024	78224	73724
375 825	**CN**	E	*SE*	RM	73325	79025	78225	73725
375 826	**CN**	E	*SE*	RM	73326	79026	78226	73726
375 827	**CN**	E	*SE*	RM	73327	79027	78227	73727
375 828	**CN**	E	*SE*	RM	73328	79028	78228	73728
375 829	**CN**	E	*SE*	RM	73329	79029	78229	73729
375 830	**CN**	E	*SE*	RM	73330	79030	78230	73730

Name (carried on one side of each MSO or TSO):

375 830 City of London

Class 375/9. Outer suburban units. 750 V DC only. DMCO–MSO–TSO–DMCO.

DMCO(A). Bombardier Derby 2003–04. 12/59. 43.4 t.
MSO. Bombardier Derby 2003–04. –/73 1T. 39.3 t.
TSO. Bombardier Derby 2003–04. –/59 1TD 2W. 35.6 t.
DMCO(B). Bombardier Derby 2003–04. 12/59. 43.4 t.

375 901	**CN**	E	*SE*	RM	73331	79031	79061	73731
375 902	**CN**	E	*SE*	RM	73332	79032	79062	73732
375 903	**CN**	E	*SE*	RM	73333	79033	79063	73733
375 904	**CN**	E	*SE*	RM	73334	79034	79064	73734
375 905	**CN**	E	*SE*	RM	73335	79035	79065	73735
375 906	**CN**	E	*SE*	RM	73336	79036	79066	73736
375 907	**CN**	E	*SE*	RM	73337	79037	79067	73737
375 908	**CN**	E	*SE*	RM	73338	79038	79068	73738
375 909	**CN**	E	*SE*	RM	73339	79039	79069	73739
375 910	**CN**	E	*SE*	RM	73340	79040	79070	73740
375 911	**CN**	E	*SE*	RM	73341	79041	79071	73741
375 912	**CN**	E	*SE*	RM	73342	79042	79072	73742
375 913	**CN**	E	*SE*	RM	73343	79043	79073	73743
375 914	**CN**	E	*SE*	RM	73344	79044	79074	73744
375 915	**CN**	E	*SE*	RM	73345	79045	79075	73745

375916	**CN**	E	*SE*	RM	73346	79046	79076	73746
375917	**CN**	E	*SE*	RM	73347	79047	79077	73747
375918	**CN**	E	*SE*	RM	73348	79048	79078	73748
375919	**CN**	E	*SE*	RM	73349	79049	79079	73749
375920	**CN**	E	*SE*	RM	73350	79050	79080	73750
375921	**CN**	E	*SE*	RM	73351	79051	79081	73751
375922	**CN**	E	*SE*	RM	73352	79052	79082	73752
375923	**CN**	E	*SE*	RM	73353	79053	79083	73753
375924	**CN**	E	*SE*	RM	73354	79054	79084	73754
375925	**CN**	E	*SE*	RM	73355	79055	79085	73755
375926	**CN**	E	*SE*	RM	73356	79056	79086	73756
375927	**CN**	E	*SE*	RM	73357	79057	79087	73757

CLASS 376   ELECTROSTAR   BOMBARDIER DERBY

Inner suburban units.

Formation: DMSO–MSO–TSO–MSO–DMSO.
System: 750 V DC third rail.
Construction: Welded aluminium alloy underframe, sides and roof with steel ends. All sections bolted together.
Traction Motors: Two Bombardier asynchronous of 200 kW.
Wheel Arrangement: 2-Bo + 2-Bo + 2-2 + Bo-2 + Bo-2.
Braking: Disc & regenerative.   **Dimensions:** 20.40/19.99 x 2.80 m.
Bogies: Bombardier P3-25/T3-25.   **Couplers:** Dellner 12.
Gangways: Within unit.   **Control System:** IGBT Inverter.
Doors: Sliding.   **Maximum Speed:** 75 mph.
Heating & ventilation: Pressure heating and ventilation.
Seating Layout: 2+2 low density facing.
Multiple Working: Within class and with Classes 375, 377, 378 and 379.

DMSO(A). Bombardier Derby 2004–05. –/36(6) 1W. 42.1 t.
MSO. Bombardier Derby 2004–05. –/48. 36.2 t.
TSO. Bombardier Derby 2004–05. –/48. 36.3 t.
DMSO(B). Bombardier Derby 2004–05. –/36(6) 1W. 42.1 t.

376001	**CN**	E	*SE*	SG	61101	63301	64301	63501	61601
376002	**CN**	E	*SE*	SG	61102	63302	64302	63502	61602
376003	**CN**	E	*SE*	SG	61103	63303	64303	63503	61603
376004	**CN**	E	*SE*	SG	61104	63304	64304	63504	61604
376005	**CN**	E	*SE*	SG	61105	63305	64305	63505	61605
376006	**CN**	E	*SE*	SG	61106	63306	64306	63506	61606
376007	**CN**	E	*SE*	SG	61107	63307	64307	63507	61607
376008	**CN**	E	*SE*	SG	61108	63308	64308	63508	61608
376009	**CN**	E	*SE*	SG	61109	63309	64309	63509	61609
376010	**CN**	E	*SE*	SG	61110	63310	64310	63510	61610
376011	**CN**	E	*SE*	SG	61111	63311	64311	63511	61611
376012	**CN**	E	*SE*	SG	61112	63312	64312	63512	61612
376013	**CN**	E	*SE*	SG	61113	63313	64313	63513	61613
376014	**CN**	E	*SE*	SG	61114	63314	64314	63514	61614
376015	**CN**	E	*SE*	SG	61115	63315	64315	63515	61615
376016	**CN**	E	*SE*	SG	61116	63316	64316	63516	61616

376017	**CN**	E	*SE*	SG	61117 63317 64317 63517 61617
376018	**CN**	E	*SE*	SG	61118 63318 64318 63518 61618
376019	**CN**	E	*SE*	SG	61119 63319 64319 63519 61619
376020	**CN**	E	*SE*	SG	61120 63320 64320 63520 61620
376021	**CN**	E	*SE*	SG	61121 63321 64321 63521 61621
376022	**CN**	E	*SE*	SG	61122 63322 64322 63522 61622
376023	**CN**	E	*SE*	SG	61123 63323 64323 63523 61623
376024	**CN**	E	*SE*	SG	61124 63324 64324 63524 61624
376025	**CN**	E	*SE*	SG	61125 63325 64325 63525 61625
376026	**CN**	E	*SE*	SG	61126 63326 64326 63526 61626
376027	**CN**	E	*SE*	SG	61127 63327 64327 63527 61627
376028	**CN**	E	*SE*	SG	61128 63328 64328 63528 61628
376029	**CN**	E	*SE*	SG	61129 63329 64329 63529 61629
376030	**CN**	E	*SE*	SG	61130 63330 64330 63530 61630
376031	**CN**	E	*SE*	SG	61131 63331 64331 63531 61631
376032	**CN**	E	*SE*	SG	61132 63332 64332 63532 61632
376033	**CN**	E	*SE*	SG	61133 63333 64333 63533 61633
376034	**CN**	E	*SE*	SG	61134 63334 64334 63534 61634
376035	**CN**	E	*SE*	SG	61135 63335 64335 63535 61635
376036	**CN**	E	*SE*	SG	61136 63336 64336 63536 61636

CLASS 377   ELECTROSTAR   BOMBARDIER DERBY

Express and outer suburban units.

Formations: Various.
Systems: 25 kV AC overhead/750 V DC third rail or third rail only with provision for retro-fitting of AC equipment.
Construction: Welded aluminium alloy underframe, sides and roof with steel ends. All sections bolted together.
Traction Motors: Two Bombardier asynchronous of 250 kW.
Wheel Arrangement: 2-Bo + 2-2 + Bo-2 or 2-Bo + 2-Bo + 2-2 + Bo-2 or 2-Bo + 2-Bo + 2-2 + Bo-2 + Bo-2.

Braking: Disc & regenerative.	**Dimensions:** 20.39/20.00 x 2.80 m.
Bogies: Bombardier P3-25/T3-25.	**Couplers:** Dellner 12.
Gangways: Throughout.	**Control System:** IGBT Inverter.
Doors: Sliding plug.	**Maximum Speed:** 100 mph.

Heating & ventilation: Air conditioning.
Seating Layout: Various, see sub-class headings.
Multiple Working: Within class and with Classes 375, 376, 378 and 379.

Class 377/1. 750 V DC only. DMCO–MSO–TSO–DMCO.
Seating layout: 1: 2+2 facing/unidirectional, 2: 2+2 facing/unidirectional (377 101–119), 3+2 (middle cars) and 2+2 (end cars) facing/unidirectional (377 120–164).

DMCO(A). Bombardier Derby 2002–03. 12/48 (s 12/56). 44.8 t.
MSO. Bombardier Derby 2002–03. –/62 (s –/70, t –/69). 1T. 39.0 t.
TSO. Bombardier Derby 2002–03. –/52 (s –/60, t –/57). 1TD 2W. 35.4 t.
DMCO(B). Bombardier Derby 2002–03. 12/48 (s 12/56). 43.4 t.

| 377101 | **SN** | P | *SN* | BI | 78501 77101 78901 78701 |
| 377102 | **SN** | P | *SN* | BI | 78502 77102 78902 78702 |

377 103		**SN**	P	*SN*	BI	78503	77103	78903	78703
377 104		**SN**	P	*SN*	BI	78504	77104	78904	78704
377 105		**SN**	P	*SN*	BI	78505	77105	78905	78705
377 106		**SN**	P	*SN*	BI	78506	77106	78906	78706
377 107		**SN**	P	*SN*	BI	78507	77107	78907	78707
377 108		**SN**	P	*SN*	BI	78508	77108	78908	78708
377 109		**SN**	P	*SN*	BI	78509	77109	78909	78709
377 110		**SN**	P	*SN*	BI	78510	77110	78910	78710
377 111		**SN**	P	*SN*	BI	78511	77111	78911	78711
377 112		**SN**	P	*SN*	BI	78512	77112	78912	78712
377 113		**SN**	P	*SN*	BI	78513	77113	78913	78713
377 114		**SN**	P	*SN*	BI	78514	77114	78914	78714
377 115		**SN**	P	*SN*	BI	78515	77115	78915	78715
377 116		**SN**	P	*SN*	BI	78516	77116	78916	78716
377 117		**SN**	P	*SN*	BI	78517	77117	78917	78717
377 118		**SN**	P	*SN*	BI	78518	77118	78918	78718
377 119		**SN**	P	*SN*	BI	78519	77119	78919	78719
377 120	s	**SN**	P	*SN*	BI	78520	77120	78920	78720
377 121	s	**SN**	P	*SN*	BI	78521	77121	78921	78721
377 122	s	**SN**	P	*SN*	BI	78522	77122	78922	78722
377 123	s	**SN**	P	*SN*	BI	78523	77123	78923	78723
377 124	s	**SN**	P	*SN*	BI	78524	77124	78924	78724
377 125	s	**SN**	P	*SN*	BI	78525	77125	78925	78725
377 126	s	**SN**	P	*SN*	BI	78526	77126	78926	78726
377 127	s	**SN**	P	*SN*	BI	78527	77127	78927	78727
377 128	s	**SN**	P	*SN*	BI	78528	77128	78928	78728
377 129	s	**SN**	P	*SN*	BI	78529	77129	78929	78729
377 130	s	**SN**	P	*SN*	BI	78530	77130	78930	78730
377 131	s	**SN**	P	*SN*	BI	78531	77131	78931	78731
377 132	s	**SN**	P	*SN*	BI	78532	77132	78932	78732
377 133	s	**SN**	P	*SN*	BI	78533	77133	78933	78733
377 134	s	**SN**	P	*SN*	BI	78534	77134	78934	78734
377 135	s	**SN**	P	*SN*	BI	78535	77135	78935	78735
377 136	s	**SN**	P	*SN*	BI	78536	77136	78936	78736
377 137	s	**SN**	P	*SN*	BI	78537	77137	78937	78737
377 138	s	**SN**	P	*SN*	BI	78538	77138	78938	78738
377 139	s	**SN**	P	*SN*	BI	78539	77139	78939	78739
377 140	t	**SN**	P	*SN*	BI	78540	77140	78940	78740
377 141	t	**SN**	P	*SN*	BI	78541	77141	78941	78741
377 142	t	**SN**	P	*SN*	BI	78542	77142	78942	78742
377 143	t	**SN**	P	*SN*	BI	78543	77143	78943	78743
377 144	t	**SN**	P	*SN*	BI	78544	77144	78944	78744
377 145	t	**SN**	P	*SN*	BI	78545	77145	78945	78745
377 146	t	**SN**	P	*SN*	BI	78546	77146	78946	78746
377 147	t	**SN**	P	*SN*	BI	78547	77147	78947	78747
377 148	t	**SN**	P	*SN*	BI	78548	77148	78948	78748
377 149	t	**SN**	P	*SN*	BI	78549	77149	78949	78749
377 150	t	**SN**	P	*SN*	BI	78550	77150	78950	78750
377 151	t	**SN**	P	*SN*	BI	78551	77151	78951	78751
377 152	t	**SN**	P	*SN*	BI	78552	77152	78952	78752
377 153	t	**SN**	P	*SN*	BI	78553	77153	78953	78753

377 154	t	**SN**	P	*SN*	BI	78554	77154	78954	78754
377 155	t	**SN**	P	*SN*	BI	78555	77155	78955	78755
377 156	t	**SN**	P	*SN*	BI	78556	77156	78956	78756
377 157	t	**SN**	P	*SN*	BI	78557	77157	78957	78757
377 158	t	**SN**	P	*SN*	BI	78558	77158	78958	78758
377 159	t	**SN**	P	*SN*	BI	78559	77159	78959	78759
377 160	t	**SN**	P	*SN*	BI	78560	77160	78960	78760
377 161	t	**SN**	P	*SN*	BI	78561	77161	78961	78761
377 162	t	**SN**	P	*SN*	BI	78562	77162	78962	78762
377 163	t	**SN**	P	*SN*	BI	78563	77163	78963	78763
377 164	t	**SN**	P	*SN*	BI	78564	77164	78964	78764

Class 377/2. 25 kV AC/750 V DC. DMCO–MSO–PTSO–DMCO. Dual-voltage units. 377 207–215 are sub-leased from Southern to Govia Thameslink Railway.
Seating layout: 1: 2+2 facing/unidirectional, 2: 2+2 and 3+2 facing/ unidirectional (3+2 seating in middle cars only).

DMCO(A). Bombardier Derby 2003–04. 12/48. 44.2 t.
MSO. Bombardier Derby 2003–04. –/69 1T. 39.8 t.
PTSO. Bombardier Derby 2003–04. –/57 1TD 2W. 40.1 t.
DMCO(B). Bombardier Derby 2003–04. 12/48. 44.2 t.

377 201		**SN**	P	*SN*	SU	78571	77171	78971	78771
377 202		**SN**	P	*SN*	SU	78572	77172	78972	78772
377 203		**SN**	P	*SN*	SU	78573	77173	78973	78773
377 204		**SN**	P	*SN*	SU	78574	77174	78974	78774
377 205		**SN**	P	*SN*	SU	78575	77175	78975	78775
377 206		**SN**	P	*SN*	SU	78576	77176	78976	78776
377 207		**FU**	P	*GT*	BF	78577	77177	78977	78777
377 208		**SN**	P	*GT*	BF	78578	77178	78978	78778
377 209		**SN**	P	*GT*	BF	78579	77179	78979	78779
377 210		**SN**	P	*GT*	BF	78580	77180	78980	78780
377 211		**FU**	P	*GT*	BF	78581	77181	78981	78781
377 212		**FU**	P	*GT*	BF	78582	77182	78982	78782
377 213		**SN**	P	*GT*	BF	78583	77183	78983	78783
377 214		**SN**	P	*GT*	BF	78584	77184	78984	78784
377 215		**SN**	P	*GT*	BF	78585	77185	78985	78785

Class 377/3. 750 V DC only. DMCO–TSO–DMCO.
Seating Layout: 1: 2+2 facing/unidirectional, 2: 2+2 facing/unidirectional.

Units built as Class 375, but renumbered in the Class 377/3 range when fitted with Dellner couplers.

DMCO(A). Bombardier Derby 2001–02. 12/48. 43.5 t.
TSO. Bombardier Derby 2001–02. –/56 1TD 2W. 35.4 t.
DMCO(B). Bombardier Derby 2001–02. 12/48. 43.5 t.

377 301	(375 311)	**SN**	P	*SN*	SU	68201	74801	68401
377 302	(375 312)	**SN**	P	*SN*	SU	68202	74802	68402
377 303	(375 313)	**SN**	P	*SN*	SU	68203	74803	68403
377 304	(375 314)	**SN**	P	*SN*	SU	68204	74804	68404
377 305	(375 315)	**SN**	P	*SN*	SU	68205	74805	68405
377 306	(375 316)	**SN**	P	*SN*	SU	68206	74806	68406

377 307	(375 317)	**SN**	P	*SN*	SU	68207	74807	68407
377 308	(375 318)	**SN**	P	*SN*	SU	68208	74808	68408
377 309	(375 319)	**SN**	P	*SN*	SU	68209	74809	68409
377 310	(375 320)	**SN**	P	*SN*	SU	68210	74810	68410
377 311	(375 321)	**SN**	P	*SN*	SU	68211	74811	68411
377 312	(375 322)	**SN**	P	*SN*	SU	68212	74812	68412
377 313	(375 323)	**SN**	P	*SN*	SU	68213	74813	68413
377 314	(375 324)	**SN**	P	*SN*	SU	68214	74814	68414
377 315	(375 325)	**SN**	P	*SN*	SU	68215	74815	68415
377 316	(375 326)	**SN**	P	*SN*	SU	68216	74816	68416
377 317	(375 327)	**SN**	P	*SN*	SU	68217	74817	68417
377 318	(375 328)	**SN**	P	*SN*	SU	68218	74818	68418
377 319	(375 329)	**SN**	P	*SN*	SU	68219	74819	68419
377 320	(375 330)	**SN**	P	*SN*	SU	68220	74820	68420
377 321	(375 331)	**SN**	P	*SN*	SU	68221	74821	68421
377 322	(375 332)	**SN**	P	*SN*	SU	68222	74822	68422
377 323	(375 333)	**SN**	P	*SN*	SU	68223	74823	68423
377 324	(375 334)	**SN**	P	*SN*	SU	68224	74824	68424
377 325	(375 335)	**SN**	P	*SN*	SU	68225	74825	68425
377 326	(375 336)	**SN**	P	*SN*	SU	68226	74826	68426
377 327	(375 337)	**SN**	P	*SN*	SU	68227	74827	68427
377 328	(375 338)	**SN**	P	*SN*	SU	68228	74828	68428

Class 377/4. 750 V DC only. DMCO–MSO–TSO–DMCO.
Seating Layout: 1: 2+2 facing/two seats longitudinal, 2: 2+2 and 3+2 facing/unidirectional (3+2 seating in middle cars only).

DMCO(A). Bombardier Derby 2004–05. 10/48. 43.1 t.
MSO. Bombardier Derby 2004–05. –/69 1T. 39.3 t.
TSO. Bombardier Derby 2004–05. –/56 1TD 2W. 35.3 t.
DMCO(B). Bombardier Derby 2004–05. 10/48. 43.2 t.

377 401	**SN**	P	*SN*	BI	73401	78801	78601	73801
377 402	**SN**	P	*SN*	BI	73402	78802	78602	73802
377 403	**SN**	P	*SN*	BI	73403	78803	78603	73803
377 404	**SN**	P	*SN*	BI	73404	78804	78604	73804
377 405	**SN**	P	*SN*	BI	73405	78805	78605	73805
377 406	**SN**	P	*SN*	BI	73406	78806	78606	73806
377 407	**SN**	P	*SN*	BI	73407	78807	78607	73807
377 408	**SN**	P	*SN*	BI	73408	78808	78608	73808
377 409	**SN**	P	*SN*	BI	73409	78809	78609	73809
377 410	**SN**	P	*SN*	BI	73410	78810	78610	73810
377 411	**SN**	P	*SN*	BI	73411	78811	78611	73811
377 412	**SN**	P	*SN*	BI	73412	78812	78612	73812
377 413	**SN**	P	*SN*	BI	73413	78813	78613	73813
377 414	**SN**	P	*SN*	BI	73414	78814	78614	73814
377 415	**SN**	P	*SN*	BI	73415	78815	78615	73815
377 416	**SN**	P	*SN*	BI	73416	78816	78616	73816
377 417	**SN**	P	*SN*	BI	73417	78817	78617	73817
377 418	**SN**	P	*SN*	BI	73418	78818	78618	73818
377 419	**SN**	P	*SN*	BI	73419	78819	78619	73819
377 420	**SN**	P	*SN*	BI	73420	78820	78620	73820

377 421	**SN**	P	*SN*	BI	73421	78821	78621	73821
377 422	**SN**	P	*SN*	BI	73422	78822	78622	73822
377 423	**SN**	P	*SN*	BI	73423	78823	78623	73823
377 424	**SN**	P	*SN*	BI	73424	78824	78624	73824
377 425	**SN**	P	*SN*	BI	73425	78825	78625	73825
377 426	**SN**	P	*SN*	BI	73426	78826	78626	73826
377 427	**SN**	P	*SN*	BI	73427	78827	78627	73827
377 428	**SN**	P	*SN*	BI	73428	78828	78628	73828
377 429	**SN**	P	*SN*	BI	73429	78829	78629	73829
377 430	**SN**	P	*SN*	BI	73430	78830	78630	73830
377 431	**SN**	P	*SN*	BI	73431	78831	78631	73831
377 432	**SN**	P	*SN*	BI	73432	78832	78632	73832
377 433	**SN**	P	*SN*	BI	73433	78833	78633	73833
377 434	**SN**	P	*SN*	BI	73434	78834	78634	73834
377 435	**SN**	P	*SN*	BI	73435	78835	78635	73835
377 436	**SN**	P	*SN*	BI	73436	78836	78636	73836
377 437	**SN**	P	*SN*	BI	73437	78837	78637	73837
377 438	**SN**	P	*SN*	BI	73438	78838	78638	73838
377 439	**SN**	P	*SN*	BI	73439	78839	78639	73839
377 440	**SN**	P	*SN*	BI	73440	78840	78640	73840
377 441	**SN**	P	*SN*	BI	73441	78841	78641	73841
377 442	**SN**	P	*SN*	BI	73442	78842	78642	73842
377 443	**SN**	P	*SN*	BI	73443	78843	78643	73843
377 444	**SN**	P	*SN*	BI	73444	78844	78644	73844
377 445	**SN**	P	*SN*	BI	73445	78845	78645	73845
377 446	**SN**	P	*SN*	BI	73446	78846	78646	73846
377 447	**SN**	P	*SN*	BI	73447	78847	78647	73847
377 448	**SN**	P	*SN*	BI	73448	78848	78648	73848
377 449	**SN**	P	*SN*	BI	73449	78849	78649	73849
377 450	**SN**	P	*SN*	BI	73450	78850	78650	73850
377 451	**SN**	P	*SN*	BI	73451	78851	78651	73851
377 452	**SN**	P	*SN*	BI	73452	78852	78652	73852
377 453	**SN**	P	*SN*	BI	73453	78853	78653	73853
377 454	**SN**	P	*SN*	BI	73454	78854	78654	73854
377 455	**SN**	P	*SN*	BI	73455	78855	78655	73855
377 456	**SN**	P	*SN*	BI	73456	78856	78656	73856
377 457	**SN**	P	*SN*	BI	73457	78857	78657	73857
377 458	**SN**	P	*SN*	BI	73458	78858	78658	73858
377 459	**SN**	P	*SN*	BI	73459	78859	78659	73859
377 460	**SN**	P	*SN*	BI	73460	78860	78660	73860
377 461	**SN**	P	*SN*	BI	73461	78861	78661	73861
377 462	**SN**	P	*SN*	BI	73462	78862	78662	73862
377 463	**SN**	P	*SN*	BI	73463	78863	78663	73863
377 464	**SN**	P	*SN*	BI	73464	78864	78664	73864
377 465	**SN**	P	*SN*	BI	73465	78865	78665	73865
377 466	**SN**	P	*SN*	BI	73466	78866	78666	73866
377 467	**SN**	P	*SN*	BI	73467	78867	78667	73867
377 468	**SN**	P	*SN*	BI	73468	78868	78668	73868
377 469	**SN**	P	*SN*	BI	73469	78869	78669	73869
377 470	**SN**	P	*SN*	BI	73470	78870	78670	73870
377 471	**SN**	P	*SN*	BI	73471	78871	78671	73871

377472	**SN**	P	*SN*	BI	73472	78872	78672	73872
377473	**SN**	P	*SN*	BI	73473	78873	78673	73873
377474	**SN**	P	*SN*	BI	73474	78874	78674	73874
377475	**SN**	P	*SN*	BI	73475	78875	78675	73875

Class 377/5. 25kV AC/750V DC. DMCO–MSO–PTSO–DMCO. Dual voltage GTR units (sub-leased from Southern). Details as Class 377/2 unless stated.

DMCO(A). Bombardier Derby 2008–09. 10/48. 43.1t.
MSO. Bombardier Derby 2008–09. –/69 1T. 40.3t.
PTSO. Bombardier Derby 2008–09. –/56 1TD 2W. 40.6 t.
DMCO(B). Bombardier Derby 2008–09. 10/48. 43.1t.

377501	**FU**	P	*GT*	BF	73501	75901	74901	73601
377502	**FU**	P	*GT*	BF	73502	75902	74902	73602
377503	**FU**	P	*GT*	BF	73503	75903	74903	73603
377504	**FU**	P	*GT*	BF	73504	75904	74904	73604
377505	**FU**	P	*GT*	BF	73505	75905	74905	73605
377506	**FU**	P	*GT*	BF	73506	75906	74906	73606
377507	**FU**	P	*GT*	BF	73507	75907	74907	73607
377508	**FU**	P	*GT*	BF	73508	75908	74908	73608
377509	**FU**	P	*GT*	BF	73509	75909	74909	73609
377510	**FU**	P	*GT*	BF	73510	75910	74910	73610
377511	**FU**	P	*GT*	BF	73511	75911	74911	73611
377512	**FU**	P	*GT*	BF	73512	75912	74912	73612
377513	**FU**	P	*GT*	BF	73513	75913	74913	73613
377514	**FU**	P	*GT*	BF	73514	75914	74914	73614
377515	**FU**	P	*GT*	BF	73515	75915	74915	73615
377516	**FU**	P	*GT*	BF	73516	75916	74916	73616
377517	**FU**	P	*GT*	BF	73517	75917	74917	73617
377518	**FU**	P	*GT*	BF	73518	75918	74918	73618
377519	**FU**	P	*GT*	BF	73519	75919	74919	73619
377520	**FU**	P	*GT*	BF	73520	75920	74920	73620
377521	**FU**	P	*GT*	BF	73521	75921	74921	73621
377522	**FU**	P	*GT*	BF	73522	75922	74922	73622
377523	**FU**	P	*GT*	BF	73523	75923	74923	73623

Class 377/6. 750V DC. DMSO–MSO–TSO–MSO–DMSO. Southern 5-car suburban units fitted with Fainsa seating. Technically the same as the 377/5s but using the slightly modified Class 379-style bodyshell.
Seating Layout: 2+2 facing/unidirectional.

DMSO. Bombardier Derby 2012–13. –/60. 44.7 t.
MSO. Bombardier Derby 2012–13. –/64 1T. 38.8 t.
TSO. Bombardier Derby 2012–13. –/46(2) 1TD 2W. 37.8 t.
MSO. Bombardier Derby 2012–13. –/66. 38.3 t.
DMSO. Bombardier Derby 2012–13. –/62. 44.7 t.

377601	**SN**	P	*SN*	SU	70101	70201	70301	70401	70501
377602	**SN**	P	*SN*	SU	70102	70202	70302	70402	70502
377603	**SN**	P	*SN*	SU	70103	70203	70303	70403	70503
377604	**SN**	P	*SN*	SU	70104	70204	70304	70404	70504
377605	**SN**	P	*SN*	SU	70105	70205	70305	70405	70505
377606	**SN**	P	*SN*	SU	70106	70206	70306	70406	70506

377607	**SN**	P	*SN*	SU	70107 70207 70307 70407 70507
377608	**SN**	P	*SN*	SU	70108 70208 70308 70408 70508
377609	**SN**	P	*SN*	SU	70109 70209 70309 70409 70509
377610	**SN**	P	*SN*	SU	70110 70210 70310 70410 70510
377611	**SN**	P	*SN*	SU	70111 70211 70311 70411 70511
377612	**SN**	P	*SN*	SU	70112 70212 70312 70412 70512
377613	**SN**	P	*SN*	SU	70113 70213 70313 70413 70513
377614	**SN**	P	*SN*	SU	70114 70214 70314 70414 70514
377615	**SN**	P	*SN*	SU	70115 70215 70315 70415 70515
377616	**SN**	P	*SN*	SU	70116 70216 70316 70416 70516
377617	**SN**	P	*SN*	SU	70117 70217 70317 70417 70517
377618	**SN**	P	*SN*	SU	70118 70218 70318 70418 70518
377619	**SN**	P	*SN*	SU	70119 70219 70319 70419 70519
377620	**SN**	P	*SN*	SU	70120 70220 70320 70420 70520
377621	**SN**	P	*SN*	SU	70121 70221 70321 70421 70521
377622	**SN**	P	*SN*	SU	70122 70222 70322 70422 70522
377623	**SN**	P	*SN*	SU	70123 70223 70323 70423 70523
377624	**SN**	P	*SN*	SU	70124 70224 70324 70424 70524
377625	**SN**	P	*SN*	SU	70125 70225 70325 70425 70525
377626	**SN**	P	*SN*	SU	70126 70226 70326 70426 70526

Class 377/7. 25 kV AC/750 V DC. DMSO–MSO–TSO–MSO–DMSO. Dual voltage Southern units, used on both the South Croydon–Milton Keynes cross-London services and on suburban services alongside the 377/6s.

DMSO. Bombardier Derby 2013–14. –/60. 45.6 t.
MSO. Bombardier Derby 2013–14. –/64 1T. 41.0 t.
PTSO. Bombardier Derby 2013–14. –/46(2) 1TD 2W. 40.9 t.
MSO. Bombardier Derby 2013–14. –/66. 39.6 t.
DMSO. Bombardier Derby 2013–14. –/62. 45.2 t.

377701	**SN**	P	*SN*	SU	65201 70601 65601 70701 65401
377702	**SN**	P	*SN*	SU	65202 70602 65602 70702 65402
377703	**SN**	P	*SN*	SU	65203 70603 65603 70703 65403
377704	**SN**	P	*SN*	SU	65204 70604 65604 70704 65404
377705	**SN**	P	*SN*	SU	65205 70605 65605 70705 65405
377706	**SN**	P	*SN*	SU	65206 70606 65606 70706 65406
377707	**SN**	P	*SN*	SU	65207 70607 65607 70707 65407
377708	**SN**	P	*SN*	SU	65208 70608 65608 70708 65408

CLASS 378   CAPITALSTAR   BOMBARDIER DERBY

These suburban Electrostars are designated Capitalstars by TfL.

Formation: DMSO–MSO–TSO–DMSO or DMSO–MSO–PTSO–DMSO.
System: Class 378/1 750 V DC third rail only. Class 378/2 25 kV AC overhead and 750 V DC third rail.
Construction: Welded aluminium alloy underframe, sides and roof with steel ends. All sections bolted together.
Traction Motors: Two Bombardier asynchronous of 200 kW.
Wheel Arrangement: 1A-Bo + 1A-Bo + 2-2 (+ Bo-1A) + Bo-1A.
Braking: Disc & regenerative.   **Dimensions:** 20.46/20.14 x 2.80 m.
Bogies: Bombardier P3-25/T3-25.   **Couplers:** Dellner 12.

Gangways: Within unit + end doors. **Control System:** IGBT Inverter.
Doors: Sliding.   **Maximum Speed:** 75 mph.
Heating & ventilation: Air conditioning.
Seating Layout: Longitudinal ("tube style") low density.
Multiple Working: Within class and with Classes 375, 376, 377 and 379.

57 extra vehicles are currently being delivered to make all units up to 5-cars.
This will be completed by the end of 2015, with 378 135–154 being done
first. The extra vehicles are numbered in the 38401–457 series and will be
inserted between the TSO and DMSO(B).

Class 378/1. 750 V DC. DMSO–MSO–TSO–DMSO. Third rail only units used
on East London Line services. Provision for retro-fitting as dual voltage.

378 150–154 are fitted with de-icing equipment.

DMSO(A). Bombardier Derby 2009–10. –/36. 43.1 t.
MSO(A). Bombardier Derby 2009–10. –/40. 39.3 t.
TSO. Bombardier Derby 2009–10. –/34(6) 2W. 34.3t.
MSO(B). Bombardier Derby 2014–15. –/40. 40.4 t.
DMSO(B). Bombardier Derby 2009–10. –/36. 42.7 t.

378 135	**LO**	QW	*LO*	NG	38035	38235	38335	38435	38135
378 136	**LO**	QW	*LO*	NG	38036	38236	38336	38436	38136
378 137	**LO**	QW	*LO*	NG	38037	38237	38337	38437	38137
378 138	**LO**	QW	*LO*	NG	38038	38238	38338	38438	38138
378 139	**LO**	QW	*LO*	NG	38039	38239	38339	38439	38139
378 140	**LO**	QW	*LO*	NG	38040	38240	38340	38440	38140
378 141	**LO**	QW	*LO*	NG	38041	38241	38341	38441	38141
378 142	**LO**	QW	*LO*	NG	38042	38242	38342	38442	38142
378 143	**LO**	QW	*LO*	NG	38043	38243	38343		38143
378 144	**LO**	QW	*LO*	NG	38044	38244	38344		38144
378 145	**LO**	QW	*LO*	NG	38045	38245	38345		38145
378 146	**LO**	QW	*LO*	NG	38046	38246	38346		38146
378 147	**LO**	QW	*LO*	NG	38047	38247	38347		38147
378 148	**LO**	QW	*LO*	NG	38048	38248	38348		38148
378 149	**LO**	QW	*LO*	NG	38049	38249	38349		38149
378 150	**LO**	QW	*LO*	NG	38050	38250	38350		38150
378 151	**LO**	QW	*LO*	NG	38051	38251	38351		38151
378 152	**LO**	QW	*LO*	NG	38052	38252	38352		38152
378 153	**LO**	QW	*LO*	NG	38053	38253	38353		38153
378 154	**LO**	QW	*LO*	NG	38054	38254	38354		38154

Class 378/2. 25 kV AC/750 V DC. DMSO–MSO–PTSO–(MSO)–DMSO. Dual
voltage units mainly used on North London Railway services. 378 201–224
built as 3-car units 378001–024 and extended to 4-car units in 2010.

378 216–220 are fitted with de-icing equipment.

Advertising livery: 378 211 and 378 221 Lycamobile (white).

DMSO(A). Bombardier Derby 2008–11. –/36. 43.4 t.
MSO(A). Bombardier Derby 2008–11. –/40. 39.6 t.
PTSO. Bombardier Derby 2008–11. –/34(6) 2W. 39.2t.
MSO(B). Bombardier Derby 2014–15. –/40. 40.4 t.
DMSO(B). Bombardier Derby 2008–11. –/36. 43.1 t.

378 201	**LO**	QW	*LO*	NG	38001	38201	38301	38401	38101
378 202	**LO**	QW	*LO*	NG	38002	38202	38302		38102
378 203	**LO**	QW	*LO*	NG	38003	38203	38303		38103
378 204	**LO**	QW	*LO*	NG	38004	38204	38304		38104
378 205	**LO**	QW	*LO*	NG	38005	38205	38305		38105
378 206	**LO**	QW	*LO*	NG	38006	38206	38306		38106
378 207	**LO**	QW	*LO*	NG	38007	38207	38307		38107
378 208	**LO**	QW	*LO*	NG	38008	38208	38308		38108
378 209	**LO**	QW	*LO*	NG	38009	38209	38309		38109
378 210	**LO**	QW	*LO*	NG	38010	38210	38310		38110
378 211	**AL**	QW	*LO*	NG	38011	38211	38311		38111
378 212	**LO**	QW	*LO*	NG	38012	38212	38312		38112
378 213	**LO**	QW	*LO*	NG	38013	38213	38313		38113
378 214	**LO**	QW	*LO*	NG	38014	38214	38314		38114
378 215	**LO**	QW	*LO*	NG	38015	38215	38315		38115
378 216	**LO**	QW	*LO*	NG	38016	38216	38316		38116
378 217	**LO**	QW	*LO*	NG	38017	38217	38317		38117
378 218	**LO**	QW	*LO*	NG	38018	38218	38318		38118
378 219	**LO**	QW	*LO*	NG	38019	38219	38319		38119
378 220	**LO**	QW	*LO*	NG	38020	38220	38320		38120
378 221	**AL**	QW	*LO*	NG	38021	38221	38321		38121
378 222	**LO**	QW	*LO*	NG	38022	38222	38322		38122
378 223	**LO**	QW	*LO*	NG	38023	38223	38323		38123
378 224	**LO**	QW	*LO*	NG	38024	38224	38324		38124
378 225	**LO**	QW	*LO*	NG	38025	38225	38325		38125
378 226	**LO**	QW	*LO*	NG	38026	38226	38326		38126
378 227	**LO**	QW	*LO*	NG	38027	38227	38327		38127
378 228	**LO**	QW	*LO*	NG	38028	38228	38328		38128
378 229	**LO**	QW	*LO*	NG	38029	38229	38329		38129
378 230	**LO**	QW	*LO*	NG	38030	38230	38330		38130
378 231	**LO**	QW	*LO*	NG	38031	38231	38331		38131
378 232	**LO**	QW	*LO*	NG	38032	38232	38332		38132
378 233	**LO**	QW	*LO*	NG	38033	38233	38333		38133
378 234	**LO**	QW	*LO*	NG	38034	38234	38334		38134
378 255	**LO**	QW	*LO*	NG	38055	38255	38355		38155
378 256	**LO**	QW	*LO*	NG	38056	38256	38356		38156
378 257	**LO**	QW	*LO*	NG	38057	38257	38357		38157

Name (carried on 38033): 378 233   Ian Brown CBE

CLASS 379   ELECTROSTAR   BOMBARDIER DERBY

Express Electrostars used on Liverpool Street–Stansted Airport and Liverpool Street–Cambridge services.

Formation: DMSO–MSO–PTSO–DMCO.
System: 25 kV AC overhead.
Construction: Welded aluminium alloy underframe, sides and roof with steel ends. All sections bolted together.
Traction Motors: Two Bombardier asynchronous of 200 kW.
Wheel Arrangement: 2-Bo + 2-Bo + 2-2 + Bo-2.

Braking: Disc & regenerative.
Bogies: Bombardier P3-25/T3-25.
Gangways: Throughout.
Doors: Sliding plug.
Heating & ventilation: Air conditioning.
Dimensions: 20.00 x 2.80 m.
Couplers: Dellner 12.
Control System: IGBT Inverter.
Maximum Speed: 100 mph.
Seating Layout: 1: 2+1 facing. 2: 2+2 facing/unidirectional.
Multiple Working: Within class and with Classes 375, 376, 377 and 378.

379013 has been converted into a trial battery-electric hybrid unit, with the
MSO vehicle being converted to a Trailer Battery Open. In early 2015 it was
being used on a trial basis on the Manningtree–Harwich branch.

DMSO. Bombardier Derby 2010–11. –/60. 42.1 t.
MSO. Bombardier Derby 2010–11. –/62 1T. 38.6 t.
PTSO. Bombardier Derby 2010–11. –/43(2) 1TD 2W. 40.9 t.
DMCO. Bombardier Derby 2010–11. 20/24. 42.3 t.

379001	**NC**	MQ	*GA*	IL	61201	61701	61901	62101
379002	**NC**	MQ	*GA*	IL	61202	61702	61902	62102
379003	**NC**	MQ	*GA*	IL	61203	61703	61903	62103
379004	**NC**	MQ	*GA*	IL	61204	61704	61904	62104
379005	**NC**	MQ	*GA*	IL	61205	61705	61905	62105
379006	**NC**	MQ	*GA*	IL	61206	61706	61906	62106
379007	**NC**	MQ	*GA*	IL	61207	61707	61907	62107
379008	**NC**	MQ	*GA*	IL	61208	61708	61908	62108
379009	**NC**	MQ	*GA*	IL	61209	61709	61909	62109
379010	**NC**	MQ	*GA*	IL	61210	61710	61910	62110
379011	**NC**	MQ	*GA*	IL	61211	61711	61911	62111
379012	**NC**	MQ	*GA*	IL	61212	61712	61912	62112
379013	**NC**	MQ	*GA*	IL	61213	61713	61913	62113
379014	**NC**	MQ	*GA*	IL	61214	61714	61914	62114
379015	**NC**	MQ	*GA*	IL	61215	61715	61915	62115
379016	**NC**	MQ	*GA*	IL	61216	61716	61916	62116
379017	**NC**	MQ	*GA*	IL	61217	61717	61917	62117
379018	**NC**	MQ	*GA*	IL	61218	61718	61918	62118
379019	**NC**	MQ	*GA*	IL	61219	61719	61919	62119
379020	**NC**	MQ	*GA*	IL	61220	61720	61920	62120
379021	**NC**	MQ	*GA*	IL	61221	61721	61921	62121
379022	**NC**	MQ	*GA*	IL	61222	61722	61922	62122
379023	**NC**	MQ	*GA*	IL	61223	61723	61923	62123
379024	**NC**	MQ	*GA*	IL	61224	61724	61924	62124
379025	**NC**	MQ	*GA*	IL	61225	61725	61925	62125
379026	**NC**	MQ	*GA*	IL	61226	61726	61926	62126
379027	**NC**	MQ	*GA*	IL	61227	61727	61927	62127
379028	**NC**	MQ	*GA*	IL	61228	61728	61928	62128
379029	**NC**	MQ	*GA*	IL	61229	61729	61929	62129
379030	**NC**	MQ	*GA*	IL	61230	61730	61930	62130

Names (carried on end cars):

379005	Stansted Express	379015	City of Cambridge
379011	Ely Cathedral	379025	Go Discover
379012	The West Anglian		

CLASS 380   DESIRO UK   SIEMENS

Used on Strathclyde area services and the Edinburgh–North Berwick route.

Formation: DMSO–PTSO–DMSO or DMSO–PTSO–TSO–DMSO.
System: 25 kV AC overhead.
Construction: Welded aluminium with steel ends.
Traction Motors: Four Siemens ITB2016-0GB02 asynchronous of 250 kW.
Wheel Arrangement: Bo-Bo + 2-2 (+2-2) + Bo-Bo
Braking: Disc & regenerative.   **Dimensions:** 23.78/23.57 x 2.80 m.
Bogies: SGP SF5000.   **Couplers:** Voith.
Gangways: Throughout.   **Control System:** IGBT Inverter.
Doors: Sliding plug.   **Maximum Speed:** 100 mph.
Heating & ventilation: Air conditioning. **Seating Layout:** 2+2 facing/unidirectional.
Multiple Working: Within class.

DMSO(A). Siemens Krefeld 2009–10. –/70. 45.0 t.
PTSO. Siemens Krefeld 2009–10. –/57(12) 1TD 2W. 42.7 t.
TSO. Siemens Krefeld 2009–10. –/74 1T. 34.8 t.
DMSO(B). Siemens Krefeld 2009–10. –/64(5). 44.9 t.

Class 380/0. 3-car units.

380 001	**SR**	E	*SR*	GW	38501	38601		38701
380 002	**SR**	E	*SR*	GW	38502	38602		38702
380 003	**SR**	E	*SR*	GW	38503	38603		38703
380 004	**SR**	E	*SR*	GW	38504	38604		38704
380 005	**SR**	E	*SR*	GW	38505	38605		38705
380 006	**SR**	E	*SR*	GW	38506	38606		38706
380 007	**SR**	E	*SR*	GW	38507	38607		38707
380 008	**SR**	E	*SR*	GW	38508	38608		38708
380 009	**SR**	E	*SR*	GW	38509	38609		38709
380 010	**SR**	E	*SR*	GW	38510	38610		38710
380 011	**SR**	E	*SR*	GW	38511	38611		38711
380 012	**SR**	E	*SR*	GW	38512	38612		38712
380 013	**SR**	E	*SR*	GW	38513	38613		38713
380 014	**SR**	E	*SR*	GW	38514	38614		38714
380 015	**SR**	E	*SR*	GW	38515	38615		38715
380 016	**SR**	E	*SR*	GW	38516	38616		38716
380 017	**SR**	E	*SR*	GW	38517	38617		38717
380 018	**SR**	E	*SR*	GW	38518	38618		38718
380 019	**SR**	E	*SR*	GW	38519	38619		38719
380 020	**SR**	E	*SR*	GW	38520	38620		38720
380 021	**SR**	E	*SR*	GW	38521	38621		38721
380 022	**SR**	E	*SR*	GW	38522	38622		38722

Class 380/1. 4-car units.

380 101	**SR**	E	*SR*	GW	38551	38651	38851	38751
380 102	**SR**	E	*SR*	GW	38552	38652	38852	38752
380 103	**SR**	E	*SR*	GW	38553	38653	38853	38753
380 104	**SR**	E	*SR*	GW	38554	38654	38854	38754
380 105	**SR**	E	*SR*	GW	38555	38655	38855	38755
380 106	**SR**	E	*SR*	GW	38556	38656	38856	38756

380 107	**SR**	E	*SR*	GW	38557	38657	38857	38757
380 108	**SR**	E	*SR*	GW	38558	38658	38858	38758
380 109	**SR**	E	*SR*	GW	38559	38659	38859	38759
380 110	**SR**	E	*SR*	GW	38560	38660	38860	38760
380 111	**SR**	E	*SR*	GW	38561	38661	38861	38761
380 112	**SR**	E	*SR*	GW	38562	38662	38862	38762
380 113	**SR**	E	*SR*	GW	38563	38663	38863	38763
380 114	**SR**	E	*SR*	GW	38564	38664	38864	38764
380 115	**SR**	E	*SR*	GW	38565	38665	38865	38765
380 116	**SR**	E	*SR*	GW	38566	38666	38866	38766

CLASS 387   ELECTROSTAR   BOMBARDIER DERBY

The 29 110 mph Class 387/1s are currently being delivered for use on the main Thameslink Bedford–Brighton route until the new Class 700s are available from 2016. They are the first units to feature 6-digit vehicle numbers.

A further 27 4-car Class 387/2s have been ordered for the Gatwick Express service (for delivery 2015–16; full details awaited). These will also be dual-voltage.

Formation: DMCO–MSO–PTSO–DMSO.
System: 25 kV AC overhead and 750 V DC third rail.
Construction: Welded aluminium alloy underframe, sides and roof with steel ends. All sections bolted together.
Traction Motors: Two Bombardier asynchronous of 250 kW.
Wheel Arrangement: 2-Bo + 2-Bo + 2-2 + Bo-2.
Braking: Disc & regenerative.   **Dimensions:** 20.00 x 2.80 m.
Bogies: Bombardier P3-25/T3-25.   **Couplers:** Dellner 12.
Gangways: Throughout.   **Control System:** IGBT Inverter.
Doors: Sliding plug.   **Maximum Speed:** 110 mph.
Heating & ventilation: Air conditioning.
Seating Layout: 2+2 facing/unidirectional. **Multiple Working:** Within class.

Class 387/1. Govia Thameslink units used on the Bedford–Brighton route.

DMCO. Bombardier Derby 2014–15. 10/46. 45.8 t.
MSO. Bombardier Derby 2014–15. –/62 1T. 41.0 t.
PTSO. Bombardier Derby 2014–15. –/44 1TD 2W. 41.5 t.
DMSO. Bombardier Derby 2014–15. –/60. 45.6 t.

387 101	**TG**	P			421101	422101	423101	424101
387 102	**TG**	P			421102	422102	423102	424102
387 103	**TG**	P			421103	422103	423103	424103
387 104	**TG**	P			421104	422104	423104	424104
387 105	**TG**	P	*GT*	BI	421105	422105	423105	424105
387 106	**TG**	P	*GT*	BI	421106	422106	423106	424106
387 107	**TG**	P	*GT*	BI	421107	422107	423107	424107
387 108	**TG**	P	*GT*	BI	421108	422108	423108	424108
387 109	**TG**	P	*GT*	BI	421109	422109	423109	424109
387 110	**TG**	P	*GT*	BI	421110	422110	423110	424110
387 111	**TG**	P	*GT*	BI	421111	422111	423111	424111
387 112	**TG**	P	*GT*	BI	421112	422112	423112	424112

387113	**TG**	P	*GT*	Bl	421113	422113	423113	424113
387114	**TG**	P	*GT*	Bl	421114	422114	423114	424114
387115	**TG**	P			421115	422115	423115	424115
387116	**TG**	P			421116	422116	423116	424116
387117	**TG**	P			421117	422117	423117	424117
387118	**TG**	P			421118	422118	423118	424118
387119	**TG**	P			421119	422119	423119	424119
387120	**TG**	P			421120	422120	423120	424120
387121	**TG**	P			421121	422121	423121	424121
387122	**TG**	P			421122	422122	423122	424122
387123	**TG**	P			421123	422123	423123	424123
387124	**TG**	P			421124	422124	423124	424124
387125	**TG**	P			421125	422125	423125	424125
387126	**TG**	P			421126	422126	423126	424126
387127	**TG**	P			421127	422127	423127	424127
387128	**TG**	P			421128	422128	423128	424128
387129	**TG**	P			421129	422129	423129	424129

Class 387/2. Govia Thameslink units on order for London Victoria–Gatwick Airport–Brighton.

DMCO. Bombardier Derby 2015–16.   t.
MSO. Bombardier Derby 2015–16.   t.
PTSO. Bombardier Derby 2015–16.   t.
DMSO. Bombardier Derby 2015–16.   t.

387201	P	421201	422201	423201	424201
387202	P	421202	422202	423202	424202
387203	P	421203	422203	423203	424203
387204	P	421204	422204	423204	424204
387205	P	421205	422205	423205	424205
387206	P	421206	422206	423206	424206
387207	P	421207	422207	423207	424207
387208	P	421208	422208	423208	424208
387209	P	421209	422209	423209	424209
387210	P	421210	422210	423210	424210
387211	P	421211	422211	423211	424211
387212	P	421212	422212	423212	424212
387213	P	421213	422213	423213	424213
387214	P	421214	422214	423214	424214
387215	P	421215	422215	423215	424215
387216	P	421216	422216	423216	424216
387217	P	421217	422217	423217	424217
387218	P	421218	422218	423218	424218
387219	P	421219	422219	423219	424219
387220	P	421220	422220	423220	424220
387221	P	421221	422221	423221	424221
387222	P	421222	422222	423222	424222
387223	P	421223	422223	423223	424223
387224	P	421224	422224	423224	424224
387225	P	421225	422225	423225	424225
387226	P	421226	422226	423226	424226
387227	P	421227	422227	423227	424227

CLASS 390   PENDOLINO   ALSTOM

Tilting units used on the West Coast Main Line.

Formations: As listed below.
Construction: Welded aluminium alloy.
Traction Motors: Two Alstom ONIX 800 of 425 kW.
Wheel Arrangement: 1A-A1 + 1A-A1 + 2-2 + 1A-A1 (+ 2-2 + 1A-A1) + 2-2 + 1A-A1 + 2-2 + 1A-A1 + 1A-A1.
Braking: Disc, rheostatic & regenerative.
Dimensions: 24.80/23.90 x 2.73 m.
Couplers: Dellner 12.
Bogies: Fiat-SIG.
Control System: IGBT Inverter.
Gangways: Within unit.
Maximum Speed: 125 mph.
Doors: Sliding plug.
Heating & ventilation: Air conditioning.
Seating Layout: 1: 2+1 facing/unidirectional, 2: 2+2 facing/unidirectional.
Multiple Working: Within class. Can also be controlled from Class 57/3 locos.

Units up to 390034 were delivered as 8-car sets, without the TSO (688xx). During 2004–05 these units were increased to 9-cars.

62 extra vehicles were built 2010–12 to lengthen 31 sets to 11-cars. On renumbering units were renumbered by adding 100 to the set number. Four new complete 11-car units were also delivered. All these extra vehicles were built at Savigliano in Italy (all original Pendolino vehicles were built at Birmingham).

390033 was written off in the Lambrigg accident of February 2007.

Advertising livery: 390 104 – Black Alstom vinyls on Virgin silver livery.

DMRFO: Alstom Birmingham/Savigliano 2001–05/2010–12. 18/–. 56.3 t.
MFO(A): Alstom Birmingham/Savigliano 2001–05/2010–12. 37/–(2) 1TD 1W. 52.3 t.
PTFO: Alstom Birmingham/Savigliano 2001–05/2010–12. 44/– 1T. 51.2 t.
MFO(B): Alstom Birmingham/Savigliano 2001–05/2010–12. 46/– 1T. 52.3 t.
(TSO: Alstom Savigliano 2010–12. –/74 1T. 49.2 t.)
(MSO: Alstom Savigliano 2010–12. –/76 1T. 52.2 t.)
TSO: Alstom Birmingham/Savigliano 2001–05/2010–12. –/76 1T. 45.5 t.
MSO(A): Alstom Birmingham/Savigliano 2001–05/2010–12. –/62(4) 1TD 1W. 52.0 t.
PTSRMB: Alstom Birmingham/Savigliano 2001–05/2010–12. –/48. 53.2 t.
MSO(B): Alstom Birmingham/Savigliano 2001–05/2010–12. –/62(2) 1TD 1W. 52.5 t.
DMSO: Alstom Birmingham/Savigliano 2001–05/2010–12. –/46 1T. 54.5 t.

Class 390/0. Original build 9-car units.
Formation: DMRFO–MFO–PTFO–MFO–TSO–MSO–PTSRMB–MSO–DMSO.

390 001	**VT**	A	*VW* MA	69101	69401	69501	69601	68801	
				69701	69801	69901	69201		
390 002	**VT**	A	*VW* MA	69102	69402	69502	69602	68802	
				69702	69802	69902	69202		
390 005	**VT**	A	*VW* MA	69105	69405	69505	69605	68805	
				69705	69805	69905	69205		
390 006	**VT**	A	*VW* MA	69106	69406	69506	69606	68806	
				69706	69806	69906	69206		
390 008	**VT**	A	*VW* MA	69108	69408	69508	69608	68808	
				69708	69808	69908	69208		
390 009	**VT**	A	*VW* MA	69109	69409	69509	69609	68809	
				69709	69809	69909	69209		

390010	**VT**	A	*VW* MA	69110 69410 69510 69610 68810
				69710 69810 69910 69210
390011	**VT**	A	*VW* MA	69111 69411 69511 69611 68811
				69711 69811 69911 69211
390013	**VT**	A	*VW* MA	69113 69413 69513 69613 68813
				69713 69813 69913 69213
390016	**VT**	A	*VW* MA	69116 69416 69516 69616 68816
				69716 69816 69916 69216
390020	**VT**	A	*VW* MA	69120 69420 69520 69620 68820
				69720 69820 69920 69220
390039	**VT**	A	*VW* MA	69139 69439 69539 69639 68839
				69739 69839 69939 69239
390040	**VT**	A	*VW* MA	69140 69440 69540 69640 68840
				69740 69840 69940 69240
390042	**VT**	A	*VW* MA	69142 69442 69542 69642 68842
				69742 69842 69942 69242
390043	**VT**	A	*VW* MA	69143 69443 69543 69643 68843
				69743 69843 69943 69243
390044	**VT**	A	*VW* MA	69144 69444 69544 69644 68844
				69744 69844 69944 69244
390045	**VT**	A	*VW* MA	69145 69445 69545 69645 68845
				69745 69845 69945 69245
390046	**VT**	A	*VW* MA	69146 69446 69546 69646 68846
				69746 69846 69946 69246
390047	**VT**	A	*VW* MA	69147 69447 69547 69647 68847
				69747 69847 69947 69247
390049	**VT**	A	*VW* MA	69149 69449 69549 69649 68849
				69749 69849 69949 69249
390050	**VT**	A	*VW* MA	69150 69450 69550 69650 68850
				69750 69850 69950 69250

Class 390/1. Original build 9-car units now extended to 11-cars, except 390154–157 which were built new as 11-cars.
Formation: DMRFO–MFO–PTFO–MFO–TSO–MSO–TSO–MSO–PTSRMB–MSO–DMSO.

390103	**VT**	A	*VW* MA	69103 69403 69503 69603 65303 68903
				68803 69703 69803 69903 69203
390104	**AL**	A	*VW* MA	69104 69404 69504 69604 65304 68904
				68804 69704 69804 69904 69204
390107	**VT**	A	*VW* MA	69107 69407 69507 69607 65307 68907
				68807 69707 69807 69907 69207
390112	**VT**	A	*VW* MA	69112 69412 69512 69612 65312 68912
				68812 69712 69812 69912 69212
390114	**VT**	A	*VW* MA	69114 69414 69514 69614 65314 68914
				68814 69714 69814 69914 69214
390115	**VT**	A	*VW* MA	69115 69415 69515 69615 65315 68915
				68815 69715 69815 69915 69215
390117	**VT**	A	*VW* MA	69117 69417 69517 69617 65317 68917
				68817 69717 69817 69917 69217
390118	**VT**	A	*VW* MA	69118 69418 69518 69618 65318 68918
				68818 69718 69818 69918 69218

390 119	**VT**	A	*VW* MA	69119	69419	69519	69619	65319	68919
				68819	69719	69819	69919	69219	
390 121	**VT**	A	*VW* MA	69121	69421	69521	69621	65321	68921
				68821	69721	69821	69921	69221	
390 122	**VT**	A	*VW* MA	69122	69422	69522	69622	65322	68922
				68822	69722	69822	69922	69222	
390 123	**VT**	A	*VW* MA	69123	69423	69523	69623	65323	68923
				68823	69723	69823	69923	69223	
390 124	**VT**	A	*VW* MA	69124	69424	69524	69624	65324	68924
				68824	69724	69824	69924	69224	
390 125	**VT**	A	*VW* MA	69125	69425	69525	69625	65325	68925
				68825	69725	69825	69925	69225	
390 126	**VT**	A	*VW* MA	69126	69426	69526	69626	65326	68926
				68826	69726	69826	69926	69226	
390 127	**VT**	A	*VW* MA	69127	69427	69527	69627	65327	68927
				68827	69727	69827	69927	69227	
390 128	**VT**	A	*VW* MA	69128	69428	69528	69628	65328	68928
				68828	69728	69828	69928	69228	
390 129	**VT**	A	*VW* MA	69129	69429	69529	69629	65329	68929
				68829	69729	69829	69929	69229	
390 130	**VT**	A	*VW* MA	69130	69430	69530	69630	65330	68930
				68830	69730	69830	69930	69230	
390 131	**VT**	A	*VW* MA	69131	69431	69531	69631	65331	68931
				68831	69731	69831	69931	69231	
390 132	**VT**	A	*VW* MA	69132	69432	69532	69632	65332	68932
				68832	69732	69832	69932	69232	
390 134	**VT**	A	*VW* MA	69134	69434	69534	69634	65334	68934
				68834	69734	69834	69934	69234	
390 135	**VT**	A	*VW* MA	69135	69435	69535	69635	65335	68935
				68835	69735	69835	69935	69235	
390 136	**VT**	A	*VW* MA	69136	69436	69536	69636	65336	68936
				68836	69736	69836	69936	69236	
390 137	**VT**	A	*VW* MA	69137	69437	69537	69637	65337	68937
				68837	69737	69837	69937	69237	
390 138	**VT**	A	*VW* MA	69138	69438	69538	69638	65338	68938
				68838	69738	69838	69938	69238	
390 141	**VT**	A	*VW* MA	69141	69441	69541	69641	65341	68941
				68841	69741	69841	69941	69241	
390 148	**VT**	A	*VW* MA	69148	69448	69548	69648	65348	68948
				68848	69748	69848	69948	69248	
390 151	**VT**	A	*VW* MA	69151	69451	69551	69651	65351	68951
				68851	69751	69851	69951	69251	
390 152	**VT**	A	*VW* MA	69152	69452	69552	69652	65352	68952
				68852	69752	69852	69952	69252	
390 153	**VT**	A	*VW* MA	69153	69453	69553	69653	65353	68953
				68853	69753	69853	69953	69253	
390 154	**VT**	A	*VW* MA	69154	69454	69554	69654	65354	68954
				68854	69754	69854	69954	69254	
390 155	**VT**	A	*VW* MA	69155	69455	69555	69655	65355	68955
				68855	69755	69855	69955	69255	

390 156	**VT**	A	*VW* MA	69156	69456	69556	69656	65356	68956
				68856	69756	69856	69956	69256	
390 157	**VT**	A	*VW* MA	69157	69457	69557	69657	65357	68957
				68857	69757	69857	69957	69257	

Names (carried on MFO No. 696xx):

390001	Virgin Pioneer	390118	Virgin Princess
390002	Virgin Angel	390119	Virgin Warrior
390005	City of Wolverhampton	390121	Virgin Dream
390006	Tate Liverpool	390122	Penny the Pendolino
390008	Virgin King	390123	Virgin Glory
390009	Treaty of Union	390124	Virgin Venturer
390010	A Decade of Progress	390125	Virgin Stagecoach
390011	City of Lichfield	390126	Virgin Enterprise
390013	Virgin Spirit	390127	Virgin Buccaneer
390016	Virgin Champion	390128	City of Preston
390020	Virgin Cavalier	390129	City of Stoke-on-Trent
390043	Virgin Quest	390130	City of Edinburgh
390040	Virgin Pathfinder	390131	City of Liverpool
390042	City of Bangor/Dinas Bangor	390132	City of Birmingham
390043	Virgin Explorer	390134	City of Carlisle
390044	Virgin Lionheart	390135	City of Lancaster
390045	101 Squadron	390136	City of Coventry
390046	Virgin Soldiers	390137	Virgin Difference
390047	CLIC Sargent	390138	City of London
390049	Virgin Express	390141	City of Chester
390050	Virgin Invader	390148	Virgin Harrier
390103	Virgin Hero	390151	Virgin Ambassador
390104	Alstom Pendolino	390152	Virgin Knight
390107	Virgin Lady	390153	Mission Accomplished
390112	Virgin Star	390154	Matthew Flinders
390114	City of Manchester	390155	X-MEN Days of Future Past
390115	Virgin Crusader	390156	Stockport 170
390117	Virgin Prince	390157	Chad Varah

CLASS 395   JAVELIN   HITACHI JAPAN

6-car dual-voltage units used on Southeastern High Speed services from St Pancras to Ashford/Dover/Margate via Ramsgate and Faversham.

Formation: PDTSO–MSO–MSO–MSO–MSO–PDTSO.
Systems: 25 kV AC overhead/750 V DC third rail.
Construction: Aluminium.
Traction Motors: Hitachi asynchronous of 210 kW.
Wheel Arrangement: 2-2 + Bo-Bo + Bo-Bo + Bo-Bo + Bo-Bo + 2-2.
Braking: Disc, rheostatic & regenerative braking.
Dimensions: 20.88/20.0 x 2.81 m.   **Couplers:** Scharfenberg.
Bogies: Hitachi.   **Control System:** IGBT Inverter.
Gangways: Within unit.   **Maximum Speed:** 140 mph.
Doors: Single-leaf sliding.   **Multiple Working:** Within class only.

Heating & ventilation: Air conditioning.
Seating Layout: 2+2 facing/unidirectional (mainly unidirectional).

PDTSO(A): Hitachi Kasado, Japan 2006–09. –/28(12) 1TD 2W. 46.7 t.
MSO: Hitachi Kasado, Japan 2006–09. –/66. 45.0t–45.7 t.
PDTSO(B): Hitachi Kasado, Japan 2006–09. –/48 1T. 46.7 t.

395001	**SB**	E	*SE*	AD	39011	39012	39013	39014	39015	39016
395002	**SB**	E	*SE*	AD	39021	39022	39023	39024	39025	39026
395003	**SB**	E	*SE*	AD	39031	39032	39033	39034	39035	39036
395004	**SB**	E	*SE*	AD	39041	39042	39043	39044	39045	39046
395005	**SB**	E	*SE*	AD	39051	39052	39053	39054	39055	39056
395006	**SB**	E	*SE*	AD	39061	39062	39063	39064	39065	39066
395007	**SB**	E	*SE*	AD	39071	39072	39073	39074	39075	39076
395008	**SB**	E	*SE*	AD	39081	39082	39083	39084	39085	39086
395009	**SB**	E	*SE*	AD	39091	39092	39093	39094	39095	39096
395010	**SB**	E	*SE*	AD	39101	39102	39103	39104	39105	39106
395011	**SB**	E	*SE*	AD	39111	39112	39113	39114	39115	39116
395012	**SB**	E	*SE*	AD	39121	39122	39123	39124	39125	39126
395013	**SB**	E	*SE*	AD	39131	39132	39133	39134	39135	39136
395014	**SB**	E	*SE*	AD	39141	39142	39143	39144	39145	39146
395015	**SB**	E	*SE*	AD	39151	39152	39153	39154	39155	39156
395016	**SB**	E	*SE*	AD	39161	39162	39163	39164	39165	39166
395017	**SB**	E	*SE*	AD	39171	39172	39173	39174	39175	39176
395018	**SB**	E	*SE*	AD	39181	39182	39183	39184	39185	39186
395019	**SB**	E	*SE*	AD	39191	39192	39193	39194	39195	39196
395020	**SB**	E	*SE*	AD	39201	39202	39203	39204	39205	39206
395021	**SB**	E	*SE*	AD	39211	39212	39213	39214	39215	39216
395022	**SB**	E	*SE*	AD	39221	39222	39223	39224	39225	39226
395023	**SB**	E	*SE*	AD	39231	39232	39233	39234	39235	39236
395024	**SB**	E	*SE*	AD	39241	39242	39243	39244	39245	39246
395025	**SB**	E	*SE*	AD	39251	39252	39253	39254	39255	39256
395026	**SB**	E	*SE*	AD	39261	39262	39263	39264	39265	39266
395027	**SB**	E	*SE*	AD	39271	39272	39273	39274	39275	39276
395028	**SB**	E	*SE*	AD	39281	39282	39283	39284	39285	39286
395029	**SB**	E	*SE*	AD	39291	39292	39293	39294	39295	39296

Names (carried on end cars):

395001	Dame Kelly Holmes	395017	Dame Sarah Storey
395002	Sebastian Coe	395018	Mo Farah
395003	Sir Steve Redgrave	395019	Jessica Ennis
395004	Sir Chris Hoy	395020	Jason Kenny
395005	Dame Tanni Grey-Thompson	395021	Ed Clancy MBE
395006	Daley Thompson	395022	Alistair Brownlee
395007	Steve Backley	395023	Ellie Simmonds
395008	Ben Ainslie	395024	Jonnie Peacock
395009	Rebecca Adlington	395025	Victoria Pendleton
395010	Duncan Goodhew	395026	Marc Woods
395011	Katherine Grainger	395027	Hannah Cockcroft
395014	THE VICTORIA CROSS	395028	Laura Trott
395016	Jamie Staff	395029	David Weir

4.2. 750 V DC THIRD RAIL EMUs

These classes use the third rail system at 750 V DC (unless stated). Outer couplers are buckeyes on units built before 1982 with bar couplers within the units. Newer units generally have Dellner outer couplers.

CLASS 442   WESSEX EXPRESS   BREL DERBY

Stock built for Waterloo–Bournemouth–Weymouth services. Previously used by South West Trains, all units now used by Southern, principally on Victoria–Gatwick Airport–Brighton services.

Formation: DTSO(A)–TSO–MBC–TSO(W)–DTSO(B).
Construction: Steel.
Traction Motors: Four EE546 of 300 kW recovered from Class 432s.
Wheel Arrangement: 2-2 + 2-2 + Bo-Bo + 2-2 + 2-2.
Braking: Disc.   **Dimensions:** 23.15/23.00 x 2.74 m.
Bogies: Two BREL P7 motor bogies (MBSO). T4 bogies (trailer cars).
Couplers: Buckeye.   **Control System:** 1986-type.
Gangways: Throughout.   **Maximum Speed:** 100 mph.
Doors: Sliding plug.   **Heating & Ventilation:** Air conditioning.
Seating Layout: 1: 2+1 facing, 2: 2+2 mainly unidirectional.
Multiple Working: Within class and Class 33/1 & 73 locos in an emergency.

DTSO(A). Lot No. 31030 Derby 1988–89. –/74. 38.5 t.
TSO. Lot No. 31032 Derby 1988–89. –/76 2T. 37.5 t.
MBC. Lot No. 31034 Derby 1988–89. 24/28. 55.0 t.
TSO(W). Lot No. 31033 Derby 1988–89. –/66(4) 1TD 1T 2W. 37.8 t.
DTSO(B). Lot No. 31031 Derby 1988–89. –/74. 37.3 t.

442 401	**GV**	A	*SN*	SL	77382	71818	62937	71842	77414
442 402	**GV**	A	*SN*	SL	77383	71819	62938	71843	77407
442 403	**GV**	A	*SN*	SL	77384	71820	62941	71844	77408
442 404	**GV**	A	*SN*	SL	77385	71821	62939	71845	77409
442 405	**GV**	A	*SN*	SL	77386	71822	62944	71846	77410
442 406	**GV**	A	*SN*	SL	77389	71823	62942	71847	77411
442 407	**GV**	A	*SN*	SL	77388	71824	62943	71848	77412
442 408	**GV**	A	*SN*	SL	77387	71825	62945	71849	77413
442 409	**GV**	A	*SN*	SL	77390	71826	62946	71850	77406
442 410	**GV**	A	*SN*	SL	77391	71827	62948	71851	77415
442 411	**GV**	A	*SN*	SL	77392	71828	62940	71858	77422
442 412	**GV**	A	*SN*	SL	77393	71829	62947	71853	77417
442 413	**GV**	A	*SN*	SL	77394	71830	62949	71854	77418
442 414	**GV**	A	*SN*	SL	77395	71831	62950	71855	77419
442 415	**GV**	A	*SN*	SL	77396	71832	62951	71856	77420
442 416	**GV**	A	*SN*	SL	77397	71833	62952	71857	77421
442 417	**GV**	A	*SN*	SL	77398	71834	62953	71852	77416
442 418	**GV**	A	*SN*	SL	77399	71835	62954	71859	77423
442 419	**GV**	A	*SN*	SL	77400	71836	62955	71860	77424
442 420	**GV**	A	*SN*	SL	77401	71837	62956	71861	77425
442 421	**GV**	A	*SN*	SL	77402	71838	62957	71862	77426

442 422	**GV**	A	*SN*	SL	77403 71839 62958 71863 77427
442 423	**GV**	A	*SN*	SL	77404 71840 62959 71864 77428
442 424	**GV**	A	*SN*	SL	77405 71841 62960 71865 77429

CLASS 444   DESIRO UK   SIEMENS

Express units.

Formation: DMCO–TSO–TSO–TSORMB–DMSO.
Construction: Aluminium.
Traction Motors: 4 Siemens 1TB2016-0GB02 asynchronous of 250 kW.
Wheel Arrangement: Bo-Bo + 2-2 + 2-2 + 2-2 + Bo-Bo.
Braking: Disc, rheostatic & regenerative. **Dimensions:** 23.57 x 2.80 m.
Bogies: SGP SF5000.   **Couplers:** Dellner 12.
Gangways: Throughout.   **Control System:** IGBT Inverter.
Doors: Single-leaf sliding plug.   **Maximum Speed:** 100 mph.
Heating & Ventilation: Air conditioning.
Seating Layout: 1: 2+1 facing/unidirectional, 2: 2+2 facing/unidirectional.
Multiple Working: Within class and with Class 450.

DMSO. Siemens Vienna/Krefeld 2003–04. –/76. 51.3t.
TSO 67101–145. Siemens Vienna/Krefeld 2003–04. –/76 1T. 40.3t.
TSO 67151–195. Siemens Vienna/Krefeld 2003–04. –/76 1T. 36.8t.
TSORMB. Siemens Vienna/Krefeld 2003–04. –/47 1T 1TD 2W. 42.1t.
DMCO. Siemens Vienna/Krefeld 2003–04. 35/24. 51.3t.

444 001	**ST**	A	*SW*	NT	63801 67101 67151 67201 63851
444 002	**ST**	A	*SW*	NT	63802 67102 67152 67202 63852
444 003	**ST**	A	*SW*	NT	63803 67103 67153 67203 63853
444 004	**ST**	A	*SW*	NT	63804 67104 67154 67204 63854
444 005	**ST**	A	*SW*	NT	63805 67105 67155 67205 63855
444 006	**ST**	A	*SW*	NT	63806 67106 67156 67206 63856
444 007	**ST**	A	*SW*	NT	63807 67107 67157 67207 63857
444 008	**ST**	A	*SW*	NT	63808 67108 67158 67208 63858
444 009	**ST**	A	*SW*	NT	63809 67109 67159 67209 63859
444 010	**ST**	A	*SW*	NT	63810 67110 67160 67210 63860
444 011	**ST**	A	*SW*	NT	63811 67111 67161 67211 63861
444 012	**ST**	A	*SW*	NT	63812 67112 67162 67212 63862
444 013	**ST**	A	*SW*	NT	63813 67113 67163 67213 63863
444 014	**ST**	A	*SW*	NT	63814 67114 67164 67214 63864
444 015	**ST**	A	*SW*	NT	63815 67115 67165 67215 63865
444 016	**ST**	A	*SW*	NT	63816 67116 67166 67216 63866
444 017	**ST**	A	*SW*	NT	63817 67117 67167 67217 63867
444 018	**ST**	A	*SW*	NT	63818 67118 67168 67218 63868
444 019	**ST**	A	*SW*	NT	63819 67119 67169 67219 63869
444 020	**ST**	A	*SW*	NT	63820 67120 67170 67220 63870
444 021	**ST**	A	*SW*	NT	63821 67121 67171 67221 63871
444 022	**ST**	A	*SW*	NT	63822 67122 67172 67222 63872
444 023	**ST**	A	*SW*	NT	63823 67123 67173 67223 63873
444 024	**ST**	A	*SW*	NT	63824 67124 67174 67224 63874
444 025	**ST**	A	*SW*	NT	63825 67125 67175 67225 63875
444 026	**ST**	A	*SW*	NT	63826 67126 67176 67226 63876

▲ Southern uses a fleet of refurbished Class 313s on the Coastway routes from Brighton. On 06/08/14 313 208 calls at Hove with the 12.09 West Worthing–Brighton. **Peter Weber**

▼ Most Class 315s are now in Greater Anglia livery. 315 858/838 arrive at Stratford with the 17.24 Shenfield–London Liverpool Street on 29/04/14. **Robert Pritchard**

▲ Angel demonstrator 317 722 passes Manor Park with the 11.45 London Liverpool Street–Ilford ecs on 10/06/14. This unit carries Greater Anglia livery on the two leading vehicles and National Express livery on the other two cars. **Antony Guppy**

▼ In the new Govia Thameslink livery, 319 010 calls at Mitcham Junction with the 09.44 St Albans–Sutton on 12/07/14. **Chris Wilson**

▲ ScotRail Saltire-liveried 320 311 passes Craigenhill with the 14.23 Lanark–Dalmuir on 18/02/13. **Robin Ralston**

▼ Greater Anglia-liveried 321 441 leads the 17.10 Southend Victoria–London Liverpool Street into Stratford on 29/04/14. **Robert Pritchard**

▲ London Midland-liveried 323 214 and 323 217 (nearest camera) leave Five Ways with the 10.57 Redditch–Four Oaks on 15/02/14. **Robert Pritchard**

▼ Royal Mail EMU 325 015 passes Wandel with the 17.49 Shieldmuir–Warrington RMT on 24/04/14. **Robin Ralston**

▲ Heathrow Express units 332 011 and 332 013 pass Royal Oak with the 08.57 Heathrow Terminal 5–London Paddington on 21/05/14. **Antony Guppy**

▼ All Class 334s are now in the ScotRail Saltire livery. 334 020 leaves Coatbridge Sunnyside with the 11.25 Helensburgh Central–Edinburgh on 02/06/13.
Robert Pritchard

▲ London Midland 350 112 calls at Atherstone with the 13.02 Crewe–London Euston on 11/08/14. **Dave Gommersall**

▼ c2c-liveried 357 007 passes Shadwell, alongside the Docklands Light Railway, with the 12.30 London Fenchurch Street–Southend Central on 15/05/14. **David Palmer**

▲ Heathrow Connect-liveried 360 201 leaves Southall with the 14.03 Hayes & Harlington–London Paddington on 23/08/14. **Antony Guppy**

▼ In the new Govia Thameslink livery, 365 517 brings up the rear of the 16.46 Peterborough–London King's Cross (led by First Capital Connect-liveried 365 501) at Hitchin on 09/05/14. **Mark Beal**

▲ 376 009 arrives at Beckenham Junction with the 11.28 special shuttle from Hayes on 06/04/12.
William Turvill

▼ One of the new Southern 5-car 377s, dual voltage 377 702, passes Hemel Hempstead with the 12.13 Milton Keynes–South Croydon on 20/08/14.
Alisdair Anderson

▲ London Overground 378 139 arrives at Haggerston with the 15.32 Highbury & Islington–Clapham Junction East London Line service on 26/07/13. **Robert Pritchard**

▼ Still in National Express livery, Greater Anglia 379 007 and 379 026 approach Cheshunt with the 11.45 Stansted Airport–London Liverpool Street on 21/07/14.
Antony Guppy

▲ ScotRail 380 101 calls at Carluke with the 13.48 Glasgow Central–Edinburgh Waverley on 12/03/14. **Robin Ralston**

▼ Virgin Trains 11-car Pendolino 390 141 arrives at Rugby with the 12.33 Birmingham New Street–London Euston on 17/07/13. **Stewart Armstrong**

▲ Southeastern High Speed 395 022 leaves Ebbsfleet International with the 14.53 Margate–London St Pancras on 08/09/14. **Antony Guppy**

▼ Gatwick Express-liveried 442 417 and 442 419 pass Coulsdon South with the 16.00 London Victoria–Gatwick Airport on 15/03/12. **Robert Pritchard**

▲ SWT white-liveried 444 016 passes Eastleigh with the 13.35 London Waterloo–Weymouth on 28/07/14. **Stewart Armstrong**

▼ SWT blue-liveried 450 076 passes Battledown working the 11.39 London Waterloo–Poole on 14/01/14. **Chris Wilson**

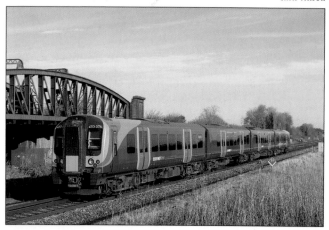

▲ Southern-liveried 455 822 leaves Mitcham Junction with the 10.47 London Victoria–Epsom on 12/07/14. **Chris Wilson**

▼ Refurbished and repainted into the South West Trains red suburban livery, 456 003 stands at Wimbledon depot on 30/06/14. **Brian Garvin**

▲ The rebuilt 5-car 458/5s slowly started to enter traffic during 2014. On 07/03/14 458 531 and 458 534 pass Vauxhall with an empty stock working from London Waterloo to Wimbledon depot following a press launch. **Robert Pritchard**

▼ Southeastern-liveried 465 042 leads a Charing Cross–Dartford service into Lewisham on 25/01/14. **Andrew Mason**

▲ A small fleet of former London Underground 1938 Stock units are used on the Isle of Wight railway, operated by South West Trains. On 18/05/14 483 006 leaves Smallbrook Junction with the 14.38 Shanklin–Ryde Pier Head. **Nigel Gibbs**

▼ New Merseyrail-liveried 507 031 leads 507 002 into Brunswick with the 12.28 Southport–Hunts Cross as 508 127 heads north on 07/09/14. **Robert Pritchard**

▲ The first of the new Thameslink Class 700s was due to arrive in Britain in 2015 following testing. On 04/09/14 12-car unit 700 101 stands at Velim station in the Czech Republic on its way to the nearby test circuit. **Quintus Vosman**

▼ One of the ten new Siemens Class 374 Eurostar Velaros, 4005/06, is seen at Mitry-Mory in France on its way to the LGV Rhin-Rhône line for tests on 24/06/14. These trains will enter traffic in 2015. **Christophe Masse**

444027	**ST**	A	*SW*	NT	63827	67127	67177	67227	63877
444028	**ST**	A	*SW*	NT	63828	67128	67178	67228	63878
444029	**ST**	A	*SW*	NT	63829	67129	67179	67229	63879
444030	**ST**	A	*SW*	NT	63830	67130	67180	67230	63880
444031	**ST**	A	*SW*	NT	63831	67131	67181	67231	63881
444032	**ST**	A	*SW*	NT	63832	67132	67182	67232	63882
444033	**ST**	A	*SW*	NT	63833	67133	67183	67233	63883
444034	**ST**	A	*SW*	NT	63834	67134	67184	67234	63884
444035	**ST**	A	*SW*	NT	63835	67135	67185	67235	63885
444036	**ST**	A	*SW*	NT	63836	67136	67186	67236	63886
444037	**ST**	A	*SW*	NT	63837	67137	67187	67237	63887
444038	**ST**	A	*SW*	NT	63838	67138	67188	67238	63888
444039	**ST**	A	*SW*	NT	63839	67139	67189	67239	63889
444040	**ST**	A	*SW*	NT	63840	67140	67190	67240	63890
444041	**ST**	A	*SW*	NT	63841	67141	67191	67241	63891
444042	**ST**	A	*SW*	NT	63842	67142	67192	67242	63892
444043	**ST**	A	*SW*	NT	63843	67143	67193	67243	63893
444044	**ST**	A	*SW*	NT	63844	67144	67194	67244	63894
444045	**ST**	A	*SW*	NT	63845	67145	67195	67245	63895

Names (carried on TSORMB):

444001	NAOMI HOUSE	444018	THE FAB 444
444012	DESTINATION WEYMOUTH	444038	SOUTH WESTERN RAILWAY

CLASS 450   DESIRO UK   SIEMENS

Outer suburban units.

Formation: DMSO–TCO–TSO–DMSO (DMSO–TSO–TCO–DMSO 450 111–127).
Construction: Aluminium.
Traction Motors: 4 Siemens 1TB2016-0GB02 asynchronous of 250 kW.
Wheel Arrangement: Bo-Bo + 2-2 + 2-2 + Bo-Bo. **Dimensions:** 20.34 x 2.79 m.
Braking: Disc, rheostatic & regenerative. **Couplers:** Dellner 12.
Bogies: SGP SF5000. **Control System:** IGBT Inverter.
Gangways: Throughout. **Maximum Speed:** 100 mph.
Doors: Sliding plug.
Heating & Ventilation: Air conditioning.
Seating Layout: 1: 2+2 facing/unidirectional, 2: 3+2 facing/unidirectional.
Multiple Working: Within class and with Class 444.

Class 450/0. Standard units.

DMSO(A). Siemens Krefeld/Vienna 2002–06. –/70. 48.0 t.
TCO. Siemens Krefeld/Vienna 2002–06. 24/32(4) 1T. 35.8 t.
TSO. Siemens Krefeld/Vienna 2002–06. –/61(9) 1TD 2W. 39.8 t.
DMSO(B). Siemens Krefeld/Vienna 2002–06. –/70. 48.6 t.

450001	**SD**	A	*SW*	NT	63201	64201	68101	63601
450002	**SD**	A	*SW*	NT	63202	64202	68102	63602
450003	**SD**	A	*SW*	NT	63203	64203	68103	63603
450004	**SD**	A	*SW*	NT	63204	64204	68104	63604
450005	**SD**	A	*SW*	NT	63205	64205	68105	63605
450006	**SD**	A	*SW*	NT	63206	64206	68106	63606

450007	**SD**	A	*SW*	NT	63207	64207	68107	63607
450008	**SD**	A	*SW*	NT	63208	64208	68108	63608
450009	**SD**	A	*SW*	NT	63209	64209	68109	63609
450010	**SD**	A	*SW*	NT	63210	64210	68110	63610
450011	**SD**	A	*SW*	NT	63211	64211	68111	63611
450012	**SD**	A	*SW*	NT	63212	64212	68112	63612
450013	**SD**	A	*SW*	NT	63213	64213	68113	63613
450014	**SD**	A	*SW*	NT	63214	64214	68114	63614
450015	**SD**	A	*SW*	NT	63215	64215	68115	63615
450016	**SD**	A	*SW*	NT	63216	64216	68116	63616
450017	**SD**	A	*SW*	NT	63217	64217	68117	63617
450018	**SD**	A	*SW*	NT	63218	64218	68118	63618
450019	**SD**	A	*SW*	NT	63219	64219	68119	63619
450020	**SD**	A	*SW*	NT	63220	64220	68120	63620
450021	**SD**	A	*SW*	NT	63221	64221	68121	63621
450022	**SD**	A	*SW*	NT	63222	64222	68122	63622
450023	**SD**	A	*SW*	NT	63223	64223	68123	63623
450024	**SD**	A	*SW*	NT	63224	64224	68124	63624
450025	**SD**	A	*SW*	NT	63225	64225	68125	63625
450026	**SD**	A	*SW*	NT	63226	64226	68126	63626
450027	**SD**	A	*SW*	NT	63227	64227	68127	63627
450028	**SD**	A	*SW*	NT	63228	64228	68128	63628
450029	**SD**	A	*SW*	NT	63229	64229	68129	63629
450030	**SD**	A	*SW*	NT	63230	64230	68130	63630
450031	**SD**	A	*SW*	NT	63231	64231	68131	63631
450032	**SD**	A	*SW*	NT	63232	64232	68132	63632
450033	**SD**	A	*SW*	NT	63233	64233	68133	63633
450034	**SD**	A	*SW*	NT	63234	64234	68134	63634
450035	**SD**	A	*SW*	NT	63235	64235	68135	63635
450036	**SD**	A	*SW*	NT	63236	64236	68136	63636
450037	**SD**	A	*SW*	NT	63237	64237	68137	63637
450038	**SD**	A	*SW*	NT	63238	64238	68138	63638
450039	**SD**	A	*SW*	NT	63239	64239	68139	63639
450040	**SD**	A	*SW*	NT	63240	64240	68140	63640
450041	**SD**	A	*SW*	NT	63241	64241	68141	63641
450042	**SD**	A	*SW*	NT	63242	64242	68142	63642
450071	**SD**	A	*SW*	NT	63271	64271	68171	63671
450072	**SD**	A	*SW*	NT	63272	64272	68172	63672
450073	**SD**	A	*SW*	NT	63273	64273	68173	63673
450074	**SD**	A	*SW*	NT	63274	64274	68174	63674
450075	**SD**	A	*SW*	NT	63275	64275	68175	63675
450076	**SD**	A	*SW*	NT	63276	64276	68176	63676
450077	**SD**	A	*SW*	NT	63277	64277	68177	63677
450078	**SD**	A	*SW*	NT	63278	64278	68178	63678
450079	**SD**	A	*SW*	NT	63279	64279	68179	63679
450080	**SD**	A	*SW*	NT	63280	64280	68180	63680
450081	**SD**	A	*SW*	NT	63281	64281	68181	63681
450082	**SD**	A	*SW*	NT	63282	64282	68182	63682
450083	**SD**	A	*SW*	NT	63283	64283	68183	63683
450084	**SD**	A	*SW*	NT	63284	64284	68184	63684
450085	**SD**	A	*SW*	NT	63285	64285	68185	63685

450086	**SD**	A	*SW*	NT	63286	64286	68186	63686
450087	**SD**	A	*SW*	NT	63287	64287	68187	63687
450088	**SD**	A	*SW*	NT	63288	64288	68188	63688
450089	**SD**	A	*SW*	NT	63289	64289	68189	63689
450090	**SD**	A	*SW*	NT	63290	64290	68190	63690
450091	**SD**	A	*SW*	NT	63291	64291	68191	63691
450092	**SD**	A	*SW*	NT	63292	64292	68192	63692
450093	**SD**	A	*SW*	NT	63293	64293	68193	63693
450094	**SD**	A	*SW*	NT	63294	64294	68194	63694
450095	**SD**	A	*SW*	NT	63295	64295	68195	63695
450096	**SD**	A	*SW*	NT	63296	64296	68196	63696
450097	**SD**	A	*SW*	NT	63297	64297	68197	63697
450098	**SD**	A	*SW*	NT	63298	64298	68198	63698
450099	**SD**	A	*SW*	NT	63299	64299	68199	63699
450100	**SD**	A	*SW*	NT	63300	64300	68200	63700
450101	**SD**	A	*SW*	NT	63701	66851	66801	63751
450102	**SD**	A	*SW*	NT	63702	66852	66802	63752
450103	**SD**	A	*SW*	NT	63703	66853	66803	63753
450104	**SD**	A	*SW*	NT	63704	66854	66804	63754
450105	**SD**	A	*SW*	NT	63705	66855	66805	63755
450106	**SD**	A	*SW*	NT	63706	66856	66806	63756
450107	**SD**	A	*SW*	NT	63707	66857	66807	63757
450108	**SD**	A	*SW*	NT	63708	66858	66808	63758
450109	**SD**	A	*SW*	NT	63709	66859	66809	63759
450110	**SD**	A	*SW*	NT	63710	66860	66810	63760
450111	**SD**	A	*SW*	NT	63901	66921	66901	63921
450112	**SD**	A	*SW*	NT	63902	66922	66902	63922
450113	**SD**	A	*SW*	NT	63903	66923	66903	63923
450114	**SD**	A	*SW*	NT	63904	66924	66904	63924
450115	**SD**	A	*SW*	NT	63905	66925	66905	63925
450116	**SD**	A	*SW*	NT	63906	66926	66906	63926
450117	**SD**	A	*SW*	NT	63907	66927	66907	63927
450118	**SD**	A	*SW*	NT	63908	66928	66908	63928
450119	**SD**	A	*SW*	NT	63909	66929	66909	63929
450120	**SD**	A	*SW*	NT	63910	66930	66910	63930
450121	**SD**	A	*SW*	NT	63911	66931	66911	63931
450122	**SD**	A	*SW*	NT	63912	66932	66912	63932
450123	**SD**	A	*SW*	NT	63913	66933	66913	63933
450124	**SD**	A	*SW*	NT	63914	66934	66914	63934
450125	**SD**	A	*SW*	NT	63915	66935	66915	63935
450126	**SD**	A	*SW*	NT	63916	66936	66916	63936
450127	**SD**	A	*SW*	NT	63917	66937	66917	63937

Names (carried on DMSO(B)):

450015 DESIRO | 450114 FAIRBRIDGE investing in the future
450042 TRELOAR COLLEGE |

Class 450/5. 28 units converted 2007–08 with First Class removed and a modified seating layout with more standing room (some Standard Class seats were taken out). First Class was refitted in 2013 but the removed Standard Class seats were not refitted so the units have kept their 450 5xx series numbers.

DMSO(A). Siemens Krefeld/Vienna 2002–04. –/64. 48.0 t.
TCO. Siemens Krefeld/Vienna 2002–04. 24/30(4) 1T. 35.5 t.
TSO. Siemens Krefeld/Vienna 2002–04. –/56(9) 1TD 2W. 39.8 t.
DMSO(B). Siemens Krefeld/Vienna 2002–04. –/64. 48.6 t.

450 543	(450 043)	**SD**	A	*SW*	NT	63243	64243	68143	63643
450 544	(450 044)	**SD**	A	*SW*	NT	63244	64244	68144	63644
450 545	(450 045)	**SD**	A	*SW*	NT	63245	64245	68145	63645
450 546	(450 046)	**SD**	A	*SW*	NT	63246	64246	68146	63646
450 547	(450 047)	**SD**	A	*SW*	NT	63247	64247	68147	63647
450 548	(450 048)	**SD**	A	*SW*	NT	63248	64248	68148	63648
450 549	(450 049)	**SD**	A	*SW*	NT	63249	64249	68149	63649
450 550	(450 050)	**SD**	A	*SW*	NT	63250	64250	68150	63650
450 551	(450 051)	**SD**	A	*SW*	NT	63251	64251	68151	63651
450 552	(450 052)	**SD**	A	*SW*	NT	63252	64252	68152	63652
450 553	(450 053)	**SD**	A	*SW*	NT	63253	64253	68153	63653
450 554	(450 054)	**SD**	A	*SW*	NT	63254	64254	68154	63654
450 555	(450 055)	**SD**	A	*SW*	NT	63255	64255	68155	63655
450 556	(450 056)	**SD**	A	*SW*	NT	63256	64256	68156	63656
450 557	(450 057)	**SD**	A	*SW*	NT	63257	64257	68157	63657
450 558	(450 058)	**SD**	A	*SW*	NT	63258	64258	68158	63658
450 559	(450 059)	**SD**	A	*SW*	NT	63259	64259	68159	63659
450 560	(450 060)	**SD**	A	*SW*	NT	63260	64260	68160	63660
450 561	(450 061)	**SD**	A	*SW*	NT	63261	64261	68161	63661
450 562	(450 062)	**SD**	A	*SW*	NT	63262	64262	68162	63662
450 563	(450 063)	**SD**	A	*SW*	NT	63263	64263	68163	63663
450 564	(450 064)	**SD**	A	*SW*	NT	63264	64264	68164	63664
450 565	(450 065)	**SD**	A	*SW*	NT	63265	64265	68165	63665
450 566	(450 066)	**SD**	A	*SW*	NT	63266	64266	68166	63666
450 567	(450 067)	**SD**	A	*SW*	NT	63267	64267	68167	63667
450 568	(450 068)	**SD**	A	*SW*	NT	63268	64268	68168	63668
450 569	(450 069)	**SD**	A	*SW*	NT	63269	64269	68169	63669
450 570	(450 070)	**SD**	A	*SW*	NT	63270	64270	68170	63670

CLASS 455   BREL YORK

Inner suburban units.

Formation: DTSO–MSO–TSO–DTSO.
Construction: Steel. Class 455/7 TSO have a steel underframe and an aluminium alloy body & roof.
Traction Motors: Four GEC507-20J of 185 kW, some recovered from Class 405s.
Wheel Arrangement: 2-2 + Bo-Bo + 2-2 + 2-2.
Braking: Disc.   **Dimensions:** 19.92/19.83 x 2.82 m.
Bogies: P7 (motor) and T3 (455/8 & 455/9) BX1 (455/7) trailer.
Gangways: Within unit + end doors (sealed on Southern units).
Couplers: Tightlock.   **Control System:** 1982-type, camshaft.
Doors: Sliding.   **Maximum Speed:** 75 mph.
Heating & Ventilation: Various.
Seating Layout: All units refurbished. SWT units: 2+2 high-back unidirectional/facing seating. Southern units: 3+2 high back mainly facing seating.
Multiple Working: Within class and with Class 456.

Class 455/7. South West Trains units. Second series with TSOs originally in Class 508s. Pressure heating & ventilation.

DTSO. Lot No. 30976 1984–85. –/50(4) 1W. 30.8 t.
MSO. Lot No. 30975 1984–85. –/68. 45.7 t.
TSO. Lot No. 30944 1979–80. –/68. 26.1 t.

5701	**SS**	P	*SW*	WD	77727	62783	71545	77728
5702	**SS**	P	*SW*	WD	77729	62784	71547	77730
5703	**SS**	P	*SW*	WD	77731	62785	71540	77732
5704	**SS**	P	*SW*	WD	77733	62786	71548	77734
5705	**SS**	P	*SW*	WD	77735	62787	71565	77736
5706	**SS**	P	*SW*	WD	77737	62788	71534	77738
5707	**SS**	P	*SW*	WD	77739	62789	71536	77740
5708	**SS**	P	*SW*	WD	77741	62790	71560	77742
5709	**SS**	P	*SW*	WD	77743	62791	71532	77744
5710	**SS**	P	*SW*	WD	77745	62792	71566	77746
5711	**SS**	P	*SW*	WD	77747	62793	71542	77748
5712	**SS**	P	*SW*	WD	77749	62794	71546	77750
5713	**SS**	P	*SW*	WD	77751	62795	71567	77752
5714	**SS**	P	*SW*	WD	77753	62796	71539	77754
5715	**SS**	P	*SW*	WD	77755	62797	71535	77756
5716	**SS**	P	*SW*	WD	77757	62798	71564	77758
5717	**SS**	P	*SW*	WD	77759	62799	71528	77760
5718	**SS**	P	*SW*	WD	77761	62800	71557	77762
5719	**SS**	P	*SW*	WD	77763	62801	71558	77764
5720	**SS**	P	*SW*	WD	77765	62802	71568	77766
5721	**SS**	P	*SW*	WD	77767	62803	71553	77768
5722	**SS**	P	*SW*	WD	77769	62804	71533	77770
5723	**SS**	P	*SW*	WD	77771	62805	71526	77772
5724	**SS**	P	*SW*	WD	77773	62806	71561	77774
5725	**SS**	P	*SW*	WD	77775	62807	71541	77776
5726	**SS**	P	*SW*	WD	77777	62808	71556	77778
5727	**SS**	P	*SW*	WD	77779	62809	71562	77780
5728	**SS**	P	*SW*	WD	77781	62810	71527	77782
5729	**SS**	P	*SW*	WD	77783	62811	71550	77784
5730	**SS**	P	*SW*	WD	77785	62812	71551	77786
5731	**SS**	P	*SW*	WD	77787	62813	71555	77788
5732	**SS**	P	*SW*	WD	77789	62814	71552	77790
5733	**SS**	P	*SW*	WD	77791	62815	71549	77792
5734	**SS**	P	*SW*	WD	77793	62816	71531	77794
5735	**SS**	P	*SW*	WD	77795	62817	71563	77796
5736	**SS**	P	*SW*	WD	77797	62818	71554	77798
5737	**SS**	P	*SW*	WD	77799	62819	71544	77800
5738	**SS**	P	*SW*	WD	77801	62820	71529	77802
5739	**SS**	P	*SW*	WD	77803	62821	71537	77804
5740	**SS**	P	*SW*	WD	77805	62822	71530	77806
5741	**SS**	P	*SW*	WD	77807	62823	71559	77808
5742	**SS**	P	*SW*	WD	77809	62824	71543	77810
5750	**SS**	P	*SW*	WD	77811	62825	71538	77812

Class 455/8. Southern units. First series. Pressure heating & ventilation. Fitted with in-cab air conditioning systems meaning that the end door has been sealed.

DTSO. Lot No. 30972 York 1982–84. –/74. 33.6 t.
MSO. Lot No. 30973 York 1982–84. –/84. 45.6 t.
TSO. Lot No. 30974 York 1982–84. –/75(3) 2W. 34.0 t.

455801	**SN**	E	*SN*	SL	77627	62709	71657	77580
455802	**SN**	E	*SN*	SL	77581	62710	71664	77582
455803	**SN**	E	*SN*	SL	77583	62711	71639	77584
455804	**SN**	E	*SN*	SL	77585	62712	71640	77586
455805	**SN**	E	*SN*	SL	77587	62713	71641	77588
455806	**SN**	E	*SN*	SL	77589	62714	71642	77590
455807	**SN**	E	*SN*	SL	77591	62715	71643	77592
455808	**SN**	E	*SN*	SL	77637	62716	71644	77594
455809	**SN**	E	*SN*	SL	77623	62717	71648	77602
455810	**SN**	E	*SN*	SL	77597	62718	71646	77598
455811	**SN**	E	*SN*	SL	77599	62719	71647	77600
455812	**SN**	E	*SN*	SL	77595	62720	71645	77626
455813	**SN**	E	*SN*	SL	77603	62721	71649	77604
455814	**SN**	E	*SN*	SL	77605	62722	71650	77606
455815	**SN**	E	*SN*	SL	77607	62723	71651	77608
455816	**SN**	E	*SN*	SL	77609	62724	71652	77633
455817	**SN**	E	*SN*	SL	77611	62725	71653	77612
455818	**SN**	E	*SN*	SL	77613	62726	71654	77632
455819	**SN**	E	*SN*	SL	77615	62727	71637	77616
455820	**SN**	E	*SN*	SL	77617	62728	71656	77618
455821	**SN**	E	*SN*	SL	77619	62729	71655	77620
455822	**SN**	E	*SN*	SL	77621	62730	71658	77622
455823	**SN**	E	*SN*	SL	77601	62731	71659	77596
455824	**SN**	E	*SN*	SL	77593	62732	71660	77624
455825	**SN**	E	*SN*	SL	77579	62733	71661	77628
455826	**SN**	E	*SN*	SL	77630	62734	71662	77629
455827	**SN**	E	*SN*	SL	77610	62735	71663	77614
455828	**SN**	E	*SN*	SL	77631	62736	71638	77634
455829	**SN**	E	*SN*	SL	77635	62737	71665	77636
455830	**SN**	E	*SN*	SL	77625	62743	71666	77638
455831	**SN**	E	*SN*	SL	77639	62739	71667	77640
455832	**SN**	E	*SN*	SL	77641	62740	71668	77642
455833	**SN**	E	*SN*	SL	77643	62741	71669	77644
455834	**SN**	E	*SN*	SL	77645	62742	71670	77646
455835	**SN**	E	*SN*	SL	77647	62738	71671	77648
455836	**SN**	E	*SN*	SL	77649	62744	71672	77650
455837	**SN**	E	*SN*	SL	77651	62745	71673	77652
455838	**SN**	E	*SN*	SL	77653	62746	71674	77654
455839	**SN**	E	*SN*	SL	77655	62747	71675	77656
455840	**SN**	E	*SN*	SL	77657	62748	71676	77658
455841	**SN**	E	*SN*	SL	77659	62749	71677	77660
455842	**SN**	E	*SN*	SL	77661	62750	71678	77662
455843	**SN**	E	*SN*	SL	77663	62751	71679	77664
455844	**SN**	E	*SN*	SL	77665	62752	71680	77666

| 455845 | **SN** | E | *SN* | SL | 77667 | 62753 | 71681 | 77668 |
| 455846 | **SN** | E | *SN* | SL | 77669 | 62754 | 71682 | 77670 |

Class 455/8. South West Trains units. First series. Pressure heating & ventilation.

DTSO. Lot No. 30972 York 1982–84. –50(4) 1W. 29.5 t.
MSO. Lot No. 30973 York 1982–84. –/84 –/68. 45.6 t.
TSO. Lot No. 30974 York 1982–84. –/84 –/68. 27.1 t.

5847	**SS**	P	*SW*	WD	77671	62755	71683	77672
5848	**SS**	P	*SW*	WD	77673	62756	71684	77674
5849	**SS**	P	*SW*	WD	77675	62757	71685	77676
5850	**SS**	P	*SW*	WD	77677	62758	71686	77678
5851	**SS**	P	*SW*	WD	77679	62759	71687	77680
5852	**SS**	P	*SW*	WD	77681	62760	71688	77682
5853	**SS**	P	*SW*	WD	77683	62761	71689	77684
5854	**SS**	P	*SW*	WD	77685	62762	71690	77686
5855	**SS**	P	*SW*	WD	77687	62763	71691	77688
5856	**SS**	P	*SW*	WD	77689	62764	71692	77690
5857	**SS**	P	*SW*	WD	77691	62765	71693	77692
5858	**SS**	P	*SW*	WD	77693	62766	71694	77694
5859	**SS**	P	*SW*	WD	77695	62767	71695	77696
5860	**SS**	P	*SW*	WD	77697	62768	71696	77698
5861	**SS**	P	*SW*	WD	77699	62769	71697	77700
5862	**SS**	P	*SW*	WD	77701	62770	71698	77702
5863	**SS**	P	*SW*	WD	77703	62771	71699	77704
5864	**SS**	P	*SW*	WD	77705	62772	71700	77706
5865	**SS**	P	*SW*	WD	77707	62773	71701	77708
5866	**SS**	P	*SW*	WD	77709	62774	71702	77710
5867	**SS**	P	*SW*	WD	77711	62775	71703	77712
5868	**SS**	P	*SW*	WD	77713	62776	71704	77714
5869	**SS**	P	*SW*	WD	77715	62777	71705	77716
5870	**SS**	P	*SW*	WD	77717	62778	71706	77718
5871	**SS**	P	*SW*	WD	77719	62779	71707	77720
5872	**SS**	P	*SW*	WD	77721	62780	71708	77722
5873	**SS**	P	*SW*	WD	77723	62781	71709	77724
5874	**SS**	P	*SW*	WD	77725	62782	71710	77726

Class 455/9. South West Trains units. Third series. Convection heating.
Dimensions: 19.96/20.18 x 2.82 m.

Vehicles 67301 and 67400 were converted from Class 210 DEMU vehicles to replace accident damaged cars.

DTSO. Lot No. 30991 York 1985. –/50(4) 1W. 30.7 t.
MSO. Lot No. 30992 York 1985. –/68. 46.3 t.
TSO. Lot No. 30993 York 1985. –/68. 28.3 t.
TSO†. Lot No. 30932 Derby 1981. –/68. 26.5 t.

5901	**SS**	P	*SW*	WD	77813	62826	71714	77814
5902	**SS**	P	*SW*	WD	77815	62827	71715	77816
5903	**SS**	P	*SW*	WD	77817	62828	71716	77818
5904	**SS**	P	*SW*	WD	77819	62829	71717	77820
5905	**SS**	P	*SW*	WD	77821	62830	71725	77822

5906		**SS**	P	*SW*	WD	77823	62831	71719	77824
5907		**SS**	P	*SW*	WD	77825	62832	71720	77826
5908		**SS**	P	*SW*	WD	77827	62833	71721	77828
5909		**SS**	P	*SW*	WD	77829	62834	71722	77830
5910		**SS**	P	*SW*	WD	77831	62835	71723	77832
5911		**SS**	P	*SW*	WD	77833	62836	71724	77834
5912	†	**SS**	P	*SW*	WD	77835	62837	67400	77836
5913	†	**SS**	P	*SW*	WD	77837	67301	71726	77838
5914		**SS**	P	*SW*	WD	77839	62839	71727	77840
5915		**SS**	P	*SW*	WD	77841	62840	71728	77842
5916		**SS**	P	*SW*	WD	77843	62841	71729	77844
5917		**SS**	P	*SW*	WD	77845	62842	71730	77846
5918		**SS**	P	*SW*	WD	77847	62843	71732	77848
5919		**SS**	P	*SW*	WD	77849	62844	71718	77850
5920		**SS**	P	*SW*	WD	77851	62845	71733	77852

CLASS 456   BREL YORK

Inner suburban units. These units are now operated by South West Trains, having previously been operated by Southern. They are currently being refurbished at Wolverton with new 2+2 Grammer seating.

Formation: DMSO–DTSO.
Construction: Steel underframe, aluminium alloy body & roof.
Traction Motors: Two GEC507-20J of 185 kW, some recovered from Class 405s.
Wheel Arrangement: 2-Bo + 2-2.   **Dimensions:** 20.61 x 2.82 m.
Braking: Disc.   **Couplers:** Tightlock.
Bogies: P7 (motor) and T3 (trailer). **Control System:** GTO Chopper.
Gangways: Within unit.   **Maximum Speed:** 75 mph.
Doors: Sliding.
Seating Layout: 3+2 facing (* 2+2 facing/unidirectional).
Heating & Ventilation: Convection heating.
Multiple Working: Within class and with Class 455.

DMSO. Lot No. 31073 1990–91. –/79 (* –/59). 41.1 t (* 43.3 t).
DTSO. Lot No. 31074 1990–91. –/73 (* –/54(5)). 31.4 t (* 32.3 t).

456 001		**SN**	P	*SW*	WD	64735	78250
456 002		**SN**	P	*SW*	WD	64736	78251
456 003	*	**SS**	P	*SW*	WD	64737	78252
456 004		**SN**	P	*SW*	WD	64738	78253
456 005		**SN**	P	*SW*	WD	64739	78254
456 006	*	**SS**	P	*SW*	WD	64740	78255
456 007		**SN**	P	*SW*	WD	64741	78256
456 008		**SN**	P	*SW*	WD	64742	78257
456 009		**SN**	P	*SW*	WD	64743	78258
456 010		**SN**	P	*SW*	WD	64744	78259
456 011		**SN**	P	*SW*	WD	64745	78260
456 012	*	**SS**	P	*SW*	WD	64746	78261
456 013		**SN**	P	*SW*	WD	64747	78262
456 014	*	**SS**	P	*SW*	WD	64748	78263

456 015	*	**SS**	P	*SW*	WD	64749 78264
456 016		**SN**	P	*SW*	WD	64750 78265
456 017		**SN**	P	*SW*	WD	64751 78266
456 018		**SN**	P	*SW*	WD	64752 78267
456 019		**SN**	P	*SW*	WD	64753 78268
456 020		**SN**	P	*SW*	WD	64754 78269
456 021		**SN**	P	*SW*	WD	64755 78270
456 022		**SN**	P	*SW*	WD	64756 78271
456 023		**SN**	P	*SW*	WD	64757 78272
456 024		**SN**	P	*SW*	WD	64758 78273

CLASS 458   JUNIPER   ALSTOM BIRMINGHAM

Outer suburban units. Between 2013 and 2015 the fleet of 30 4-car Class 458 units and the former Gatwick Express fleet of eight 8-car Class 460 units is being combined to form a fleet of 36 5-car Standard Class only Class 458/5s. The work is being carried out at Wabtec Doncaster and Brush Loughborough. Former Class 460 driving cars 67901/903/907/908 are not included in this programme and are shown in the EMUs Awaiting Disposal section of this book.

The first six units to be completed were 458 531–536, which use all former Class 460 vehicles. These are being followed by 8001–30 which are being augmented to 5-cars. All of the spare 460 vehicles to be added to 458s are listed at the end of this section, with a space left in the formations of 8001–30 for them to be inserted.

After lengthening each unit is being renumbered into the 458 5xx series. All individual vehicles retain their original numbers.

Formation: DMCO–TSO–MSO–DMCO (as built) or 5-cars DMSO–TSO–TSO–MSO–DMSO.
Construction: Steel.   **Dimensions:** 21.16 or 21.06 x 2.80 m.
Traction Motors: Two Alstom ONIX 800 asynchronous of 270 kW.
Wheel Arrangement: 2-Bo + 2-2 (+ 2-2) + Bo-2 + Bo-2.
Braking: Disc & regenerative.   **Control System:** IGBT Inverter.
Bogies: ACR.   **Doors:** Sliding plug.
Gangways: Throughout.
Couplers: Scharfenberg AAR (458/5 Voith 136).
Maximum Speed: 75 mph (original 458/0s are 100 mph).
Heating & Ventilation: Air conditioning. **Multiple Working:** Within class.
Seating Layout: 1: 2+2 facing, 2: 3+2 facing/unidirectional (458/5 units Standard Class only, 2+2 facing/unidirectional).

DMCO(A). Alstom 1998–2000. 12/63 (458/5 –/60). 46.4 t/45.7 t.
TSO (ex-460): Alstom 1998–99. 458 531–536 –/52 1T (for 458 501–530 –/56). 34.4 t.
TSO. Alstom 1998–2000. –/54(6) 1TD 2W (458/5 –/42 1TD 2W). 34.6 t/34.1 t.
MSO. Alstom 1998–2000. –/75 1T (458 531–536 –/56, 458 501–530 –56 1T). 42.1 t/39.3 t.
DMCO(B). Alstom 1998–2000. 12/63 (458/5 –/60). 46.4 t/45.7 t.

458501	**SD**	P	*SW*	WD	67601 74431 74001 74101 67701
458502	**SD**	P	*SW*	WD	67602 74421 74002 74102 67702
458503	**SD**	P	*SW*	WD	67603 74441 74003 74103 67703
458504	**SD**	P	*SW*	WD	67604 74451 74004 74104 67704
8005	**ST**	P	*SW*	WD	67605 74005 74105 67705
8006	**ST**	P	*SW*	WD	67606 74006 74106 67706
8007	**ST**	P	*SW*	WD	67607 74007 74107 67707
8008	**ST**	P	*SW*	WD	67608 74008 74108 67708
8009	**ST**	P	*SW*	WD	67609 74009 74109 67709
8010	**ST**	P	*SW*	WD	67610 74010 74110 67710
8011	**ST**	P	*SW*	WD	67611 74011 74111 67711
8012	**ST**	P	*SW*	WD	67612 74012 74112 67712
8013	**ST**	P	*SW*	WD	67613 74013 74113 67713
8014	**ST**	P	*SW*	WD	67614 74014 74114 67714
8015	**ST**	P	*SW*	WD	67615 74015 74115 67715
8016	**ST**	P	*SW*	WD	67616 74016 74116 67716
8017	**ST**	P	*SW*	WD	67617 74017 74117 67717
8018	**ST**	P	*SW*	WD	67618 74018 74118 67718
8019	**ST**	P	*SW*	WD	67619 74019 74119 67719
458520	**SD**	P	*SW*	WD	67620 74401 74020 74120 67720
8021	**ST**	P	*SW*	WD	67621 74021 74121 67721
8022	**ST**	P	*SW*	WD	67622 74022 74122 67722
8023	**ST**	P	*SW*	WD	67623 74023 74123 67723
8024	**ST**	P	*SW*	WD	67624 74024 74124 67724
8025	**ST**	P	*SW*	WD	67625 74025 74125 67725
8026	**ST**	P	*SW*	WD	67626 74026 74126 67726
8027	**ST**	P	*SW*	WD	67627 74027 74127 67727
8028	**ST**	P	*SW*	WD	67628 74028 74128 67728
8029	**ST**	P	*SW*	WD	67629 74029 74129 67729
458530	**SD**	P	*SW*	WD	67630 74411 74030 74130 67730

The following Class 460 vehicles will be added to the above units during 2015.

74402	74403	74404	74405	74406	74407	74408	74412	74422
74423	74424	74425	74426	74427	74428	74432	74433	74434
74435	74436	74437	74438	74442	74452

The following units have been converted from Class 460s.

458531	**SD**	P	*SW*	WD	67913 74418 74446 74458 67912
458532	**SD**	P	*SW*	WD	67904 74417 74447 74457 67905
458533	**SD**	P	*SW*	WD	67917 74413 74443 74453 67916
458534	**SD**	P	*SW*	WD	67914 74444 74444 74454 67918
458535	**SD**	P	*SW*	WD	67915 74415 74445 74455 67911
458536	**SD**	P	*SW*	WD	67906 74416 74448 74456 67902

CLASS 465   NETWORKER

Inner/outer suburban units.

Formation: DMSO–TSO–TSO–DMSO.
Construction: Welded aluminium alloy.
Traction Motors: Hitachi asynchronous of 280 kW (Classes 465/0 and 465/1) or GEC-Alsthom G352BY (Classes 465/2 and 465/9).
Wheel Arrangement: Bo-Bo + 2-2 + 2-2 + Bo-Bo.
Braking: Disc & rheostatic and regenerative (Classes 465/0 and 465/1 only).
Bogies: BREL P3/T3 (465/0 and 465/1), SRP BP62/BT52 (465/2 and 465/9).
Dimensions: 20.89/20.06 x 2.81 m.
Control System: IGBT Inverter (465/0 and 465/1) or 1992-type GTO Inverter.
Gangways: Within unit.   **Couplers:** Tightlock.
Doors: Sliding plug.   **Maximum Speed:** 75 mph.
Seating Layout: 3+2 facing/unidirectional.
Multiple Working: Within class and with Class 466.

64759–808. DMSO(A). Lot No. 31100 BREL York 1991–93. –/86. 39.2t.
64809–858. DMSO(B). Lot No. 31100 BREL York 1991–93. –/86. 39.2t.
65734–749. DMSO(A). Lot No. 31103 Metro-Cammell 1991–93. –/86. 39.2t.
65784–799. DMSO(B). Lot No. 31103 Metro-Cammell 1991–93. –/86. 39.2t.
65800–846. DMSO(A). Lot No. 31130 ABB York 1993–94. –/86. 39.2t.
65847–893. DMSO(B). Lot No. 31130 ABB York 1993–94. –/86. 39.2t.
72028–126 (even nos.) TSO. Lot No. 31102 BREL York 1991–93. –/90. 27.2t.
72029–127 (odd nos.) TSO. Lot No. 31101 BREL York 1991–93. –/86 1T. 28.0t.
72787–817 (odd nos.) TSO. Lot No. 31104 Metro-Cammell 1991–92. –/86 1T. 28.0t.
72788–818 (even nos.) TSO. Lot No. 31105 Metro-Cammell 1991–92. –/90. 27.2t.
72900–992 (even nos.) TSO. Lot No. 31102 ABB York 1993–94. –/90. 27.2t.
72901–993 (odd nos.) TSO. Lot No. 31101 ABB York 1993–94. –/86 1T. 28.0t.

Class 465/0. Built by BREL/ABB.

465001	**SE**	E	*SE*	SG	64759	72028	72029	64809
465002	**SE**	E	*SE*	SG	64760	72030	72031	64810
465003	**SE**	E	*SE*	SG	64761	72032	72033	64811
465004	**SE**	E	*SE*	SG	64762	72034	72035	64812
465005	**SE**	E	*SE*	SG	64763	72036	72037	64813
465006	**SE**	E	*SE*	SG	64764	72038	72039	64814
465007	**SE**	E	*SE*	SG	64765	72040	72041	64815
465008	**SE**	E	*SE*	SG	64766	72042	72043	64816
465009	**SE**	E	*SE*	SG	64767	72044	72045	64817
465010	**SE**	E	*SE*	SG	64768	72046	72047	64818
465011	**SE**	E	*SE*	SG	64769	72048	72049	64819
465012	**SE**	E	*SE*	SG	64770	72050	72051	64820
465013	**SE**	E	*SE*	SG	64771	72052	72053	64821
465014	**SE**	E	*SE*	SG	64772	72054	72055	64822
465015	**SE**	E	*SE*	SG	64773	72056	72057	64823
465016	**SE**	E	*SE*	SG	64774	72058	72059	64824
465017	**SE**	E	*SE*	SG	64775	72060	72061	64825
465018	**SE**	E	*SE*	SG	64776	72062	72063	64826
465019	**SE**	E	*SE*	SG	64777	72064	72065	64827

465 020	**SE**	E	*SE*	SG	64778	72066	72067	64828
465 021	**SE**	E	*SE*	SG	64779	72068	72069	64829
465 022	**SE**	E	*SE*	SG	64780	72070	72071	64830
465 023	**SE**	E	*SE*	SG	64781	72072	72073	64831
465 024	**SE**	E	*SE*	SG	64782	72074	72075	64832
465 025	**SE**	E	*SE*	SG	64783	72076	72077	64833
465 026	**SE**	E	*SE*	SG	64784	72078	72079	64834
465 027	**SE**	E	*SE*	SG	64785	72080	72081	64835
465 028	**SE**	E	*SE*	SG	64786	72082	72083	64836
465 029	**SE**	E	*SE*	SG	64787	72084	72085	64837
465 030	**SE**	E	*SE*	SG	64788	72086	72087	64838
465 031	**SE**	E	*SE*	SG	64789	72088	72089	64839
465 032	**SE**	E	*SE*	SG	64790	72090	72091	64840
465 033	**SE**	E	*SE*	SG	64791	72092	72093	64841
465 034	**SE**	E	*SE*	SG	64792	72094	72095	64842
465 035	**SE**	E	*SE*	SG	64793	72096	72097	64843
465 036	**SE**	E	*SE*	SG	64794	72098	72099	64844
465 037	**SE**	E	*SE*	SG	64795	72100	72101	64845
465 038	**SE**	E	*SE*	SG	64796	72102	72103	64846
465 039	**SE**	E	*SE*	SG	64797	72104	72105	64847
465 040	**SE**	E	*SE*	SG	64798	72106	72107	64848
465 041	**SE**	E	*SE*	SG	64799	72108	72109	64849
465 042	**SE**	E	*SE*	SG	64800	72110	72111	64850
465 043	**SE**	E	*SE*	SG	64801	72112	72113	64851
465 044	**SE**	E	*SE*	SG	64802	72114	72115	64852
465 045	**SE**	E	*SE*	SG	64803	72116	72117	64853
465 046	**SE**	E	*SE*	SG	64804	72118	72119	64854
465 047	**SE**	E	*SE*	SG	64805	72120	72121	64855
465 048	**SE**	E	*SE*	SG	64806	72122	72123	64856
465 049	**SE**	E	*SE*	SG	64807	72124	72125	64857
465 050	**SE**	E	*SE*	SG	64808	72126	72127	64858

Class 465/1. Built by BREL/ABB. Similar to Class 465/0 but with detail differences.

465 151	**SE**	E	*SE*	SG	65800	72900	72901	65847
465 152	**SE**	E	*SE*	SG	65801	72902	72903	65848
465 153	**SE**	E	*SE*	SG	65802	72904	72905	65849
465 154	**SE**	E	*SE*	SG	65803	72906	72907	65850
465 155	**SE**	E	*SE*	SG	65804	72908	72909	65851
465 156	**SE**	E	*SE*	SG	65805	72910	72911	65852
465 157	**SE**	E	*SE*	SG	65806	72912	72913	65853
465 158	**SE**	E	*SE*	SG	65807	72914	72915	65854
465 159	**SE**	E	*SE*	SG	65808	72916	72917	65855
465 160	**SE**	E	*SE*	SG	65809	72918	72919	65856
465 161	**SE**	E	*SE*	SG	65810	72920	72921	65857
465 162	**SE**	E	*SE*	SG	65811	72922	72923	65858
465 163	**SE**	E	*SE*	SG	65812	72924	72925	65859
465 164	**SE**	E	*SE*	SG	65813	72926	72927	65860
465 165	**SE**	E	*SE*	SG	65814	72928	72929	65861
465 166	**SE**	E	*SE*	SG	65815	72930	72931	65862
465 167	**SE**	E	*SE*	SG	65816	72932	72933	65863
465 168	**SE**	E	*SE*	SG	65817	72934	72935	65864

465 169	**SE**	E	*SE*	SG	65818	72936	72937	65865
465 170	**SE**	E	*SE*	SG	65819	72938	72939	65866
465 171	**SE**	E	*SE*	SG	65820	72940	72941	65867
465 172	**SE**	E	*SE*	SG	65821	72942	72943	65868
465 173	**SE**	E	*SE*	SG	65822	72944	72945	65869
465 174	**SE**	E	*SE*	SG	65823	72946	72947	65870
465 175	**SE**	E	*SE*	SG	65824	72948	72949	65871
465 176	**SE**	E	*SE*	SG	65825	72950	72951	65872
465 177	**SE**	E	*SE*	SG	65826	72952	72953	65873
465 178	**SE**	E	*SE*	SG	65827	72954	72955	65874
465 179	**SE**	E	*SE*	SG	65828	72956	72957	65875
465 180	**SE**	E	*SE*	SG	65829	72958	72959	65876
465 181	**SE**	E	*SE*	SG	65830	72960	72961	65877
465 182	**SE**	E	*SE*	SG	65831	72962	72963	65878
465 183	**SE**	E	*SE*	SG	65832	72964	72965	65879
465 184	**SE**	E	*SE*	SG	65833	72966	72967	65880
465 185	**SE**	E	*SE*	SG	65834	72968	72969	65881
465 186	**SE**	E	*SE*	SG	65835	72970	72971	65882
465 187	**SE**	E	*SE*	SG	65836	72972	72973	65883
465 188	**SE**	E	*SE*	SG	65837	72974	72975	65884
465 189	**SE**	E	*SE*	SG	65838	72976	72977	65885
465 190	**SE**	E	*SE*	SG	65839	72978	72979	65886
465 191	**SE**	E	*SE*	SG	65840	72980	72981	65887
465 192	**SE**	E	*SE*	SG	65841	72982	72983	65888
465 193	**SE**	E	*SE*	SG	65842	72984	72985	65889
465 194	**SE**	E	*SE*	SG	65843	72986	72987	65890
465 195	**SE**	E	*SE*	SG	65844	72988	72989	65891
465 196	**SE**	E	*SE*	SG	65845	72990	72991	65892
465 197	**SE**	E	*SE*	SG	65846	72992	72993	65893

Class 465/2. Built by Metro-Cammell. **Dimensions:** 20.80/20.15 x 2.81 m.

465 235	**SE**	A	*SE*	SG	65734	72787	72788	65784
465 236	**CN**	A	*SE*	SG	65735	72789	72790	65785
465 237	**SE**	A	*SE*	SG	65736	72791	72792	65786
465 238	**SE**	A	*SE*	SG	65737	72793	72794	65787
465 239	**CN**	A	*SE*	SG	65738	72795	72796	65788
465 240	**SE**	A	*SE*	SG	65739	72797	72798	65789
465 241	**SE**	A	*SE*	SG	65740	72799	72800	65790
465 242	**SE**	A	*SE*	SG	65741	72801	72802	65791
465 243	**SE**	A	*SE*	SG	65742	72803	72804	65792
465 244	**SE**	A	*SE*	SG	65743	72805	72806	65793
465 245	**SE**	A	*SE*	SG	65744	72807	72808	65794
465 246	**CN**	A	*SE*	SG	65745	72809	72810	65795
465 247	**SE**	A	*SE*	SG	65746	72811	72812	65796
465 248	**SE**	A	*SE*	SG	65747	72813	72814	65797
465 249	**CN**	A	*SE*	SG	65748	72815	72816	65798
465 250	**SE**	A	*SE*	SG	65749	72817	72818	65799

Class 465/9. Built by Metro-Cammell. Refurbished 2005 for longer distance services, with the addition of First Class. Details as Class 465/0 unless stated.
Formation: DMCO–TSO(A)–TSO(B)–DMCO.
Seating Layout: 1: 2+2 facing/unidirectional, 2: 3+2 facing/unidirectional.

65700–733. DMCO(A). Lot No. 31103 Metro-Cammell 1991–93. 12/68. 39.2t.
72719–785 (odd nos.) TSO(A). Lot No. 31104 Metro-Cammell 1991–92. –/76 1T 2W. 30.3t.
72720–786 (even nos.) TSO(B). Lot No. 31105 Metro-Cammell 1991–92. –/90. 29.5t.
65750–783. DMCO(B). Lot No. 31103 Metro-Cammell 1991–93. 12/68. 39.2t.

465 901	(465 201)	**CN**	A	*SE*	SG	65700	72719 72720	65750
465 902	(465 202)	**SE**	A	*SE*	SG	65701	72721 72722	65751
465 903	(465 203)	**SE**	A	*SE*	SG	65702	72723 72724	65752
465 904	(465 204)	**SE**	A	*SE*	SG	65703	72725 72726	65753
465 905	(465 205)	**SE**	A	*SE*	SG	65704	72727 72728	65754
465 906	(465 206)	**CN**	A	*SE*	SG	65705	72729 72730	65755
465 907	(465 207)	**SE**	A	*SE*	SG	65706	72731 72732	65756
465 908	(465 208)	**CN**	A	*SE*	SG	65707	72733 72734	65757
465 909	(465 209)	**CN**	A	*SE*	SG	65708	72735 72736	65758
465 910	(465 210)	**SE**	A	*SE*	SG	65709	72737 72738	65759
465 911	(465 211)	**CN**	A	*SE*	SG	65710	72739 72740	65760
465 912	(465 212)	**SE**	A	*SE*	SG	65711	72741 72742	65761
465 913	(465 213)	**SE**	A	*SE*	SG	65712	72743 72744	65762
465 914	(465 214)	**SE**	A	*SE*	SG	65713	72745 72746	65763
465 915	(465 215)	**SE**	A	*SE*	SG	65714	72747 72748	65764
465 916	(465 216)	**SE**	A	*SE*	SG	65715	72749 72750	65765
465 917	(465 217)	**SE**	A	*SE*	SG	65716	72751 72752	65766
465 918	(465 218)	**SE**	A	*SE*	SG	65717	72753 72754	65767
465 919	(465 219)	**SE**	A	*SE*	SG	65718	72755 72756	65768
465 920	(465 220)	**SE**	A	*SE*	SG	65719	72757 72758	65769
465 921	(465 221)	**SE**	A	*SE*	SG	65720	72759 72760	65770
465 922	(465 222)	**SE**	A	*SE*	SG	65721	72761 72762	65771
465 923	(465 223)	**SE**	A	*SE*	SG	65722	72763 72764	65772
465 924	(465 224)	**SE**	A	*SE*	SG	65723	72765 72766	65773
465 925	(465 225)	**SE**	A	*SE*	SG	65724	72767 72768	65774
465 926	(465 226)	**CN**	A	*SE*	SG	65725	72769 72770	65775
465 927	(465 227)	**SE**	A	*SE*	SG	65726	72771 72772	65776
465 928	(465 228)	**SE**	A	*SE*	SG	65727	72773 72774	65777
465 929	(465 229)	**SE**	A	*SE*	SG	65728	72775 72776	65778
465 930	(465 230)	**SE**	A	*SE*	SG	65729	72777 72778	65779
465 931	(465 231)	**SE**	A	*SE*	SG	65730	72779 72780	65780
465 932	(465 232)	**SE**	A	*SE*	SG	65731	72781 72782	65781
465 933	(465 233)	**SE**	A	*SE*	SG	65732	72783 72784	65782
465 934	(465 234)	**CN**	A	*SE*	SG	65733	72785 72786	65783

CLASS 466   NETWORKER   GEC-ALSTHOM

Inner/outer suburban units.

Formation: DMSO–DTSO.
Construction: Welded aluminium alloy.
Traction Motors: Two GEC-Alsthom G352AY asynchronous of 280 kW.
Wheel Arrangement: Bo-Bo + 2-2.   **Couplers:** Tightlock.
Braking: Disc, rheostatic & regen.   **Control System:** 1992-type GTO Inverter.
Dimensions: 20.80 x 2.80 m.   **Maximum Speed:** 75 mph.
Bogies: BREL P3/T3.   **Doors:** Sliding plug.
Gangways: Within unit.   **Seating Layout:** 3+2 facing/unidirectional.
Multiple Working: Within class and with Class 465.

DMSO. Lot No. 31128 Birmingham 1993–94. –/86. 40.6 t.
DTSO. Lot No. 31129 Birmingham 1993–94. –/82 1T. 31.4 t.

466 001	**SE**	A	*SE*	SG	64860	78312
466 002	**SE**	A	*SE*	SG	64861	78313
466 003	**SE**	A	*SE*	SG	64862	78314
466 004	**SE**	A	*SE*	SG	64863	78315
466 005	**SE**	A	*SE*	SG	64864	78316
466 006	**SE**	A	*SE*	SG	64865	78317
466 007	**SE**	A	*SE*	SG	64866	78318
466 008	**SE**	A	*SE*	SG	64867	78319
466 009	**SE**	A	*SE*	SG	64868	78320
466 010	**SE**	A	*SE*	SG	64869	78321
466 011	**SE**	A	*SE*	SG	64870	78322
466 012	**SE**	A	*SE*	SG	64871	78323
466 013	**SE**	A	*SE*	SG	64872	78324
466 014	**SE**	A	*SE*	SG	64873	78325
466 015	**SE**	A	*SE*	SG	64874	78326
466 016	**SE**	A	*SE*	SG	64875	78327
466 017	**SE**	A	*SE*	SG	64876	78328
466 018	**SE**	A	*SE*	SG	64877	78329
466 019	**SE**	A	*SE*	SG	64878	78330
466 020	**SE**	A	*SE*	SG	64879	78331
466 021	**SE**	A	*SE*	SG	64880	78332
466 022	**SE**	A	*SE*	SG	64881	78333
466 023	**SE**	A	*SE*	SG	64882	78334
466 024	**SE**	A	*SE*	SG	64883	78335
466 025	**SE**	A	*SE*	SG	64884	78336
466 026	**SE**	A	*SE*	SG	64885	78337
466 027	**SE**	A	*SE*	SG	64886	78338
466 028	**SE**	A	*SE*	SG	64887	78339
466 029	**SE**	A	*SE*	SG	64888	78340
466 030	**SE**	A	*SE*	SG	64889	78341
466 031	**SE**	A	*SE*	SG	64890	78342
466 032	**SE**	A	*SE*	SG	64891	78343
466 033	**SE**	A	*SE*	SG	64892	78344
466 034	**SE**	A	*SE*	SG	64893	78345
466 035	**SE**	A	*SE*	SG	64894	78346

466036	**SE**	A	*SE*	SG	64895	78347
466037	**SE**	A	*SE*	SG	64896	78348
466038	**SE**	A	*SE*	SG	64897	78349
466039	**SE**	A	*SE*	SG	64898	78350
466040	**SE**	A	*SE*	SG	64899	78351
466041	**SE**	A	*SE*	SG	64900	78352
466042	**SE**	A	*SE*	SG	64901	78353
466043	**SE**	A	*SE*	SG	64902	78354

CLASS 483   METRO-CAMMELL

Built 1938 onwards for LTE. Converted 1989–90 for the Isle of Wight Line.

Formation: DMSO–DMSO.
System: 660 V DC third rail.
Construction: Steel.
Traction Motors: Two Crompton Parkinson/GEC/BTH LT100 of 125 kW.
Braking: Tread.   **Dimensions:** 16.15 x 2.69 m.
Bogies: LT design.   **Couplers:** Wedglock.
Gangways: None. End doors.
Control System: Pneumatic Camshaft Motor (PCM).
Doors: Sliding.   **Maximum Speed:** 45 mph.
Seating Layout: Longitudinal or 2+2 facing/unidirectional.
Multiple Working: Within class.
Notes: The last three numbers of the unit number only are carried.

Former London Underground numbers are shown in parentheses.

DMSO (A). Lot No. 31071. –/40. 27.4 t.
DMSO (B). Lot No. 31072. –/42. 27.4 t.

483002	**LT**	SW		RY	122	(10221)	225	(11142)	RAPTOR
483004	**LT**	SW	*SW*	RY	124	(10205)	224	(11205)	
483006	**LT**	SW	*SW*	RY	126	(10297)	226	(11297)	
483007	**LT**	SW	*SW*	RY	127	(10291)	227	(11291)	
483008	**LT**	SW	*SW*	RY	128	(10255)	228	(11255)	
483009	**LT**	SW	*SW*	RY	129	(10229)	229	(11229)	

CLASS 507   BREL YORK

Formation: BDMSO–TSO–DMSO.
Construction: Steel underframe, aluminium alloy body and roof.
Traction Motors: Four GEC G310AZ of 82.125 kW.
Wheel Arrangement: Bo-Bo + 2-2 + Bo-Bo.
Braking: Disc & rheostatic.   **Dimensions:** 20.18 x 2.82 m.
Bogies: BX1.   **Couplers:** Tightlock.
Gangways: Within unit + end doors. **Control System:** Camshaft.
Doors: Sliding.   **Maximum Speed:** 75 mph.
Seating Layout: All refurbished with 2+2 high-back facing seating.
Multiple Working: Within class and with Class 508.

Advertising livery: 507 002 Liverpool Hope University (white).

BDMSO. Lot No. 30906 1978–80. –/56(3) 1W. 37.0 t.
TSO. Lot No. 30907 1978–80. –/74. 25.5 t.
DMSO. Lot No. 30908 1978–80. –/56(3) 1W. 35.5 t.

507 001	**MY**	A	*ME*	BD	64367	71342	64405
507 002	**AL**	A	*ME*	BD	64368	71343	64406
507 003	**MY**	A	*ME*	BD	64369	71344	64407
507 004	**ME**	A	*ME*	BD	64388	71345	64408
507 005	**MY**	A	*ME*	BD	64371	71346	64409
507 006	**MY**	A	*ME*	BD	64372	71347	64410
507 007	**ME**	A	*ME*	BD	64373	71348	64411
507 008	**ME**	A	*ME*	BD	64374	71349	64412
507 009	**ME**	A	*ME*	BD	64375	71350	64413
507 010	**MY**	A	*ME*	BD	64376	71351	64414
507 011	**MY**	A	*ME*	BD	64377	71352	64415
507 012	**MY**	A	*ME*	BD	64378	71353	64416
507 013	**MY**	A	*ME*	BD	64379	71354	64417
507 014	**MY**	A	*ME*	BD	64380	71355	64418
507 015	**MY**	A	*ME*	BD	64381	71356	64419
507 016	**MY**	A	*ME*	BD	64382	71357	64420
507 017	**MY**	A	*ME*	BD	64383	71358	64421
507 018	**MY**	A	*ME*	BD	64384	71359	64422
507 019	**MY**	A	*ME*	BD	64385	71360	64423
507 020	**MY**	A	*ME*	BD	64386	71361	64424
507 021	**MY**	A	*ME*	BD	64387	71362	64425
507 023	**MY**	A	*ME*	BD	64389	71364	64427
507 024	**ME**	A	*ME*	BD	64390	71365	64428
507 025	**MY**	A	*ME*	BD	64391	71366	64429
507 026	**MY**	A	*ME*	BD	64392	71367	64430
507 027	**MY**	A	*ME*	BD	64393	71368	64431
507 028	**MY**	A	*ME*	BD	64394	71369	64432
507 029	**MY**	A	*ME*	BD	64395	71370	64433
507 030	**MY**	A	*ME*	BD	64396	71371	64434
507 031	**MY**	A	*ME*	BD	64397	71372	64435
507 032	**MY**	A	*ME*	BD	64398	71373	64436
507 033	**ME**	A	*ME*	BD	64399	71374	64437

Names:

507 004	Bob Paisley
507 008	Harold Wilson
507 009	Dixie Dean
507 023	Operations Inspector Stuart Mason
507 033	Councillor Jack Spriggs

CLASS 508   BREL YORK

Formation: DMSO–TSO–BDMSO.
Construction: Steel underframe, aluminium alloy body and roof.
Traction Motors: Four GEC G310AZ of 82.125 kW.
Wheel Arrangement: Bo-Bo + 2-2 + Bo-Bo.
Braking: Disc & rheostatic.   **Dimensions:** 20.18 x 2.82 m.
Bogies: BX1.   **Couplers:** Tightlock.
Gangways: Within unit + end doors.   **Control System:** Camshaft.
Doors: Sliding.   **Maximum Speed:** 75 mph.
Seating Layout: All refurbished with 2+2 high-back facing seating.
Multiple Working: Within class and with Class 507.

Advertising livery: 508 111 Beatles Story (blue).

DMSO. Lot No. 30979 1979–80. –/56(3) 1W. 36.0 t.
TSO. Lot No. 30980 1979–80. –/74. 26.5 t.
BDMSO. Lot No. 30981 1979–80. –/56(3) 1W. 36.5 t.

508 103	**MY**	A	*ME*	BD	64651	71485	64694
508 104	**ME**	A	*ME*	BD	64652	71486	64695
508 108	**MY**	A	*ME*	BD	64656	71490	64699
508 110	**MY**	A	*ME*	BD	64658	71492	64701
508 111	**AL**	A	*ME*	BD	64659	71493	64702
508 112	**ME**	A	*ME*	BD	64660	71494	64703
508 114	**MY**	A	*ME*	BD	64662	71496	64705
508 115	**MY**	A	*ME*	BD	64663	71497	64706
508 117	**MY**	A	*ME*	BD	64665	71499	64708
508 120	**MY**	A	*ME*	BD	64668	71502	64711
508 122	**MY**	A	*ME*	BD	64670	71504	64713
508 123	**MY**	A	*ME*	BD	64671	71505	64714
508 124	**MY**	A	*ME*	BD	64672	71506	64715
508 125	**ME**	A	*ME*	BD	64673	71507	64716
508 126	**MY**	A	*ME*	BD	64674	71508	64717
508 127	**ME**	A	*ME*	BD	64675	71509	64718
508 128	**MY**	A	*ME*	BD	64676	71510	64719
508 130	**MY**	A	*ME*	BD	64678	71512	64721
508 131	**ME**	A	*ME*	BD	64679	71513	64722
508 134	**ME**	A	*ME*	BD	64682	71516	64725
508 136	**MY**	A	*ME*	BD	64684	71518	64727
508 137	**MY**	A	*ME*	BD	64685	71519	64728
508 138	**MY**	A	*ME*	BD	64686	71520	64729
508 139	**MY**	A	*ME*	BD	64687	71521	64730
508 140	**ME**	A	*ME*	BD	64688	71522	64731
508 141	**MY**	A	*ME*	BD	64689	71523	64732
508 143	**MY**	A	*ME*	BD	64691	71525	64734

Names:

508 123 William Roscoe
508 136 Wilfred Owen MC

4.3. DUAL VOLTAGE THAMESLINK UNITS

The large fleet of EMUs currently under construction for the Thameslink routes have been designated Class 700. The first of these units will be delivered for testing in 2015 and the fleet will enter traffic between early 2016 and the end of 2018. They are being financed by Cross London Trains (a consortium of Siemens Project Ventures, Innisfree Ltd and 3i Infrastructure Ltd) and will be based at new depots being constructed at Three Bridges and Hornsey. The units have 6-digit vehicle numbers. Full details awaited.

CLASS 700   DESIRO CITY   SIEMENS

Formations (8-car): DMCO–PTSO–MSO–TSO–TSO–MSO–PTSO–DMCO or **(12-car):** DMCO–PTSO–MSO–MSO–TSO–TSO–TSO–TSO–MSO–MSO–PTSO–DMCO.
Systems: 25 kV AC overhead/750 V DC third rail.
Construction: Aluminium.
Traction Motors:
Wheel Arrangement (8-car): Bo-Bo + 2-2 + Bo-Bo + 2-2 + 2-2 + Bo-Bo + 2-2 + Bo-Bo. **(12-car):** Bo-Bo + 2-2 + Bo-Bo + Bo-Bo + 2-2 + 2-2 + 2-2 + 2-2 + Bo-Bo + Bo-Bo + 2-2 + Bo-Bo.
Braking: **Dimensions:** 20.0 m x 2.80 m.
Bogies: Siemens SF7000 inside-frame. **Couplers:**
Gangways: Within unit.   **Control System:** IGBT Inverter.
Doors: **Maximum Speed:** 100 mph.
Heating & ventilation: Air conditioning.
Seating Layout: 2+2 facing/unidirectional.
Multiple Working: Within class.

Class 700/0. 8-car units.

DMCO(A). Siemens Krefeld 2014–18. 26/16(3).   t.
PTSO. Siemens Krefeld 2014–18. –/54 1T.   t.
MSO. Siemens Krefeld 2014–18. –/64.   t.
TSO. Siemens Krefeld 2014–18. –/56.   t.
TSO. Siemens Krefeld 2014–18. –/40(8) 1TD 2W.   t.
MSO. Siemens Krefeld 2014–18. –/64.   t.
PTSO. Siemens Krefeld 2014–18. –/54 1T.   t.
DMCO(B). Siemens Krefeld 2014–18. 26/16(3).   t.

700 001	401001	402001	403001	406001
	407001	410001	411001	412001
700 002	401002	402002	403002	406002
	407002	410002	411002	412002
700 003	401003	402003	403003	406003
	407003	410003	411003	412003
700 004	401004	402004	403004	406004
	407004	410004	411004	412004

700 005	401005	402005	403005	406005
	407005	410005	411005	412005
700 006	401006	402006	403006	406006
	407006	410006	411006	412006
700 007	401007	402007	403007	406007
	407007	410007	411007	412007
700 008	401008	402008	403008	406008
	407008	410008	411008	412008
700 009	401009	402009	403009	406009
	407009	410009	411009	412009
700 010	401010	402010	403010	406010
	407010	410010	411010	412010
700 011	401011	402011	403011	406011
	407011	410011	411011	412011
700 012	401012	402012	403012	406012
	407012	410012	411012	412012
700 013	401013	402013	403013	406013
	407013	410013	411013	412013
700 014	401014	402014	403014	406014
	407014	410014	411014	412014
700 015	401015	402015	403015	406015
	407015	410015	411015	412015
700 016	401016	402016	403016	406016
	407016	410016	411016	412016
700 017	401017	402017	403017	406017
	407017	410017	411017	412017
700 018	401018	402018	403018	406018
	407018	410018	411018	412018
700 019	401019	402019	403019	406019
	407019	410019	411019	412019
700 020	401020	402020	403020	406020
	407020	410020	411020	412020
700 021	401021	402021	403021	406021
	407021	410021	411021	412021
700 022	401022	402022	403022	406022
	407022	410022	411022	412022
700 023	401023	402023	403023	406023
	407023	410023	411023	412023
700 024	401024	402024	403024	406024
	407024	410024	411024	412024
700 025	401025	402025	403025	406025
	407025	410025	411025	412025
700 026	401026	402026	403026	406026
	407026	410026	411026	412026
700 027	401027	402027	403027	406027
	407027	410027	411027	412027
700 028	401028	402028	403028	406028
	407028	410028	411028	412028
700 029	401029	402029	403029	406029
	407029	410029	411029	412029

700 030	401030	402030	403030	406030
	407030	410030	411030	412030
700 031	401031	402031	403031	406031
	407031	410031	411031	412031
700 032	401032	402032	403032	406032
	407032	410032	411032	412032
700 033	401033	402033	403033	406033
	407033	410033	411033	412033
700 034	401034	402034	403034	406034
	407034	410034	411034	412034
700 035	401035	402035	403035	406035
	407035	410035	411035	412035
700 036	401036	402036	403036	406036
	407036	410036	411036	412036
700 037	401037	402037	403037	406037
	407037	410037	411037	412037
700 038	401038	402038	403038	406038
	407038	410038	411038	412038
700 039	401039	402039	403039	406039
	407039	410039	411039	412039
700 040	401040	402040	403040	406040
	407040	410040	411040	412040
700 041	401041	402041	403041	406041
	407041	410041	411041	412041
700 042	401042	402042	403042	406042
	407042	410042	411042	412042
700 043	401043	402043	403043	406043
	407043	410043	411043	412043
700 044	401044	402044	403044	406044
	407044	410044	411044	412044
700 045	401045	402045	403045	406045
	407045	410045	411045	412045
700 046	401046	402046	403046	406046
	407046	410046	411046	412046
700 047	401047	402047	403047	406047
	407047	410047	411047	412047
700 048	401048	402048	403048	406048
	407048	410048	411048	412048
700 049	401049	402049	403049	406049
	407049	410049	411049	412049
700 050	401050	402050	403050	406050
	407050	410050	411050	412050
700 051	401051	402051	403051	406051
	407051	410051	411051	412051
700 052	401052	402052	403052	406052
	407052	410052	411052	412052
700 053	401053	402053	403053	406053
	407053	410053	411053	412053
700 054	401054	402054	403054	406054
	407054	410054	411054	412054

700 055	401055	402055	403055	406055
	407055	410055	411055	412055
700 056	401056	402056	403056	406056
	407056	410056	411056	412056
700 057	401057	402057	403057	406057
	407057	410057	411057	412057
700 058	401058	402058	403058	406058
	407058	410058	411058	412058
700 059	401059	402059	403059	406059
	407059	410059	411059	412059
700 060	401060	402060	403060	406060
	407060	410060	411060	412060

Class 700/1. 12-car units.

DMCO(A). Siemens Krefeld 2013–18. 26/20.   t.
PTSO. Siemens Krefeld 2013–18. –/54 1T.   t.
MSO. Siemens Krefeld 2013–18. –/60 (3).   t.
MSO. Siemens Krefeld 2013–18. –/56 1T.   t.
TSO. Siemens Krefeld 2013–18. –/64.   t.
TSO. Siemens Krefeld 2013–18. –/56.   t.
TSO. Siemens Krefeld 2013–18. –/37(8) 1TD 2W.   t.
TSO. Siemens Krefeld 2013–18. –/64.   t.
MSO. Siemens Krefeld 2013–18. –/56 1T.   t.
MSO. Siemens Krefeld 2013–18. –/60(3).   t.
PTSO. Siemens Krefeld 2013–18. –/54 1T.   t.
DMCO(B). Siemens Krefeld 2013–18. 26/20.   t.

700 101	401101	402101	403101	404101	405101	406101
	407101	408101	409101	410101	411101	412101
700 102	401102	402102	403102	404102	405102	406102
	407102	408102	409102	410102	411102	412102
700 103	401103	402103	403103	404103	405103	406103
	407103	408103	409103	410103	411103	412103
700 104	401104	402104	403104	404104	405104	406104
	407104	408104	409104	410104	411104	412104
700 105	401105	402105	403105	404105	405105	406105
	407105	408105	409105	410105	411105	412105
700 106	401106	402106	403106	404106	405106	406106
	407106	408106	409106	410106	411106	412106
700 107	401107	402107	403107	404107	405107	406107
	407107	408107	409107	410107	411107	412107
700 108	401108	402108	403108	404108	405108	406108
	407108	408108	409108	410108	411108	412108
700 109	401109	402109	403109	404109	405109	406109
	407109	408109	409109	410109	411109	412109
700 110	401110	402110	403110	404110	405110	406110
	407110	408110	409110	410110	411110	412110
700 111	401111	402111	403111	404111	405111	406111
	407111	408111	409111	410111	411111	412111
700 112	401112	402112	403112	404112	405112	406112
	407112	408112	409112	410112	411112	412112

700 113	401113 402113 403113 404113 405113 406113
	407113 408113 409113 410113 411113 412113
700 114	401114 402114 403114 404114 405114 406114
	407114 408114 409114 410114 411114 412114
700 115	401115 402115 403115 404115 405115 406115
	407115 408115 409115 410115 411115 412115
700 116	401116 402116 403116 404116 405116 406116
	407116 408116 409116 410116 411116 412116
700 117	401117 402117 403117 404117 405117 406117
	407117 408117 409117 410117 411117 412117
700 118	401118 402118 403118 404118 405118 406118
	407118 408118 409118 410118 411118 412118
700 119	401119 402119 403119 404119 405119 406119
	407119 408119 409119 410119 411119 412119
700 120	401120 402120 403120 404120 405120 406120
	407120 408120 409120 410120 411120 412120
700 121	401121 402121 403121 404121 405121 406121
	407121 408121 409121 410121 411121 412121
700 122	401122 402122 403122 404122 405122 406122
	407122 408122 409122 410122 411122 412122
700 123	401123 402123 403123 404123 405123 406123
	407123 408123 409123 410123 411123 412123
700 124	401124 402124 403124 404124 405124 406124
	407124 408124 409124 410124 411124 412124
700 125	401125 402125 403125 404125 405125 406125
	407125 408125 409125 410125 411125 412125
700 126	401126 402126 403126 404126 405126 406126
	407126 408126 409126 410126 411126 412126
700 127	401127 402127 403127 404127 405127 406127
	407127 408127 409127 410127 411127 412127
700 128	401128 402128 403128 404128 405128 406128
	407128 408128 409128 410128 411128 412128
700 129	401129 402129 403129 404129 405129 406129
	407129 408129 409129 410129 411129 412129
700 130	401130 402130 403130 404130 405130 406130
	407130 408130 409130 410130 411130 412130
700 131	401131 402131 403131 404131 405131 406131
	407131 408131 409131 410131 411131 412131
700 132	401132 402132 403132 404132 405132 406132
	407132 408132 409132 410132 411132 412132
700 133	401133 402133 403133 404133 405133 406133
	407133 408133 409133 410133 411133 412133
700 134	401134 402134 403134 404134 405134 406134
	407134 408134 409134 410134 411134 412134
700 135	401135 402135 403135 404135 405135 406135
	407135 408135 409135 410135 411135 412135
700 136	401136 402136 403136 404136 405136 406136
	407136 408136 409136 410136 411136 412136
700 137	401137 402137 403137 404137 405137 406137
	407137 408137 409137 410137 411137 412137

700 138	401138 402138 403138 404138 405138 406138
	407138 408138 409138 410138 411138 412138
700 139	401139 402139 403139 404139 405139 406139
	407139 408139 409139 410139 411139 412139
700 140	401140 402140 403140 404140 405140 406140
	407140 408140 409140 410140 411140 412140
700 141	401141 402141 403141 404141 405141 406141
	407141 408141 409141 410141 411141 412141
700 142	401142 402142 403142 404142 405142 406142
	407142 408142 409142 410142 411142 412142
700 143	401143 402143 403143 404143 405143 406143
	407143 408143 409143 410143 411143 412143
700 144	401144 402144 403144 404144 405144 406144
	407144 408144 409144 410144 411144 412144
700 145	401145 402145 403145 404145 405145 406145
	407145 408145 409145 410145 411145 412145
700 146	401146 402146 403146 404146 405146 406146
	407146 408146 409146 410146 411146 412146
700 147	401147 402147 403147 404147 405147 406147
	407147 408147 409147 410147 411147 412147
700 148	401148 402148 403148 404148 405148 406148
	407148 408148 409148 410148 411148 412148
700 149	401149 402149 403149 404149 405149 406149
	407149 408149 409149 410149 411149 412149
700 150	401150 402150 403150 404150 405150 406150
	407150 408150 409150 410150 411150 412150
700 151	401151 402151 403151 404151 405151 406151
	407151 408151 409151 410151 411151 412151
700 152	401152 402152 403152 404152 405152 406152
	407152 408152 409152 410152 411152 412152
700 153	401153 402153 403153 404153 405153 406153
	407153 408153 409153 410153 411153 412153
700 154	401154 402154 403154 404154 405154 406154
	407154 408154 409154 410154 411154 412154
700 155	401155 402155 403155 404155 405155 406155
	407155 408155 409155 410155 411155 412155

4.4. EUROSTAR UNITS

The original Eurostar Class 373 units were built for and are normally used on services between Britain and continental Europe via the Channel Tunnel. SNCF-owned units 3203/04, 3225/26 and 3227/28 have been removed from the Eurostar pool and were used on Paris–Lille services, but have now been withdrawn. As they are not now permitted through the Channel Tunnel they are not listed here.

Each Class 373 train consists of two 10-car units coupled, with a motor car at each driving end. All units are articulated with an extra motor bogie on the coach adjacent to the motor car.

All Class 373 sets can be used between London St Pancras and Paris, Brussels and Disneyland Paris. Certain sets (shown *) are equipped for 1500 V DC operation and are used for the winter service to Bourg Saint Maurice and the summer service to Avignon.

Seven 8-car Class 373 sets were built for Regional Eurostar services, but all except one power car (3308) and one half set are on long-term hire to SNCF for use on French internal services so are not listed here. They were taken out of traffic in 2014. The spare half set (from 3308/07) is stored at Temple Mills depot.

The second generation Eurostar trains, Class 374s, are currently being delivered and will replace most of the Class 373s.

CLASS 373   "THREE CAPITALS" EUROSTARS

10-car half-sets. Built for services starting from or terminating in London Waterloo (now St Pancras). Individual vehicles in each set are allocated numbers 373xxx0 + 373xxx1 + 373xxx2 + 373xxx3 + 373xxx4 + 373xxx5 + 373xxx6 + 373xxx7 + 373xxx8 + 373xxx9, where 3xxx denotes the set number.

At the time of writing power cars 3015 and 3016 are carrying the numbers 3212 and 3211 respectively, as they are running with the trailers from set 3211/12.

Formation: DM–MSO–4TSO–RB–2TFO–TBFO. Gangwayed within pair of units. Air conditioned.
Construction: Steel.
Supply Systems: 25 kV AC 50 Hz overhead or 3000 V DC overhead (* also equipped for 1500 V DC overhead operation).
Control System: GTO–GTO Inverter on UK 750 V DC and 25 kV AC, GTO Chopper on SNCB 3000 V DC.
Wheel Arrangement: Bo-Bo + Bo–2–2–2–2–2–2–2–2–2.
Lengths: 22.15 m (DM), 21.85 m (MSO & TBFO), 18.70 m (other cars).
Couplers: Schaku 10S at outer ends, Schaku 10L at inner end of each DM and outer ends of each sub set.
Maximum Speed: 186 mph (300 km/h)
Built: 1992–93 by GEC-Alsthom/Brush/ANF/De Dietrich/BN Construction/ACEC.
DM vehicles carry the set numbers indicated below.

373xxx0 series. DM. Lot No. 31118 1992–95. 68.5 t.
373xxx1 series. MSO. Lot No. 31119 1992–95. –/48 2T. 44.6 t.
373xxx2 series. TSO. Lot No. 31120 1992–95. –/56 1T. 28.1 t.
373xxx3 series. TSO. Lot No. 31121 1992–95. –/56 2T. 29.7 t.
373xxx4 series. TSO. Lot No. 31122 1992–95. –/56 1T. 28.3 t.
373xxx5 series. TSO. Lot No. 31123 1992–95. –/56 2T. 29.2 t.
373xxx6 series. RB. Lot No.31124 1992–95. 31.1 t.
373xxx7 series. TFO. Lot No. 31125 1992–95. 39/– 1T. 29.6 t.
373xxx8 series. TFO. Lot No. 31126 1992–95. 39/– 1T. 32.2 t.
373xxx9 series. TBFO. Lot No. 31127 1992–95. 25/– 1TD. 39.4 t.

3001	**EU**	EU	*EU*	TI		3107	**EU**	SB	*EU*	FF
3002	**EU**	EU	*EU*	TI		3108	**EU**	SB	*EU*	FF
3003	**EU**	EU	*EU*	TI		3201 *	**EU**	SF	*EU*	LY
3004	**EU**	EU	*EU*	TI		3202 *	**EU**	SF	*EU*	LY
3005	**EU**	EU	*EU*	TI		3205	**EU**	SF	*EU*	LY
3006	**EU**	EU	*EU*	TI		3206	**EU**	SF	*EU*	LY
3007	**EU**	EU	*EU*	TI		3207 *	**EU**	SF	*EU*	LY
3008	**EU**	EU	*EU*	TI		3208 *	**EU**	SF	*EU*	LY
3009	**EU**	EU	*EU*	TI		3209 *	**EU**	SF	*EU*	LY
3010	**EU**	EU	*EU*	TI		3210 *	**EU**	SF	*EU*	LY
3011	**EU**	EU	*EU*	TI		3211	**EU**	SF	*EU*	LY
3012	**EU**	EU	*EU*	TI		3212	**EU**	SF	*EU*	LY
3013	**EU**	EU	*EU*	TI		3213 *	**EU**	SF	*EU*	LY
3014	**EU**	EU	*EU*	TI		3214 *	**EU**	SF	*EU*	LY
3015	**ER**	EU	*EU*	TI		3215 *	**EU**	SF	*EU*	LY
3016	**ER**	EU	*EU*	TI		3216 *	**EU**	SF	*EU*	LY
3017	**EU**	EU	*EU*	TI		3217	**EU**	SF	*EU*	LY
3018	**EU**	EU	*EU*	TI		3218	**EU**	SF	*EU*	LY
3019	**EU**	EU	*EU*	TI		3219	**EU**	SF	*EU*	LY
3020	**EU**	EU	*EU*	TI		3220	**EU**	SF	*EU*	LY
3021	**EU**	EU	*EU*	TI		3221	**EU**	SF	*EU*	LY
3022	**EU**	EU	*EU*	TI		3222	**EU**	SF	*EU*	LY
3101	**EU**	SB		TI		3223 *	**EU**	SF	*EU*	LY
3102	**EU**	SB		TI		3224 *	**EU**	SF	*EU*	LY
3103	**EU**	SB	*EU*	FF		3229 *	**EU**	SF	*EU*	LY
3104	**EU**	SB	*EU*	FF		3230 *	**EU**	SF	*EU*	LY
3105	**EU**	SB	*EU*	FF		3231	**EU**	SF	*EU*	LY
3106	**EU**	SB	*EU*	FF		3232	**EU**	SF	*EU*	LY

Spare Regional Eurostar DM:

3308	**EU**	EU		LB

Spare DM:

3999	**EU**	EU	*EU*	TI

Names:

3001/02	Tread Lightly/Voyage Vert	3013/14	LONDON 2012
3003/04	Tri-City-Áthlon 2010	3207/08	MICHEL HOLLARD
3007/08	Waterloo Sunset	3209/10	THE DA VINCI CODE
3009/10	REMEMBERING FROMELLES		

CLASS 374   SIEMENS VELARO e320

8-car half-sets. Currently being delivered for Eurostar. These units are similar to the DB Class 407 ICE sets, with distributed power rather than a power car at either end like the Class 373s. They will enter service in late 2015 ahead of a proposed St Pancras–Amsterdam service starting in 2016.

The initial order was for ten units (4001–20) and this was then increased by another seven (4021–34) in late 2014. An option exists for a further six units.

Formation (provisional): DMFO–TBFO–MFO–TSO–TSO–MSO–TSO–MSORB. Gangwayed within pair of units. Air conditioned.
Construction: Aluminium.   **Control System:** IGBT Inverter.
Supply Systems: 25 kV AC 50 Hz overhead, 1500 V DC overhead and 3000 V DC overhead.
Continuous rating: 8000 kW (AC), 4200 kW (DC).
Wheel Arrangement: Bo-Bo + 2-2 + Bo-Bo + 2-2 + 2-2 + Bo-Bo + 2-2 + Bo-Bo.
Lengths: 26.035 m (DMFO), 24.775 m (other cars).
Couplers: Dellner 12.   **Maximum Speed:** 200 mph (320 km/h).
Built: 2012–16 by Siemens, Krefeld, Germany.

DM vehicles carry the full 12-digit EVNs as indicated below. For example set 4001/02 carries the numbers 93 70 3740 011-9 + 93 70 3740 012-7 + 93 70 3740 013-5 + 93 70 3740 014-3 + 93 70 3740 015-0 + 93 70 3740 016-8 + 93 70 3740 017-6 + 93 70 3740 018-4 + 93 70 3740 028-3 + 93 70 3740 027-5 + 93 70 3740 026-7 + 93 70 3740 025-9 + 93 70 3740 024-2 + 93 70 3740 023-4 + 93 70 3740 022-6 + 93 70 3740 021-8.

93 70 3740 xx1-c series. DMFO. Siemens Krefeld 2012–16. 40/– (1). 58.0 t.
93 70 3740 xx2-c series. TBFO. Siemens Krefeld 2012–16. 36/– 2T. 59.0 t.
93 70 3740 xx3-c series. MFO. Siemens Krefeld 2012–16. 34/– (2) 1TD 2W. 59.0 t.
93 70 3740 xx4-c series. TSO. Siemens Krefeld 2012–16. –/76 2T. 53.0 t.
93 70 3740 xx5-c series. TSO. Siemens Krefeld 2012–16. –/76 2T. 53.0 t.
93 70 3740 xx6-c series. MSO. Siemens Krefeld 2012–16. –/76 2T. 58.0 t.
93 70 3740 xx7-c series. TSO. Siemens Krefeld 2012–16. –/76 2T. 57.0 t.
93 70 3740 xx8-c series. MSORB. Siemens Krefeld 2012–16. –/32 2T. 58.0 t.

4001	**ER**	4018	
4002	**ER**	4019	
4003	**ER**	4020	
4004	**ER**	4021	
4005	**ER**	4022	
4006	**ER**	4023	
4007	**ER**	4024	
4008	**ER**	4025	
4009	**ER**	4026	
4010	**ER**	4027	
4011	**ER**	4028	
4012	**ER**	4029	
4013		4030	
4014		4031	
4015		4032	
4016		4033	
4017		4034	

4.5. SERVICE EMUS

The following unit is used by Network Rail for ERTMS testing on the Hertford
Loop. The unit has been heavily modified from its original condition, and
now includes a toilet.

313121   **Y**   BN   *GB*   WN   62549   71233   62613

4.6. EMU VEHICLES IN INDUSTRIAL SERVICE

This list comprises EMU vehicles that have been withdrawn from active
service but continue to be used in industrial service.

Cl. 390	69133	69833	Virgin Trains Training Centre, Westmere Drive, Crewe, Cheshire
Cl. 390	69633	69733	The Fire Service College, Moreton-in-Marsh, Gloucestershire
Cl. 390	69933		Safety & Accident Investigation Centre, Cranfield University, Cranfield, Bedfordshire
Cl. 508	64649	64712	Emergency Services Training Centre, Seacombe, Merseyside
Cl. 508	64681	71511 64724	The Fire Service College, Moreton-in-Marsh, Gloucestershire

4.7. EMUS AWAITING DISPOSAL

This list comprises vehicles awaiting disposal which are stored on the
national railway network.

25 kV AC 50 Hz OVERHEAD UNITS:

Cl. 309	**RR**	WC	CS	71758
Cl. 365	**N**	X	ZN	65919

750 V DC THIRD RAIL UNITS:

Cl. 460	**GV**	P	ZB	67901	67903	67907	67908
Cl. 508	**CN**	A	ZG	64667	64680	64723	
Cl. 508	**CN**	A	ZI	64710	64720		

5. ON-TRACK MACHINES

These machines are used for maintaining, renewing and enhancing the infrastructure of the national railway network. With the exception of snowploughs all can be self-propelled, controlled either from a cab mounted on the machine or remotely. They are permitted to operate either under their own power or in train formations throughout the network both within and outside engineering possessions. Machines only permitted to be used within engineering possessions, referred to as On-Track Plant, are not included. Also not included are wagons included in OTM consists.

For each machine its Network Rail registered number, owner or responsible custodian and type is given, plus its name if carried. In addition, for snow clearance equipment and breakdown cranes the berthing location is given. Actual operation of each machine is undertaken by either the owner/ responsible custodian or a contracted responsible custodian.

Machines were numbered by British Rail with either six-digit wagon series numbers or in the CEPS (Civil Engineers Plant System) series with five prefixed digits. Recently delivered machines have been numbered in the EVN series. Machines may also carry additional identifying numbers which are shown as "xxxx". Machines are listed here in CEPS/wagon series order. Those with EVN numbers are included where they would have been if allocated CEPS numbers.

(S) after the registered number designates a machine that is currently stored (the storage location of each is given at the end of this section).

DYNAMIC TRACK STABILISERS

| DR 72211 | BB | Plasser & Theurer DGS 62-N |
| DR 72213 | BB | Plasser & Theurer DGS 62-N |

TAMPERS

DR 73108	CS	Plasser & Theurer 09-32-RT	Tiger
DR 73109	SK	Plasser & Theurer 09-3X-RT	
DR 73110	SK	Plasser & Theurer 09-3X-RT	PETER WHITE
DR 73111	NR	Plasser & Theurer 09-3X-Dynamic	Reading Panel 1965–2005
DR 73113	NR	Plasser & Theurer 09-3X-Dynamic	DAI EVANS
DR 73114	NR	Plasser & Theurer 09-3X-Dynamic	Ron Henderson
DR 73115	NR	Plasser & Theurer 09-3X-Dynamic	
DR 73116	NR	Plasser & Theurer 09-3X Dynamic	
DR 73117	NR	Plasser & Theurer 09-3X Dynamic	
DR 73118	NR	Plasser & Theurer 09-3X Dynamic	
DR 73803	SK	Plasser & Theurer 08-32U-RT	Alexander Graham Bell
DR 73804	SK	Plasser & Theurer 08-32U-RT	James Watt
DR 73805	CS	Plasser & Theurer 08-16/32U-RT	
DR 73806	CS	Plasser & Theurer 08-16/32U-RT	Karine
DR 73904	SK	Plasser & Theurer 08-4x4/4S-RT	Thomas Telford
DR 73905	CS	Plasser & Theurer 08-4x4/4S-RT	Eddie King

DR 73906	CS	Plasser & Theurer 08-4x4/4S-RT	Panther
DR 73907	CS	Plasser & Theurer 08-4x4/4S-RT	
DR 73908	CS	Plasser & Theurer 08-4x4/4S-RT	
DR 73909	CS	Plasser & Theurer 08-4x4/4S-RT	Saturn
DR 73910	CS	Plasser & Theurer 08-4x4/4S-RT	Jupiter
DR 73911	CS	Plasser & Theurer 08-16/4x4C-RT	Puma
DR 73912	CS	Plasser & Theurer 08-16/4x4C-RT	Lynx
DR 73913	CS	Plasser & Theurer 08-12/4x4C-RT	
DR 73914	SK	Plasser & Theurer 08-4x4/4S-RT	Robert McAlpine
DR 73915	SK	Plasser & Theurer 08-16/4x4C-RT	William Arrol
DR 73916	SK	Plasser & Theurer 08-16/4x4C-RT	First Engineering
DR 73917	BB	Plasser & Theurer 08-4x4/4S-RT	
DR 73918	BB	Plasser & Theurer 08-4x4/4S-RT	
DR 73919	CS	Plasser & Theurer 08-16/4x4C100-RT	
DR 73920	CS	Plasser & Theurer 08-16/4x4C80-RT	
DR 73921	CS	Plasser & Theurer 08-16/4x4C80-RT	
DR 73922	CS	Plasser & Theurer 08-16/4x4C80-RT	John Snowdon
DR 73923	CS	Plasser & Theurer 08-4x4/4S-RT	Mercury
DR 73924	CS	Plasser & Theurer 08-16/4x4C100-RT	Atlas
DR 73925	CS	Plasser & Theurer 08-16/4x4C100-RT	Europa
DR 73926	BB	Plasser & Theurer 08-16/4x4C100-RT	Stephen Keith Blanchard
DR 73927	BB	Plasser & Theurer 08-16/4x4C100-RT	
DR 73928	BB	Plasser & Theurer 08-16/4x4C100-RT	
DR 73929	CS	Plasser & Theurer 08-4x4/4S-RT	
DR 73930	CS	Plasser & Theurer 08-4x4/4S-RT	
DR 73931	CS	Plasser & Theurer 08-16/4x4C100-RT	
DR 73932	SK	Plasser & Theurer 08-4x4/4S-RT	
DR 73933	SK	Plasser & Theurer 08-16/4x4/C100-RT	
DR 73934	SK	Plasser & Theurer 08-16/4x4/C100-RT	
DR 73935	CS	Plasser & Theurer 08-4x4/4S-RT	
DR 73936	CS	Plasser & Theurer 08-4x4/4S-RT	
DR 73937	BB	Plasser & Theurer 08-16/4x4C100-RT	
DR 73938	BB	Plasser & Theurer 08-16/4x4C100-RT	
DR 73939	BB	Plasser & Theurer 08-16/4x4C100-RT	Pat Best
DR 73940	SK	Plasser & Theurer 08-4x4/4S-RT	
DR 73941	SK	Plasser & Theurer 08-4x4/4S-RT	
DR 73942	CS	Plasser & Theurer 08-4x4/4S-RT	
DR 73943	BB	Plasser & Theurer 08-16/4x4C100-RT	
DR 73944	BB	Plasser & Theurer 08-16/4x4C100-RT	
DR 73945	BB	Plasser & Theurer 08-16/4x4C100-RT	
DR 73946	VO	Plasser & Theurer Euromat 08-4x4/4S	
DR 73947	CS	Plasser & Theurer 08-4x4/4S-RT	
DR 73948	CS	Plasser & Theurer 08-4x4/4S-RT	

99 70 9128 001-3 SK Plasser & Theurer Unimat 09-4x4/4S Dynamic "928001"

DR 75301	VO	Matisa B 45 UE	
DR 75302	VO	Matisa B 45 UE	
DR 75303	VO	Matisa B 45 UE	Gary Wright
DR 75401	VO	Matisa B 41 UE	
DR 75402	VO	Matisa B 41 UE	
DR 75403	VO	Matisa B 41 UE	

DR 75404	VO	Matisa B 41 UE
DR 75405	VO	Matisa B 41 UE
DR 75406	CS	Matisa B 41 UE
DR 75407	CS	Matisa B 41 UE
DR 75408	BB	Matisa B 41 UE
DR 75409	BB	Matisa B 41 UE
DR 75410	BB	Matisa B 41 UE
DR 75411	BB	Matisa B 41 UE
DR 75501	BB	Matisa B 66 UC
DR 75502	BB	Matisa B 66 UC

Eric Machell

BALLAST CLEANERS

DR 76323	NR Plasser & Theurer RM95-RT	
DR 76324	NR Plasser & Theurer RM95-RT	
DR 76501	NR Plasser & Theurer RM-900-RT	*(works with DR 76703/DR 92285/ DR 92286)*
DR 76502	NR Plasser & Theurer RM-900-RT	*(works with DR 76702/DR 92331/ DR 92332)*
DR 76503	NR Plasser & Theurer RM-900-RT	*(works with DR 76701/DR 76801/ DR 92431/DR 92432)*

VACUUM PREPARATION MACHINES

DR 76701	NR Plasser & Theurer VM80-NR	*(works with DR 76503/DR 76801/ DR 92431/DR 92432)*
DR 76702	NR Plasser & Theurer VM80-NR	*(works with DR 76502/DR 92331/ DR 92332)*
DR 76703	NR Plasser & Theurer VM80-NR	*(works with DR 76501/DR 92285/ DR 92286)*
DR 76710 (S)	NR Plasser & Theurer VM80-TRS	
DR 76711 (S)	NR Plasser & Theurer VM80-TRS	

RAIL VACUUM MACHINES

99 70 9515 001-4	RC	Railcare 1800/500-UK RailVac
99 70 9515 002-2	RC	Railcare 1800/500-UK RailVac
99 70 9515 003-0	RC	Railcare 1800/500-UK RailVac

BALLAST TRANSFER MACHINES

| DR 76750 | NR Matisa D75 | *(works with DR 78802/DR 78812/ DR 78822/DR 78832)* |
| DR 76751 | NR Matisa D75 | *(works with DR 78801/DR 78811/ DR 78821/DR 78831)* |

CONSOLIDATION MACHINE

| DR 76801 | NR Plasser & Theurer 09-CM-NR | *(works with DR 76503/DR 76701/ DR 92431/DR 92432)* |

FINISHING MACHINES & BALLAST REGULATORS

| DR 77001 | SK | Plasser & Theurer AFM 2000-RT Finishing Machine |
| DR 77002 | SK | Plasser & Theurer AFM 2000-RT Finishing Machine |

DR 77315 (S)	BB	Plasser & Theurer USP 5000C Regulator
DR 77316 (S)	BB	Plasser & Theurer USP 5000C Regulator
DR 77322	BB	Plasser & Theurer USP 5000C Regulator
DR 77327	CS	Plasser & Theurer USP 5000C Regulator
DR 77336 (S)	BB	Plasser & Theurer USP 5000C Regulator
DR 77801	VO	Matisa R 24 S Regulator
DR 77802	VO	Matisa R 24 S Regulator
DR 77901	CS	Plasser & Theurer USP 5000-RT Regulator
DR 77903	NR	Plasser & Theurer USP 5000-RT Regulator Frank Jones
DR 77904	NR	Plasser & Theurer USP 5000-RT Regulator
DR 77905	NR	Plasser & Theurer USP 5000-RT Regulator
DR 77906	NR	Plasser & Theurer USP 5000-RT Regulator
DR 77907	NR	Plasser & Theurer USP 5000-RT Regulator
DR 77908	SK	Plasser & Theurer USP 5000-RT Regulator

TWIN JIB TRACK RELAYERS

DRP 78213	VO	Plasser & Theurer Self-Propelled Heavy Duty
DRP 78215	SK	Plasser & Theurer Self-Propelled Heavy Duty
DRP 78216	BB	Plasser & Theurer Self-Propelled Heavy Duty
DRP 78217 (S)	SK	Plasser & Theurer Self-Propelled Heavy Duty
DRP 78218 (S)	BB	Plasser & Theurer Self-Propelled Heavy Duty
DRP 78219	SK	Plasser & Theurer Self-Propelled Heavy Duty
DRP 78221	BB	Plasser & Theurer Self-Propelled Heavy Duty
DRP 78222	BB	Plasser & Theurer Self-Propelled Heavy Duty
DRP 78223 (S)	BB	Plasser & Theurer Self-Propelled Heavy Duty
DRP 78224 (S)	BB	Plasser & Theurer Self-Propelled Heavy Duty
DRC 78226	CS	Cowans Sheldon Self-Propelled Heavy Duty
DRC 78229	NR	Cowans Sheldon Self-Propelled Heavy Duty
DRC 78231	NR	Cowans Sheldon Self-Propelled Heavy Duty
DRC 78234	NR	Cowans Sheldon Self-Propelled Heavy Duty
DRC 78235	CS	Cowans Sheldon Self-Propelled Heavy Duty
DRC 78237 (S)	NR	Cowans Sheldon Self-Propelled Heavy Duty

NEW TRACK CONSTRUCTION
TRAIN PROPULSION MACHINES

| DR 78701 | BB | Harsco Track Technologies NTC-PW |
| DR 78702 | BB | Harsco Track Technologies NTC-PW |

TRACK RENEWAL MACHINES

Matisa P95 Track Renewals Trains
DR 78801+DR 78811+DR 78821+DR 78831 NR *(works with DR 76751)*
DR 78802+DR 78812+DR 78822+DR 78832 NR *(works with DR 76750)*

RAIL GRINDING TRAINS

Loram SPML 15
DR 79200A + DR 79200B + DR 79200C   NR

Loram SPML 17
DR 79201A + DR 79201B   NR

Speno RPS-32
DR 79221 + DR 79222 + DR 79223 + DR 79224 + DR 79225 + DR 79226   SI

Loram C21
DR 79231 + DR 79232 + DR 79233 + DR 79234 + DR 79235 + DR 79236 + DR 79237   NR
DR 79241 + DR 79242 + DR 79243 + DR 79244 + DR 79245 + DR 79246 + DR 79247   NR
DR 79251 + DR 79252 + DR 79253 + DR 79254 + DR 79255 + DR 79256 + DR 79257   NR

Names: DR 79241/247   Roger South *(one plate on opposite sides of each)*
       DR 79257   Martin Ellwood

Harsco Track Technologies RGH20C
DR 79261 + DR 79271   NR
DR 79262 + DR 79272   NR
DR 79263 + DR 79273   NR
DR 79264 + DR 79274   NR
DR 79265 (S)   NR   *spare vehicle*
DR 79267 + DR 79277   NR

STONEBLOWERS

DR 80200 (S)	NR	Pandrol Jackson Plain Line
DR 80201	NR	Pandrol Jackson Plain Line
DR 80202 (S)	NR	Pandrol Jackson Plain Line
DR 80203 (S)	NR	Pandrol Jackson Plain Line
DR 80204 (S)	NR	Pandrol Jackson Plain Line
DR 80205	NR	Pandrol Jackson Plain Line
DR 80206	NR	Pandrol Jackson Plain Line
DR 80207 (S)	NR	Pandrol Jackson Plain Line
DR 80208	NR	Pandrol Jackson Plain Line
DR 80209	NR	Pandrol Jackson Plain Line
DR 80210	NR	Pandrol Jackson Plain Line
DR 80211	NR	Pandrol Jackson Plain Line
DR 80212 (S)	NR	Pandrol Jackson Plain Line
DR 80213	NR	Harsco Track Technologies Plain Line
DR 80214	NR	Harsco Track Technologies Plain Line
DR 80215	NR	Harsco Track Technologies Plain Line
DR 80216	NR	Harsco Track Technologies Plain Line
DR 80217	NR	Harsco Track Technologies Plain Line
DR 80301	NR	Harsco Track Technologies Multi-purpose Stephen Cornish
DR 80302	NR	Harsco Track Technologies Multi-purpose
DR 80303	NR	Harsco Track Technologies Multi-purpose

CRANES

DRP 81505	BB	Plasser & Theurer 12 tonne Heavy Duty Diesel Hydraulic
DRP 81507 (S)	BB	Plasser & Theurer 12 tonne Heavy Duty Diesel Hydraulic
DRP 81508 (S)	BB	Plasser & Theurer 12 tonne Heavy Duty Diesel Hydraulic
DRP 81511 (S)	BB	Plasser & Theurer 12 tonne Heavy Duty Diesel Hydraulic
DRP 81513 (S)	BB	Plasser & Theurer 12 tonne Heavy Duty Diesel Hydraulic
DRP 81517	BB	Plasser & Theurer 12 tonne Heavy Duty Diesel Hydraulic
DRP 81519 (S)	BB	Plasser & Theurer 12 tonne Heavy Duty Diesel Hydraulic
DRP 81522	BB	Plasser & Theurer 12 tonne Heavy Duty Diesel Hydraulic
DRP 81525	BB	Plasser & Theurer 12 tonne Heavy Duty Diesel Hydraulic
DRP 81532	BB	Plasser & Theurer 12 tonne Heavy Duty Diesel Hydraulic
DRK 81601	VO	Kirow KRC 810UK 100 tonne Heavy Duty Diesel Hydraulic
DRK 81602	BB	Kirow KRC 810UK 100 tonne Heavy Duty Diesel Hydraulic
DRK 81611	BB	Kirow KRC 1200UK 125 tonne Heavy Duty Diesel Hydraulic
DRK 81612	CS	Kirow KRC 1200UK 125 tonne Heavy Duty Diesel Hydraulic
DRK 81613	VO	Kirow KRC 1200UK 125 tonne Heavy Duty Diesel Hydraulic
DRK 81621	VO	Kirow KRC 250UK 25 tonne Diesel Hydraulic
DRK 81622	VO	Kirow KRC 250UK 25 tonne Diesel Hydraulic
DRK 81623	SK	Kirow KRC 250UK 25 tonne Diesel Hydraulic
DRK 81624	SK	Kirow KRC 250UK 25 tonne Diesel Hydraulic
DRK 81625	SK	Kirow KRC 250UK 25 tonne Diesel Hydraulic

Names:

DRK 81601	Nigel Chester		DRK 81611	Malcolm L. Pearce

LONG WELDED RAIL TRAIN PROPULSION MACHINES

DR 89005	NR	Cowans Boyd PW
DR 89006 (S)	NR	Cowans Boyd PW
DR 89007	NR	Cowans Boyd PW
DR 89008	NR	Cowans Boyd PW
DR 89009 (S)	NR	Cowans Boyd PW

BALLAST SYSTEM PROPULSION MACHINES

DR 92263	NR	Plasser & Theurer MFS-PW
DR 92264	NR	Plasser & Theurer NB-PW
DR 92285	NR	Plasser & Theurer PW-RT *(works with DR 76501/DR 76703/ DR 92286)*
DR 92286	NR	Plasser & Theurer NPW-RT *(works with DR 76501/DR 76703/ DR 92285)*
DR 92331	NR	Plasser & Theurer PW-RT *(works with DR 76502/DR 76702/ DR 92332)*
DR 92332	NR	Plasser & Theurer NPW-RT *(works with DR 76502/DR 76702/ DR 92331)*
DR 92431	NR	Plasser & Theurer PW-RT *(works with DR 76503/DR 76701/ DR 76801/DR 92432)*
DR 92432	NR	Plasser & Theurer NPW-RT *(works with DR 76503/DR 76701/ DR 76801/DR 92431)*

TELESCOPIC BREAKDOWN CRANES

ADRC 96710	NR	Cowans Sheldon 75 tonne Diesel Hydraulic	Wigan Springs Branch
ADRC 96713	NR	Cowans Sheldon 75 tonne Diesel Hydraulic	Wigan Springs Branch
ADRC 96714	NR	Cowans Sheldon 75 tonne Diesel Hydraulic	Knottingley Depot
ADRC 96715	NR	Cowans Sheldon 75 tonne Diesel Hydraulic	Wigan Springs Branch

GENERAL PURPOSE VEHICLES

DR 97001	H1	Eiv de Brieve DU94BA TRAMM with Crane "DU 94 B 001 URS"
DR 97011	H1	Windhoff MPV (Modular)
DR 97012	H1	Windhoff MPV (Modular)
DR 97013	H1	Windhoff MPV (Modular)
DR 97014	H1	Windhoff MPV (Modular)
DR 98008	NR	Windhoff MPV Twin-cab with test equipment

DR 98215A + DR 98215B	BB	Plasser & Theurer GP-TRAMM with Trailer
DR 98216A + DR 98216B	BB	Plasser & Theurer GP-TRAMM with Trailer
DR 98217A + DR 98217B	BB	Plasser & Theurer GP-TRAMM with Trailer
DR 98218A + DR 98218B	BB	Plasser & Theurer GP-TRAMM with Trailer
DR 98219A + DR 98219B	BB	Plasser & Theurer GP-TRAMM with Trailer
DR 98220A + DR 98220B	BB	Plasser & Theurer GP-TRAMM with Trailer

DR 98305 (S) NR	Geismar GP-TRAMM VMT 860 PL/UM
DR 98306 (S) NR	Geismar GP-TRAMM VMT 860 PL/UM

DR 98307A + DR 98307B (S) CS	Geismar GP-TRAMM VMT 860 PL/UM with Trailer
DR 98308A + DR 98308B (S) CS	Geismar GP-TRAMM VMT 860 PL/UM with Trailer

DR 98901 + DR 98951	NR	Windhoff MPV Master & Slave
DR 98902 + DR 98952	NR	Windhoff MPV Master & Slave
DR 98903 + DR 98953	NR	Windhoff MPV Master & Slave
DR 98904 + DR 98954	NR	Windhoff MPV Master & Slave
DR 98905 + DR 98955	NR	Windhoff MPV Master & Slave
DR 98906 + DR 98956	NR	Windhoff MPV Master & Slave
DR 98907 + DR 98957	NR	Windhoff MPV Master & Slave
DR 98908 + DR 98958	NR	Windhoff MPV Master & Slave
DR 98909 + DR 98959	NR	Windhoff MPV Master & Slave
DR 98910 + DR 98960	NR	Windhoff MPV Master & Slave
DR 98911 + DR 98961	NR	Windhoff MPV Master & Slave
DR 98912 + DR 98962	NR	Windhoff MPV Master & Slave
DR 98913 + DR 98963	NR	Windhoff MPV Master & Slave
DR 98914 + DR 98964	NR	Windhoff MPV Master & Slave
DR 98915 + DR 98965	NR	Windhoff MPV Master & Slave
DR 98916 + DR 98966	NR	Windhoff MPV Master & Slave
DR 98917 + DR 98967	NR	Windhoff MPV Master & Slave
DR 98918 + DR 98968	NR	Windhoff MPV Master & Slave
DR 98919 + DR 98969	NR	Windhoff MPV Master & Slave
DR 98920 + DR 98970	NR	Windhoff MPV Master & Slave
DR 98921 + DR 98971	NR	Windhoff MPV Master & Slave
DR 98922 + DR 98972	NR	Windhoff MPV Master & Slave

DR 98923 + DR 98973	NR	Windhoff MPV Master & Slave
DR 98924 + DR 98974	NR	Windhoff MPV Master & Slave
DR 98925 + DR 98975	NR	Windhoff MPV Master & Slave
DR 98926 + DR 98976	NR	Windhoff MPV Master & Powered Slave
DR 98927 + DR 98977	NR	Windhoff MPV Master & Powered Slave
DR 98928 + DR 98978	NR	Windhoff MPV Master & Powered Slave
DR 98929 + DR 98979	NR	Windhoff MPV Master & Powered Slave
DR 98930 + DR 98980	NR	Windhoff MPV Master & Powered Slave
DR 98931 + DR 98981	NR	Windhoff MPV Master & Powered Slave
DR 98932 + DR 98982	NR	Windhoff MPV Master & Powered Slave

Names:

| DR 97012 | Geoff Bell |
| DR 98926+DR 98976 | John Denyer |

ELECTRIFICATION VEHICLES

DR 98001		NR	Windhoff MPV with Piling Equipment
DR 98002 (S)		NR	Windhoff MPV with Piling Equipment
DR 98003		NR	Windhoff MPV with Overhead Line Renewal Equipment
DR 98004		NR	Windhoff MPV with Overhead Line Renewal Equipment
DR 98005 (S)		NR	Windhoff MPV with Piling Equipment
DR 98006		NR	Windhoff MPV with Piling Equipment
DR 98007		NR	Windhoff MPV with Piling Equipment
DR 98009		NR	Windhoff MPV with Overhead Line Renewal Equipment
DR 98010		NR	Windhoff MPV with Overhead Line Renewal Equipment
DR 98011		NR	Windhoff MPV with Overhead Line Renewal Equipment
DR 98012		NR	Windhoff MPV with Overhead Line Renewal Equipment
DR 98013		NR	Windhoff MPV with Overhead Line Renewal Equipment
DR 98014		NR	Windhoff MPV with Overhead Line Renewal Equipment

99 70 9131 001-8	NR	Windhoff MPV with Piling Equipment	"DR 76901"
99 70 9131 003-4	NR	Windhoff MPV with Piling Equipment	"DR 76903"
99 70 9131 005-9	NR	Windhoff MPV with Piling Equipment	"DR 76905"
99 70 9131 006-7	NR	Windhoff MPV with Concrete Equipment	"DR 76906"
99 70 9131 010-9	NR	Windhoff MPV with Concrete Equipment	"DR 76910"
99 70 9131 011-7	NR	Windhoff MPV with Structure Equipment	"DR 76911"
99 70 9131 013-3	NR	Windhoff MPV with Structure Equipment	"DR 76913"
99 70 9131 014-1	NR	Windhoff MPV with Overhead Line Equipment	"DR 76914"
99 70 9131 015-8	NR	Windhoff MPV with Overhead Line Equipment	"DR 76915"
99 70 9131 018-2	NR	Windhoff MPV with Overhead Line Equipment	"DR 76918"
99 70 9131 020-8	NR	Windhoff MPV with Overhead Line Equipment	"DR 76920"
99 70 9131 021-6	NR	Windhoff MPV with Overhead Line Equipment	"DR 76921"
99 70 9131 022-4	NR	Windhoff MPV with Final Works Equipment	"DR 76922"
99 70 9131 023-2	NR	Windhoff MPV with Final Works Equipment	"DR 76923"

Names:

DR 98003	ANTHONY WRIGHTON 1944–2011
DR 98004	PHILIP CATTRELL 1961–2011
DR 98009	MELVYN SMITH 1953–2011
DR 98010	BENJAMIN GAUTREY 1992–2011
99 70 9131 001-8	BRUNEL

MOBILE MAINTENANCE SYSTEM UNITS

Robel Type 69.70

99 70 9481 001-4 + 99 70 9559 001-1 + 99 70 9580 001-4 NR "DR 97501/601/801"
99 70 9481 002-2 + 99 70 9559 002-9 + 99 70 9580 002-2 NR "DR 97502/602/802"
99 70 9481 003-0 + 99 70 9559 003-7 + 99 70 9580 003-0 NR "DR 97503/603/803"
99 70 9481 004-8 + 99 70 9559 004-5 + 99 70 9580 004-8 NR "DR 97504/604/804"
99 70 9481 005-5 + 99 70 9559 005-2 + 99 70 9580 005-5 NR "DR 97505/605/805"
99 70 9481 006-3 + 99 70 9559 006-0 + 99 70 9580 006-3 NR "DR 97506/606/806"
99 70 9481 007-1 + 99 70 9559 007-8 + 99 70 9580 007-1 NR "DR 97507/607/807"
99 70 9481 008-9 + 99 70 9559 008-6 + 99 70 9580 008-9 NR "DR 97508/608/808"

SNOWPLOUGHS

ADB 965203	NR	Independent Drift Plough	Tees Yard
ADB 965206	NR	Independent Drift Plough	York Parcels Sidings
ADB 965208	NR	Independent Drift Plough	Motherwell Depot
ADB 965209	NR	Independent Drift Plough	Bristol Barton Hill Depot
ADB 965210	NR	Independent Drift Plough	Tonbridge West Yard
ADB 965211	NR	Independent Drift Plough	March Depot
ADB 965217	NR	Independent Drift Plough	Edinburgh Slateford Depot
ADB 965219	NR	Independent Drift Plough	Edinburgh Slateford Depot
ADB 965223	NR	Independent Drift Plough	Margam Wagon Works
ADB 965224	NR	Independent Drift Plough	Carlisle Kingmoor Depot
ADB 965230	NR	Independent Drift Plough	Carlisle Kingmoor Depot
ADB 965231	NR	Independent Drift Plough	Bristol Barton Hill Depot
ADB 965234	NR	Independent Drift Plough	Inverness Millburn Yard
ADB 965235	NR	Independent Drift Plough	Margam Wagon Works
ADB 965236	NR	Independent Drift Plough	Tonbridge West Yard
ADB 965237	NR	Independent Drift Plough	March Depot
ADB 965240	NR	Independent Drift Plough	Motherwell Depot
ADB 965241	NR	Independent Drift Plough	York Turntable Sidings
ADB 965242	NR	Independent Drift Plough	Tees Yard
ADB 965243	NR	Independent Drift Plough	Inverness Millburn Yard
ADB 965576	NR	Beilhack Type PB600 Plough	Doncaster West Yard
ADB 965577	NR	Beilhack Type PB600 Plough	Doncaster West Yard
ADB 965578	NR	Beilhack Type PB600 Plough	Carlisle Kingmoor Yard
ADB 965579	NR	Beilhack Type PB600 Plough	Carlisle Kingmoor Yard
ADB 965580	NR	Beilhack Type PB600 Plough	Crewe Gresty Bridge Depot
ADB 965581	NR	Beilhack Type PB600 Plough	Crewe Gresty Bridge Depot
ADB 966098	NR	Beilhack Type PB600 Plough	Doncaster West Yard
ADB 966099	NR	Beilhack Type PB600 Plough	Doncaster West Yard

SNOWBLOWERS

ADB 968500	NR	Beilhack Self-Propelled Rotary	Edinburgh Slateford Depot
ADB 968501	NR	Beilhack Self-Propelled Rotary	Edinburgh Slateford Depot

INFRASTRUCTURE MONITORING VEHICLES

999800 (S) NR   Plasser & Theurer EM-SAT 100/RT Track Survey Car
999801 (S) NR   Plasser & Theurer EM-SAT 100/RT Track Survey Car

Name: 999800   Richard Spoors

ON-TRACK MACHINES AWAITING DISPOSAL

Tampers
DR 73105   Plasser & Theurer 09-32 CSM   Rugby Depot
DR 73503   Plasser & Theurer 08-16/90 ZW   Ashford OTM Depot
DR 75201   Plasser & Theurer 08-275 S&C   Hither Green Depot
DR 75202   Plasser & Theurer 08-275 S&C   Hither Green Depot

Ballast Cleaners
DR 76304   Plasser & Theurer RM74   Plasser UK, West Ealing
DR 76318   Plasser & Theurer RM74   Plasser UK, West Ealing

Twin Jib track relayer
DRB 78123 British Hoist & Crane Non-Self-Propelled   Polmadie DHS

LOCATIONS OF STORED ON-TRACK MACHINES

The locations of machines shown above as stored (S) are shown here.

DR 76710	Crewe Gresty Lane Sidings	DRP 81507	Ashford OTM Depot
DR 76711	Taunton Fairwater Yard	DRP 81508	Ashford OTM Depot
DR 77315	Ashford OTM Depot	DRP 81511	Ashford OTM Depot
DR 77316	Ashford OTM Depot	DRP 81513	Ashford OTM Depot
DR 77336	Hither Green Depot	DRP 81519	Woking OTM Depot
DRP 78217	Glasgow Rutherglen Depot	DR 89006	York Klondyke Yard
DRP 78218	Ashford OTM Depot	DR 89009	York Klondyke Yard
DRP 78223	Ashford OTM Depot	DR 98002	York Holgate Works
DRP 78224	Hither Green Depot	DR 98005	York Holgate Works
DRC 78237	York Holgate Works	DR 98305	Eastleigh Works
DR 79265	Eastleigh Works	DR 98306	Eastleigh Works
DR 80200	East Dereham	DR 98307A+	
DR 80202	Eastleigh Works	DR 98307B	Rugby Depot
DR 80203	Eastleigh Works	DR 98308A+	
DR 80204	East Dereham	DR 98308B	Rugby Depot
DR 80207	Eastleigh Works	999800	Eastleigh Works
DR 80212	Eastleigh Works	999801	Eastleigh Works

6. UK LIGHT RAIL & METRO SYSTEMS

This section lists the rolling stock of the various light rail and metro systems in Great Britain. Passenger carrying vehicles only are covered (not works vehicles). This listing does not cover the London Underground network.

6.1. BLACKPOOL & FLEETWOOD TRAMWAY

Until the opening of Manchester Metrolink, the Blackpool tramway was the only urban/inter-urban tramway system left in Britain. The infrastructure is owned by Blackpool Corporation, and the tramway is operated by Blackpool Transport Services Ltd. The 11 miles from Fleetwood to Starr Gate reopened in spring 2012 following rebuilding as a modern light rail system with a new fleet of 16 Bombardier Flexity 2 trams: these are now used on all scheduled services.

System: 600 V DC overhead.
Depot & Workshops: Starr Gate and Rigby Road (heritage fleet).
Standard livery: Flexity 2s and **F**: White, black & purple.

FLEXITY 2   5-SECTION TRAMS

These 16 articulated Supertrams are the trams used in normal daily service.

Built: 2011–12 by Bombardier Transportation, Bautzen, Germany.
Wheel arrangement: Bo-2-Bo.
Traction Motors: 4 x Bombardier 3-phase asynchronous of 120 kW.
Dimensions: 32.2 x 2.65 m.   **Seats:** 70 (4).
Doors: Sliding plug.   **Couplers:**
Weight: 40.9 t.   **Maximum Speed:** 43 mph.
Braking: Regenerative, disc and magnetic track.

Advertising livery: 016 Fleetwood Freeport (blue).

001	005	009	013
002	006	010	014
003	007	011	015
004	008	012	016 **AL**

Name: 002 "Alderman E.E. Wynne"

"BALLOON" DOUBLE DECKERS   A1-1A

The nine cars listed have partial exemption from the Rail Vehicle Accessibility Regulations and have been fitted with wider doors. However all except 700 and 711 were stored in 2014.

Built: 1934–35 by English Electric.
Traction Motors: 2 x EE305 of 40 kW. **Seats:** 94 (*† 92).

* Rebuilt with a flat front end design and air-conditioned cabs.

Advertising liveries:

707: Coral Island: The Jewel on the Mile (black) | 718: Madame Tussaud's (purple & red)
709: Blackpool Sealife Centre (blue) | 720: Walls ice cream (red)
713: Houndshill Shopping Centre (purple & white) | 724: Lyndene Hotel (blue)

700	**F**		711 †	**F**		719	**F** (S)
707 *	**AL** (S)		713	**AL** (S)		720	**AL** (S)
709 *	**AL** (S)		718 *	**AL** (S)		724 *	**AL** (S)

Name: 719   Donna's Dream House

HERITAGE FLEET of VINTAGE CARS

The following trams have exemption from the RVAR for Heritage use. They normally see use during the autumn Illuminations season or for private excursions.

Blackpool & Fleetwood 40	Single-deck Fleetwood Box car	Built: 1914
Bolton 66	Bogie double-decker	Built: 1901
Blackpool 147 MICHAEL AIREY	Standard double-decker	Built: 1924
Blackpool 227 (602)	Open boat car	Built: 1934
Blackpool 230 (604) GEORGE FORMBY OBE	Open boat car	Built: 1934
Blackpool 272+T2 (672+682)	Progress Twin Car	Rebuilt: 1960
Blackpool 304	Coronation Class single-decker	Built: 1952
Blackpool 600 THE DUCHESS OF CORNWALL	Open boat car	Built: 1934
Blackpool 631	Brush car	Built: 1937
Blackpool 642	Centenary car	Built: 1986
Blackpool 648	Centenary car	Built: 1987
Blackpool 701	Balloon double-decker	Built: 1934
Blackpool 706 PRINCESS ALICE	Balloon open-top double-decker	Built: 1934
Blackpool 717 WALTER LUFF	Balloon double-decker	Built: 1935
Blackpool 723	Balloon double-decker	Built: 1935

Illuminated cars

Blackpool 733	Western Train loco & tender	Rebuilt: 1962
Blackpool 734	Western Train coach	Rebuilt: 1962
Blackpool 736	"Warship" HMS Blackpool	Rebuilt: 1965
Blackpool 737	Illuminated Trawler – "Fisherman's Friend"	Rebuilt: 2001

STORED VEHICLES

The following vehicles are stored at Rigby Road depot.

Blackpool 8 (S)	BCT One Man Car	Rebuilt: 1974
Blackpool 143 (S)	Standard double-decker	Built: 1924
Blackpool 259 (S)	Brush car	Built: 1937
Blackpool 279 (S)	English Electric Railcoach	Rebuilt: 1960
Blackpool 622 (S)	Brush car	Built: 1937
Blackpool 632 (S)	Brush car	Built: 1937
Blackpool 660 (S)	Coronation Class single-decker	Built: 1953
Blackpool 663 (S)	Coronation Class single-decker	Built: 1953
Blackpool 675+685 (S)	Progress Twin Car	Rebuilt: 1958/60
Blackpool 676+686 (S)	Progress Twin Car	Rebuilt: 1958/60
Blackpool 704 (S)	Balloon double-decker	Built: 1934
Blackpool 715 (S)	Balloon double-decker	Built: 1935
Blackpool 732 (S)	Rocket illuminated car	Built: 1961
Blackpool 761 (S)	Jubilee Class double-decker	Rebuilt: 1979

6.2. DOCKLANDS LIGHT RAILWAY

This system runs for a total of approximately 23 route miles from termini at Bank and Tower Gateway in central London to Lewisham, Stratford, Beckton and Woolwich Arsenal. A new line from Canning Town to Stratford International also opened in 2011. The first part of the network opened in 1987 from Tower Gateway to Island Gardens. Originally owned by London Transport, it is now part of the London Rail division of Transport for London and operated Keolis/Amey. Cars are normally driven automatically using the Alcatel Seltrack moving block signalling system.

Original P86 and P89 Class vehicles 01–21 were withdrawn from service in 1991 (01–11) and 1995 (12–21) and sold for use in Essen, Germany. 55 new cars from Bombardier in Germany entered traffic between 2008 and 2010. These new vehicles enabled 3-unit trains to operate on all routes.

System: 750 V DC third rail (bottom contact). High-floor.
Depots: Beckton (main depot) and Poplar.
Livery: Red with a curving blue stripe to represent the River Thames.

CLASS B90   2-SECTION UNITS

Built: 1991–92 by BN Construction, Bruges, Belgium. Chopper control.
Wheel Arrangement: B-2-B.   **Traction Motors:** 2 x Brush 140 kW.
Seats: 52 (4).   **Weight:** 37 t.
Dimensions: 28.80 x 2.65 m.   **Braking:** Rheostatic.
Couplers: Scharfenberg.   **Maximum Speed:** 50 mph.
Doors: Sliding. End doors for staff use.

22	26	30	34	38	42
23	27	31	35	39	43
24	28	32	36	40	44
25	29	33	37	41	

CLASS B92   2-SECTION UNITS

Built: 1992–95 by BN Construction, Bruges, Belgium. Chopper control.
Wheel Arrangement: B-2-B.   **Traction Motors:** 2 x Brush 140 kW.
Seats: 52 (4).   **Weight:** 37 t.
Dimensions: 28.80 x 2.65 m.   **Braking:** Rheostatic.
Couplers: Scharfenberg.   **Maximum Speed:** 50 mph.
Doors: Sliding. End doors for staff use.

45	53	61	69	77	85
46	54	62	70	78	86
47	55	63	71	79	87
48	56	64	72	80	88
49	57	65	73	81	89
50	58	66	74	82	90
51	59	67	75	83	91
52	60	68	76	84	

CLASS B2K   2-SECTION UNITS

Built: 2002–03 by Bombardier Transportation, Bruges, Belgium.
Wheel Arrangement: B-2-B.   **Traction Motors:** 2 x Brush 140 kW.
Seats: 52 (4).   **Weight:** 37 t.
Dimensions: 28.80 x 2.65 m.   **Braking:** Rheostatic.
Couplers: Scharfenberg.   **Maximum Speed:** 50 mph.
Doors: Sliding. End doors for staff use.

92	96	01	05	09	13
93	97	02	06	10	14
94	98	03	07	11	15
95	99	04	08	12	16

CLASS B07   2-SECTION UNITS

Built: 2007–10 by Bombardier Transportation, Bautzen, Germany.
Wheel Arrangement: B-2-B.   **Traction Motors:** 2 x Brush 140 kW.
Seats: 52 (4).   **Weight:** 37 t.
Dimensions: **Braking:** Rheostatic.
Couplers: Scharfenberg.   **Maximum Speed:** 50 mph.
Doors: Sliding. End doors for staff use.

101	111	120	129	138	147
102	112	121	130	139	148
103	113	122	131	140	149
104	114	123	132	141	150
105	115	124	133	142	151
106	116	125	134	143	152
107	117	126	135	144	153
108	118	127	136	145	154
109	119	128	137	146	155
110					

6.3. EDINBURGH TRAMWAY

The new Edinburgh tramway finally opened in May 2014, after years of delays. The scheme was dogged by construction problems, with the originally planned terminus of Newhaven in the north of the city later cut back to York Place in the city centre. In the west side of the city trams operate to Edinburgh Airport, the complete route being 8½ miles long.

The tramway is operated by Edinburgh Trams Ltd, a publicly owned company that works in partnership with Lothian Buses, as part of the Transport for Edinburgh Group.

The trams are the longest to operate in the UK, although only around nine of the 27 are normally required to operate the off-peak service (but all are used as cars are rotated in traffic).

System: 750 V DC overhead.
Platform Height: 350 mm.
Depot & Workshops: Gogar.
Livery: White, red & black.

CAF   7-SECTION TRAMS

Built: 2009–11 by CAF, Irun, Spain.
Wheel Arrangement: Bo-Bo-2-Bo. **Traction Motors:** 12 x CAF 80 kW.
Seats: 78.   **Weight:** 56.25 t.
Dimensions: 42.8 x 2.65 m.   **Braking:** Regenerative & electro hydraulic.
Couplers: Albert.   **Maximum Speed:** 50 mph.
Doors: Sliding plug.

251	257	263	268	273
252	258	264	269	274
253	259	265	270	275
254	260	266	271	276
255	261	267	272	277
256	262			

6.4. GLASGOW SUBWAY

This circular 4 ft gauge underground line is the smallest metro system in the UK, running for just over six miles. Operated by Strathclyde PTE the system has 15 stations. The entire passenger railway is underground, contained in twin tunnels, allowing for clockwise operation on the "outer" circle and anti-clockwise operation on the "inner" circle.

Trains are formed of 3-cars – either three power cars or two power cars sandwiching one of the newer trailer cars.

System: 600 V DC third rail.
Depot & Workshops: Broomloan.
Livery: Orange & grey Subway livery.

SINGLE POWER CARS

Built: 1977–79 by Metro-Cammell, Birmingham. Refurbished 1993–95 by ABB Derby.
Wheel Arrangement: Bo-Bo.
Traction Motors: 4 x GEC G312AZ of 35.6 kW.

Seats: 36.	**Dimensions:** 12.81 m x 2.34 m.
Couplers: Wedglock.	**Doors:** Sliding.
Weight: 19.6 t.	**Maximum Speed:** 33.5 mph.

101	108	115	122	128
102	109	116	123	129
103	110	117	124	130
104	111	118	125	131
105	112	119	126	132
106	113	120	127	133
107	114	121		

INTERMEDIATE BOGIE TRAILERS

Built: 1992 by Hunslet Barclay, Kilmarnock.

Seats: 40.	**Dimensions:** 12.70 m x 2.34 m.
Couplers: Wedglock.	**Doors:** Sliding.
Weight: 17.2 t.	**Maximum Speed:** 33.5 mph.

201	203	205	207	208
202	204	206		

6.5. GREATER MANCHESTER METROLINK

Metrolink was the first modern tramway system in the UK, combining street running with longer distance running over former BR lines. The system opened in 1992 from Bury to Altrincham with a street section through the centre of Manchester and a spur to Piccadilly station. A second line opened in 2000 from Cornbrook to Eccles.

A short spur off the Eccles line to MediaCityUK opened in September 2010 whilst the first part of the South Manchester Line to Chorlton and St Werburgh's Road opened in July 2011. This was followed by a further extension to East Didsbury in May 2013. In June 2012 the former National Rail line from Manchester to Oldham Mumps opened as a Metrolink line and this was extended to Shaw & Crompton in December 2012 and to Rochdale station in February 2013. The East Manchester Line reached Droylsden in February 2013 and this was followed by Droylsden–Ashton-under-Lyne in October 2013, Oldham town centre (January 2014), Rochdale town centre (March 2014) and finally St Werburgh's Road–Manchester Airport in November 2014, extending the total route mileage to 57½ miles.

Work is currently taking place on a second city crossing in Manchester, this is due to open in 2017.

Operator: RATP Dev.
System: 750 V DC overhead. High floor.
Depot & Workshops: Queens Road and Trafford.

T68 1000 SERIES   2-SECTION TRAMS

All T68 trams have now been withdrawn and those remaining in Manchester are awaiting disposal.

Built: 1991–92 by Firema, Italy. Chopper control.

Wheel Arrangement: Bo-2-Bo.	**Traction Motors:** 4 x GEC 130 kW.
Dimensions: 29.0 x 2.65 m.	**Seats:** 82 (4).
Doors: Sliding.	**Couplers:** Scharfenberg.
Weight: 45 t.	**Maximum Speed:** 50 mph.

Braking: Regenerative, disc and emergency track.

Liveries: White, dark grey & blue with light blue doors.
M: Silver & yellow.

(S) Stored at Trafford depot (except 1003 at Queens Road).

1003 is reserved for the Greater Manchester Fire & Rescue Service.

1007 and 1020 are reserved for Heaton Park Tramway.

Stored 1016, 1022, 1024 and 1026 have been moved to Long Marston for use in UKTram development work.

```
1003  M (S)
1007    (S)  EAST LANCASHIRE RAILWAY
1020    (S)
1023    (S)
```

T68 2000 SERIES   2-SECTION TRAMS

Built: 1999 by Ansaldo, Italy. Chopper control.

Wheel Arrangement: Bo-2-Bo.	**Traction Motors:** 4 x GEC 130 kW.
Dimensions: 29.0 x 2.65 m.	**Seats:** 82 (4).
Doors: Sliding.	**Couplers:** Scharfenberg.
Weight: 45 t.	**Maximum Speed:** 50 mph.

Braking: Regenerative, disc and magnetic track.

Livery: White, dark grey & blue with light blue doors.

```
2001   (S)
```

3000 SERIES   FLEXITY SWIFT   2-SECTION TRAMS

120 Bombardier M5000 "Flexity Swift" trams are currently being delivered.
These trams now operate all services, having replaced the T68 series trams.
They operate either singly or in pairs. Deliveries had reached 3093 by the
start of 2015 and all 120 will be delivered by 2016. Trams from 3075 upwards
have 8 more seats.

Built: 2009–16 by Bombardier, Vienna, Austria.
Wheel Arrangement: Bo-2-Bo.
Traction Motors: 4 x Bombardier 3-phase asynchronous of 120 kW.
Dimensions: 28.4 x 2.65 m.   **Seats:** 52 or 60 (3075–3120).
Doors: Sliding.   **Couplers:** Scharfenberg.
Weight: 39.7 t.   **Maximum Speed:** 50 mph.
Braking: Regenerative, disc and magnetic track.

Livery: Silver & yellow.

3001–3004 have been fitted with special "ice-breaking" pantographs.

3001	3025	3049	3073	3097
3002	3026	3050	3074	3098
3003	3027	3051	3075	3099
3004	3028	3052	3076	3100
3005	3029	3053	3077	3101
3006	3030	3054	3078	3102
3007	3031	3055	3079	3103
3008	3032	3056	3080	3104
3009	3033	3057	3081	3105
3010	3034	3058	3082	3106
3011	3035	3059	3083	3107
3012	3036	3060	3084	3108
3013	3037	3061	3085	3109
3014	3038	3062	3086	3110
3015	3039	3063	3087	3111
3016	3040	3064	3088	3112
3017	3041	3065	3089	3113
3018	3042	3066	3090	3114
3019	3043	3067	3091	3115
3020	3044	3068	3092	3116
3021	3045	3069	3093	3117
3022	3046	3070	3094	3118
3023	3047	3071	3095	3119
3024	3048	3072	3096	3120

Names:

3009   50th Anniversary of Coronation Street 1960–2010
3020   LANCASHIRE FUSILIER

6.6. LONDON TRAMLINK

This system runs through central Croydon via a one-way loop, with lines radiating out to Wimbledon, New Addington and Beckenham Junction/ Elmers End, the total route mileage being 18½ miles. It opened in 2000 and is now operated by Transport for London. Six new Stadler trams entered traffic in spring 2012 and four more are on order.

System: 750 V DC overhead.   **Platform Height:** 350 mm.
Depot & Workshops: Therapia Lane, Croydon.

Livery: Light grey & lime green with a blue solebar.

Advertising liveries:

2531 – McMillan Williams Solicitors (black).
2534 – McMillan Williams Solicitors (white & red).
2542 – Turkish Airlines (red)

BOMBARDIER   3-SECTION TRAMS

Built: 1998–99 by Bombardier, Vienna, Austria.
Wheel Arrangement: Bo-2-Bo.   **Traction Motors:** 4 x 120 kW.
Dimensions: 30.1 x 2.65 m.   **Seats:** 70.
Doors: Sliding plug.   **Couplers:** Scharfenberg.
Weight: 36.3 t.   **Maximum Speed:** 50 mph.
Braking: Disc, regenerative and magnetic track.

2530		2534	**AL**	2538	2542	**AL**	2546	2550
2531	**AL**	2535		2539	2543		2547	2551
2532		2536		2540	2544		2548	2552
2533		2537		2541	2545		2549	2553

Name: 2535 STEPHEN PARASCANDOLO 1980–2007

STADLER   5-SECTION TRAMS

Six new Variobahn trams entered traffic in 2012.
Built: 2011–12 by Stadler, Berlin, Germany.
Wheel Arrangement: **Traction Motors:** 8 x 45 kW.
Dimensions: 32.4 x 2.65 m.   **Seats:** 74.
Doors: Sliding plug.   **Couplers:** Albert.
Weight: 41.5 t.   **Maximum Speed:** 50 mph.
Braking: Disc, regenerative and magnetic track.

Advertising livery: 2554 – Love Croydon (purple & blue)

2554	**AL**	2555	2556	2557	2558	2559

On order and due for delivery 2015–16:

2560	2561	2562	2563

6.7. NOTTINGHAM EXPRESS TRANSIT

This light rail system opened in 2004. Line 1 runs for 8¾ miles from Station Street, Nottingham (alongside Nottingham station) to Hucknall, including a short spur to Phoenix Park. There is around three miles of street running through Nottingham. Extensions are under construction to Clifton Lane (Line 2) to the south of Nottingham, and Toton Lane (Chilwell) via Beeston to the west (Line 3) and these are due to open in spring/summer 2015.

22 new Alstom Citadis trams are now being delivered for these extensions. The first of these new trams entered service on Line 1 in July 2014.

The system is operated by the Tramlink Nottingham consortium (formed of Alstom Transport, Keolis, Wellglade, Meridiam Infrastructure, InfraVia and VINCI Construction).

System: 750 V DC overhead.   **Platform Height:** 350 mm.
Depot & Workshops: Wilkinson Street.
Livery: Silver & green with black window surrounds.

BOMBARDIER INCENTRO   5-SECTION TRAMS

Built: 2002–03 by Bombardier, Derby Litchurch Lane Works.
Wheel Arrangement: Bo-2-Bo.   **Traction Motors:** 8 x 45 kW wheelmotors.
Dimensions: 33.0 x 2.4 m.   **Seats:** 54 (4).
Doors: Sliding plug.   **Couplers:** Not equipped.
Weight: 36.7 t.   **Maximum Speed:** 50 mph.
Braking: Disc, regenerative and magnetic track for emergency use.

Advertising liveries:

206 – e.on (red).
207 – PayPoint (white & yellow).
209 – Trent Barton Mango tickets (lime green).
211 – Alstom (pale blue).

201		Torvill and Dean	209	**AL**	Sid Standard
202		DH Lawrence	210		Sir Jesse Boot
203		Bendigo Thompson	211	**AL**	Robin Hood
204		Erica Beardsmore	212		William Booth
205		Lord Byron	213		Mary Potter
206	**AL**	Angela Alcock	214		Dennis McCarthy
207	**AL**	Mavis Worthington	215		Brian Clough
208		Dinah Minton			

ALSTOM CITADIS 402   5-SECTION TRAMS

All of these trams had been delivered to Nottingham by the end of 2014 but are only seeing limited use on Line 1, but will be required once the new extensions open in 2015.

Built: 2013–14 by Alstom, Barcelona, Spain.

Wheel Arrangement: Bo-2-Bo.   **Traction Motors:** 4 x 120 kW.
Dimensions: 32.0 x 2.4 m   **Seats:** 58 (10).
Doors: Sliding plug.   **Couplers:** Not equipped.
Weight: 40.8 t.   **Maximum Speed:** 50 mph.
Braking: Disc, regenerative and magnetic track for emergency use.

216	Julie Poulter	227	
217	Carl Froch	228	
218	Jam Taylor	229	
219	Alan Sillitoe	230	
220		231	
221		232	
222		233	
223		234	
224		235	
225		236	
226		237	

6.8. MIDLAND METRO

Opened in 1999 and operated by Travel West Midlands, Midland Metro consists of a 12½ mile line from Birmingham Snow Hill to Wolverhampton along the old GWR route to Wolverhampton Low Level. Approaching Wolverhampton it leaves the old railway for street-running to the St George's terminus.

An extension is currently under construction from Snow Hill through the centre of Birmingham to New Street station, and this will open in 2015. Future extensions are planned – to Centenary Square and Edgbaston and also eventually to the new Curzon Street HS2 station.

20 CAF trams are currently being delivered to replace the Ansaldo trams and also to serve the New Street extension. There is an option for a further five vehicles.

System: 750 V DC overhead.   **Platform Height:** 350 mm.
Depot & Workshops: Wednesbury.

ANSALDO   2-SECTION TRAMS

All of these trams are due to be stored by spring 2015. They will be stored at Long Marston for potential future use if required.

Built: 1998–99 by Ansaldo Transporti, Italy.

Wheel Arrangement: Bo-2-Bo.	**Traction Motors:** 4 x 105 kW.
Dimensions: 24.00 x 2.65 m.	**Seats:** 52.
Doors: Sliding plug.	**Couplers:** Not equipped.
Weight: 35.6 t.	**Maximum Speed:** 43 mph.

Braking: Regenerative, disc and magnetic track.

Standard livery: Dark blue & light grey with a green stripe & red front end.

MW: Network West Midlands silver & pink.
0: Original Birmingham Corporation tram livery (cream & blue).

01, 02, 07, 13, 14 and 15 are stored at Long Marston (14 is being used for UKTram development work). The other stored trams are at Wednesbury depot.

01	(S)			09	**MW**	JEFF ASTLE
02	(S)			10	**MW**	JOHN STANLEY WEBB
03	(S)		RAY LEWIS	11	(S) **0**	THERESA STEWART
04	(S)		SIR FRANK WHITTLE	12		
05	(S)	**MW**	SISTER DORA	13	(S)	
06			ALAN GARNER	14	(S)	
07		**MW**		15	(S)	
08	(S)		JOSEPH CHAMBERLAIN	16		GERWYN JOHN

CAF URBOS 3   5-SECTION TRAMS

These cars are currently being delivered and the first entered traffic in September 2014.

Built: 2013–14 by CAF, Zaragoza, Spain.

Wheel Arrangement: Bo-2-Bo.	**Traction Motors:** 8 x 65 kW.
Dimensions: 32.96 x 2.65 m.	**Seats:** 52.
Doors: Sliding plug.	**Couplers:** Albert.
Weight: 41.0 t.	**Maximum Speed:** 43 mph.

Braking: Regenerative, disc and magnetic track.

Livery: Network West Midlands silver & pink.

17	21	25	29	33
18	22	26	30	34
19	23	27	31	35
20	24	28	32	36

6.9. SHEFFIELD SUPERTRAM

This system opened in 1994 and has three lines radiating from Sheffield City Centre. These run to Halfway in the south-east, with a spur from Gleadless Townend to Herdings Park, to Middlewood in the north with a spur from Hillsborough to Malin Bridge and to Meadowhall Interchange in the north east, adjacent to the large shopping complex. The total length is 18 miles. The system is a mixture of on-street and segregated running.

The cars are owned by South Yorkshire Light Rail Ltd, a subsidiary of South Yorkshire PTE. The operating company, South Yorkshire Supertram Ltd, is contracted to Stagecoach who operate the system as Stagecoach Supertram.

Because of severe gradients in Sheffield (up to 1 in 10) all axles are powered on the vehicles, which have low-floor outer sections.

System: 750 V DC overhead.   **Platform Height:** 450 mm.
Depot & Workshops: Nunnery.
Standard livery: Stagecoach (all over blue with red & orange ends).

Non-standard/Advertising liveries:

111 and 116 – East Midlands Trains (blue).
120 – Original Sheffield Corporation tram livery (cream & blue).

SIEMENS   3-SECTION TRAMS

Built: 1993–94 by Siemens-Duewag, Düsseldorf, Germany.
Wheel Arrangement: B-B-B-B.
Traction Motors: 4 x monomotor drives of 250 kW.
Dimensions: 34.75 x 2.65 m.   **Seats:** 80 (6).
Doors: Sliding plug.   **Couplers:** Not equipped.
Weight: 52t.   **Maximum Speed:** 50 mph.
Braking: Regenerative, disc and emergency track.

101	106	110	114	118	122
102	107	111 **AL**	115	119	123
103	108	112	116 **AL**	120 **0**	124
104	109	113	117	121	125
105					

6.10. TYNE & WEAR METRO

The Tyne & Wear Metro system covers 48 route miles and can be described as the UK's first modern light rail system.

The initial network opened between 1980 and 1984, consisting of a line from South Shields via Gateshead and Newcastle Central to Bank Foot (extended to Newcastle Airport in 1991) and the North Tyneside loop (over former BR lines) serving Tynemouth and Whitley Bay with a terminus at St James. A more recent extension was from Pelaw to Sunderland and South Hylton in 2002, using existing heavy rail infrastructure between Heworth and Sunderland.

The system is owned by Nexus (the Tyne & Wear PTE) and operated by DB Regio.

System: 1500 V DC overhead.   **Depot & Workshops:** South Gosforth.

METRO-CAMMELL   2-SECTION UNITS

Built: 1978–81 by Metropolitan Cammell, Birmingham (Prototype cars 4001 and 4002 were built by Metropolitan Cammell in 1975 and rebuilt 1984–87 by Hunslet TPL, Leeds).

Fleet refurbishment is currently taking place at Wabtec, Doncaster but this will only include 86 cars. The work commenced in 2010 and is due to be completed by mid 2015. As part of this work the number of seats is reduced from 68 to 64. Refurbished cars are shown as **TW**.

Wheel Arrangement: B-2-B.
Traction Motors: 2 x Siemens of 187 kW each.
Dimensions: 27.80 x 2.65 m.   **Seats:** 68 (**TW** = 64).
Doors: Sliding plug.   **Couplers:** BSI.
Weight: 39.0 t.   **Maximum Speed:** 50 mph.
Braking: Air/electro magnetic emergency track.

Standard livery: Red & yellow unless otherwise indicated.
0 (4001) Original 1975 Tyne & Wear Metro livery of yellow & cream.
0 (4027) Original North Eastern Railway style (red & white).
TW New Tyne & Wear Metro (grey, black & yellow).

Advertising liveries:

4002 – Tyne & Wear Metro (orange & black).
4040 and 4083 – Emirates Airlines (red).
4045 – Newcastle International Airport – 75 years (purple).
4080 – South Shields market (white).

4001	**0**	4016	**TW**	4031	**TW**	4046	**TW**	4061	**TW**	4076	**TW**
4002	**AL**	4017	**TW**	4032	**TW**	4047	**TW**	4062	**TW**	4077	
4003	**TW**	4018	**TW**	4033	**TW**	4048		4063	**TW**	4078	**TW**
4004	**TW**	4019	**TW**	4034	**TW**	4049	**TW**	4064	**TW**	4079	**TW**
4005	**TW**	4020	**TW**	4035	**TW**	4050	**TW**	4065	**TW**	4080	**AL**
4006	**TW**	4021	**TW**	4036	**TW**	4051	**TW**	4066	**TW**	4081	**TW**
4007	**TW**	4022	**TW**	4037	**TW**	4052	**TW**	4067	**TW**	4082	**TW**
4008	**TW**	4023	**TW**	4038	**TW**	4053	**TW**	4068	**TW**	4083	**AL**
4009	**TW**	4024	**TW**	4039	**TW**	4054	**TW**	4069	**TW**	4084	**TW**
4010	**TW**	4025		4040	**AL**	4055	**TW**	4070	**TW**	4085	
4011	**TW**	4026		4041	**TW**	4056	**TW**	4071	**TW**	4086	**TW**
4012		4027	**0**	4042	**TW**	4057	**TW**	4072	**TW**	4087	**TW**
4013	**TW**	4028	**TW**	4043	**TW**	4058	**TW**	4073	**TW**	4088	**TW**
4014	**TW**	4029	**TW**	4044	**TW**	4059	**TW**	4074	**TW**	4089	**TW**
4015	**TW**	4030	**TW**	4045	**AL**	4060	**TW**	4075	**TW**	4090	**TW**

Names (to be removed on refurbishment):

4026   George Stephenson | 4077   Robert Stephenson

7. CODES

7.1. LIVERY CODES

Livery codes are used to denote the various liveries carried. It is impossible to list every livery variation which currently exists. In particular items ignored for this publication include:

• Minor colour variations.
• Omission of logos.
• All numbering, lettering and brandings.

Descriptions quoted are thus a general guide only. Logos as appropriate for each livery are normally deemed to be carried. The colour of the lower half of the bodyside is stated first.

Code Description

1	"One" (metallic grey with a broad black bodyside stripe. White National Express/Abellio Greater Anglia "interim" stripe as branding).
AB	Arriva Trains Wales/Welsh Government sponsored dark blue.
AG	Arlington Fleet Services (green).
AI	Aggregate Industries (green, light grey & blue).
AL	Advertising/promotional livery (see class heading for details).
AN	Anglia Railways Class 170s (white & turquoise with blue vignette).
AR	Anglia Railways (turquoise blue with a white stripe).
AV	Arriva Trains (turquoise blue with white doors & a cream "swish").
AW	Arriva Trains Wales/Welsh Government sponsored dark & light blue.
AZ	Advenza Freight (deep blue with green Advenza brandings).
B	BR blue.
BB	Balfour Beatty Rail (white & blue).
BG	BR blue & grey lined out in white.
BL	BR Revised blue with yellow cabs, grey roof, large numbers & logo.
BP	Blue Pullman ("Nanking blue & white).
CC	BR Carmine & Cream.
CD	Cotswold Rail (silver with blue & red logo).
CE	BR Civil Engineers (yellow & grey with black cab doors & window surrounds).
CH	BR Western Region/GWR (chocolate & cream lined out in gold).
CL	Chiltern Railways Mainline Class 168 (white & silver).
CM	Chiltern Railways Mainline loco-hauled (two-tone grey & silver with blue stripes).
CN	Connex/Southeastern (white with black window surrounds & grey lower band).
CR	Chiltern Railways (blue & white with a red stripe).
CS	Colas Rail (yellow, orange & black).
CU	Corus (silver with red logos).
CX	Connex (white with yellow lower body & blue solebar).
DB	DB Schenker (Deutsche Bahn red with grey roof & solebar).
DC	Devon & Cornwall Railways (metallic silver).
DG	BR Departmental (dark grey with black cab doors & window surrounds).
DI	New DRS {Class 68 style} (deep blue & aquamarine with large compass logo).

DR   Direct Rail Services (dark blue with light blue or dark grey roof).

DS   Revised Direct Rail Services (dark blue, light blue & green. "Compass" logo).

E   English Welsh & Scottish Railway (maroon bodyside & roof with a broad gold bodyside band).

EB   Eurotunnel (two-tone grey with a broad blue stripe).

EC   East Coast (silver or grey with a purple stripe).

ECR   Euro Cargo Rail (light grey).

EG   "EWS grey" (as **F** but with large yellow & red EWS logo).

EL   Electric Traction Limited (silver & red).

EP   European Passenger Services (two-tone grey with dark blue roof).

EM   East Midlands Trains {Connect} (blue with red & orange swish at unit ends).

ER   Revised Eurostar (deep blue & two-tone grey).

EU   Eurostar (white with dark blue & yellow stripes).

EX   Europhoenix (silver, blue & red).

F   BR Trainload Freight (two-tone grey with black cab doors & window surrounds. Various logos).

FA   Fastline Freight (grey & black with white & orange stripes).

FB   First Group dark blue.

FD   First Great Western & First Hull Trains "Dynamic Lines" (dark blue with thin multi-coloured lines on the lower bodyside).

FE   Railfreight Distribution International (two tone-grey with black cab doors & dark blue roof).

FER   Fertis (light grey with a dark grey roof & solebar).

FF   Freightliner grey (two-tone grey with black cab doors & window surrounds. Freightliner logo).

FG   First Group InterCity (indigo blue with a white roof & gold, pink & white stripes).

FH   Revised Freightliner {PowerHaul} (dark green with yellow cab ends & grey stripe/buffer beam).

FI   First Great Western "Local Lines" DMU (varying blue with local visitor attractions applied to the lower bodyside).

FL   Freightliner (dark green with yellow cabs).

FP   Old First Great Western (green & ivory with thin green & gold stripes).

FO   BR Railfreight (grey bodysides, yellow cabs & red lower bodyside stripe, large BR logo).

FR   Fragonset Railways (black with silver roof & a red bodyside band lined out in white).

FS   First Group (indigo blue with pink & white stripes).

FT   First TransPennine Express "Dynamic Lines" (varying blue with multi-coloured lines).

FU   First Group "Urban Lights" (varying blue or uniform indigo blue with pink, white & blue markings on the lower bodyside).

FY   Foster Yeoman (blue & silver. Cast numberplates).

G¹   BR Green (plain green, with white stripe on main line locomotives).

G²   BR Southern Region/SR or BR DMU green.

GA   Abellio Greater Anglia (white with red doors & black window surrounds).

GB   GB Railfreight (blue with orange cantrail & solebar stripes, orange cabs).

GC   Grand Central (all over black with an orange stripe).

GG   BR two-tone green.

GIF   GIF (Spain) (light blue with a dark blue band).

GL   First Great Western locomotives (green with a gold stripe).

GN   Great North Eastern Railway {modified} (dark blue with a white stripe).
GS   Royal Scotsman maroon.
GV   Gatwick Express EMU (red, white & indigo blue with mauve & blue doors).
GW   Great Western Railway (green, lined out in black & orange).
GX   Gatwick Express InterCity (dark grey/white/burgundy/white).
GY   Eurotunnel (grey & yellow).
HA   Hanson Quarry Products (dark blue/silver with oxide red roof).
HB   HSBC Rail (Oxford blue & white).
HC   Heathrow Connect (grey with a broad deep blue bodyside band & orange doors).
HE   Heathrow Express (silver with purple doors and black window surrounds). Red advertising for Vodaphone.
HN   Harry Needle Railroad Company (orange with a black roof and solebar).
IC   BR InterCity (dark grey/white/red/white).
K   Black.
LH   BR Loadhaul (black with orange cabsides).
LM   London Midland (white/grey & green with broad black stripe around the windows).
LN   LNER Tourist (green & cream).
LO   London Overground (all over white with a blue solebar & black window surrounds).
LT   London Transport maroon & cream.
M   BR maroon (maroon lined out in straw & black).
MA   Maintrain/East Midlands Trains blue.
ME   Merseyrail (metallic silver with yellow doors).
ML   BR Mainline Freight (aircraft blue with a silver stripe).
MY   New Merseyrail (all over yellow or all over grey (alternate sides)).
N   BR Network SouthEast (white & blue with red lower bodyside stripe, grey solebar & cab ends).
NB   Northern all over dark blue.
NC   National Express white (white with blue doors).
NO   Northern (deep blue, purple & white). Some units have area-specific promotional vinyls (see class headings for details).
NP   Northern purple {Class 319 style} (all over purple with dark blue ends and doors).
NR   Network Rail (blue with a red stripe).
NX   National Express (white with grey ends).
O   Non-standard (see class heading for details).
P   Porterbrook Leasing Company (white or grey & purple).
PB   Porterbrook Leasing Company blue.
PC   Pullman Car Company (umber & cream with gold lettering lined out in gold).
RB   Riviera Trains Oxford blue.
RG   BR Parcels (dark grey & red).
RK   Railtrack (green & blue).
RM   Royal Mail (red with yellow stripes above solebar).
RP   Royal Train (claret, lined out in red & black).
RR   Regional Railways (dark blue & grey with light blue & white stripes, three narrow dark blue stripes at vehicle ends).
RS   RMS Locotec blue.
RV   Riviera Trains Great Briton (Oxford blue & cream lined out in gold).
RX   Rail Express Systems (dark grey & red with or without blue markings).

RZ   Royal Train revised (plain claret, no lining).
SB   Southeastern High Speed (all over blue with black window surrounds).
SC   Strathclyde PTE (carmine & cream lined out in black & gold).
SD   South West Trains outer suburban {Class 450 style} (deep blue with red doors & orange & red cab sides).
SE   Southeastern (all over white with black window surrounds, light blue doors and (on some units) dark blue lower bodyside stripe).
SN   Southern (white & dark green with light green semi-circles at one end of each vehicle. Light grey band at solebar level).
SR   ScotRail – Scotland's Railways (dark blue with Scottish Saltire flag & white/light blue flashes).
SS   South West Trains inner suburban {Class 455 style} (red with blue & orange flashes at unit ends).
ST   Stagecoach {long-distance stock} (white & dark blue with dark blue window surrounds and red & orange swishes at unit ends).
TG   Govia Thameslink interim {Class 387} (white with dark green doors).
TL   Govia Thameslink (light grey & white with blue stripe).
TT   Transmart Trains (all over green).
U   White or grey undercoat.
V   Virgin Trains (red with black doors extending into bodysides, three white lower bodysides stripes).
VP   Virgin Trains shunters (black with a large black & white chequered flag on the bodyside).
VN   Belmond Northern Belle (crimson lake & cream lined out in gold).
VT   Virgin Trains silver (silver, with black window surrounds, white cantrail stripe & red roof. Red swept down at unit ends).
WA   Wabtec Rail (black).
WC   West Coast Railway Company maroon.
XC   CrossCountry (two-tone silver with deep crimson ends & pink doors).
Y   Network Rail yellow.
YR   West Yorkshire PTE/Northern EMUs (red, lilac & grey).

7.2. OWNER CODES

The following codes are used to define the ownership details of the locomotives or rolling stock listed in this book. Codes shown indicate either the legal owner or "responsible custodian" of each vehicle.

20	Class 20189	AV	Arriva UK Trains
40	Class 40 Preservation Society	BA	British American Railway Services
47	Stratford 47 Group		
50	Class 50 Alliance	BB	Balfour Beatty Rail Infrastructure Services
56	Class 56 Locomotives		
62	The Princess Royal Class Locomotive Trust	BE	Belmond (UK)
		BK	The Scottish Railway Preservation Society
70	7029 Clun Castle		
71	71A Locomotives	BN	Beacon Rail
2L	Class 20 Locomotives	BT	Bombardier Transportation UK
A	Angel Trains	CR	The Chiltern Railway Company
AI	Aggregate Industries	CS	Colas Rail
AM	Alstom	DB	DB Schenker Rail (UK)

DP	Deltic Preservation Society
DR	Direct Rail Services
DT	The Diesel Traction Group
E	Eversholt Rail (UK)
EL	Electric Traction Limited
EM	East Midlands Trains
EP	Europhoenix
ET	Eurotunnel
EU	Eurostar International
FG	First Group
FL	Freightliner
FW	First Great Western (assets of the Greater Western franchise)
GB	GB Railfreight
H1	Network Rail (High Speed)
HA	Hanson Group
HD	Hastings Diesels
HE	British Airports Authority
HJ	Howard Johnston
HN	Harry Needle Railroad Company
LF	Lombard Finance
LS	Locomotive Services
LM	London Midland
MG	Mid Glamorgan County Council
MQ	Macquarie Group
MW	Beaver Sports (Yorkshire)
NB	Neil Boden
NM	National Museum of Science & Industry
NR	Network Rail
NS	Nemesis Rail
NY	North Yorkshire Moors Railway Enterprises
P	Porterbrook Leasing Company
PP	Peter Pan Locomotive Company
QW	QW Rail Leasing
RA	Railfilms
RC	RailCare UK
RE	Railway Vehicle Engineering
RL	Rail Management Services (trading as RMS Locotec)
RM	Royal Mail
RP	Rampart Engineering
RV	Riviera Trains
SB	SNCB/NMBS (Société Nationale des Chemins de fer Belges/ Nationale Maatschappij der Belgische Spoorwegen)
SF	SNCF (Société Nationale des Chemins de fer Français)
SG	South Glamorgan County Council
SI	Speno International
SK	Swietelsky Babcock Rail
SM	Siemens Transportation
SR	ScotRail
SN	Southern
SW	South West Trains
TT	Transmart Trains
UR	UK Rail Leasing
VI	Virgin Trains
VL	Voyager Leasing (Lloyds Banking Group/Angel Trains)
VO	VolkerRail
VT	Vintage Trains
WA	Wabtec Rail Group
WC	West Coast Railway Company
X	Sold for scrap/further use and awaiting collection

7.3. LOCOMOTIVE POOL CODES

Locomotives are split into operational groups ("pools") for diagramming and maintenance purposes. The official codes used to denote these pools are shown in this publication.

ACAC	Electric Traction Limited locomotives
ACXX	Electric Traction Limited locomotives for static depot use.
ATLO	Alstom Class 08.
AWCA	West Coast Railway Company operational locomotives.
AWCX	West Coast Railway Company stored locomotives.
CFOL	Class 50 Operations locomotives.
COFS	Colas Rail Class 56.
COLO	Colas Rail Classes 47, 60, 66 & 70.
COLS	Colas Rail stored locomotives.

COTS	Colas Rail Class 37.
DFGH	Freightliner Heavy Haul Class 70.
DFGI	Freightliner Intermodal Class 70.
DFHG	Freightliner Heavy Haul low emission Class 66.
DFHH	Freightliner Heavy Haul Class 66.
DFIM	Freightliner Intermodal Class 66.
DFIN	Freightliner Intermodal low emission Class 66.
DFLC	Freightliner Intermodal Class 90.
DFLH	Freightliner Heavy Haul Class 47.
DFLS	Freightliner Class 08.
DFMC	Freightliner Intermodal Class 86/5.
DFNC	Freightliner Intermodal Class 86/6.
DHLT	Freightliner locomotives awaiting maintenance/repair/disposal.
EFOO	First Great Western Class 57.
EFPC	First Great Western Class 43.
EFSH	First Great Western Class 08.
EHPC	CrossCountry Class 43.
EJLO	London Midland Class 08.
ELRD	East Lancashire Railway-based main line registered locomotives.
EMPC	East Midlands Trains Class 43.
EMSL	East Midlands Trains Class 08.
EPEX	Europhoenix locomotives for export.
EPUK	Europhoenix UK locomotives.
ETLO	Electric Traction Limited Class 87.
GBBR	GB Railfreight Class 73/9.
GBCM	GB Railfreight Class 66. General.
GBDF	GB Railfreight Class 47.
GBDR	GB Railfreight Class 66. Locomotives from Germany.
GBED	GB Railfreight Class 73.
GBEE	GB Railfreight Class 20. On hire from Harry Needle/Class 20189.
GBET	GB Railfreight Class 92.
GBFM	GB Railfreight Class 66. RETB fitted.
GBNB	GB Railfreight Class 66. New build.
GBNL	GB Railfreight Class 66. Locomotives from the Netherlands.
GBRT	GB Railfreight Class 66. Network Rail duties.
GBSD	GB Railfreight Class 66.
GBWM	GB Railfreight Class 08/09.
GBYH	GB Railfreight Class 59.
GCHP	Grand Central Class 43.
GPSS	Eurostar (UK) Class 08.
HBSH	Wabtec hire shunting locomotives.
HNRL	Harry Needle Railroad Company hire locomotives.
HNRS	Harry Needle Railroad Company stored locomotives.
HTLX	British American Railway Services locomotives.
HWSU	Southern Class 09.
HYWD	South West Trains Class 73.
IANA	Greater Anglia Class 90.
IECA	East Coast Class 91.
IECP	East Coast Class 43.
MBDL	Non TOC-owned diesel locomotives.
MBED	Non TOC-owned electro-diesel locomotives.

MBEL	Non TOC-owned electric locomotives.
MOLO	Class 20189 Ltd Class 20s.
MRSO	RMS Locotec Class 08.
NRLO	Nemesis Rail locomotives.
QADD	Network Rail diesel locomotives.
QCAR	Network Rail New Measurement Train Class 43.
QETS	Network Rail Class 37.
RFSH	Wabtec Rail locomotives.
RTLO	Riviera Trains Class 47.
RVLO	Rail Vehicle Engineering locomotives.
WAAC	DB Schenker Class 67.
WABC	DB Schenker Class 67. RETB fitted.
WACC	DB Schenker Class 67 for hire to Chiltern Railways.
WAWC	DB Schenker Class 67 for hire to Arriva Trains Wales.
WBAI	DB Schenker Class 66. Locomotives being fitted with "stop-start" technology.
WBAK	DB Schenker Class 66. Locomotives fitted with "stop-start" technology.
WBAT	DB Schenker Class 66.
WBBT	DB Schenker Class 66. RETB fitted.
WBLT	DB Schenker Industrial Class 66. Dedicated locomotives for Lickey Incline banking duties.
WBTT	DB Schenker Class 66. Fitted with tripcocks.
WCAT	DB Schenker Class 60.
WCBT	DB Schenker Class 60. Extended-range fuel tanks.
WDAM	DB Schenker Class 59.
WEAC	DB Schenker Class 90.
WEDC	DB Schenker Class 90 for hire to DRS.
WFAC	DB Schenker Class 92.
WFBC	DB Schenker Class 92 with commissioned TVM430 cab signalling equipment for use on High Speed 1.
WFCC	DB Schenker Class 92 for hire to DRS.
WGEE	DB Schenker Class 92 for export.
WQAA	DB Schenker stored locomotives Group 1A (short-term maintenance).
WQBA	DB Schenker stored locomotives Group 2 (unserviceable).
WQCA	DB Schenker stored locomotives Group 3 (unserviceable).
WQDA	DB Schenker stored locomotives Group 4 (awaiting disposal).
WSGC	DB Schenker Class 08/09. GSMR fitted.
WSRC	DB Schenker Class 08/09. Remote control fitted.
WSSC	DB Schenker Class 08/09.
XHAC	Direct Rail Services Classes 37/4, 47 & 57/3.
XHCE	Direct Rail Services Class 68 for hire to Chiltern Railways.
XHCK	Direct Rail Services Class 57/0.
XHHP	Direct Rail Services locomotives – holding pool.
XHIM	Direct Rail Services locomotives – Intermodal traffic.
XHNB	Direct Rail Services Class 47 for use on the Northern Belle.
XHNC	Direct Rail Services locomotives – nuclear traffic/general.
XHSS	Direct Rail Services stored locomotives.
XHVE	Direct Rail Services Class 68.
XHVT	Direct Rail Services Class 57/3 for hire to Virgin Trains.
XYPA	Mendip Rail Class 59/1.
XYPO	Mendip Rail Class 59/0.

7.4. OPERATOR CODES

Operator codes are used to denote the organisation that facilitates the use of that vehicle, and may not be the actual Train Operating Company which runs the train. Where no operator code is shown, vehicles are currently not in use.

62	The Princess Royal Class Locomotive Trust		HE	Heathrow Express
AW	Arriva Trains Wales		HT	First Hull Trains
BK	The Scottish Railway Preservation Society		LO	London Overground
			LM	London Midland
BP	Belmond British Pullman		ME	Merseyrail
C2	c2c		NB	Belmond Northern Belle
CR	Chiltern Railways		NO	Northern
CS	Colas Rail		NY	North Yorkshire Moors Railway
DB	DB Schenker		RP	Royal Train
DR	Direct Rail Services		RS	The Royal Scotsman (Belmond)
EC	East Coast		RV	Riviera Trains
EM	East Midlands Trains		SE	Southeastern
EU	Eurostar (UK)		SN	Southern
GA	Abellio Greater Anglia		SR	ScotRail
GB	GB Railfreight		ST	Statesman Rail
GC	Grand Central		SW	South West Trains
GT	Govia Thameslink Railway		TP	TransPennine Express
GW	First Great Western		VT	Vintage Trains
HC	Heathrow Connect		VW	Virgin Trains
HD	Hastings Diesels		WC	West Coast Railway Company
			XC	CrossCountry

7.5. ALLOCATION & LOCATION CODES

Allocation codes are used in this publication to denote the normal maintenance base ("depots") of each operational locomotive, multiple unit or coach. However, maintenance may be carried out at other locations and may also be carried out by mobile maintenance teams.

Location codes are used to denote common storage locations whilst the full place name is used for other locations. The designation (S) denotes stored.

Code	Depot	Operator
AD	Ashford (Kent)	Hitachi
AK	Ardwick (Manchester)	Siemens
AL	Aylesbury	Chiltern Railways
AN	Allerton (Liverpool)	Northern
BA	Basford Hall Yard (Crewe)	Freightliner
BD	Birkenhead North	Merseyrail
BF	Bedford Cauldwell Walk	Govia Thameslink Railway
BH	Barrow Hill (Chesterfield)	Barrow Hill Engine Shed Society
BI	Brighton Lovers Walk	Southern
BL*	Shackerstone, Battlefield Line	*Storage location only*
BM	Bournemouth	South West Trains
BN	Bounds Green (London)	East Coast
BO	Burton-upon-Trent	Nemesis Rail

Code	Location	Operator
BQ	Bury (Greater Manchester)	East Lancashire Rly Trust/Riley & Son (Railways)
BS	Bescot (Walsall)	DB Schenker Rail (UK)
BT	Bo'ness (West Lothian)	The Bo'ness & Kinneil Railway
BY	Bletchley	London Midland
BZ	St Blazey (Par)	Storage location only
CD	Crewe Down Holding Sdgs	Riviera Trains
CE	Crewe International	DB Schenker Rail (UK)
CF	Cardiff Canton	Arriva Trains Wales/Colas Rail
CH	Chester	Alstom
CK	Corkerhill (Glasgow)	ScotRail
CL*	Crewe LNWR Heritage	LNWR Heritage Company
CM	East Cranmore	Cranmore Railway Company
CO	Coquelles (France)	Eurotunnel
CP	Crewe Carriage Shed	Arriva TrainCare
CR	Crewe Gresty Bridge	Direct Rail Services
CS	Carnforth	West Coast Railway Company
CZ	Central Rivers (Barton-under-Needwood)	Bombardier Transportation
DY	Derby Etches Park	East Midlands Trains
EC	Edinburgh Craigentinny	East Coast
EH	Eastleigh	Arriva TrainCare
EM	East Ham (London)	c2c
EX	Exeter	First Great Western
FA	Fawley (Hampshire)	Storage location only
FF	Forest (Brussels)	SNCB/NMBS
GW	Glasgow Shields Road	ScotRail
HA	Haymarket (Edinburgh)	ScotRail
HE	Hornsey (London)	Govia Thameslink Railway
HT	Heaton (Newcastle)	Northern
IL	Ilford (London)	Abellio Greater Anglia
IS	Inverness	ScotRail
KM	Carlisle Kingmoor	Direct Rail Services
KR	Kidderminster	Severn Valley Railway
KY	Knottingley	DB Schenker Rail (UK)
LA	Laira (Plymouth)	First Great Western
LB	Loughborough Works	Wabtec Rail
LD	Leeds Midland Road	Freightliner Engineering
LE	Landore (Swansea)	First Great Western
LG	Longsight (Manchester)	Northern
LM	Long Marston (Warwickshire)	Motorail Logistics
LR	Leicester	UK Rail Leasing
LT	Longport (Stoke-on-Trent)	ElectroMotive Diesel Services
LY	Le Landy (Paris)	SNCF
MA	Alstom Longsight (Manchester)	Alstom
MD	Merehead	Mendip Rail
ME	Mossend Yard	DB Schenker Rail (UK)
MI*	Minehead	West Somerset Railway
MH	Millerhill (Edinburgh)	DB Schenker Rail (UK)
MN	Machynlleth	Arriva Trains Wales
NC	Norwich Crown Point	Abellio Greater Anglia
NG	New Cross Gate (London)	London Overground
NH	Newton Heath (Manchester)	Northern

NL	Neville Hill (Leeds)	East Midlands Trains/Northern
NM	Nottingham Eastcroft	East Midlands Trains
NN	Northampton King's Heath	Siemens
NT	Northam (Southampton)	Siemens
NY	Grosmont (North Yorkshire)	North Yorkshire Moors Railway Enterprises
OH	Old Oak Common Heathrow	Heathrow Express
OO	Old Oak Common HST	First Great Western
PM	St Philip's Marsh (Bristol)	First Great Western
PZ	Penzance Long Rock	First Great Western
RG	Reading	First Great Western
RM	Ramsgate	Southeastern
RR	Doncaster Roberts Road	ElectroMotive Diesel Services
RU	Rugby	Colas Rail
RY	Ryde (Isle of Wight)	South West Trains
SA	Salisbury	South West Trains
SE	St Leonards (Hastings)	St Leonards Railway Engineering
SG	Slade Green (London)	Southeastern
SH	Southall (London)	West Coast Rly Co/Locomotive Services
SJ*	Stourbridge Junction	Parry People Movers
SK	Swanwick Junction (Derbyshire)	Midland Railway Enterprises
SL	Stewarts Lane (London)	Southern/Belmond
SO	Soho (Birmingham)	London Midland
SP	Spings Branch (Wigan)	DB Schenker Rail (UK)
SU	Selhurst (Croydon)	Southern
TI	Temple Mills (London)	Eurostar International
TJ	Tavistock Junction Yard (Plymouth)	*Storage location only*
TM	Tyseley Locomotive Works	Birmingham Railway Museum
TN	Thornton (Fife)	John Cameron
TO	Toton (Nottinghamshire)	DB Schenker Rail (UK)
TS	Tyseley (Birmingham)	London Midland
TW*	Tonbridge West Yard	GB Railfreight
WB	Wembley (London)	Alstom
WD	Wimbledon (London)	South West Trains
WE	Willesden Brent sidings	*Storage location only*
WH*	Washwood Heath (Birmingham)	Boden Rail Engineering/RMS Locotec
WN	Willesden (London)	London Overground
WO*	Wolsingham, Weardale Railway	RMS Locotec
XW	Crofton (Wakefield)	Bombardier Transportation
YK	National Railway Museum (York)	National Museum of Science & Industry
ZA	RTC Business Park (Derby)	Railway Vehicle Engineering
ZB	Doncaster Works	Wabtec Rail
ZC	Crewe Works	Bombardier Transportation UK
ZD	Derby Works	Bombardier Transportation UK
ZG	Eastleigh Works	Arlington Fleet Services
ZH	Springburn Depot (Glasgow)	Knorr-Bremse Rail Systems (UK)
ZI	Ilford Works	Bombardier Transportation UK
ZJ	Stoke-on-Trent Works	Axiom Rail (Stoke)
ZK	Kilmarnock Works	Wabtec Rail Scotland
ZN	Wolverton Works	Knorr-Bremse Rail Systems (UK)
ZR	York (Holgate Works)	Network Rail

*= unofficial code.

7.6. ABBREVIATIONS

The following general abbreviations are used in this book:

AC	Alternating Current (ie Overhead supply)
AFD	Air Force Department
BAA	British Airports Authority
BR	British Railways
BSI	Bergische Stahl Industrie
CRDC	Component Recovery & Disposal Centre
C&W	Carriage & Wagon
DC	Direct Current (ie Third Rail)
DEMU	Diesel Electric Multiple Unit
DERA	Defence Evaluation & Research Agency
DfT	Department for Transport
Dia	Diagram number
DMU	Diesel Multiple Unit (general term)
DSDC	Defence Storage & Distribution Centre
DRS	Direct Rail Services
EMU	Electric Multiple Unit (general term)
GWR	Great Western Railway
FLT	Freightliner Terminal
H-B	Hunslet-Barclay
hp	Horse power
HNRC	Harry Needle Railroad Company
Hz	Hertz
kN	Kilonewtons
km/h	Kilometres per hour
kW	Kilowatts
lbf	Pounds force
LT	London Transport
LUL	London Underground Limited
m	Metres
mm	Millimetres
mph	Miles per hour
NPCCS	Non Passenger Carrying Coaching Stock
PTE	Passenger Transport Executive
RCH	Railway Clearing House
rpm	Revolutions per minute
RR	Rolls Royce
RSL	Rolling Stock Library
SR	BR Southern Region and Southern Railway
t	Tonnes
T	Toilet
TD	Toilet suitable for disabled passengers
TDM	Time Division Multiplex
TOPS	Total Operations Processing System
V	Volts
W	Wheelchair space

7.7 BUILDERS

These are shown in class headings. The workshops of British Railways and the pre-nationalisation and pre-grouping companies were first transferred to a wholly-owned subsidiary called "British Rail Engineering Ltd", abbreviated to BREL. These workshops were later privatised, BREL then becoming "BREL Ltd". Some of the works were then taken over by ABB, which was later merged with Daimler-Benz Transportation to become "Adtranz". This company has now been taken over by Bombardier Transportation, which had taken over Procor at Horbury previously. Bombardier also builds vehicles for the British market in Brugge, Belgium.

Other workshops were the subject of separate sales, Springburn, Glasgow and Wolverton becoming "Railcare" and Eastleigh becoming "Wessex Traincare". All three were sold to GEC-Alsthom (now Alstom) but Eastleigh Works closed in 2006, although the site is now used as a storage and refurbishment location.

Part of Doncaster works was sold to RFS Engineering, which became insolvent and was bought out and renamed RFS Industries. This is now part of Wabtec Rail Group.

The builder details in the class headings show the owner at the time of vehicle construction followed by the works as follows:

Ashford	Ashford Works (now Ashford Rail Plant depot). This is not the same location as the now closed Chart Leacon Works.
Birmingham	The former Metro-Cammell works at Saltley, Birmingham.
Cowlairs	Cowlairs Works, Glasgow.
Derby	Derby Carriage Works (also known as Litchurch Lane).
Doncaster	Doncaster Works.
Eastleigh	Eastleigh Works
Swindon	Swindon Works.
Wolverton	Wolverton Works.
York	York Carriage Works.

Other builders are:

Alexander	Walter Alexander, Falkirk.
Barclay	Andrew Barclay, Caledonia Works, Kilmarnock (now Wabtec Rail Scotland).
BRCW	Birmingham Railway Carriage & Wagon, Smethwick.
CAF	Construcciones y Auxiliar de Ferrocarriles, Zaragosa, Spain.
Cravens	Cravens, Sheffield.
Gloucester	Gloucester Railway Carriage & Wagon, Gloucester.
Hunslet-Barclay	Hunslet-Barclay, Caledonia Works, Kilmarnock (now Wabtec Rail Scotland).
Hunslet TPL	Hunslet Transportation Projects, Leeds.
Lancing	SR, Lancing Works.
Leyland Bus	Leyland Bus, Workington.
Metro-Cammell	Metropolitan-Cammell, Saltley, Birmingham
Pressed Steel	Pressed Steel, Linwood.
Charles Roberts	Charles Roberts, Horbury Junction, Wakefield.
SGP	Simmering-Graz-Pauker, Austria (now owned by Siemens).
Siemens	Siemens Transportation Systems (works in Germany (Krefeld), Austria (Vienna) and the Czech Republic (Prague).
SRP	Specialist Rail Products Ltd (A subsidiary of RFS).